MOON HANDBOOKS®
NEVADA

SEVENTH EDITION

DEKE CASTLEMAN

Ⓡ AVALON TRAVEL

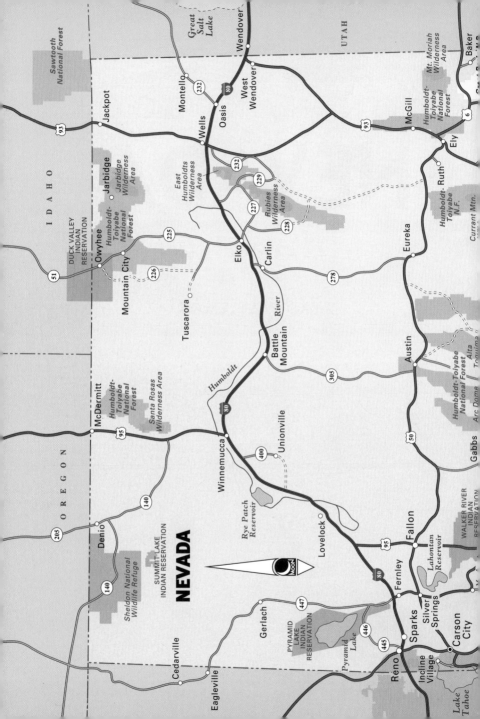

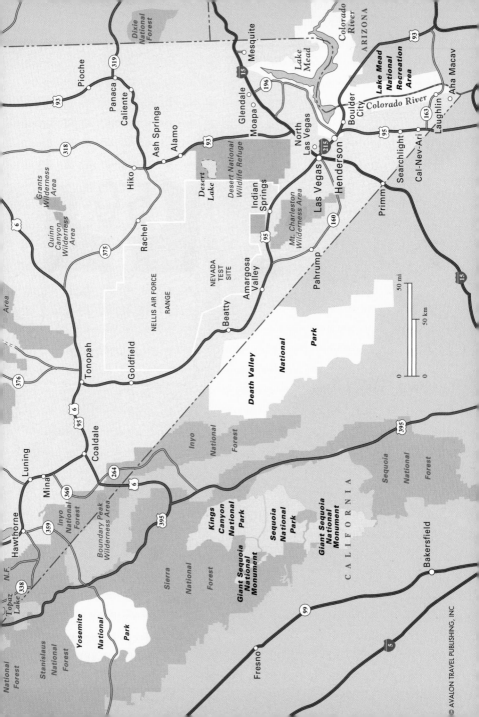

CONTENTS

Discover Nevada

Explore Nevada

Know Nevada

MAPS

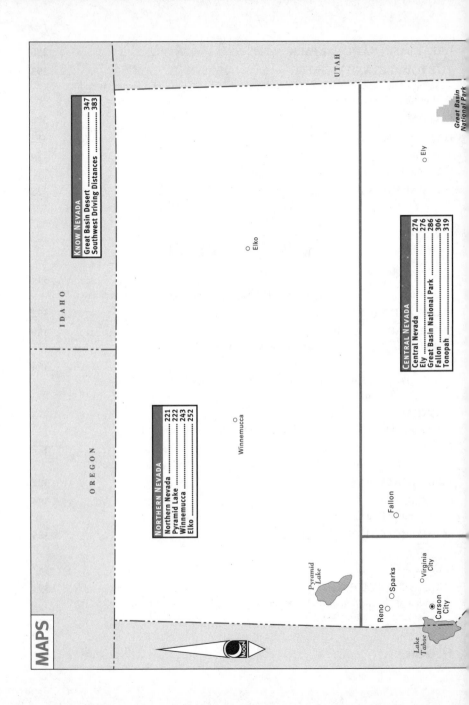

OREGON

IDAHO

UTAH

Lake
Tahoe

Reno ○ Sparks

Carson
City

Virginia
City

Fallon

Pyramid
Lake

Winnemucca

Elko

Ely

Great Basin
National Park

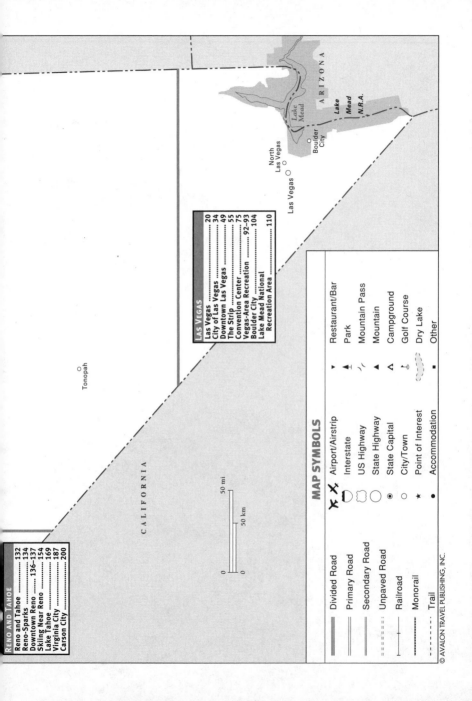

CALIFORNIA

Tonopah

Las Vegas

North
Las Vegas

Boulder
City

Lake
Mead

ARIZONA

*Lake
Mead
N.R.A.*

50 mi

0

50 km

0

MAP SYMBOLS

Divided Road	Airport/Airstrip		Restaurant/Bar
Primary Road	Interstate		Park
Secondary Road	US Highway		Mountain Pass
Unpaved Road	State Highway		Mountain
Railroad	State Capital		Campground
Monorail	City/Town		Golf Course
Trail	Point of Interest		Dry Lake
	Accommodation		Other

Discover Nevada

Stare long enough at a large blank map of Nevada, just the outline of the state boundaries, and it starts to look like a cartoon balloon, emanating from the mouth of a caricature of, say, Mark Twain, exclaiming, "And so! Ho for Washoe!" Now paint the balloon with Nevada's colors: the sandy brown of its great western deserts, the silvery green of its sage and creosote carpet, the carob hue of its mountains, stippled with forests and snow. Imbue the western and southern borders with ovals of deep blue. Now tilt the picture horizontally so that the whole thing is a pitted wedge, high end at the north, with a long slow slope to the south. Draw on a few bold black highways (with a yellow stripe down the middle) and thin gray byways. Finally, spotlight the cities and border towns with bright neon and blinking bulbs; sprinkle in the streetlights of the small towns and remote highway junctions; and add a soundtrack of coins jangling, crowds jostling, and machines shrieking—and you have Nevada in a nutshell.

Encompassing 110,000 square miles, Nevada is the seventh largest state in the union. It's home to most of the country's remaining wild horses, and boasts more than 200 individual mountain ranges, half a dozen rivers to nowhere, and huge hunks of the Great Basin and Mojave Desert. It was the last piece of the West to be claimed and conquered by Europeans; the first contact with native peoples happened only some 200 years ago.

Since then we've changed everything. We grabbed the land, put a political boundary around it, sliced it into jigsaw pieces, dug into it, dumped on it, dammed it up, even detonated all over it. We've grazed it, paved it, run our wires and pipes over and under it, and filled up the airwaves. We've bought, sold, traded, and inherited tiny parcels of it. And the transformation continues unabated.

Yet in spite of all that, Nevada contains the most rugged and remote wild country in the contiguous United States. You can hike clear across a mountain range and not see another soul for days. In the middle of the driest land on the continent, you can fish for huge trout, houseboat among hidden coves, and ride whitecaps. You can search for wildlife galore, from pelicans to pronghorns, from falcons to mountain lions. And you can get as wild indoors as out, winning or losing fortunes on the turn of a card or the spin of a wheel.

Most people, however, drive across Nevada east and west on long dull stretches of highway, never noticing its subtle beauty, great variety, or electric excitement. Too many people believe in the stereotypes of the state: that "there's nothing there" except land suitable only for the testing of atomic bombs and smoky casinos filled with degenerate gamblers. But if you give Nevada a chance, you'll find it to be perhaps the most unusual, exotic, and inviting state of them all.

LAS VEGAS

Luxor: This dramatic pyramid houses the world's largest atrium.

Forum Shops at Caesars: For a fun break, check out the two animatronic shows at this shopping complex.

Bellagio: The fountain show and conservatory gardens offer a more refined take on Las Vegas extravagance.

New York–New York: Hop aboard the roller coaster for a whirlwind tour of this little Big Apple.

Paris: Even at half the size of the original, this Eiffel Tower dazzles visitors.

Venetian: Take a gondola ride on its canals—it's almost as romantic as the real thing.

Golden Nugget: The mammoth gold nugget on display will remind you how Nevada's embarrassment of riches got its start.

Mirage: No it's not a mirage: This casino's stunning aquarium really is in the middle of a desert.

Buffets: No trip to Las Vegas would be complete without a gluttonous helping at the Rio, Fiesta, Texas Station, or Main Street Station.

Views: All the action on the streets is even more thrilling to witness from the top of the Stratosphere and from the tower at the Rio.

NEAR LAS VEGAS

Mount Charleston: It's 15–20 degrees cooler than the Strip on the hottest day and snowy enough on the coldest for downhill skiing.

Valley of Fire State Park: The sandstone here is so colorful, so unusual, and so enormous, that words fail.

Hoover Dam: The behemoth buttress of Black Canyon features a 60-story elevator ride to the bottom, with Lake Mead, the largest manmade lake in the country, behind it.

Laughlin: A follow-up to or a reprieve from Las Vegas, this gambling mecca on the Colorado River serves up bright casinos, cheap room and board, water taxis, and blast-furnace heat.

RENO AND TAHOE

Views: The best sight of downtown Reno is from the Top restaurant on the 21st floor of the Golden Phoenix. Two good "cheap aerials" of Lake Tahoe are from Llewellyn's/Peak Lounge at the top of Harveys at Stateline and from the fire lookout in Crystal Bay on the north shore. The best views of Virginia City require a little more effort: Just climb straight up Mt. Davidson.

Parks: Mills Park in Carson, and of course Lake Tahoe–Nevada State Park are all worth some quality time.

Museums: The best in the area are Nevada State Historical Society Museum, National Automobile Museum, Wilbur D. May Museum and Arboretum, and Liberty Belle Saloon in Reno; the Castle and Fourth Ward School in Virginia City; and Nevada State Museum and Stewart Indian Museum in Carson City.

Casinos: The ones not to miss are Reno Hilton, Club Cal-Neva, and the Peppermill in Reno; John Ascuaga's Nugget in Sparks; Bucket of Blood and Delta Saloon in Virginia City; Carson Station and Cactus Jack's in Carson, Sharkey's in Gardnerville; and Harveys (south shore) and the Cal-Neva Resort Spa and Casino (north shore) on Lake Tahoe.

© CRAIG JONES

beached on Lake Tahoe

NORTHERN NEVADA

Pyramid Lake: This is perhaps the most beautiful desert lake in the world; if you have the chance, spend a night anywhere on the lakeshore (especially at the Great Stone Mother on the east side).

Black Rock Desert: This is the most mind-bending stretch of desert in a state that's composed of mostly mind-bending desert.

Sheldon National Wildlife Refuge: The refuge hosts the most concentrated numbers of wildlife in Nevada; travel through at sunrise to see countless pronghorn antelope and birds.

Buckaroo Hall of Fame and Western Heritage Museum: Worth a stop is this shrine to cowboys and the Old West, appropriately sited in Winnemucca.

Western Folklife Center: A superb overview of cowboy culture, this museum is one of the many attractions in Elko, one of country's most livable small towns.

Ruby Crest Trail: South of Elko is the stunning Lamoille Canyon in the incomparable Ruby Mountains; a leisurely seven-day stroll along this 45-mile trail is a highlight.

CENTRAL NEVADA

Bristlecone Convention Center: This Ely institution displays a section of "Prometheus," a tree that dates back to the time of Moses.

Nevada Northern Railway: Tour the museum and then take a joyride on this thrilling, working short-line railroad near Ely.

Cave Lake State Park: This is a gorgeous plot of treed land for camping, hiking, and biking.

Ward Charcoal Ovens: Trace the history of charcoal making in this other-worldly location.

Lehman Caves: Twenty million years of geology are bound up in these caves. Be sure to tour them while visiting Great Basin National Park.

Central Nevada Museum: This Tonopah collection offers a vast and thorough overview of mining.

Outdoors

PARKS AND WILDERNESS

Nevada has one national park, Great Basin, which is 65 miles east of Ely near the Utah border. It encompasses a part of the Snake Range, which includes Wheeler Peak, Lehman Caves, and a fair amount of backcountry wilderness.

Nevada has 13 official Wilderness Areas, encompassing 733,400 acres. Other than the Mt. Charleston Wilderness, less than one hour from Las Vegas, and the Mt. Rose Wilderness, less than one hour from Reno, all of the areas are fairly remote, untouched, and primitive. The vast majority of the protected acreage is so underused that no permits are even required to hike, backpack, or camp on it.

Twenty-four state parks, historic sites, and recreation areas occupy nearly 150,000 acres. The largest and oldest (and one of the most spec-

COURTESY OF THE NEVADA COMMISSION ON TOURISM

Nevada's only national park, Great Basin

tacular) is Valley of Fire State Park northeast of Las Vegas, at 46,000 acres. The smallest is Belmont Courthouse State Historic Site, at a single solitary lonesome acre. The newest, the Big Bend of the Colorado State Recreation Area, on the shores of the Colorado River five miles south of Laughlin, opened in 1993. *The Sierra Club Guide to the Natural Areas of New Mexico, Arizona, and Nevada,* by John and Jane Perry, covers 82 sites in Nevada of the authors' choosing.

Any way you look at it, there's a lot of outdoors in the Silver State.

RESPECTING THE LAND AND THE PEOPLE

When you're anywhere outdoors, especially in the backcountry, make it your objective to leave no trace of your passing. Litter is pollution. Whenever you are tempted to leave garbage behind, think of how you feel when you find other people's plastic bags, tins, or aluminum foil in *your* yard. If you packed it in, you can pack it out. Burying garbage is useless as animals soon dig it up. Be a caretaker by picking up trash left by less conscientious visitors. In this way, in part, you thank the land for the experiences it has provided you.

Human wastes should be disposed of at least 100 feet from any trail or water source. Bury wastes and carefully burn the toilet paper, if possible. Extreme care should be taken with fire everywhere. As you explore, remember that Nevadans are fiercely independent people who value their privacy. They can also be overwhelmingly hospitable if you treat them with respect.

SPORTS
WINTER SPORTS

As one would expect, downhill ski resorts, along with the numerous cross-country operations, abound in the Lake Tahoe area. But you can find a couple in more remarkable locations, including the Lee Canyon Ski Resort, 45 minutes from Las Vegas, and the Elko Snowbowl. Heli-skiing is a big attraction in the Ruby Mountains.

You can ice skate indoors at the Santa Fe Ice Arena (at the Santa Fe Hotel-

Casino). Outdoor options include the Squaw Valley Olympic Ice Pavilion (highest year-round ice rink in the world), Davis Creek Park in Washoe Valley, Elko City Park, and Winnemucca Sports Complex. In Reno, the city puts up a portable outdoor ice skating rink somewhere near the Truckee River, usually in Wingfield or Idlewild Parks.

Have inner tube, will slide down a snowy hill in the state. Snowmobiles are for rent at Zephyr Cove and near Truckee.

BIKING

Riding mountain bikes off-road and racing bikes on the streets of Nevada is a special treat. The surfaces on- and off-road are excellent; you have your choice of flat and hilly terrain. In most places you can see forever—or at least to the next mountain range; the bird-watching can be exciting. As inviting as all this sounds, certain precautions are mandatory to have an experience that's not only comfortable but safe as well. In the spring-to-fall desert heat and searing sunshine, riding is best in the early morning and evening. Though it might be tempting to wear short shorts and a T-shirt, adequate protection for your tender skin is a must, as are sunglasses to cut the potentially blinding glare. Carry twice as much water as you think you'll need, and when you run out of water earlier than you'd expected, cut your ride short. Take along tools and a first-aid kit, and wear a helmet.

© CYNTHIA DELANY YARNELL/COURTESY OF THE NEVADA COMMISSION ON TOURISM

ideal biking conditions in Lamoille Canyon

BOATING

Boating? In Nevada? The state department of wildlife lists many of the sites for boating, and some of them aren't even reservoirs. Nevada has boating from row-boating on Jiggs Reservoir to houseboating in Lake Mead. For a complete run-down of all the lakes and reservoirs, public and private, in Nevada, along with the numerous state boating laws and regulations, and tips on water safety, equip-ment, waterway markers, etc., contact the Nevada Division of Wildlife, 1100 Val-ley Rd., Reno, 755/688-1558, and ask for the *Nevada Boating Access Guide.*

GOLF

Nevada has more than 100 golf courses, with a couple of dozen in Las Vegas alone and over a dozen in Reno. *Nevada* magazine publishes an annual direc-tory and guide to all the golf courses in the state. It's available for the asking: contact *Nevada* at 775/687-5416, www.nevadamagazine.com.

FISHING AND HUNTING

For the official word, contact the Nevada Division of Wildlife, in Reno (755/688-1558), in Las Vegas (702/486-5127), or in Elko (775/738-5332).

For the expert look at the whole range of fishing opportunities in the state of Nevada, pick up *Nevada Angler's Guide — Fish Tails in the Sagebrush,* by Renoite Richard Dickerson. You'll have yourself a guide to everything you'd ever need to know to enjoy a lifetime of fishing in Nevada.

BALLOONING

Reno hosts the state's largest hot-air-balloon event the second weekend in September. For information on the Reno Balloon Race, call 775/826-1181 or visit www.renoballoon.com.

For balloon rides year-round, in the Reno area try Mountain High, 888/GO-ABOVE. To balloon right over Lake Tahoe there's Lake Tahoe Balloons, 800/872-9294 or 530/544-1221. In Las Vegas, try D&R Balloons, 702/248-7609.

Festivals and Events

What follows is a list of Nevada's major annual festivals and events. Sometimes events' dates can be changed, or ongoing events can be cancelled. Before you use this list to make travel plans, be sure to check current schedules.

The statewide Nevada Commission on Tourism has current information on these and hundreds of other events around the state. They publish a Calendar of Events, and also list events on their website: 800/237-0774 or 775/687-4322, www.travel-nevada.com. So does *Nevada* magazine: www.nevadamagazine.com. Local tourist information centers and chambers of commerce, mentioned throughout this book, also have current information on events in their areas.

JANUARY

Laughlin Desert Challenge: A 165-mile off-road race along the banks of the Colorado River; 800/227-5245.

Las Vegas International Marathon and Half-Marathon: Attracts more than 7,500 runners from all 50 states and 40 other countries for the annual 26.2 and 13.1-mile races. Event includes a 5K "friendship run" the day before, and on race day an international food festival and health and fitness expo; 702/240-2722.

Cowboy Poetry Gathering: Largest gathering in the country (reserve early); weeklong concerts, readings, workshops and other activities. Last week in January, held in Elko; 775/738-7508.

FEBRUARY

Nevada Shakespeare Festival: Reno celebrates the Bard; 775/324-4198.

Walker Lake Fishing Derby: Competition for cash prizes, on Walker Lake, 12 miles north of Hawthorne; 775/945-5896.

MARCH

North Lake Tahoe Snow Festival: Mountain Mardi Gras with serious and offbeat ski races, outdoor parties, concerts, parades, bonfire, ice carvings, snow sculptures, polar bear swim, snowshoe races, torchlight parade. First week of March, at area ski resorts; 530/583-5605.

Virginia City Mountain Oyster Fry: Chefs compete for best recipe made with this ranch delicacy. Mid-March; 775/847-0311.

Shooting the West: Professional and amateur photographers meet for inspiring symposium that includes top-notch speakers, critiques, and photography outings. Usually mid-March, in Winnemucca; 800/962-2638.

Ranch Hand Rodeo: Ranch hands compete in such working events as wild-cow milking and others, in Winnemucca; 775/623-2220.

APRIL

Invitational Native American Arts Festival: Demonstrations, dance and music performances, lectures and films, outdoor Native American arts and crafts market, and food vendors. Early April, Clark County Heritage Museum, Henderson; 702/455-7955.

Clark County Fair and Rodeo: PRCA Rodeo, concert, entertainment, carnival, junior livestock judging and auction, juried art show, and antique farm equipment displays. Second weekend of April, Fairgrounds, Logandale; 888/876-FAIR.

Loon Festival: Boat tours of Walker Lake during the loons' migration season. Third weekend in April, Walker Lake, 12 miles north of Hawthorne, 775/945-8243.

Laughlin River Run: The West Coast's largest motorcycle event featuring displays, trade show exhibits, custom bike show, and concerts; 800/357-8223.

MAY

Cinco de Mayo: Large Hispanic celebrations throughout the state. Las Vegas's celebration attracts thousands of Mexican nationals. Virginia City's celebration is a Cinco de Mayo Chili Cook-Off; 775/847-0311.

The X Rides: Fully supported bicycle rides include a 40-mile evening ride and a 27-mile mountain bike ride. Early May, in Rachel; 775/588-9658.

Spring Wings Festival: Birders flock to this portion of the Pacific Flyway for workshops, field trips, and a banquet. Early May, Stillwater Wildlife Refuge, near Fallon; 775/428-6452.

Reno River Festival: Kayakers compete on Reno's new Truckee River Whitewater Park; 800/FOR-RENO.

Comstock Historic Preservation Weekend: Lectures, tours, concerts, and fashion shows. Mid-May, in Virginia City; 775/847-0975.

Jim Butler Days: Parade, barbecue, and other events honor Tonopah's founder. Memorial Day weekend; 775/482-3859.

JUNE

Laughlin River Days: Boat races on the Colorado River. Early June; 800/227-5245.

Carson City Rendezvous: Civil War re-enactment and living history camps. Second weekend, at Mills Park; 800/NEVADA-1.

Carson Valley Days: Music, food, rodeo. Mid-June, in Gardnerville; 775/783-1143.

Gridley Days: Parade, entertainment, exhibits, crafts, vendor booths, barbecue, pancake breakfast, and mountain bike rally. Mid-June, in Austin; 775/964-2200.

Winnemucca Basque Festival: Parade, games of strength, and traditional music and food. Mid-June; 800/962-2638.

Reno Rodeo: Major PRCA rodeo with a cattle drive, parade, carnival, and entertainment. Third week in June, Livestock Events Center; 775/329-3877.

COURTESY OF THE NEVADA COMMISSION ON TOURISM

rodeo time in Reno

JULY

Independence Day: Fireworks displays and other celebrations throughout the state, especially in Las Vegas and Reno.

National Basque Festival: Entertainment, games of skill and strength, dancing, food, and drink. First weekend in July, fairgrounds and City Park, Elko; 775/738-1240.

Silver State International Rodeo: Parade, booths. Week of July 4, Churchill County Fairgrounds, Fallon; 775/423-4674.

Celebrity Golf Championship: Sports and entertainment stars compete in golf tournament. Early July, Edgewood Tahoe, Stateline; 530/544-5050.

Artown: Summer arts festival with performances and exhibits throughout Reno; 775/322-1538.

Incline Village: Lake Tahoe Shakespeare Festival: The Bard's plays are presented on the beach with Lake Tahoe as a backdrop. Mid-July through August, Sand Harbor, Incline Village, 800/74-SHOWS.

Fallon All-Indian Rodeo and Powwow: Rodeo, Native American dancers, handgames, arts and crafts, dance, parade, food booths. Mid-July, Regional Park; 775/423-2544.

Reno Basque Festival: Traditional food, dance, games, Mass, barbecue. Mid-July, Wingfield Park; 775/787-3039.

Renaissance Fair: Arts and crafts, antiques, actors, jugglers, jousters, and rapier fighters. Late July, Genoa; 775/782-4951.

AUGUST

Lake Tahoe Shakespeare Festival: The Bard's plays are presented on the beach with Lake Tahoe as a backdrop. Mid-July through August, Sand Harbor, Incline Village; 800/74-SHOWS.

Reno–Tahoe Open: Golf tournament featuring top PGA players. Montreux Golf and Country Club, Reno; 775/322-3900.

Hot August Nights: Hot rods, music of the '50s and '60s, dances, concerts. First week of August, Reno and Victorian Square, Sparks; 775/356-1956, www.hot augustnights.net.

Silver Dollar Car Classic: Street dance, custom cars, poker run, barbecue, and entertainment. Early August, Mills Park, Carson City; 775/687-7410.

Pony Express 100: Open road race from Austin to Battle Mountain, also car show, dance, parade. Mid-August, Battle Mountain; 775/635-1112.

Old Spice Festival in the Pit: Town honors its distinction by the Washington Post as the "armpit of the nation" with such tongue-in-cheek events as an armpit beauty pageant. Mid-August, Battle Mountain; 775/635-1112.

Nevada State Fair: Livestock exhibits and auction, creative living competition, food booths, carnival, and entertainment. Fourth week of August, Livestock Events Center, Reno; 775/688-5767.

Spirit of Wovoka Days Powwow: Native American dance, food, arts, crafts. Fourth weekend of August, in Yerington; 775/463-2350.

SEPTEMBER

Best in the West Nugget Rib Cook-Off: World-class event featuring the West's best rib cookers competing for fame and the crowd's acclaim, with entertainment and arts and crafts fair. Labor Day weekend, Victorian Square and John Ascuaga's Nugget; Sparks, 800/843-2427.

Hearts of Gold Cantaloupe Festival: Labor Day weekend, in Fallon; 775/423-2544.

Pioche Labor Day: Electric light parade, crafts, golf tournament, and fireworks. Labor Day weekend; 775/962-5876.

Burning Man Festival: Counterculture event culminating in the burning of a giant wooden sculpture. Labor Day week and weekend, in the Black Rock Desert; www.burningman.com.

Virginia City International Camel Races: Camel, ostrich, and water buffalo races, specialty acts, daily parades, and food. Second weekend in September, Camel Arena; 775/847-0311 or 775/847-7500.

Great Reno Balloon Race: A top ballooning event that draws 120,000 people.

Early morning rally has been voted one of Nevada's best events. Second weekend in September, Rancho San Rafael Park; 775/826-1181.

National Championship Air Races: Four classes of racers, plus military displays and aerobatics. Third weekend in September, Reno; 775/972-6663.

Silver State Classic Challenge: Ninety-mile open road car race on Route 318 from Lund to Hiko, with pre-race activities in Ely. Third weekend in September; 775/631-6166.

Genoa Candy Dance: Annual arts and crafts fair featuring more than 300 fine arts and crafts booths; dinner and dance on Saturday night. Third weekend in September; 775/782-TOWN.

Street Vibrations: Motorcycle tours, entertainment, ride-in shows, parade, poker run/walk, vendors, and concerts. Late September, Reno; 800/648-6992.

OCTOBER

World Outhouse Races: Hand-constructed outhouses are raced to the finish line, in Virginia City; 775/847-0311.

Great Italian Festival: Grape-stomp, spaghetti-eating contest, food booths, entertainment. First weekend in October, Eldorado Hotel, Reno; 800/648-5966.

Nevada Day Celebration: Parade, carnival, midway games, entertainment, food booths, arts and crafts, and dance bands. Weekend nearest October 31, Carson City; 800/NVDAY-4U.

NOVEMBER

National Senior Pro Rodeo: Veterans compete, in Reno; 775/688-5751.

Rhymers Rodeer Cowboy Poetry: Cowboy poetry tribute, in Minden; 775/783-6679.

Fisherman's Holiday Fish Derby: Anglers compete for cash prizes. Fourth weekend in November, Walker Lake, 12 miles north of Hawthorne; 775/945-5896.

DECEMBER

National Finals Rodeo: Top 120 rodeo contestants compete for more than $4.5

million in prize money. First week in December, Thomas and Mack Center, Las Vegas; 702/260-8605, www.lasvegasevents.com.

Lake Mead Parade of Lights: Annual parade of 50 decorated boats on Lake Mead, starts at Lake Mead Marina, 322 Lakeshore Rd., off Highway U.S. 93., Boulder City. Early December; 702/457-2797.

New Year's Eve: Outdoor public celebrations in Las Vegas and Reno.

Explore Nevada

Las Vegas

From the first glimpse of neon glowing in the middle of empty desert, Las Vegas seduces the senses. An island of glittering marquees, endless buffets, feathered showgirls, chiming slot machines, and grand re-creations, the city surrounds visitors—all 35 million of them each year—with its unique concept as a monument to fantasy. Here, you can stroll the streets of Paris, float down a Venetian canal, lie on a tropical beach, pretend the King is alive, and most of all, feel as though tremendous riches are within your reach.

Those riches may be the most unattainable of all the fantasies, for odds overwhelmingly favor the house. But the slim chance at fortune is powerful enough to have lured vacationers into the southern Nevada desert for more than seven decades, ever since the Silver State legalized gambling in 1931. At first, the cowboy casinos that dotted downtown's Fremont Street were the center of action, but they soon faced competition from a resort corridor blooming to the south on Route 91. Los Angeles nightclub owner Billy Wilkerson dubbed it "The Strip" after that city's

Sunset Strip, and together with Bugsy Siegel, built the Flamingo, the first upscale alternative to frontier gambling halls. Their vision left a legacy that came to define Las Vegas hotel-casinos. This shift was only one of the many reinventions Las Vegas has gone through—city of sleaze, family destination, upscale resort town—each leaving its mark even as the next change takes hold.

So today, under one roof you can indulge in a five-star dinner, attend spectacular productions, dance until dawn with the beautiful people, and browse in designer boutiques. If there's still time you can get a massage and ride a roller coaster, too. The buffet, a fitting metaphor for the city that has everything to offer, still rules in many regulars' hearts. But an influx of celebrity chefs is turning the town into a one-stop marketplace of the world's top names in dining. Similarly, cutting-edge performers such as Blue Man Group and Cirque du Soleil have taken up residence alongside such beloved showroom fixtures as Wayne Newton and *Folies Bergere*. These hip offerings are drawing a younger, more stylish crowd that hearkens back to the swinging '60s, when Las Vegas was a pure adult recreation and celebrity magnet.

Some say Old Vegas is as hard to find as a game of single-deck blackjack. It's true that you can't have your picture taken in front of the Rat Pack's old haunts, but the artifacts of their heyday can be found in impersonators and tribute shows, low-lit lounges, and old-school casinos. Nor has Las Vegas lost its sense of humor or its unique brand of kitsch. Elvis impersonators (or "stylists," as some prefer to be called) will always have a place on the entertainment scene, and pedestrians still roam the Strip and Fremont Street sipping from oversized novelty drinks in the shape of the Eiffel Tower or a football.

Perhaps Vegas's most enduring legacy is its hospitality. Everyone from the lowest roller to the biggest spender can count on being treated like a VIP. Valets open car doors, waiters offer food and wine recommendations like it's inside information, and nearly everyone wishes you luck. Beating the odds may be a statistical miracle, but here, they've perfected the art of easing the blow.

THE LAND

The most famous and flamboyant resort city in the world spreads out over a small harsh low-desert valley in an unlikely corner of the American Southwest. Some of the most inhospitable terrain imaginable provides a patented hospitality to more than 35.5 million visitors a year and another nearly two million locals, and the numbers keep growing. Sitting as it does in the middle of the minor Mojave Desert, with the northern edge of the great Sonoran Desert and the southern edge of the even greater Great Basin Desert hemming it in on all sides, Las Vegas is one of the hottest and driest urban areas in the United States. It's also one of the country's most remote cities. Yet refer to any map of the southwestern United States and you'll soon realize that Las Vegas is a perfectly situated playground. Located almost precisely in the geographical center of California, Nevada, Arizona, and Utah, Las Vegas is only a five-hour drive from Los Angeles (272 miles away), and less than a two-hour flight from Phoenix (285 miles), Reno (446 miles), San Francisco (570 miles), and Salt Lake City (419 miles).

All these people, all this attention, are zeroing in on the heart of Las Vegas Valley, a relatively flat 18- by 26-mile strip oriented northeast to southwest, cutting diagonally across Clark County. The Spring Mountain Range to the west, which includes Mt. Charleston, eighth highest in the state (11,910 feet), and Sunrise and Frenchman's peaks to the east rise sharply from the smooth, gently sloping valley floor. Ten miles southeast of town is the lowest point, the Vegas Wash, which drains the valley's meager surface water into Lake Mead. Other nearby topographical features of note include Valley of Fire State Park, Red Rock Canyon, and the interminable desert.

Orientation

The city of Las Vegas huddles around the intersection of the three main highways that slices through southern Nevada: I-15, which hacks a wide gash from northeast (Mesquite) to southwest (the state line); US 95, which slices a thin

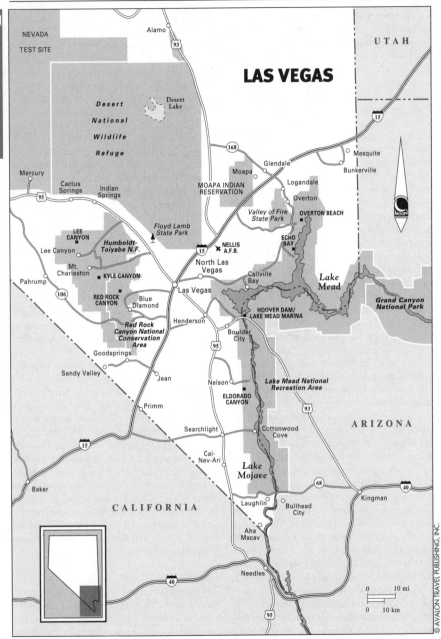

LAS VEGAS

UTAH

NEVADA
TEST SITE

Alamo

93

15

Mesquite

*Desert
National
Wildlife
Refuge*

Desert
Lake

168

Glendale

Bunkerville

Mercury

Cactus
Springs

Indian
Springs

Moapa

MOAPA INDIAN
RESERVATION

Logandale

95

Overton

LEE
CANYON

*Humboldt-
Toiyabe N.F.*

Floyd Lamb
State Park

Valley of Fire
State Park

OVERTON BEACH

Lee Canyon

NELLIS
A.F.B.

ECHO
BAY

Mt.
Charleston

KYLE CANYON

15

North Las
Vegas

Callville
Bay

*Lake
Mead*

Pahrump

106

RED ROCK
CANYON

Blue
Diamond

Las Vegas

*Grand Canyon
National Park*

*Red Rock
Canyon National
Conservation
Area*

Henderson

HOOVER DAM/
LAKE MEAD MARINA

Goodsprings

Boulder
City

95

Sandy Valley

Jean

Nelson

*Lake Mead National
Recreation Area*

ARIZONA

Primm

ELDORADO
CANYON

93

Searchlight

Cottonwood
Cove

15

Cal-
Nev-Ari

*Lake
Mojave*

68

Kingman

40

Baker

Laughlin

Bullhead
City

Aha
Macav

CALIFORNIA

Needles

40

95

0   10 mi

0   10 km

slash northwest (Beatty) to south (Laughlin); and US 93, which cuts a thick wedge northeast (Caliente) to southeast (Boulder City). Together they make a huge X through central Las Vegas, like the mark on a map that pinpoints Buried Treasure—Dig Here.

Similarly, Main Street–Las Vegas Boulevard and Fremont Street–Rancho Road make a smaller, rougher X downtown, which delineates the cardinal sectioning of the city. The corner of Main and Fremont Streets in the heart of downtown, at the Plaza Hotel, is ground zero: all street numbers and directions fan out from here. Everything east and west of the Main Street–Las Vegas Boulevard artery is labeled thus.

North and south are a bit trickier. Fremont Street (all of which is technically *East* Fremont, since it dead-ends at Main) separates north from south until it intersects Charleston (which runs due east from there, unlike Fremont, which cuts south). East of the corner of Fremont, Charleston then separates north from south streets.

The west side is even more vague. Here the Las Vegas Expressway (also know as Oran K. Gragson Expressway and US 95) defines north and south, even though it's not itself a street. To further complicate matters, US 95 is a major highway that runs north-south from Canada to Mexico, but in Las Vegas cuts due east (south) and west (north).

Thoroughly confused? Actually, five minutes spent comparing these notes with any street map will make all this clear. And if it doesn't? Many visitors never venture half a block in either direction of Las Vegas Boulevard South between Sahara and Tropicana, more popularly known as the Strip. For that matter, some never even step out of Caesars Palace, Circus Circus, or the MGM Grand.

Most tourists, however, do manage to find their way between the Strip and downtown. One good reason to know your way around a little is that rush hour throughout Las Vegas extends from about 6 to 10 A.M. and 3 to 7 P.M., and is particularly brutal on Las Vegas Boulevard. Use Paradise and Swenson Roads (a long block or two to the east) and Industrial Road and the freeway (a block west) as alternatives.

Watch for speed bumps, which erupt from most parking lots and some side streets; a few, like at the airport, are so wide that they're painted yellow and used for crosswalks. Also, slow down for flashing yellow lights and speed-limit signs at school zones; Nevadans take these 15-mph limits quite seriously, as do the police and courts (fines up to hundreds of dollars). Also, make extra certain to turn on your headlights at night, especially downtown and on the Strip. You'll notice more unlit cars in Las Vegas than anywhere else you've ever been.

Finally, take extra care driving around this town. So many drivers are visitors in rental cars, or locals in a daze from the casinos, or visitors and locals full of free booze, that Las Vegas has some of the highest accident and car-insurance rates in the country.

Climate

Though Las Vegas is now a large city with every amenity you could possibly want or imagine, it is still located in the center of an otherwise dangerous land. For at least half the year, air-conditioning is a must as summer temperatures fluctuate between 80°F and 115°F. And Las Vegas keeps getting warmer. Why? Locally, the building and population boom has its thermal counterpart: During the day, heat from the sun is absorbed by concrete and asphalt, then released at night. The hot air rises till it meets, and is trapped by, cooler air, creating a "heat island."

Wintertime temperatures are mild, averaging 45°F, occasionally dropping into the 20s at night, and often hovering daytime in the 60s. Las Vegas's mean annual temperature is a comfortable 67°F. To say this city is a year-round destination is a laughable understatement. Las Vegas has no off-season, period. Even the formerly slack weeks between Thanksgiving and Christmas are now booked solid, and prices don't come down anywhere near what they used to.

Las Vegas has the least precipitation and lowest relative humidity (20 percent) of all metropolitan areas in the country. Average local rainfall is only 4.19 inches annually, fairly evenly distributed by month throughout the year, with the most rain in January and August, the least in

May and June. It's a desert out there, dry as Death Valley sand, and during the summer you'll know every snack bar, Coke machine, and water fountain in your sphere of operations. Cyclonic storms in summer are accompanied by cloudbursts that can drop an inch in an hour, rendering the danger of flash flooding real and worrisome—locals call it the "typhoon" season. Winds that carry in the summer storms have been known to shift all the sand from the west side of town to the east, and vice versa. But any time of year, the winds can be so strong that a giant 30-foot flag on W. Tropicana stands proudly at a perfect right angle to the pole; you have to hang on tight to Caesars Palace's people movers so as not to get blown off; and miniature golfing at Scandia Fun Center is a riot.

WATER

Underneath the valley is a major system of artesian aquifers. Groundwater has been tapped at levels as shallow as 40 feet and as deep as 1,000 feet. This underground lake is recharged by rain running off the ranges. Before the drastic depletion of the reservoir between the early 1900s and the 1940s, artesian pressure forced this water up into the valley as a series of springs, creating an oasis. The first Spanish explorers stumbled upon this life-saving lea and named it *Las Vegas,* "the Meadows."

Because of the conservative growth policies of the original Las Vegas Land and Water Company and a rapidly increasing population, the wildcat Vegas Artesian Water Syndicate began tapping into the artesian system almost immediately after the railroad town was founded in 1905. The Company watered only the 40 blocks of the town it had planned; the Syndicate dug wells for everybody outside the perimeter. By 1911, 100 artesian wells had been drilled, and the "mining" of Las Vegas Valley water was fully underway. For the next 25 years, acute water crises were a way of life for Las Vegans; throughout the late '30s and most of the '40s, water shortages, inadequate pressure, broken mains, and clogged sewers had turned the acute crises into a chronic condition. The problem was only alleviated in 1948 by piping water from new Lake Mead behind Hoover Dam.

Though the piping quenched the immediate thirst, the expense and the less-than-optimal water quality initially discouraged dependence

You won't find water from this lake being used in the luxuries of Las Vegas.

on it. Nearly 20 years later, only 20,000 acre-feet per year were used (one acre-foot is equivalent to 325,872 gallons, about what the average single family uses in two years). But by 1987, Las Vegans were using 130,000 acre-feet yearly, out of their annual 300,000 acre-feet allotment And only five years later, the remaining water allotted to Nevada (between 58,000 and 106,000 acre-feet, depending on how return-flow is calculated) was finally allocated to the Southern Nevada Water Authority.

The Present and Future

No more Lake Mead water is available for Las Vegas backyard swimming pools, fruit trees, fountains, man-made lakes and bays, volcanoes, golf courses, lawns, etc. What's more, in times of drought, Lake Mead allotments are substantially reduced.

Which is why, for the past few years, Las Vegas water officials have been eyeing the water in Lincoln, Nye, and White Pine counties—totaling nearly a million acre-feet. In a plan hatched secretly in the traditional fashion of Western water schemes, suddenly Las Vegas was filing hundreds of claims to "unappropriated" water north and east for a couple of hundred miles and proposing to dam the Virgin River and pipe the water into town which, predictably, touched off a flurry of fury that has yet to subside. Of course, that was just a ploy, even a smokescreen for the real water games: redivvying up "the law of the river," or the allocation of Colorado River water among seven Western states and Mexico.

Nevada is allocated the least amount of water of the eight separate entities, two-thirds less than Wyoming and New Mexico. The imperative for changing the compact is the change in demographics over the past century—from an agricultural to a primarily urban population. Indeed, the damming of the Colorado River was to provide irrigation water for farmers, at a time when you could count Las Vegans by the hundreds and Los Angelenos by the thousands. It's a very different world now, and the Las Vegas Valley Water Authority has taken to wheeling and dealing downstream water rights, such as paying Arizona farmers not to grow crops in exchange for future water credit.

Conservation is not a possibility. There are more than 100,000 hotel rooms (with thousands more being planned and constructed each year), which means 100,000 showers, not to mention whirlpool suites and megapools, plus the spas, backyard pools, and showers of all the houses (being built at a rate of about 15,000 a year). Or lakes around the Mirage, Treasure Island, and Bellagio, not to mention canals at the Venetian. Or the lakes that the most exclusive gated-community mansions are built around. The vaguest stirrings of the concept of conservation are barely noticeable to the trained observer; in fact, Las Vegans have the highest rate of water consumption in the country (therefore the world), though they live in the driest spot on the continent: roughly 300 gallons per person per day. That's twice as high as Phoenix, four times as high as Philadelphia.

Meanwhile, experts disagree vocally on how many years Las Vegas and vicinity can expect to maintain water in the taps given the current growth rates and the finite amount of water. Most prognosticators seem to agree that Las Vegas will run out of water sometime between 2006 and 2014—but Las Vegas, true to form, will have found more by then.

HISTORY

Early human habitation in Las Vegas Valley varied with the climate. Although excavations around Tule Springs in the eastern valley have uncovered 11,000-year-old hearths, fluted arrow and spear points, scrapers, and scarred and charred animal bones, experts consider the era between 7000 and 3000 B.C. too arid for settlement in the area. After 2500 B.C., however, the climate changed to nearly what it is today: cool and damp enough, relatively speaking, to support an evolving Indian society. Known as the Archaic or Desert period, this era hosted a forager culture, whose members adapted to the use of resources such as the desert tortoise, bighorn sheep, screwbean mesquite, canyon grape, and cholla fruit. They built rock shelters and roasting pits and used the atlatl (a primitive but remarkably efficient arrow-throwing stick), mortars and pestles, flaked knives, and hammerstones. These

Archaic people could be considered the behavioral ancestors of the later Paiute people.

Anasazi and Paiute

Whether the Archaic people evolved into or were absorbed or evicted by the Basket Makers is unclear, but around 300 B.C., a new people appeared in the Las Vegas area. Also hunter-gatherers, these early Basket Makers were more sophisticated than their predecessors in only one respect. They lived in pit houses: three- to four-foot-deep excavations with mud floors and walls, brush roofs supported by strong poles, and a central fireplace. By about A.D. 500, the Modified Basket Maker period had arrived; within a couple of hundred years, these Anasazi (Navajo for "Enemies of our Ancestors") were settled permanently in the fertile river valleys of what is now southeastern Nevada. They cultivated maize, beans, squash, and cotton, wove intricate baskets, fashioned handsome black-and-white pottery, constructed large adobe pit houses, and hunted with bows and arrows.

As their agricultural techniques became more refined and their population increased, the Anasazi entered the peak of their civilization: the Classic Pueblo or Lost City period (850–1050). They lived in a sizable urban metropolis known as Pueblo Grande, in the fertile delta between the Muddy and Virgin Rivers (roughly 60 miles northeast of Las Vegas, near present-day Overton). The Anasazi were intricately linked to trading centers throughout the Southwest, and travelers carried back not only products but new agricultural and technological information, along with religious and social ideas. During the population explosion of the Lost City period, Las Vegas Valley supported an outpost of Lost City Anasazi—its only known prehistoric architecture.

By the year 1050, Pueblo Grande had become Nevada's first ghost town. The Anasazi simply packed up and headed out, dispersing throughout the Southwest. They probably returned to the center of their civilization, becoming the ancestors of today's Hopi and Zuni.

Why would such a sophisticated and successful civilization abandon a major city? Theories include stress from overpopulation, natural disasters

(such as several seasons of drought followed by flooding, which would strip the topsoil), and encroachment by the Southern Paiute. One eminent archaeologist insists that the swampy river bottomland was a prime breeding ground for malarial mosquitoes; after too many deaths, the people simply moved. A recent, provocative theory holds that the disintegration of this extensive Southwestern society coincided with the collapse of Mexico's vast Toltec empire. Deprived of primary trading links and suffering urban and ecological stress, the Anasazi confederacy unraveled.

For the next 700 years, the nomadic Paiute occupied the territory in southern Nevada abandoned by the Anasazi. These Indians called themselves Tudinu, "Desert People," and spoke an Uto-Aztecan variety of the Shoshonean language, which indicates that they probably arrived from the northeast. The Paiute had some contact with the Anasazi, but the Paiute seem to have been peaceful; there's no evidence of confrontation between the immigrants and emigrants.

The Paiute knew the land and its resources and developed a successful culture. They cultivated squash and corn and traveled seasonally to hunt and harvest wild foods. They roamed on foot in small flexible family units. They had no chiefs, only heads of families. No formal structures linked the families, though annual spring and fall game drives and pine-nut harvests united bands for several days.

Missionaries and Explorers

The Paiute's first contact with Europeans occurred in 1776, when two Franciscan friars were establishing both ends of the Old Spanish Trail. Father Silvestre Escalante blazed the eastern end of the trail from Santa Fe, New Mexico, to the southwestern corner of Utah. From the other end, Father Francisco Garces traveled through California and Arizona. Garces encountered southern Nevada Paiute, who by all accounts treated him hospitably. But it was another 50 years before further Paiute–European contact.

Before Mexico gained its independence from Spain in 1822, the Spanish government had enforced strict laws against trespassing. After independence, the first wave of eastern fur trappers and mountainmen penetrated the previously unknown Southwest. In 1826–27, famed trader and explorer Jedediah Smith became the first Anglo-European explorer to travel through what is now southern and central Nevada, and he too made contact with Paiute. Three years later, Antonio Armijo, a Mexican trader, set out from Santa Fe on the Spanish Trail. An experienced scout in Armijo's party, Rafael Rivera, discovered a shortcut on the route by way of Las Vegas's Big Springs, thereby making him the first nonindigenous person to set foot on what would become Las Vegas—and at the same time decisively sealing the doom of the southern Nevada Paiute. Within 25 years of contact, the Paiute were a broken people, and dependence became a new way of life.

By the time John Frémont, legendary surveyor and cartographer for the Army Topographical Corps, passed through Las Vegas Valley in 1845, the Old Spanish Trail had become the most traveled route through the Southwest. Las Vegas by then was a popular camping spot, the nearest grass and water to the Muddy River, a withering 55-mile march to the northeast. Frémont's exploration preceded by only three years the mass migration, in 1847, of persecuted Latter-day Saints, led by Brigham Young, to Salt Lake Valley, at that time still claimed by Mexico. Only a year later, however, the Mexican-American War and subsequent Treaty of Guadalupe Hidalgo wrested control of the vast Far West into American hands. Utah Territory was created, colonized, and administered by Young and his disciplined followers.

By 1854, the section of the Old Spanish Trail from central Utah to Los Angeles had been so tamed by Mormon guides and wagon trains that it came to be called the Mormon Trail. A monthly mail service and regular freight trains traveled between Salt Lake City and the coast. Only the 55 miles from the Muddy River to the Las Vegas Springs remained risky; it became so littered with abandoned emigrant implements and pack-animal skeletons that it was labeled "Journada de Muerta." Las Vegas constituted exquisite relief from the harrowing desert, and its name became synonymous with refreshment and hospitality.

In 1855, Brigham Young dispatched a party of missionaries to establish a community at Las Vegas. The ill-fated colony was plagued from the start. A vast desert surrounded the Meadows; the climate proved almost unbearable; millable timber had to be hauled from 20 miles away; and the isolation sapped what little morale existed. Still, the missionaries erected a fort, dug irrigation ditches, cultivated farms, and managed to befriend some native peoples. They might have succeeded, but the colonists' reports of lead deposits nearby prompted Young to send a party of miners to Las Vegas to extract and refine the ore. The missionaries' meager rations were soon stretched to the breaking point by the miners' demands. As was so often the case in early Nevada settlements, deep-seated tensions between miners and Mormons often erupted into bitter disputes—even at Las Vegas, where the miners *were* Mormons. Their disagreements, compounded by the other problems, finally caused the mission to be abandoned in 1858, leaving the second ghost town in Nevada.

Miners and Migrants

Soon after the Mormons abandoned the mission, discovery of the Comstock Lode triggered a backwash of miners and migrants east from California. The Latter-day Saints' lead mine, Potosi, was reprospected and found to average $650 in silver per ton, attracting hundreds of fortune seekers. Some enterprising growers sold produce to the new locals. Many prospectors fanned out from Potosi, and discovered gold along the Colorado River. Among the gold miners was Octavius Decatur Gass who, in 1865, took his small stake and high hopes to Las Vegas and built a ranch house and a blacksmith shop inside the decaying Mormon stockade. The Gass family irrigated 640 acres, and raised grain, fruit, vegetables, and cattle. By the mid-1870s, Gass had bought up or inherited most of the homesteaded land in the Meadows, and he owned the rights to most of the water.

Gass was an enlightened and active pioneer, who treated the local Paiute with respect and generosity and extended hospitality to all who desired it. Stanley Paher, in his outstanding *Las*

RED-LIGHT DISTRICT

At the turn of the 20th century, red-light districts were common in small towns and large cities throughout the country. They were confined and adequately policed. By the time Las Vegas was founded in 1905, Nevada's own tradition of flesh peddling in boomtowns was nearly 50 years old, as old as the state itself.

Las Vegas's original sex market, known as Block 16 (downtown between 1st, 2nd, Ogden, and Stewart streets), was typical. A mere block from the staid and proper First State Bank, the Block was established in 1905 by conservative town planners working for the San Pedro, Los Angeles, and Salt Lake Railroad, as the predictable by-product of the company's liquor-containment policy. Immediately after investors bought Block 16 lots at the railroad's town site auction, saloons erupted from the desert downtown, with hastily erected cribs out back. Within a year or so, rooms upstairs from the bars were added, all in a "line" facing 2nd Street. The Block, sleepy and deserted during the daytime, woke up at night, when its well-known vices, gambling and whoring, temporarily banished the small-town desolation.

In a twilight zone not quite illegal, Block 16 was not quite legal either. In the earliest years, barkeeps operating brothels were required to buy a $500 license. Later, regular raids and shakedowns helped finance local government. The 40 or so "darlings of the desert" were required to undergo weekly medical exams; charging at $2 per exam, the city physician held a plum position. Law and order were maintained by the steely eyes and quick fists of six-foot-three, 250-pound Sam Gay; the one enduring character from the Block, he went from bouncer to five-term sheriff.

Even with an occasional spirited campaign to eliminate Block 16, its activities were barely interrupted by the state's 1911 ban on gambling. It also managed to survive the tidal wave of red-light-district shutdowns nationwide during the 1910s. The Block fared well during the tricky years of Prohibition, with booze provided by bootleggers. And even during the years of Boulder Dam and the New Deal, amorality thrived, and Block 16 housed more than 300 working girls without undue interference.

Ironically, the relegalization of wide-open gambling in 1931 foreshadowed an end to the "line" and kindled the strong and enduring opposition to blatant prostitution of casino operators, who felt that it could do Las Vegas—and therefore gambling—no good. Still, to the dismay of local boosters, the prosaically named Block began to gain a measure of fame as word spread about this last holdout of the Wild West, and tourists to the dam site and Lake Mead visited Las Vegas to rubberneck the saloons, casinos, and bordellos.

What finally killed Block 16 was World War II. The War Department had many reasons to want open prostitution closed, not the least of which included sexually transmitted disease epidemics and the vocal opposition of military wives. The commander of the Las Vegas Aerial and Gunnery Range simply threatened to declare the whole city off-limits to servicemen, and local officials immediately revoked the liquor licenses and slot-machine permits of the casinos on Block 16. These fronts financed the prostitution, and the Block finally ran out of juice.

Today, what was once Block 16 is a parking lot for Binion's Horseshoe. Near the corner of Ogden and 1st is a 20-foot-tall bronze statue of old man Benny Binion, sitting atop his trusty steed, presiding over all the human drama and lust that transpired and expired under his feet so many years ago.

Vegas, writes, "Most travelers had come to Las Vegas dirty, weary, and in need of provisions, some even with sick children, but they left refreshed, clean, and happy." Gass traveled extensively to fulfill his duties as justice of the peace and legislator from Pah-Ute County, which encompassed Las Vegas, in newly formed Arizona Territory.

In May 1866, the U.S. Congress extended Nevada's boundaries to include Pah-Ute County, renamed Lincoln County, a move that Gass bitterly contested, especially when back taxes were levied on the new Nevadans. In the mid-1870s, Gass found himself overextended, and took a loan from Archibald Stewart, a wealthy Pioche rancher. When he couldn't repay the loan, Stewart foreclosed and took Gass's Las Vegas Ranch. In 1884, Stewart was fatally shot by a ranch hand. Stewart's wife, Helen, managed the ranch for another 20 years, till the advent of the railroad.

From Ragtown to Boomtown

In the early 20th century, William Clark's San Pedro, Los Angeles, and Salt Lake Railroad merged with E. H. Harriman's Oregon Short Line, and track from Salt Lake City to Los Angeles was completed, the first railroad line across southern Nevada. The right-of-way ran through Helen Stewart's 2,000 acres, and in preparation, she hired J. T. McWilliams to survey her property, which she subsequently sold to the railroad for $55,000. McWilliams discovered and immediately claimed 80 untitled acres just west of the big ranch. Thanks to its strategic location and plentiful water, Las Vegas had already been designated as a division point for crew changes, a service stop for through trains, and an eventual site for repair shops. McWilliams platted a town site on his 80 acres and began selling lots to a steadfast group of Las Vegas sooners. In 1904, tracks converged on Las Vegas Valley from the southwest and northeast. In January 1905, the golden spike was driven into a tie near Jean, Nevada, 23 miles south of town.

By the time the first train had traveled the length of the track, McWilliams's Las Vegas town site, better known as Ragtown, boasted 1,500 residents, brickyards, weekly newspapers, a bank,

an ice plant, a tent hotel, and mercantiles. In April 1905, with the start of regular through service, the San Pedro, Los Angeles, and Salt Lake Railroad organized the subsidiary Las Vegas Land and Water Company, platted its own town site, and bulldozed all the desert scrub from a 40-block area. The railroad advertised heavily in newspapers on both coasts and transported speculators and investors to Las Vegas from Los Angeles ($16) and Salt Lake City ($20)—fares deducted from the deposit on a lot. The company was immediately buried in applications for choice lots. Railroad officials knew a gift horse when it smiled, and they quickly scheduled an auction to pit eager settlers against Los Angeles real estate speculators and East Coast investors—gamblers all. It's fitting that the real Las Vegas (the old town site shortly dried up and blew away) was founded on the principles that would sustain it to the present.

In two scalding days of auctioneering on the site of today's Plaza Hotel, 1,200 lots sold for a cool quarter of a million. Immediately, the proud new owners searched out the stakes marking property boundaries sticking out from the desert sand and erected makeshift shelters. Hotels, saloons, gambling halls, restaurants, warehouses, banks, a post office, and a school were built in Las Vegas's first month on the map. The Las Vegas Land and Water Company lived up to its commitment to grade and gravel city streets, construct curbs, and lay water mains, hydrants, and pipes, but only within the boundaries of the railroad's own town site. The nightlife and red-light district centered on the infamous Block 16, between Ogden and Stewart and 1st and 2nd. By the time revelers rang in 1906 at the Arizona Club in Block 16, Las Vegans already numbered 1,500.

This boom resonated for the first year or so, until initial euphoria gave way to the dismal demands of domesticating a desert. Service policies of the railroad management were conservative and bureaucratic. Flash floods tore up track and delayed trains. The usual fires, conflicts, and growing pains of a new company town dampened local optimism. Even so, William Clark's new Las Vegas and Tonopah Railroad reached the boomtown of Beatty in late 1906, furthering Las Vegas's ambitions as a crossroads.

From 1906 through 1909, the issue of dividing vast Lincoln County in two raised the political climate almost as high as when Arizona's Pah-Ute County became Nevada's Lincoln County in 1866. The distance from Searchlight, the county's southernmost settlement, to Pioche, the county seat, was 235 miles—a serious hardship for far-flung citizens needing to appear at the county courthouse. Furthermore, Pioche was without a bank; all county funds were deposited in Las Vegas. Worse, Lincoln County officials had already amassed a $500,000 debt. After the hotly contested 1909 election, officials supporting division pushed a bill through the state Legislature. Named for the railroad magnate, Clark County officially came into existence in July 1909.

Further cause for celebration that year arrived on the heels of the railroad's decision to construct a large maintenance yard at Las Vegas. Then disaster struck: An enormously destructive flood on New Year's Day, 1910, ripped up more than 100 miles of track, plus trestles and buildings, curtailing train service until May.

The hot, little railroad town rebounded quickly. When completed in 1911, the locomotive repair shops created new jobs. The population doubled to 3,000 between 1911 and 1913, two years marked by growing prosperity and progress. A milestone was reached in 1915, when around-the-clock electricity was finally supplied to residents.

But the 10-year crescendo of the first boom had climaxed, and Las Vegas went into a slow but steady slide. In 1917, the Las Vegas and Tonopah Railroad suspended operations; hundreds of workers were laid off and left. By 1920, the population had dropped to 2,300. A year later, an elderly William Clark sold his interest in the railroad to Union Pacific, which closed the Las Vegas repair shops, eliminating hundreds more jobs and residents. Up until the late 1920s, Las Vegas remained at its lowest and remotest.

By 1931, the Great Depression was in full swing. The Volstead Act, enforcing the Temperance Movement's pet pitbull Prohibition, had entered its second decade. Nevada's economy was faring only marginally better than the nation's, thanks in large part to vice-starved visitors flocking to the state's libertarian attractions: prevalent bootlegging, prizefights, quickie three-month divorces, liberal prostitution laws, and ubiquitous backroom gambling. But when Governor Fred "Ballsy" Balzar signed legislation that legalized gambling and cut the divorce waiting period to six weeks, Nevada found itself the country's undisputed "Sin Central." Even so, it took the state's largest population center, Reno, many years to accept front-room gambling as respectable; Las Vegas, on the other hand, benefited from a fortuitous event that dovetailed perfectly with the new state-sanctioned sin-centered excitement.

Hoover Dam and the New Boom

The key to Las Vegas's resurrection lay just 40 miles away, at the Colorado River. By 1924, the Bureau of Reclamation had narrowed locations for a dam on the Colorado to Black and Boulder Canyons, east of Las Vegas. Anticipation alone began to fuel noticeable growth. By the end of the decade, Las Vegas had long-distance phone service, a federal highway from Salt Lake City to Los Angeles, regularly scheduled airmail and air-passenger services, more than 5,000 residents, and one of the world's most colossal engineering projects about to begin just over the next rise.

More than 5,000 workers labored for five years, often inventing and installing the necessary technology as they went along, to finish Hoover Dam by 1935. Las Vegas benefited not only from the influx of workers and their families, but also from the massive worldwide publicity of the monumental undertaking. The *Las Vegas Review-Journal* adopted for its masthead the slogan, "Everybody knows Las Vegas is the best town by a damsite."

Though an expected exodus of dam builders put late-1930s Las Vegas in the doldrums, secondary effects foreshadowed the area's commercial eruption in the early '40s. First, 20,000 people attended the dedication ceremonies of Hoover Dam in September 1935, with a speech by President Roosevelt and a parade down Fremont Street. Second, the dam, and Lake Mead filling up behind it, quickly became major tourist and recreational destinations. Hotels and casinos began springing up to accommodate the expected horde of visitors. Third, with the dam completed and ready to supply endless water and power, the federal government, gearing up for World War II, began again focusing its attention on southern Nevada.

In 1940, with the population at 8,500, city officials teamed up with the Civil Aeronautics Agency and the Army Air Corps to expand the original airport into a million-acre training school for pilots and gunners. Over the next five years, the Las Vegas Aerial Gunnery School trained tens of thousands of military personnel; the school eventually expanded to three million acres. In 1942, a monster metal-processing plant, Basic Magnesium Inc., was constructed halfway between Las Vegas and Boulder City—large enough to eventually process more than 100 million tons of magnesium, vital to the war effort for flares, bomb housings, and airplane components. At its peak in 1944, BMI employed 10,000 factory workers, many of whom lived nearby in housing projects at the new town site of Henderson. Las Vegas's population doubled in five years, from 8,500 in 1940 to 17,000 in 1945.

Bugsy Siegel

Right after the war ended, while the rest of the United States entered an era of prosperity, moral decency, and babies, Las Vegas entered an era of organized crime. The 1920s, 1930s, and World War II had witnessed the evolution of the underworld from a loose agglomeration of family businesses into a unified illegal empire. In 1919, New York City street toughs were poised to exploit the prohibition of alcohol. Boyhood buddies Benjamin "Bugsy" Siegel—tall, handsome, and fearless—and Meyer Lansky—a genius for figuring, planning, and manipulating—hooked up with Frank Costello and Charlie "Lucky" Luciano. Together they developed the organized crime's signature modus operandi—disciplined gang action, strong-arm persuasion and ruthless revenge, and careful financial accounting patterned after big business.

In 1938, Lansky dispatched Bugsy to Los Angeles to consolidate the California mob and to

muscle in on the bookmakers' national "wire" in Las Vegas. That accomplished, he bought into several downtown Las Vegas casinos, and began to implement his vision of an opulent hotel-casino-resort in the desert—the highest-class casino for the highest-class clientele. Over the next several years, Siegel managed to raise a million dollars for his Flamingo Hotel.

Bugsy hired the Del Webb Company of Phoenix to put up the Flamingo, and construction began in 1946. But building materials were scarce after the war, and Siegel's extravagance was limitless, matched only by his inability to stick to a budget. Overruns, faded by his old pal Lansky, finally reached a healthy (or unhealthy, as it turned out) five million bucks, and the project began to exact a heavy toll on Siegel's already questionable nerves, not to mention his silent partners' notorious impatience. According to conventional mob history (which is based more on legend and hearsay than any other type of American history), at a meeting of the bosses in Havana on Christmas Day 1946, a vote was taken. If the Flamingo were a success, Siegel would be reprieved and given a chance to pay back the huge loan. If it failed. . . *muerta.* But according to Robert Lacey in his exhaustive biography of Meyer Lansky, *Little Man,* Siegel was killed by his local Las Vegas associates for being a madman who might endanger Nevada's role as the gamblers' promised land.

The hotel opened the next day. Movie stars attended, headliners performed, but the half-finished hotel—miles out of town, rainy and cold the night after Christmas—flopped. Worse, the casino suffered heavy losses, which the bosses suspected to be further skim. In early January 1947, the Flamingo closed. It reopened in March and started showing a profit in May, but Siegel's fate had been sealed. In Virginia Hill's Beverly Hills's mansion in June 1947, Bugsy Siegel was hit. Before his body was cold, Phoenix boss gambler Gus Greenbaum had taken over the Flamingo.

The Mob and the Media

So began 20 years of the Italian-Jewish crime-syndicate's presence in Las Vegas. And 10 years of the biggest hotel-building boom that the country had ever seen. It also triggered an increasing uneasiness among state officials who quickly moved to assume further regulatory responsibilities from the counties, which had overseen the casinos since gambling was legalized in 1931. And then the feds began to apply their patented pressure.

In November 1950, the Committee to Investigate Organized Crime, led by Tennessee Senator Estes Kefauver, came to town. The Kefauver Commission revealed beyond any shadow of a doubt that Las Vegas had completed its transition from a railroad company town to a gambling company town. The biggest gamblers—criminals in every other state in the country—were in charge. On the 20th anniversary of legalized gambling in 1951, the state, the feds—everyone—publicly woke up to the questionable histories of the people waist-deep in counting-room gambling revenues.

The Kefauver hearings triggered two additional, unexpected, though typical, events. First, it created a media hysteria that flooded the rackets divisions of police departments around the country with funds and guns to wipe out the illegal gambling operations within their jurisdictions. This, of course, engendered a large migration to Las Vegas of expert casino owners, managers, and workers, all sticking a thumb into the perfectly legal, largely profitable, and barely policed pie. Black money from the top dons of the Syndicate and their fronts and pawns poured in from the underworld power centers of New York, New England, Cleveland, Chicago, Kansas City, New Orleans, Miami, and Havana. Netween 1951 and 1958, 11 major hotel-casinos opened in Las Vegas, nine on the Strip and two downtown, all but one generally believed to be financed with underworld cash.

Two months after Kefauver blew through town, another type of federal heat fell down on Las Vegas. The Atomic Energy Commission conducted its first above-ground nuclear test explosion in the vast uninhabited reaches of the old gunnery range, which now encompassed the Nellis Air Force Base and the Nuclear Test Site. For the next 10 years, nearly a bomb a month was detonated into the atmosphere 70 miles northwest of Las Vegas. For most blasts, the AEC erected realistic "Doom Town" sets to measure destruction, and thousands of soldiers were posted within a tight radius to be purposefully exposed to the radiation. Locals worried which way the wind blew, and seemed to contract a strange "atom fever"—marketing everything from atomburgers to cheesecake frames of Miss Atomic Blast. But mostly, Las Vegans reveled in the AEC and military payrolls, in a notoriety approaching cosmic dimensions, and in the neon-fireworks-thermonuclear aspects of the whole extravaganza.

But of all the heat—local, state, federal—felt in Las Vegas in the 1950s and '60s, the strongest came from the media. A bandwagon of invective, everything from "corrupt, vile, venal, and immoral" to "gang-controlled, crime-ridden, whore-ridden, and rotten" was unleashed into the public consciousness by the scandal-obsessed press. Known as the Diatribe, it started when Siegel's contract expired in the spring of 1947, gathered steam with the Kefauver investigation in 1950, gained momentum when the Thunderbird Hotel's license was removed in 1955 (because of hidden underworld ownership), and was already out of control when, according to Gabriel Vogliotti, in his brilliant and incisive *Girls of Nevada*, "In 1963, Nevada was hit by the book that would start the change in its gambling, its laws, and its history"—*Green Felt Jungle*. "It remains the greatest excoriation of an American state in the English language." The front-cover copy on the Pocket Book edition reads, "The shocking documented truth about Las Vegas. . . lays bare a corrupt jungle of iniquity." Vogliotti notes, "It became a worldwide bestseller, [and a] desk manual for American editors."

Even so, during this period, Las Vegas was sucking up gamblers, tourists, migrators, movie stars, soldiers, prostitutes, petty crooks, musicians, preachers, and artists like a vacuum cleaner. Between 1955 and 1960, the city's population mushroomed from 45,000 to 65,000 (a 44 percent jump), with another 20,000 people living in Henderson and Boulder City.

Howard Hughes

Enter Howard Hughes—through the back door, at midnight, incognito, with a tractor-trailer full of Kleenex, and an entire floor of the Desert Inn reserved for him and his faithful LDS advisers. By the time this part of Las Vegas history was transpiring, Hughes had been a recluse for five years and had a paranoid aversion to germs and a well-developed craving for codeine and valium. His legendary idiosyncrasies notwithstanding, the man's command of highest finance was still quite intact in 1966 while he perched on the ninth floor of the Desert Inn. The story of his official entry onto the scene is pure Las Vegas, and combines all the divergent elements of the Hughes myth. Apparently, Howard grew so comfortable at the Desert Inn that he didn't feel like moving out in time for Christmas, when the hotel needed the ninth-floor suites for its high rollers. Hughes had just sold his interest in TWA for a cool half-*billion* dollars, and had to spend some. So he paid Desert Inn owner Moe Dalitz $13 million for the hotel—and he didn't have to move.

But he moved his cash in a big way, embarking on the most robust buying binge in Nevada history. When the dust finally settled, Hughes's Summa Corporation owned the Landmark, Silver Slipper, Sands, Castaways, and Frontier hotels, in addition to the Desert Inn. He also acquired most of the available acreage along the Strip, $10 million worth of mining claims, the North Las Vegas Airport, a TV station, and an airline. In all, Hughes dropped $300 million.

And suddenly, according to conventional chronology, Las Vegas was swept clean of its entire undesirable element by the huge broom of corporate respectability. Although Hughes ultimately contributed nothing to the Las Vegas skyline or industrial sector, the presence alone of the master financier added an enormous degree of long-needed legitimacy to the city's tarnished image. Hughes's investments stimulated an unprecedented speculation boom. Also, the special dispensations Hughes received from the Nevada gambling industry regulators paved the way for the Nevada Corporate Gaming Acts of 1967 and 1969, which allowed publicly traded corporations to acquire gambling licenses. (Before Hughes, every stockholder in a casino had to be individually licensed, which effectively eliminated corporations, with their millions of stock-holders.) Hilton, Holiday Inn, MGM, and others quickly secured financing from legitimate sources to build their own hotels. Best of all for Las Vegas, the Diatribe ended, and the mob story finally passed out of the spotlight.

But did it really? Actually, some original connections continued to play themselves out. In 1973, for example, past owners of the Flamingo pleaded guilty to a hidden interest by Meyer Lansky from 1960 to 1967. In 1976, the Audit Division of the Gaming Control Board uncovered a major skimming operation that amounted to a full 20 percent of slot revenues at the Stardust. In 1979, four men were convicted in Detroit of concealing hidden mob ownership in the Aladdin, which had been funded with $37 million of Teamsters' money. Also in 1979, casino and hotel executives of the Tropicana became embroiled in an underworld-related scandal. Finally, by the mid-'80s, Tony "the Ant" Spilotro, the Chicago mob's ruthless enforcer on the Las Vegas streets, had been killed in a power struggle of the Midwest mob, and experts agreed that Las Vegas was as free of mob involvement as was apparently detectable.

Las Vegas Today

In early 1980s, the emergence of Atlantic City as the East Coast's casino center, along with the deep recession of the early Reagan years, considerably reduced visitor volume and gambling revenues. A terrible fire at the MGM Grand (now Bally's) left 84 dead and nearly 700 injured; the Grand closed from November 1980 to July 1981. A fire at the Las Vegas Hilton in February 1981 took another eight lives. Las Vegas staggered through the rest of the 1980s, until one monumental event rang out the old decade and rang in the new: the Mirage opened in November 1989 and launched the biggest boom this world has ever seen.

More than 20 major hotel-casinos have opened since the Mirage, giving Las Vegas a total of more than 120,000 hotel rooms, the most of any city in the world. More than 30 million visitors have been showing up annually since 1995, and the influx shows no signs yet of slowing. Visitor numbers skyrocketed to more than 35 million in 2000.

Las Vegas can also lay claim to 9 of the 10 largest hotels in the world (the Ambassador City in Jomtien, Thailand, is the only non–Las Vegas hotel on that list). Meanwhile, the population of the Las Vegas Metropolitan Statistical Area (MSA) now stands at 1.3 million (the whole state only surpassed a million people in 1987.) Las Vegas has remained the fastest growing city in the country for nearly a decade now, with roughly 5,000 people a month exchanging out-of-state for Nevada drivers' licenses. Las Vegas also continues to issue more building permits (per capita) than anywhere else in the country, averaging 1,500 a month.

Since 1998, five new mammoth resort casinos, averaging close to 3,000 rooms a piece, have thrust themselves onto the Vegas skyline, and there are no fewer than half a dozen new megaprojects in some stage of development. When Mirage Resorts debuted Bellagio, their $1.4 billion monument to extravagance, excess, and decadence, it was the first in a new wave of destination casinos that strove to present themselves as first-class luxury hotels where gaming comes secondary. Signature chef restaurants supplant all-you-can eat buffets. Don't be fooled. Every major complex, however new, still boasts tens of thousands of square feet devoted to gambling. The Venetian has risen from the rubble where the Sands fell (in November 1996), boasting over 3,000 rooms, every one a 700-square-foot suite, along with gondola-plying canals, a giant shopping mall, and a vast nongambling entertainment center. Just south of Bally's is Las Vegas's version of Paris, a 2,900-room French-themed upscale Hilton (Hilton acquired Bally's for $3.2 billion in 1995), complete with a 50-story half-scale Eiffel Tower. The Aladdin has re-ceived a $1.4 billion face-lift that includes a 2,500-room Arabian Nights–themed resort and casino complex that rubs shoulders with its new neighbor Desert Passage, 500,000 square feet of elaborately detailed retail space. And Mandalay Bay, a 3,000-room Circus Circus affair that evokes the South Pacific, has gone in where the Hacienda went down (in January 1997).

And that's just for starters. The latest market segment that Las Vegas hopes to fill in the next few years is the luxury niche. Recently launched are THE Hotel, yet another companion hotel to Mandalay Bay; a Ritz-Carlton (currently being built next to the MGM Grand); and a Hyatt and Grand Bay, two 400- to 500-room hotels at Lake Las Vegas, the most exclusive development in southern Nevada, located just east of Henderson.

And it doesn't stop there. A handful of other hotels are on the drawing boards. Plans for a San Francisco–themed casino have been floating around for a while; it's rumored to be going in where the Frontier now sits. Black Entertainment Television has gone into partnership with Hilton to build a 1,000-room resort. Plus a gaggle of locals' casinos are planned for the suburban neighborhoods where the Las Vegans (heavy gamblers themselves) live and play. And those are the ones most likely to succeed. Another half dozen are too speculative to mention.

At press time, the MGM Mirage (majority owned by Kirk Kerkorian) made a successful bid to buy the Mandalay Resort Group for nearly $5 billion in cash, which would mean a total of 11 hotel-casinos would be owned by one corporation. This development will make it interesting to see where this takes Las Vegas development in the future.

Entertainment

It's impossible to be bored in Las Vegas. The city's entertainment offerings are staggering: a dozen arenas and concert halls hosting everything from headliners to prizefights and rock 'n' roll to rodeos, plus nearly 20 Las Vegas–style revues, more than 50 lounges, and at least a dozen discos, nightclubs, and country-western saloons. Plus there are a handful of comedy clubs, along with new high-tech motion simulators, virtual reality, and interactive video. Combine that with laser shows, dancing waters, people-watching, bargain movies, amusement parks, local theater, dance, music, and art performances and exhibitions, and you've got something for everyone.

The primary hotels with showrooms where the major headliners appear are Aladdin, Bally's, Bellagio, Caesars Palace, Mandalay Bay, and MGM Grand. MGM Grand has both a showroom (700 seats) and an arena (15,000 seats). The showroom hosts acts such as Randy Travis, Rita Rudner, and Carrot Top; the arena has the giants, such as Bette Midler, Barbra Streisand, and the Rolling Stones. Other performing artists— mostly pop and rock—appear at the Hard Rock's 1,400-seat concert venue called the Joint.

Unless the performer is a perennial sell-out, you should be able to get into any show that's in town when you are. Check out the shows as soon as you settle in, and make reservations immediately. If you'd like to know who's going to be performing in the upcoming three months, subscribe to the *Las Vegas Advisor,* which publishes a complete list of performances.

PRODUCTION SHOWS

Production shows are the classic Las Vegas–style entertainment, the kind that most people identify with the Entertainment Capital of the World. An American version of French burlesque, the Las Vegas production show has been gracing various stages around town since the late 1950s. Of course, most of the shows have been updated over the years; only Folies Bergere is a throwback to the naughty old days of the French imports. Jubilee is a more contemporary version.

The shows fall into several categories: Broadway, burlesque, extravaganza, illusion, superstar imitators, and female impersonators. The sets are lavish, the costumes dazzling, and the special effects surprising. Then there are the specialty acts: magicians, jugglers, comics, daredevils, acrobats and aquabats, musclemen and musclewomen, marionetteers, and indescribable gimmicksters.

The big shows, since they're so expensive to produce, are fairly reliable, and you can count on them being around for the life of this edition. They do, on occasion, change. The smaller shows come and go with some frequency, but unless a show bombs and is gone in the first few weeks, it'll usually be around for at least a year or so.

Folies Bergere

Folies epitomizes the old-fashioned excess of the extravaganza: elaborate song-and-dance production numbers with performers costumed in anything from the skimpiest G-string to the most outrageous 20-pound headgear; taped music accompanies some combination of nostalgic tunes (in this case, 150 years worth), cabaret classics, and the requisite can-can). The GI generation will fully appreciate *Folies;* others might find it slow and dated. At the Tropicana, Mon., Wed., Thurs., Sat. 7:30 and 10 P.M. and Tues. and Fri. 8:30 P.M. You must be 16 or older to attend; $52–64, 702/739-2411 or 800/829-9034.

Jubilee

Donn Arden took the old-time French burlesque and pumped it full of steroids. Full many years, *Jubilee,* and Arden's other productions were the most extravagant and expensive on Las Vegas (and Reno) stages. But Arden died in 1993 and shows such as Cirque du Soleil and Blue Man Group have upped the ante by tens of millions of dollars. Still, this remains an exciting show, if only in terms of the sheer volume of gorgeous flesh-a cast of 100, with 60 to 70 bodies on stage at any given time. The sets are imaginative, the

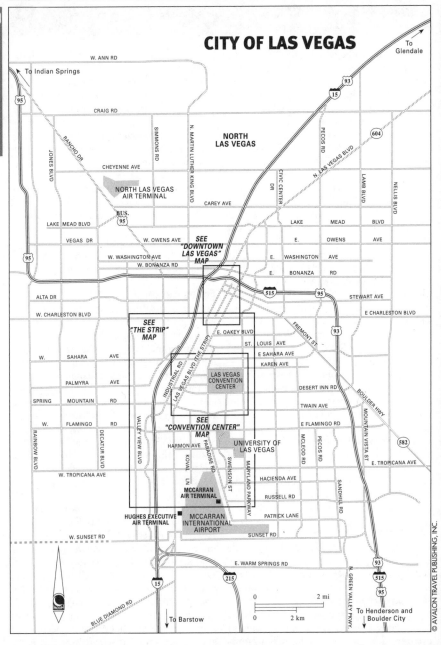

CITY OF LAS VEGAS

To Glendale

To Indian Springs

W. ANN RD

CRAIG RD

NORTH LAS VEGAS

CHEYENNE AVE

NORTH LAS VEGAS AIR TERMINAL

CAREY AVE

LAKE MEAD BLVD

VEGAS DR

W. OWENS AVE

SEE "DOWNTOWN LAS VEGAS" MAP

W. WASHINGTON AVE

W. BONANZA RD

ALTA DR

W. CHARLESTON BLVD

SEE "THE STRIP" MAP

E. OAKEY BLVD

ST. LOUIS AVE

W. SAHARA AVE

E SAHARA AVE

KAREN AVE

PALMYRA AVE

LAS VEGAS CONVENTION CENTER

DESERT INN RD

SPRING MOUNTAIN RD

TWAIN AVE

W. FLAMINGO RD

SEE "CONVENTION CENTER" MAP

E FLAMINGO RD

UNIVERSITY OF LAS VEGAS

HARMON AVE

W. TROPICANA AVE

HACIENDA AVE

MCCARRAN AIR TERMINAL

RUSSELL RD

HUGHES EXECUTIVE AIR TERMINAL

MCCARRAN INTERNATIONAL AIRPORT

PATRICK LANE

W. SUNSET RD

SUNSET RD

E. WARM SPRINGS RD

To Barstow

BLUE DIAMOND RD

To Henderson and Boulder City

RANCHO DR

JONES BLVD

SIMMONS RD

N. MARTIN LUTHER KING BLVD

CIVIC CENTER DR

PECOS RD

N. LAS VEGAS BLVD

LAMB BLVD

NELLIS BLVD

LAKE   MEAD   BLVD

E.   OWENS   AVE

E.   WASHINGTON   AVE

E.   BONANZA   RD

STEWART AVE

E CHARLESTON BLVD

FREMONT ST

BOULDER HWY

MOUNTAIN VISTA ST

MCLEOD RD

PECOS RD

SANDHILL RD

E. TROPICANA AVE

N. GREEN VALLEY PKWY.

INDUSTRIAL RD

LAS VEGAS BLVD (THE STRIP)

VALLEY VIEW BLVD

DECATUR BLVD

RAINBOW BLVD

PARADISE RD

KOVAL LN

SWENSON ST

MARYLAND PARKWAY

BUS. 95

0   2 mi

0   2 km

© AVALON TRAVEL PUBLISHING, INC.

song and dance is entertaining, and images of the show will stay with you a long time. At Bally's, Sat.–Thurs. 7:30 and 10:30 P.M., 18 and up only, $57.50–71.50, 800/237-7469.

KA

Cirque du Soleil shows its flexibility once again with the troupe's newest show to debut among the MGM properties, "KA," at TI. This show, which opened in November 2004, incorporates martial arts, acrobatics, and plenty of flashy visuals involving pyrotechnics. "KA" also weaves a cinematic element by introducing a storyline based on a tale of separated twins who endure numerous perils as their destinies unite. As with all Cirque productions, the costumes and sets are lavish, the effects are technologically advanced, and the performers are amazingly flexible and talented. The show's title was inspired by the ancient Egyptian belief in "ka," in which every human has a spiritual duplicate. At TI, Fri.-Tues. 7 and 10:30 p.m., $100–$150. 800/929-1111.

Mama Mia

A mother, a daughter, three possible dads, and a trip down the aisle lead to some madcap action during which fans of the 1980s enjoy singing along to the more than 20 hit songs of Abba. This show has played to more than 10 million show-goers around the world and is now a big hit on the Strip. Mandalay Bay, Mon.–Thurs. 7 P.M., Sat. and Sun. 5 P.M. and 9 P.M. $45–100, 877/632-7400.

Mystere

At first glance, *Mystere* is like a circus. But it also plays on other performance archetypes, from classic Greek theater to surrealism. A cross between theater and art, this production dazzles audiences who are looking for more than the standard Vegas fare. At Treasure Island, Wed.–Sun. 7:30 P.M., Sun. at 4:30 P.M., $61–155, 702/894-7722 or 800/392-1999.

An Evening at La Cage

A re-creation of the famous namesake show in New York and Los Angeles, the long-running *La Cage* features some of the world's most ac-

complished female impersonators in the world, highlighted by Frank Marino as a memorable Joan Rivers. At the Riviera, nightly (except Tues.) 7:30 P.M., $40, 702/794-9433.

O

Bellagio likes to do everything bigger, better, and more extravagant, and *O* is no exception. This Vegas Cirque de Soleil incarnation involves a $90 million set, 74 artists, and a 1.5-million-gallon pool of water. The title comes from the French word for water, *eau,* and is pronounced like the letter O. The production involves both terrestrial as well as aquatic feats of human artistry and athleticism. It truly needs to be seen to be believed, and if you can stomach the splurge, it's worth it. It's breathtaking. Wed.–Sun. 7:30 and 10:30 P.M., $99–150, 702/796-9999 or 888/488-7111.

Blue Man Group

Bald, blue, and silent (save for homemade musical instruments). Who knew that this combination would be one of the hottest things to hit the Strip in years? Hip, ground-breaking, thought-provoking, and hilarious, this unlikely trio of performance artists from New York City is definitely not what you expected. Longtime Vegas veterans Penn & Teller were the first to suggest to the Blue Man Group that they take their successful, if eccentric, New York act to the encourage to the Vegas Strip. Anyone with a quirky sense of humor should see this outrageous show. At the Luxor, Wed.–Sun. 7 and 10 P.M., $75–$85, 702/262-4400.

Midnight Fantasy

Midnight Fantasy is a basic yet provocative revue with a collection of dancers and comedian tap-dancing sensation Lindell Blake. At the Luxor, Tues., Thurs., and Sat. 8:30 and 10:30 P.M., Wed. and Fri. 10:30 P.M., and Sun. 8:30 P.M., $34.95, 702/262-4400.

Zumanity

This show is fast becoming the hot ticket on the Strip. Blending human sensuality and eroticism, *Zumanity* is the latest offering from Cirque du Soleil. The show consists of 50 performers and musicians who masterfully integrate human voices, beautifully sculpted bodies, and exotic rhythms. For ages 18 and over. At New York–New York, Fri.–Tues. 7 and 10 P.M., $75–190, 702/740-6815.

A New Day . . . Starring Celine Dion

Caesars is banking on the very bankable Canadian songstress to lure showgoers with strong performances from the very talented Celine, a powerful international cast, and an elaborate production in the Colosseum, a $95 million state-of-the-art showroom custom-built for Celine. So far, the formula seems to be working: Fans are filing into the 4,000-seat theater, which hosts other headliners when Celine's show is dark. Room and dinner/show packages available. At Caesars Palace, Wed.–Sun. 8:30 P.M., $87.50, 866/276-9468.

Splash

If it's relentless variety that you're after, this is the show for you. *Splash* combines the usual song-and-dance production numbers with the most specialty acts of any show in town: ice skating couples, performing birds, comedians, jugglers, motorcycle daredevils (cover your ears!), trained sea lions, break dancers, and a water ballet in a 20,000-gallon tank. This show will leave your head spinning. At the Riviera, Tues.–Thurs. and Sat. 8 P.M. and 10:30 P.M., and Sun.–Mon. 8 P.M., $60–75, 702/794-9301.

Danny Gans— The Man of Many Voices

Danny Gans is an impressionist par excellence, and he does roughly 65 characters during his 90-minute show—everyone from Elvis, Frank, and Dino to Dr. Ruth, Homer Simpson, and Kermit the Frog. He not only does the voices, he does the moves, gestures, and facial expressions, too; his comedic timing is impeccable. The show is a breathtaking performance by a virtuoso entertainer and his tight three-piece band. Gans only performs five times a week, so seats are at a premium; reserve early. At the Mirage, nightly at 8 P.M. except Mon. and Fri., $100, 702/792-7777.

Legends in Concert

This is a long-running and fun superstar-impersonator show, where lookalike performers pretend to be major entertainers dead and alive. There's a rotating roster of celebrities—Madonna, Blues Brothers, Buddy Holly, Michael Jackson, Roy Orbison, Marilyn Monroe, Janis Joplin, Cher, and others—but the Elvis impersonator always closes the show with a rousing patriotic finale. If the Liberace character is on the schedule, he'll blow you away. (One time, Kenny Rogers, who lives in Las Vegas, appeared as himself on stage and everyone in the audience commented how realistic the impersonator seemed!) It's a little strange watching imitators, but if you can suspend your disbelief, this show will leave you singing and dancing. At the Imperial Palace, nightly 7 and 10 P.M., dark Sun., $39.95, 702/794-3261.

American Superstars

This is the other celebrity-impersonator show. It's a little less polished and effective than Legends, but it has its charms. The Charlie Daniels fiddle-sawing character burns down the house, and the Michael Jackson character is great. Look for discount coupons in the freebie magazines. At the Stratosphere, Sun.–Tues. 7 P.M., Wed.–Sat. 6:30 P.M. and 8:30 P.M., $38, 702/382-4446.

Clint Holmes

Las Vegas favorite Clint Holmes performs a musical variety show with the help of a 12-piece band, appearing in the Clint Holmes Theatre (a true mark that a performer is there to stay). The music is a mix of updated classics and new hits. Playing at Harrah's Las Vegas, Mon.–Sat. 7:30 P.M., $67, 800/392-9002 ext. 5222.

La Femme

La Femme is an import from one of the hottest nightspots in the world, the original Paris's Crazy Horse, which has been creating productions that celebrate beautiful women and the art of the nude since 1951. The show uses a combination of light effects, film, and projections to create dramatic, often sensual but some humorous, effects. The 12 dancers in the cast are members of the original Crazy Horse dance troupe, trained in how to integrate ballet and their movements with textured light designs and colors. Must be at least 21 years of age. At the MGM Grand, Wed.–Sun. 8 P.M. and 10:30 P.M., $59, 702/891-7777.

Lance Burton, Master Magician

The terminally youthful-looking magician headlines in the $27 million theater built and named in his honor at the Monte Carlo. He immerses audiences in a world where gloves turn into doves, and burning candles appear in his hands. It's a classic Las Vegas magic show that has broad appeal. At the Monte Carlo, Tues. and Sat. 7 and 10 P.M., Wed.–Fri. 7 P.M., $65, 702/730-7160.

Penn & Teller

These well-traveled, off-beat magicians have settled into their own space at the Rio, where they have found a home for their edgy comedy-magic show. It's a show that might be an acquired taste, especially for purists, who are shocked by the duo's seemingly laid-back approach and the irreverent divulgence of how some magic tricks work. But overall, the show is entertaining and fun to watch. At the Rio, daily at 9 P.M. except Tues., $70, 888/746-7784.

LOUNGES

Lounges are another Las Vegas institution: Several dozen of the major hotels have live entertainment in bars usually located right off the casino. These acts are listed in the tabloids and magazines, but unless you're familiar with the performers, it's potluck. Some groups are hot; others absorb more energy than they supply. But it's generally a good value, since there's no cover and rarely a drink minimum.

The "good old days" of the late '50s and '60s, when up-and-coming stars earned $10,000 a week to hone their acts in the lounges on their climb to the showrooms, are over. Gone are the comedians doing a fourth show at three in the morning; gone are the singers sitting in with their friends in other lounges; gone is the Rat Pack, any one to six of

whom could invade a performance and treat the crowd to a night it would never forget. The stars and singers all work the headliner rooms, comedians appear at the clubs, and the novelty acts are incorporated into the extravaganzas.

The Vegas icons are Keely Smith and Sam Butera (Louis Prima is long dead), but there's a veritable subculture of hip Las Vegas twenty- and thirtysomethings who're really into the fringe and cult entertainment scenes of the '50s through the '70s. It's all quite retro and ironic, but these youngsters have a hold of some wild old music, movies, and personalities, and weirdness.

For the rest of us, the show lounges of yesterday have been turned into the keno lounges of today. The show lounges of today are mostly meant to be Muzak to the slots.

COMEDY

Comedy is still king in Las Vegas, and fans of the genre will find both comedy clubs as well as comedians with permanent showroom gigs. Rita Rudner appears at **New York–New York** Sat.–Thurs. 8 P.M., and Fri. 9 P.M., $50, 702/740-6815. For the traditional comedy club there's **The Improv** at Harrah's, Tues.–Sun. 8:30 P.M. and 10:30 P.M., $25, 702/369-5500; the **Riviera Comedy Club,** 8:30 and 10:30 P.M. daily, $18, 702/794-9433; and the **Comedy Stop,** Tropicana, $20, 702/739-2714 or 800/829-9034. The **Comedy Zone** is at the Plaza nightly at 9 P.M. except Mon., 702/992-7970. The infamous Second City Improv group from Chicago appears nightly at the **Flamingo,** Thurs.–Tues. 8 P.M. with Mon., Thurs., Fri, and Sat. additional 10:30 P.M. shows, $30, 702/733-3333. **Laugh Trax Comedy Club** at the Palace Station offers a different comedian every night, Tues.–Thurs. 7:30 P.M. and Fri. and Sat. 7:30 and 10 P.M., $12.95, 702/547-5300.

THEME PARKS AND THRILL RIDES

As if the aural and visual stimuli of millions of neon tubes and blinking lights and screaming slot machines doesn't thrill enough, Las Vegas is flush with amusement parks and roller coasters. Some have height restrictions, but even those who mean the requirements might not want to take the gamble—some of these rides will push you to the limit.

Top of the Tower

The Stratosphere offers some of the Strip's most heart-stopping thrills, thanks to the perch at almost 100 feet above the ground. The thrill rides include the Big Shot, X Scream, and the High Roller roller coaster. The High Roller coaster is the world's highest roller coaster. Situated at 909 feet, it rockets around the tower pad on 840 feet of track. At 866 feet, the X Scream is shaped like a giant teeter-totter that propels riders head-first 27 feet over the edge of the Stratosphere Tower at 30 mph and then dangles them weightlessly above the Strip. The Big Shot is the big attraction. You're launched 160 feet up the needle, squeezed by gravitational forces equal to four times your weight until you reach the apex of the ascent. Hey, great view! All of a sudden you drop like a rock, but you don't weigh a thing—it's zero-gravity. Then you're bounced back up, but this second time it's only about twice your weight, and dropped back down, like half a rock. The feeling stays with you for hours. The rides run Sun.–Thurs. 10 A.M.–1 A.M., Fri.–Sat. until 2 A.M. Tower admission is $9, the Big Shot and X Scream are $8, and the High Roller is $4.

Manhattan Express

Manhattan Express is the roller coaster that circles New York–New York. You catch the ride inside the building at the back of the video arcade on the second floor. Your car begins its chug toward the top, 17, 18, 19, 20 stories above the backstreet of New York. And then you're over the top and diving down a 75-foot drop. It's a great rush, but merely the warm-up sensation for the big 55-degree 144-foot fall, reaching speeds of 67 miles per hour. Then you hang a quick left behind the Statue of Liberty at the corner of Tropicana Avenue and the Strip, with unbelievable views of lions, castles, tropical islands, and pyra-

mids. The first loop is a 360-degree over-the-head somersault. Then comes the one-of-a-kind "heartline twist and dive," the half-curl, barrel-roll, upside-down rigamarole that's unique to Manhattan Express. Finally, the car is put through a dizzying succession of high-banked turns and camel-back hills, plus a 540-degree spiral, before the brakes are slammed on and you roll slowly through the casino roof and into the station. The ride lasts 3 minutes and 50 seconds, and it's a bumpy, neck-jarring ride. Manhattan Express runs Sun.–Thurs. 10 A.M.–10 P.M., Fri.–Sat. until midnight, $10. It shuts down during periods of rain and high winds. You must be 46 inches tall to ride.

Adventuredome

The big pink dome behind Circus Circus has been through a number of changes since it opened in August 1994 and now can be called an amusement park. The main adult attractions are the Canyon Blaster roller coaster (largest indoor coaster in the world at speeds up to 55 mph; pretty rough) and the Rim Runner flume ride (big drop, big splash; you walk around wet the rest of the day, there is a 48-inch height requirement for this ride). The other rides and midway games are geared toward children ages 2–8. The price structure here changes about once a month; these days, admission is $5, which includes one ride, or you can buy a ride-all-day wristband for $22 adults, $14 kids 4–9, free for ages 3 and under. Open Mon.–Thurs. 10 A.M.–6 P.M. and Fri.–Sun. 10 A.M.–midnight; 702/794-3939.

Speed: The Ride

So you want to go fast? The Sahara's foray into the roller coaster market brings us this jaw-dropping high-speed adrenaline producer. The ride wraps its way around the Sahara Hotel, curls in a loop, and climbs over 200 feet above the Strip. You pause at this vantage point for one breathtaking moment and then hurtle back the way you came, backwards. Speed is found in front of the NASCAR Cafe at the Sahara Hotel. Open Mon.–Thurs. 11 A.M.–10 P.M., Fri.–Sat. until 1 A.M., $10, 702/734-7223.

Amusement Parks

Even if you're in Las Vegas for only a day or two in the summer, it's hard to resist an interlude at **Wet'n Wild**, 2635 Paradise Rd., 702/737-7873, open May–late Aug., 10 A.M.–8 P.M.; July 10 A.M.–10 P.M., and Sept.–Oct. 10 A.M.–6 P.M., $27.99 adults, $20 kids 3–12. Look for discount coupons everywhere. The thrills are nonstop and never-ending. The Blue Niagara is the beast along the Strip—six stories high and 300 feet of "blue innerspace." The 75-foot-long Der Stuka right next to it gives you the sensation of free fall. The Wave Pool has four-foot-high surf. You can also float around the Lazy River; Hydra-Maniac, Banzai Boggan, Raging Rapids, Bubble Up, and Flumes will keep you and your kids wet and wild all day long.

Scandia Family Fun Center, 2900 Sirius Rd. right next to the freeway (off Valley View), 702/364-0071, open year-round 10 A.M. to at least 11 P.M., offers some variety for the kids. A creative 18-hole miniature golf course is $4.50 per person, racecars and bumper boats are $5 per person, or get an unlimited wristband for $17.50. It also has automated pitching machines, video arcade, and snack bar. Its Super-Saver coupons are a good value.

Luxor's Theaters

Three theater presentations on the Attractions (upper) level follow a thin plot line in which the heroes are an archaeologist who discovers an ancient Egyptian civilization directly below Luxor and teams up with a local developer to preserve it for posterity and peace. The bad guys are a military agent who's trying to secure the area for the government and a mad scientist who wants to exploit the magical powers of the ancient technology. Theater One, In Search of the Obelisk, consists of two high-impact motion simulators: The first is a freight elevator that gets sabotaged and becomes a runaway; the second is a high-speed chase through the vast subterranean temple. Both are a pretty good thrill. Specific films change every few months, so be sure to check frequently.

If you want the whole experience, by all means follow the story from beginning to end and buy the package for a $2 discount. If you're just into the tech, you could probably skip the movie and get away with $5 for the motion and $4 for the three-dimensional. But do check out at least one of the attractions up here; this is state-of-the-art entertainment. Call 702/262-4000 for current times and prices.

Las Vegas Cyber Speedway

The most extensive and sophisticated virtual-reality attraction in Las Vegas is at the Sahara. The $15 million, 40,000-square-foot Speedworld consists of two three-dimensional motion theaters (depicting an Indy race and an off-road race), along with 24 three-quarter-scale Indy-racecar simulators, each in its own private bay. The cars are mounted on hypersensitive hydraulic platforms, surrounded by 20-foot-wide, 133-degree, wrap-around screens of the racecourse and 15 speakers. The screen displays the track whizzing by as you speed around it. The sound effects include the roar of acceleration, the screech of rubber against pavement, even the crunch of metal against metal). If you're the kind that has to experience all the latest high-tech thrill rides, this is the new one for you. Open Mon.–Thurs. noon–9 P.M., Fri.–Sat. until 10 P.M., and Sun. 11 A.M.–9 P.M. The 3-D motion show costs $15, the race costs $10 (it's eight minutes long).

Cinema Ride

The newest type of motion simulator combines seats that move in synchronization to the action with a three-dimensional screen. You climb into a compact theater, then go for a three-minute thrill ride on a computer-generated animated chase. There are six different software packages, of which a couple are showing at any given time. Cinema Ride is on the basement arcade level at the Forum Shops at Caesars. Open daily 10 A.M.–midnight, $4.

Race for Atlantis

This is the most sophisticated digital thrill in Las Vegas: state-of-the-art motion simulation, three-dimensional computer graphics, and the largest dome-shaped IMAX screen ever built. Located in the new wing of the Forum Shops at Caesars, you enter a five-story lobby with a 30-foot tall statue of Neptune battling a sea dragon to buy your tickets, then climb some stairs and follow a corridor around to the Heavens Room. This is a 6,000-square-foot antechamber with a cloud-simulating fog machine, otherworldly sculpture, lightning and thunder, and a bridge with fiber-optic cables. From there you're ushered into an inner sanctum for a five-minute pre-show orientation to the headgear and plot. The headset comes with a personal sound system and special goggles that receive a synchronized infrared signal from the IMAX projection system that enhances the three-dimensional effects. Then it's into the theater. You strap in, don the headset, and the ride begins. The hydraulics are tight for the 27-seat six-axis platforms. The immersion in the virtual space is total: vents even blow air to further simulate motion. If you can only catch one of the digital thrill rides in Las Vegas, this is the one. Open Sun.–Thurs. 10 A.M.–11 P.M., Fri.–Sat. 10 A.M.–midnight; $9.50.

Time Traveler 3D at The Venetian

The Venetian has hopped on the cinema ride bandwagon. Escape from Venice takes riders for eight-and-a-half minutes back through time to a secret carnival in old Venice. From there, it's on to Egypt to try and defeat the curse of King Tut's Tomb. Besides Time Traveler: The 3D Ride, there are four additional 3D adventures. Blue Magic is a 16-minute underwater romp with fish, stingrays, and other creatures. It's the only nonmotion ride, which is good for those who like 3-D but not motion simulators. Other rides include Red Hot Planet, a journey to Mars; Escape from Nemo, an underwater expedition, and the haunting Doomed Castle. Open daily 10 A.M.–11 P.M. and until midnight on weekends. Tickets are $7 each; combination packages are available, 702/733-0545.

Merlin's Magic Motion Machine Film Ride

Located in the Fantasy Faire Midway at Excalibur, Merlin offers an interactive ride-movie for kids of all ages (you must be 42-inches tall to ride though). Open daily 11 A.M.–10:30 P.M., closed 8–9 P.M., $4.

Star Trek: The Experience

The Paramount-Hilton Star Trek attraction is a combination museum, motion simulator, and interactive shows. Buy your tickets up to three days in advance from ticket windows in the Hilton's futuristic Space Quest Casino. You enter a Star Trek museum, winding around a long corridor (which doubles as the line for the ride); check out the Star Trek timeline, exhibits and displays, and clips on video monitors large and small. With four television series and eight movies produced over the past 30-some years, the range of depth of the Star Trek universe is amazing. The "ride" consists of five separate environments (including two motion simulators); the premise is that you've been kidnapped by Klingons and beamed onto the bridge of the Enterprise; it's up to the crew (live actors) to get you home. The Experience also continues to keep a current stardate with Trekkies by opening new attractions. The new Borg Invasion 4D attraction is an interactive state-of-the-art theater that incorporates both live actors and on-screen effects to "assimilate" spectators into the Borg Collective. Open daily 11 A.M.–11 P.M. $24.99.

LIGHT SHOWS

Las Vegas and light shows are synonymous. Glitter Gulch downtown is so bright that you can't tell day from night. The five-mile-long stretch of neon art against the black desert sky along the Strip is, of course, the famous cliche. Long neon tubing, in brilliant reds, whites, blues, and pinks, borders the edges of shopping centers, car washes, apartments, and restaurants. And it's not just the designs and colors and size and intensity of the lights. The latest and brightest rage is electronic billboards—programmable colors, graphics, dissolves and splashes, and animated effects. And topping it all off are the huge, square, black-on-white marquees, advertising everything from buffets to burlesque. And all the outside glass reflects the effects in a cosmic double exposure.

Fremont Street Experience

The greatest light show of them all, in Las Vegas and arguably the world, is known as the Fremont Street Experience. Picture this: It's nighttime in downtown Las Vegas, and splashy neon signs illuminate what looks like a street carnival in Glitter Gulch. A crowd of bystanders mills around, waiting. People stream out of the casinos onto Fremont Street to join the throng—everyone peering or pointing skyward, in anticipation. Suddenly, somewhere, someone flicks a switch and Glitter Gulch's whole flamboyant facade is simply shut off. For a moment, it's dark. But then a multisensory high-fidelity kaleidoscopic fanfaronade kicks on. A colossal overhead graphic-display system delivers state-of-the-art animation and acoustic effects via two million lightbulbs and 540,000 watts of sound.

The whole high-tech hullabaloo consists of a four-block-long, 90-foot-tall silver canopy supported by 16 columns and 43,000 struts, 2.1 million polychromatic lightbulbs, and 208 concert-quality speakers. In addition to the canopy, FSE has a pedestrian mall, complete with food and merchandise booths, and a 1,500-car parking garage. The main attraction is the collection of four different six-minute musicals, performed on the hour between 6 and 11 P.M. For a recording of all the special events scheduled for the promenade in conjunction with the light show, call 702/678-5777.

Another good light show in a historic vein is the Neon Museum, ostensibly an outdoor collection of old neon that no longer has a home atop a Las Vegas casino or building. Las Vegas doesn't often hold onto its past, so this little walking tour of old signs such as the Hacienda Horse and Rider is an intriguing sight—and it's free. The museum is located at the Fremont Street Experience; 702/387-NEON, www.neonmuseum.org.

Animatronic Shows

Free shows combine animatronics (moving statues) with lasers, film and video, and dancing waters; The **Festival Fountain** at the Forum Shops opens with laser lightning and stereo thunder that awakens Bacchus, god of wine. He introduces Plutus, who infuses the dancing waters with merry-go-round music; Venus, who blots out the sun and conjures laser constellations on the ceiling; and Apollo, who strums his fiberoptic lyre strings. Finally, Bacchus bows out with a burp.

The **Atlantis** show in the Forum Shops is qualitatively superior to the Festival Fountain. There are four animatronic characters (the king of Atlantis, his son and daughter, and a monster); the movements of the son and daughter are more fluid and lifelike than the Festival statues. The special effects, as well, are more fully rendered: steam and mist, 20-foot flames, 30-foot dancing waters, and 18 overhead screens.

Another show worth the trek is encased at Sam's Town's spectacular Central Park indoor atrium. The **Sunset Stampede** is presented at 2, 6, 8, and 10 P.M. The dancing waters flare over 100 feet high, synchronized with lasers and a stirring soundtrack. The animatronic wolf steals the show.

Fire and Water Shows

The quintessential show is the 54-foot manmade **volcano** that fronts the Mirage, which erupts every 15 minutes nightly (as long as it's not too windy) from 7 P.M. to midnight. Flames spew from the crater, big speakers roar, and red water flows down the slopes.

Next door at Treasure Island is the new **Sirens of TI** show, which replaced the tired Pirate show. Twenty stuntmen and scantily clad women manning two 60-foot-tall ships duke it out nightly (again, weather cooperating) every 90 minutes starting at 7 P.M. and continuing through 11:30 P.M. Arrive 30 minutes early for a good viewing spot.

Another traffic-stopper is the commanding water feature at the Bellagio, in which dancing fountains are choreographed to opera, classical, and whimsical music. The waters at Bellagio erupt every half hour daily from 3 P.M.–7 P.M., then every 15 minutes from 7 P.M.–midnight.

Sky Parade

Las Vegas's newest free spectacle, the Masquerade Show in the Sky, happens every hour daily from

3 P.M. to 9:30 P.M. in the Masquerade Village wing of the Rio. Singers, dancers, stiltwalkers, and bungee swingers, all decked out in outrageous Mardi Gras–style costumes, perform on the main stage, while parade floats—riverboat, teacup, hot-air balloon, swan gondola, and giant interactive two-faced head—circle the casino suspended from a track on the ceiling. You might feel like Hunter S. Thompson at Circus Circus in 1970, pop-eyed from the Big Top bedlam overhead in the midst of which high-stakes players gamble oblivious to the ambient madness.

Best Views

The "cheap aerials" have improved dramatically over the last few years. Before, your best overviews were found at the **Centerstage Restaurant,** in a tinted dome in the front of Plaza Hotel, with seats looking straight down Glitter Gulch; and the **Ranch Steakhouse** on the 24th floor of the Horseshoe hotel tower, complete with a outdoor glass elevator.

These days, you can get really high on the panoramas. Seen from all over the valley is the observation pod at the top of the Stratosphere Tower (850 feet high). The best way to take it all in is to eat at the **Top of the World** restaurant on the 106th floor, a 360-seat and 360-degree revolving restaurant. You can hop a ride on the high-speed double-decker elevators to the top for $6, or you can make a reservation for dinner at the restaurant ($15 minimum) and ride up the special-guest elevator for free. And as long as you're up there for the view, you might as well ride the Big Shot.

An even better view—lower, closer, more central—awaits at the top of the new Rio hotel tower on the bilevel decks outside the **Voodoo Cafe** restaurant and bar. It's free just to ride the outdoor glass elevator for the view.

The newest aerial highlight to hit the Strip is Paris's Eiffel Tower Experience. Nine dollars ($12 on weekends) buys you the right to be whisked up 50 stories in a glass elevator, to an observation deck offering jaw-dropping views. At a lower elevation, but still affording an excellent panorama, the Eiffel Tower Restaurant hovers 100 feet above the Strip and features a piano bar and Parisian fare that doesn't come cheap.

MUSEUMS, VEGAS-STYLE

As with everything in Las Vegas, the museum scene ranges from high-brow to high-camp. This is the home of both the Guggenheim and Liberace. You can find some of the finest art in the world at one place, then walk next door and fill up on kitsch. Touring museums in Vegas is anything but boring.

Liberace Museum

Liberace embodies the heart and soul of Las Vegas, in life and in death. Born in Wisconsin in 1919, third of four children in a musical family, Walter Valentino Liberace (who legally assumed the one name, Liberace, in 1950, and was known as "Lee" to his friends) was a prodigy pianist at age seven, a concert boy wonder at 14, and first played Sin City at 23. From then on, he was a one-man walking advertisement for the extravagance, flamboyance, and uninhibited tastelessness usually associated with the town he loved so much. Like Las Vegas's surface image, Liberace's costumes began as a means of standing out; then he had to keep topping himself with increasingly outrageous gimmicks. Along the way, he became one of the most popular entertainers of all time: "Mr. Showmanship" racked up six gold records.

The Liberace Museum is the most popular tourist attraction in Las Vegas, outside of the casinos. The main building preserves Liberace's costumes: Uncle Sam hot pants; suits made of ostrich feathers, rhinestones, and beads; and massive fur capes. Also on display is the world's largest rhinestone (50 pounds). The library building houses family photos, miniature pianos, silver, china, cut glass, gold records, and historical data. The gallery contains several antique pianos, a 50,000-rhinestone Baldwin, a mirror-tiled Rolls Royce, a rhinestone car (with matching toolbox), and a 1940s English taxi.

A gift shop in the main building sells Liberace albums, tapes, videos, postcards, photos, and other memorabilia. The museum is located at 1775 E. Tropicana just east of Maryland Pkwy., 702/798-5595. Open Mon.–Sat. 10 A.M.–5 P.M., Sun. noon–4 P.M. Admission is $12, $8 seniors and children under 12—steep, but tax-deductible as a contribution to the nonprofit Libèrace Foundation for Creative and Performing Arts.

Guggenheim Hermitage Museum

The Venetian on the Las Vegas Strip hosts the Guggenheim Hermitage Museum, a joint venture of the world renowned State Hermitage Museum in St. Petersburg, Russia, and the Solomon R. Guggenheim Foundation in New York. The gallery houses masterpieces drawn from their permanent collections from around the world.

The exhibits rotate, but past shows included the work of such masters as Rubens, Velasquez, Picasso, Renoir, Gauguin, Monet, Pollack, Van Gogh, Chagall, and others. Check www.venetian.com/guggenheim for the current exhibit or call 702/414-2440. Admission is $15 for adults, $12 seniors and Nevada residents, $11 for students with ID, and $7 for children 6–12, free for kids under 6. An audio guide is included with the price of admission. Open daily 9:30 A.M.–8:30 P.M. The museum sometimes closes early for special events. If you plan to visit the museum on a particular date, call 702/414-2493 to check for that day's closing time.

Bellagio Gallery of Fine Art

Located in an elegant setting at the Bellagio Hotel, this gallery features exhibits from various collections throughout the country on a rotating basis. The exhibit hours are typically 9 A.M.–9 P.M. daily, but be sure to call in advance. Located inside the Bellagio, 3600 Las Vegas Blvd. S., 702/693-7871. Admission is $15 for adults and $12 for students, children, and seniors.

The Wynn Collection of Fine Art

Steve Wynn's private collection of fine art has made more Las Vegas re-appearances than Lance Burton. The latest home for the multimillion dollar collection is being built as part of the massive new Wynn Las Vegas Resort, set to open in April 2005 (on the site of the old Desert Inn). The collection includes works by Matisse, Van Gogh, Cezanne, Modigliani, Gauguin, and Warhol. An audio tour gives patrons background information about each piece in the collection. While hours and admission prices have yet to be set, previously the collection was viewable daily for $6 to $10. For more information, call 702/733-4300 or visit www.wynnlasvegas.com.

Madame Tussaud's

More than 100 celebrities with fixed waxen smiles await the visitor at this spin-off of the famous London Museum. The likenesses are truly amazing; in some instances the wax figure looks more alive than the real thing. Set in five different theatrical settings ranging from sports arenas to concert venues, the museum provides a nice diversion before hitting the slots and attempting to win your own fame and fortune. The museum, located at the entryway to The Venetian, 702/367-1847, is open daily 10 A.M.–10 P.M., $19.95 adults; $14.50 seniors, students and Nevada residents.

Guinness World of Records Museum

This small museum on the Strip features photographic, typographic, video, audio, and slide-show exhibits of world records: the tallest, fattest, oldest, and most-married men; longest-necked women; smallest bicycle; videos of dominoes; slides of the greatest engineering projects; and an informative display of Las Vegas firsts and foremosts, among others. The museum is located at 2780 Las Vegas Blvd. S., just north of Circus Circus, 702/792-0640, open daily 9 A.M.–5 P.M., $6.50 adults; $5.50 seniors, military and students; $4.50 for children 4–12; free for children under 4.

Elvis-A-Rama Museum

Elvis has definitely not left this building. This museum is devoted to $3.5 million worth of Elvis memorabilia. This quirky spot, featuring Elvis's customized purple Lincoln, his army uniform, and his peacock jumpsuit, rates high on the kitsch factor, but can be a kick for true Elvis fans. Concert footage, photos, and costumes chronicle the King's life from the early beginnings to his washed-up Vegas days. Be sure to time your visit to catch a live Elvis tribute performance, daily at 2 P.M., 4 P.M., and 7 P.M. The museum is open daily 10 A.M.–8 P.M. It's located one block off the Strip behind Fashion Show Mall at 3401 Industrial Rd., 702/309-7200.

Admission is $9.95, $7.95 seniors; performances cost an extra $10, but combination packages are available.

Casino Legends Hall of Fame

If you're looking for some gaming history, the Casino Legends Hall of Fame at the Tropicana is a good place to start. The museum traces the history of the Las Vegas Strip, showcasing the world's largest collection of casino memorabilia that ranges from rare celebrity photos and video clips to costumes and jewels. Open daily 9 A.M.–9 P.M., admission is $6.95 for adults and $5.95 for seniors.

KIDS STUFF

While Las Vegas is a big playground for adults, it also has some good fun for the children. Some of it is even—gasp!—educational. Just don't let the kids know.

M&M's World

This museum of sorts is located on the Strip in the Showcase Mall, next to the MGM Grand; most kids find the twinkling M&M's perched out front too tough to resist. While there's plenty of merchandise, you'll also find some eye candy, including a free 3-D movie shown every 20 minutes and other of interactive exhibits. Open Sun.–Thurs. 9 A.M.–6 P.M. and Fri.–Sat. 9 A.M.–8 P.M.

Game Works

This entertainment complex offers a wide variety of activities for game lovers of all ages. The multithemed attraction areas offer more than 200 of the hottest games, a high-energy bar area, and a restaurant. Located inside the Showcase Mall next to the MGM, open Sun.–Thurs. 10 A.M.–midnight, Fri.–Sat. 10 A.M.–2 A.M.; admission is free and rides cost $0.50–3 each.

Lion Habitat

A pride of magnificent lions lounge in a terrarium-type habitat overlooking the MGM casino in this eye-catching attraction. The big cats seem non-plussed as visitors stroll up to and under the glass, where the lions yawn, play, and mostly sleep in

their attractive, albeit artificial, environment. Longtime cat handler, trainer, and expert Keith Evans oversees the group of up to six cats that are escorted into and out of the environment (the cats actually live at Evans' private habitat). The see-through tunnel under the exhibit is one of the most popular spots for cat-watching, and, naturally, there's a gift shop attached. At the MGM Grand, open daily 11 A.M.–11 P.M., free.

Siegfried and Roy's Secret Garden and Dolphin Habitat

There are two distinct attractions here: the Secret Garden, where you might catch the white tigers and lions lounging in a lush tropical atmosphere; and the 2.5-million-gallon dolphin habitat, a more education-oriented endeavor in which dolphins are studied rather than taught to perform for the public. The white cats in the habitat remain a popular attraction, despite the mauling of Roy Horn by one of the cats during a show in 2004. Visitors also will catch a glimpse of a four-ton elephant and other cats, such as panthers and leopards.

Educational programs and guided tours are available. Admission is $12, free for children under 10. Open daily 10 A.M.–5:30 P.M. For a free glimpse at the tigers, check out the open-air White Tiger Habitat inside the casino, where the cats frolic in their pool and lounge on the white rocks.

Las Vegas Mini Gran Prix

This place is packed with Gran Prix Cars, Sprint cars, and even kiddie cars (for tots ages 4 and under). There's also a huge slide, arcade games, and inexpensive food. Located at 1401 N. Rainbow Blvd., 702/259-7000, $5.50.

Shark Reef at Mandalay Bay

Big-fish lovers can explore the depths of Shark Reef, which houses 100 different species of sharks, including a sand tiger nurse, lemon, and blacktip reef. The latest addition is a hammerhead (a rarity for captivity), but the extensive attraction also has rays, a massive collection of colorful tropical fish, and reptiles. Located inside Mandalay Bay, open daily 10 A.M.–11 P.M. Admis-

Mars family cactus garden

sion is $16 for adults, $10 children 12 and younger, 702/632-4555.

Ethel M's Desert (and Dessert)

The M stands for *Mars,* as in Mars bars (along with Milky Ways, 3 Musketeers, and M&M's). The Mars family of Las Vegas is consistently ranked in the top five richest families in the world by Forbes, with around $9 billion worth of assets. If you feel like taking a ride after lunch or dinner, head out to this chocolate factory and cactus garden (way out E. Tropicana, right on Mountain Vista, left on Sunset Way, left onto Cactus Garden Dr.). The inside tour (self-guided, free) takes you past big picture windows overlooking the bright factory, with workers and machines turning and churning, then out into the tasting room. Outside is an enjoyable 2.5-acre cactus garden, with indigenous desert flora: purple pancake, horse crippler, hedgehog, saguaro, yucca, cholla, Spanish bayonet, and 345 other species. Check out the Home Demonstration Garden for ideas on starting one, then make your purchases at the Cactus Shoppe. Ethel M's is open daily 8:30 A.M.–7 P.M.; it makes the chocolate weekday mornings; 702/458-8864 or 702/435-2655 (chocolate shop).

Las Vegas Demonstration Gardens at the Springs Preserves

More than 1,000 varieties of plants and rock gardens are on display at this 2.5-acre botanical garden, the most beautiful desert landscaping in the city. The Las Vegas Valley Water District, which supplies most of Las Vegas with its water, has designed and created the Demonstration Gardens as a means of instructing people in the art of Xeriscaping, or the conservation of water through efficient landscaping. Here you can inspect plants in 11 themed gardens; it'll quickly dispel the mistaken belief that desert landscaping is limited to cactus and rock. The gardens also host a variety of wildlife, including nighttime visits by a kit fox searching for a meal, numerous birds feeding on the insect life, and three varieties of lizard. The gardens average 1,000 visitors a week; when you visit, don't forget to sign the guest register, as the funding for this beautiful depends on the number of visitors that make it through its doors.

The most common thing to do here is to take the 20-minute self-guided tour, but the gardens also have an amphitheater where classes and other community events are held. The resource center also offers Xeriscape-design workshops, landscaping classes and lectures, irrigation workshops, experts to answer all your landscaping questions, and group tours. Free pamphlets and information sheets are available. Located at 3701 W. Alta Dr. (one block east of Valley View Blvd.), 702/258-3205. Open daily 8 A.M.–5 P.M.

The Old Fort

This tiny museum is the oldest building in Las Vegas. The adobe remnant, constructed by Mormon missionaries in 1855, was part of their original settlement, which they abandoned in 1858. It then served as a store, barracks, and shed on the Gass/Stewart Ranch. After that, the railroad leased the old fort to various tenants, including the Bureau of Reclamation, which stabilized and rebuilt the shed to use as a concrete-testing laboratory for Hoover Dam. In 1955, the railroad sold the old fort to the Elks, who in 1963 bulldozed the whole wooden structure (except the little remnant) into the ranch swimming pool and torched it. The shed was bought back by the city in 1971.

Since then a number of preservation societies have helped keep the thing in place. A tour guide presents the history orally, while display boards give it to you visually. The Old Fort is at the corner of Las Vegas Blvd. N. and Washington (in the northwest corner of the Cashman Field parking lot), 702/382-6510; open daily 8 A.M.–4:30 P.M., $2. Your special effort to visit this place will not go unrewarded—it's immensely refreshing to see some preservation of the past in this city of the ultimate now.

Lied Discovery Children's Museum

This museum features 130 exciting, thought-provoking, and fun exhibits. Highlights include a human-performance area with ski, baseball, and football machines to test athletic skills; a money display to teach about savings accounts, writing checks, and using ATMs; and telescopes atop the eight-story science tower. At the What Can I Be exhibit, kids can look at and play with career ideas. A radio and TV station, a newspaper office, a bubble machine, a space shuttle display, and 120 other attractions, along with a museum

store and restaurant, are all contained in the 40,000-square-foot facility. The museum is within the Las Vegas Central Library building, 833 N. Las Vegas Blvd., 702/382-3445; open Tues.–Sun. 10 A.M.–5 P.M. Admission is $6 adults, $5 for kids and seniors.

Las Vegas Natural History Museum

Across the street from the Lied is this wildlife museum, which displays a large collection of stuffed animals in realistic dioramas: North American predator species, African prey species, a whole room full of birds, another whole room full of dinosaurs and hands-on exhibits such as a fossil sandbox, and a live shark exhibit. Two leopard sharks and a banded cat shark swim in a 3,000-gallon aquarium; they're fed shrimp and squid Monday, Wednesday, and Saturday at 2 P.M. Kids chosen from the crowd help feed them. A new exhibit depicts wildlife found within 100 miles of Las Vegas with mounted animals in dioramas, murals, and landscapes. The museum is at 900 Las Vegas Blvd. N., 702/384-3466; open daily 9 A.M.–4 P.M. Admission is $6 adults, $5 military and senior, $3 children 4–12.

Southern Nevada Zoological Park

This could be the "wildest" place in Las Vegas, a shaded very personal little zoo, with an offbeat charm and a lot of heart. Lion, tiger, cougar, monkeys, bird boutique, fine arts gallery, petting zoo with pygmy goats—all just off a busy street in northwest Las Vegas, with Siegfried and Roy's mission-style mansion just around the corner (4200 Vegas Dr. at Valley). The zoo is located at 1775 N. Rancho Dr., 702/648-5955; open daily 9 A.M.–4:30 P.M., $7 adults, $2 children under 12 and seniors.

Marjorie Barrick Museum of Natural History

This museum on the university grounds is a good place to bone up on local flora, fauna, and artifacts. First study the local flora in the arboretum outside the museum entrance, then step inside for the fauna: small rodents, big snakes, lizards, tortoises, gila monster, iguana, chuckwalla, gecko, spiders, beetles, cockroaches, the most extensive collection of birds in Nevada, even a polar bear. Wander through the art gallery into some graphic Las Vegas history, such as the famous painting of Frémont at Las Vegas Springs in 1844, the view of Las Vegas Creek both in 1900 and 1978, and Miss Atomic Blast 1957. Display cases are full of native baskets, kachinas, masks, weaving, pottery, and jewelry. There are also Mexican dance masks, traditional Guatemalan textiles, and an extensive exhibit of Tom and Jerry cels, backgrounds, and musical scores (donated by creator Chuck Jones). The centerpiece is a rough skeleton of an ichthyosaur, a whale-sized marine dinosaur (Nevada's state fossil). The museum, 702/895-3381, is open Mon.–Fri. 8 A.M.–4:45 P.M., Sat. 10 A.M.–2 P.M., donations appreciated. To find it, drive onto the UNLV campus on Harmon Street and follow it around to the right, then turn left into the museum parking lot (signposted).

Nevada State Museum and Historical Society

This is a comfortable and enjoyable place to spend a hour or two studying Mojave and Spring Mountains ecology, southern Nevada history, and local art. Three changing galleries might be exhibiting anything from photography of the neon night or black-and-white desert to Nevada textiles or early telephone technology. The Hall of Biological Science shows interesting exhibits on life in the desert: butterflies, cholla and cactus, reptiles, and the bighorn sheep centerpiece. Also learn here how the Spring Mountains (Mt. Charleston) are a "biological island surrounded by a sea of desert." The Hall of Regional History contains breezy graphic displays on mining and atomic testing, and eye-catching photos of nuclear tests, blasts, holes, Hoover Dam construction, politics, ranching, and native Americans. The museum is in the southwest corner of Lorenzi Park, off Twin Lakes Drive, 702/486-5205. Open daily 9 A.M.–5 P.M.; admission $4 adults, $3 seniors.

Imperial Palace Auto Collection

IP owner Ralph Engelstad acquired much of this collection, once owned by Bill Harrah, when Holiday Inn Corp. bought Harrah's and sold off the majority of Harrah's cars in the early '80s. Among

some real interesting cars here are the custom 1928 Delage limousine built for King Rama VII of Siam (Thailand) and the 1948 Chrysler convertible with the cowhead-and-horn emblem. The 1947 Tucker has a third-eye headlight that turns with the steering wheel, and the 1955 Mercedes sports car comes with factory-fitted luggage. You'll ho-hum over all the Rolls-Royces, Cadillacs, and Duesenbergs, but Hitler's bulletproof Mercedes parade car will raise some eyebrows, as will the half-dozen prototype motorcycles. Of course, the curators couldn't forget the 1954 Chrysler Imperial. Some of these cars are restored by prison convicts in a program introduced by the administrator of the collection; some "graduates" of the program are hired once paroled. Walk through the Imperial Palace casino past the elevators and go all the way to the back; other elevators whisk you up to the collection, on the fifth floor of the parking structure; 702/731-3311. Open daily 9:30 A.M.–8 P.M.; free coupons are ubiquitous (even at the entrance to the hotel), so you probably won't have to pay the $6.95 adult admission, $3 and up or 12 and under and seniors.

Nevada Banking Museum

All large industries should follow First Interstate's lead and provide such free, informative displays of historical tools of their trades. The exhibits trace banking in Nevada, from checks written before statehood to consolidation in 1981 of 16 original Farmers and Merchants, and Nation banks into First Interstate Bank of Nevada. The main display exhibits currency issued by local Nevada banks in the early 1900s. No less thought-provoking are the collections of letterheads, passbooks, liberty bonds, CDs, financial statements, silver commemorative bars, gaming tokens and chips, Carson City coins, and old teller machines. Don't miss this one. Located at 3800 Howard Hughes Pkwy., in the landmark First Interstate building, off Sands Ave. at the corner of Paradise; 702/791-6373. Open 9 A.M.–4 P.M.; free.

Las Vegas Chinatown Plaza

This pleasant little shopping and dining complex is a good place to absorb some non-casino culture. The Asian architecture of the plaza is packed with nine authentic Chinese restaurants, herbal shops, jade stores, furniture, and many other retail outlets. The 99 Ranch Market features Asian delicacies and spices. The plaza also hosts a number of special events, the most notable of which is the celebration of the Chinese New Year. Located at 4255 Spring Mountain Rd., 702/221-8448, www.lvchinatown.com.

Casinos

DOWNTOWN

Jackie Gaughan's Plaza

Start your tour of downtown Las Vegas at Jackie Gaughan's Plaza, a 1,000-room hotel-casino (second largest downtown) with a stunning location facing Glitter Gulch. This is the "zero-zero" point, where the original town site auction was held in 1905, and from which all street numbers and directions emanate, as well as the site of the original art-deco Union Pacific railroad depot. The Amtrak depot is tucked away in the back; a large railroad mural is painted on the wall between the depot and casino. The Greyhound station is next door. The Centerstage Restaurant overlooks the Fremont Street Experience light show. Here are the best nickel video poker in Las Vegas; penny slots provide the locals an easy place to cash in their jars of copper. 1 Main Street at Fremont, 702/386-2110 or 800/634-6575, double room rates $40–90.

Las Vegas Club

Across the street on the northwest corner of Main and Fremont is this venerable casino, which was opened by Southern California gamblers right after gambling was legalized in 1931. A 224-room hotel tower was added in 1980, and as part of downtown's expansion boom triggered by the Fremont Street Experience, a 200-room tower, new casino wing, and two new restaurants were opened in late 1996. The Las Vegas Club also advertises the most liberal blackjack rules in town. You can double down on any two, three, or four cards. You can split and resplit any pairs, and surrender half your bet on the first two cards. And you win on any six cards that don't bust. The Las Vegas Club also displays a large collection of sports memorabilia. 18 East Fremont St., 702/385-1664 or 800/634-6532, double room rates $45–150.

Golden Gate

Miller's Hotel, across the street on the opposite corner of Fremont and Main from the Las Vegas Club, was the first downtown establishment to receive water in 1905. Fifty years later, this casino became the Golden Gate. The Gate is famous for it's $0.99 shrimp cocktails, a concept introduced in 1959. It's the best, and most venerable, meal deal in Vegas. The Gate has been restored to its original condition; it's the only place in town where you get the feeling you're staying in a real old-fashioned downtown. The 106 small rooms are tastefully decorated, comfortable, and affordable. 1 Fremont St., 702/382-6300 or 800/426-1906, double room rates $35–80.

Golden Nugget

When Steve Wynn (Las Vegas's top celebrity owner) bought, renovated, and expanded it in the 1970s, the 1940s Golden Nugget once again became downtown's centerpiece, as well as its largest hotel (with 1,900 rooms spread over two blocks). The exterior features polished white marble and brass trim. The lobby showcases marble and etched and leafed glass. The highlight here is the 61-pound, 11-ounce gold nugget (displayed around the corner from the front desk by the boutique entrance)—largest in public view in the world. Right under it is the second largest; both were found in Victoria, Australia. The buffet is one of the best in town, and Lillie Langtry's serves gourmet Szechuan and Cantonese cuisine. And the pool is the biggest and best downtown with personal cabanas available. In early 2004, the Golden Nugget changed hands again (this time to Travelocity.com entrepreneurs), but it appears the property will continue to shine downtown. 129 East Fremont St., 702/385-7111 or 800/634-3454, double room rates $65–350.

Las Vegas

DOWNTOWN
LAS VEGAS

MAIN STREET STATION
CALIFORNIA
VEGAS VIC
BINION'S HORSESHOE
GOLDEN GATE
GOLDEN NUGGET
FREMONT
FOUR QUEENS
FITZGERALDS
LADY LUCK
NEONOPOLIS
FREMONT STREET EXPERIENCE
PLAZA

0   500 yds
0   500 m

P Parking Structure

© AVALON TRAVEL PUBLISHING, INC.

GAMBLING

While gaudy shows and kitschy museums are certainly part of the Vegas experience, the main attraction in town is gambling. All over town, casinos post the notice, "Know when to stop before you start," but too few people heed the warning. A strategy that works for many is setting aside a certain amount of money each day for gambling. Unfortunately, it's very hard to stop; most of the games are fun, bordering on addictive, and the urge to keep playing until you win is hard to resist. Once you've played a few hands or spun a few reels on slot machines at the major casinos on the Strip, you may want to try your luck at a couple of the casinos frequented by locals, like those run by the Station chain (Green Valley Ranch, Palace Station, etc.). Many of them advertise looser slots and offer promotions such as two-for-one dinners or inexpensive buffets to attract gamblers to their off-the-Strip locations.

Whether you decide to gamble at a casino on the Strip, downtown, or elsewhere, it helps to be familiar with the variety of games. Many casinos offer free lessons on how to play blackjack, craps, roulette, poker, and baccarat. The following is a rundown of the major games you will find at all casinos.

Baccarat and Mini-Baccarat

Baccarat is played with eight decks of cards. It tends to be a high-stakes game with minimums starting at $20 and up. It's usually played in an upscale area of the casino with dealers wearing tuxedos. The game is played with six to eight cards dealt from a shoe. Before cards are dealt, players bet on the player or the banker, and each gets two cards. The hand closest to nine is the winner, and zero (baccarat) is the worst score. There is no win on a tie.

Mini-baccarat is played at a blackjack-style table with smaller minimum bets. It's played like baccarat except the bettor doesn't deal the cards. Wagers can be made on the player, the banker, or for a tie.

Big Six Wheel

The Big Six Wheel is the game you are least likely to win. Looking like a big carnival wheel with dollar bills inserted, it offers players a chance to bet a dollar and up on $1, $2, $5, $10, and $20 symbols. You may also place a bet on the joker and house symbols. If your number comes up after the spin, you win that amount. In the unlikely event you happen to hit a joker or house logo, it pays 40-to-1.

Blackjack

Also called 21, blackjack is the most popular casino table game. The object is to have your cards total closer to 21 than the dealer, without going over. Players play against the house, rather than against each other. It's one of the best games to play since your odds of winning are greater than if you play a slot machine, roulette, or other game of chance. According to conventional strategy, if the dealer has 7, 8, 9, 10, or ace showing on his or her hand, it's advisable to hit (take additional cards) until your hand reaches 17. If the dealer has 2, 3, 4, 5 or 6 showing, don't hit if you have 12–16, or you could bust (go over 21). If you are dealt a pair (two 7s, two 9s, whatever) you can split them and play two separate hands if you choose. This doubles your stake so that you have two separate bets on each hand. Numerous books have been published on blackjack strategy, but one of the most important rules you need to know is that casinos frown on card counters. If you are caught counting cards, you may be barred from playing in that particular casino.

Craps

Craps is one of the more social games in the casino as groups of players gather around a table and whoop and scream as numbers come up on the dice. A shooter rolls two dice, and if the dice totals 7 or 11, those on everyone who has a bet on Pass wins automatically, and everyone with a bet on Don't Pass loses. (A pass line bet pays even money.) If the come-out roll is 2, 3, or 12, the shooter and all Pass bettors lose. Any other come-out roll becomes "the point," and a marker is placed in that position on the table. The shooter must then throw the point again before throwing a 7. If he succeeds, Pass wins and Don't Pass loses. (Betting on the Don't Pass Line is the opposite of betting on the Pass Line.) Don't Pass bettors win on 2 or 3. If the first roll is a 12, no one wins. After the come-out roll, players can also bet on Come and Don't Come. The next throw becomes the Come number, and a Come bet wins if the thrower throws that number before throwing a 7. To fully understand Pass Lines, points and other rules, it's best to take one of the instruction courses offered by the casinos. There are lots of betting options which makes craps one of the more interesting table games.

Keno

Keno may be played in the casino or in most Las Vegas coffee shops. Every 10 or 15 minutes a machine selects 20 out of 80 possible winning numbers. To play you must fill out a form for each game you wish to play and pick the numbers you hope will turn up on the keno board. A keno ticket is divided into numbers 1–40 on top and 41–80 on the bottom. You can pick 1–15 numbers on a straight ticket. Depending on what the payout table indicates, you could win $9 on a $1 bet if five out of eight numbers match, and more matching numbers mean more winnings. (The higher value you place on your bet, the more you win if your numbers come up.) A replay ticket simply uses the same numbers you played on the previous ticket. With a split ticket, you can bet different amounts on two or more groups of numbers. The amount you bet is divided among the number of groups you are playing. A keno runner will take your bet and return with your winning or losing ticket. Many people play $2 or $4 bets while they are having breakfast or lunch. The odds are heavily in favor of the house, but it can be a fun way to pass the time. There are myriad ways of picking numbers, splitting your bet, etc. The rules are posted at all tables with keno forms.

Let It Ride

Growing in popularity, Let It Ride can be played on tables with a dealer or at some video machines. Players play a basic five-card poker hand with the goal of getting the best possible hand. (In this game the dealer doesn't have a hand.) A player places three chips of equal value on the table and is dealt three cards. Two community cards are placed face down in the center. If you like your three cards you can place them under the first chip. If you are not happy with your cards, you can indicate to the dealer that you are taking back your bet by scraping the cards on the table toward you, or making a

brushing motion with your hand. If you let your bet ride, then it becomes part of your total bet for the hand. When all players have made a decision on their three cards, the dealer flips over the first community card, which counts as each player's fourth card. The procedure is repeated with the second community card completing everyone's hand. A pair of 10s pays even money, two pairs two-to-one, etc. A royal flush pays 1,000 to one.

Poker

Poker is one of the more popular casino games, and it's played much the same as you may play with your friends. But in Vegas the stakes are usually quite a bit higher. The dealer handles shuffling and dealing, and the house takes in 1–10 percent of each jackpot. Variations of poker include Seven-Card Stud, Hi-Lo Split, Hold-Em, Pai-Gow, and Caribbean Stud. In Pai-Gow, the joker is a wild card that can be used to complete a straight, flush, or royal flush. In Caribbean Stud, there is often a progressive jackpot that allows you to place a side bet separate from your hand.

Race and Sports Book

Sports betting in Vegas is huge. Bets on the Super Bowl alone account for $70 million annually. Most of the major casinos have large areas where players can bet on horse races and sports events. Horse races are broadcast live from many tracks, and fans can follow the action on large-screen televisions.

Roulette

One of the simpler games, roulette features a big wheel with numbers 00 through 36 marked in red and black. The 0 and 00 are green. It's possible to bet on 0 or 00 but neither counts as red or black, or odd or even, so they are colored green on the wheel. Players can bet on individual numbers, groups of numbers, red or black, or odd or even. Most roulette wheels in Vegas have a 00 layout. Choosing the right number pays off at 35 to 1. Choosing a pair of numbers pays 17 to 1, a block of three pays 11 to 1, etc. Experts advise against betting on 0, 00, 1, 2 and 3, which pay 5 to 1 and offer the worst odds on the table. Many gamblers say it is better to take part in fewer spins,

continued on next page

GAMBLING (cont'd)

place what you can afford to risk on an even money bet (odd/even or red/black) and walk away whether you win or lose. Roulette chips are purchased in stacks of 20 and you decide the value of each. Most roulette tables have a minimum value of each chip, such as $1. When you buy your chips, you tell the dealer if you want the value to be $1, $5, $20, etc.

Slots
Every casino has thousands of slot machines, and they've become even more popular since slot manufacturers introduced interactive games with bonus rounds based on popular games and TV shows like Monopoly, Wheel of Fortune, and The Munsters. Reel-type machines, also called one-arm bandits, have also been modernized to allow more extra spins, bells, and whistles. Some casinos offer penny and two-cent slots, but nickel, quarter, and dollar machines are the most widely played. Casinos also set aside high roller slot areas for those willing to pay $5 and up per pull. The odds of winning at a slot machine are set by the casino and vary widely depending on the establishment and machine. Your chance of hitting the jackpot at a $0.25 slot machine is likely to be 1 in 10,000 or smaller. The house advantage on slots varies 2–25 percent. Generally dollar machines pay back at a higher percentage than quarter or nickel machines, but you may win smaller sums (like $50–100) more frequently on nickel and quarter slots. Nonprogressive machines have fixed payback amounts for different winning combinations and pay lower bonuses more frequently. Progressive machines are linked to networks of other machines throughout Nevada and have the potential to pay off in millions of dollars but offer payouts less frequently.

If you plan to play the slots, take the time to join each casino's slot club. Even if you aren't a heavy gambler or big winner, the time you play can earn points toward free meals, free rooms, and other promotions that you will receive in the mail. Some casinos offer a percentage of money back for your first 30 minutes of play or they mail a certificate redeemable for $5–10 in free play on your next visit. Many of the casinos under the same management, such as MGM Mirage and ParkPlace Entertainment, have slot cards that may be used at sister casinos for cumulative points and rewards.

Video Poker
Video poker is played like regular poker, except you are playing against a machine. Several variations include Jacks or Better, Bonus Poker, Double Down, and Deuces Wild. Many of the machines allow players to choose the denomination played—$.05–1.00 per hand. Basically you are dealt a hand, choose which cards to keep or discard, and rack up winnings or losses depending on the cards you are dealt. One of the appeals to this game is that there isn't as much pressure playing a machine as sitting around a table with a bunch of other players.

Binion's Horseshoe Hotel
The city-block-long Horseshoe Hotel, which was opened in 1951 by Benny Binion, a bootlegger and boss gambler in Texas before achieving a certain legitimacy in Nevada. Benny Binion died in 1990 at the age of 85. His son Jack now runs the place. The Horseshoe is the quintessential old-time gambling hall, with low-limit blackjack, one of the top two poker rooms and the largest crap pit (14 tables) in town, food comps literally for the asking, and no house limit ($250,000 bets at the crap tables are not uncommon). The Horseshoe also sponsors the World Series of Poker ($10,000 buy-in for the finals and $1 million first prize).

The old Mint Hotel next door was acquired by the Horseshoe in 1988; the connecting casinos provide an interesting contrast between the Wild West motif of the early 1950s and the glitz of the mid-1960s. Ride the glass elevator to the Ranch Steakhouse on the 24th floor for the view.

The two snack bars, open daily 10 A.M.–10 P.M., serve some of the best and cheapest counter food anywhere (try the $2.99 turkey breast sandwich and the $1.49 bean soup of the day, which comes with a big slab of cornbread). 128 East Fremont St., 702/382-1600 or 800/237-6537, double room rates $45–70.

The Fremont

The Fremont epitomizes the old downtown carpet joint—a wonderfully long and narrow row of table games, crowded noisy slots, with red neon border lighting heightening the effect. Stand at one end and watch the players watch the cards, the dealers watch the players, the floormen watch the dealers, the pit bosses watch the floormen. The black eye-in-the-sky watches you. The Fremont opened in 1956 and was the tallest building in Nevada at the time. It embodied a combination of Strip classiness and downtown sensibility. Tony Roma's is there, and the Second Street Grill gourmet room is a real sleeper— excellent California-Hawaiian cuisine and rarely longer than a 15-minute wait even without reservations. 200 East Fremont St., 702/385-3232 or 800/634-6182, double room rates $35–85.

Four Queens

Across from the Fremont, the Four Queens opened in 1965, named for the owner's four daughters; it declared bankruptcy in 1995 and was taken over by the management team that rescued the Riviera from a similar fate a few years earlier. Twin 19-story towers boast 690 rooms, including some whirlpool-tub suites. 202 East Fremont St., 702/385-4011 or 800/634-6045, double room rates $60–200.

Fitzgeralds

Fitzgeralds started out as the Sundance Hotel, built in 1980 by Moe Dalitz when he was 84 years old. At 33 stories, it was the tallest building in Nevada for 14 years, until the Stratosphere Tower surpassed it. The Fitzgeralds Group bought it in 1987, and the casino was bought and completely remodeled in 1996 by the Holiday Inn franchise. It has two interesting views of the Fremont Street Experience: one from the wall of windows fronting the McDonald's on one side, the other from a unique second-story balcony, complete with patio furniture. 301 East Fremont St., 702/388-2400 or 800/274-LUCK, double room rates $50–100.

El Cortez

This hotel opened in late 1941 at the corner of Fremont and 6th, at a time when the downtown sidewalks stopped at 3rd. It had 71 rooms and a Wild West motif to compete with the first Strip resort, the El Rancho Vegas. Bugsy Siegel and the Berman brothers owned it for a while in the mid-1940s. The hotel changed hands a few times, until Jackie Gaughan acquired it in the early '80s. Though it's been expanded, the casino wing at the southwest corner is original—ancient history in Las Vegas; it also has the oldest original casino in Nevada. The king crab, steak, prime rib, and lobster dinners at Roberta's restaurant are good and cheap. 600 East Fremont St., 702/385-5200 or 800/634-6703, double room rates $25–60.

Lady Luck

This casino has grown from a tiny slot joint (opened in 1964) into a major downtown property. It's a comfortable place to gamble—bright, airy, with big picture windows on two sides. Its funbook is one of the best in town: Show an out-of-state ID and get a giant hot dog (free), plus gambling coupons, dining discounts, and a free room night. The Lady is also the best casino for low-limit comps. Put up $1,000 in the cage and bet $50 a hand for eight hours for a comped suite and meals. The Burgundy Room is recommendable. 206 N. 3rd St., 702/477-3000 or 800/523-9582, double room rates $45–120.

California

This is the original Boyd Group casino, opened in 1975, the same year that Sam Boyd, the late elder statesman of Las Vegas, organized his friends and family into the Boyd Group, now the Boyd Gaming Corporation, which runs Main Street Station, Sam's Town, the Stardust, the Fremont, and Joker's Wild and the Eldorado in Henderson. The California caters almost exclusively to the Hawaiian market and has a noticeably relaxed aloha vibe. It has almost 800 guest rooms, but the hotel is still booked solid 365 nights a year. The Pasta Pirate is one of the best restaurants downtown, with a great filet mignon special; the Redwood Bar and Grill is also excellent, with a 16-ounce porterhouse special. 12 Ogden Ave., 702/385-1222 or 800/634-6255, double room rates $50–70.

Main Street Station

This hotel has gone through a lot of changes over the years. The last incarnation named it Main Street Station, as it was opened in early 1992 by Bob Snow, the owner of the popular Church Street Station in downtown Orlando, Florida. Snow sunk millions into stained-glass, brass, marble, and hardwood appointments, plus a collection of antiques unequaled in Nevada casinodom, including Buffalo Bill Cody's private rail car. Unfortunately, Main Street Station lasted only eight months before it went into receivership. Boyd Corp. bought it a couple of years later. Main Street Station could be the most aesthetically interesting and attractive casino in Las Vegas. While you're checking it out, have a meal in the gorgeous and top-notch buffet, a beer in the microbrewery, and a cigar and cognac in the smoking car in the Pullman Grill steakhouse. 200 N. Main St., 702/387-1896 or 800/465-0711, double room rates $35–60.

UPPER STRIP

Stratosphere Hotel, Tower & Casino

Stratosphere, which opened in April 1996 and occupies the site of the old Bob Stupak's Vegas World, is the tallest building west of the Mississippi and the tallest observation tower in the United States. It boasts the world's two highest thrill rides, a revolving restaurant on the 106th floor, 1,500 rooms, a shopping mall, a showroom and lounge, six restaurants and several fast-food outlets, and a 97,000-square-foot casino with some of the best odds in Las Vegas. You'll see signs all over the joint insisting that the better odds—98 percent return on dollar slots, positive video poker, good two-deck blackjack, single-zero roulette, and 100X odds at craps—are "certified."

Take the escalator upstairs, mosey through the mall, then catch the high-speed double-decker elevators up to the observation pod, where the 360-degree view of Las Vegas Valley and environs will take your breath away. The Top of the World restaurant makes a complete 360-degree revolution once every 80 minutes or so. The roller coaster and the Big Shot will take a few years off your life, but they're worth it. 2000 Las Vegas Blvd. S., 702/380-7777 or 800/99-TOWER, double room rates $40–250.

Sahara

Building started on the Sahara in 1952, and over the next four decades, two more towers and 600 rooms were added. William Bennett, CEO and chairman of the board of Circus Circus for more than 20 years, bought the Sahara in 1995. Since then, he has renovated the Sahara, adding a Moroccan facade, casino wing, new buffet, and parking garage. The latest Circus Circus–inspired influence is Speed—The Ride, a roller coaster that wraps its way around the building and climbs over 200 feet above the Strip. The Sahara makes for an excellent conventioneer's hotel, being a very short ride to the convention center. 2535 Las Vegas Blvd. S., 702/737-2111 or 800/634-6666, double room rates $50–150.

Circus Circus

This was opened in 1968 by Jay Sarno, best known as the originator of the Caesars Palace concept, and thus the trendsetter for themed hotels. This property, however, was unsuccessful until William Bennett took over in 1974. Bennett turned Circus Circus Enterprises into one of the most profitable hotel-casino companies in the world, before resigning in 1994.

Circus also owns Slots-A-Fun next door, and Silver City across the street. The eponymous casino is *always* packed, as you might expect, since it offers cheap rooms, rock-bottom food prices, and caters to families. Free circus acts are presented continuously throughout the day and evening, and the well-known mezzanine midway offers every kind of dime-tossing, quarter-pitching, ball-rolling, hoop-ringing, balloon-busting, clown-drenching, camel-chasing, milkcan-downing, and rubber chicken–propelling carnie trick known to man. The Adventuredome, a five-acre indoor amusement park behind the hotel, features another midway, kiddie rides, and the world's largest indoor roller coaster. 2880 Las Vegas Blvd. S., 702/734-0410 or 800/634-3450, double room rates $40–200.

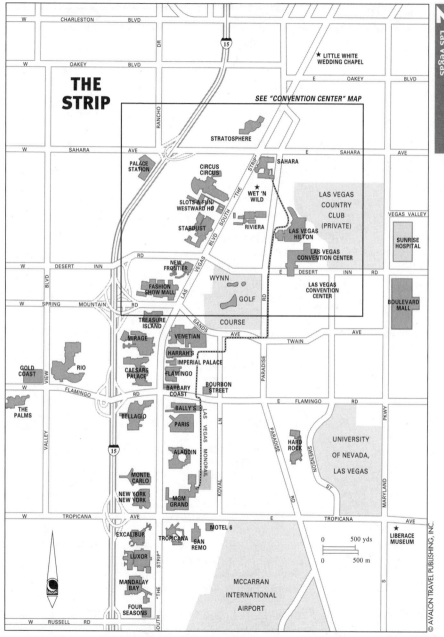

Las Vegas

LAS VEGAS HOTEL CHRONOLOGY

1904 . . . . Ladd's Hotel
1905 . . . . Hotel Las Vegas, Miller's Hotel
1932 . . . . Apache Hotel
1941 . . . . El Rancho Vegas, El Cortez
1942 . . . . Last Frontier
1946 . . . . Flamingo
1948 . . . . Thunderbird
1950 . . . . Desert Inn (closed)
1951 . . . . Horseshoe
1952 . . . . Sahara, Sands (closed)
1954 . . . . Showboat (closed)
1955 . . . . Riviera, Dunes (closed), New Frontier
1956 . . . . Fremont, Hacienda
1957 . . . . Tropicana
1958 . . . . Stardust
1965 . . . . Four Queens
1966 . . . . Aladdin, Caesars Palace
1968 . . . . Circus Circus
1969 . . . . Landmark (closed), International Hilton
1970 . . . . Royal Las Vegas
1971 . . . . Union Plaza
1972 . . . . Holiday
1973 . . . . MGM Grand (Bally's)
1975 . . . . Continental, California, Marina (closed)
1977 . . . . Maxim, Golden Nugget
1979 . . . . Sam's Town, Barbary Coast, Imperial Palace, Vegas World
1980 . . . . Sundance (Fitzgeralds), Las Vegas Club, Lady Luck
1984 . . . . Alexis Park, Paddlewheel
1986 . . . . Gold Coast
1988 . . . . Bourbon Street, Boardwalk, Arizona Charlie's
1989 . . . . San Remo, Mirage
1990 . . . . Rio, Excalibur
1992 . . . . Main Street Station
1993 . . . . Luxor, Treasure Island, MGM Grand
1994 . . . . Boomtown, Fiesta, Casino Royale, Boulder Station
1995 . . . . Hard Rock
1996 . . . . Barley's, Stratosphere, Monte Carlo, Main Street Station, Orleans
1997 . . . . New York: New York, Sunset Station
1998 . . . . Reserve (closed), Bellagio
1999 . . . . Venetian, Paris, Mandalay Bay, Four Seasons
2000 . . . . Aladdin, Suncoast
2001 . . . . Green Valley Ranch and Spa, The Palms
2003 . . . . Westin Casuarina

Riviera

The Riviera was the first high-rise on the Strip, starting out in 1955 with nine stories. It weathered a celebrated connection with the Chicago underworld and a succession of front men, a couple of bankruptcies, and a number of expansions. Today, the Riv is a masterpiece of tacked-on towers, leap-frogging cubes of rooms, and a maze of casino wings. Its casino is among the largest in the world at 125,000 square feet. And a magnificent casino it is, bright, open, and airy—for a maze! The Riviera has the most concentrated shows in town, with the big production revue Splash, along with La Cage female impersonators, and a comedy club. 2901 Las Vegas Blvd. S., 702/734-5110 or 800/634-6753, double room rates $65–200.

Las Vegas Hilton

Kirk Kerkorian opened this huge hotel over the July 4th weekend in 1969, but had to sell out to Hilton a short while later to extricate himself from a financial jam. Hilton added another 1,500 rooms in 1973. Elvis made his comeback in the 2,000-seat showroom, and performed there exclusively up until his death in 1977. The 46 video screens in the sports book are an overwhelming spectacle even for Las Vegas. Among the eight restaurants is Benihana, itself consisting of three dining rooms and four bars, set in a veritable Japanese village with three-story palace, lush gardens, stone lanterns, waterfalls, running streams, and nightly special effects. Le Montrachet is no slouch either, and the buffet features king crab legs. The Nightclub lounge is one of the largest (and rockinest) in town. Star Trek: The Experience is a virtual reality adventure sure to appeal to Trekkies and kids. 3000 Paradise Rd., 702/732-5111 or 800/732-7117, double room rates $100–300.

Renaissance Las Vegas

Taking the "What happens in Vegas, stays in Vegas" mantra to heart, the Renaissance Las Vegas, scheduled to open in December 2004, will be catering to guests looking to sample the wares of Sin City. Located adjacent to the Las Vegas Convention Center, the 548-room hotel is blending, according to marketing materials, "a confident and cool style with a slightly rebellious and irreverent attitude." Rather than a concierge, the hotel offers an "activities accomplice." Upon

COURTESY OF THE LAS VEGAS NEWS BUREAU

the Riviera

COURTESY OF THE LAS VEGAS NEWS BUREAU

Wayne Newton's second home, the Stardust

arrival, guests are given cards printed with seven "subtle" sins—at they end of their stay, they toss the card into the Confessions Cauldron for absolution (there won't be a casino on site, so the proposed sins will hopefully involve some creativity). 866/352-3434, room rates will range from $169 for standards and $399–850 for suites.

Westward Ho

This place claims to be the largest motel in the world with 1,000 rooms, none up more than one flight of stairs. It is a sprawling affair, which stretches from the Strip sidewalk all the way back to Industrial Road a good half-mile west. The casino is famous for its excellent video poker and snack bar, which serves cheap sandwiches and a legendary strawberry shortcake ($1.50). 2900 Las Vegas Blvd. S., 702/731-2900 or 800/634-6803, double room rates $35–75.

Stardust

Since its inception in 1955 till quite recently, the Stardust has stepped gingerly through a minefield of high explosives. It all started in the feverish dreams of Anthony Cornero, who embarked on a crusade to build the biggest and most lavish

hotel in the history of the world. He actually raised $6 million, personally selling stock in the company, and had the hotel half-completed when he dropped dead from a massive coronary while shooting dice at a Desert Inn crap table. Cornero's story alone could be the basis for a novel; the Stardust's subsequent story easily suffices as a sequel. Max Factor's brother, Jake the Barber, fronted the cash to finish the hotel for Sam Giancana and the Chicago mob, which pulled the strings for nearly a quarter century until state gaming regulators discovered that "owner" Allen Glick was running a massive slot-skimming operation for the Midwest syndicate. When the Boyd Group bought the Stardust in 1985, Las Vegas was finally free of the old-time mob influence. The 1995 movie, *Casino,* with Robert DeNiro and Sharon Stone and directed by Martin Scorsese, based on a book by Nicholas Pileggi, chronicles a part of this era.

The Stardust sign—188 feet tall, with 26,000 bulbs and 30 miles of wiring—*says* Las Vegas more clearly than any other image in town. Las Vegas legend Wayne Newton headlines 40 weeks per year at the Stardust. And Ralph's Diner is a fun place to eat. 3000 Las Vegas Blvd. S.,

702/732-6111 or 800/824-6033, double room rates $40–350.

The New Frontier

The Last Frontier was the second rancho-style resort to open on the Strip, in 1942, a year after the El Rancho Vegas. It was Las Vegas's first real tourist-attraction hotel. Last Frontier Village was a theme park next door, an entire town site filled with authentic western artifacts collected over the years by Doby Doc Caudill. The Little Chapel of the West, for example, was built for the Village in 1942. In 1955, the Last Frontier closed and the New Frontier opened next door. The New had a Stardust-like outer-space theme, about as different from the Last as it was possible to be. Howard Hughes watched the new hotel go up from the window of his penthouse suite across the street in the Desert Inn and bought it in 1967. Hughes's Summa Corporation sold the Frontier in 1988 to the Elardi family. It appears that the Frontier's days are once again numbered, as this is the proposed sight for the new San Francisco–themed casino.

The Elardis built a 14-story Atrium Suites tower that's unique in Las Vegas: open to the sky and overlooking a lagoon, a creek, and a courtyard. All the accommodations are two-room suites with wet bars and mini-fridges. The food at the Frontier is uniformly good and cheap, with a $2.99 steak and eggs and good specials at Margarita's. 3120 Las Vegas Blvd. S., 702/794-8200 or 800/421-7806, double room rates $40–90.

Wynn Las Vegas Resort

Currently under construction on 20 acres, on the site of the old Desert Inn, is Steve Wynn's latest creation. The $2.5-billion project is expected to be completed in April 2005. It will feature 2,700 luxury rooms and suites, 18 restaurants and an 18-hole golf course.

LOWER STRIP

The Venetian

The Sands opened in 1952 and was *the* in place in Las Vegas for glamorous entertainment throughout the freewheeling '50s. Frank Sinatra and Dean Martin owned points; they and their Rat Pack friends and colleagues performed in the Copa Room and relaxed in the health club. Howard Hughes bought the Sands in 1967 (and cut off Sinatra's credit). In 1988, Hughes's Summa Corporation sold the Sands to Sheldon Adelson of the Interface Group, a trade-conference company that at the time sponsored Comdex, Las Vegas's largest convention. Interface added a million square feet of convention center, before imploding the Sands in November 1996 to make room for the Venetian.

The Venetian is big. The Venetian offers 4,000 of some of the world's largest standard suites, nearly double the size of the average Strip hotel room. Each suite is 700 square feet, with a sitting room, a large bedroom (two queen-size beds), and a large bathroom (shower stall and tub, phone next to the toilet). Gondolas ply canals, passing the Campanile and Clock Tower and the Rialto Bridge, and dramatic reproductions of Venetian art grace the walls and ceiling. A peek at the sumptuous baroque hotel lobby alone merits a visit. It features a 200,000-square-foot casino, the 1.6-million-square-foot Sands Convention Center, a 140-store mall, and an entertainment-dining complex. Wolfgang Puck and Emeril Lagasse are only two of the six signature chefs gracing the kitchens of The Venetian's 13 dining establishments. The price tag? A mere $2 billion. 3355 Las Vegas Blvd. S., 702/414-1000 or 888-2-VENICE, double room rates $110–1,000.

Harrah's

This hotel went up on the Strip in 1972 as the Holiday Inn, one of the first major hotel chains to build in Las Vegas after Hughes had paved the way for corporate casino ownership. It opened with 1,000 rooms; a 735-room expansion, put into service in late 1989, rendered it the largest Holiday Inn in the world. The name was changed in 1992 to Harrah's and a complete remodeling transformed the hotel into the "Ship on the Strip," with a riverboat facade. The riverboat bit got old after four years so Harrah's spent another $250 million renovating it again. It now sports an elegant yet generic French Quarter front, with Mardi Gras decor throughout. The Carnival

Court Plaza features Ghirardelli's Old-Fashioned Chocolate Shop and Jackpot, Harrah's logo shop. The Range Steakhouse is a gorgeous restaurant with big picture windows overlooking the Strip. 3475 Las Vegas Blvd. S., 702/369-5000 or 800/ HARRAHS, double room rates $60–375.

Imperial Palace

With nearly 2,700 rooms, the IP is one of the largest hotels in the world, though you'd never know it by looking at the facade on the Strip. The hotel-casino and parking structure completely fill the narrow slice of land it occupies between Harrah's and the Flamingo. The Asian theme consists mostly of dragons. The IP is Nevada's largest employer of disabled people and consistently wins awards and praise for its personnel policies. The big news here, however, is the automobile collection. The casino is a sprawling affair on the ground floor; upstairs are the showroom, with a new unique experience: celebrity impersonator dealers. The steakhouse, Embers, has a good reputation, well deserved. 3535 Las Vegas Blvd. S., 702/731-3311 or 800/634-6441, double room rates $55–300.

Westin Casuarina Las Vegas

Formerly the Maxim, this property underwent a $75 million renovation and upgrade. The hotel now under the Westin brand offers 825 luxury guest rooms and suites just off the Strip. The Silver Peak Grill is the hotel's 24-hour restaurant, and comedian David Brenner performs nightly at 8 P.M. in the hotel's 200-seat showroom. 160 E. Flamingo Rd., 702/836-9775.

Flamingo Hilton

This is the house that Bugsy built, in 1946, with millions of mob dollars. It wasn't the first hotel on the L.A. Highway (contrary to public perception, Bugsy no more invented the Strip than Bugs Bunny invented the cartoon); the western-themed El Rancho Vegas and Last Frontier preceded it by half a decade. But it was the first gangster hotel, with architecture direct from Miami and a market targeted right at Hollywood. The fabulous Flamingo opened the sluice gates to a flood of black money from all around the country and changed the course of Las Vegas history forever. Kirk Kerkorian bought it to use as a training facility for the core staff of his megalith International (now Las Vegas Hilton) Hotel. In

the Imperial Palace

1970, shortly after the International opened, Kerkorian found himself in a cash crunch, partially due to the Flamingo's shady past: the SEC wouldn't approve a public stock offering Kerkorian needed to pay off the International unless he turned over the Flamingo's financial archives (which he refused to do). So Kirk had to sell both of his hotels to Hilton for half of what they were worth.

Since then, Hilton has erected five massive towers, expanding the hotel to 3,500 rooms. Chicago's Second City Improv troupe perform in Bugsy's Theatre, and Gladys Knight headlines in the cozy Flamingo showroom. The Flamingo Room has one of the best salad bars in town. The 15-acre pool and waterpark in the central courtyard rivals the one at the Tropicana.

Don't come here looking for any evidence of Bugsy. The last vestige of him, the Oregon Building where he had his office and suite, was torn down in 1994 to make room for the waterpark and a timeshare tower. A small shrine, however, stands on the side of the pool area. 3555 Las Vegas Blvd. S., 702/733-3111 or 800/732-2111, double room rates $75–300.

The Barbary Coast

Between the Flamingo Hotel and Flamingo Avenue sits this small hotel-casino owned by Michael Gaughan, son of Las Vegas gaming pioneer Jackie Gaughan (who owns the El Cortez, Gold Spike, and Plaza downtown). It opened in 1979 and now has 200 rooms and a great turn-of-the-20th-century San Francisco feel. The 30-foot Tiffany-style stained-glass mural, *Garden of Earthly Delights,* is advertised as the world's largest; the stained-glass signs are also works of art. Even the McDonald's marquee is tasteful. The Strip Western Union office is here, as is Michael's, one of the most exclusive gourmet restaurants in the world. Michael Gaughan and his partners also own the Gold Coast and the Orleans. 3595 Las Vegas Blvd. S., 702/737-7111 or 888/BARBARY, double room rates $45–150.

Treasure Island

This $450 million, 3,000-room hotel is a scaled-down version of its sister hotel next door, the Mirage. Though Treasure Island and the Mirage have the same number of rooms, TI does it in half the space, which makes this place twice as crowded, if that's possible. Add to it the hordes that make up the audience for *Sirens of TI* out front four times a night and what you have here is gridlock central on the Strip. It gets so ferocious that on a busy Saturday night, foot traffic slows, stalls, then stops completely for a total of 15 minutes at showtime. Hold onto your valuables! This is the second most popular venue for pickpockets in Las Vegas. (Strip buses are first.)

The inside of the casino is pretty classy, what you can see of it beyond the people, that is. Attention to detail is meticulous; no expense was spared. You won't find the show-stopping aquarium or tiger habitat of the Mirage, but check out the Buccaneer Bay restaurant and solid-bronze-skull door handles. Cirque du Soleil's *Mystere,* featuring some of the most amazing feats of human acrobatics in town, plays here. 3300 Las Vegas Blvd. S., 702/894-7111 or 800/944-7444, double room rates $65–300.

The Mirage

The scale of the Mirage is almost unfathomable. A 3-million-square-foot building on 100-acre site, the Mirage contains more than 2,700 rooms in three 29-story, Y-shaped, gold-mirrored wings. Outside visitors flock to the 54-foot-high manmade volcano, and wander the grounds—waterfalls, lagoons, grottoes, and a thousand or so giant palm trees. Inside is a nearly 100-foot-high glass-domed atrium, housing royal and canary palms, banana trees, elephant ears, orchids. The front desk is backed by a huge aquarium: 20,000 gallons, 53 feet long, six feet deep, with sharks, rays, wrasses, groupers, surgeonfish, puffers, angelfish, and triggerfish. The casino decor is rich and tropical: carved teakwood, bamboo, thatch, marble, rattan. The white Bengal tigers in a show-biz habitat from Siegfried and Roy's former show are eye-catching. Several dolphins cavort in a million-gallon saltwater pool. There are Japanese, Chinese, French, Italian, steak and seafood, and buffet restaurants, plus slots, table games, monumental sports book, all served by nearly 5,000 employees. 3400 Las Vegas Blvd. S.,

702/791-7111 or 800/627-6667, double room rates $90–450.

Caesars Palace

Since it opened in 1966, Caesars has earned its place as one of the most famous hotels in the world. Start your tour from the 20-foot statue of Augustus Caesar, hailing a cab, at the driveway to the main entrance; beyond are fountains spewing 35-foot-high columns of water in front of 50-foot-tall Italian cypresses. Pause at the four-faced and eight-armed Brahma nearby to light some incense and kneel in meditation on the prayer cushions. Grab one of the two people movers (the south one, next to the Mirage, forces you to go through the Forum Shops).

Once inside, wander through the sprawling Roman and Olympic casinos. Stroll past Cleopatra's Barge dance lounge and a replica of Michelangelo's *David.* Peek into Empress Court

THE WORLD'S LARGEST HOTELS

1. MGM Grand, Las Vegas—5,005 rooms
2. Ambassador City, Jomtien, Thailand—4,631 rooms
3. Luxor, Las Vegas—4,407 rooms
4. Excalibur, Las Vegas—4,008 rooms
5. Circus Circus, Las Vegas—3,770 rooms
6. Mandalay Bay, Las Vegas—3,646 rooms
7. Flamingo Hilton, Las Vegas—3,600 rooms
8. Las Vegas Hilton, Las Vegas—3,174 rooms
9. The Mirage, Las Vegas—3,044 rooms
10. The Venetian, Las Vegas—3,036 rooms
11. Bellagio, Las Vegas—3,005 rooms
12. Monte Carlo, Las Vegas—3,002 rooms
13. Paris, Las Vegas—2,916 rooms
14. Treasure Island, Las Vegas—2,885 rooms
15. Opryland USA, Nashville—2,881 rooms
16. Bally's, Las Vegas—2,814 rooms
17. Imperial Palace, Las Vegas—2,700 rooms
18. Harrah's, Las Vegas—2,601 rooms
19. Aladdin, Las Vegas—2,567 rooms
20. Rio, Las Vegas—2,563 rooms

(the most expensive Chinese food you will ever see), and Primavera restaurants; La Piazza is the most upscale food court in town and the Palatium is one of the fanciest buffets (the food is okay). Check out the NASA-esque sports book, and if you wander around far enough, you might even stumble into the hotel lobby.

The **Forum Shops at Caesars** connects to the Olympic Casino. The original 250,000-square-foot wing opened in summer 1992; it was doubled in size in summer 1997. At press time, the Forum was adding even more haute retail space. Nearly everything for sale is Italian designer, French chic, American yuppie, or just plain dear, guaranteed to raise the eyebrows of even the highbrows. Get your designer sunglasses for $700 and your burlap coffeesack jackets for $400. The galleries have some of the finest art within 400 miles.

The restaurant food here is divine. You've got Spago, the Palm, Bertollini's, Stage Deli, Boogie Diner, Chinois (Wolfgang Puck's Chinese restaurant), and the Cheesecake Factory.

The mall itself is also is a visual and sensual extravaganza; what Caesars is to casinos, the Forum is to malls. The details are exquisite and Roman: columns and arches, railing-lined balconies, statues, marble floors, and a Mediterranean sky that changes from sunrise to sunset in three hours. The main entertainment is at the Festival Fountain and the Atlantis Fountain. 3570 Las Vegas Blvd. S., 702/731-7110 or 800/634-6661, double room rates $100–350.

Bellagio

The Dunes, which consisted of 164 acres of sprawling casino, two hotel towers, courtyard bungalows, and a golf course, was built in 1955. In 1992, the whole bankrupt property was sold to Steve Wynn of Mirage Resorts. Wynn proceeded to take down the casino and tear out the bungalows, and the first tower was imploded in a huge public explosion that coincided with the opening of Treasure Island up the street.

When the dust settled, Bellagio was born, Mirage Resorts's $1.4 billion monument devoted to all the luxury money can buy. Before you even set foot in Bellagio, you are treated to one of the best free shows Las Vegas has to offer: More than one thousand fountains dance in the 12-acre lake in front. The water ballet is choreographed to everything from opera to Broadway hits, with jets of water soaring more than 200 feet into the air. The show takes place Mon.–Fri. every 30 minutes 3 P.M.–7 P.M. and Sat.–Sun. noon–7 P.M.; daily from 7 P.M.–11:45 P.M. the show is increased to every 15 minutes.

Bellagio strives to be a first-class retreat, attracting everyone from high-rollers to nongamblers interested in buying Gucci bags and dining in top-notch restaurants. Judging from the hotel's occupancy rate and celebrity guest list, it has succeeded. And it truly is a stunning, beautiful affair. Make your way to the lobby and turn your eyes upward to enjoy the extraordinary glass parasol chandelier, *Fiori di Como,* created by famed glass sculptor Dale Chihuly. While gazing upward, an overwhelming floral scent will undoubtedly draw you to the 13,500-square-foot conservatory garden, where a staff of 115 horticulturists cultivates a floral display worthy of a royal wedding.

Everything about Bellagio carries a high price tag. Via Bellagio's retail district carries Prada, Armani, Giorgio, and Tiffany & Co., while the restaurant selections include Marc Poidevin's Le Cirque and Mark Lo Russo's Aqua. In a theater designed to emulate Paris's Opera House, Cirque de Soleil's newest production, O, takes place on a $90 million stage. With over 3,000 hotel rooms and a rack rate starting at $225 a night (families with children will be encouraged to find accommodations elsewhere), Bellagio has raised the bar for grand-scale indulgence. 3600 Las Vegas Blvd. S., 702/693-7111 or 888/987-3456, double room rates $225–1600.

Bally's

This was originally called the MGM Grand. In 1980, a terrible fire raged through the Grand, killing 84 people. A couple of years later, it was sold to Bally's, and then to Hilton in 1995. Bally's is the 15th largest hotel in the world, with 2,814 rooms in two towers, one of which is 25 stores high. Its 500-square-foot guest rooms are among the most spacious accommodations on the Strip.

Its land area totals more than 70 acres, with 3.25 million square feet. Its huge casino, along with six restaurants, full resort facilities, 40-store shopping mall, two showrooms, and two lounges, conspire to eliminate any reason to leave.

Bally's teamed up with MGM Grand to build a $25 million milelong monorail that has connected the two properties since 1995 (free). The long-running Donn Arden extravaganza, Jubilee, plays in the theater. 3645 Las Vegas Blvd. S., 702/739-4111 or 800/634-3434, double room rates $100–1,000.

Paris

When Hilton bought Bally's, it inherited a vacant lot just south on the Strip, along with three-year-old plans to build a 3,000-room, $785 million megaresort. In 1999, Paris made its entrée onto the Strip, giving Las Vegas another landmark of colossal proportions: the Eiffel Tower. Using Gustav Eiffel's original 1889 drawings, architects took painstaking care—even going so far as to match the paint color and lighting system—to ensure that this half-size replica mirrored the original City of Light's tower, save for the 85,000-square-foot casino sprawled beneath its legs. Other signature Parisian touches are a replica of the Arc de Triomphe and the Pont Alexandre III, along with facades of the Paris Opera House and the Louvre.

Featuring no fewer than eight French restaurants, the creators seem confident that France's renown for gastronomic *savoir-faire* will draw diners. Guests at Paris may enjoy the two-acre rooftop swimming pool and a 25,000-square-foot European spa. 3655 Las Vegas Blvd. S., 702/946-7000 or 888/BONJOUR, double room rates $150–1500.

Aladdin

This hotel, between Bally's and the MGM Grand on the Strip, was opened on New Year's Day 1966 by Milton Prell, who'd sold his points in the Sahara a few years previously to Del Webb. Prell was a personal friend of Elvis's (Priscilla and the King were married in Prell's private suite in 1967)—the Aladdin's 15 minutes of fame. Prell suffered a heart attack shortly thereafter, and the

Aladdin was sold to a succession of owners who drove it right into the ground. A Las Vegas developer, Jack Sommers, bought it out of receivership in 1994 and got it back on its feet, only to close it in November 1997. In August of 2000, it reopened with $1.4 billion dollars worth of cosmetic surgery and 2,600 rooms. With its completely revamped 1,00l Arabian Nights ornamentation comes a 50-foot-tall lamp bar where you can drown your sorrows should all your wishes not be fulfilled in the 100,000-square-foot casino. 3667 Las Vegas Blvd. S., 702/736-7114 or 877/333-WISH, double room rates $100–800.

Blending seamlessly with Aladdin's decor, one of the newest shopping extravaganzas to hit the Strip is **Desert Passage,** 500,000 square feet of retail shops, restaurants, and performance space. Two "gates" lead into the shopping area: India Gate and Morocco Gate. Exotic music wafts overhead as you shop your way into the "Lost City," where belly dancers and acrobats perform regularly in front of the central fountain and food court. En route, you'll pass the Merchant's Harbor, where torrential rainstorms occur every 15 minutes in front of Ben & Jerry's ice cream store. Or you may have a veiled woman apply a henna tattoo to your hand before you make your way into Banana Republic. Whether you're a shopper or not, a visit to the Desert is a kick.

MGM Grand

Kirk Kerkorian likes building the largest hotels in the world: the International, the original Grand, and in 1993 this monolith. But this one takes the cake. With 5,034 rooms' worth of guests and 8,000 employees, the Grand is larger than most towns in Nevada. It also boasts a 16-valet-lane porte cochere, a 171,000-square-foot casino, a 15,000-seat arena, a 1,200-seat theater, seven major restaurants, plus a buffet, coffee shop, and fast-food court, a convention center, a double-Olympic-sized pool, a giant video arcade, a big daycare center, 9,000-space parking garage, 90 elevators, four theaters, and a dozen eateries. Still going? Well then head to Studio 54, where the bold and beautiful shake their groove thang until the wee hours of the morning. It's best to tackle the Grand after a full night's sleep; by the time you're done with the place, you'll be ready for

You'll find more people in the MGM Grand than in many towns in Nevada.

THE FOUR CORNERS

For more than 30 years, the Tropicana alone occupied the far southern end of the Las Vegas Strip. Built in 1957 and expanded several times over the following three decades, it wasn't until 1989 that the Trop got any company—and competition—on its corner, when the 300-room San Remo opened next door. In 1990, the massive 4,000-room Excalibur arrived across the street, and in 1993, both the 2,500-room Luxor (since expanded to nearly 4,500 rooms) and the 5,005-room MGM Grand were built at the Tropicana's intersection on the Strip. In June 1996, the 3,000-room Monte Carlo opened and six months later, in early January 1997, the 2,054-room New York–New York joined the crowd.

Today, this corner boasts 4 of the 10 largest hotels in the world. Altogether, the seven hotels combine for more than 21,000 hotel rooms, 50 restaurants, 15,000 slot machines, 12 showrooms and theaters with a total of 23,000 seats, and a "population" at any given of approximately 75,000 employees, guests, showgoers, conventioneers, and sightseers. By comparison, those 75,000 people would make up the fifth-largest town in Nevada, larger even than the state capital at Carson City.

bed again. The notable eateries include Emeril Lagasse's New Orleans Fish House (very creative, unusual, and expensive seafood) and Craftsteak.

In 1997 the Grand underwent a complete renovation. A highly touted visitor attraction is the Lion Habitat. Smack dab in the middle of the casino, the "habitat" has thick glass walls that allow gamblers to gawk at lions and cubs as they pace around their living room. Well-coiffed handlers routinely feed the lions bits of steak right up against the window for maximum viewing pleasure, while lion roars are piped over the speakers. The attraction is free, and you may wander through the glass tunnel for a better look at the felines. At the end of the tunnel is a gift shop where you can buy any size of stuffed MGM lion you desire. 3799 Las Vegas Blvd. S., 702/891-1111 or 800/929-1111, double room rates $75–300.

Tropicana

When the Trop opened in 1958, it was the ninth hotel on the Strip, the fifth to open in three years, and the most expensive up to that time, costing $15 million. It was initially so exquisite that it earned the nickname "Tiffany of the Strip." After the early mob owners were forced out, a series of new owners oversaw the deterioration of the Trop's aura, until Ramada Corporation bought it in 1979, and gradually reinvested the property

with much of its original glory. More than an acre of the stunning five-acre centerpiece, the Island Waterpark, is water: three swimming pools, one 75 by 300 feet; glass doors slide shut in winter, transforming one side into an indoor pool, creating the town's most delightfully *humid* public room. There's also a water slide, and the lush landscaping makes it easy to pretend you're at a resort in Polynesia.

The casino's main pit is under a magnificent 4,000-square-foot leaded stained-glass dome (which the engineers had to suspend on pneumatic shock absorbers to account for building vibrations from the air-conditioning; the ceiling remains stationary and the building vibrates around it). The 425-foot people mover between the towers passes through a bright tunnel full of macaws, parrots, and coral aquariums. The glass-elevator ride to the top of the Island Tower is fun. The Trop is also known for its Sunday brunch, Mizuno's teppanyaki restaurant, and Folies Bergere, the longest-running and one of the last true Las Vegas–style extravaganzas. 3801 Las Vegas Blvd. S., 702/739-2222 or 800/634-4000, double room rates $55–200.

Monte Carlo

This gorgeous $350 million, 3,000-room megaresort, built by Circus Circus, opened in June 1996. Modeled after the opulent Place du Casino in Monaco, the Las Vegas version of Monte Carlo replicates its fanciful arches, chandeliered domes, ornate fountains, marble floors, gas-lit promenades, and Gothic glass registration area overlooking the lush pool area. And it all took 14 months—from groundbreaking to grand opening—to put together. Amazing.

Within Monte Carlo are a beautiful casino that combines European elegance and American informality; five restaurants, a microbrewery, and a fast-food court; Circus Circus's signature high-tech arcade; a big bingo parlor upstairs; a waterpark consisting of adult and children pools, whirlpool tubs, and a wave pool and "lazy river" combo; and the Lance Burton Theater, a 1,200-seat showroom featuring the world-class illusionist, which is modeled after European opera houses and is one of a kind in Las Vegas. 3770 Las Vegas Blvd. S., 702/730-7777 or 800/311-8999, double room rates $80–200.

New York–New York

Andy Warhol would have been proud: This is the single most monumental piece of pop art the world has ever seen. This $460 million, 2,000-room megaresort sets a new standard for thematic accomplishment in Las Vegas. The mini-skyline re-creates a half-size Statue of Liberty and Empire State Building, along with the Chrysler, Seagrams, and CBS buildings, the New York Public Library, New Yorker Hotel, Grand Central Station, and Brooklyn Bridge, among others. A Coney Island–style roller coaster runs completely around the property. The interior is no less realized thematically than the exterior. Everywhere you look there's a clever replica of another New York icon: New York Stock Exchange, New York Racetrack, New York Public Library.

The pièce de résistance is the simulation of Greenwich Village. Narrow, crooked, and of course crowded reproductions of Bleecker Street, Hudson Street, Broadway, and others all frame the Village Eateries area. The floors are brick, with faux manhole covers inset here and there. Multistory townhouses line the streets, complete with brown stone, fire escapes, and ivy trellises. The roller coaster rumbles overhead like an elevated commuter train.

The most realistic thing about New York–New York is the cramped space. The owners, MGM Grand and Primadonna Resorts, stuffed a big megaresort into a postage-sized lot, much like Manhattan is a huge city jammed into a 200-by 12-block island. For comparison purposes, Monte Carlo next door occupies a 66-acre parcel; New York–New York fills 20 acres. Get ready for a high-population density. 3790 Las Vegas Blvd. S., 702/740-6969 or 800/NYFORME, double room rates $150–250.

Excalibur

A stroll through this 4,000-room hotel (each one redecorated in 1999) is a lesson in medieval architecture and culture: 14 spires, with turrets and parapets in the battlements, and cones topped by steeples and spikes. The drawbridge crosses the moat, beyond which a cobblestone foyer is draped with velvet, satin, and gold heraldic banners, and a three-story-high fountain sports lion heads and stone frogs. Upstairs is the medieval village, where magicians, jugglers, mimes, court jesters, belly dancers, contortionists, even a harpist entertain on the floor and various stages. Knights, lords, maidens, serfs, ladies-in-waiting, gypsies, even wenches provide the service in appropriate uniforms. Downstairs on the Fantasy Faire level, turret pitch, flagon toss, great racing knights, topple the towers, knock out the knaves' teeth, and William Tell darts make up the Renaissance midway. Eat at The Steakhouse at Camelot, Sir Galahad's, Sherwood Forest Café, even Robin Hood's Snack Bar. Not quite in keeping with Excalibur theme, WCW's Nitro Grill just opened on the casino level and features both planned and spontaneous visits from wrestling stars. Better yet, take the kids to the Tournament of Kings hosted in King Arthur's Arena.

Finally, there's the anomalous casino, with its neon, stained glass, gold-capped columns, huge wood beams, and the most lethal-looking chandeliers you've ever seen. Bottom line? Excalibur is fun, silly, both totally larger than life and attentive to the merest details, inviting of exploration, an amusement park with rooms and a casino. 3850 Las Vegas Blvd. S., 702/597-7777 or 800/937-7777, double room rates $80–300.

Luxor

Luxor is by far one of the most dramatic architectural influences on the Las Vegas Strip (designed by Veldon Simpson, who also designed MGM Grand and Excalibur). You can't help but pick it right out of the lineup of hotels on the Strip: a sleek bronze pyramid in the midst of stark gray boxes. And the closer you get, the better it looks, until you're standing right at the base of one of the walls, staring straight up into infinity, and you get the idea of what those old Egyptian mathematicians had in mind.

This 30-story pyramid-shaped Circus Circus property opened in October 1993. Since then Circus has added another 2,000 rooms in two ziggurat towers (with 4,500 rooms, it's now the second largest hotel in Las Vegas, third in the world), a shopping mall, a 1,700-seat showroom, and a large and luxurious spa. The futuristic Egyptian dance club, Ra, frequently tops the polls as the best place to dance in Vegas. Pulsating music, flashing strobes and expensive drinks all round out the experience.

The pyramid's interior occupies 29 million cubic feet of open space, the world's largest atrium. The casino is round, roomy, and airy (the ventilation system is world-class). On the second-floor attractions level you get the full effect the enormous atrium. Also upstairs, the video arcade is on two levels, with interactive racecars, small motion simulators, state-of-the-art video, and a roomful of air-hockey games. 3900 Las Vegas Blvd. S., 702/262-4000 or 800/288-1,000, double room rates $80–300.

Mandalay Bay

The Hacienda opened in 1956. It was so far off the beaten Strip that it did its own thing through the 1960s. But after the original owners died, Chicago-mob front-man Allen Glick added it to his stable of hotels in the 1970s, then sold out to Paul Lowden, who also once owned the Sahara and now owns the Santa Fe. Lowden sold the Hacienda to Circus Circus in 1995, completing the casino giant's Miracle Mile, which stretches from the Excalibur past the Hacienda property all the way to the corner of Russell Road.

Circus imploded the Hacienda on New Year's Eve 1996 and constructed a 3,000-room homage to Polynesia in its place. While of course it has the requisite wedding chapels, casino floor, and lounges, the real fun of Mandalay Bay lies in all the somewhat gimmicky extras. In the lobby, hundreds of fish writhe in a 3,000-gallon circular tank. And don't miss Shark Reef, a colossal aquarium filled to the gills with more than 100 varieties of sharks, as well as rays, reptiles, and fish. Need more water? Mandalay Bay boasts an 11-acre waterpark with four pools, hot tubs, a lazy river, and a continual "wave" for body surfing.

Since its debut, Mandalay Bay has been earning rave reviews for its eccentric dining and entertainment options. Cocktails, dinner and dancing await behind the wall of fire at Rumjungle: provided, that is, that you can get in the door—there's always a long line. Slam frozen vodka shots at Red Square next door and contemplate the irony of a Soviet restaurant set in defiantly capitalistic Vegas. For more sedate, but equally delicious, dining options, choose Wolfgang Puck's Trattoria del Lupo or Charlie Palmer's Aureole. Big name acts and Creole cuisine are the main draw at the House of Blues. 3950 Las Vegas Blvd. S., 702/632-7777 or 877/632-7000.

Four Seasons Las Vegas

Literally on top of Mandalay Bay, occupying floors 36 through 39 but maintaining a completely separate identity, is the Four Seasons Las Vegas. While many of the larger, gaudier Vegas resorts claim that they are classy, this is the real deal. One of the few nongaming hotels on the Strip, the Four Seasons offers 400 pricey guest rooms, a Charlie Palmer steakhouse, and a private, lushly landscaped swimming pool. The hotel also hosts an afternoon tea. 3960 Las Vegas Blvd. S., 702/632-5000, double room rates $150–700.

THE Hotel

For hipsters who find the Four Seasons a bit stuffy, Mandalay Bay opened yet another adjoining satellite called THE Hotel. The resort-next-to-a-resort offers 1,120 luxurious suites with such amenities as separate living/sleeping areas, posh, modern furnishings, 42-inch plasma televisions, and wet bars. The Bathhouse Spa reflects the same minimalist feel. 3950 Las Vegas Blvd. S., 877/632-7800, room rates $159–420.

LOCALS' CASINOS

You might've heard that people who live in Las Vegas don't gamble—that they never go near the Strip or downtown and they'd never be caught dead inside a casino. Yeah, right. Locals casinos, which cater to the residents, are some of the busiest and most successful in Las Vegas. They're also proliferating at an equal pace to the population. In fact, the latest trend is for five-star hotel and resort companies to throw up ultra-posh 400- to 500-room hotel-casinos in the expensive subdivisions: Seven Circle in Summerlin, the Hyatt and Grand Bay at Lake Las Vegas, and the Ritz-Carlton at Mountain Spa.

Locals' casinos combine neighborhood locations, plenty of parking, excellent restaurants, good gambling, and exemplary service. Neighborhood casinos attract the locals with full-pay video poker opportunities, active promotional campaigns (such as paycheck cashing, drawings for cash, cars, even houses, and direct-mail offers like restaurant and show discounts during slow periods), and strong slot clubs. Many of the savviest out-of-towners frequent the locals' casinos for the best deals in town.

Castaways Hotel, Casino and Bowling Center

Formerly the Showboat is one of a half-dozen baby-boomer hotel-casinos that opened in the '50s that haven't been imploded yet. Dating from 1954, this casino out among the creosote on the Boulder Highway was far enough away from the mainstream that it could steer its own course along the tricky current of Las Vegas hotel competition. It eventually found its niche with bowling and bingo and has enjoyed mostly smooth sailing ever since. The bowling alley is the largest in the country. 2800 East Fremont St., 702/385-9123 or 800/826-2800, double room rates $40–150.

Boulder Station

This hotel, which opened in August 1994, is the fraternal twin of the west side's Palace Station, the original locals' casino. The parent company, Station Casinos, took the highly successful Palace Station formula and improved on it. The decor is a bit upgraded, with rich hardwood and brick floors, stained glass galore, and much higher ceilings. The restaurants serve the same great food at great prices, and even have fast-food outlets on the side that dispense the same great food at even greater prices. The Broiler has what could be the best salad bar in town. Boulder Station caters to the locals in many other ways, too. It was the first casino to attach a movie theater to it (an 11-plex at that); it also has Kid's Quest, a large, efficient, and convenient child-care center. 4111 Boulder Hwy., 702/432-7777 or 800/683-7777, double room rates $50–2500.

Sam's Town

This hotel opened in 1979 way out on Boulder Highway, almost to Henderson, with a hundred or so rooms. It remained a small, eastside-locals' casino with a country-and-western theme for the next 15 years. In 1994, Sam's Town unveiled its spectacular $100 million expansion. The centerpiece is a nine-story glass-roof atrium full of live foliage, a rock waterfall, babbling brooks, and animatronic wildlife. The laser-dancing-waters-western-music show (free) is presented daily at 2, 6, 8 and 10:30 P.M. The Final Score sports bar has more diversions than the Bureau of Reclamation. Sam's is surrounded by two 500-space RV parks. Make an effort to get out to Sam's Town to see the atrium and show, and while you're out here, have a steak at Diamond Lil's or a burger at Ralph's Diner, and check out the Western Emporium, selling every country consumable under the sun. 5111 East Fremont St., 702/456-7777 or 800/634-6371, double room rates $55–300.

Texas Station

Texas Station is another Stations casino, following in the highly successful footsteps of Palace and Boulder Stations: sprawling parking lots, big casino and small hotel, seven restaurants and six bars; this one also has a 12-screen movie complex. The theme is in the details. The custom carpeting is full of wagon wheels, 10-gallon hats, cow skulls, lone stars, and cattle brands. The deli sells barbecue brisket sandwiches. The cashier's cage is behind a Bank of Texas facade. A longhorn Cadillac sits 15 feet above the Texaco bar on a gas station hoist. And a 200-pound reflective disco armadillo rotates above the Honky Tonk Dance Hall. It also has one of the top buffets in town. 2140 North Rancho Dr., 702/631-1000 or 800/944-7444, double room rates $60–125.

Fiesta

Fiesta could be the quintessential locals' casino: tons of parking, food specials galore (late-night cheap eats for $2.99, and one of the best buffets in town), promotion-crazy (especially if you have lots of slot club points), and jam-packed with video poker. Indeed, Fiesta calls itself the Royal Flush Capital of the World, and apparently has the goods to prove it. Fiesta also has a drive-up sports betting window—you don't even have to get out of the car to lay a wager on your favorite team. 2400 North Rancho Dr., 702/631-7000 or 800/731-7333, double room rates $60–150.

Santa Fe

The original "Rancho Strip" joint, the Santa Fe owned the northwest market for nearly four years, and still packs in the local residents. Santa Fe is the only casino in Nevada with an ice-skating rink attached; there's also bowling, bingo, and a 16-screen movie theater directly across the street. And there's usually some passable entertainment in the lounge. 4949 Rancho Blvd., 702/658-4900 or 800/872-6823, double room rates $40–75.

Gold Coast

Next door to the Rio is this Coast Hotel (sister to Barbary Coast and the Orleans), opened in 1986 by Michael Gaughan. In its first five years of operation, the Gold Coast expanded three times, most recently in 1990 with a 10-story, 400-room tower. Locals love this place for its distance from the Strip, along with its big bowling alley, bingo

parlor, first-run movie theater, ice cream parlor, video poker payouts, and meal deals, especially the $9.95 one-pound T-bone with a veritable ton of carbohydrate sides, served 24 hours in the coffee shop. The sports book is wise-guy central, and the slot club boasts more than 300,000 members (almost all locals), largest in Las Vegas. In addition, the Gold Coast has a popular lounge from which live big-band music emanates day and night, and has a dance hall and saloon, featuring the largest dance floor in town. 4000 West Flamingo Rd., 702/367-7111 or 888/402-6278, double room rates $50–80.

Sun Coast

Michael Gaughan's latest Coast property opened in 2000. Four hundred rooms, a 64-lane bowling alley, a 16-screen movie theater and day care for the tykes make this new venture popular with locals and visiting families alike. 9090 Alta Dr., 702/636-7111 or 887/677-7111, double room rates $60–90.

Orleans

Another fine locals' casino from Coast Hotels, the Orleans opened in December 1996 to rave reviews. The Orleans seems to be trying to compete with the Rio, and is doing a fair job of it. The showroom features headliners, two lounges offer live big band, jazz, and zydeco bands; there's a big bowling alley upstairs; the buffet serves up some great Cajun and Creole; and the video poker machines are often monopolized by the professionals taking advantage of positive situations. The Orleans is unique among locals' casinos in that it has 800 hotel rooms; locals don't often need rooms, so the Orleans has trouble keeping them all filled, which means great deals. And if you're thirsty, a (strange) line-up of eight stainless-steel water fountains awaits on the second floor. 4500 West Tropicana Rd., 702/365-7111 or 800/675-3267, double room rates $75–100.

Palace Station

Palace Station is a very popular casino with both locals and visitors, off the Strip about a mile west on Sahara Avenue. The parking lot is always packed. Palace Station lays claim to having the largest (though not tallest) sign in town—and therefore the world. It offers consistently excellent room deals, consistently has the best dinner deals in town along with a great $0.99 margarita, and its Feast Buffet is a perennial favorite. 2411 West Sahara Ave., 702/367-2411 or 800/634-3101, double room rates $45–350.

Arizona Charlie's

Opened in 1988, Charlie's services the western suburbs, on Decatur Boulevard a half-block north of Charleston. It was overhauled in 1994, and now has a seven-story tower (400 rooms total), three restaurants, saloon, big sports book and deli, and, of course, great video poker. The casino decorations and names have finally added a little slice of Alaska to Las Vegas; Arizona Charlie, after all, made his name and fortune as a saloon owner and impressario in Dawson during the Klondike. The Sourdough Cafe has some of the best deals in town. 740 South Decatur Blvd., 702/258-5200 or 800/342-2695, double room rates $40–75.

OFF THE STRIP

Rio

This hotel opened in late 1990 with 400 suites. Then, the Rio's claims to fame were its stunning sign, which finally beat out the Stardust's for best neon in Las Vegas, its sandy beach by the pool, and its cocktail waitress uniforms. All three are still famous, but today the Rio is perhaps the most exciting casino in Las Vegas. A second tower was added in 1994, a third tower was completed in early 1995, and a fourth, stand-alone, 42-story tower opened in early 1997, giving the Rio a total of 2,500 suites. All the rooms are mini-apartments, with a large bedroom-sitting area, floor-to-ceiling picture windows, and luxurious his and hers dressing areas. The Rio's Carnival World Buffet was the first, and is still one of the best, of the new-style "mini-food-city" smorgasbords. The other restaurants—13 in all—are equally fantastic, right down to the sports book deli. There's also a free show, the Sky Parade, in the casino Masquerade Village casino wing. Penn & Teller perform nightly except Tuesday. 3700

COURTESY OF THE LAS VEGAS NEWS BUREAU

large rooms, nice neon, good buffet: the Rio

West Flamingo Rd., 702/252-7777 or 800/ PLAYRIO, double room rates $60–350.

Hard Rock

The world's only Hard Rock Hotel and Casino opened in March 1994 and has been in a world of its own ever since. It's definitely one of the hippest (in a rock 'n' roll kind of way) casino in Las Vegas. The small casino features tons of pop memorabilia, slot machines have guitar-neck handles, table-game layouts are customized with rock lyrics and art, and the casino employees all look like they're straight off the set of a soap opera. There's the requisite logo shop, a cool pool area with sandy beach, only 300 rooms (thousands are turned away), and a 1,200-seat concert venue. For a little nongaming night action, there's Baby's, a cutting-edge, hipster nightclub that flies D.J.s in from around the country to spin the latest in electronica and house music in an underground den of retro-cool. Dining options include a pricey steakhouse (A.J.s), modern Japanese cuisine (Nobu), and a Mexican restaurant boasting Nevada's best tequila bar (Pink Taco). If you're under 55, you'll want to at least see the Hard Rock, if not hang here. 4455 Paradise Ave., 702/693-5000 or 800/HRD-ROCK, double room rates $150–350.

Palms

Arguably one of the hippest new hotels in town, the Palms, established by the Maloof brothers, has become the place to see all the pretty people and be seen (if you happen to be one of the pretty people). The 447-room resort, which opened in November 2001, was the infamous site of MTV's Real World: Las Vegas (the suite is available for rent). Aside from the standard rooms," the hotel also offers NBA Suites, with furnishings made to fit taller patrons, as well as the Playrooms, fashioned in retro '60s style and complete with dancer poles, dance floors, and premium sound systems. Young Hollywood types seem to congregate at the hotel's high-profile nightspots, such as Ghostbar, Skin Pool Lounge, and Rain Nightclub. 4321 West Flamingo Rd., 775/942-7064 or 866/725-6773, www.palms.com, double room rates $79–409.

Accommodations

With more than 70 major hotels and 200 motels, Las Vegas boasts a grand total of 120,294 places to sleep indoors. But if that makes it sound easy to find the one perfect room with your name on it, think again. More than 34 million visitors occupy those 202,000 beds every year; that's roughly 88,000 a night. In addition, every weekend of the year either sells out or comes close to. Long weekends and holidays (especially New Year's Eve, Valentine's Day, Memorial Day, 4th of July, Labor Day, and Thanksgiving, along with international holidays such as Cinco de Mayo and Mexican Independence Day, and Chinese New Year's) are sold out weeks in advance. Special events, such as concerts, title fights, the Super Bowl, the Final Four, and the National Finals Rodeo, are sold out months in advance. Reservations are made for the biggest conventions (Comdex, Consumer Electronics, Men's Apparel, Broadcasters, etc.) a year ahead of time.

In short, this town fills up fast—especially the top hotels, the best-value hotels, and the cheapest motels. What's more, the crowds are relentless; Las Vegas rarely gets a break to catch its breath. There are some minor quiet times, such as the three weeks before Christmas and a noticeable downward blip in July and August when the mercury isn't see fit to drop below 90 degrees. Also, Sunday through Thursday when there aren't any large conventions or sporting events are a little less crazy than usual; almost all the room packages and deep discounts are only available Sunday through Thursday. Weekends are dealless. In fact, most of the major hotels don't even let you check in on a Saturday night. You can stay Friday night of Friday and Saturday, but not Saturday by itself.

Of course, your hotel or motel room is where you'll spend the *least* time during your stay in Las Vegas, so remember the old travelers' axiom:

Eat sweet, pay for play, but sleep cheap. Otherwise, as always, it's best to make your reservations far in advance to ensure the appropriate kind, price, and location of your room.

HOTELS
Orientation

Basically, Las Vegas hotels congregate in three locations: downtown, the Strip, and off-Strip. The Fremont Street Experience unifies the majority of downtown hotels into one multifarious attraction. Downtown's rooms are uniformly less expensive, the food is also cheaper with no loss of quality, the gambling can be more positive if you know what you're looking for, and the cast of characters is far more colorful. Henderson has stepped up to the plate with the expansive and luxurious hotels at Lake Las Vegas and a few others in the Green Valley area.

The Strip has the biggest, newest, most themed, and most crowded hotels. Twelve of the 15 largest hotels in the world are along a four-mile stretch on Las Vegas Boulevard South between Sahara and Tropicana Avenues. These hotels are self-contained mini-cities, and though you never have to leave them, you're also somewhat captive in them: it's often hard to find your way out; the distance from your car to your room can be daunting; the distances between the hotels can be prohibitive; and the lines to do anything—eat, drink, play blackjack, see a show, or catch a cab—can drive you to distraction. But if you want to be right in the thick of the gambling action, the Strip's the ticket.

The off-Strip hotels have the popular casinos, but they often have a minimum of rooms. A Nevada ordinance requires new casinos to open with a minimum of 200 hotel rooms, and that's all they often have. They're mostly for out-of-towners who particularly like them and for relatives of locals who live nearby. But you can often find good room deals at them, because even with so few rooms, the locals' casinos often have trouble filling them. Most visitors want to be in the thick of the neon—on the Strip or downtown.

Rates

No two people pay the same amount for a seat on the same airline, and no two people pay the same amount for a hotel room in Las Vegas. If you have to fly somewhere at the last minute, and can't arrange for any advance purchase, charter, or discount fares, you'll pay retail for your seat, often upwards of four, five, even six times more than someone who reserves a week in advance. The same holds true of reserving a hotel room in Las Vegas, but here it's not a matter of time. It's more a matter of juice (who you know). If you have to call hotel reservations for your room, you'll pay top dollar (if you can even get a room). That's because the hotel reservations departments are set up to ream the visitor off the street via the rack rate, which is one of the most expensive room rates that's charged. (Probably the most expensive rate is the convention rate; never tell a hotel reservations agent that you're coming for a convention.)

How does the Las Vegas room system work? First, Las Vegas hotel room rates change minute to minute, and the range of rates can be spectacular. Imperial Palace, for example, charges $300 a night for a standard room during huge conventions, and $30 a night for the same room on selected dates starting a week later, between Thanksgiving and Christmas. A number of variables determine the rates for a room, but it mainly boils down to the great free-market motivator of supply and demand. When it's crowded, rooms are expensive. When it's slow, rooms are given away. A good option these days is to try an online reservations service, such as www.vegas.com.

Another factor that comes into play is the operative through which you secure your room. There are four or five different departments within the hotel, as well as a number of outside agents, that are allocated rooms to sell (or give away); the system is large and complex. Depending on whom you book your room through, your rate on any given day of the year can range from free (room comps issued by the casino) up to top-dollar (last-minute reservations through the front desk).

The best way to get a free or deeply discounted room in Las Vegas is to stay where you play. If you play table games with an average bet of at least $25, you should be able to get the "casino rate" (usually a 40–50 percent discount off the rack rate) for any room in Las Vegas except for the high-roller casinos, such as Caesars, Mirage, the Venetian, Bellagio, and MGM Grand, where an average bet of $50–100 is required. That same bet at the medium-priced casinos, like the Stardust, New Frontier, Tropicana, and downtown places, should get you a free room. If you play slots or video poker, it behooves you to join the slot club at the casino that sees most of your action. The more slot club points you accumulate in your account, the more free rooms (and other free stuff) you're entitled to. Two excellent books cover the room situation in detail. *Comp City* by Max Rubin shows you all the tricks if you're a table game player; *The Las Vegas Advisor Guide to Slot Clubs* by Jeffrey Compton is for slot and video poker players.

Other departments also handle rooms. Sales and marketing control blocks of rooms for special events (slot tournaments, sporting events such as prizefights or the Super Bowl, conventions, and wedding parties). And rooms are blocked off for the use of travel packagers and wholesalers. Discounts on rooms can often be obtained by finding a good "package," either one that the hotel itself is offering or that a tour-and-travel packager has put together or that a travel wholesaler is advertising. Look for package deals (often air–room, but sometimes room only) advertised in the Sunday travel supplement of the newspaper of the largest city near you. If you can, get a hold of the *Los Angeles Times* Sunday Calendar; that's where most Las Vegas hotels advertise their deals. Travel clubs, such as the Entertainment Book, often contain 50 percent-off coupons for Las Vegas hotel rooms. Your travel agent might have a connection with some discounted room deal, but don't count on it. Because Las Vegas rooms are relatively inexpensive to begin with, travel agents don't make too hefty a commission for booking them. Other discounts might be offered by the hotel, such as corporate, AAA, military, or senior.

Also, most Las Vegas hotels have a variety of rooms at different rates. At the older places, two classes of rooms are standard: "garden" (low-rise motel-style rooms from the '50s and '60s; cheaper) and "tower" (newer high-rise; more ex-

pensive). Some offer mini-suites and suites (though these are often reserved for room comps and upgrades by the casino). "Casino rate" is another discount, generally 35–50 percent of rack, that's given to gamblers whose action doesn't quite merit a fully comped room, but is good enough for half off.

Bottom line, however, is that because casino profits subsidize the other revenue-producing departments, Las Vegas hotels can afford to discount their rooms 20 percent, 40 percent, 60 percent, up to a whopping 80 percent at times over the standard rates at *all* other resort destinations around the country.

Reservations

Booking a room at a major Las Vegas hotel can be as simple as calling the 800 reservations number, agreeing to pay rack rate, and guaranteeing arrival with a credit card number. In this scenario, all you have to worry about is getting the kind of room you want at the location you desire at the price you're willing to pay. One word to the wise here: It's always wise to make a few calls to Las Vegas hotels *before* you make a final determination on the dates of your vacation to find out if something is going on in town (convention, event, holiday) for which you'll be reamed for your room. (You can also call the Las Vegas Convention and Visitors Authority at 702/892-0711 and ask what conventions are scheduled for the dates that you'll be in town.)

However, for those of you who like to get the best deal humanly possible on everything, and are willing to travel during the low seasons, Sunday through Thursday, and maybe even play a little to see if you can win your room, the booking of Las Vegas hotel rooms will send you straight to bargain-hunter heaven. There's no doubt about it: The supply of Las Vegas hotel rooms is up, and it's going even higher. When the demand is low, they're giving 'em away.

Las Vegas room reservation services come and go (and sometimes take your money with them), but one that's been in business for 15 years is **Las Vegas Travel,** 702/794-2061. Mitchell Group, the program director, claims that Las Vegas Travel is the largest room wholesaler and reservation service that sells rooms only in the Las Vegas market, with an availability of 500 rooms daily in all the top hotels. Call Las Vegas travel to see what kind of room deals they're offering when your dates are firm.

Specials

As previously mentioned, the last two weeks in July, the first two weeks in August, and the period from after Thanksgiving to just before Christmas are the (relatively) slow seasons in Las Vegas. These are the only times of year when Las Vegas's hotel rooms are readily available—so available, in fact, that the hotels nearly bribe you to stay in them, to keep the casinos busy and the profits flowing. If you can come to Las Vegas the first or second week of December, and you do a marginal amount of research, such as checking the *Los Angeles Times* Calendar section or ordering the December issue of the *Las Vegas Advisor,* you'll be hard pressed to spend more than $10 a night for a room.

MOTELS

Many travelers prefer motels to hotels. Since you'll be spending very little time in your room, the quality of amenities isn't particularly critical. A bed, shower, TV, heater/air-conditioner, and a good lock on the door are the salient features; the rest is luxury. Price is another consideration, since motels are generally 25–75 percent less expensive than hotel rooms. Distance is also a factor; at a motel you can pull a car right up to your door and don't have to navigate large parking lots or garages, crowded casinos, slow elevators, and long halls.

On the other hand, most Las Vegas motels tend to be older, less hygienic, and more run-down than their high-rise counterparts. They're also generally in funkier neighborhoods. They have thinner walls, flimsier beds, smaller bathrooms, and shabbier carpet. You need a little sense of adventure to stay in them.

Downtown: East Fremont

Glitter Gulch fills up Fremont Street from Main to 4th, but beyond that, and on side streets, bargain-basement motels are numerous. Dozens of

places are bunched together in three main groupings. It's not the best part of town, but it's certainly not the worst, and security is usually seen to by the management (but check). Generally speaking, the motels along Las Vegas Boulevard North and East Fremont are the least expensive. Motels between downtown and the Strip on Las Vegas Boulevard South are slightly more expensive and in a slightly better neighborhood.

East Fremont between 7th Street and the Castaways Hotel has the most motels, grouped sometimes one right next to another, or separated by car dealers and bars. On the other side of the Castaways the motels are a little farther apart. It's a few minutes' drive to the downtown casinos, and an excursion to the Strip, but the Castaways is on one end and Sam's Town and Nevada Palace on the other, so it's not too far to just gamble. Also, this is RV country, with RV parks lining the highway past motel row, and big parking lots at the casinos. And with so many possibilities out here, it's a good stretch to cruise if you don't have reservations and most No Vacancy signs are lit. Two reliable standards in this neighborhood, with rooms generally under $50 are **Lucky Cuss,** 702/457-1929, and **Ponderosa,** 702/457-0422.

Downtown: North

Las Vegas Boulevard North from Fremont to Bonanza, along with North Main and the north numbered streets from 6th to 13th, are also packed with motels one after the other. Stay on the lighted streets. It might be a little unnerving to deal with the front desk person through bars, but Glitter Gulch is very handy if that's where you want to spend your time, and these rooms can be amazingly reasonable, if a room is not where you want to spend your money. Weekly rates here, especially without kitchenette, could be as little as $15 a night. Both the **Golden Inn,** 702/384-8204, and the **Travel Inn,** 702/384-3040, offer the basics with rates starting at $35 for a double room with two beds and climbing to $100 during peak seasons.

Downtown: South

The motels on Las Vegas Boulevard South between downtown and the north end of the Strip at

Sahara Ave. have the most convenient location if you like to float between downtown and the Strip, or if you're getting married in one of the wedding chapels that line this stretch of the boulevard. It's also brighter and busier. You're right on the main bus routes. Most of these motels also offer weekly room rates, with or without kitchenettes. The **High Hat,** 702/382-808, has been around for several years and offers double rooms for $35–95.

Upper Strip

Several good-value motels congregate on Las Vegas Boulevard South between the Stratosphere and the Sahara; these places are also good to try for weekly rooms with kitchenettes. These are handy places to stay in the summer with kids, who'll be able to run right over to Wet 'n Wild. They're also within walking distance (though these blocks are very long) to the Sahara, Riviera, and Circus Circus (and the Adventuredome). **Fun City,** 702/731-3155, is within walking distance of the Sahara and offers clean doubles for $35–100.

Lower Strip

Motels along the lower Strip, between Bally's below Flamingo Avenue and all the way out to the Mandalay Bay at the far south end of the Strip, are well placed to visit all the new big-band casino resorts, but have prices that match the cheaper places north of downtown.

Convention Center

Another group of motels clings to the south side of the convention center, on Paradise and Desert Inn Roads, as well as the west side, between Paradise and

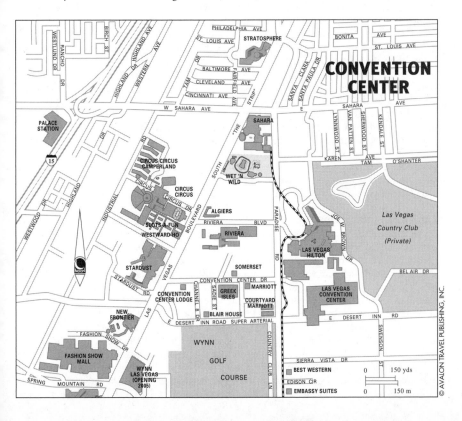

the Strip on Convention Center Drive. If you're attending a convention here and plan well in advance, you can reserve a very reasonable and livable room at any of several motels within a five-minute walk of the convention floor; most of them have plenty of weekly rooms with kitchenettes, which can save you a bundle. It's a joy to be able to leave the convention floor and walk over to your room, and back again if necessary—the shuttle buses to the far-flung hotels are very often crowded, slow, and inconvenient. Even if you're not attending a convention, this is a good part of town to stay in: off the main drag but in the middle of everything.

Rates

Like hotel rooms, motel room rates have more ups and downs than an elevator operator. During the summer, the price will be 10–20 percent higher. Weekend rates can be double weekdays; on holidays they can go up by another 25 percent. Conventions? Forget it. Sometimes a reservationist will leaf through the Las Vegas Convention and Visitor Authority's schedule of conventions to see if there are any in town at the time of your arrival before quoting a price. Occasionally he or she will ask you if you're coming to town for a convention. Again, deny it with authority. Often the rate quoted beforehand is for one type of room but when you arrive, only a more expensive room is available. Most motels have refundable key deposits (usually $5). Always add the 9 percent room tax to the price (10 percent downtown).

Las Vegas International Hostel

It's hard to beat this place for budget accommodations. The Las Vegas International Hostel has accommodations for 60 people in four-bed dorms and six private rooms reserved for couples. The hostel has a common kitchen and RV room; each dorm has its own bathroom with shower. Check in between 7 A.M. and 11 P.M. You get your own key and you can come and go as you please. A bed for the night is $12 with a· membership card, $14 without; private rooms are $26 with, $28 without. Beds are usually available but it's not a bad idea to reserve. Located at 1208 Las Vegas Blvd. S., a bit north of Vegas

World right on the bus line, 702/385-9955. Another option is the Las Vegas Backpacker's Resort offers private bathrooms, swimming pool, whirlpool tub, full common kitchen and high-speed internet connections for $15–21. It's located at 1522 Fremont St., 702/385-1150.

CAMPING AND RV PARKING

Camping

The nearest government tent campgrounds to Las Vegas are at Red Rock Canyon, Callville Bay on Lake Mead (around 20 miles east of Las Vegas), and up on Mt. Charleston (40 miles north of town).

Casino RV Parking

A number of casinos have attached RV parks. Other casinos allow RVs to park overnight in their parking lots, but have no facilities. Below are descriptions of both.

Circusland, 500 Circus Circus Dr., 702/733-9707 or 800/634-3450, is a prime spot for RVers, especially those with kids, who want to be right in the thick of things, but also want to take advantage of very good facilities. The big park is all paved, with a grassy island here and a shade tree there. The convenience store is open 24 hours. Ten minutes spent learning the Industrial Road back entrance will save hours of sitting in traffic on the Strip. The park has 370 spaces. All have full hookups (20-, 30-, and 50-amp receptacles); 280 are pull-throughs. Tents are not allowed. Accessible restrooms have flush toilets and hot showers; there's also a laundry, game room, fenced playground, heated swimming pool, children's pool, spa, and sauna, and groceries are available. The fee is $17–25 for two people.

KOA Las Vegas, 3333 Blue Diamond Rd., 702/263-7777 or 800/588-7711, opened in May 1994. It's the second largest RV park in Las Vegas, with 460 spaces, all with full hookups (20-, 30-, and 50-amp receptacles), of which 260 are pull-throughs. It's also the nicest in Las Vegas. The spaces are ample, providing room for two RVs where most other parks would squeeze four, maybe five. Each has a pine tree and a verdant square of grass. There's also a two-acre grassy picnic area and two pools, one for adults and the other for children, complete with a play apparatus and fountains. There's also a rec room and groceries. Accessible restrooms have flush toilets and hot showers. To top it all off, this place is a bona fide Las Vegas–style bargain: the fee is $15–20 per vehicle (Good Sam discount available). Tents are not allowed. Maximum stay is 14 days. Reservations are recommended September through April.

Sam's Town Boulder RV Park, 5225 Boulder Hwy., 702/456-7777 or 800/634-6371, is one small step above a parking lot, with little shade. But it's fairly roomy and is only a two-minute walk across the auto parking lot to the casino. It has 291 spaces, all with full hookups (20-, 30-, and 50-amp receptacles), of which 93 are pull-throughs. Tents are not allowed. Accessible restrooms have flush toilets and hot showers; there's also a laundry, limited groceries, heated swimming pool, and spa. The maximum stay is 14 days. The fee is $14 for two people. Open year-round

Sam's Town Nellis RV Park, 4040 South Nellis Blvd., 702/456-7777 or 800/634-6371, has 207 spaces for motor homes, all with full hookups (20-, 30-, and 50-amp receptacles), of which 14 are pull-throughs. It's mostly a gravel parking lot with spacious sites, a heated pool, and a spa; the rec hall has a pool table and kitchen. This is the snowbird park, which closes down in the summer. The minimum stay to qualify for the snowbird rate ($335) is three months, the maximum stay is six months. Tents are not allowed. The fee is $16 for two people. Open Sept.–May.

Arizona Charlie's East, 4445 Boulder Hwy., 702/951-5911, has 239 spaces for $20 nightly. **Nevada Palace VIP Travel Trailer Park,** at 5325 Boulder Hwy., 702/451-0232, has 170 spaces that go for $15 per night. **Mahoney's Silver Nugget** at North Las Vegas Blvd. and Civic Center Dr., 702/649-7439, offers 152 spaces with full hookups for $15 per night.

Non-Casino RV Parking

Twenty private RV parks are sprinkled throughout the city, but 10 of them are for long-term stays and are a little rough for overnighters. The three best of the visitor RV parks are described below (in order of preference). These are a bit more expensive than the casino RV parks.

Las Vegas KOA, 4315 Boulder Hwy., 702/451-5527, is a well-established RV park/campground, pleasantly rustic around the edges. The trees, oleander, and pool area are large and the sites aren't at all cramped. A little less than half the spaces are taken up by residential units, but the rest are reserved for transients. Tenters are welcome here, the closest place to downtown and the Strip to pitch a little A-frame or dome (60 tent spaces). Boulder Station is right up the street on the same side. A casino shuttle runs back and forth to the Strip. There are 180 spaces, most with full hookups (20-, 30-, and 50-amp receptacles), all pull-throughs. Accessible restrooms have flush toilets and hot showers; there are also a laundry, groceries, game room, playground, two heated swimming pools, wading pool, spa, and RV wash. The fees are $22 for tenters and $24–26 for two RVers.

Destiny's Oasis RV Park is at 2711 West Windmill, 702/260-2000 or 800/566-4707, directly across the interstate from Silverton. (Take the Blue Diamond exit, three miles south of Russell Road, and go east to Las Vegas Blvd. South. Turn right and drive one block to West Windmill, then turn right to the park.) Opened in January 1996, Oasis's 707 spaces make it the second largest RV park in all of Nevada. All have full hookups (20-, 30-, and 50-amp receptacles); roughly 500 are pull-throughs. Five rows of towering date palms usher you from the park entrance to the cavernous clubhouse, 24,000 square feet of it. Each space is wide enough for a car and motor home, and comes with a picnic table and patio. The horticulture is plentiful, though it needs a few years to mature. Be sure to grab a map from the front desk; this is Nevada's easiest RV park to get lost in. Tents are allowed. Accessible restrooms have flush toilets and hot showers; there is also a laundry, grocery store, bar and lounge, arcade, exercise room, putting course, and heated swimming pool. Maximum stay is 30 days. The fee is $12–27 per vehicle.

Boulder Lakes RV Resort, 6201 Boulder Hwy.,

702/435-1157, is a mile south of the corner of Russell Road and Boulder Highway. A long and winding road leads from the highway to this large residential park, of which a portion is reserved for overnighters. There are 417 total spaces here, 75 held for overnight motor homes, all with full hookups (20- and 30-amp receptacles). There are no pull-throughs. Tents are not allowed. Accessible restrooms have flush toilets and hot showers; there are also laundry facilities, limited groceries, rec hall, and 4 heated swimming pools. The fee is $20 for two people. The **Las Vegas International RV Resort,** 6900 East Russell Rd., 877/977-1700, offers 224 sites with private phone lines at each for $24 per day. The **Las Vegas Motorcoach Resort,** 8175 Arville St., 702/897-9300 or 866/897-9300, offers a clubhouse with a pool and a spa with its hookups. Rates are in the $40 range.

Food

Think of dining Las Vegas style and you're likely to conjure up free hot dogs, $0.99 shrimp cocktails, $1.99 breakfast specials, $3.99 lunch buffets, and $4.99 prime rib dinners. True, Las Vegas deserves its reputation for good food at rock-bottom prices, but it also boasts enough gourmet, ethnic, trendy, themed, celebrity-chef, meat-and-potatoes, and hole-in-the-wall restaurants to delight the most sophisticated and discriminating tastes.

Most major hotels have a 24-hour coffee shop and a buffet, along with some combination of Italian, Japanese, Chinese, Mexican, steakhouse, and fast food. Non-casino restaurants around town are also proliferating quickly. Best of all, menu prices, like room rates, are consistently less expensive in Las Vegas than any other major city in the country.

Why? Because almost all Las Vegas hotel-casino food and beverage departments lose money. Food, like every other hotel amenity, is a loss leader for the casino, where the real profits are accrued. And the non-casino restaurants have to compete with the casino restaurants, so they're forced to hold the line on prices.

At first glance, you can easily believe that the casinos take a loss on their buffets, $1.99 breakfasts, $7 prime rib, $10 steaks, and $12 lobsters. But the prices in the gourmet and ethnic restaurants, and even the coffee shops, might surprise you if you've always heard that casino restaurant food is dirt cheap. How do casinos lose money on $15 chicken dinners, $12 Mexican meals, $10 spaghetti, and $6.95 bacon and eggs? Easy. They lose it on comps. At any given time in any casino restaurant, perhaps only 50–75 percent of the patrons in a restaurant are paying for their food. Sure, the comped customers risked their money at the tables and machines and probably spent way more than $10 for the spaghetti dinner they're scarfing in the coffee shop, but the gambling losses are the price of admission for the entertainment, and the free food is part of the bargain.

Of course, don't feel too sorry for the casinos that have to give away all that food to attract players. That's why the prices on the menus are so high. The casinos have it wired from every which way: By charging big-city prices, the comped customers feel they're getting their money's worth in food for the losses they've sustained; the paying customers help subsidize the comped customers; and the casino can write off comp expenses at retail, even though they're paying wholesale.

MEAL DEALS
Shrimp Cocktail
The Golden Gate restaurant downtown began serving a San Francisco–style shrimp cocktail in 1955, and more than 30 million have been served since. The price up until a few years ago was only $0.49, but it's still a number-one value at $0.99. In fact, it's the oldest meal deal in Las Vegas—appropriate for the oldest hotel in Las Vegas. It goes great with a draft beer ($1); a piano player serenades patrons. At the Deli, open 24 hours, 702/385-1906.

Bacon and Eggs
Most places, you can't even get a cup of coffee for a dollar anymore. But at El Cortez, a dollar buys

you two eggs, two strips of bacon, toast, hash browns, and all the coffee you can drink. It's worth coming back for. Open 24 hours, 702/385-5200.

Porterhouse

The $9.95 porterhouse might be the best meal deal in Las Vegas. This giant 16-ounce slab of red meat is served in the Monterrey coffee shop at the Gold Coast casino on West Flamingo. It comes with salad, crisp potatoes, onion rings, baked beans, rolls, and a glass of draft beer (must be 21 or older). It's not advertised anywhere, not even on the Gold Coast marquee, so it's not particularly well known, but it is featured prominently on the coffee shop menu, so you don't have to ask the waitperson if it exists. Best of all, it's served 24 hours a day. Polish one off at 8 A.M., then go out and run a marathon. Open 24 hours, 702/367-7111.

Steak and Shrimp

It's not on the menu, but if you ask for it at Mr. Lucky's coffee shop in the Hard Rock Hotel, they'll be happy to serve it to you. You can enjoy an eight-ounce steak, three grilled jumbo shrimp, salad, roll and a potato for $7.77. Open 24 hours, 702/693-5000.

Free Drinks

The most common comp of them all (other, perhaps, than free parking) is free drinks to all players. Got a nickel? Sit at a slot machine and wait for the cocktail waitress to happen by. Don't wanna wait? Head over to Palace Station and get yourself a 16-ounce margarita for a mere $0.99, or go to Slots-A-Fun for an imported beer in the bottle for $0.75 (popcorn is free, too).

CASINO RESTAURANTS

Buffets

The Las Vegas buffet was inaugurated in the late 1940s, when the El Rancho Vegas put out a big spread between midnight and 4 A.M. to keep patrons in the casino after the late headliner show. A lavish feast, it cost $1, and it was called a "chuck wagon." The chuck wagon caught on and soon all the big casinos laid out major midnight smorgasbords. In the mid-1950s, weekend chuck wagon hours were extended to encompass breakfast, the forerunners of today's Saturday and Sunday champagne brunch. By the late 1960s, the chuck wagon was served at most of the major casinos for all three meals. It wasn't until the early '80s that chuck wagons became buffets. And today, Las Vegas is the buffet capital of the world.

Las Vegas buffets are one small step up from fast food in quality, one giant leap down in price, and in a class all their own worldwide in quantity. For the cost of satisfying a Big Mac attack, you can shovel home, on average, 23 choices of chow. Breakfast presents the usual fruits, juices, croissants, steam-table scrambled eggs, sausage, potatoes, and pastries. Lunch is salads and cold cuts. Dinner is salads, steam-table mook, vegetables, and potatoes, and usually either a baron of beef, shoulder of pork, leg of lamb, saddle of mutton, breast of turkey, whole rotisserie chicken, or barbecued ribs.

Prices are standard, with a few extremes at either end: breakfast $8–10; lunch $9–12; dinner $10–20. Quality has less to do with price than you might imagine. If you're really starving and must have food *now,* go to the nearest buffet and load up. You can also buffet shop, simply by walking in and sneaking a peek. Otherwise, plan ahead and try to be at the right place at the right time. And those with young children, don't forget: The buffet is your best friend in Las Vegas.

Buffet times and prices are quite changeable, so it's wise to check the buffet listings in the free visitors guides or the Weekend section of Friday's *Review-Journal.* Generally, breakfast is served 7–10 A.M., lunch 11 A.M.–3 P.M., and dinner 4–10 P.M., give or take a half hour.

The best buffet in Las Vegas is, without a doubt, the **Village Seafood Buffet** at the Rio. Here, you have an incredible choice of seafood preparations. The Mongolian barbecue grills up whitefish, scallops, shrimp, mussels, and calamari with assorted vegetables and sauces. At the American station you can load up on seafood salads, snow crab legs, oysters on the half shell, peel-and-eat shrimp, seafood gumbo, grilled salmon, blackened scallone, broiled swordfish, oysters Rockefeller, poached roughy, steamed clams, and lobster tails. Then come the ethnic ocean entrées, such as seafood fajitas, squid chow fun, kung pao scallops, and cioppino. The Village Buffet also has the best selection of the highest-quality after-dinner goodies in town. The pies come in chocolate cream, coconut cream, coconut pineapple, lemon meringue, key lime, apple, blueberry, pecan, cherry, peach, and more; there's also assorted pound cakes, cheesecakes, pastries, tortes, mousses, chocolate decadence, and cookies. It's expensive at $34.99 for dinner, but it's worth it. 702/252-7777.

As for the best regular buffet, a lot of people still vote for the **Carnival World** at the Rio, the original big buffet. Carnivores swear by the **Festival Buffet** at the Fiesta, which features a Mongolian barbecue and one of the largest open-pit barbecues in the west; if you can grill it, you'll find it at the Fiesta (702/631-7000). The **Market Street Buffet** at Texas Station (702/631-1000) is a perennial favorite; it has a Texas chili bar with a dozen different concoctions, along with cooked-to-order fajitas, pizza, and stirfries. Another attractive option is the **Garden Court** at Main Street Station (702/387-1896).

Other interesting buffets are found at the **French Market Buffet** at the Orleans (702/365-7111), which features good Cajun and Creole dishes; **Las Vegas Hilton** (702/732-5111), where you can get all the cold king crab legs you can eat; **Treasure Island** (702/894-7111), for peel-and-eat shrimp; and **Golden Nugget** (702/385-7111), where the bread pudding is world renowned.

Panorama and Pageantry

Top of the World, the 360-seat, 360-degree restaurant, on the 106th floor of Stratosphere Tower over 800 feet above the Strip, makes a complete revolution once every 80 minutes or so. The view of Vegas defies description, and the food is a recommendable complement. Try the charbroiled portobella mushrooms, pan-seared peppersteak, or lobster linguine, and be sure to save room for Chocolate Stratosphere, which is nearly as tall as the tower. Entrées average $28.

Open Sun.–Thurs. 6–11 P.M., Fri.–Sat. until midnight, 702/380-7777.

Paris' **Eiffel Tower Restaurant** hovers 100 feet above the Strip. The bilingual culinary staff masters delicate French culinary feats, while a romantic piano bar rounds out the Parisian experience. Located on the 11th floor of the Eiffel Tower, 702/739-4111, reservations suggested. Open daily 5:30–10:15 P.M.

Voodoo Cafe requires a mini thrill ride to the top of the newest Rio tower on the glass elevator. The Rio contends that the restaurant is on the 51st floor and the lounge is on the 52nd floor, even though they're really on the 42nd and 41st floors, respectively; Rio management dropped floors 40–49-something having to do with a superstition. Whatever floors they're on, the Voodoo double-decker provides the great view of the Strip. The food and drink are expensive and a bit tame, but the fun is in the overlook, especially if you eat or drink outside on the decks. Open daily 5–11 P.M., 702/252-7777.

Another glass elevator delivers you to the **Ranch Steakhouse,** at the top of the Horseshoe tower downtown; they say it's the 24th floor and it is. Before Stratosphere opened, this was the best view in Las Vegas, and it's still fine. Steaks are the play here—filet, porterhouse, New York—and the prime rib is as thick as a Michener novel. Most of the people up here are comped. Entrées average $16–22. Open daily 6–10 P.M., 702/382-1600, reservations required.

This spectacle of a restaurant, at Las Vegas Hilton, **Benihana** consists of a cocktail lounge out front, with musical waters, and an animated bird show with stuffed-animal entertainers, reminiscent of Chuck E. Cheese. Hibachi tableside and *robata* barbecue rooms feature similar menus, with dinners from $15–35, mostly meat, fish, and veggies. For just the show, though, sit in the lounge and sip some steaming sake (performances on the hour starting at 5:30 P.M.). Open 5:30–10:30 P.M., 702/732-5755.

Centerstage is a combination steakhouse and coffee shop, a very effective concept for its location. Without a doubt the room with the best neon view in town, the Centerstage sits in a tinted dome looking straight down Glitter Gulch, with the lighted Plaza Hotel tower soaring above. When you make reservations, specify seating at a front-window table. Open 4:30–11 P.M., 1 Main St., 702/386-2512.

Ristorante Italiano at the Riviera is known for its wall-length mural behind glass and its veal: osso buco, saltimbocca, piccata, and scaloppine ($18–20). Pasta $11–12, chicken $15–16, steaks $25, lobster $35. Open Fri.–Tues. 5:30–11 P.M., 702/794-9363.

Kokomo's sits under hut-like canopies within the rain forest of the Mirage's domed atrium. It's slightly noisy from the casino and the waterfalls, but the hubbub quickly becomes part of the unusual atmosphere. Try the Dungeness crab cakes ($16), salmon ($18), filet mignon ($16–22), prime rib ($18–28), or lobster tail ($34). Open 5–10 P.M., 702/791-7111.

Next door to Kokomo's is **Moongate,** which replicates a Chinese village square, with a big lilac tree in the middle, pagoda roofs, and scalloped walls. The food is as pleasing as the environment, and the prices are reasonable. Satay beef, mu shu pork, tea-smoked duck, and strawberry chicken all go for $14, and scallops, shrimp, and lobster are under $20. Open 5:30–10 P.M., 702/791-7111.

Pound on the table with your goblet while you eat medieval-style (that is, without utensils) and cheer for the jousting knights on horseback at Excalibur's **Tournament of Kings.** Twice nightly at 6 P.M. and 8:30 P.M., $50 buys you a Cornish game hen dinner, unlimited soft drinks, and the chance to hiss at fire-breathing dragons and listen to Merlin recount a somewhat modified legend of King Arthur. While a bit hokey, the horsemanship is impressive, and kids will love the noise and excitement: a definite family winner.

Gourmet

While just a few years ago, there were only two four-star/diamond restaurants in Las Vegas, this category is quickly proliferating. Bellagio alone boasts seven James Beard award–winning chefs. Its **Picasso** is among only 18 restaurants in North America to win the Mobil Five-Star Award. Under the tutelage of chef Julian Serrano, the kitchen dishes up amazing twists on Mediterranean

French cuisine. Pablo's artwork fittingly graces the walls and Pablo's son designed the carpet and furniture for the rustically sumptuous restaurant. Open Wed.–Mon. 6–9:30 P.M., 702/693-7111.

When Las Vegas' first five-star dining establishment closed, the Desert Inn's Monte Carlo room, maitre d' David Orvin sought out a second home where he could take his passion for legendary service to a new level. And he feels right at home in the Luxor's **Isis.** Egyptian artifacts, intimate booths, and a ceiling landscape of desert stars set the stage for chef Bradley Aug's classically traditional fare with an emphasis on fresh seafood. Open Thurs.–Mon. 5:30–10:30 P.M., 702/262-4773.

Mandalay Bay's **Aureole** is as remarkable for its architecture and catwalk-entry as for chef Charlie Palmer's seasonally inspired American cuisine. Sweet tooths will want to save room for the warm chocolate–peanut butter liquid-center torte, with caramel-pecan ice cream and peanut brittle, one of Aureole's signature decadent desserts. The four-story wine cellar is a sight to behold, and the wine selection covers virtually every continent on the globe. If what you want isn't in reach, a black-garbed acrobat with climbing gear will scale the tower to find the appropriate bottle. Open nightly 6–10 P.M., 702/632-7401.

Downtown, **Hugo's Cellar** at the Four Queens is perhaps the best gourmet room for the money. The cellar location, though right off the casino, is well insulated from the upstairs hubbub; all the ladies receive a red rose upon entering. The salad is brought around on a cart and prepared tableside, sherbet cones are served between courses. The house appetizer is the Hot Rock, which you have to see to believe. Entrées are $20–30—try the duck, snapper, or tournedos. Open 5:30-10:30 P.M., 702/385-4011.

Many Las Vegas veterans consider **Michael's,** a dark little room at the Barbary Coast, to be the best restaurant in town. The entrées are $30–70 and strictly à la carte; a party of two will run up a $200 tab without trying. But the intimate surroundings, the quality of the food, and the show put on by the wait staff is more than worth it. This restaurant is not advertised anywhere and is run exclusively for the high rollers at the Barbary and Gold Coasts, but reservations are taken starting at 3:30 P.M. when the count of comped customers has been taken. Open daily 6–11 P.M., 702/737-7111.

Steakhouses

Perhaps the essence of the Las Vegas steakhouse can be experienced at Circus Circus's aptly named **THE Steakhouse.** Wind your way through the permanent crowds of grinds and kids toward the buffet and tower elevators; cow portraits lead to the meat locker where sides of beef hang. The split-level dining area surrounds the grill, which lends an authentic, slightly smoky air to the room. Chicken for $12, top sirloin for $15, filet $20, surf and turf $20. Open daily 5:30–10 P.M., 702/794-3767.

Similarly, the large mesquite grill and line area of the **All-American Bar and Grille** at the Rio Hotel faces the downstairs dining room; upstairs are additional tables, along with a quite unusual collection of antique slot machines. Order your meat—top sirloin for $14, New York for $18, filet for $19—and then choose your sauce: bearnaise, dijon, peppercorn, mushroom, horseradish. The prime rib could be the largest cut you've ever seen—you won't be able to finish it, and you'll need a trailer to carry the thing out. Open daily 11 A.M.–11 P.M., 702/252-7777.

Gallagher's Steakhouse at New York–New York has been an institution in New York City since 1927. You'll understand the reputation after sampling their famed dry-aged beef, as well as their notable seafood selection. Open Mon.–Thurs. 4–10 P.M. and Fri.–Sun. until midnight, 702/740-6450.

Seafood

For variety and quantity in food fish, head straight for the Village Seafood Buffet at the Rio.

Bring your credit cards to **Emeril's New Orleans Fish House** in the MGM Grand, because this place is expensive and worth every dollar. The menu changes when award-winning celebrity-chef Emeril Lagasse feels like it, but appetizers have included smoked trout wontons, ragout of duck pastrami, sushi with softshell crab roll and salmon tartar, and spiced artichoke stuffed with assorted boiled shellfish (all in the $8–14 range).

The lobster comes in cheesecake, a dome (covered with baked puff pastry), sauce, Creole gazpacho, and a "study" (variations on the theme). There's also Louisiana softshell crab with crawfish jambalaya, oyster stew with andouille sausage, salmon tartar, tuna steak with fresh foie gras, potato-crusted Gulf pompano with lump crabmeat, along with Louisiana campfire steak and Mississippi chicken (entrées average $26 or so). Did someone say dessert? How about praline cheesecake, peanut butter–chocolate pie, bread pudding with whiskey sauce, or banana cream pie with banana crust (averaging $10)? You've probably gotten the idea that Emeril's is exotic—especially for Las Vegas. Open daily 11 A.M.–2:30 P.M., 5:30–10:30 P.M., 702/891-7777.

The Bellagio brings San Francisco's renowned seafood haven, **Aqua,** to Las Vegas with flair. To celebrate the opening, two paintings were commissioned by Robert Rauschenberg and everything about the restaurants speaks to great taste: both literal and figurative. Chef Mark Lo Russo adds an amazing, if rather expensive ($70 for a five-course menu), French influence to traditional seafood cuisine. The restaurant is found off the botanical conservatory near the lobby, open daily 5:30–9:30 P.M., 702/693-7223.

The Rio, with 13 restaurants, is known for both its variety and quality of food offerings, and **Buzio's** is its seafood showcase (unlike the seafood buffet, which is its seafood pig-out). First, it's a beautiful room that overlooks the pool area and has a seaworthy canvas ceiling; there's also an oyster bar for informal counter seating and quicker service. Secondly, the fish: fresh oysters, lobster, clams, and catch of the day from all over the world; pan roasts, stews, cioppino, and bouillabaisse; salads and louies and cocktails; all served with bread fresh baked on the premises and soup or salad. This place gets hectic, so make reservations and arrive early. Open daily 5 A.M.–11 P.M., 702/252-7697.

"American contemporary with a Pacific Rim flair" is how the **Second Street Grill** describes its food, and its menu is a successful combination of international influences. You can get steaks, chops, and veal (there's a $10.95 porterhouse that's a bargain), but the play here is the denizens of the deep:

Mongolian seafood pot, ahi sashimi, Maryland crab cakes, seared sea scallops to start; then wok-charred salmon with king crab hash, pound-and-a-half of king crab legs in a ginger-lime sauce (skip the sauce), and the usual Chilean sea bass and swordfish steak. The Grill is a sleeper of a downtown restaurant and you can almost always get a table even on a busy night without a reservation. The *Las Vegas Advisor* coupon book has a 50 percent-off coupon for the whole meal. Open Thurs.–Mon. 5–10 P.M., Fri.–Sat. until 11 P.M.

Another option worth checking out is **Aqua-Knox** at the Venetian, which bills its cuisine as "California-inspired seafood." There's a water-encased wine cellar and an extensive raw bar. Open nightly from 5:30–11 P.M., Fri.–Sat. until 11:30 P.M., 702/414-3772.

Delis and Food Courts

For a little slice of New York, stop in at the **Stage Deli** in your wanderings around the Forum Shops at Caesars, which serves specialty meats and desserts flown in from the Big Apple daily. Allow a few minutes to choose from the more than 300 menu items, such as brisket, stuffed cabbage, knishes, potato pancakes, chicken soup with matzoh balls, "skyscraper" sandwiches (literally 10–12 layers) named after celebrities, and egg creams. You'll spend $7–12 for entrées. There's also a Stage Deli fast-food counter at the MGM Grand next to the race and sports book. Open daily 8 A.M.–11 P.M., 702/893-4045.

La Piazza is to fast-food courts what Caesars is to casinos, which is fitting, since it the fast-food court at Caesars. You can get deli, Mexican, Chinese, pasta and Italian, burgers, and beer and wine here; there's also a salad bar where you pay by the plate. The dining area overlooks the casino. Open daily 8:30 A.M.–11 P.M., 702/731-7731.

Italian

One of the best hotel restaurants in Las Vegas is **Pasta Pirate** at the California Hotel downtown. Designer pasta is an alternative: First "you picka you pasta, then you picka you sauca," as the menu instructs. Huge kids' plates of spaghetti are under $5. The grill is out front, and those

cooks move. The decor is early rustic—vents, pipes, shelves—plus neon. Open daily 5:30–11:30 P.M., 702/385-1222.

Pasta Palace at Palace Station on West Sahara frequently has a pizza and beer special, and the pasta dishes are all less than $10. For example, try the ravioli *fra diavolo* ($9.95); you'll be hard pressed to finish it. Open daily 5–10 P.M., 702/367-2411.

Asian

Empress Court at Caesars Palace is the fanciest, most exotic, and most expensive Chinese restaurant you'll ever eat in. Try the bird's nest (not a soup), $13–19 depending on side dishes, or the shark fin (also not a soup), $16–24, also depending on what goes along. Open Thurs.–Mon. 5–11 P.M., 702/731-7731.

Moongate at the Mirage is in a beautiful setting: a footbridge over a brook, a tranquil courtyard in front, and a rounded entry. Here, the shark's fin is in a soup ($30); the rest of the menu is the usual kung pao, mu shu, Peking duck, and nutty chicken. Next door is the equally elegant and expensive **Mikado**. Open daily 5:30–10:30 P.M., 702/791-7111.

Voted one of the Zagat's favorite restaurants in Vegas, **China Grill** is another one of Mandalay Bay's architecturally arresting designer restaurants. Signature specialties include lamb ribs and exotic twists on traditional Chinese favorites. Open nightly 5:30–11 P.M., 702/632-7404. After hours, usually around 1 A.M., the lights go down and the deep house music starts pumping, when China Grill transforms itself nightly into the Red Dragon Lounge. More traditional, expensive, and classic is China Grill's next-door neighbor, **Shanghai Lilly.** Here Cantonese and Szechwan creations reign supreme and the decor is understated and elegant. Open nightly 5–10:30 P.M., 702/632-7409.

Other high-end options include **Pearl** at the MGM Grand, which specializes in creative Asian seafood dishes, open nightly 6–10:30 P.M., 702/693-7223; and **Little Buddha** at the Palms, a beautiful dining room offering sushi and other Asian specialties, open nightly 5:30–11 P.M., Fri.–Sat. until midnight, 702/942-7778.

NON-CASINO RESTAURANTS

Old-time Favorites

In 1933, J.S. Fong opened the Silver Cafe at 106 N. 1st St. next to the Silver Club. He advertised American food, with $0.25 breakfasts and $0.35 dinners, and was the only Las Vegas café serving Chinese food, by request, until 1941. In 1955, the Silver Cafe changed its name to **Fong's** when it relocated to the present site on East Charleston. You can't miss it: Big neon pagoda-roof signs grace the entrance. Inside are red booths, large paintings, and a rock shrine, along with the same American and Chinese food this family has been dishing up for decades. 2021 E. Charleston, 702/382-1644. Open Tues.–Sun. 4 P.M.–midnight.

El Sombrero has been in the same location since 1951, when it was opened by Clemente Greigo; his nephews Jose and Zeke Aragon are now in charge. The best thing about this adobe restaurant is that this stucco cantina, with six booths, six tables, and a completely Mexican jukebox, looks its age and has certainly seen it all, but retains its baby-boomer vitality and devotion to service and quality. Small dinners are $5, combo dinners are $8, and the service is no-nonsense. 807 S. Main St., 702/382-9234. Open Mon.–Sat. 11 A.M.–9 P.M., closed Sun.

You wouldn't recognize it from the unremarkable exterior, but this **Golden Steer** steakhouse, in the same location since 1962, is one of the most popular and elegant restaurants in Las Vegas, usually jammed with locals and visitors in the know. In the front room is the spectacular woody, glassy bar surrounded by comfy living room furniture. The three dining rooms are no less inviting. And the food? Well, the filet mignon is truly the "Aristocrat of Tenderness," and the New York pepper-steak is the best in town. Dinners start at $17. Reservations a must at prime time. 308 West Sahara, 702/384-4470. Open daily 11 A.M.–11 P.M.

Breakfast

Coffee Pub is the power-breakfast spot on the west side, with an ambience and menu that you might expect to see more at a ski resort or a mountain retreat than the Las Vegas flatlands. Big, hearty breakfasts are served indoors or outside on a patio with spray misters. 2800 West Sahara, 702/367-1913. Open daily 7 A.M.–3 P.M.

Las Vegas is a great town for bagels, lox, matzo brie, and designer cream cheese. **Bagelmania** is one of the best places to get all of that. 855 East Twain, 702/369-3322. Open Mon.–Sat. 6:30 A.M.–5 P.M., Sun. until 3 P.M.

Jamie's is a classic diner with great food and cheap prices. 2405 East Tropicana, 702/435-8100. Open Mon.–Fri. 7 A.M.–8 P.M., Sat. until 6 P.M., Sun. until 4 P.M.

Brazilian

Yolie's Steakhouse is the only place in Nevada to get marinated meat, mesquite-broiled, *rodizio*-style, sliced continuously from the skewer onto your plate by the waiter in the fashion of a true *churrascaria* (Brazilian house of meat). Sausage, turkey, brisket, lamb, pork, along with salad, soup, and sides, come for a set price of $28.95. The room is soft and inviting, the bar is big and comfortable, and the service attentive. 3900 Paradise, 702/794-0700. Open Mon.–Fri. 11 A.M.–3 P.M., daily 5:30–11 P.M.

Chinese

At **Chin's**, eggrolls are $5, other appetizers up to $14, vegetable plate $8, and chicken, seafood, pork, and beef dishes start at $15. Fashion Show Mall, 3200 Las Vegas Blvd., South Las Vegas, 702/733-8899. Open daily 11 A.M.–9:30 P.M.

Don't let the humble setting in a storefront in a Flamingo Avenue strip mall deter you: **Bamboo Gardens** has some of the most original preparations anywhere. The clams **dou chi** are out of this world; also try the Mongolian lamb, firecracker beef, and Hunan eggplant. The Szechuan string beans over steamed rice is a meal in itself. 4850 W. Flamingo, 702/871-3262. Open Mon.–Sat. 11 A.M.–8 P.M., Sun. 5–10 P.M.

Sitting right on the edge of the bluff out Spring Mountain Avenue overlooking the Strip, **Cathay House** has the view and the food to go with it. This is *the* spot for a dim sum lunch. Dinner dishes include orange beef, cashew scallops, garlic chicken, crystal shrimp, shark's fin soup, and Szechuan pork. 5300 West Spring Mountain Ave., 702/876-3838. Open daily 10:30 A.M.–10 P.M.

Continental/French

Pamplemousse is French for "grapefruit," but it might as well mean "ultimate." The cuisine is so fresh that the menu is spoken, not printed: your waiter describes the nightly fare in detail (be sure to ask about prices to avoid surprises). Specialties include bay scallops sautéed in grapefruit roux, medallions of veal with baked apple, rack of lamb, and filet mignon. The small house, converted into a country inn, only seats 70, so reserve as far in advance as possible. Entrées average $21. 400 East Sahara, 702/733-2066. Open daily 5:30–9:30 P.M.

Award-winning **Andres** is downtown in a strange neighborhood, but once you're inside the converted house, you'll forget all about the outside world. Plan on a couple of hours and a couple hundred dollars to enjoy a full meal at chef Andre Rochat's restaurant, including a bottle from the extensive wine list to accompnay salmon tartar with cucumber salad, macadamia-crusted sea scallops, sautéed duck, rabbit loin, and the like. The vegetable-medley accompaniment is always excellent, and the fruit tarts for dessert are recommended. Entrées average $30. 401 South 6th St., 702/385-5016. Open Mon.–Sat. 6–10 P.M. (Andres also has a location at the Monte Carlo.)

You wouldn't expect to find a fine Continental dining room attached to a bowling alley in Green Valley, but in Las Vegas nothing is as it seems. It's worth the effort to find **Renata's**, which serves imaginative combinations of food, such as salmon with lentil salsa, prawn salad, chicken in a tequila cream, even meat loaf with mashed potatoes. Also, Renata's isn't as expensive as the other fancy places, with entrées in the $17–22 range. 4451 East Sunset, Henderson, 702/435-4000. Open Mon.–Sat. 5–11 P.M.

Italian

Battista's Hole In The Wall: Family-style meals (antipasto, garlic bread, minestrone, all-you-can-eat pasta on the side, and all-you-can-drink red wine) start at $10.95 for spaghetti and meatballs and go all the way up to $30 for cioppino. Classic Italian restaurant decor. Walking distance of the Strip next to the Barbary Coast near the corner of Flamingo Avenue. 4041 Audrie, 702/732-1424. Open 5–10:30 P.M.

Carluccio's Tivoli Gardens is Liberace's old restaurant, and the decor (glittery ceiling, bar designed like a grand piano) remains to prove it. The food is workman-like Italian, with the usual pasta in red or clam sauce, eggplant parmesan, chicken, veal, and beef plates. Try the crab-stuffed shrimp. Workman-like prices, too: two can escape for under $20. 1775 East Tropicana, 702/795-3236. Open Tues.–Sun. 4:30–10 P.M.

North Beach Cafe gets some buzz from the locals, for its great service and light Italian fare. Try the linguine with your choice of shellfish or chicken cognac. The swordfish preparation is also recommendable. Entrées run in the $10–18 range. 2605 South Decatur, 702/247-9530. Open daily 5–11 P.M.

Bootlegger is a cozy, family-run spot with great service, reasonable prices, and tasty food; try the pizzas, calzone, veal saltimbocca. There's also a variety of vegetarian and low-calorie selections. Lunches are $4–7, dinners $9–17. Bootlegger also has a call-in joke line at 702/736-8661. 5025 South Eastern, 702/736-4939. Open 24 hours.

Japanese

Ginza is always occupied by at least several tourists from Tokyo. Ten à la carte dishes, in true Japanese style, will run $40. 1000 East Sahara, 702/732-3080. Open daily 5:30 P.M.–1 A.M.

Osaka is another nice Japanes spot. 4205 West Sahara, 702/876-4988. Open Mon.–Fri. 11:30 A.M.–3 P.M., daily 5 P.M.–midnight.

At the annual Consumer Electronics Show, Japanese exhibitors line up out the door and down the block, waiting to get in **Tokyo** to eat. 953 East Sahara, 702/735-7070. Open Mon.–Fri. 11:30 A.M.–2:30 P.M., daily 5 P.M.–1.A.M.

Mexican

Dona Maria's has good and inexpensive food. The tamale with green enchilada sauce is a lip-smacker. 910 Las Vegas Blvd. S., 702/382-6538. Open 8 A.M.–10 P.M. A perennial local favorite, **Viva Mercado's** features traditional Mexican and Southwestern cooking with no animal fat or lard used in the preparation. The langostino enchiladas are prime; also try the steak with stir-fried cactus. The ceviche is recommendable, as is the build-your-own fajitas. Entrées are in the $8–15 range. 6182 West Flamingo, 702/871-8826. Open Sun.–Thurs. 11 A.M.–9:30 P.M., Fri.–Sat. until 10:30 P.M.

Lindo Michoacan is the eastsiders' choice. It's a bustling noisy open restaurant that stuffs lots of people into two open rooms. Try the steak cilantro, chicken with cactus, *camarones rancheros,* and tequila shrimp. You'll pay $8–15 for entrées. 2655 East Desert Inn, 702/735-6828. Open 11 A.M.–11 P.M.

Thai

Thai Spice is the best Thai restaurant in town; the soups, noodle dishes, and traditional curries, pad thai, mee krob, and egg roll are all well prepared

and cost $7–14. Tell your waiter how hot you want your food on a scale of 1 to 10. 4433 West Flamingo, 702/362-5308. Open Mon.–Sat. 11:30 A.M.–10 P.M.

Vegetarian

Slim pickin's in this town. **Wild Oats** grocery stores are in two locations, one east and one west. Both stores have cafés, which serve good wholesome food (some meat) and have big salad and soup bars. 6720 West Sahara, 702/253-7050, and 3455 East Flamingo, 702/434-8115. Open 10 A.M.–7 P.M. **Shalimar** Indian food has a number of vegetarian dishes. 3900 Paradise, 702/796-0302. Open daily 5:30–10:15 P.M.

Information and Services

Information Bureaus

The **Chamber of Commerce,** 3720 Howard Hughes Pkwy., 702/735-4515, open weekdays 8 A.M.–5 P.M., has a bunch of brochures and general fact sheets to give away, and sells maps and some books (*Las Vegas Perspective* on area statistics, updated every year), and has a computerized phone line. The John L. Goolsby Visitor Center on the first floor is the best spot for brochure hunting and other services.

The **Las Vegas Convention and Visitors Authority,** 3150 Paradise Rd., 702/892-0711, also dispenses flyers and brochures and sometimes coupons in its visitor info center right inside the front door of the convention center. One of the LVCVA's priorities is filling up hotel rooms—call its reservations service at 877/VISITLV. You can also call the same number for convention schedules and for an entertainment schedule. The LVCVA's website is pretty good: www.lasvegas24hours.com.

Las Vegas Advisor

This 12-page monthly newsletter is a must for serious and curious Las Vegas visitors. The *Advisor* takes a close and objective look (no advertising or comps accepted) at every particular of consumer interest in the Las Vegas firmament, from an entire megaresort to a shrimp cocktail. It also tracks

important local trends, local and national gambling news, new gambling publications and products, Las Vegas restaurants, shows, theme parks, meal deals, gambling promotions, tournaments, entertainment options, coupon opportunities, and probably its most valuable information, Las Vegas's Top Ten Values. A year's subscription ($50) includes exclusive coupons worth up to $800. One trip to Las Vegas and two coupons more than pay for the annual sub price. *Advisor* subscribers have an industrial-strength edge over the tens of millions of Las Vegas visitors *and* locals. Highly recommended. To subscribe, call 800/244-2224, or write to Huntington Press, 3687 South Procyon Ave., Las Vegas, NV 89103, 702/252-0655.

Visitors Guides and Magazines

Nearly a dozen free periodicals for visitors are available in various places around town; racks in motel lobbies and by the bell desks of the large hotels are the best bet. They all cover basically the same territory—showrooms, lounges, dining, dancing, buffets, gambling, sports, events, coming attractions—and most have numerous ads that will transport coupon clippers to discount heaven.

Today in Las Vegas is a 32-page weekly minimag bursting its staples with listings, coupons, 20 pages of restaurants, and a good column on free casino lessons. For a sample copy, write or call Lycoria Publishing, 3226 McLeod Dr. #203, Las Vegas, NV 89121, 702/385-2737.

What's On provides comprehensive information, plus articles, calendars, phone numbers, and lots of ads. Its Las Vegas maps are by far the best of the lot. Single issues cost send $4.95; call 800/4WHATSON or go to www.ilovevegas.com.

The 150-page **Showbiz Weekly** spotlights performers and has listings and ads for shows, lounges, and buffets, plus television and movie times; get a complimentary issue by calling 702/383-7185.

Libraries

The **Clark County Library** main branch is at 1401 East Flamingo, 702/507-3400. **The Las Vegas Public Library** main branch is at 833 Las Vegas Blvd. N., 702/507-3500, open Mon.–Thurs. 9 A.M.–9 P.M., Fri.–Sun. 10 A.M.–6 P.M.

The **Lied Library,** 505 Maryland Pkwy., 702/895-2111, at the university is relatively new. **Special Collections,** on the third floor of the Lied library, includes hundreds of computer entries under Las Vegas—everything from Last Frontier Hotel promotional material (1949) and mobster biographies to screenplays for locally filmed movies and the latest travel videotapes. Also in Special Collections is the Gaming Research Center, largest and most comprehensive gambling research collection in the world. It covers business, economics, history, psychology, sociology, mathematics, police science, and biography, all contained in books, periodicals, reports, promo material, photographs, posters, memorabilia, and tape.

Bookstores

Las Vegas is not renowned as a literary town. In fact, the word "book" around here, 90 percent of the time, is a verb. One books reservations, rooms, tickets, criminals; "to book" also means to accept and record wagers. "Book" as a noun generally refers to the room, counter, or big board where wagers on sports events and races are recorded. One exception is **The Reading Room,** an independent bookstore tucked amid the high-end shops at Mandalay Place, located on the sky bridge connecting Mandalay Bay and the Luxor. Proba-

bly the only place in town where bookmaking has anything to do with publishing is at the **Gambler's Book Club,** open Mon.–Sat. 9 A.M.–5 P.M. This cramped space is crowded with all the books on every form of wagering extant, from craps to video machines, from jai alai to dog racing. It also has a large case devoted to Mafia books and biographies, lots of local fiction, history, travel guides, books on probability theory, casino management, gambling and the law, magic, and a room in the back full of used books. It's at 630 South 11th St. near Charleston, 702/382-7555 or 800/522-1777.

The only bona fide bookstore on the Strip is **Waldenbooks** in the Fashion Show Mall, 702/733-1049. Waldenbooks is also at the Meadows Mall, 702/870-4914, and has a superstore across the street from the Boulevard Mall, 702/369-1996.

Barnes & Nobles are found at several locations, including 2191 North Rainbow Blvd., 702/631-1775. **Borders** has three stores in Las Vegas: 2323 South Decatur, 702/258-0999; 1445 West Sunset Rd., 702/433-6222; 2190 North Rainbow, 702/638-7866.

Book Magician, 2202 West Charleston, 702/384-5838, is a great used bookstore, with some excellent deals on classic Nevadana.

Maps

Front Boy sells state-by-state Rand McNallys, raised-relief maps of Las Vegas and southern Nevada ($15 each), and USGS topographical maps in different scales ($5). Ask for the stunning USGS Landsat photo of Las Vegas and Lake Mead. Front Boy also sells a street-map book of the city ($18.95). 3340 West Sirius, 702/876-7822, open Mon.–Fri. 9 A.M.–5 P.M.

Services

In emergencies, if you need the police, the fire department, or an ambulance, dial **911.**

If you need a doctor, call the **Clark County Medical Society,** 702/739-9989, to get a referral. For a dentist referral, contact the **Clark County Dental Society,** 702/733-8700. In a dental emergency, you'll need to contact the emergency room of a hospital to see if there's a dentist on duty.

University Medical Center, 1800 West

Charleston Blvd. at Shadow Ln., 702/383-2000, has a 24-hour emergency service with outpatient and trauma-care facilities. **Sunrise Hospital,** 3186 South Maryland Pkwy., 702/731-8000) also has an emergency room.

If you need to fill a prescription in the wee hours, try **White Cross Drug,** 1700 Las Vegas Blvd. S., 702/382-1733), near the Stratosphere and is open 7 A.M.–1 A.M., with a pharmacy that stays open until 9 P.M.

Transportation

By Air

Las Vegas is one of the easiest cities in the world to fly to. The number of airlines keeps fares competitive, and charter companies can bring airfare down even more. Package deals can be an especially good value, if you're only staying the usual three or four days, but you might have to do your own research to get the best deals. A good way to start is to look in the Sunday travel supplement from the largest daily newspaper in your area, where many of the airlines, wholesalers, packagers, and hotel specials are advertised. Also, look in the travel supplements of the Los Angeles, Chicago, Dallas, and New York newspapers if you can; though the advertised tour operators and wholesalers might not serve your area, sometimes you can get in on the air-only or room-only part of their packages. Given the popularity of Las Vegas, it's best to make your reservations as early as possible: last-minute deals are few and far between, and you'll pay through the nose to fly to Vegas on a whim. Unless your travel agent specializes in Las Vegas, don't count on him or her to help much. Las Vegas prices are so cheap that agents don't make much money on selling it, and therefore don't have much incentive to stay up on the deals, which change with the wind.

McCarran International Airport reportedly handles a greater percentage of passengers per capita than any other airport in the world. The wide-eye rubbernecking that this town is famous for kicks in the moment you step into the terminal, with its slots, palm sculptures, maze of people movers, escalators, elevators, and, of course, advertisements full of showgirls, neon, and casinos.

Las Vegas Transit buses now serve the airport. You can catch one of two buses, the 108 that runs up Swenson (the closest it comes to Las Vegas Blvd. is the corner of Paradise and Sahara), the 109 runs east of that, up Maryland Parkway. To get to the Strip, you have to transfer at the large cross streets onto westbound buses that cross the Strip. Both buses wind up at the Downtown Transportation Center; if you're headed downtown, stay on the bus till the end of the line. The buses ($2 exact fare) run from 5 A.M. to 1 A.M.; be sure to ask for a transfer so you can switch buses at no charge. The Strip bus runs 24 hours a day. Call 702/228-7433 for more information.

You can take a **Gray Line** airport shuttle van to your Strip ($4.75 one-way), downtown ($5.75 one-way), or outlying ($6 one-way) destination. These shuttles run continually (you shouldn't have to wait any longer than 20 minutes) throughout the day and evening; you'll find them outside the baggage claim area. You don't need reservations from the airport, but you will need reservations from your hotel to return to the airport. Call 702/384-1234 24 hours in advance to reserve a spot on an airport-bound shuttle.

A taxi ride should run no more than $9–12 to the convention center and south and central Strip hotels, $12–15 for upper Strip hotels, and $15–18 for downtown.

By Rental Car

Las Vegas crowds around the intersection of I-15, US 95, and US 93. The interstate runs from Los Angeles (272 miles, four to five hours' drive) to Salt Lake City (419 miles, six to eight hours). US 95 meanders from Yuma, Arizona, on the Mexico border, up the western side of Nevada, through Coeur D'Alene, Idaho, all the way up to Golden, British Columbia. US 93 starts in Phoenix and hits Las Vegas 285 miles later, then merges with I-15 for a while, only to fork off and shoot straight up the east side of Nevada, and continue due north all the way to Jasper, Alberta.

Renting a car provides an opportunity to experience some real thrills while you travel around town. If you're visiting Las Vegas for the first time on a package deal at a Strip hotel and don't plan on going off the beaten track, you probably don't need a car; just ride the Strip buses or trolleys or grab a cab. But if you've been here before and want to peel out a little, or see more of stunning southern Nevada, why not do it in the style to which you've always wanted to become accustomed? Check with your insurance agent at home about coverage on rental cars; often your insurance covers rental cars (minus your deductible) and you won't need the rental company's. If you rent a car on most credit cards, you get automatic rental-car insurance coverage.

Rental car rates change even faster than hotel room rates in Las Vegas and the range can be astounding. When you call around to rent, be sure to ask what the *total* price of your car is going to be. With sales tax, use tax, airport fees, and other miscellaneous charges, you can pay upwards of 21 percent over and above the quoted rate.

Generally, the large car-rental companies have desks at the baggage pick-up room at the airport. Those that don't have courtesy phones there; they send their shuttles out to get you, and bring you to their properties, most around the corner of Paradise Road and Harman Avenue.

Allstate, 702/736-6147, has pickups, 4X4s, and passenger and cargo vans. **Rent-a-Vette,** 702/736-8016, rents Corvettes, Ferraris, Jaguars, BMWs, and Lexus. **Rebel Rent-A-Car,** 702/597-1707, rents mopeds and motorcycles. **Lloyd's,** 702/736-2663, rents Corvettes, Cadillacs, Lincolns, and vans. **Sunbelt,** 702/731-3600, rents convertible BMWs, Jaguars, Miatas, and Mustangs. The usuals—Hertz, Dollar, Payless, Enterprise, Thrifty, Budget,and Alamo—also all rent cars in Las Vegas.

Las Vegas Monorail

The future is now in Las Vegas. The mod Las Vegas Monorail in 2004 connected the Sahara on the north end of the Strip with the MGM Grand on the south end, now stopping at seven other resorts and the convention center in-between. More than 27 major resorts are now within easy transit along the Strip, all without a car or taxi. Reaching speeds up to 50 miles per hour, the monorail glides above traffic to cover the four-mile one-way route in about 14 minutes. Nine trains with air-conditioned cars carry up to 152 riders along the elevated track running on the east side of the strip, Stopping every few minutes between the seven stations. The stations include the Sahara, Las Vegas Hilton, Las Vegas Convention Center, Harrah's/Imperial Palace, Flamingo/Caesars Palace, Bally's/Paris, and the MGM Grand. The Las Vegas Monorail runs daily, 8 A.M.–midnight. Tickets start at $3 for a single ride, with discounts for multiple-trip tickets. One- and three-day passes are also available for $15 and $40 respectively. Tickets are available at vending machines at each station as well as at station properties. For more information, call 702/699-8200 or visit www.lvmonorail.com.

By Bus and Trolley

Citizen Area Transit (CAT), the public bus system, is managed by the Regional Transportation Commission and is financed by a 0.25 percent cut of the sales tax and passenger fares. CAT services a couple of dozen routes all over Las Vegas Valley between 5:30 A.M. and 1:30 A.M.; only the Strip buses run 24 hours a day. All buses depart from and return to the Downtown Transportation Center (DTC), at Stewart Street and Casino Center Blvd. behind the post office. The fares are $1.25–2 on the Strip for adults, $1 on the Strip for children 5–17 and seniors over 65. Call 702/228-7433 for recorded information on fares, times, and routes; stay on the line to talk to a CAT representative who can help you plan your route through the city.

Bus service has improved considerably over the past few years, and we no longer hear as many complaints about them. (Watch your wallets and purses, however; the Strip buses are the number-one sphere of operations for pickpockets.) Another way to get around, besides your own two feet, is on the local trolleys (702/382-1404). These custom vehicles travel up and down the Strip like the buses, but they pull right up to the front door of the hotels, passing every 15 minutes or so from 9:30 A.M. to 1:30 A.M., $1.75, exact change. They also tool around downtown. Both lines terminate at the Stratosphere, so you can now connect from the Strip to downtown on the trolley. It's a good alternative to public buses, especially from Friday afternoon to Sunday night.

The **Greyhound depot** is right next door to the Plaza Hotel (south side), at 200 South Main St.; 702/384-9561. These buses arrive and depart frequently throughout the day and night from and to all points in North America, and are a reasonable alternative to driving or flying. Advance purchase fares are extremely inexpensive, and with extended travel passes you can really put the miles on.

By Taxi

Except for peak periods, taxis are numerous and quite readily available, and the drivers are good sources of information (not always accurate) and entertainment (not always politically correct)—the information is often more on the entertainment level. Of course, Las Vegas operates at peak period most of the time, so if you're not at a taxi zone right in front of one of the busiest hotels, it might be tough. They cost $2.20 for the flag drop and $1.50 per mile ($3.70 for the first mile); it's also $0.35 per minute waiting time. That's why it's wiser to take the surface streets from the airport to where you're going, rather than the freeway, which is several miles longer.

Cab companies include **Ace Cab,** 702/736-8383; **Checker,** 702/873-2000; **Western,** 702/382-7100; **Whittlesea,** 702/384-6111; and **Yellow,** 702/873-2000.

By Limo

With a local fleet of more than 200 limousines, **Bell Trans** can handle anything you might dream up. Its rates are most reasonable too: $39 an hour for a standard limo (seats five), $50 for a stretch (one-hour minimum, seats six, TV, VCR, CD, unstocked bar), and $76 for a superstretch (one-hour minimum, seats six, real leather, moon roof, two TVs). Bell also does the airport limo transfers; 702/385-LIMO.

Presidential Limousine, 702/731-5577,

charges $50 an hour for its stretch six-seater, and $75 an hour for the superstretch eight-seater; both include TVs/VCRs, mobile telephones, champagne, and roses for the ladies.

Tours

The ubiquitous **Gray Line,** 702/384-1234 or 800/634-6579, offers tours of the city, Hoover Dam, and Grand Canyon. City tours last three hours; tours beyond the area are all-day affairs. Gray Line will pick you up at your hotel and return you to it at the end of the tour. Tours run from $40 (nightly tour of the Strip) to $149 (Grand Canyon). Reservations can be made by telephone at any hour.

Key Tours, 702/362-9355, offers trips from Las Vegas to Laughlin, a gambling town that is about 90 miles from Las Vegas on the Colorado River at the Arizona state line, from $5 a person and a four-hour Hoover Dam tour for $25.

To Grand Canyon

Las Vegas is the gateway to the Grand Canyon, and a handful of **flightseeing companies** offer excursions from McCarran Airport. Some deals are air only: the planes don't land. Other longer excursions fly over the city, Boulder City, Hoover Dam and Lake Mead, and the West and South rims, and land at the canyon airport. From there, ground transportation covers the 12 miles to the South Rim services where, depending on the tour, you have from two to four hours for sightseeing, photography, hiking, lunch, the museum, or an IMAX movie.

These flights have become controversial lately, for two reasons. First, the feds, prompted by complaints from hikers and campers, are considering discontinuing Grand Canyon flightseeing altogether, reasoning that they disturb the "natural peace" of the national park. Operators, on the other hand, wonder how one would quantify "quiet" and argue that flightseeing has much less impact than hiking and camping, since flightseers don't touch the canyon at all. Second, fatal crashes of the small aircraft are not uncommon. Meanwhile, the flights go on and here are the vitals.

All the tours depart from the Grand Canyon Tour Center at the Scenic Airline center near

Koval and Reno Streets. They all pick you up and drop you off at your hotel.

Scenic Airlines, 702/638-3300, provides a 90-minute round-trip flight to the West Rim for $180, and an eight-hour round-trip excursion with a two hour coach tour of the South Rim and a buffet lunch for $230.

Sundance Helicopter, 702/597-5505, does a 10-minute helicopter tour of the Las Vegas Strip for $80 per person, as well as a thrilling two-and-a-half hour ride over Las Vegas, Hoover Dam, and Lake Mead, then halfway down into the Canyon to land on a private plateau. The chopper ride is a once-in-a-lifetime experience; $300 per person.

Vegas-Area Recreation

All the glitter and glitz of Vegas can lead to sensory overload. Thankfully, there is abundant natural beauty within a hour's drives of the Strip, where you unwind. Wander a wildlife refuge, hike to the mountain's summit, and scramble red rock, and you'll forget how close you are to the biggest adult playland in the world.

FLOYD LAMB STATE PARK

Roughly 15 miles north of Las Vegas on US 95, drive past the Las Vegas Shed Company, noticeable for its 100-foot-tall antenna, turn right at Durango Road, and follow the signs around to this oasis in the desert. The park is open 8 A.M.–5 P.M. daily (later during summer) and it costs $6 to get in, 702/486-5413. Signboards at the entrance detail the history of the area and present information on Desert National Wildlife Refuge, desert wildlife, and news clippings about the park.

Some of the oldest and most complete and well-known archaeological evidence in the country was discovered at this water hole, originally known as Tule Springs. Between 14,000 and 11,000 B.C., giant ground sloths, mammoths, prehistoric horses, American camels, and condors all congregated around the tules; perhaps as early as 13,000 B.C., but definitely by 11,000 B.C., humans were present, hunting the big game.

Tule Springs shows up in the early history of Las Vegas, but it wasn't until 1941 that there was any development here. The property was purchased by Prosper Goumond, who owned a casino on Fremont Street. Over the next 15 years, Goumond turned the springs into a self-sufficient ranch and dude ranch. He built the big

hay barns, water tower, pump house and well, foreman's house, root cellar, and coops, stables, and storages. He also welcomed dudes to the ranch, especially socialites waiting out their six-week residency for a divorce, and built guest-houses, a bathhouse and pool, and gazebo. Activities included fishing, canoeing, swimming, tennis, horseback riding, trap shooting, hayrides, and dances.

Goumond died in 1957 and the city bought the property in 1964 to use as Tule Springs Park. The name was changed in 1977 to honor Floyd Lamb, a state senator who was later convicted of taking a bribe in a federal sting operation. The city transferred ownership to the state shortly thereafter.

At the front gate pick up a brochure, which identifies all the buildings in the historic area, including the adobe hut (in ruins behind a cyclone fence) built in 1916 by Burt Nay. Then explore the lush grounds: domesticated peacocks by the foreman's house, the occasional roadrunner scurrying by, big cottonwoods, oleanders, screwbean mesquites, and tules surrounding four ponds. The largest, Tule Springs Lake, is stocked with catfish during the summer and rainbows in the winter. Fishing is definitely the main activity here, being the nearest fishing hole to Las Vegas. Picnicking is also popular, with sheltered tables all around the ponds, and a group picnic area with volleyball at the back end of the park. The Las Vegas Gun Club takes target practice right on the other side of the park fence.

In 1999, Las Vegas Assemblywoman Kathy Von Tobel attempted to change park's name back to Tule Springs. This move was prompted both because Lamb's name was somewhat

Las Vegas

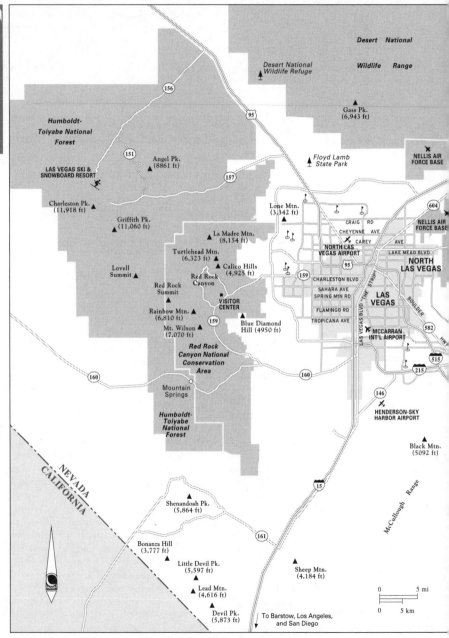

Desert National

Wildlife Range

Desert National
Wildlife Refuge

156

95

Gass Pk.
(6,943 ft)

Humboldt-
Toiyabe National
Forest

151

Angel Pk.
(8861 ft)

Floyd Lamb
State Park

NELLIS AIR
FORCE BASE

LAS VEGAS SKI &
SNOWBOARD RESORT

157

Lone Mtn.
(3,342 ft)

NELLIS AIR
FORCE BASE

604

Charleston Pk.
(11,918 ft)

CRAIG   RD

CHEYENNE   AVE

Griffith Pk.
(11,060 ft)

CAREY   AVE

La Madre Mtn.
(8,154 ft)

NORTH LAS
VEGAS AIRPORT

LAKE MEAD BLVD

NORTH
LAS VEGAS

Turtlehead Mtn.
(6,323 ft)

Calico Hills
(4,925 ft)

159

CHARLESTON BLVD

Lovell
Summit

Red Rock
Canyon

SAHARA AVE

SPRING MTN RD

LAS
VEGAS

Red Rock
Summit

VISITOR
CENTER

FLAMINGO RD

THE STRIP

Rainbow Mtn.
(6,810 ft)

159

Blue Diamond
Hill (4950 ft)

TROPICANA AVE

BOULDER HWY

Mt. Wilson
(7,070 ft)

McCARRAN
INT'L AIRPORT

582

Red Rock
Canyon National
Conservation
Area

LAS VEGAS BLVD

515

160

160

215

Mountain
Springs

146

HENDERSON-SKY
HARBOR AIRPORT

Humboldt-
Toiyabe
National
Forest

Black Mtn.
(5092 ft)

NEVADA
CALIFORNIA

15

Shenandoah Pk.
(5,864 ft)

McCullough Range

Bonanza Hill
(3,777 ft)

161

Little Devil Pk.
(5,597 ft)

Sheep Mtn.
(4,184 ft)

Lead Mtn.
(4,616 ft)

Devil Pk.
(5,873 ft)

To Barstow, Los Angeles,
and San Diego

0   5 mi

0   5 km

MOON

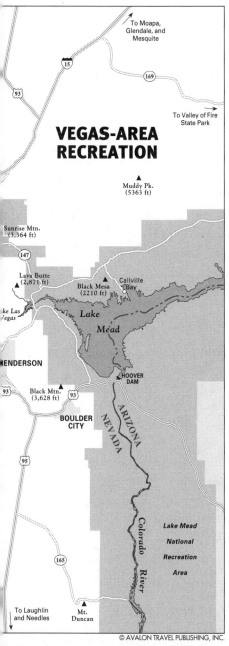

VEGAS-AREA RECREATION

To Moapa, Glendale, and Mesquite

To Valley of Fire State Park

Muddy Pk. (5363 ft)

Sunrise Mtn. (3,364 ft)

Lava Butte (2,871 ft)

Black Mesa (2210 ft)

Callville Bay

ke Las Vegas

Lake Mead

HENDERSON

Black Mtn. (3,628 ft)

HOOVER DAM

BOULDER CITY

ARIZONA

NEVADA

Colorado River

Lake Mead

National

Recreation

Area

To Laughlin and Needles

Mt. Duncan

© AVALON TRAVEL PUBLISHING, INC.

tainted in the eyes of some residents due to his being forced to resign his office in 1983 after being convicted of attempted extortion, as well as because it relates to the geographic features of the park. As of September of 2004, however, the name remains the same.

GILCREASE WILDLIFE SANCTUARY

Named for William Gilcrease, a kindly elderly gent and owner of the property, Gilcrease Wildlife Sanctuary contains five acres dedicated to the care and rehabilitation of wildlife of all kinds. Bill can be seen rambling around the sanctuary at all hours, usually talking to or nurturing one or another of the animals. The Sanctuary has been in operation since the late 1970s and has been the headquarters for the Wildwing Project since 1992.

The sanctuary is located at 8103 Racel Rd.; open Wed.–Sun. 10 A.M.–3 P.M. A tax-deductible donation of $4 ($1 for children under 6) gets you inside. To get there, go north on US 95 just past Las Vegas Shed Co. with the huge antenna, turn right on Durango Rd., turn right on Racel Rd., and turn right on Silk Purse Rd. For additional information, call the sanctuary at 702/645-4224.

MT. CHARLESTON AND THE DESERT NATIONAL WILDLIFE REFUGE

Another five or so miles north on US 95 is Route 157; turn left (west) and head straight into **Kyle Canyon,** one of many short, narrow, and sheer gashes in the massive Spring Mountain Range, which hems in Las Vegas Valley to the west for 50 miles. Most of this range, well placed for Las Vegans, is administered by the Bureau of Land Management, but the elevations above 7,000 feet are managed by the Las Vegas Ranger District of the Humboldt-Toiyabe National Forest, under the designation of the Spring Mountains National Recreation Area. Within that is the 43,000-acre Mt. Charleston Wilderness Area. The picnic areas, campgrounds, trails, overlooks, and ski slopes accommodate nearly a million visitors a year. Some commercial logging is conducted on

Mount Charleston is a world away from nearby Las Vegas.

this Forest Service land, and the nearly 30 inches of precipitation grabbed by the Springs's high peaks are extremely important for the watersheds of the Las Vegas Valley to the east and Pahrump Valley to the west.

Being high and wet, and surrounded by low and dry, the Spring Mountains approximate "a garden island poking out of a sea of desert." In fact, the local flora and fauna have become biologically isolated; 30 species of plants are endemic. Additionally, these mountains support a system of five distinct life zones; ascending from Las Vegas to Mt. Charleston in terms of altitude is the equivalent of traveling from Mexico to Alaska in terms of latitude. Good roads take you up to 8,500 feet, within 45 minutes of downtown Las Vegas, and it can be 20–30°F cooler here.

Kyle Canyon

A little more than 10 miles from US 95, Route 157 climbs into the forest and gets canyony. First

stop is **Mt. Charleston Hotel,** 2 Kyle Canyon Rd., 702/872-5500 or 800/794-3456, which has a large, lodgelike lobby complete with roaring fireplace, bar and big dance floor, and spacious restaurant. Built in 1984, this is one of the most romantic spots in southern Nevada, a perfect place to propose (you can then return to Las Vegas and get married an hour or two later). Two arcades house slots and video games. The lodge has 63 rooms, which start at $79 during the week, and go up to $200 for a suite on a Friday or Saturday.

Beyond the hotel, Route 157 continues another four miles. You first pass **Kyle Canyon Campground** at 7,100 feet. This is the lowest of five high-mountain campgrounds in the vicinity, roughly 5,000 feet higher in elevation than downtown Las Vegas (and usually at least 20 degrees cooler). It's also the closest, a mere 45 minutes away. It has big sites, fairly far apart. Most are shaded by tall pines, with plenty of greenery in between. Here you'll find 24 campsites for tents or self-contained motor homes up to 40 feet. Piped drinking water, vault toilets, picnic tables, grills, and fire pits are provided. There's also a campground host. Some reservations are accepted for the multi-family sites, while others are first-come first-served. The fee is $15 for single family, $25 for multi-families. The maximum stay is 14 days. It's open May through September, depending on snowfall. Contact the Spring Mountain National Recreation Area Visitor Center, 877/444-6777.

A little farther along is **Mt. Charleston village,** with a few residences and a U.S. Forest Service district office. Next to it is **Fletcher View Campground,** with 11 sites (it can accommodate self-contained motor homes up to 32 feet). This one is smaller and more compact than the Kyle Canyon Campground down the street, just one road in and out. Sites are a little closer together and a bit shadier. If both campgrounds are full, Kyle RV area is across the road, just a parking lot with room for about a dozen rigs. No reservations are taken; the fee is $10.

The road ends at **Mt. Charleston Lodge,** 702/872-5408 or 800/955-1314, the main action on the mountain. This is a funky alpine operation, with rustic cabins and a restaurant. The cabins come in two sizes, basic (one bed and a hide-a-bed, $125–150) and deluxe (two kings and a hide-a-bed, $190–220). The bar and restaurant are open 24 hours. Pull into the parking lot above the lodge for the half-mile Little Falls Trail is easy going, the three-quarter-mile Cathedral Rock Trail is moderately steep, with sheer drops but great views, and the North Loop Trail covers nine hard miles to the peak.

Backtracking on Route 157 to just before the hotel, Route 158 heads off to the left and connects in six miles with Route 156, the Lee Canyon Road. **Robbers Roost** is a short easy hike to a large rock grotto that once sheltered local horse thieves. A mile north is **Hilltop Campground,** at 8,400 feet. Hilltop was completely renovated in 1994 and has new asphalt pavement complete with curb, new picnic tables and grills, wide staircases from parking areas to uphill tent sites, and Mr. Clean restrooms. This aptly named campground is situated high up on a bluff; a few sites have a fine view over the valley floor, but little shade. Other sites have more shade but less view. It's also cooler and breezier than the two campgrounds down in Kyle Canyon. There are 35 campsites for tents or self-contained motor homes up to 40 feet. Piped drinking water, flush toilets, picnic tables, grills, and fire rings are provide, and there's a campground host. Reservations are accepted for the multi-family sites, the rest are first-come first-served. The fee is $14 for single family, $20 for multi-families. The maximum stay is 16 days. It's open May through mid-October, depending on snowfall. Call 702/515-5400.

Up the road you'll find the access for the southern loop of the **Charleston Peak Trail,** and two picnic areas: **Mahogany Grove** is for groups, reservations required ($112.50 with a maximum of 75 people); **Deer Creek** is a one-quarter-mile stroll in from the road. In another couple of miles is **Desert View Trail,** a brief enjoyable nature walk with incomparable views of the surrounding desert.

National Desert Wildlife Refuge

Drive out US 95 past the Kyle Canyon turnoff to Mt. Charleston. The road leading into the refuge is easily missed, so keep a sharp eye. About three miles after you pass the Kyle Canyon turnoff (but before you get to the turnoff for Lee Canyon), you'll see a sign on the right side of the road indicating the turn for the Desert National Wildlife Range.

Turn right and drive four miles down this well-graded dirt and gravel road to the **Corn Creek Field Station,** at the entrance to the refuge. Stop at the kiosk; pick up maps and a brochure. If you're planning on traveling into the interior of the refuge, sign the guest book and trip log. If you're just out for the day, take a tour around the Field Station and surrounding springs.

Archaeologists have found evidence of campfires at the dunes site to the north between 4,000 and 5,000 years ago. Around the turn of this century, this area housed a way station on the Las Vegas & Tonopah Railroad. The area was named for Corn Creek Springs, which feeds the small stream and ponds in this beautiful desert oasis. Today, Corn Creek Springs, with its lush environment, three spring-fed ponds, woodland, and pasture, is a fantastic place to have a picnic, view wildlife, or just stroll amidst quiet and clean air and meditate on the beauty of a very unusual desert oasis. More than 240 species of birds have been observed at the springs, including a great blue heron and a pair of red-tailed hawks. Well-cared-for trails entwine the springs and surrounding environs. Early mornings and evenings are the best time to spot rabbits, squirrel, an occasional mule deer, coyote, badger, and fox ranging about the field station.

The refuge was established in 1936 to protect the overhunted desert bighorn sheep. It encompasses approximately 1.5 million acres (2,200 square miles) of the Mohave Desert, making it the largest National Wildlife Refuge in the Lower 48. About half the Refuge overlaps the Nellis Air Force Bombing Range, which is prohibited to public access. Only native wildlife and the Air Force are permitted entry.

If you go into the refuge, drive only on designated roads; no unlicensed off-road vehicles are allowed in the Range. All camps (except backpack camps) must be located within 100 feet of designated roads. Camping within a quarter mile or within sight of any waterhole or spring is prohibited for protection of the wildlife. There is no potable no water on the refuge, so you must bring your own. In an emergency, spring or storage water can be used, but it must be boiled or purified first. Campfires are permitted in designated camping areas. Only dead and down wood may be used for fires and no wood may be removed from the range for any reason. All firearms and other weapons are prohibited and shooting is outlawed.

Just past the entrance kiosk, a sign shows mileage along two routes through the Refuge from this junction. Alamo Road, the longest route, wends up a wide playa on the western slope of the Sheep Mountains, skirts the edge of the Nellis Air Force Range, and rambles for 72 miles through some fairly scenic Joshua forest before dropping down to the 3,000-foot-level and exiting at Pahranagat National Wildlife Refuge Headquarters on US 93. Mormon Well Road, the shorter of the two routes and by far the more scenic and historic, climbs slowly to an elevation of 6,500 feet and ends 47 miles later at US 93 about halfway to Pahranagat.

About four miles up Mormon Well Road, the surrounding mountains offer the best bighorn habitat in the entire range. The precipitous terrain allows these spectacular desert bighorn a quick escape from predators, and the shrub-covered ledges offer good forage. Bighorn visit this area early and late in the year when it is cooler. However, since there are no watering holes nearby, the sheep descend to lower elevations to drink at numerous springs and catch basins. During the hot dry summer months, the sheep move to the northern portion of the range, closer to perennial springs. Their coats blend well with the rugged terrain, so watch the high crags and pinnacles for movement or their telltale white muzzle.

About a mile farther you come to ancient roasting pits used by natives to slow-cook their meat and vegetables. Agave was placed in a bed of hot coals and limestone cobbles, then covered with vegetable material or earth and left to slowly roast.

Some 17 miles from the junction, you come to Peek-A-Boo Canyon. Watch for the natural cave located at the mouth of the canyon. In another

11 miles is a road to the left leading to Mormon Well Spring and the Mormon Well Corral. This road, closed to vehicles, is worth the short third-of-a-mile hike to visit the spring and corral, which served as a stopover during the old horse and buggy days and was later used to water livestock. The old corral on the north side of the spring is listed in the National Register of Historical Places. Storage facilities have been installed at the spring to ensure an adequate water supply for wildlife during the summer when the local springs dry up. Make your visit short to avoid keeping mule deer, bighorn sheep, and other wildlife from this critical watering place.

A little beyond Mormon Well Spring you come to an established picnic area. Stop for lunch, relax, and enjoy the scenery. This rest area is at 6,000 feet, so the weather is generally cool in the summer. After a leisurely lunch, continue north on Mormon Well Road for another 14 miles to where it joins US 93, or return to US 95 the way you came. Either way is an enjoyable trip, and going back the same way you came will seem like an entirely new trip. Contact the refuge manager at 702/646-3401.

Lee Canyon

Hang a left onto Lee Canyon Road (Route 156). It's 3.5 miles to the end of the road. Just before you get to the parking lot for the Las Vegas Ski and Snowboard Resort, you'll pass two campgrounds. **McWilliams Campground** is 1,500 feet higher (8,500 feet) than the ones at Kyle Canyon. Here, the trees are still tall but sparser and there's less undergrowth, so there's more space between sites. It's less in the canyon, so the sky is bigger. The sites are all off one large loop; the ones in the middle are most private. There are 40 campsites, one flush toilet and 4 vault toilets, piped drinking water, picnic tables, grills, fire rings, and a campground host. The maximum stay is 16 days. Reservations are accepted for the multi-family sites, the rest are first-come first-served. The fee is $14 for single family, $24 for multiple families. It's open May through September, depending on snowfall. Slightly up the hill is **Dolomite Campground,** similar to McWilliams but with 31 sites; the ones at the back (and highest point) of the campground are prime (also $14 per night). Open mid-May to mid-October.

Finally you come to the ski resort. Only 45 miles (and 6,500 feet) away from sizzling Sin City, "Ski Lee" has been operated since 1962 by the Highfield family. With the advent of snowboarding, they changed their name in 1995 to The Las Vegas Ski & Snowboard Resort, and in 2000 they added a terrain park and half-pipe for hot-doggers. Base elevation is 8,500 feet and the top of the chairlift is another 1,000 feet higher—thin air. But cliff walls towering above the slope protect skiers from biting westerlies. A beginner chairlift (and ski school) feeds the bunny slope; three double chairlifts ferry skiers to the intermediate Strip and to runs called Keno, Blackjack, and Slot Alley that cover 40 acres. Get here early on the weekends!

Also here are a day lodge with a coffee shop and lounge, a ski shop that rents equipment (702/645-2754), and a ski school. The slopes are open daily 9 A.M.–4 P.M. from Thanksgiving to Easter, and snow machines ensure packed and groomed slopes all winter. There's also night skiing on Saturday 4:30–10 P.M., along with a ski school, rental shop, coffee shop, and cocktail lounge in the day lodge. Lift tickets are $33 for all day, $25 kids and seniors. Call 702/645-2754 for general information, 702/593-9500 for snow conditions, 702/486-3116 for the road conditions report.

Down the mountain a bit from the ski area are plentiful places for tubing, sledding, snowmobiling, and cross-country skiing. The best Nordic is on north-facing slopes, in open meadows above 8,000 feet (2,438 meters). Scott Canyon, Mack's Canyon, and the Bristlecone Pine Trail are popular. Next nearest skiing to Las Vegas is Brian Head, Utah, four hours away. During the summer the resort offers scenic chairlift rides ($10 for adults, $6 for children), summer concerts, and barbecues.

SPRING MOUNTAIN RANCH STATE PARK

Not far from spectacular Red Rock Canyon is Spring Mountain Ranch State Park. Watch for wild burros along the stretch of Route 159 between Red Rock Canyon and the state park; it's easy to tell the males from the females. Some might be very friendly, but don't feed them. Not only is it bad for the burros, it's against the law.

Pay at the gate ($6 per carload) to enter the state park, nestled at the base of the Wilson Cliffs, sheer buff-colored sandstone bluffs still within the official confines of Red Rock Canyon. The area's cooler temperatures, plentiful water, bountiful land, and gorgeous setting have attracted travelers since the 1830s. By 1869 a ranch had been established with a stone cabin and blacksmith shop (both still standing). Three generations of Wilsons owned the land from 1876 till 1948, after which it was sold several times, once to Vera Krupp (ex-wife of a German industrialist) and once to Howard Hughes. The State Parks Division finally acquired the 528-acre ranch in 1974; by then it was worth more than $3 million.

The long green lawns, bright white picket fences, and New England–style red ranch house make an idyllic setting for picnics, football or frisbee tossing, daydreaming, and snoozing, as well as for concerts, musicals, and kids' events put on in summer. Stroll around the grounds, and up to the reservoir, which waters the ranch via gravity-fed pipes. The main ranch house doubles as the visitors center; pick up a self-guiding tour brochure. Concerts and plays are held here during the summer. Sunsets are incomparable.

Admission to Spring Mountain is $6 per carload. The park is open daily 8 A.M.–7 P.M. The ranch house is open daily 10 A.M.–4 P.M. Walking tours of the old ranch are conducted weekdays at 1 and 2 P.M. and on weekends at noon, 1, 2, and 3 P.M. Call 702/875-4141 for more information.

Cathedral Canyon

A project begun in 1972 by a former Clark County District Attorney is one of the most unusual sites in southern Nevada. As you drive out Route 160 toward Pahrump, you come to a road to the west (left) marked Tecopa. This is the Old Spanish Trail Highway. Drive three miles west on this road till you come to another sign marked Cathedral Canyon and turn right. Though the terrain is desolate and sun-baked and dry, you suddenly come upon a small picnic

RED ROCK CANYON—ANTIDOTE TO LAS VEGAS

West of Las Vegas, stretching across the sun-setting horizon and hemming in the valley, are the mighty and rugged Spring Mountains. Smack in the center of this range is Red Rock Canyon, a multicolored sandstone palisade so close to Las Vegas that it competes with, or better yet complements, the electrified cityscape. Less than 15 miles from the world's greatest concentration of indoor recreation await 196,000 acres of outdoor splendor—as dramatic a contrast as imaginable. The transition from city and suburb to expanding sprawl and then wilderness, is unforgettable. A mere 10 miles from downtown Las Vegas on West Charleston Boulevard, you're on open road through the outback Mojave. The view—thick stands of Joshua trees, backdropped by the precipitous Spring Mountain walls, with Red Rock Canyon standing sentinel—has been known to leave even *National Geographic* photographers speechless.

In 20–30 minutes you take a right into the Bureau of Land Management's southern Nevada showcase.

Start with the enormous expanse of the semicircle scenery, swallowing crowds and dwarfing climbers. Then superimpose the gorgeous colors of the sandstone—yellow, orange, pink, red, purple—all overlaid by the stalwart and tempered gray of older limestone. Then add the narrow, steep-walled canyons, moist, cool, lush gashes between the cliffs for wonderland hiking, and the contoured, inviting boulders that have turned Red Rock Canyon into an international climbing destination. Finally, tack on the cooperative year-round climate, close proximity to the city, and the excellent visitor center, and it's safe to say that the 28 million or so tourists who don't make it to Red Rock Canyon every year simply don't see Las Vegas.

Red Rock Canyon clearly reveals the limestone formed when most of Nevada lay under a warm shallow sea, and the massive sand

COURTESY OF THE LAS VEGAS NEWS BUREAU

Red Rock Canyon

area with tables, barbecue grills, chairs, and a suspension bridge over a very deep arroyo.

The arroyo was created by the rare rains that fall on the flood plain above, then drain into the gorge. Over centuries, these floods gradually carved a miniature canyon, sculpting fantastic and strangely beautiful crevices along the rim of the caliche hardpan.

Take a walk across the suspension bridge, which is hung by cables from steel girders. Looking down, you'll see crevices and caves sheltering stained-glass windows, oil paint-

ings, and images from many different religions. You can also see a walkway into the canyon, which leads you to a more intimate encounter with this unusual "cathedral," enhanced by ex-DA Roland Wiley. Once there, sign the guest book and continue to wander through the canyon, following the fenced path. Climb up a few of the alcoves to get a closer look at dunes that later covered this desert. Chemical and thermal reactions "petrified" the dunes into polychrome sandstone; erosion sculpted it into strange and wondrous shapes. When the land began faulting and shifting roughly 100 million years ago, the limestone was thrust up and over the younger sandstone, forming a protective layer that inhibited further erosion. Known as the Keystone Thrust, the contact between the limestone and sandstone is as precise as a textbook illustration and accounts for the bands of contrasting colors in the cliffs. Except for the spectacular canyons carved from runoff over the past 60 million years, the 15-mile-long, 3,000-foot-high sandstone escarpment today remains relatively untouched by the march of time.

The BLM visitor center is situated near the beginning of the Scenic Loop road at the lower end of the wide oval that encompasses all this glowing Aztec sandstone. Take a while and orient yourself to the area at the center's excellent 3-D exhibits of geology, flora and fauna, and recreational opportunities, then walk along the short nature trail out back. The 13-mile loop road is open 7 A.M.–dusk and features half a dozen overlooks, picnic sites, and trails leading to springs, canyons, quarries, and *tinajas* (tanks). With any luck, you'll see hikers and climbers dotted along the rock to demonstrate the amazing scale of the fiery walls. A nice long lens for your camera would be helpful. Across the highway is 13-Mile Campground, which charges $10 per night for individual sites and $25 per night for group sites.

You can easily spend an entire day exploring the edges of the loop road. Be sure to stop at both Calico Vista points, with huge 6,323-foot Turtle Head Mountain leaning high and limy over the Calico Hills. A short trail from the second vista gets you into the territory. Another trail enters Sandstone Quarry, where red and white sandstone for buildings was mined from 1905–1912. Absorb the view of the Madre Mountains, a dramatic limestone ridge line of the Spring Range, then swing around south past the White Rock Hills, Bridge and Rainbow mountains, and Mt. Wilson. Hikes enter Lost Creek, Icebox, and Pine Creek canyons. You could then spend another six days hiking around the 16-by 10-mile park, or devote a lifetime to climbing the 1,500 known routes up the red rock. The whole park, in fact, is a favorite rock-climbing destination for international climbers, who appreciate the cooperative clime. The BLM website has a map of the area's hiking trails.

For more details, contact the visitor center (702/363-1921) or the BLM district office, 4765 W. Vegas Dr. (P.O. Box 26569), Las Vegas, 702/647-5000, www.redrockcanyon.blm.gov. The visitor center is open daily 8:30 A.M.–4:30 P.M. except Christmas Day.

some of the art that decorates this anomalous marvel. At night, classical symphonies and arias pour forth from hidden speakers, filling the canyon with eeriness. Necklaces of colored lights adorn niches, caves, and crevices, adding to the surreal surroundings.

Wiley's purpose in creating this experience is summed up in his dedication. "I wanted to leave something for everyone of all faiths to enjoy and be inspired by to seek new ways to fulfill their own lives while they, too, are on this earth." Entrance fee is $3.

ASH MEADOWS NATIONAL WILDLIFE REFUGE AND VICINITY

Ash Meadows National Wildlife Refuge is unique to the planet. The surface discharge point for a huge underground aquifer that liberates 10,000 gallons of water every minute into 30 different springs and seeps, it's home to more than 20 plants and animals found nowhere else on Earth. Ash Meadows is so important it has been designated as one of the

15 Wetlands of International Importance in the United States.

To reach this unique refuge, continue through Pahrump on Route 160 to Belle Vista Road, turn left, and head up into the pass. About 24 miles along Belle Vista, you come to the dirt road into Ash Meadows. Turn right and follow the signs that guide you around the Refuge and to Refuge headquarters. As you progress toward HQ, passing through meadows and springs, note the green mineral deposits throughout the area. In spite of a close resemblance to cyanide, this mineral is actually nontoxic and highly useful. Called zeolite, it's heavily mined throughout the Amargosa Desert for such purposes as cat litter and landscaping, and for its unique ability to absorb deadly radiation.

Once at Refuge headquarters, the staff, when available, are always happy to answer questions, discuss refuge management, or arrange guided tours (with advance notice). Call Ash Meadows National Wildlife Refuge at 775/372-5436 for more information. If no one is there, pick up a pamphlet describing the Refuge and take a short stroll along a recently completed wood-planked walkway to Crystal Spring. Take the time to walk among the tules, rushes, and spring-watered growth, but don't step off the walkway (swimming and wading are not allowed in the spring pools). The Refuge is home to one-of-a-kind three-foot-tall poppy flowers that have taproots reaching 10 feet down into the desert soil to find water. It's also home to the entire known population of a water beetle that survives in creeks smaller than the length of a football field. Ash Meadows is also the sole home to the unique Devil's Hole pupfish, whose ancestors swam around the feet of mastodons and saber-tooth tigers.

The best times to visit the refuge are spring and fall, when the temperatures are pleasant and the variety of wildlife affords the most advantageous viewing opportunities. In spring, the Ash Meadows pupfish, which inhabits many of the springs and pools, turn silvery blue and dart around the spring pools defending territories and laying eggs on the algae and sand. Also in spring, you'll see a plethora of migrating shorebirds that rest and feed here. Winters in the refuge can be sunny and mild, or windy and wet, depending on the vagaries of Mother Nature, but it's still the best time to catch a glimpse of long-legged herons and egrets hunting for fish at the water's edge, a dozen different species of ducks and goose diving for food, and even a few bald eagles that spend the winter here.

The clear blue springs are the refuge's most stunning sites. Both Peterson and Crystal Reservoirs are easily accessible and good places to view ducks and other water birds. If you're up for a hike, you can walk to Horseshoe Reservoir or Lower Crystal Marsh; the latter is particularly good for shorebirds in late summer. Longstreet Spring, harboring pupfish, is four miles north of Refuge headquarters. The remains of frontiersman Jack Longstreet's stone cabin are also located at this site.

Two kinds of mesquite grow here: one with corkscrew-shaped and the other with string-bean shaped pods. Wild grapes and saltgrass also flourish near the water.

Death Valley National Monument

Devil's Hole is a holdover from tens of thousands of years ago when much of the area was covered by Ice Age lakes. At the time, a tiny little-known breed of fish called the pupfish existed throughout the area. As the waters receded, much of this "fossil water" (so-called because it's thousands of years old) seeped deep into the groundwater system (all of the springs in the Ash Meadows NWR are fed by this huge underground reserve of fossil water). Springs eventually erupted in this area, where the underground fossil aquifer comes close to the surface, which managed to preserve the few remaining pupfish from that era. The pupfish you spot today are the direct progeny of those ancient ancestors.

Devil's Hole had its first recorded visit by William L. Manly in 1849 when he conducted his exploration party through this section of Nevada. In later years, a tent station, with sleeping tents and a saloon, was established at the site by "Dad" Fairbanks, a freighter who ran between Las Vegas and Beatty. The springs eventually became a source of water for the mining town of Greenwater, California. Today, Devil's Hole is a noncontiguous portion of Death Valley National Park located in the middle of Ash Meadows refuge. The limestone crevice, which is open to sunlight, contains a deep warm-water spring, the top 60 feet of which is inhabited by the entire natural population of the Devil's Hole pupfish. These inch-long fish, an endangered species, live in one of the most restrictive and isolated environments of any animal in the world. Call 760/786-3200.

Hoover Dam/Lake Mead Vicinity

The old road east out of Las Vegas is Boulder Highway, which is the extension of Fremont Street from downtown. You can hook up with Boulder Highway by heading east on Sahara, Desert Inn, Flamingo, and Tropicana (then take a right). The new road east is I-515, which has been extended as far as a little past Henderson. US 93 and 95 travel along with I-515 till it ends, then continue over Railroad Pass and down into Eldorado Valley. There, US 95 turns off south toward Laughlin and Needles, California, while US 93 continues east into Boulder City.

HENDERSON

Only four years after the completion of Hoover Dam, the Germans commenced raining terror down on England in the form of bombs whose deadly incendiary properties were attributed to magnesium, till then a little-known metal. In addition, lightweight magnesium was discovered in various components of downed German airplanes. A year later, Allied scientists and engineers had analyzed the qualities of this metal, and geologists had located huge deposits near Gabbs, Nevada. Since vast amounts of electrical power are required to process magnesium, a site halfway between Hoover Dam and Las Vegas was selected for the magnesium processing plant, and in September 1941 construction commenced on a massive factory known as Basic Magnesium. More than 10,000 workers spent only a few months erecting the plant, the town, and the transportation systems necessary to aid the war effort. By early 1942, 5,000 people lived in "Basic," and by 1943, 16 million pounds of magnesium had been produced. By 1944, so much magnesium had been shipped from Basic that the government had a surplus; with the war in Europe winding down, the plant was closed.

For the next few years, this metal-heavy town was on the verge of becoming yet another ghost in the Nevada desert. But then the federal government agreed to turn over the property and facilities to the state. The town, renamed to honor Albert Henderson, a local politician and judge who was pivotal in the takeover negotiations, received a new lease on life. By the early 1950s, the huge manufacturing complex had been subdivided to accommodate smaller private industry, and by the early 1980s, Henderson claimed half of the entire state's nontourist industry output. The town made the national news in May 1988 when a huge explosion leveled Pacific Engineering, which manufactures ammonia perchlorate, the oxydizer in solid rocket fuel, and Kidd's Marshmallow company next door (subsequently relocated a safe distance away).

Henderson is aesthetically. . . uh. . . interesting—with its huge industrial complex set off from fast-growing residential and commercial districts. It's not only fast growing, it has plenty of room to expand; a little less than half of the space within the city limits remains undeveloped. In early 1994, Henderson joined the Nevada 100,000 Club, an exclusive group of towns with more than 100,000 residents (now 235,000, to be exact, along with Las Vegas and Reno). Henderson is one of the fastest-growing cities in the fastest-growing state in the country. Reflecting this accelerated growth are a handful of new casinos strung along Boulder Hwy. and the upscale Lake Las Vegas area. Finally, its excellent location is undeniable—only 15 minutes from the Lake Mead, and close enough to Las Vegas to enjoy the benefits, while far enough away to outdistance the disadvantages.

Las Vegas (sidebar)

Along Boulder Highway

Boulder Station and Sam's Town are covered under Las Vegas casinos. Down the road a little ways, just north of Tropicana, is **Nevada Palace,** 702/458-8810, is a small locals' joint with a tradition of good cheap grub. The **Longhorn,** 702/435-9170, is another small locals' casino, with the usual good video poker, $1 blackjack, a 24-hour $1.95 breakfast special, and lots of parking.

On Sunset Road near Boulder Hwy. is the **Skyline,** 702/565-9116, with one whole long roomful of breakeven video poker machines, a $0.99 margarita, and a good $1 shrimp cocktail. The coffee shop is a five-room maze; sit at the counter and have a good prime rib special.

Finally is **Joker's Wild,** just before the intersection with Water St., 702/564-8100, a Boyd Group property. This full-service casino has no hotel, with blackjack, Caribbean stud, craps, roulette, a coffee shop, a buffet, and a lounge with a large screen.

Around Town

Turn right into Henderson on Water Street at the big signs for town off Boulder Highway or go left from the end of the Expressway on Lake Mead Dr., then take a right on Water Street. Either way, you'll go right by the old BMI plant, now housing the big chemical companies, such as Timet ("Making Our Lives Better Through Titanium Technology"), Pepcon, Kerr McGee, Chemstar, and many others, as well as small manufacturing and construction companies.

Downtown are two main casinos and one minor casino. The **Eldorado,** 140 S. Water, 702/564-1811, is a typical Boyd Group property (like the Stardust, California, Sam's Town, Joker's Wild, etc.): a large, bright, classy place, with a large pit full of blackjack, crap, and roulette tables, along with a sports book, keno, bingo, a couple of bars, a 24-hour coffee shop, and Mariana's Mexican restaurant. The 80-foot old neon marquee in front, big letters stacked vertically spelling Gambling with a star on top, dominates downtown. There's a waterfall out back.

Next door the **Rainbow Club,** 122 S. Water, 702/565-9776, is as claustro as the Eldorado is agora. With its low mirrored ceilings, startling neon border lights, and crowds around the slots and video poker, the Rainbow has the unmistakable signature of a Peppermill. The 24-hour coffee shop serves a $0.99 breakfast special around the clock.

Past downtown on Water Street are the convention center, a library, and a park; Water runs around to the left and joins Major Street, which heads right back out to Boulder Highway. The **Chamber of Commerce** is right at 100 E. Lake Mead Dr., right at the corner of Boulder Hwy., 702/565-8951, open Mon.–Fri. 8 A.M.–5 P.M.

Classing up the accommodations offerings in Henderson is the **Green Valley Ranch,** the latest, and most upscale, of the Station Casinos properties. Located on I-215 just west of town, the upscale property offers a lavish spa and attractive rooms packed with amenities, such as doorbells and down comforters. The pool area offers private cabanas and infinity dipping pools. Guests also will find upscale dining, headliner entertainment, eye-catching bars (the Whiskey Bar is worth checking out), and even a 10-screen cinema. Located at 2300 Paseo Verde Dr., 702/617-7777 or 866/782-9487, 201 rooms in the $180–200 range.

Lake Las Vegas

Henderson has always been considered the much less attractive step-sister of Las Vegas, but a new development is changing its less-than-stellar perception. Lake Las Vegas, the ultraposh housing and resort development seven miles east of Henderson, is establishing the area as the playground for the rich and pampered. Resembling a small-scale Mediterranean city, Lake Las Vegas features a 320-acre lake surrounded by golf courses, shopping, resort condominiums, and resort hotel-casinos, including the Ritz-Carlton and the Hyatt Regency. The centerpiece is the MonteLago Village, which offers lakeside restaurants, upscale boutiques, and a casino. Gondola rides and other activities are offered on the lake. The Ritz-Carlton, 29 Grand Mediterra Blvd., 702/568-6858 or 800/241-3333, has 350 rooms and suites for $180–450 that serve the Ritz reputation well. The Hyatt Regency, 101 Montelago Blvd., 702/567-1234 or 800/55-HYATT, offers 496 rooms in the $115–345 range. Both offer lavish spas.

Clark County Museum

As you continue east on Boulder Highway, the next attraction is this extensive and fascinating museum, 1830 S. Boulder Hwy. two miles beyond Henderson, 702/455-7955, open daily 9 A.M.–4:30 P.M., admission $1.50 adults, $1 for 55-over and 15-under. The main museum exhibit is now housed in the new pueblo building. The fine displays trace Indian cultures from the prehistoric to the contemporary and chronicle white exploration, settlement, and industry: Mormons, military, mining, ranching, railroading, riverboating, and gambling, up through the construction of Hoover Dam and the subsequent founding of Henderson.

The old depot that houses the collection has been restored. Also be sure to stroll down to the Heritage Street historical residential and commercial buildings: the **Townsite House,** built in Henderson in the 1940s; the 1890s print shop; the **Babcock and Wilcox House,** one of 12 original residences built in Boulder City in early 1933; and the pièce de résistance **Beckley House,** a simple yet stunning example of the still-popular California bungalow style, built for $2,500 in 1912 by Las Vegas pioneer and entrepreneur Will Beckley.

Other displays include a ghost town trail, a nature trail, and a mining and railroad display. The gift shop sells some interesting items, such as books, magazines, minerals, jewelry, beads, pottery, textiles, even Joshua tree seeds.

Henderson Bird Viewing Preserve

Southern Nevada's natural side isn't always easy to find, but when you peel back the neon, the discoveries are often surprisingly rich. A good example is the Henderson Bird Viewing Preserve. Situated on 140 acres at the city's water treatment center, the preserve is home to hundreds of hummingbirds, ibis, ducks, eagles, roadrunners, and numerous other species. The park, which is managed by the City of Henderson, offers nine ponds with both paved and dirt paths. Throughout the year, birders can attend a number of educational programs for feathered fans of all ages. The preserve is located at 2400 B Moser Dr., near the intersection of Sunset Rd. and Boulder

Hwy., 702/267-4180. Entry is free, and the park is open 6 A.M.–3 P.M.

Railroad Pass

US 93/95 continues southwest up and over a low gate between the River Mountains and the Black Hills known as Railroad Pass (2,367 feet), named for the Union Pacific route to Boulder City and the dam. **Railroad Pass Hotel and Casino** sits at the top, at 2800 Boulder Hwy., 702/294-5000, with a full-service and red casino, coffee shop and buffet, and $39–59 rooms. Just beyond is the junction: US 95 cuts right (south) down to west of Laughlin, and US 93 heads straight (east) into Boulder City.

BOULDER CITY

In 1930, when Congress appropriated the first funds for the Boulder Canyon Project, the Great Depression was in full swing, the country was embarking on its first massive reclamation effort, the dam was to be one of the largest single engineering and construction tasks ever undertaken, and urban architects were increasingly leaning toward the social progressiveness of the Community Planning Movement. Boulder City was born of these unique factors and remains the most unusual town in Nevada. In July 1930, the Commissioner of Reclamation, Dr. Elwood Mead, hired Saco R. DeBoer, a highly regarded 35-year-old landscape architect from Denver, to develop the Boulder City Master Plan. DeBoer set the government buildings at the top of the site's hill, within a greenbelt of parks. The town radiated out like a fan, with the main commercial and residential sections concentrated around three through streets that converged symmetrically at the handle. Secondary roads conformed to the contours of the land, and parks, plazas, and perimeters enclosed the neighborhoods in pleasant settings.

Construction of the town began in March 1931, only a month before work commenced at the dam site. The increasing influx of workers, most of whom were housed in a cluster of temporary tent cabins known as Ragtown, forced the government to accelerate the building. Most of DeBoer's more grandiose elements (neighborhood greenbelts,

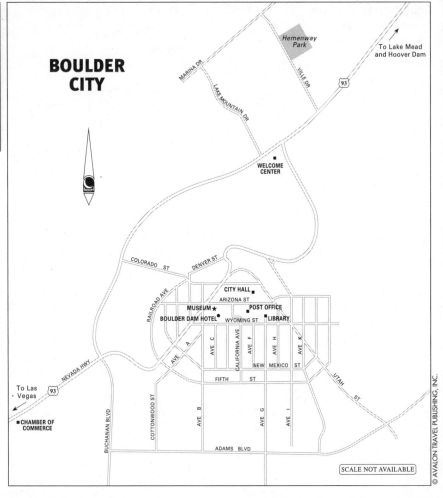

BOULDER CITY

Hemenway Park

To Lake Mead and Hoover Dam

MARINA DR

LAKE MOUNTAIN DR

VILLE DR

93

MOON

WELCOME CENTER

COLORADO ST

DENVER ST

RAILROAD AVE

CITY HALL

ARIZONA ST

MUSEUM ★

POST OFFICE

BOULDER DAM HOTEL

WYOMING ST

LIBRARY

AVE A

AVE C

CALIFORNIA AVE

AVE F

AVE H

AVE K

NEW MEXICO ST

NEVADA HWY

FIFTH ST

UTAH ST

To Las Vegas

93

CHAMBER OF COMMERCE

BUCHANAN BLVD

COTTONWOOD ST

AVE B

AVE G

AVE I

ADAMS BLVD

SCALE NOT AVAILABLE

© AVALON TRAVEL PUBLISHING, INC.

large single-family houses) were abandoned in favor of a more economical and expedient approach (dormitories and small cottages). Still, Boulder City became a prettified all-American oasis of security and order in the midst of a great desert and the Great Depression. The Bureau of Reclamation controlled the town down to the smallest detail; a city manager, answerable directly to the federal Commissioner of Reclamation, oversaw operations, and his authority was near total.

After the dam was completed, the town master plan was further dismantled, as workers left and company housing was moved or torn down for materials. For a while thereafter, Boulder City seemed in a little danger of turning into a ghost, but visitors to the dam and Lake Mead had a different idea, and the town became a service center for the recreation area. For 30 years the federal government owned the town and all its buildings, but in early 1960, an act of Congress established Boulder City as an independent municipality. Officials drew up a city charter, the feds began to sell property to the long-time residents, and alcohol sales were allowed for the first time in Boulder City. Gambling, however, remains disallowed—the only town in the state with laws against it. Boulder City today might be far from the government's squeaky clean and De-Boer's grandly green. But it retains an air of its own—especially in contrast to the rest of southern Nevada.

Sights

Coming into Boulder City on US 93 (Nevada Hwy.) is more like entering a town in Arizona or New Mexico, with Indian and Mexican gift shops and a number of galleries, as well as crafts, jewelry, antique, and collectibles stores along the downtown streets, and no casinos.

Across the street at 1305 Arizona St., 702/293-3510, have a look around the 65-year-old **Boulder Dam Hotel,** restored in 1980 and the town's main landmark. Though its elegant dining, private baths, and air conditioning were rarities in southern Nevada in the early '30s, the hotel over the years had fallen into disrepair. In late 1993 Boulder City's Chamber of Commerce, arts council, and historical society raised $560,000 and bought the place; the Chamber of Commerce and the Hoover Dam Museum subsequently moved in. Matteo's restaurant is open for breakfast, lunch and dinner, and the hotel offers 22 rooms with vintage decor that rent for $89–159 per night (includes a full breakfast). The lobby looks exactly the same as it did in 1933 when it was constructed, as you can see for yourself in the black and whites. Matteo's is open 7 A.M.–8 P.M.; three sets of double French doors open onto the al fresco patio, with a view of the distinctive white brick and gumwood exterior. Downstairs in the cellar is the Underground Lounge, a subterranean affair with a stone wall in back of the bar, where 1930s celebrities and dignitaries drank and gambled, both of which were illegal in the government town.

Inside the hotel be sure to check out the **Boulder City/Hoover Dam Museum,** 702/294-1988, open Mon.–Sat. 10 A.M.–5 P.M. and Sun. noon–5 P.M., $2 admission for adults (admission to the museum is free if you stay at the hotel). Inside are interesting black-and-white prints from the '30s, such as the Six Companies' rec hall, and high scalers working high up on the canyon walls. Also look for the high-scaler bosun's chair. And pick up Dennis McBride's excellent book on Boulder City.

After visiting the hotel, make sure to pull out your walking tour brochure and stroll up Arizona Street, then down Nevada Highway, to get a feel for the history and design significance of downtown. Then continue on the residential and public-building walks to get an intimate glimpse of DeBoer's imagination—as modified by government work. You can also head back toward Henderson on Nevada Hwy. to the Frank T. Crowe Memorial Park (named for the chief dam engineer, immortalized in *Big Red*), and take a right there onto Cherry Street to see the fine row of original bungalows from the '30s.

Railroad buffs can climb aboard the train rides on the **Nevada Southern Railway** at the Boulder City's branch of the Nevada State Railroad Museum. The renovated historic cars make treks along the old Boulder Branch Line on selected weekends. The Pullman coaches, some of which date back to 1911, take passengers for a seven-mile, 45-minute journey across the stark Mojave Desert. All of the cars and engines have been refurbished, and the indoor cars have been retrofitted with air conditioning. The spur used for the excursion was donated to the Nevada State Railroad Museum in 1985, and the train still chugs along the original tracks. The ride goes as far as the Railroad Pass Casino, and along the way, passengers can expect to see jackrabbits, bighorn sheep, a variety of desert plant life, and a few historic sites along the way. Rides begin at the Nevada State Railroad Museum's new station and platform, located in Boulder City at the intersection of the Boulder Highway and Yucca Street. Departure times (subject to change) are daily 9 A.M., 10:30 A.M., noon, and 1:30 P.M. Fares are $5 for adults, $4 for seniors, and $3 for ages 6–11, 702/486-5933.

Practicalities

Boulder City has a handful of motels, all strung along Nevada Highway (US 93) as you enter town.

From west to east are: **Starview,** 1017 Nevada Hwy., 702/293-1658, $25–75; **Nevada,** 1009 Nevada Hwy., 702/293-2044, $30–55; **Sands,** 809 Nevada Hwy., 702/293-2589, $37–50; **Flamingo,** 804 Nevada Hwy., 702/293-3565, $27–60; **Desert Inn,** 800 Nevada Hwy., 702/293-2827, $30–90; **El Rancho,** 725 Nevada Hwy., 702/293-1085, $60–150; and **Super 8,** 704 Nevada Hwy., 702/293-8888 or 800/800-8000, $40–50. There's also the **Lighthouse Inn and Resort,** 110 Ville Dr., 702/293-6444, $70–80.

Canyon Trail RV Park, 1200 Industrial Rd., 702/293-1200, is the only RV park in Boulder City. It's mostly residential, with permanent mobiles, but there're plenty of overnight spots. There's no shade and precious little greenery, but craggy sandstone mountains rise from the rear of the place. It has 156 spaces, all with full hookups, or which 86 are pull-throughs. Tents are not allowed. The fee is $15 for two people (Good Sam discount). To get there, from the traffic light in Boulder City, take the truck route one block to Canyon Road. Turn left on Canyon Road, drive to the end, and turn left on Industrial Road. Drive half a block and turn right into the RV park.

The **Chamber of Commerce,** 1305 Arizona St. in the Boulder Dam Hotel, 702/293-2034, open Mon.–Fri. 9 A.M.–5 P.M., has all the local brochures and can answer questions about the town, the dam, and the lake.

To the Dam

To get to the dam (eight miles away), cut off to the left on the truck route (at Buchanan Blvd.) before town, or continue through town along Nevada Highway to join up with it. At the junction of the truck route with Nevada Highway is a state **Welcome Center,** 702/294-1252, for all the visitors coming in from Arizona over the dam. Pick up your handful of brochures and visitors guides; if the center is closed, read the signboards out front.

At the corner of US 93 and Ville Street (at the Texaco station), take a left and go two blocks to **Hemenway Park.** Don't be surprised by all the signs about bighorn sheep. In the summer, these wild creatures (the state animal), which are nor-

mally extremely skittish and retiring, come down from the hills for water and grass at this park.

In a mile or so you enter **Lake Mead National Recreation Area,** and arrive at the junction of US 93 and Route 166 (Lakeshore Dr.). Taking a left on the state route brings you right to the **Alan Bible Visitor Center,** 702/293-8906, and park headquarters for the recreation area. Named after a popular Nevada U.S. senator, this modern facility is open daily 8:30 A.M.–5 P.M., has a 15-minute movie on the lake and flora (shown 9 A.M.–4 P.M.), and sells postcards, videos, books, and maps.

Across Lake Shore Drive from the visitor center is a parking lot for the trailhead to the **U.S. Government Construction Railroad Trail.** The 2.6-mile one-way route follows an abandoned railroad grade along a ledge overlooking the lake. It passes through four tunnels blasted through the hills and ends at the fifth tunnel, which is sealed. This is an enjoyable level stroll that anyone can do. Mountain bikers can check out the Bootleg Canyon Mountain Bike Trail, which has 36 miles of cross-country and downhill runs (the "Elevator Shaft" has a 22 percent grade). Trailhead access is off Yucca or Canyon Streets.

Another trail to consider in Boulder City is the **River Mountain Hiking Trail,** a five-mile round-trip hike built originally by the Civilian Conservation Corps in 1935 and recently restored, with good views of the lake and the valley. The trailhead is on the truck bypass, just beyond the traffic light in downtown Boulder City, on the left as you're heading toward the dam.

On the way to the dam, up the hill from the visitor center, is the **Hacienda,** 800/245-6380, with 375 rooms going for $29–64 (it replaced the Gold Strike Inn, which burned down in 1999). The hotel-casino offers extensive slot and video machines as well as such standards as a buffet.

On the other side of the Hacienda you enter some wild canyonlands in the rugged mountains above the Colorado River, with a massive parade of supernatural superstructures: cosmic-erector-set towers; alien electrical generators, transformers, and capacitors; neuro-planetary high-tension cables and inductive coils—in short, *the grid*—like some alien invasion force straight out of the imagination of George Lucas. Cyclone fencing keeps the humans away.

HOOVER DAM

The 1,400-mile Colorado River has been carving and gouging great canyons and valleys with red *(colorado)* sediment-laden waters for nearly 10 million years. For 10,000 years, Indian, Spanish, and Mormon settlers coexisted with the fitful river, which often overflowed with spring floods and then tapered off in the fall to a muddy trickle. By the turn of the 20th century, irrigation ditches and canals had diverted some of the river water into California's Imperial Valley, west of its natural channel. But in 1905, a wet winter and abnormal spring rains combined to drown everything in sight: flash floods deepened the manmade canal and actually changed the course of the river to flow through California's low-lying valley. For nearly two years engineers and farmers fought the Colorado back into place; the Salton Sea, which had been 22 square miles, grew to 500 square miles, and remains today more than 200 square miles, nearly 95 years later. But the message was clear to the dam-building, river-diverting, nature-conquering federal overseers: the Rio Colorado had to be tamed.

Enter the Bureau of Reclamation, established only three years earlier, the brainchild of Nevada Senator Francis Newlands. Over the next 15 years, the bureau began to "reclaim" the West, primarily by building dams and canals. Its first was Derby Dam, a few miles east of Reno; it also built Lahontan Dam, a few miles west of Fallon. By 1920, Reclamation had narrowed the possible dam sites on the Colorado from 70 to 2, Boulder and Black canyons. It took another three years to negotiate an equitable water distribution among the affected states (and Mexico) and another six for Congress to pass the Boulder Canyon Project Act, authorizing funds for Boulder Dam to be constructed in Black Canyon (the dam's name was eventually changed to honor Herbert Hoover, then secretary of commerce).

The immensity of the undertaking still boggles the brain. The closest civilization was at a sleepy railroad town, 40 miles west, called Las Vegas, and the nearest large power plant was in San Bernardino, more than 200 miles away. Tracks had to be laid, a town built, men hired, equipment shipped in—just to prepare for construction. And then! The

the impressive Hoover Dam

mighty Colorado had to be diverted. The project began in April 1931. Workers hacked four tunnels, each 56 feet across, through the canyon walls. They loosened, carried off, and dumped thousands of tons of rock every day for 16 months. Finally, in November 1932, the river water was rerouted around the dam site.

Then came the concrete.

Over the course of the next two years, eight-cubic-yard buckets full of cement were lowered into the canyon (five million of them) till the dam—660 feet thick at the base, 45 feet thick at the crest, 1,244 feet across, and 726 feet high—had swallowed 3.2 million cubic yards, or seven million tons, of the hardening stuff. The top of the dam was built wide enough to accommodate a two-lane highway. Inside this Pantagruelian wedge were placed 17 gargantuan electrical turbines. The cost of the dam surpassed $175 million. At the peak of construction, more than 5,000 workers toiled day and night to complete the project, under the most extreme conditions of heat and dust, and danger from heavy equipment, explosions, falling rock, heights, etc. (An average of 50 injuries per day and a total of 94 deaths were recorded over the 46 months of construction.)

The largest construction equipment yet known to the world had to be invented, designed, fabricated, and installed on the spot. Yet miraculously, the dam was completed nearly two years *ahead* of schedule. In February 1935, the diversion tunnels were closed, and Lake Mead began to fill up behind the dam, which was dedicated eight months later by President Franklin Roosevelt. A month after that, the first turbine was turned, and electricity started flowing as the water was finally controlled.

Today, the Colorado River system has several dams and reservoirs, storing roughly 60 million acre-feet of water (an acre-foot is just under 326,000 gallons, about as much water as an average American household uses in two years). California is allotted 4.4 million acre-feet, Arizona gets 2.8 million, Nevada 300,000, and Mexico 1.5 million. Hoover Dam, meanwhile, supplies four billion kilowatt-hours of electricity annually (enough to power half a million homes).

Sights and Tours

In 1977, the Bureau of Reclamation decided to build a new and improved visitor center to accommodate the 700,000 visitors the dam receives yearly (more than 32 million visitors have taken the tour of the most heavily visited dam in the country). Estimates in 1983 tagged the cost at $32 million. Well, in what turned out to be one of the biggest federal boondoggles in recent memory, the 44,000-square-foot visitor center and five-story 450-car parking garage (wedged into a ravine in the mountain) cost upwards of $120 million and were finally completed and opened in the summer of 1995. Construction of the visitor center weathered three presidential administrations, four regional directors of Reclamations, and five congressional elections. Financed over 50 years, the new visitor center is expected to cost $435 million when all is said and done. Luxor cost only $375 million.

Anyway, it's a pretty nice visitor center. It has some exhibits, a movie on the Colorado River, and elevators that take you into the bowels of the dam. Buy tickets for the 35-minute dam tour ($6, open 9 A.M.–5 P.M. Memorial Day to Labor Day, 9 A.M.–4 P.M. winter), then get in line and wait (arriving as early as possible will shorten the waiting time in line). Eventually you'll take the 75-second elevator ride to the bottom of the dam (it's like descending from the 53rd floor of a skyscraper). Tunnels lead you to a monumental room housing the monolithic turbines. Next you step outside, where a hundred necks crane to view the top of the dam. Next you walk through one of the diversion tunnels to view a 30-foot-diameter waterpipe. The guides pack hours of statistics and stories into the short tour. Parking at the dam costs $5. For more info, call the visitor center at 702/293-8321 (you'll also find more enchanced tours, too).

River Tours

Black Canyon Rafting Company, 800/455-3490, offers river trips year-round. The tours leave at 9–10 A.M.; you're bused to the restricted side of the dam, where you board rafts that can hold 35 people, for a 3.5-hour ride through Black Canyon down the Colorado 12 miles to Willow

Beach. You're served lunch, then driven back around 3:30 (call for departure location). The cost is $72.95 for adults, $69.95 for ages 13–15, $45 for 5–12.

The *Desert Princess* is a 250-passenger Mississippi-style sternwheeler and its little sister, the Desert Princess Too cruises Lake Mead out of the Lake Mead Cruises Landing, 702/293-6180. Daily 90-minute cruises leave at noon, 2, and 4 ($20 adults, $9 children); a two-hour dinner cruise departs Thurs.–Sun. at 5:30 ($44/$21); a three-hour dinner-dance cruise departs Sat. at 7:30 P.M. ($54, adults only); and a two-hour brunch cruise departs Sat.–Sun. at 9:30 A.M. ($32.50/$15). Lake Mead Marina is off US 93; take a right at the sign just before the Alan Bible Visitor Center.

Back to Las Vegas

Head back toward Boulder City from the dam, but take a right at the fork onto Route 166 (Lakeshore Dr.). In a couple of miles you come to **Boulder Beach,** a typical Lake Mead settlement, with trailer parks, marinas, picnic areas, and a two-mile-long beach. Colorful Fortification Hill stands out on the other side of the lake; a basalt

formation, the reddish rocks around the base are known as the Paint Pots. Continue north on Lakeshore Dr. between the lake on the east and the rugged River Range on the west. In another seven miles the road curves around left (west), where it turns into Route 147 toward Henderson. But take a right (north) on Route 147 and cross **Las Vegas Wash,** an amazing little creek that drains Las Vegas Valley into the Colorado River system. At the intersection with North Shore Drive, follow Route 147 around to the left (west). This turns into Lake Mead Boulevard, passing behind and through Frenchman's and Sunrise mountains, to enter Las Vegas from the northeast.

LAKE MEAD NATIONAL RECREATION AREA

Hoover Dam began detaining the Colorado and Virgin rivers in 1935. By 1938, Lake Mead was full: three years' worth of river water braced by the Brobdingnagian buttress at Black Canyon. Largest man-made lake in the West, Lake Mead measures 110 miles long and 500 feet deep, has 822 miles of shoreline, and contains 28.5 million acre-feet of water (or just over nine trillion gallons), a

boating on Lake Mead

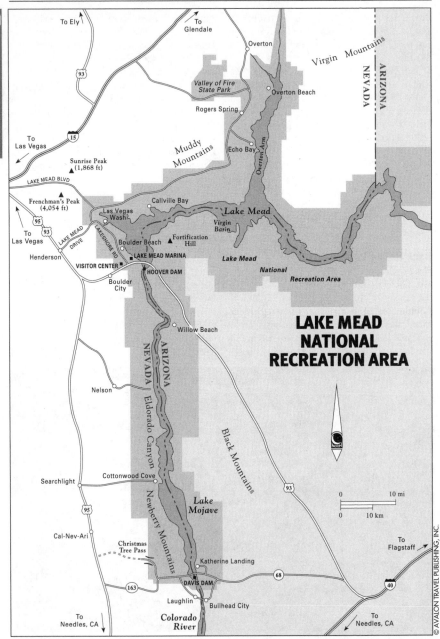

To Ely

To Glendale

Overton

Virgin Mountains

NEVADA

ARIZONA

93

Valley of Fire State Park

Overton Beach

Rogers Spring

To Las Vegas

15

Muddy Mountains

Echo Bay

Overton Arm

Sunrise Peak (1,868 ft)

LAKE MEAD BLVD

Frenchman's Peak (4,054 ft)

Callville Bay

Lake Mead

95

Las Vegas Wash

Virgin Basin

To Las Vegas

93

LAKE MEAD DRIVE

LAKESHORE RD

Boulder Beach

Fortification Hill

Lake Mead

Henderson

VISITOR CENTER

LAKE MEAD MARINA

National

Boulder City

HOOVER DAM

Recreation Area

Willow Beach

LAKE MEAD NATIONAL RECREATION AREA

NEVADA

ARIZONA

Nelson

Eldorado Canyon

Black Mountains

Searchlight

Cottonwood Cove

95

93

0   10 mi

0   10 km

Cal-Nev-Ari

Newberry Mountains

Lake Mojave

Christmas Tree Pass

To Flagstaff

Katherine Landing

Davis Dam

68

40

163

Laughlin

Bullhead City

To Needles, CA

Colorado River

To Needles, CA

little less than half the water reserved along the entire Colorado River system. The reservoir irrigates 2.25 million acres of land in the U.S. and Mexico and supplies water for more than 14 million people. Nine million people each year use Lake Mead as a recreational resource; it's the fourth most visited Park Service-managed area in the country.

For all this, Lake Mead is only a sidelight to the dam's primary purpose: flood and drought control. In addition, Lake Mead is only the centerpiece of the 1.5-million-acre Lake Mead National Recreation Area, which includes Lake Mojave and the surrounding desert from Davis Dam to the south and Grand Canyon National Park in the east, all the way north to Overton—the largest Department of Interior recreational acreage in the country, outside of Alaska.

And recreation it certainly provides. **Swimming** is the most accessible, and requires the least equipment: a bathing suit. Boulder Beach, only 30 miles from Las Vegas and just down the road from the Alan Bible Visitor Center, is the most popular swimming site. For **divers,** visibility averages 30 feet, the water is stable, and sights of the deep abound: the yacht *Tortuga* rests at 50 feet near the Boulder Islands; Hoover Dam's asphalt factory sits on the canyon floor nearby; the old Mormon town of St. Thomas, inundated by the lake in 1938, has many a watery story to tell; Wishing Well Cove has steep canyon walls and drop-offs, caves, and clear water; Ringbolt Rapids, an exhilarating drift dive, is for advanced divers only; and the Tennis Shoe Graveyard, near Las Vegas Wash, is one of many footholds of hidden treasure.

Boating on the vast lake is even more varied. Power boats skip across the surface, houseboats putter toward hidden coves, and sailing and windsurfing are year-round thrills.

For **anglers,** largemouth bass, rainbow, brown, and cutthroat trout, catfish, and black crappie have been the mainstays for decades. These days, though, striped bass provide the sport. Five marinas in Nevada provide camping, restaurants and bars, fishing supplies, and boat rentals. Two of these offer showers, houseboats, and motels.

Recreation is also abundant at **Lake Mojave,**

created downstream by Davis Dam in 1953. This lake backs up almost all the way to Hoover Dam, like an extension of Lake Mead. The two lakes are similar in climate, desert scenery, vertical-walled canyon enclosures, and a shoreline digitated with numerous private coves. It offers excellent trout fishing at Willow Beach on the Arizona side, where the water, too cold for swimming, is perfect for serious angling. Marinas are found at Cottonwood Cove just north of the widest part of the lake and at Katherine Landing just north of Davis Dam.

LAKESHORE AND NORTHSHORE ROADS

Three roads provide access to the NRA: one urban loop road that connects to two lakeside drives. Route 147 is the loop road; the northern section is called Lake Mead Boulevard, the southern section Lake Mead Drive. Lake Mead Boulevard runs east through North Las Vegas (pick it up off I-15 or Las Vegas Boulevard North, climbs into the Sunrise Mountains, and enters the rugged Lake Mead Recreation Area. Lake Mead Drive runs northeast through Henderson (pick it up off I-215 or Boulder Hwy.) and passes Lake Las Vegas, the most exclusive subdivision in southern Nevada. From Lake Mead Boulevard, take a left at the stop sign onto Route 167 toward Callville Bay and Overton, or a right onto Route 166 toward Lake Mead Marina and Boulder Beach. From Lake Mead Drive, take a right onto Route 167 toward Callville Bay and Overton or just follow the road around to the left (Route 166) for Lake Mead Marina and Boulder Beach.

Lakeshore Road

About a mile north on Lakeshore Road is the **Lake Mead RV Village,** which is mostly for permanent mobiles and trailers, but has a compact area near the entrance dedicated to transient RVers (register at the office near the entrance). There are 85 spaces for overnight motor homes, all with electricity. Some tent sites available. Laundromat and groceries are available. Reservations are accepted up to one year in advance.

SOUTHEASTERN NEVADA TOUR

With proper promotion and packaging, southeastern Nevada would make a perfect one-week bus tour. More historic, scenic, artistic, and recreational attractions are concentrated between Las Vegas and Ely than in any other comparable stretch in the state. Start with two nights in Las Vegas, one of the easiest places in the world to fly to, and an exciting destination itself.

On the third morning, head straight over to Lake Mead, and take North Shore Road by the bays, marinas, and springs; have a rest stop at Echo Bay or Overton Beach. Serve a box picnic at Valley of Fire State Park, and visit the Lost City Museum in Overton after lunch. Then settle down to a two-hour bus ride up US 93 to Alamo and Ash Springs (rest, snack, and swimming stop). Arrive an hour later in Caliente to get settled into motel rooms and have dinner. Afterward, meet at the Spanish railroad depot to hear historian Mary Ellen Sadovich and artist Rett Hastings talk about their stunning mural depicting southern Nevada history. Then enjoy cocktails in Rainbow Canyon at sunset, and finish up with an evening at the Hot Springs Motel, with its large private mineral Roman tubs and swimming pool.

The fourth day, have breakfast in Caliente, take a short swing through Mormon Panaca, one of the oldest towns in the state, then spend the rest of the morning hiking around the unique, accessible, and thrilling Cathedral Gorge State Park. Picnic there, then run up to Pioche for massive mining remains, two museums, shops, rest stop, and snack. Next, sit back for an afternoon ride to Ely. Stop at a motel, eat dinner, and tour the city that evening.

On the fifth morning, take the tour through the Nevada Northern's freight yards, then ride the Ghost Train to Ruth or McGill. If there's time, the group could easily go to Cave Lake State Park up in the mountains, or the Ward Charcoal Ovens in the desert.

The sixth morning leave for Great Basin National Park and Lehman Caves. Take the cave tour, drive up the mountain, have a picnic lunch, spend the afternoon hiking, head down to Baker for dinner at the Outlaw, then drive back to the motels in Ely. The seventh day, bus down to Las Vegas (250 miles) on NV 318 via Preston, Lund, and Hiko, which parallels US 93 mile for mile, only one valley east. There the group can disband, and the people can fly out at their convenience. Options out of Las Vegas for further travel are manifold.

The fee is $24 for two people. Call 702/293-2540 for information.

You turn right off Lakeshore Road into the entrance and right to the trailer village. If you take a left at the entrance, you enter **Boulder Beach Campground,** a sprawling and somewhat rustic campground with plenty of shade under cottonwood and pines. There are 150 campsites for tents or self-contained motor homes up to 35 feet. Piped drinking water, flush toilets, sewage disposal, picnic tables, and grills are provided. There is a campground host. The maximum stay is 30 days. No reservations; $10 per site. It's a three-minute walk down to the water (by car, a half-mile drive north on Lakeshore Drive). They don't call it Boulder Beach for nothing: the bottom is rocky and hard on the feet (bring your sandals). But the water is bathtub warm, 80°F

or so all summer long. Sheltered picnic tables and restrooms are available waterside.

Seven miles beyond Boulder Beach is **Las Vegas Bay Campground.** Turn right into the Las Vegas Marina, then take your first left; the campground is about a mile down the spur road. The campground sits on a bluff over the lake; it's not quite as shady or large as Boulder Beach. Also, you've got to climb down a pretty steep slope to get the water, but even when you get there, there's no real beach here. There are 86 campsites for tents or self-contained motor homes up to 35 feet. Piped drinking water, flush toilets, picnic tables, grills, and fire pits are provided. There is a campground host. The maximum stay is 30 days. No reservations; $8 per site; contact: National Park Service, 601 Nevada Hwy., 702/293-8907. The marina is a bit of a trek (a mile and a half by vehicle). It has a convenience store, restaurant, and bar.

Continuing north you follow Lakeshore Road around to the left (southwest), then take a right onto Northshore Road (Route 167). In another few miles, go right at the intersection with Lake Mead Blvd. (Route 147). In another seven miles is the turnoff for Callville Bay.

Callville Bay

From the highway, you rock and roll four miles down to the marina, which is green from oleanders, Russian olives, yucca, palms, and pines. Callville Bay is the site of Callville, founded by Anson Call in 1865 in response to a directive from Brigham Young. Callville flourished briefly in the 1860s as a landing for Colorado River steamboats and an army garrison, but the post office closed in 1869. The stone ruins of Call's warehouse today rest under 400 feet of Lake Mead water and 10 feet of Lake Mead silt.

As you come into the marina, the first left is to **Callville Bay Trailer Village,** most of which is occupied by permanent mobiles and trailers. There are only five spaces for overnight motor homes, all with full hookups and three pull-throughs. Tents are not allowed. Laundromat and groceries are available at the marina. Reservations are recommended, especially on weekends; 702/565-8958. The fee is $17 for two people; register at the Administration office by the marina. RVs can also park without hookups at the campground across the way. (Better yet, drive another 30 minutes to Echo Bay, the best RV parking on the lake.)

Callville Bay Campground is a little farther down the access road. A beautiful grassy area greets you at the entrance, with stone picnic benches under shelters and a restroom. The sites closer to the front have the taller shade-giving oleanders; those toward the rear are more exposed. A half-mile trail climbs from the dump station near the entrance to a sweeping panorama of the whole area. There are 170 campsites for tents or self-contained motor homes up to 35 feet. Piped drinking water, flush toilets, picnic tables and grills are provided. There is a campground host. The maximum stay is 90 days. No

reservations; the fee is $8. Contact the National Park Service at 702/293-8907.

Continuing toward the marina, you'll encounter the visitor center in a gray trailer in the upper parking lot, open Fri.–Sun. 10 A.M.–2 P.M. Pick up the requisite ton of brochures and check out the photo of Callville's stone ruins and the geology poster. Volunteers answer your questions and sell you books about the desert. Restrooms are next door. A sign at the edge of the lower parking lot points down to a swimming area in a little inlet (no lifeguard).

The marina has a grocery store with snack bar (bacon and eggs $4–5, burgers $4, sandwiches $5) and a bar-restaurant with a wall of big picture windows overlooking the lake. Down at the boat launch you can rent houseboats (from about $250 a night between November and May up to $500 a night between June and September). You can also hop on Forever Resorts' Lake Mead tour boats. Callville attracts the lion share of the crowds from Las Vegas, and has no beach to speak of. It's worth it to drive another 24 miles to Echo Bay.

Back on Route 167, continue east. It's rugged country out here, with the Black Mountains between you and the lake and the dark brooding Muddy Mountains to the left. In a while is the **Redstone Picnic Area,** just a big old pile of Aztec sandstone in the middle of nowhere, with picnic tables, pit toilets, and a one-mile trail through the monoliths, complete with interpretive signs. Just past Redstone, the road turns north and aims straight toward the east edge of the Muddy Mountains. The turnoff to Echo Bay, 24 miles from Callville, is on the right.

Echo Bay

You rock and roll four miles down Bitter Spring Valley to Echo Bay. This resort has a similar layout to Callville Bay, but is much larger. The first left is to **Echo Bay Trailer Village** the best RV park on Lake Mead's Nevada side. Spaces are nice and wide, with telephone-pole stumps separating them. Every site has a tree or two. And there are no permanents: all the mobiles and trailers are across the way, and this lot is only for RVs. There are 35 spaces for motor homes, all with full hookups, but no pull-throughs. Tents are not allowed. Restrooms have flush toilets and hot showers; public phone, sewage disposal, laundry, and groceries are available. Reservations are accepted; 702/394-4000. The fee is $12 per vehicle in winter, $18 per vehicle in summer. Register at the front desk of Echo Bay Seven Crowns Resort.

Or go left into **Echo Bay Campground.** There's an upper and a lower campground. The lower campground overlooks the houseboating area and is closer to the marina action, and has 20-foot tall oleander bushes that give much-needed shade to the sites in the hot summer afternoons. There are 155 campsites for tents or self-contained motor homes up to 35 feet. Piped drinking water, flush toilets, sewage disposal, picnic tables, and grills are provided. The maximum stay is 90 days. No reservations; the fee is $10. Contact the National Park Service in Boulder City, 702/394-4066.

A little past the campground turnoff is a self-service information center, open daily 8 A.M.–4 P.M. Outside is a desert garden with labeled plants; inside are displays on fishing (including record catches) and the town of St. Thomas, inundated by Lake Mead in June 1938.

Continue down toward the marina; just before the big boat-repair building is the right turn into the lower campground. You pass the boat buildings and Park Service administrative offices and residences, then come to Echo Bay's Seven Crowns Resort, 702/394-4000. Rooms at the inn are $60 in winter and $90, $105, and $115 in summer depending on the room's size and view. The restaurant next door is open 8 A.M.–8 P.M. (an hour earlier and later on weekends), serving bacon and eggs and omelettes for $4.75, salads and sandwiches for $6, and steaks, chicken, fish, and stir-fries for $10–15. The windows overlook the parking lot.

The store and Texaco gas station are open daily 8 A.M.–5 P.M. You can rent houseboats, a variety of fishing and ski boats, and Sea-Doos, too.

But the great thing about Echo Bay is the beach: the best and most easily accessible beach on the Nevada side of the lake. There's no shade to speak of, but it's a sandy beach (unlike the rocks at Boulder Beach), and you'll pretty much own the place. The bay is shallow for a long distance out, so the swimming is safe (no lifeguard).

Overton Beach

Back on North Shore Road, you continue north for a little ways, skirting the east edge of the Muddies. In less than a mile is **Rogers Spring,** which bubbles up clear and warm in a wash that runs east from the Muddy Mountains into Roger's Bay in the Overton Arm of Lake Mead. The warm turquoise pool, which is outlined by towering palms and old sturdy cottonwoods, overflows into a bubbling creek which meanders down a tree-lined course toward Lake Mead. The high mineral content of the water give the pool a beautiful blue color and makes its depth deceptive. Transplanted tropical fish dart in the shallows and thrive in its warm waters. This spring has long been a favorite camping spot of southern Nevadans; in fact, it was originally developed by the Civilian Conservation Corps in the 1930s under the direction of Col. Thomas W. Miller, the same colonel who was instrumental in developing the first facilities at nearby Valley of Fire State Park. The National Park Service has plans, when the money is available, to develop some 250 campsites with water, sewer and power. For now, there're only chemical toilets and picnic shelters. A sign cautions swimmers not to put their heads in the water. The trailhead for a mile-long trail to an overlook is across the bridge over the stream.

A mile up the road from Rogers is **Blue Point Spring,** from where you have a grand view of Lake Mead on one side and the back of Valley of Fire on the other.

In another mile is the turnoff to **Overton Beach,** a three-mile straight shot to the top of Overton Arm of Lake Mead. Overton Beach is the farthest resort from the dam. The best fishing on Lake Mead is up here, thanks to its location three miles from both the Muddy and Virgin rivers (which dump a lot of fish food into the lake). **Overton Beach RV Park** is on the right. Every one of the 54 spaces has a view of the lake and is a two-minute walk to the water. There are 12 pull-throughs. Tents are allowed. Restrooms have flush toilets and hot showers ($1 for non-campers); public phone, sewage disposal, laundry, groceries, gas dock, marina, and swim beach are available. Reservations are accepted; the fee is $19 for two people; 702/394-4040.

The marina has a convenience store and café, selling the usual groceries, sundries, and T-shirts, along with $2 hot dogs at the snack bar. The beach is a bearable combination of stone and sand. The eastern entrance to Valley of Fire is less than a mile west of the turnoff to Overton Beach; instead of going right to the lake, you take a left onto Route 169. This intersection is 93 miles from Las Vegas.

Virgin Basin

Just above the Overton Beach, two rivers, the Virgin to the northeast and the Muddy to the northwest, empty into Lake Mead. The Virgin Basin is a widening of the Virgin River just before it merges with the reservoir. It's a primary habitat for numerous species of wildlife, including mammals, waterfowl, birds of prey, fish, and reptiles and amphibians. In the fall and spring, for example, numerous migrating species use the Virgin Basin as a resting place on their way. Some species, including numerous bald eagles, spend the winter in the Virgin Basin. Because it's accessible only by boat, the Virgin Basin is well protected and offers wildlife a habitat safe from most human intervention. If you're careful, the basin provides an excellent opportunity to view and photograph wildlife in one of the few wilderness river areas left near the lake. To get there, you have to boat in from the Overton Arm. Most of the time there isn't enough water in the Virgin River below Riverside (just south of Mesquite) to float anything but an innertube.

BLACK CANYON

Black Canyon, which starts at the base of Hoover Dam and extends downriver to Katherine, is the nearest river running to Las Vegas. If you want to take a commercial raft trip, call Black Canyon Raft Tours. If you're looking to run the river from the base of the dam on your own, you have to get a permit from the U.S. Department of Interior's Bureau of Reclamation for access via Portal Road on dam property. The Bureau of

Reclamation only allows two groups of 15 people each to access the river per day: one at 8 A.M. and the second at 10:30 A.M. All popular dates, such as weekends and holidays, are booked up a year or more in advance. You can acquire a permit to put in at Portal Road during the week with a mere two or three weeks' notice, and you may also be able to snag a cancellation. For more information on accessing the Colorado River from Portal Road, call the Reclamation reservation department at 702/293-8204, Mon.–Fri. 10:30 A.M.–5 P.M. PST, or if there's no response at that number, contact the Hoover Dam Visitor's Center Manager at 702/294-3513. The 24-hour emergency phone number is 702/293-8932. The fees are $10 plus a $3 national park fee.

Other put-in and take-out points include Cottonwood Cove and Eldorado Canyon on the Nevada side, Willow Beach and Katherine Landing on the Arizona side. Once on the river, there are many exciting places to visit and things to do. Our river tour will begin at the base of the dam as if you had launched at Portal Road. If you launch from any other point you can come upriver to enjoy these locations.

Life jackets must be worn during the entire trip down Black Canyon to Chalk Cliffs at marker 43. The water below the dam is 53°F all year, warming up as it goes farther downriver toward Eldorado Canyon, where it widens out and is warm enough for swimming in the summer. Navigational markers (day boards) are posted on the shores of the river: red triangles with even numbers on the Arizona side, green squares with odd numbers on the Nevada side. These markers indicate the approximate distance, in miles, from Davis Dam at the extreme southern end of Lake Mohave. Also look for bighorn sheep on the cliffs along the river throughout Black Canyon. Sighting them provides the sharp-eyed observer a special opportunity to see these majestic animals in their natural environment.

Remember that the water level in the canyon can fluctuate considerably during the day, sometimes as much as four-six vertical feet, depending on releases from Hoover Dam. When stopping to camp, picnic, or explore, small craft should be pulled well up out of the water and larger craft should be well anchored on shore above any highwater marks to prevent being stranded.

Sights

There are hundreds of interesting places in Black Canyon. Below are some of the best.

Sauna Cave: A few hundred yards below the Portal Road launch site on the Nevada side of the river is a long gravel spit with tamarisk bushes. At the end of a lagoon just past the spit are some rain caves on the west wall. Some drops of water are hot, while others are cold. During the construction of Hoover Dam, workers started to drill a tunnel at this site; however, they encountered hot water (122°F) and had to abandon the site.

Goldstrike Canyon: At the entrance to the lagoon on the left is a small very hot spring (123°F). The mouth of Goldstrike Canyon is 50 yards below the entrance to the lagoon on the Nevada side. A short walk up this canyon leads to hot pools and a hot waterfall that is about as hot as a person can stand. Various algae are responsible for the vivid green colors on the rocks. The rock formations are spectacular and there are many hot pools. The rocks and pebbles in the hot stream are sharp and tennis shoes are advised. (**Caution:** *Naegleria fowleri,* an amoeba common to thermal pools, can enter the human body through the nose, causing a rare infection and possible death. Do not allow water from the hot springs or associated streams to enter your nose. Do not dive into or submerse your head in any thermal water in this recreation area.)

After leaving Goldstrike Canyon, inexperienced boaters, especially canoeists, should line their craft past the rock reef, or paddle upstream far enough to get over to the Arizona side, where the water is less turbulent.

A hot waterfall is located within a few feet of the river about 100 yards below Goldstrike Canyon on the Arizona side. This waterfall is larger and not as hot as the one in Goldstrike Canyon. Just past the waterfall is a palm tree. The palm, which is not native to Black Canyon, was planted around 1970 by G. W. Paulin, who loved these canyons and spent much time exploring the river.

Boy Scout Canyon: About a third of a mile

south of the Mile 62 marker is a sandy beach at the mouth of a large canyon on the Nevada side. Hot springs and hot pools are about a half mile up the canyon. The stream goes underground before it reaches the river.

Ringbolt Rapids: When approaching Ringbolt Rapids, watch for a large iron ring set into the rock on the Arizona side about 50 yards above the rapids (marker 60) and 15–20 feet above the high-water mark. This is one of many ringbolts that were placed in the canyon walls and used to winch steamboats up through the rapids from 1865 to 1890. The construction at Davis Dam, 60 miles downstream and the resulting Lake Mohave significantly tamed these rapids, which at one time were one of the most challenging on the Colorado River. These rapids are adjacent to White Rock Canyon and the Arizona Hot Springs on the Arizona side of the river (see entry for White Rock Canyon.)

Gauging Station: An old gauging station can be seen clinging to the Nevada canyon wall at mile 54.25 The gauging station was used prior to and during construction of Hoover Dam for monitoring the water levels, flow rate, and silt content of the Colorado. A cable car provided access to the gauging station from the Arizona side. Just across the river on the Arizona side is the trail and catwalk used by the resident engineers who were responsible for gathering the data at the gauging station to travel from their residence to the Station. The catwalk can be seen high up on the sheer walls above the river and is unsafe for access. A second cable car across a side canyon enabled the engineers to go from the trail over to the catwalk. The foundations of the gauger's house and garage are located just down the river at about mile 53.

Willow Beach Fish Hatchery: The buildings on the Arizona bank just before mile 52 are a part of the Willow Beach National Fish Hatchery. The buoys floating on the Arizona shore mark an area that is closed to all watercraft including canoes and kayaks (see entry for Willow Beach.) The Willow Beach area extends for about a half mile along the Arizona shore. If you're terminating your trip at Willow Beach, boat to the south end at the harbor past the marinas, and bring your vessel to shore at the south end of the parking lot. There is convenient vehicle access to this location and you will not come into conflict with other boaters as you remove your boat from the water. South of Willow Beach the river is still narrow and cold; it continues flowing through the deep canyon for about 3.5 miles. Life jackets must still be worn while underway.

Monkey Hole: The point where the river widens is known as Monkey Hole. With a bit of imagination, the rock formation high on the Arizona shore kinda sorta resembles a monkey. Just below Monkey Hole and mile 48, the Mead-Liberty powerlines cross the river.

Windy Canyon: The stretch of river between mile 45 and 44A is known as Windy Canyon. On occasion up-river winds become quite strong in this area, when this canyon more than earns its name. Canoes and other small boats are recommended to check the wind currents before venturing below Willow Beach, the last take-out point before Windy Canyon. Below mile 44A, the river spreads out into Copper Basin; several canyons open out in this area, providing good places to camp.

Chalk Cliffs: Just below Squaw Peaks on the Nevada side are the Chalk Cliffs. A navigational light and marker 43 high on the Nevada side mark the mouth of Black Canyon. Life jackets are not required to be worn below this point, but their continued use is strongly recommended as the river current is still strong at this point.

Eldorado Canyon: Eldorado Canyon is on the Nevada side at about Mile 39. The take-out point used is a quarter-mile-long uphill portage to the road. This was the site of a large flash flood in 1974 that wiped out the facilities at Eldorado Canyon; they were never replaced.

For those intrepid boaters who wish to continue south of Eldorado Canyon, be prepared for open water, possible very windy conditions, and extreme temperature ranges. Cottonwood Cove is 17 miles distant and Katherine Landing is 40 miles.

VALLEY OF FIRE STATE PARK

At this stunning piece of Olympian sculpture, the gods had miles of fire-red rock to carve, and 150 million years to fill in the details. Like Red Rock Canyon, this valley, six miles long and three to four miles wide, is another spectacular ancestral hall of the Navajo Formation, a continuum of Mesozoic sandstone that stretches from southern Colorado through New Mexico, Arizona, Utah, and Nevada. Its monuments—arches, protruding jagged walls, divine engravings and human etchings, all in brilliant vermilion, scarlet, mauve, burgundy, magenta, orange, and gold—more than any other characteristic are representative of the great American Southwest.

The highest and youngest formations in the park are mountains of sand deposited by desert winds 140 million years ago—the familiar, by now, Aztec sandstone. These dunes were petrified, oxidized, and chiseled by time, sun, water, and chemical reactions into their psychedelic shapes and colors. Underneath the Aztec is a 5,000-foot-deep layer of brown mud, dating back at least 250 million years, when uplift displaced the inland sea. The gray limestone below represents another 200 million years of deposits from as long as 550 million years ago, from the Paleozoic marine environment.

This stunning valley was venerated by Indians, as evidenced by numerous petroglyphs in the soft rock, and was part of the old Arrowhead Trail through southern Nevada. It was originally included in lands set aside by the federal government for construction of Boulder Dam in the 1920s, then donated to the state in 1931 as a state park. Nevada had little money to spend on development, so the feds sent in the Civilian Conservation Corps, which built the road, campgrounds, and some cabins.

Meanwhile, Nevada designated Valley of Fire a state park in 1935, one of the four original Nevada state parks. Eager locals jumped the gun and held an unofficial celebration on Easter Sunday 1935 for the completion of the road, which is how Valley of Fire came to be considered Nevada's first state park.

Sights

A turnout near the entrance to the park has a self-service fee station: $6 admission for cars, $1 for bicycles, $14 for camping. Here is also an information shelter with a description of **Elephant Rock,** one of the best and most photographed examples of eroded sandstone in the park. A short trail leads to it. Continue west past signs for the Arrowhead Trail and petrified logs to the **Cabins,** built for travelers out of sandstone bricks by the CCC in 1935. Farther in, the **Seven Sisters** are stunning sentinels along the road.

The **visitors center** has a truly spectacular setting under a mountain of fire. Outside is a demonstration garden and inside is the finest set of exhibits at a Nevada state park. Signboards by the front window describe the complex 550-million-year-old geological history of the view. You can spend another hour reading all the displays on the history, ecology, archaeology, and recreation of the park, along with browsing in the changing exhibit gallery and at the bookshelf by the information desk. Don't miss the colorful signboard of the most popular features in Valley of Fire: Cobra Rock, Indian Marbles, Grand Piano, Beehive, Balancing Rock, Mouse's Tank, Duck Rock, Rock of Gibraltar, Silica Dome, Limestone Hoodoos, and more. And don't forget to pick up a map of the park. For info, contact Valley of Fire State Park at 702/397-2088.

From the visitor center, take the spur road to **Petroglyph Canyon Trail,** and dig your feet into some red sand. A trail guide introduces you to the local flora. **Mouse's Tank** is a basin that fills up with water after a rain; a fugitive Indian, Mouse, hid here in the late 1890s. The spur road continues through the towering canyon and peaks at **Rainbow Vista,** which has a parking area and spectacular overlook.

The road used to dead-end here, but in summer 1994, the state opened a new four-mile extension all the way to Silica Dome. This is one of the most fun roads in Nevada, not only for its incomparable views, but for its twists and turns and ups and downs; a maniac on a motorcycle could catch *big* air—before being arrested by a ranger. The rare red-rocky and riotous relief will rally you to rants, raves, and high crimes of alliteration. Finally, you arrive at **Silica Dome,** where you can park your car and marvel, open-mouthed, at the walls and pillars and peaks of sparkling white rock.

Heading west again on the through road,

Route 169, you come to a quarter-mile loop trail to fenced-in **petrified wood,** the most common local fossil. On the other side of the highway, another spur road goes to the campgrounds and the high staircase up to petroglyphed and sheer **Atlatl Rock.** This is the tallest outdoor staircase in the state, more than 100 steps up to the face of the rock. You'll wonder how whoever inscribed the face got up and stayed up here.

Atlatl Rock is between the two separate and prosaically named campgrounds. **Campground A** is the larger; thus it's more crowded with RVers; three walk-in campsites are in the rear of the campground. Sites here have gravel pads for tent camping, picnic tables under shelters, barbecue grills, and running water; the restrooms have showers. **Campground B** is more compact and scenic; the back campsites, under the fiery red cliffs, are the most spectacular in Nevada. Together the two combine for 51 campsites for tents or self-contained motor homes up to 30 feet. Both have piped drinking water. Campground A has flush toilets and shower, Campground B has vault toilets. Campground A is open year-round, Campground B is closed for two to three months every summer (to regenerate). Picnic tables under ramadas, grills, and fire rings are provided. The maximum stay is 14 days. No reservations; the fee is $14 per vehicle.

The loop road continues back to the highway, though the pavement ends. It's hard red gravel, bumpy and rocky, but it's not too far back to smooth sailing.

Take a right and continue west to the **Beehives,** worth a look. From here you can turn around, return to the east entrance, and take a left on Route 169 up to Overton. Or you can head to the west end of the park and back to Las Vegas (55 miles). Or you can take a 28-mile detour on a BLM Back Country Byway Trail, winding up on Northshore Road near Echo Bay.

BITTER SPRINGS BACK COUNTRY BYWAYS TRAIL & BUFFINGTON POCKETS

The Bitter Springs Back Country Byways Trail to Buffington Pockets and beyond is a worthwhile scenic trip through brightly colored red and tan sandstone bluffs. The 28-mile drive is a challenging adventure that can be made in a dependable vehicle with decent ground clearance. However, you should stay on the main road and avoid side trips into the many canyons unless you have a 4WD vehicle. The beginning of the Bitter Springs Byway is 4.5 miles east of the Valley of Fire exit on I-15; follow the sign for Bitter Springs to the left (south).

You start out cutting through the foothills of the Muddy Mountains, then travel through several dry washes and past numerous abandoned mining operations, before ending up on Northshore Drive. Along the way you have the opportunity to view lush streams that provide a strong contrast to the surrounding desert and access for viewing geologic formations that are very rare for this region of Nevada. Frequent evidence of the borax mining that was once a dominant economic force in the region is obvious everywhere. Landforms are colorful, complex, and add to the feeling of isolation. Among the more striking scenes you'll encounter is Bitter Ridge, a sweeping arc that cuts for eight miles across a rolling valley. Geology buffs will appreciate the features of this tilt fault with its rugged vertical southern face looming several hundred feet off the desert floor.

Moving past rolling landforms of red, brown, black, and white, you drop into Bitter Valley, where burnt-red buttes stand like silent sentinels in the middle of the desert floor. These formations are rare, as are others found near the western edge of the Byway after driving across creosote flatlands and through a gray limestone canyon. Emerging from the canyon, you'll be captivated by the sight of the brilliantly colored sandstone hills of Buffington Pockets and Color Rock Quarry.

Continue to wind through a field of sandstone boulders; you'll soon arrive at the entrance to Hidden Valley, tucked away a short distance from the road up a deep, winding, boulder-choked canyon. Confined within the valley's walls, which soar hundreds of feet into the desert sky, are numerous sandstone windows, arches, and spires. Stop and take a short hike up into the valley. Early humans were apparently awed by

the grandeur here, as demonstrated by an unusually high concentration of pictographs and petroglyphs marking various sights.

Remnants of mining man can be seen when you come across the remains of the American Borax mining operation. Several mine buildings still stand, and the ground is marked by 30-foot-deep cisterns that once held water. Mine tunnels and adits (horizontal passages) are also abundant in the area, along with the debris generally associated with old mining districts. Be very careful around the old mines. Cave-ins, rattlesnakes, and other dangers lurk in dark corners and around unseen bends. Obey all signs and fencing that have been installed for your protection.

There are no services along this isolated road, so make sure your vehicle is in good repair and running on sound tires, and don't forget to let a responsible person know where you're going and when you'll be back. Just in case. Maps of this area are available from the local BLM office, 702/515-5000. Ask for the Nevada Back Country Byway guide for Bitter Springs Trail.

MOAPA VALLEY

Over a rise awaits the Muddy River Wash, at the outlet of Moapa Valley. Lake Mead terminates here and a thin strip of rich agricultural green escorts the road up the river valley. The Anasazi Indians were farming successfully here a thousand years ago, and built the Pueblo Grande de Nevada, or Lost City, on the fertile delta between the Muddy and Virgin rivers. Paiute replaced Pueblo, and when the Mormons began to colonize the valley in 1864, the Paiute were still there. The Mormons' efforts were successful, and today this well-tended plot is their legacy. Settlement extends the six miles north, up the irrigated green Moapa Valley, surrounded on three sides by crew-cut buttes, to Logandale.

Overton

Overton is a compact agricultural community whose downtown is strung along several blocks of Route 169, also known as Moapa Valley Boulevard and Main Street. The main action in town is at **Sugars,** 702/397-8084. The restaurant serves $5 bacon and eggs, $4.50–6 burgers (including the Sugar Burger: cheeseburger and polish sausage). There's also a sports bar with bartop video poker and sports memorabilia, some from the Moapa Valley Pirates. The **Inside Scoop,** 702/397-2055, has 32 flavors of Dreyers and sandwiches for $3, baked potatoes for $2.50, and nachos for $3–4. A nice big map of Moapa Valley graces the side wall. You can also stop at the Red Rooster Bar, a pizza place, and the Chevron station.

If you take a right at the sign, across the street from Foodtown, you'll come to **Overton Community Park.** It has a playground with swings and slides, picnic tables under shelters with grills, big trees, basketball courts, and a baseball field.

Fun & Sun RV Park, 280 N. Cooper, Overton, 702/397-8894, has 112 spaces, 66 of which are pull-throughs. Tents are not allowed. Restrooms have flush toilets and hot showers; public phone, sewage disposal, laundry, rec room, and heated swimming pool and spa are available. Reservations are accepted; the fee is $18 for two people.

Lost City Museum

A glimpse of the Anasazi legacy is found at the Lost City Museum, just south of the small farming town of Overton, 50 miles northeast of Las Vegas. The museum houses an immense collection of Pueblo artifacts, including an actual pueblo foundation, and a fascinating series of black-and-white photos covering the site's excavation in 1924. In an incisive article in *Nevada* magazine (November 1976), David Moore made the point that the Lost City wasn't so much lost as simply overlooked; Jedediah Smith cited the site during his travels through southern Nevada in the 1820s, and another expedition reported these "ruins of an ancient city" in the *New York Tribune* in 1867. But it was Nevada governor James G. Scrugham, a mining engineer who, in 1924, initiated the official dig. Some of the Anasazi ruins were drowned by Lake Mead, but even today, the Overton–Logandale area of the delta remains one of the country's "finest bottomless treasure chests of ancient history," according to Moore. Residents who till their yards or replace septic tanks uncover scads of shards: In

1975 an entire ancient village was revealed by workmen digging a leach line.

The exterior of the museum, reminiscent of an adobe pueblo, was constructed by the CCC in 1935; climb down the log ladder into the authentic pit house in front. Stroll around back for petroglyphs, more pueblos, picnic tables, and a pioneer monument.

The museum is open daily 8:30 A.M.–4:30 P.M., $3 adults, $2 for seniors, 18 and under free; call 702/397-2193 for more information.

Logandale

If you head north on Route 169 from Overton, you pass a string of ranches on your way into Logandale. On the site of St. Joseph, one of the original (1865) Mormon towns in southern Nevada, this ranching village is mostly east of the road nearer the Muddy River. Along the road are the post office, a grocery store, and cows.

Glendale and Moapa

You cross the Muddy River and continue north for another few miles, untill the road dead-ends at the interstate. Down the frontage road is **Glendale Motel,** and its café, grocery store, and bar, 702/864-2277, charging $35–45 for the night. The restaurant serves burgers and shakes and malts. The lounge has bartop video poker and a pool table.

Take a right at the corner onto Route 168 and drive north, crossing the Muddy River again and passing BJ's restaurant and bar, a hardware store, a school, and the district court. The power plant on the edge of town belches white smoke into the purple sky toward the orange orb. Go up the road a few miles and take a left into the Moapa Paiute Reservation. The tribal store is behind the administrative offices. Alfalfa fields abut the small settlement.

MESQUITE

Thirty miles east of the Glendale exit of I-15 is Mesquite, on the Arizona border. A 13-mile spur road (Route 170) leaves I-15 10 miles west of Mesquite and drops fast into Virgin Valley, heading straight toward the high Virgin Mountains.

The road crosses the Virgin River at Rancho Riverside, then continues along the Virgin River Valley, through dairy land, past Bunkerville, another Mormon settlement from the 1870s, and into Mesquite through the back door.

This border town is quickly turning itself into Nevada's answer to Palm Desert (in California), at the center of a major population and economic boom. For years, Mesquite was known for, and dominated by, the Peppermill Hotel-Casino, first gambling in Nevada for westbound travelers along I-15. From a population of 900 in 1980, Mesquite, thanks to the Peppermill, added 1,000 people in the 1980s, closing out the decade with nearly 1,900. Between 1990 and 1997, Mesquite exploded, with the population more than tripling, to 6,500. In 2003 the estimate was 13,2777. Projections suggest that Mesquite will soon be home to over 20,000 residents. New commercial centers were thrown up along Mesquite Blvd., with names such as Sun Valley Plaza, Mesquite Business Park, and Mesquite Plaza. Condos, town homes, and custom houses popped up in developments named Rising Star, Rock Springs, Ventana, Silvercrest, and Las Palmas. A new post office was built; it was supposed to take into account potential growth over the next decade, but has already run short of post office boxes. The town has three major hotel-casinos: the Virgin River, CasaBlanca, and the Oasis. In addition, a country club is centered around two new Arnold Palmer–designed 18-hole championship golf courses. What we have here is yet another Nevada border boomtown, centered around gambling and resort living, right in the middle of its making.

Casinos

The Peppermill went through a management reorganization in 1993 and emerged known as the **Oasis Hotel-Casino**, 702/346-5232 or 800/621-0187. The Peppermill core casino remains, stylistically the same as the ones in Reno, Sparks, and Wendover with a predominance of red and blue border neon and millions of dollars of silk trees, flowers, and ferns. But the place underwent a $100 million expansion completed in 1995, which added Peggy Sue's Family Fun Center, a 300-room hotel tower and 60 upscale suites, new casino

space, and a parking garage across the street, connected by a pedestrian walkway over Mesquite Boulevard. The Oasis offers all the usual casino hysteria, including bingo and sports book, plus a steakhouse, buffet, coffee shop, diner, arcade, and miniature golf. The Oasis also owns Arvada Ranch, nearby in Arizona, with three golf courses, horseback riding, hunting, and target shooting.

Virgin River, 702/346-7777 or 800/346-7721, is on the other (east) side of town. It's smaller and more crowded, with the usual games, plus bingo, a two-screen movie theater, buffet and coffee shop, and 724 rooms. A 300-room tower is going up behind the hotel, and the new country club is across the street.

In July 1994, Player's International (Merv Griffin's casino company) opened **Player's Island** across from the Oasis on the west part of town, with a view east of the Virgin Mountains. Spending $85 million, Player's put up a gorgeous property, with 500 rooms, an attractive casino, lounge, showroom, coffee shop, buffet, steakhouse, and large pool area. The pièce de résistance was an extensive European-style health spa, complete with warm and hot pools, a watsu pool, mud baths (Virgin River mud), steam room and sauna, and all kinds of massage and skin therapies. Very upscale and luxurious. Player's marketed their Island hard, but a little more than a year later, the hotel-casino had lost so much money that it was put up for sale. In March 1997, Player's Island was sold to the Black family, owners of the Virgin River across town, for a bargain-basement $30 million. Since then, the name has been changed to the **CasaBlanca,** 950 W. Mesquite Blvd., 877/771-2777.

While all this was happening, in February 1997, Holiday Inn came to town and built a $35 million 215-room hotel-casino with a 45,000-square-foot casino called the **Eureka Casino and Hotel,** up the hill from the Virgin River at 275 Mesa Blvd., 702/346-4600 or 800/346-4611.

Accommodations

Mesquite's lodging situation has been growing as fast as the rest of the town. There are now about 3,000 rooms.

The biggest place is the **Oasis,** 1137 Mesquite Blvd., 702/346-5232 or 800/621-0187, with 1,000 rooms at $39–69. Next largest is **Virgin River,** 915 N. Mesquite Blvd., 702/346-7777 or 800/346-7721, with 724 rooms at $22–50. Then there's **Eureka Casino Hotel,** 301 Mesa Blvd., 702/346-4600 or 800/346-4611, with 210 rooms at $34–79. There's also a **Budget Suites** at the east exit, 702/346-7444 or 800/463-6302, with 67 suites (two rooms and a kitchenette) going for $40–125. The Ramada Inn Falcon Ridge Resort has 83 rooms at 1030 W. Pioneer Blvd., 702/346-2200, $49–89.

The little digs include: **Desert Palms,** Mesquite Blvd., 702/346-5756, $27–50; **Mesquite Springs,** 580 Mesa Blvd., 702/346-4700 or 800/319-2935, $420–575 per week (weeklies only); and **Valley Inn,** 773 W. Mesquite Blvd., 702/346-5281, $34–89.

Rvers have three parks to choose from in Mesquite. **Oasis RV Park** has 91 spaces for motor homes, all with full hookups; 30 are pull-throughs. Tents are not allowed. There's a Laundromat, grocery store, game room, and heated swimming pool. Reservations are accepted and recommended. The fee is $12.50 per vehicle (Good Sam discount available); 702/346-5232 or 800/621-0187.

Virgin River RV Park is small, sparse, and clean—separated from the hotel parking lot by a low retaining wall. Register at the front desk of the ho702/It has 47 spaces for motor homes, all with full hookups, but no pull-throughs. Tents are not allowed. A Laundromat and heated swimming pool are available. Reservations are accepted and recommended; the fee is $10 per vehicle; 702/346-7777 or 800/346-7721.

Casablanca RV Park has what could be the widest parking spaces in the state, wide enough to fit a big motor home, slide-out, and car. Or two cars and a motor home. Or a trailer, pickup truck, and car. The RV park is all asphalt with young trees, but has a fine view of the Virgin Mountains across the Virgin Valley. There are 45 spaces for motor homes, all with full hookups; 16 are pull-throughs. Tents are not allowed. Reservations are accepted and recommended. The fee is $16.20 daily for people under 50, and $12.96

weekdays for people over 50. 930 Mesquite Blvd., 702/346-7529 or 800/896-4567. The **Desert Skies RV Resort** just on the Arizona side has golf, horseback riding, and a heated pool. Rates are $35 and up; 928/347-6000.

Food

The Oasis and Virgin River have three-meal buffets and 24-hour coffee shops; Carollo's is also open 24 hours. Mesquite also has a McDonald's (across from the Oasis) and a Burger King (near the Virgin River).

The **Virgin River** has a couple of breakfast specials: two eggs and bacon or sausage for $2.22 or ham and eggs for $2.79, 24 hours a day. A cart in the sports lounge sells good hot dogs for $1.25 that come with sauerkraut and chili—a meal in itself.

The fine dining in Mesquite is at **Charmaine's Steakhouse** in the Oasis. Dinner is served 5–10 P.M. in the $11–20 range. Steaks, veal, king crab, chicken, seafood, and surf and turfs regularly go for $17–21. The hotel also offers an ice cream parlor, a buffet, and a coffee shop.

If you don't want to eat with a casino full of slots clanging in your ear, try the **Chalet Cafe,** in the middle of town, open daily 6 A.M.–10 P.M. It's cozy and local, and serves $4 bacon and eggs, $3–5 sandwiches, $10 eight-ounce New York steak, and shakes and malts for less than $2.

Virgin Canyon

The Virgin River remains the only wild river left in southern Nevada. It ends in Lake Mead across from Overton, creating a silted marshland where waterfowl prowl for fish, frogs, and mud-turtles. The headwaters of the Virgin River, one of the main tributaries feeding the Colorado River and Lake Mead, are in Utah's Dixie National Forest, where winter ice and snow and summer rainstorms feed the 300-mile long river. Occasionally violent deluges flood out the valleys below Dixie, ripping out forests and sending enormous walls of water sweeping through canyons that are six feet wide and 300 feet deep at Zion National Park.

By the time the Virgin reaches the Virgin River Canyon, or Virgin Gorge as it has come to be known (in the far northwest corner of Arizona; I-15 runs through it), its waters are somewhat tamer, but during heavy rain years, they can still get cantankerous and dangerous. During calmer times of the year, many people have explored sections of the Virgin River in canoes, kayaks, on foot and swimming, depending on the time of year, the specialty of the explorer, and the nature of the terrain.

Some of the most beautiful parts of the Virgin River Gorge are accessible by driving up I-15 past the Nevada–Arizona border to the area near the Arizona–Utah border. A public campground is just off I-15 above Exit 18 to Beaver Dam Mountains Wilderness and the Paiute Wilderness. Much of the Virgin River Gorge is still pristine and explorable. Contrary to what a few old-timers maintain, the construction of I-15 has made the gorge more accessible to the average visitor.

Among some of the treasures you'll find in the gorge are extensive hikes to places where ancient Indians carved petroglyphs in rock wall. When you get tired, you can relax on soft sandy river banks under salt cedars and watch the happy birds hunting fat insects or contemplate what these rock walls have seen during the last 50 million years. Caves abound along the riverbanks. Inside some of them you will find large trunks of trees, pounded inside caves by the force of a raging torrent in times past. In some places the granite walls are polished smooth by water levels of thousands of years ago. In other caves, high up on the face of the cliffs, you can see where campfires of ancient natives blackened the ceiling. Deer and other small game abound in the gorge, one of the few wild places left in this kind of country.

Laughlin

What it is about godforsaken patches of the Nevada desert that gives men visions of booming metropolises is hard to say. Abe Curry bought a tiny trading post in Eagle Valley to launch the capital city of a state that didn't even exist. Myron Lake bought a collapsing bridge and proceeded to found the world's biggest little city. And Don Laughlin bought a bankrupt bait shop and built, in a few short years, one of the largest gambling centers in the country. Maybe it's water. All three pioneers had rivers—the Carson, Truckee, and Colorado—in common. Maybe it's heat—the scorching, absorbing, blinding swelter that gives rise to sugar-plum fairies, pink elephants, and mirages of gold mines. Probably it's destiny—the Great Basin and Mojave are littered with the ghosts of hundreds of boomtowns whose founding fathers dreamed of the prosperity and posterity that only a select few have achieved. Whatever it is, Don Laughlin came, invested, and conquered, giving life to a namesake town site the likes of which Nevada hasn't seen for exactly 100 years.

Don Laughlin was born in 1933 and grew up in Owatonna, Michigan. By the time he was in the ninth grade, he already had a successful business supplying pinball machines, jukeboxes, and slots (legal at the time) to nearby bars and restaurants. He moved to Las Vegas at the age of 21 and worked as a bartender and dealer for a couple of years, then bought the 101 Club, a small bar in North Las Vegas that afforded him the opportunity to get a gaming license. In 1966 he sold the bar and began looking around for a place to start an empire—a predictable ambition for any 33-year-old entrepreneur with Las Vegas cash and a gaming license burning a hole in his pocket. Soon he'd spotted Sandy Point, a small beach on the Colorado River where the southern tip of Nevada wedges between California and Arizona in the fierce Sonoran desert. At the time the only business was a baked and bankrupt bait shop, familiar only to a handful of anglers from broiling Bullhead City, Arizona, across the river. Laughlin bought six acres of land at the end of a sandy road for $250,000 ($35,000 down). Along with the land came the bait shop, an eight-room motel (Laughlin's family occupied half of it), and a six-seat bar. But it was his unrestricted gaming license that put Laughlin in the black, and an Irish postal official who put "Laughlin" on the map. According to legend, the inspector, O'Reilly, listened to Laughlin's suggestions of Riverside and Casino for the name of the town, but settled on Laughlin instead, for the Irish ring of it. Today Don jokes that Laughlin was named after his mother.

The Riverside

Both Laughlins struggled for the first decade or so; banks laughed at the Don's loan applications. But Southern California Edison built a coal-fired power plant just up the hill from the river, expanding the population base. Slowly, people from Needles, Kingman, Lake Havasu, and even as far away as San Bernardino and Flagstaff began frequenting the homegrown little river resort-casino as an alternative to corporate Las Vegas. By 1976, the Riverside Hotel had expanded to 100 rooms and 300 slots. The growth of Bullhead City, Arizona, right across the Colorado River, kept pace; its population increased from 600 in 1966 to more than 6,000 in 1976, as employees, retirees, and snowbirds moved in, attracted by the weather, the water, and the wagering. In 1982, the Colorado River Commission began developing housing and recreational facilities nearby, then Clark County installed water and sewer systems, and growth rapidly snowballed, so to speak.

By 1984, the Riverside was a 14-story, 350-room hotel, accompanied by half a dozen other casinos lining the river—and little else. In that year Laughlin had a grand total of 95 residents—the temp. still higher than the pop. and one casino for every 16 townspeople! The rest of the 3,000 employees lived on the Arizona side (by then Bullhead City had surpassed the 15,000 mark), commuting across the river by way of the Davis Dam bridge or the casino ferries, and gaining an hour in the process (Arizona is on Mountain Time, but unlike Jackpot and Wendover, Laughlin sticks to Pacific Time).

The Boom

But the mid-'80s was just the beginning of the boom. Don Laughlin proceeded to spend more than a million of his own dollars in road improvements, $3 million to build the new bridge from Bullhead City to his hotel (then had a little trouble getting Nevada to take it over), and $6

million to expand the airport across the river. Meanwhile, developers began throwing up condos, apartments, shopping centers, even a school and library. And the casinos kept coming: Sam's Town Gold River opened in 1985 (the name was changed, along with the management, in 1992 to Gold River Resort; and then again in 1998 to River Palms Resort); Circus Circus's Colorado Belle opened in July 1987, right next door to its sister the Edgewater. Harrah's gorgeous Del Rio Hotel opened in mid-1988, and a big Flamingo Hilton opened in August 1990. Steve Wynn paid $40 million for Del Webb's Nevada Club (now the Golden Nugget and owned by MGM-Mirage), vastly improved the interior, and built a 300-room tower. Parking garages have now been built at every joint.

The Flamingo is the largest hotel with 1,912 rooms; Harrah's is second largest, having expanded to 1,616. Ramada Express has a total of 1,500, and Don Laughlin's own Riverside has a total of 1,440.

Gambling revenues began dropping slightly in Laughlin in 1994, due to intense competition from the new megajoints on the Las Vegas Strip, but it's too early to wonder if it will become an ongoing trend. More competition has arrived, however, and not from the north, but from the south. The Fort Mojave Tribe opened the Avi Hotel-Casino 10 miles south of Laughlin right on the state line. The new boomtown is called Aha Macav.

Laughlin is one of the hottest spots in the country, logging in with the second-highest record temperatures, right behind Laredo, Texas. On June 29, 1994, the official thermometer at Laughlin's Clark County Fire Department station registered a sizzling 125°F, breaking Nevada's highest recorded temperature (in 1954) by two degrees. But in another way, Laughlin is pretty cool. You'll immediately notice how airy and bright the casinos are, thanks to the big picture windows overlooking the river. Their more comfortable and less claustrophobic atmosphere makes you wonder what Las Vegas has against natural light. Also, inside the Riverside and Del Rio casinos, you can snap pictures to your heart's content. The hotel rooms can be 50 percent cheaper than comparable ones in Las Vegas. And food here, like the cheap hotel rooms, expansive casinos, cooperative weather, and playful river, is user-friendly.

CASINOS

From the Nevada corner of the Laughlin bridge it's exactly a mile to the traffic light at the Ramada Express, then another mile exactly to Harrah's Del Rio. Between March and November, unless you're a camel it's a long sweaty walk from one end to the other, even if you take the fine river-walk behind the casinos between the Riverside and the Golden Nugget. You can take the public bus, the Silver Rider, which runs along the Strip ($1.50). You can also catch a water taxi to any of the hotels ($3 one way). Or grab a cab to where you want to go. But easiest, as always, is to drive. You can park in the Riverside lot to see it, then park in the Flamingo structure to see the Hilton, Ramada Express, Edgewater, Colorado Belle, Pioneer, and Golden Nugget, then drive to River Palms Resort, and on to Harrah's.

Riverside

Start your tour, naturally enough, at Don Laughlin's front-runner Riverside Hotel. The Riverside, being Laughlin's first, has the Greyhound bus depot, a movie theater (newly expanded to six cinemas), a showroom and headliner room, and the old post office. It's an older establishment, comparatively speaking, so it's somewhat claustrophobic and always *very* crowded with regulars. It has one of the state's only scenic pits—which runs along the back of the casino, over the sunken bar, looking out the big picture windows onto the Colorado.

The Riverside has a 24-hour coffee shop, buffet, snack bar, and prosaically but practically named Prime Rib Room and Gourmet Room. The showroom features headliners and traveling productions, such as "Legends in Concert." Something a little wild is almost always going in Loser's Lounge: rock 'n' roll, drinking. Check out the big poster of the famous Las Vegas horror movie, *Attack of the 50-Foot Woman.* There's also a Western dance hall, where a DJ spins the country tunes, the local country station holds contests and country-and-western fans learn to line dance.

Flamingo Laughlin

This 2,000-room hotel, with its trademark purple and pink neon, and nearly 8,000 pink-tinted windows, opened in August 1990. Its casino, in the Laughlin tradition, is wide open and airy, with high ceilings and good ambient light. Club Flamingo is a good-sized lounge with 400 seats; you can almost see, and clearly hear, the performers from the casino; lately from fall through spring, It's a Really Big Shew, a tribute to Ed Sullivan, has been playing here. May through August the showroom turns into the Comedy Stop.

Edgewater

This Circus Circus hotel grew to nearly 1,500 rooms when its 1,000-room tower, right on the river, opened in 1992. The casino is about 50 times larger inside than it looks from the outside: sprawling, airy, roomy. Downstairs are the buffet, 24-hour coffee shop, and a typical Hickory Pit steakhouse in the Circus Circus mold. A new Sports Bar has opened next to the buffet and will feature sports memorabilia. The snack bar is a great place to get big sandwiches, shrimp cocktails, and strawberry shortcake.

Colorado Belle

Another Mandalay Resort Group establishment, this hotel-casino is an anomaly in Nevada: a riverboat casino actually right on a river. The smokestacks soar 21 stories (with 1,177 remodeled rooms and suites), strobe lights turn the paddlewheel, and a bridge over a little moat fronts the main entrance. Inside is red-flocked wallpaper, riveted stacks for beams, fancy cut-glass chandeliers, major period murals and paintings, and a sweeping staircase with wood and brass banisters. The big Riverboat Lounge at the south end gets the boat rocking at night.

The hotel offers 12 restaurants, including the Boiler Room Microbrewery, as well as a new full-service spa and salon, a fitness room, an intriguing koi pond (said to be the largest privately owned koi pond in Nevada) that doubles as a moat, plus a gift shop, a candy shop, and an arcade.

Pioneer

This is the other grind joint in Laughlin with low ceilings, closely packed slots, dark, crowded. The Pioneer has a buffet that, especially on the weekends, lines them up out the back door, along with Granny's Gourmet Room upstairs from the main desk. The big neon River Ric, third in the unholy trinity of Vegas Vic and Wendover Will, waves with both arms, winks with one eye, and puffs on the perfect cigarette.

Ramada Express

Across the street sits this big hotel-casino, the only hotel (so far) on the east side of the Strip. Catch Old No. 7, "the Gambler," at the new depot in front of the hotel for a 10-minute three-quarter-mile ride around the parking lot. The trip takes you fairly high above the action and supplies convenient transportation from the covered parking lot down to the casino and street. It runs every 15 minutes on the quarter hour 10 A.M.–10 P.M. (until 11 on weekends); cost of your ticket is one smile. A fog machine simulates smoke from the stack and engine; sound effects, such as the roar of fire in the engine's boiler and whoosh of air brakes, add to the effect.

Cameras are welcome inside. The original casino wing is set up like a giant depot. The whole joint is full of railroad memorabilia; employees are called "the crew," the gift shop is train-oriented, the carpet looks like railroad track, and the bus boys greet you with "Welcome aboard." When the slot attendants announce their wares, it sounds like "Train! Train!" until you finally figure out they're saying "Change! Change!"

The air in the casino actually *circulates,* thanks to hundreds of ceiling fans, and track lighting (along with the eyes-in-the-sky) is suspended from black pipe from the high round ceiling. The acoustics are so muffled that you can have a conversation with the crap dealer, and there's even a water fountain right in the front vestibule. Ramada Express has taste and good designers.

Be sure to also check out the Veterans Museum, a good place to wander and take in a tribute to those who've served. The museum offers a variety of memorabilia from World War II,

Korea, and Vietnam. A film, The American Spirit, is a 15-minute, uplifting tribute to veterans. Admission is free.

Golden Nugget

You walk in through a familiar tropical atrium that was inspired by (or left over from) the Las Vegas Mirage: verdant foliage, curvy palms, rocky waterfalls—humid. Duck down the alleyway to the right for the Gilded Cage, in which five animated birds do French showtunes every 15 minutes 10 A.M.–10 P.M. It's about as tasteful as such a thing can be (though you still feel pretty silly standing there watching it). Have a coconut cocktail at Tarzan's Nightclub, which generally showcases the best lounge bands in Laughlin and doubles as a comedy club (all free).

River Palms Resort

You walk through the front doors onto the mezzanine level, overlooking the casino and looking out over a slew of neon signs of mines. Up here are slots, a bar, and an ice cream parlor. Down a level you'll find the main casino, the Lodge restuarant, the buffet, Palace Theater, Gaming Society slot club, the Bermuda Club, front desk, bingo parlor, sports book, and bake shop that, altogether, are larger than Cal-Nev-Ari. On the lowest (river) level are Pasta Cucina, the video arcade, and the doors to the dock.

Harrah's Laughlin

Harrah's Mexican-theme hotel, Laughlin's southernmost hotel-casino so far, is in a league all its own—as classy as you would expect a Harrah's to be. Opened in the summer of 1988, Harrah's simple white walls, painted with green and purple flora, the strolling mariachi bands, and the overhead decorations create a festive south-of-the-border feel. The resort also offers a separate nonsmoking casino.

Catch a good view of the sports book at Margaritaville or sip cocktails in Rosa's Cantina in the main casino. This is also one of the best places to sample a Laughlin buffet: The Fresh Market Buffet received a $6 million facelift that was unveiled in May 2004 (look for a sushi-making "robot" and a chocolate fountain. Harrah's also boasts the only official swimming beach along the Strip on the Nevada side, and it's open to the public.

Bay Shore Inn

Newest lodging in Laughlin, this 100-room hotel on Casino Drive near the intersection with the Needles Highway offers mostly video poker and the Lazy River Lounge.

Avi Resort and Casino

Ten miles south of Laughlin is the 455-room Avi Resort, owned and operated by the Fort Mojave Indian tribe. Avi is a sprawling and scenic resort situated along an attractive stretch of the Colorado River, but the main draw here is the Mojave Resort Golf Club, a challenging championship golf course surrounded by purple mountains and sand dunes. Whether or not you're here for the golf, the resort offers some good amenities, including a decent sandy beach for watersports and lounging, a Kids Quest play center (where you can actually drop off the kids for a spell), numerous dining options, and a movie theater.

PRACTICALITIES

Accommodations

At last count, there were nearly 11,000 rooms in Laughlin itself, and another goodly amount in Bullhead City across the river. Though around 4,000 of them have opened in the past few years, the total rooms still don't go very far in accommodating nearly 500,000 visitors a month. And the season here is year-round, with older snowbirds in the winter and younger river rats in the summer (120°F notwithstanding!). Also, the hotel rooms can be amazingly cheap, which ensures vacancy rates that you need a micrometer to measure. So, as always, make your reservations early. If you can't get one, call over to the Bullhead City Chamber of Commerce (928/763-9400) for a motel room (also see *Moon Handbooks Arizona* by Bill Weir).

Colorado Belle, 2100 Casino Dr., 702/298-4000 or 800/47-RIVER, $29–105; **Edgewater,** 2020 Casino Dr., 702/298-2453 or 800/67-RIVER, $25–85; **Flamingo Laughlin,** 1900 Casino Dr., 702/298-5111 or 800/FLAMING,

$24–199; **River Palms Resort,** 2700 Casino Dr., 702/298-2242 or 800/835-7903, $24–65; **Golden Nugget,** 2300 Casino Dr., 702/298-7111 or 800/237-1739, $25–199; **Harrah's,** 2900 Casino Dr., 702/298-3023 or 800/427-7247, $25–100; **Pioneer,** 2200 Casino Dr., 702/298-2442 or 800/634-3469, $25–95; **Ramada Express,** 2100 Casino Dr., 702/298-6403 or 800/2-RAMADA, $22–119; **Riverside,** 1650 Casino Dr., 702/298-2535 or 800/227-3849, $22 and up; **Avi,** 10000 Aha Macav Pkwy., 702/535-5555 or 800/430-0721, $19–129.

Airport

The Laughlin/Bullhead International Airport, located east of the Colorado River, is a full-service regional airport with daily flights from numerous cities. Call 928/754-2134.

Camping and RVing

On the Nevada side, there is one RV park, **Riverside RV Park,** just up Laughlin Cutoff Rd., 702/298-2535. It charges $22–23 a night for one of 600 spaces with full hookups, has showers and a laundry on the property, and allows the use of all the Riverside Hotel's resort amenities.

In Arizona, **Davis Camp Park** is a mile or so south of Davis Dam—go right on AZ 68 and follow it around to the left; 928/754-7250. Enter and pay at the guard station: $17 for one of 95 spaces and full hookups, $10 for tent camping, $2 for day use (8 A.M.–8 P.M.). Take a right to get to the tent and beach area, a left for the RV park and day-use picnic facilities. This is a 355-acre Mohave County park, a relaxing place to meet people, eat, breathe, watch the river go by, get into the river, and dig the view of the strip. Highly recommended. Bullhead City also has a KOA and three private RV parks.

Food

Food in Laughlin is good, plentiful, cheap, and has some variety, with a major in meat and a minor in Italian and Mexican. Also, Laughlin buffets are ubiquitous and usually inexpensive.

The nicest restaurant in town for ambience is the **Lodge** at River Palms Resort, 702/835-7904, open 5–10 P.M. (11 P.M. Friday and Saturday), with tasteful stone and log architecture, a comfortable bar with piano, and outside seating. Caesar salad is $4; clams casino $7; blackened redfish, red snapper, halibut, shrimp, chicken, game hen, and duck are $11–15, steaks, blackened filet, and cioppino are $16–20. **Pasta Cucina,** downstairs at River Palms Resort, serves $5–6 pasta, $6 pizza, $7–9 chicken and veal parmesan, and $10 New York steak (a good deal is the $5.99 all-you-can-eat soup, salad, and pasta dinner). River Palms Resort also has a coffee shop, a buffet, Subway shop, and Java Joe's Coffee Company.

Ramada Express is proud of its promenade, where you can duck into **Ramada Expresso, Passaggio Italian Gardens,** and the **Steakhouse.** Passaggio offers Italian sandwiches, pasta, pizza, chicken, veal, and eggplant in the $8–12 range. The Steakhouse features Caesar salad for $3.75 and a good lobster and shiitake mushroom appetizer for $6.75; salads are served from the gambling-train salad cart, with entrées of chicken, swordfish, veal, and steaks $13–20, and rack of lamb, lobster thermidor, and king crab $20–25. Ramada Express also has a 24-hour coffee shop, a buffet, and a snack bar.

Stefano's Italian restaurant has singing waiters to serve your pasta at the Golden Nugget. There's also a good deli with New York–style sandwiches for around $3.50. Or head downstairs for the buffet and 24-hour coffee shop.

Harrah's has **The Range Steakhouse** with everything from escargot ($9) to filet mignon ($35). Also there are the Margaritaville Bar, Baja Blue Mexican restaurant, a buffet, and a 24-hour coffee shop.

The Edgewater's **Deli** has an awesome shrimp cocktail served on a paper plate for $1.29, plus a $2 hot dog, $1.50 bowl of chili, and big $3 sandwiches.

Upstairs at the Colorado Belle are **Mark Twain's,** serving barbecue chicken and ribs in the $7.50–10 range; **Mississippi Lounge,** serving oysters and clams on the half shell for $5.50, seafood sampler $10, steamed clams $10 a dozen, crab melt sandwich $5; the **Orleans Room** steakhouse, serving steak and seafood in the $12–19 range; and a buffet.

The **Alta Villa** and **Beef Barron** are at the

Flamingo; the former is like an Italian town square, with pasta, chicken, beef, and fish $10–17; the latter serves ribs, prime rib, steaks, and barbecue chicken for $9–15. The Flamingo also has a 24-hour coffee shop, a buffet, a '50s-style diner, and Burger King.

Fishing

Striped bass are the big thing around here—30 pounds isn't uncommon. The world's record (inland) striper was landed at Bullhead City: 59.5 pounds. May is the best time to fish for them; they run north from Lake Havasu starting in March. There's a bass derby all summer on the river and a few rainbows might be lurking in the cold water right below the dam. Or head down to Katherine Landing and strike up a conversation about the crappies, carpies, and catfish.

Tours

Three tour boats cruise the Colorado, as long as there's enough water downriver—the Bureau of Reclamation controls the levels, often not to the liking of the tour-boat operators. Laughlin River Tours run the *Fiesta Queen* and the *Celebration,* both of which offer three to five sightseeing cruises per day; 800/228-9825. The *Fiesta Queen* is docked at the Edgewater, and the *Celebration* is at the Flamingo Laughlin. Rates are adults $11, children $6, kids under 3 are free. The **USS-Riverside** is a luxury casino cruiser designed to be able to pass under the Laughlin Bridge for a look at Davis Dam. It departs from the Riverside dock for 75-minute cruises 10:30 A.M.–6:30 P.M. (and 8:30 P.M. on Saturday); $10/$6.

Shopping

The Horizon Outlet Center is the big game in town with 55 stores, stocked with factory-discounted merchandise, such as Gap Outlet, Levi's, and Van Heusen. There is also a food court and market as well as a nine-screen movie theater. Open Mon.–Sat. 9 A.M.–8 P.M. and Sun. 10 A.M.–6 P.M.; 702/298-4497.

Outdoors

Big Bend of the Colorado State Park, five miles south of Laughlin on the Needles Highway,

702/298-1859, is a pleasant spot for camping, boating, picnicking, and hiking along the river. Fee is $3 to enter, $9 for camping and $8 for boating. Be sure to bring sunscreen and swim gear—temperatures can get steamy in the summer.

Christmas Tree Pass and Grapevine Canyon, seven miles west of Davis Dam, is a scenic area for picnicking, hiking, camping, and sightseeing (be on the lookout for Indian petroglyphs on canyon walls). Contact the Bureau of Land Management's Las Vegas office, 702/515-5000.

Golfers aren't neglected here, either. There are two golf courses: the **Emerald River Country Club** in town (702/298-0061) and the **Mojave Resort Golf Club** near the Avi Casino (702/535-4650).

Information

Most of the real-life activities take place in or around the **El Mirage Shopping Center,** five miles from the strip inland. The library, a post office, a supermarket, and a video store, are in the vicinity.

The Laughlin Chamber of Commerce/Convention and Visitors Authority **visitor center** is in a building across from the Flamingo, 1725 Casino Dr., 702/298-2214 or 800/4-LAUGH-LIN, www.visitlaughlin.com; the Bullhead City **Chamber of Commerce** is on US 95 just next door (south) to Bullhead Community Park for some good brochure hunting, 928/754-4121 or 800/987-7457.

Reno and Tahoe

In *Fear and Loathing in Las Vegas,* Hunter S. Thompson describes Reno as a "mom and pop store," compared to the megamall that is Las Vegas. In the last 50 years or so, Las Vegas has eclipsed Reno to the extent that when asked their impressions of Nevada, many people (especially those from the East) describe a vast desert wasteland, with the neon blaze of Glitter Gulch scorching a swath right through the middle of it. In their mental cartography, Las Vegas fills up the Nevada desert from border to border. At the very least, Las Vegas sits smack in the center of it, its capital and only city.

The fact is, Reno is the *original* Las Vegas. Las Vegas could never have become Las Vegas if Reno hadn't been Reno first. But Reno made a deliberate conscious decision *not to become* Las Vegas. While Las Vegas is arguably one of the littlest big cities in the world, Reno is still, to those in the know, the Biggest Little City in the World.

A short drive to the west, is another original—Lake Tahoe. This immense lake is the dazzling crown of western Nevada. Its air is so crisp and clean, its water is so clear and colorful, its mountains are so craggy and close, and its people are so crowded and condo-ized that the crown's gemstones are either splendor or spectacle, beauty or vanity. It's as if Mother Nature has created a

perfect optical illusion: Do you see the white setting or the black development? For example, you can swim and sunbathe in seclusion, hike and climb so far and high that you just have to reach up to kiss the sky, and sleep for free among the pine needles and longtail weasels, as if you're Sam Clemens in 1861. Or, you can get your instant tan under sunlamps in December, strut from blackjack to video poker, and then take the elevator to your two-bathroom, three-telephone, four-TV, five-star suite, complete with butler, bar, and choice of pillows, as if you're Donald Trump. This perfectly balanced pendulum swings only, of course, on the *Nevada* side of Tahoe, between the south wall of Harveys (at Stateline) and the north wall of Cal-Neva (at Crystal Bay), with stunning Lake Tahoe State Park in between. With all of the wilderness, you never have to step indoors if you don't want to, and with all the high-rise hotel-casinos, you never have to step outside. But you're a winner either way. Because you get to keep the crown.

Reno

Reno began its life as a crude bridge across the capricious Truckee River and grew initially into a crossroads settlement for the Comstock Lode. The arrival of the transcontinental railroad gave Reno a brief bask in the local limelight; the arrival of the Virginia & Truckee Railroad from Virginia City gave it a cut of the Comstock riches. For more than 30 years, the mainline ensured a steady flow of people, products, and progress, even after the Comstock finally played out. Even so, Reno remained a whistlestop, fighting river flooding, economic stagnation, and the day-to-day struggles of all northern Nevada railroad towns.

But just after the turn of the 20th century, Reno was "discovered"—as a divorce destination. Suddenly, the little outpost found itself at the center of a national controversy between social conscience and license. On the one hand, rich and public figures or their wives graced Reno with their presence for six months while awaiting divorce decrees. On the other hand, it took another 15 years for Reno to fully embrace its growing national notoriety. But once it did, Reno wasted little time solidifying its celebrity as the country's sexiest town.

Millionaires, movie stars, socialites, and artists—unhappily married all—flocked to the Reno "clinic" to take the "cure"; throughout the nation, newspaper society pages covered them daily, rendering Reno a household word. The daily train became known as the Divorcée Special, the county courthouse as the Separator. The mayor of Reno himself set the record for the number of clients granted divorce decrees in one day. In addition, the political and financial power brokers all moved to Reno from the waning mining excitement of Tonopah and Goldfield in central Nevada. And to cap it off, a national exposition celebrating the completion of the transcontinental Victory and Lincoln Highways was held in Reno, prompting the exultant residents to install an arch at the entrance to downtown with the proud slogan, "Biggest Little City in the World."

In 1927, the divorce residency requirement was reduced from six months to three, and in 1931 to a scandalous six weeks. Now, everyday people could afford a glamorous Reno divorce. That year, nearly 5,000 divorces were granted in Reno, roughly 20 every working day of the year. By then, however, the divorce trade had some competition not only from several other states, but also from little Las Vegas, the southern Nevada railroad town with aspirations to take on its big-sister city to the north.

Luckily for Reno, wide-open legal gambling and instant marriages quickly filled in the gap. Throughout the 1930s and '40s, the Smith family's national advertising campaign for Harold's Club and William Harrah's classy carpet casino kept Reno firmly in its familiar limelight. In addition, California's and Utah's marriage restrictions (waiting periods and blood tests) triggered a boom of wartime weddings—which led to a miniboom of postwar divorces—in Reno.

By the mid-1950s, as hotels rose regularly

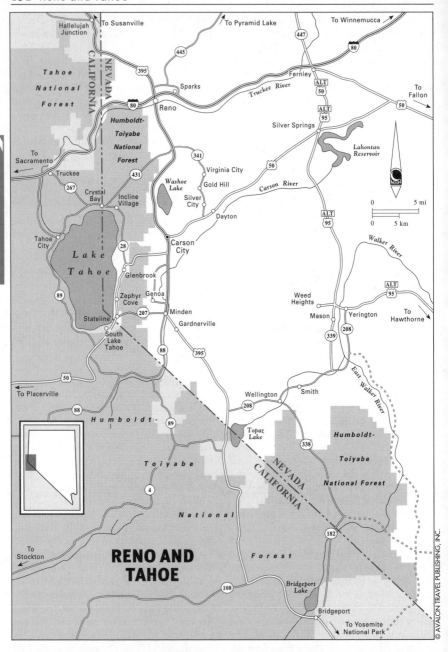

Reno and Tahoe

To Susanville
Hallelujah Junction
To Pyramid Lake
To Winnemucca
447
445
80
395
Tahoe National Forest
CALIFORNIA
NEVADA
80
Fernley
ALT 50
Truckee River
To Fallon
Sparks
Reno
ALT 95
50
Silver Springs
Humboldt-Toiyabe National Forest
Lahontan Reservoir
To Sacramento
Truckee
341
Virginia City
267
431
Washoe Lake
Gold Hill
Carson River
Crystal Bay
Incline Village
Silver City
50
ALT 95
Tahoe City
Dayton
28
Carson City
89
Lake Tahoe
Glenbrook
Genoa
Weed Heights
ALT 95
Zephyr Cove
207
Minden
Mason
Yerington
To Hawthorne
Stateline
Gardnerville
339
208
South Lake Tahoe
88
395
50
To Placerville
Wellington
Smith
East Walker River
88
208
89
Topaz Lake
338
Humboldt-Toiyabe National Forest
Humboldt-
409
Toiyabe
4
NEVADA
CALIFORNIA
National
182
RENO AND TAHOE
Forest
To Stockton
108
Bridgeport Lake
Bridgeport
To Yosemite National Park

0   5 mi
0   5 km

MOON

RENO'S CLIMATE

Reno reflects the Great Basin's general climate conditions: cool, semi-arid, continental. It may not feel like it on a 95°F day in July or an 18° night in January, but Reno's weather is often referred to as "mild." The average annual high temperature is 67°, the low 32°, with 51 days reaching above 90° and nine days dropping below 32°. The sun shines 306 days a year (80 percent), and there are 47 days of measurable precipitation. Lying right in the middle of the Sierra Nevada rainshadow, Reno receives only seven yearly inches (half of it snow), and that's in a normal year. For the past several years, western Nevada has received less than half its expected precipitation. In a good year, Mt. Rose, only 20 miles south (and 5,000 feet higher), gets 200–300 inches of snow. The Sierra snowpack is critical to western Nevada's water supply: most snowmelt in the Tahoe basin runs off into Lake Tahoe: source of the Truckee River, total source of the water for the Reno–Sparks area and Pyramid Lake fisheries, and partial source for Fernley and Fallon farmers, and Stillwater reservation and wildlife refuge.

The winds come primarily from the north in the winter, from the south and southwest in the summer. The coldest and wettest month is January, with an average high of 45° and an average low of 20°. July and August are the hottest, driest months, with average highs around 90°; average lows around 50° at night, however, make the nights not only bearable, but enjoyable. During these months humidity hovers around 20 percent. John Townley, in his book *Tough Little Town on the Truckee: Reno,* comments that in the summer, "the valley's con-sumption of hand-lotion is second only to beer." In fact, the high altitude and low humidity make both high and low temperatures quite bearable.

In the summer, occasional hot storms blow in from the north, bringing major cloudbursts and the real threat of flash floods. But the climate's harshest element is the wind, the famous Washoe Zephyrs which, funneling through Truckee Canyon, can reach 100 mph in April and May, and 70 mph anytime throughout the rest of the year. Yet the Zephyrs are more often gentle, gusty at worst, and are locally appreciated for blowing away the smog inversions that settle over the Meadows during the occasional calm air.

Here's a high/low temperature chart for the area spanning Reno–Sparks, Carson City, and Washoe Valley.

	High*	Low
January	46	16
February	51	22
March	56	25
April	65	30
May	73	35
June	80	40
July	91	46
August	90	44
September	83	38
October	71	30
November	57	22
December	48	18

* Temperatures are in °F.

along the new Las Vegas Strip, Reno had seen it all for more than a half-century. City planners, officials, and downtown interests witnessed Las Vegas's unbridled growth (and evolving notoriety) and decided to slap a "redline" around the gambling district, content to allow Las Vegas to sustain the type of attention from which Reno was only recently recovering. While the new Nevada boomtown to the south experienced its adolescent growing pains, a mature Reno could sit back and observe from a safe distance, and concen-trate on principles and values that had less to do with reputation or visitor volume and more to do with local quality of life.

By the late 1970s, however, Reno got a little jealous of its brazen sibling, and officials removed the redline. A major casino boom ensued, accompanied by a substantial population increase throughout the '80s. But Reno couldn't shake a lingering ambivalence about growth, trying to protect itself from, and at the same time compete with, the Las Vegas urban situation. Reno has

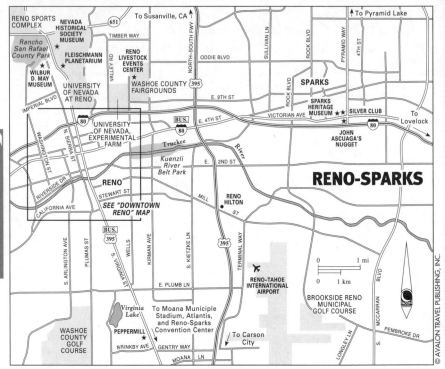

been attempting, over the past 20 years or so, to adopt an identity, a unifying design and marketing theme, that will remind potential visitors that Nevada consists of more than just Las Vegas and the desert.

But with its celebrated history of mining, divorce, gambling, and hospitality, its full slate of current events such as balloon, air, and Grand Prix races, rib and chili cook-offs, Hot August Nights and Harley-Davidson gatherings, and a surrounding wonderland of mountains, lakes, and desert, Reno would do well simply to remain what it is and always has been: the Biggest Little City in the World.

ORIENTATION

The Truckee River runs west to east right through the heart of downtown Reno. First Street parallels the Tahoe-to-Pyramid waterway as it flows under Virginia Street. The intersection of 1st and Virginia, roughly where Myron Lake had his bridge and inn, is the "00" point for Reno's numbering system. Everything east and west of Virginia Street and north and south of 1st Street is labeled such. The higher the number, the farther away from downtown. The "downtown core" is a five-block stretch of Virginia between 2nd and 6th Streets. I-80 cuts an east-west swath a block north of there, separating high-rise downtown from the mostly low-rise buildings of the University of Nevada–Reno campus on Virginia, which sits on a bluff overlooking downtown.

Between 2nd and 6th Streets are souvenir and pawn shops, clothing and jewelry stores, residence hotels, the famous Reno Arch, and hotel-casinos, which boast 4,000 rooms, a score of restaurants, hundreds of gambling tables, and thousands of slot machines. Countless hordes of hopefuls disappear through the yawning entrances. Inside, they gamble, drink, and generally forget about the world. Outside though, the world awaits. Be careful when visiting downtown Reno. The sidewalks and thoroughfares are narrow and crowded. Often pedestrians stagger out of dim or flashy casinos into the bright day (or night), and suddenly they're in the middle of the street. More than a few people perambulate in a casino or alcohol daze. Many drivers are from out of town and don't know where they're going. Walking or driving—stay on your toes.

Truckee Meadows

US 395 drifts down from California to the northwest; several miles north of the college, N. Virginia Street branches off the freeway to become Business Highway 395. From there, the freeway turns due south at N. McCarran Boulevard two miles east of downtown (near the Reno–Sparks boundary), bypasses the business district, and reconnects with S. Virginia Street near the Mt. Rose–Virginia City intersection roughly eight miles south of downtown. Thus, US and Business 395 make a banana-shaped oblong around Reno's high-density center.

McCarran Boulevard surrounds the suburbs, making a complete 23-mile loop around Reno–Sparks. In fact, a 45-minute drive on McCarran Boulevard is an enjoyable way to get instantly oriented to the different faces of Truckee Meadows: mountains, desert, river, industry, commerce, and suburbs. There are some superb views of downtown with a variety of backdrops, and the fastest growing residential areas in Reno–Sparks are along McCarran. Since you'll be covering the compass, it's advisable to do this in midday; otherwise you'll have the sun in your eyes at one or the other end.

From downtown, head north on N. Virginia, pass the college, and take a left (west) on McCarran. You drive right by the big white-washed "N" for Nevada, maintained by UNR students, on Peavine Mountain (elev. 8,266 feet), northernmost peak of the Carson Range of the Sierra Nevada; the Basque Monument of Rancho San Rafael Park provides a stark green contrast. From there you're into the desert—sand, sage,

hills—continuing west before turning to the south and entering the newest expansion zone of Reno. The western subdivisions are the fastest growing neighborhoods in Truckee Meadows, having expanded 100 percent in the last 10 years. The high Sierra are close by to the west, and 4th Street, old US 40, cuts between Mt. Rose on the left and the Peavine drainage on the right. The developments continue on the other side of the Truckee River, where sprawling new suburbs have taken over most of the old Caughlin Ranch.

When you cross Mayberry Street, you're on the newest section of McCarran, opened in 1990. On the other side of Plumb Lane are the southwestern foothills of Reno. At the summit is Caughlin Crest and the southern edge of the onetime Caughlin Ranch, which is now one of the largest and most expensive subdivisions in Truckee Meadows.

There, the road twists and turns down the hills to south Reno, through the ritzy Lakeridge subdivision. At the bottom of the hill, back in the basin, a rapidly expanding shopping area is emerging. From there, you go under US 395, past Virginia Street, and between Smithridge Plaza and Meadowood Mall in the big shopping district of south Reno. Next up is Longley Lane; to the right (south) about a mile is Double Diamond Ranch, site of an 1,800-acre development that will eventually consist of nearly 5,000 residential units and a 200-acre golf course, the largest single housing project ever proposed in the Reno area. Just north of Double Diamond is the site of the industrial park where Lockheed is building a 400-acre research facility.

Just before Mira Loma Park you turn north. Beyond the park are most of the last wide-open spaces within the McCarran loop. Cows graze along the flat fields, backdropped by the rugged line of the Virginia Range to the east. A bit north you come to the University of Nevada–Reno's Main Agricultural Experimental Station, with green and white farm buildings, stables, barns, silos, and stock pens sandwiched between Clean Water Drive and the Truckee River.

Cross the Truckee River and enter Sparks proper. The big white-washed "S" rests on a foothill to the east. The transition from the pastoral to the industrial is palpable. Immediately you're into Sparks's freeport zone, with its sprawling warehouses and truck yards; the overpass provides a wide view of railroad tracks, fuel tanks, and entrepôts. After passing under I-80 you're into a world of truck stops and shopping centers, then the fast-growing northeast Sparks residential area.

Just before butting up against the northern hills, McCarran Boulevard swings west. Beyond Pyramid Way, you wind up into the hills, crest a rise, and get one of the best views of downtown

Reno, backdropped by the stunning Sierra. In a few miles, you're back to the corner of N. Virginia and McCarran, where you started.

CASINOS
Silver Legacy

When the plans were unveiled in 1993, this new megaresort, a joint venture between Circus Circus and the Eldorado, was going to be a 16th-century Spanish seaport theme, complete with 2,000 rooms in three curved hotel tow-

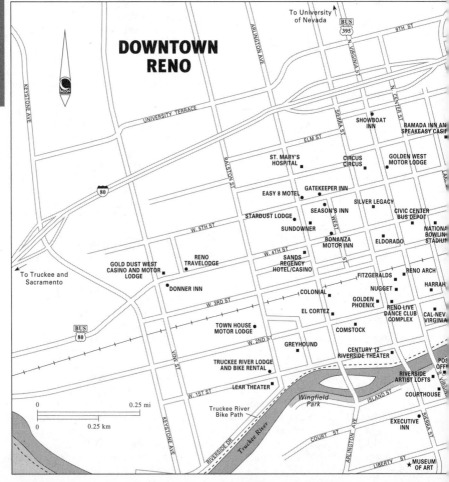

DOWNTOWN RENO

ers, a Spanish castle inside a 200-foot-tall dome, a galleon amusement ride on a river through the property, and 60,000 square feet of casino space. It was supposed to be completed by April 1995. However, the Castillian harbor concept proved too difficult to anchor in reality, and the theme was changed to the Old West. The legend to go with the theme owes a large debt to Circus Circus's Luxor in Las Vegas: Sam Fairchild, also known as "Old Silver," hit a silver lode directly under the megaresort and built a resort to end all resorts on top of it.

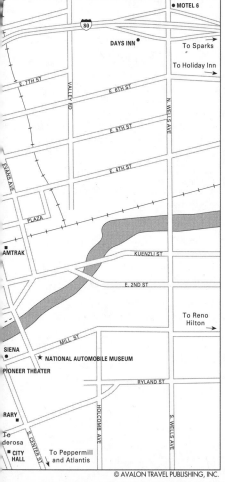

Opened in June 1995, Silver Legacy is downtown Reno's answer to the Las Vegas Strip. (Of course, even though it boasts 1,720 rooms—second largest in Reno, and covers two full city blocks—it would still only be the 21st largest hotel in Vegas.) Its main claim to fame is Reno's only Las Vegas–type spectacle, housed in the world's largest composite dome, with a surface area of 75,000 square feet: a 120-foot-tall mining rig, a cross between a train trestle, a mining headframe, and a Mr. Magoo machine that is the star of an hourly light show.

Skywalks connect the Legacy with the Eldorado on one side and Circus Circus on the other. The skywalks might remind New Yorkers of around Grand Central Station. You can now walk more than four city blocks in downtown Reno without stepping foot outside, by parking in the Circus garage at West and 6th and heading over to the Eldorado at Virginia and Plaza. 407 N. Virginia St., 775/329-4777 or 800/687-8733, www.silverlegacy.com, double room rates $49–250.

Harrah's

Harrah's dominates downtown Reno, as it has for 55 years. Like Harold's Club before it, Harrah's is also the result of a Nevada gambling pioneer's success story. William Harrah arrived in Reno in 1937 and opened two ill-fated bingo parlors before beginning his steady journey to fame and fortune by acquiring five bar-casinos before 1942. He opened Harrah's at its original location in 1946 and continued his expansion downtown, culminating in the purchase of the Golden Hotel in 1966. Harrah also bought the old Gateway Club at the south shore of Lake Tahoe in 1956. When he died in 1978, his hotels had 7,000 employees and the reputation for being the cleanest, classiest, and best managed in the gaming industry.

Harrah's Reno is a perennial four-star place. It expanded many times over the decades, and finally gained a foothold on Virginia Street in 1991 when it took over and remodeled the old bank building on the corner of 2nd Street where George Wingfield once had his offices. The casino takes a strong stand on customer satisfaction, offering cheerful employees, expanded nonsmoking areas

Reno and Tahoe

HAROLD'S CLUB OR BUST

At 250 North Virginia Street, Harold's Club was once the point of emanation of the modern Nevada boom, and therefore of the whole nationwide madness over gambling. Raymond "Pappy" Smith, a carnival operator, sent his son Harold to Reno to open a little roulette concession (one wheel, two nickel slots) in 1935, at a time when gambling, though legal, was still very much a Douglas Alley, back-room, scam-riddled affair. That first little excursion into legal gambling proved profitable, so the Smiths expanded, and in the process proceeded to change the face of casino gambling forever. They not only ushered gambling into the daylight of Virginia Street and jettisoned the old-time flotsam from their club, but they also launched a campaign to improve the image of legalized casino gambling in the national consciousness, which also, of course, reflected on the image of Harold's Club and Reno. In so doing, the Smiths set the ground rules for Nevada's incipient gambling industry, by showing the first generation of casino operators how to make gambling palatable to the middle-class masses. Without them, Meyer Lansky and Ben Siegel could never have envisioned their own resort hotel in Las Vegas. And it would've been a very different world today.

In the late 1930s, the slogan "Harold's Club or Bust" suddenly loomed from billboards, played on radio, and appeared in newspapers all over the country, introducing locals and non-Nevadans to the novel concept that gambling was good,, clean fun. The Smiths implemented sophisticated safeguards against cheating perpetrated on both sides of the table, inventing them as they went along—the original eye-in-the-sky, one-way-glass, and catwalk system, for example. Harold's Club was first to offer free drinks, comps, and junkets, and to charter trains and planes for its customers. Harold's was the first to hire female dealers, during the man shortage of World War II, further enhancing casino respectability. The whole strategy worked so well that it immediately became standard casino operating procedure and has remained so ever since.

The distinctive mural above the main entrance on Virginia Street was painted in 1949 to commemorate the centennial of the Gold Rush. The Smiths were also the first to implement a sophisticated leaseback sales arrangement for the club that became popular throughout the state with casino owners.

Pappy Smith, who's been called the Henry Ford of Nevada gambling, died in 1967. The Club was sold to Howard Hughes's Summa Corporation in 1970. Summa expanded the casino in 1979. When Fitzgeralds bought Harold's Club from Summa in 1988, it was the last casino property that Summa had to sell, thereby ending the 20-odd-year presence of Howard Hughes's corporation in Nevada. (Fitzgeralds also bought the Sundance in Las Vegas in 1987, thereby ending Moe Dalitz's nearly 40-year reign as that city's King of Juice.) Fitzgeralds tried to sell the unprofitable casino for years, and finally had to shut it down in 1995. It remained dark for a couple of years, until a discount store moved in. There's nothing symbolic about that.

of its casinos and restaurants, and good perks for its slot-club members. A non-casino Hampton Inn opened next door in 1996. 219 N. Center St., 775/786-3232 or 800/HARRAHS, www.harrahs.com, double room rates $39–169.

Fitzgeralds

Like Pappy Smith and William Harrah, Lincoln Fitzgerald was an early Reno casino operator, who opened the Nevada Club in 1947. Fitzgeralds, named after him, opened in the boom year of 1979 and has been going strong ever since. The thing to do here is to take the escalator to the second floor and follow the footlights to Lucky Forest. Walk by the queue waiting to sign up for something and just take in the exhibit: horseshoe, Leprechaun's cave, Ho Tei (Chinese god of good fortune), Aladdin's lamp, wishing well, blarney stone, rabbit's foot, and Abraxas (supreme Egyptian deity)—maybe some of the luck will rub off on you. Then again, so might some of the bad-luck display! Can't have one without the other—the old yin and yang of risk. 255 N. Virginia St., 775/785-3300 or 800/535-LUCK, www.fitzgeraldsreno.com, double room rates $18–250.

Eldorado

The Eldorado is owned and operated by the Carano family. Don Carano's great-grandfather Bernardo Ferrari emigrated from Italy and wound up as a cook in Virginia City during the Comstock boom. His daughter married Ben Carano, whose son Louis worked in Reno as a clerk for the Southern Pacific Railroad. Ben Carano invested in a 50-foot parcel on Virginia Street at 4th just north of the Arch, in 1929. The family added on to the property with land purchases over the years. Louis's son Don was born in the pivotal year of 1931, when gambling was legalized. He became a Reno lawyer, which introduced and taught him the casino business, and he held an interest in the Pioneer and Boomtown before building the Eldorado, which opened in 1973 with 282 rooms and a 10,000-square-foot casino. Another 129 rooms were added in 1978 during Reno's great expansion phase, and the hotel was again expanded in 1985 to 800 rooms and a 40,000-square-foot casino. The Eldorado casino has an interesting roulette table, with three separate wheels and layouts.

The Caranos partnered up with Circus Circus to build Silver Legacy, which fits snugly between them. And it expanded in 1996, adding 12-story all-suites tower, a showroom, a brewpub, a health spa, and an expanded buffet.

The Eldorado is revered locally for its fine hotel restaurants and buffet. The Caranos also operate a $6 million winery on a 60-acre ranch in Sonoma, California, called Ferrari-Carano. 345 N. Virginia St., 775/786-5700 or 800/648-5966, www.eldoradoreno.com, double room rates $29–750.

Club Cal-Neva

In 1947, the Cal-Neva opened on the site of the old Fortune Club, which had occupied the southeast corner of Virginia and 2nd since the 1930s. In 1955, Leon Nightingale, a downtown bar owner, bought it from Sanford Adler, then sold it in 1957, then bought it back in 1961. Nightingale and his partners, including Warren Nelson, remodeled the club and had a big grand opening in 1962, still fondly remembered by old-timers. Cal-Neva expanded with the rest of them in 1978, and the casino now occupies nearly an entire city block, even though it doesn't have any hotel rooms. Leon Nightingale mined a lot of gold from the club and donated fortunes to the university for scholarships, to the city for culture, and to private charities. He owned it until his death in 1990. Now Warren Nelson and the other original partners carry on the tradition. It's a rare occurrence in Nevada: the same owners for 35 years.

Warren Nelson has been a fixture on the Reno casino scene since the 1930s, when he started Nevada's first keno game at the old Palace Club. He adapted a Chinese lottery by giving it a horse-racing theme. The numbers represented jockeys; he played racetrack music and announced the numbers as in a race. (To this day, keno games are called "races.") A short time later, he witnessed a game in southern California played with ping-pong balls drawn from a cage and applied it to horserace keno.

Cal-Neva sports many interesting features.

Trains frame the slots in the Railroad Express casino; the balcony on the second floor provides a good overlook. On the third floor is the hot and sweaty (and smoky) action, with machines galore, a rammin' jammin' pit, the poker room, and sports and race books. In fact, the race and sports books account for 25 percent of the total casino floor space, and the managers also operate sports books at several other casinos around town.

Cal-Neva (no relation to Cal-Neva Lodge in Crystal Bay) also offers some of the best food deals in the vicinity. 150 N. Virginia St., 775/954-4540 or 887/777-7303, www.clubcal-neva.com, double room rates $19–129.

Golden Phoenix

Del Webb built the 21-story, 604-room Reno Sahara on the block between Sierra, West, 2nd, and Commercial, and sold it to Hilton in 1981. It transformed into the Flamingo Hilton in 1989 and is now the Golden Phoenix. The Flamingo name is gone, but the unmistakable plumage neon still lights the front entrance. The casino is bright yet claustrophobic and has one of the biggest lounge stages in town. You take an overhead walkway across Sierra Street, bypassing the traffic hazards below. The Top restaurant, with its lounge, nightclub, and fine dining, is the highest dining room in town and offers a view of the twinkling lights of Reno. 255 N. Sierra St., 775/785-7100 or 800/648-1828, www.goldenphoenixreno.com, double room rates $35 and up.

Holiday

The Holiday has been a fixture on the Truckee River just east of Virginia Street for more than 30 years. Since the National Auto Museum was built across the street, it's closer to downtown than ever. It recently had a $1.5 million facelift, including lights on trees along the riverbank, and of course new carpeting and slot carousels. 1000 E. 6th St., 775/786-5151 or 800/648-4877, double room rates $59–89.

Reno Nugget

This Nugget, one of a dozen in the state, was

free popcorn at the Reno Nugget!

opened by Dick Graves, the Idaho restaurateur also responsible for the Sparks and Carson City Nuggets, in the mid-1950s. John Ascuaga worked here for Graves then, before moving over to Sparks. Jim Kelley, another Idahoan, bought this Nugget from Graves, then sold it to Rick Heaney, who owns it today. The Reno Nugget has 200 slots and one low-limit blackjack table. At this very same table, blackjack guru Stanford Wong counted down his first deck of cards in a Nevada casino, a few days after his 21st birthday around three decades ago. The Nugget serves $0.99 margaritas, $1 draft beers, and free popcorn; the diner in the rear is a classic. 233 N. Virginia St., 775/323-0716, no accommodations.

Circus Circus

Circus Circus, with its big-top acts performed continuously throughout the day and its consistent crowds of low rollers, tourists, and kids, is the best place for cheap thrills, people-watching, and free entertainment in Reno. The concept of an actual circus-in-a-casino was first imagined by Jay Sarno, who is also credited with the idea for Caesars Palace. Amazingly enough, Sarno conceived of Circus Circus as an attraction for high rollers and actually charged admission when the first Circus opened in Las Vegas in 1968. After a few years of dismal business (and some ridicule), Sarno sold out to William Bennett, an Arizona furniture mogul and Del Webb casino executive, who turned the operation into one of the largest casino companies in the world. Today, Mandalay Resort Group owns hotel.

The low table limits, high occupancy rates, circus acts and midway, monorail shuttle between towers, and perpetual crush of crowds have become this hotel's trademarks. The hip restaurant here is Art Gecko's, serving Southwestern cuisine; it also houses Kokopelli's Sushi. 500 N. Sierra St., 775/329-0711 or 800/648-5010, www.circus-reno.com, double room rates $34–130.

Siena

Perched right on the bank of the Truckee River, the Siena brought a new understated elegance to downtown Reno when it opened in July 2001. With its Tuscan architecture, notable lack of neon,

and emphasis on relaxation and service, the 214-room boutique hotel is obviously courting a different crowd. The resort includes an extravagant day spa with myriad beauty and relaxation treatments. The coffee shop and gourmet room overlook the Truckee—a surprisingly unusual feature for a resort town surrounding a river. Wine lovers also rejoice here at Enoteca, downtown Reno's first full-blown wine bar. The casino also echoes the Italian theme, with massive archways and pillars accenting the 23,000-square-foot room packed with slots and table games. 1 S. Lake St., 775/32-SIENA or 877/743-6233, www.sienareno.com, double room rates $119–169.

Sands Regency

Just a few blocks off the strip on 4th Street, the Sands has the classic Las Vegas–type look of a casino that's grown up piecemeal, with original (1964) low-rise motel units surrounding its first pool, towers rising above, and three or four different wings to the casino. Owned by the Cladianos family, the Sands opened a new hotel wing and an enlarged casino in 1989. The Sands is popular with locals for the franchise approach to food service: Mel's: The Original diner; Arby's; Pizza Hut; Tony Roma's; and others. Nearly three out of every four overnight customers arrive on package trips from the Pacific Northwest and Canada. 345 N. Arlington Ave., 775/348-2200 or 800/233-4939, www.sandsregency.com, double room rates $39–129.

Sundowner

This hotel, farthest from Virginia Street in downtown, is casual, making no bones about its top priority: catering to a devoted clientele. The uniforms are basic Western ware, and the well-worn crap table is often crowded with locals. For a break, ride an elevator to the 20th floor of the tower and catch the long view south from the big front picture windows. 450 N. Arlington Ave., 775/786-7050 or 800/648-5490, double room rates $30–159.

Peppermill

About a mile south of downtown is Reno's most psychedelically impressive (or oppressive—depending on your tolerance for psychoactive sensations) casino. In fact, stop by if only for a

Take it or leave it, but at least check out the Peppermill.

hallucination check: The place either sucks you in or spits you out. There's enough indoor neon and noise for *five* casinos, but the plush red-velvet chairs at the slots are *so* comfortable. The dealer uniforms are suitably glittery. The bar is big and boisterous. The upstairs phone booths would've made Clark Kent's day; call home and then stretch out for 40. The casino also displays at least a million dollars in silk flowers, leaves, ferns, and trees.

The original Peppermill on this site opened in 1971 as a small motel and restaurant (a lone Peppermill coffee shop remains on the Las Vegas Strip near the Riviera). Its expansions have included a 632-room tower, a 300-room tower, a sports book, and a parking garage. Its Sierra Mountain pool complex, with a 60-foot faux mountain with waterfall, hosts a 10-minute show featuring five animatronic animals and a 10,000-watt sound system. 2707 S. Virginia St., 775/826-2121 or 800/648-6992, www.peppermillcasinos.com, double room rates $49–399.

Atlantis

Like the Peppermill, the Atlantis started out as a small motel, the Golden Road, in the early 1970s,

and has expanded many times since. A 300-room tower was built in 1994, complete with an 18-story glass atrium and glass elevators (fun little thrill ride with a good view). The tower makes Atlantis the seventh-largest hotel in Reno, just behind the Peppermill.

Atlantis has capitalized on its location—the only lodging and gambling within walking distance of the Reno–Sparks Convention Center—to become a major player in the Reno casino firmament. The casino features a tropical setting, including a 30-foot waterfall and thatched roofing over the pits, and an underwater theme for its fancy eponymous restaurant. The resort also has a spa and salon—a good place to get pampered before dining at the resort's most romantic, fabulously wine-stocked restaurant, Monte Vigna Italian Ristorante. 3800 S. Virginia St., 775/825-4700 or 800/723-6500, www.atlantiscasino.com, double room rates $49–375.

Reno Hilton

This memorable monument, Nevada's largest hotel-casino outside of Las Vegas, was built by master financier Kirk Kerkorian in 1978 and opened as the MGM Grand. After a turbulent history and several changes of hands, it became a Hilton. (The resort is now part of the massive Caesars Entertainment empire, which owns Caesars, Bally's, Paris, the Hilton, and the Flamingo in Las Vegas.)

To get the full effect, approach it from the south heading up US 395, and exit at Mill Street, in effect the Hilton's own driveway off the freeway. Park in one of the 5,000 spaces and walk through one of the 20 front doors into this 2.5-million-square-foot hotel, whose 2,003 rooms (including 418 suites) account for just under 10 percent of Reno–Sparks's total accommodations. The 100,000-square-foot casino was at one time the largest in the world. It is so big that, even with the 1,160 slot machines, 68 blackjack tables, 10 craps tables, four roulette wheels, baccarat, Big Six wheel, poker tables, 275-seat race and sports book, 150-seat keno lounge, two bars, and restaurant row, you can still hear yourself think.

In addition, it could easily take you an entire afternoon to see, let alone partake of, the Hilton's restaurants and buffet, headliner entertainment, 50-lane bowling alley, 20-shop arcade, Fun Quest arcade and virtual-reality attraction, thrill ride, go-karts, eight tennis courts, his-and-her health clubs—and you'd never even have to step outside, except to get to the Olympic-sized swimming pool, the 33-acre Hilton Bay driving range, or the 452-space RV park. It takes so long to really experience the place that you might as well sleep here; its one- and two-night package plans are reasonable. 2500 E. 2nd St., 775/789-2000 or 800/648-5080, www.renohilton.com, double room rates $59–200.

ENTERTAINMENT

Reno has plenty of nongambling entertainment, and many different publications can help you plan when you want to visit, according to how you prefer to be entertained.

The daily *Reno Gazette-Journal* has a special entertainment section in its Thursday edition called "Best Bets," which covers the headliners, big-name bands, comedians, and lounge groups at the hotels, plus an up-to-date chart with listings of all enter-tainment, club acts, and events in the area. It also has blurbs on parks, museums, outdoor activities, and local recreation. You'll often see "Best Bets" on giveaway racks. Or visit www.rgj.com.

The weekly *Reno News and Review* is published on Thursday and distributed free on news racks around town. It reviews of local arts, movies, restaurants, and clubs, and prints a weekly calendar of events. Visit www.newsreview.com.

Casino Showrooms and Lounges

Almost all the major hotel-casinos have at least one lounge, cabaret, show bar, or bandstand with groups entertaining the masses.

Harrah's renamed its showroom Sammy's Showroom after Sammy Davis Jr., one of the most venerable and best-loved performers in Reno, died in 1991. Also there is the newer The Plaza, for free concerts and other entertainment. Call 775/788-3773 for times, prices, and reservations.

The **Golden Phoenix** offers comedy, music, and magic in its showroom. Call 775/785-7100 for reservations. The **Eldorado** has four entertainment venues: the Brew Brothers, Bistro Roxy, the BuBinga Lounge, and the Eldorado Showroom. Call 775/786-5700 for more information.

John Ascuaga's Nugget has the 750-seat Celebrity Showroom, plus the Rose Ballroom, Casino Cabaret, and Trader Dick's. Call 775/356-3300 for reservations. The **Peppermill** has two entertainment venues: the Convention Showroom and the Cabaret; 775/826-2121.

At the **Reno Hilton** is the 2,000-seat Hilton Showroom. The Hilton has long offered room and show packages. The Garage offers more entertainment in a retro garage club. In the summer the hotel's 8,500-seat outdoor amphitheater offers such names as Reba McEntire, Rod Stewart, and Deep Purple as well as various music festivals; call 775/789-2285 for prices and reservations.

Circus Circus, of course, has continuous entertainment under the big top. Free circus acts are presented every day, noon–midnight; 775/329-0711.

For stand-up comedy, **Just for Laughs** is at the Sands Regency, 775/348-2200; **Catch a Rising Star** is at the Silver Legacy, 775/325-7452.

Nightclubs

These places come and go almost as fast as first-run movies. Check the chart in the *Gazette-Journal's* entertainment section for all the latest.

The **Metropolis Nightclub** contains four dance clubs: Club 2000 for Top 40 dancing, The Blast Room with hits from the '70s and '80s, The Lounge with pool tables and a jukebox, and the downstairs Fusion Room with house, techno, and trance music. There's also The Basement downstairs, for live concerts. On Thursday nights, the whole complex is open to ages 18 and up, and no alcohol is served in the building. The management emphasizes that this is a place where women are safe to relax and enjoy a night out; reportedly, the club has the most bouncers of any nightclub in the USA. It's on the corner of Sierra and 2nd Sts., opposite the Golden Phoenix casino, 775/329-1950. Open nightly, starting at 9 P.M.

Another popular Reno dance venue is the up-market, lavishly decorated **BuBinga Lounge** at the Eldorado, which starts off each night with sophisticated jazz or piano early in the evening, followed by live music or cutting-edge DJs for dancing. Opens 4:30 P.M. nightly. The **Brew Brothers** offers live music as well as hand-crafted beers and a late-night menu. **Roxy's** is a bit more intimate, with its menu of 102 martinis and live piano music nightly; 775/786-5700.

For a more intimate setting, Harrah's Reno has the **Sapphire Lounge;** opens nightly except Monday at 5 P.M. A more raucous affair is **The Virg,** which offers rock headliners as well as some impromptu jam sessions. Virginia and 2nd Sts., 775/788-2900. Open Fri. and Sat. at 7:30 P.M.

The Silver Legacy offers **Rum Bullions Island Bar,** which packs them in with exotic (and often flaming) rum drinks as well as live entertainment, such as dueling pianos; 800/687-8733.

For country music fans there's the **Haywire Country Night Club,** with live country bands, country DJs, and free dance lessons Wed.–Sat. nights. Here you can dance to all your favorite country hits, on the largest hardwood dance floor in Reno. 701 S. Virginia St., 775/337-2345. Opens nightly at 5 P.M.

Performing Arts

If you've had enough drinking, eating, and losing money, and want some routine escapism, take in a first-run flick at the **Century 14 Riverside Theater,** 11 N. Sierra St. beside the Truckee River, 775/786-7469; **Century Theaters 16,** 210 E. Plumb Ln., 775/824-3333; or the **Century 14 Cinema,** 1250 Victorian Ave., Sparks, 775/353-7440. Or check out the current presentation at the giant-screen **IMAX theater** in the National Bowling Stadium, 775/334-2634. For a more retro experience check out the **El Rancho Drive-In,** 555 El Rancho Dr.; 775/358-6920. The drive-in parking lot also doubles as a swap meet.

The historic **Lear Theater,** on the corner of 1st and Ralston Sts. facing the Truckee River, offers theater and other performances. Other performing arts venues and companies in the Reno area include the **Bruka Theater,** 775/323-3221; the **Nevada Opera,** 775/786-4046; **Pioneer Center for the Performing Arts,** 100 S. Virginia St., 775/686-6600; the **Reno Chamber Orchestra,** 775/348-9413; the **Reno Little Theater,** 775/329-0661; the **Reno Philharmonic Association,** 775/323-6393; the **Sierra Arts Foundation,** 775/329-2787; and **University of Nevada Performing Arts,** 775/784-4046.

SIGHTS

The revitalization of downtown hasn't only been about the big-ticket national Bowling Stadium and Siena resort. Smaller piecemeal development is noticeable: The Truckee River Whitewater Park officially opened to kayakers in 2004; the **River Walk** development opened 20,000 square feet of new retail space; and the financial district has been given a half-million-dollar facelift, with cobblestone sidewalks, trees, and benches. Still, the Reno core lacks a unifying characteristic, such as downtown Las Vegas's Fremont Street Experience, or even downtown Sparks's Victorian Square.

Riverfront Plaza

The $7.7 million two-tiered Raymond I. Smith Truckee River Walk, on the river side of the Riverside, was completed in July 1991. The plaza beautifies a city block between the Virginia and Sierra Streets bridges with an attractive and low-maintenance granite deck, benches, shelters, and bandshell. Arts and crafts shows, performing groups, and special events, such as the popular Celebrate the River festival, are held on the plaza. In 1992, the River Walk was extended one block west toward Wingfield Park on Island Avenue.

Truckee River Whitewater Park at Wingfield

Kayakers, tubers, and rafters can make a splash in downtown Reno at this newest outdoor attraction in Reno. Winding along 2,600 feet past casinos, parks, bridges, abundant birdlife, and anglers, the course offers 11 drop pools, boulders, year-round water flow, and plenty of obstacles to keep all levels interested. Some casinos are even getting on-board by offering "kayak–hotel room" packages to lure canoe-minded guests.

Truckee River Bridges

The Virginia Street bridge is only eight feet upstream from where hapless Charles Fuller built his original log structure in 1859. Reno founder Myron Lake bought the span in 1861, com-

pletely rebuilt it, and collected his tolls for 10 years, until his license expired (and wasn't renewed) in 1871. In 1877 the county replaced the wood with iron, matching the railroad bridge just downriver. In 1905, the reinforced concrete bridge standing today (146 feet by 56 feet) was constructed. Now a century old, its design and strength have enabled it to survive numerous floods, including the horrendous flood of January 1997, which inundated 20 blocks of downtown Reno with river water.

The Center Street bridge, one block east, however, was poorly constructed when it went up in 1926. In 1994 it was in such bad shape that the sidewalks were closed. Reconstruction commenced in fall 1996, but was interrupted by the flood. The bridge was finally completed, to the tune of $3.1 million, in May 1998.

Reno Arch

Reno's main arch, which spans Virginia Street at 3rd, is one of the four most famous arches in the United States (along with St. Louis's, Devil's, and McDonald's). Its slogan, "The Biggest Little City in the World," is among the most recognized in the country. The first arch was erected in 1926 to

Reno's downtown arch

COURTESY OF THE NEVADA COMMISSION ON TOURISM

Reno and Tahoe

celebrate the completion of the transcontinental Victory and Lincoln Highways. It cost $5,500 and read Reno Transcontinental Highway Exposition. Afterwards, when it was decided to leave the arch standing over N. Virginia Street downtown, Mayor Roberts challenged Renoites to create a permanent slogan. The winning slogan was lifted from the ad campaign for the 1910 Jim Jeffries–Jack Johnson prizefight in Reno, which was "Biggest Little City on the Map." The sign consisted of nearly 1,000 bulbs and cost $30 a month to operate, which proved too rich for the Depression budget, so it was shut off in 1932. A great hue and cry erupted over the cost-saving measure, and downtown businessmen paid the electric bill to keep the arch lit for the duration.

A new improved arch was erected in 1934, reinforced with steel and lit with neon, which read, simply, Reno. This change was again universally condemned and in 1936 the old slogan was returned to the arch (that arch now stands outside the National Automobile Museum at Lake and Mill Streets). The next time someone tried to monkey with the archway was in 1956, when Mayor Ken Harris proposed to change the slogan; it nearly cost him his job.

In 1963, a new arch was installed in preparation for Nevada's centennial. The fourth and current arch was unveiled in front of a jam-packed Virginia Street crowd in August 1987. It was designed by Charles Barnard of Ad Art Company, Stockton, California, who is also responsible for the sizzling light show outside the Stardust Hotel in Las Vegas. Young Electric Sign Company (YESCO) built the arch for $99,000, charging the city for the materials only. It uses 800 feet of tubing and 1,600 light bulbs.

National Bowling Stadium

This $35 million stadium, the only one of its kind anywhere, has made Reno the bowling capital of the world. It features 80 lanes, a 100-seat geodesic Omnimax theater (in the shape of a bowling ball), a '50s-style diner and dance hall, and the downtown visitor center. Ten major bowling tournaments sponsored by the American Bowling Congress and the Women's International Bowling Congress are already contracted to

be held in Reno over the next 15 years, pumping at least $1 billion into the local economy. Ironically, Reno's main competition for bowlers comes from Las Vegas, where there are well over 400 lanes, most of which are spread among five hotel-casinos. The National Bowling Stadium is at 300 N. Center St., 775/334-2600.

Reno-Tahoe Gaming Academy

This dealer and gambling school, 1313 S. Virginia St., 775/329-5665, is the oldest dealer school in the USA. The academy offers classes for careers in the pit: 21, craps, mini-baccarat, roulette, poker and pai-gow poker, plus pit supervisor and bartender courses. The academy offers 30 different program combinations, with classes all year round; programs of study can last anywhere from two weeks to six months, and cost anywhere from $600 to $5,000, depending which games and skills are chosen. Job placement assistance and some financial assistance are available. The student dealers receive intensive training, and practice against each other, until they are proficient enough to assume "pre-casino break-in status" by dealing to tourists and visitors who pay $15 for a 90-minute lesson in the game or games of their choice in a behind-the-scenes gaming tour. You probably can't *learn* all the fine points of either blackjack, craps, roulette, and pai-gow, in a hour and a half, but if you read up a little beforehand, you can get over your first-time shyness about the tables at this mostly realistic (for the players *and* the dealers) setting. The tour of the academy includes a fine display of antique gaming equipment and memorabilia, some of it available for sale. The classes and the gaming tour are by appointment only.

Newlands Heights

Much of the great wealth from the Tonopah and Goldfield mines began to show up in Reno around 1908, as speculators, lawyers, bankers, physicians, merchants, and laborers migrated from the mining frontier back to civilization. The richest of them gravitated to a bluff above the Truckee River a short walk from downtown Reno. Frederic DeLongchamps, Nevada's most famous architect, designed many of the homes in this historic district, which you can reach by heading south on Sierra Street, crossing the river, and taking a right on Court Street.

The house on the corner of Arlington, **247 Court Street,** is one of the oldest in the district, built in 1907 for the Frisch family. Roy Frisch was a cashier in George Wingfield's bank who agreed to testify against bad guys Graham and McKay in their prosecution for federal mail fraud. Frisch disappeared before the trial and was never seen again. The houses at 401, 421, 435, 457, 491, and 514 Court are almost a century old.

The house at **617 Court,** completed in 1890, was once the Queen Anne office of Francis Newlands, the powerful U.S. senator from Nevada at the turn of the 20th century; **7 Elm Court** was the Newlands's house. The house at **4 Elm Court** was built by DeLongchamps personally as a honeymoon cottage.

Follow Lee and Ridge Streets around to California and take a right. The house at **631 California** was George Nixon's, built in 1906 for his move to Reno from Winnemucca. The house at **825 California** was designed by DeLongchamps for Mrs. William Johnson, Newlands's daughter and the granddaughter of William Sharon, Comstock mogul and U.S. senator.

Downtown Parks

Three blocks west of Virginia Street along the Truckee River is **Wingfield Park,** on an island in the middle of a bulge in the river, connected to the mainland by walking bridges. The amphitheater there was completed in June 1992 at a cost of $810,000. Some concert, comedy, or gathering occurs here nearly every day in the summer, always free. In winter, the city installs an 85- by 200-foot outdoor ice skating rink—sometimes here, opposite the amphitheater, and sometimes a bit further downriver at Idlewild Park.

Surrounding the island on both riverbanks is **Riverside Park,** three acres of grass, with a playground and tennis and basketball courts. It's a good place to stroll from downtown day or night to clear your head of all the mind games and guessing games of gaming.

Continue west along the north side of the river (or motor out Riverside Drive and follow the signs) to **Idlewild Park.** Just under a mile from downtown, this park, originally developed for the Transcontinental Highway Exposition in 1927, is one of the oldest and prettiest city parks in the state. It boasts a large duck pond and outdoor swimming pool, picnic pavilions, baseball fields, volleyball courts, a playground, stately old trees, a rose garden, and Peter Toth's Nevada sculpture, *53rd Whispering Giant,* looking down from 30 feet to whisper something important (and different) into every visitor's ear. The kiddie amusement park opens daily at 11 A.M. May through Labor Day, weekends and holidays (weather permitting) the rest of the year. The rides are perfect for preschoolers; tickets go for $0.70 apiece (or 20 for $12). The merry-go-round, kiddie choochoo, airplane, and octopus charge one ticket, while the roller-coaster and tilt-a-whirl charge two. It's $0.50 for popcorn to feed the duckies.

VW Beetle

One of the most unusual sights in Reno is an 18-foot-tall, 30-foot-wide horror-movie spider made out of a Volkswagen body and irrigation pipe. It was created by artist David Fambrough in 1978 as "fun art," and has occupied a number of locations around town. In 1994, it settled atop the six-story pink fire building just east of the Wells Street bridge near 6th Street and has been there ever since.

National Automobile Museum

This downtown museum, opened in November 1989, is about as evocative of automotives as a 100,000-square-foot building could ever be. The curvaceous design has been described as "latterday Modern, with metallic skin colored heatherfire mist set off with chrome bands," which "might bring to mind an airflow Chrysler or a '50s dream car." And the tinted glass all around adds considerably to the effect.

Inside it's no less imaginative. The wide hallways or "streets" are interesting sets suggestive of the period encompassed by each of four galleries. The first gallery starts with the one-of-a-kind 1890 Philion and displays a Locomobile, Rolls, Cadillacs, and winds up with the 1913 Stutz. The second contains cars from 1914 to

1931, including one of the first station wagons (a sign explains the etymology of the term), plus two working cutaway engines. The third has the wildest vehicles, from the 1934 Dymaxion and 1938 Phantom Corsair to the 1954 Buick, including an unusual Airomobile, and what's probably the classiest car in the collection: a 1936 Mercedes. Gallery four has the familiar Mustangs and Chevys, along with unfamiliar European models, and some speed demons such as the Flying Caduceus and 1962 Maserati (which inspired Joe Walsh's lyric "My Maserati does one-eighty-five/I lost my license, now I don't drive"). Of course, no collection would be complete without a '59 Edsel or one of Elvis's Cadillacs.

The collection is just a small percentage of the 1,000 or so cars amassed by the late William F. Harrah. After Harrah died and his company was sold, the new owners auctioned off nearly 75 percent of the cars, many of which were bought by Ralph Engelstad, owner of the Imperial Palace in Las Vegas, and displayed in the auto collection there. The remainder was donated to the museum foundation.

A 22-minute multimedia presentation is shown in the museum theater, in which cars roll on and off the screen, and two banks of 12 video screens present dazzling, though hard-to-see, effects. Wheels Cafe is in a separate building, with outdoor seating right on the river's edge. You can partake of hot dogs, burgers, soup and salad, and drinks. The gift shop has a great stock of auto-related paraphernalia, including models, wooden toys, books, T-shirts, knickknacks, car cups, chocolate cars, road signs, cards, stationery, magazines, and trucks. Check out the phone cars.

The museum, 10 S. Lake St. at the corner of Mill and Lake Sts., 775/333-9300, is open Mon.–Sat. 9:30 A.M.–5:30 P.M., Sun. 10 A.M.–4 P.M. Admission is $7.50 adults, $6.50 seniors, $2.50 ages 6–18, under 5 free. Look for dollar-off coupons on the back of the museum brochure, available at the visitor center in the National Bowling Stadium.

Nevada Museum of Art

For more than 10 years, this museum occupied the Hawkins House, built on Court Street by Nevada banking pioneer Prince Hawkins. His family lived there until the Art Society bought it in 1978. But in early 1990, the museum (the only state-operated museum for fine art) opened in its new, spacious, and attractive building. Inside, the floors and ceiling are stark black, and the walls are bright white. The effect nicely highlights the colorful paintings and photographs in the three galleries. The front two house the changing exhibits; the back gallery has the permanent collection.

The museum store sells books, posters, prints, art magnets, jewelry, cards, pottery, T-shirts, and some sculpture. 160 W. Liberty St., next to the Porsche Building two blocks west of Virginia, 775/329-3333, www.nevadamuseumofart.org, Tues.–Sun. noon–6 P.M., admission $5 adult, $3 seniors and students, $1 for ages 6–12.

Nevada State Historical Society Museum

At the north end of the UNR campus, this is one of the best historical museums in the state. Its walls and floor are so packed with artifacts, photographs, cartographs, and typographs that to absorb it all will take hours. In fact, you might want to leave halfway through and come back to finish.

Follow its well-organized timeline from the primitive immigrants of 13,000 years ago and the Desert Archaic culture of 8000–1000 B.C., through the Paiute, Shoshone, Washo, and Anasazi evolution, up to initial contact with Europeans in the 1820s. Learn how the earliest explorers, the first wagon trains from the east, the original settlers, and finally the Comstock strike and Pyramid Lake battles managed, in only 25 years, to disrupt, co-opt, and completely overwhelm the native cultures. Finish up reading about the mining boom, military arrival, Pony Express, telegraph, railroad, and 20th-century politics and progress. If you still have any feeling in your feet, look through the books in the gift shop and the changing art display in the side room.

The adjoining research department houses a huge collection of historical black-and-white photographs, books, manuscripts, diaries, brochures, pamphlets, newspapers, phone books, directories, death and census records, site files, maps, even the collection of William Stewart, one of Nevada's first two U.S. senators. 1650 N. Virginia St., 775/688-1190, Mon.–Sat., 10 A.M.–5 P.M. Admission is $2 for ages 18 and over, free for those under 18. The research department is open Tues.–Sat. noon–4 P.M.

Fleischmann Planetarium and Science Center

Next door is Fleischmann Planetarium and Science Center, where it's easy to get lost in space among the thought-provoking exhibits: globes of the Earth and moon, large relief map of the Sierra area, clouds display, and a collection of meteorites found in Nevada and elsewhere, one weighing more than a ton. Stick a nickel in the gravity well and play (gently) with the instruments in the gift shop. Admission to the main building is free. You can also catch a multimedia planetarium star show and a superwide-angle dome movie (both changeable) in the dome theater ($7 adults, $5 kids and seniors). A small permanent observatory next to the planetarium, with a 12-inch reflecting telescope, is open for free public viewing on clear evenings from 9:30 to 10:30 P.M.

Public showings are always a double feature, pairing a SkyDome large-format film with a planetarium show. Shows and schedules vary throughout the year. The planetarium is open daily with shows starting at 2:30, 4, 5:30, and 7 P.M. with additional shows on Sat. and Sun. at 11 A.M. and 1 P.M. Call 775/784-4811 for recorded show information, 775/784-4812 for reservations and further information, or 775/784-1-SKY for current sky and star information.

Wilbur D. May Museum and Arboretum

This amazing man (1898–1982), though physically challenged from birth, led a charmed and charming life. Heir to the May Department Store fortune, young Wilbur was already quite financially successful in his own right when, just before he left for Africa in early 1929, he liquidated all his stocks for cash and government bonds. Upon his return later that year, after the Crash, he bought everything back for 10 cents on the dollar, and it's safe to say that he enjoyed the fruits of his remarkable foresight for the 63 years left of his life. He was a pilot, world traveler, art and artifact collector, big-game hunter, composer (his tune "Pass a Piece of Pizza, Please" sold 100,000 copies), philanthropist (mostly for children's organizations), and rancher, living on a 2,600-acre spread outside of Reno.

And as this gem of a museum amply illustrates, May not only had money, he had excellent taste; he collected treasures during more than 40 trips around the world. Tour the replicated rooms from May's ranch house: tack room, living room, trophy room, and bedroom. Watch the 20-minute video of his life—great travel and wildlife footage. Notice his passports, a spine-chilling shrunken head, and weavings, glass, silver, masks, ivory, pottery, from all corners of the globe. Compare all the horned, antlered, fanged, and wild-eyed creatures in the living room to the identification chart.

Relax at the indoor arboretum, with its ponds (stocked with poi) and waterfall. Then ask at the desk for the attractive brochure with the layout of the arboretum out back and wander through the large variety of gardens: energy conservation, Xeriscape, songbird, fragrant, rock, desert, rose, and many others.

An extra treat for the kids is the **Great Basin Adventure** historical theme park next door, which whisks kids back to pioneer days. Hands-on "exhibits" include gold panning, mining, and flume and pony rides. There are also farm animals, a petting zoo, a dinosaur play area, and a pond. It's open 10 A.M.–5 P.M. summer only (closed Mon.), 775/785-4064; $2.50 adults, $1.50 kids and seniors.

The museum, 1595 N. Sierra St. at the south end of Rancho San Rafael Park, 775/785-5961, is open in summer Mon.–Sat. 10 A.M.–5 P.M., Sun. noon–5 P.M. (same hours, except closed Mon., in winter); admission $6.50 adults, $5 children and seniors.

Liberty Belle Saloon

Any slot player with the slightest curiosity about the machines should not leave town without visiting the Liberty Belle Saloon & Restaurant, for

THE FOUNDER OF RENO

Myron Lake, like Carson City's Abe Curry, surveyed a patch of godforsaken desert in western Nevada and foresaw, somehow, a booming metropolis. They both embodied the necessary aptitudes for vision and business, faith and acuity, to triumph in such a grand undertaking. However, while Curry had a civic-minded, people-oriented, generous spirit of ambition, Myron Lake, it turned out, was interested in one thing and one thing only: Myron Lake.

Even though Curry and Lake both donated land and sold buildings to the government, almost everything Curry did is remembered with favor; indeed, Curry was appointed first superintendent for both the prison and mint after he'd finished building them. Almost nothing that Lake did, however, is remembered for any reason other than his own profit and aggrandizement.

In 1871, Lake subdivided land on the south side of his bridge for housing and the county courthouse. Naturally, people had to use Lake's Crossing to get from the town on the north side of the river to the new seat of government and south addition. Lake had already made tens of thousands of dollars by 1869 when the Central Pacific arrived, charging $1 for each horse-drawn vehicle, $0.10 for pedestrians, and three cents for every pig, sheep, and horse that crossed his bridge. In fact, in 1869, county commissioners forced Lake to reduce his tolls up to 25 percent. But as late as 1872, Lake still charged the full toll each way for delivery wagons using his bridge.

In 1872, the Virginia & Truckee railroad bridge was built a few hundred feet east of Lake's Crossing, and people walked over it to avoid the tolls. When the county commissioners declared the railroad bridge a public thoroughfare, Lake responded by withholding taxes on his tolls. And a year later, when Lake's 10-year toll franchise was not renewed, he closed the gate and guarded the bridge with a shotgun. Lake was arrested, and though he eventually won the court battle, he lost the bridge.

But his troubles were far from over. In 1879, Jane Lake, his wife of 15 years, sued for divorce, claiming extreme mental and physical cruelty, which included beatings and threat of murder. Myron Lake in turn accused Jane of infidelity. The vicious court battle dragged on for years, and seemed to take the spirit from Lake. He died two years later, in 1884, a rich, powerful, unpopular, and unhappy man.

its outstanding exhibit on the development of this seductive pastime. The owners, Marshall and Frank Fey, are the grandsons of Charlie Fey, 16th child of a Bavarian schoolmaster. This adventurous and industrious young man left home at 15, arrived in San Francisco in 1885, and promptly redesigned the first gambling machines, which had just come on the San Francisco bar scene a few years earlier, revolutionizing the young industry. From his prototype three-reel Liberty Belle, more than a million similar slots have been produced. Fey also invented the five-card poker reel in 1901, and the dollar slot in 1929 (both on display).

Just walking into the Liberty Belle is a historical experience: The heavy brass doors were salvaged from William Ralston's famous Palace Hotel after the San Francisco earthquake. Buy a drink at the bar, then settle in for a long look at one of the finest collections and accompanying descriptions of antique slot machines and gaming devices anywhere.

Fey's first slot is on display, as are the first dollar slot and early five-card poker reels. Check out the original reel strips and read how the fruits—cherries, lemons, strawberries—corresponded to the flavor of gum delivered as prizes. Other pay schedules list the number of winning cigars. Don't miss the old map and big photographs of historical Reno in the front alcove.

Finally, fish out some of that gambling change and buy *Slot Machines,* a gorgeous, oversize coffee-table book ($29.95) by the heirs of the inventor of the machines that now earn Nevada casinos more than three billion dollars each year in profits—more than all table games combined. The restaurant here has reasonable prices on meat and fish for lunch and dinner, and a congenial atmosphere. It's always packed when there's a convention in town, and usually packed with locals most other times.

You can stop by the saloon to see the collection any time the restaurant is open. 4250 S. Virginia St. (right in front of the convention center), 775/825-1776. The restaurant is open for lunch Mon.–Fri., 11 A.M.–2:30 P.M. Dinner hours are Mon.–Sat. 5–10 P.M., Sun. 4–9 P.M.

Lake Mansion

While you're down in this neck of the woods, take in this restored mansion, home of Reno's founder, Myron Lake. He bought a toll bridge across the Truckee River in 1861, then donated land to the Central Pacific Railroad to ensure the perpetual prosperity of what was then known as Lake's Crossing. His house originally sat at Virginia and California Streets: Reno's first address. You only tour the first floor and few of the furnishings are original, but in the dining room check out the painting by McClellan of Lake's bridge. And the pink bathroom off the downstairs bedroom might have contributed to the undoing of the Lakes's marriage; Jane Lake filed for divorce right after Myron bought the place in 1879. Upstairs are offices of the March of Dimes and a couple of other community organizations. 4598 S. Virginia St., on the far southern corner of the convention center parking lot, 775/829-1868, Mon.–Fri., 9 A.M.–4 P.M.; donation optional.

W. M. Keck Minerals Museum

On the University of Nevada–Reno campus is the Mackay Mining School (775/784-4528), with a statue of the famous and generous miner, John Mackay, who became Bonanza King of the Comstock and later endowed the university. The building, constructed in 1908, has recently been renovated for earthquake-proofing. It now rests an eighth of an inch off the ground on 66 high-tech rubber bearings and 43 Teflon slider plates. The museum entrance is on the first floor of the

building; it's open Mon.–Fri. 8 A.M.–4 P.M., admission free. Here you can see all the gold, silver, copper, lead, uranium, turquoise, magnesite, magnesium, mercury, gypsum, and borax that you've been hearing and reading about around the state. Not to mention the sulfides, oxides, haloids, quartzites, geodes, silicates, phosphates, psychedelic jasper, infamous black hydrocarbons (and argilite). Historical black-and-white photos of many mining boomtowns grace the walls, and Mackay's own vault houses two dozen rocks from the Comstock itself. Upstairs on the mezzanine is a geological breakdown of minerals and some fossils from around the world, plus miners' tools, machines, scales, and diagrams.

Oxbow Nature Study Area

Head west on 2nd Street and bear left on Dickerson Road just before the railroad underpass about two miles west of town. You might think you're in the wrong neighborhood to be looking for a park, with all the auto body shops, apartment complexes, used furniture stores, moving and storage warehouses, and truck lettering shops. But it's all just to enhance the surprise with a bit of relief by arriving at the portal to this unusual city park.

An oxbow is a former river channel diverted from the main flow by sediment deposition. This 30-acre park along the Truckee encompasses a large oxbow area. A flood on New Year's Day 1997 completely changed the face of the park, and it took three years to rebuild. But the park naturalist says the redesigned park is even better now than it was before, sporting a half-mile boardwalk interpretive trail (wheelchair and stroller accessible) winding through 18 acres of interesting features, including ponds and riparian (or wetlands) flora and fauna, and a large deck right out over the river, great for bird-watching. Grasses, sedges, tules, cattails, wild rose, alder, and cottonwood, along with beaver, muskrat, great blue herons, geese, and other birds, naturally inhabit this environment. The sage and rabbitbrush identify the areas that have been high and dry for some time.

Most of the year, most of what you see here are local flora and birds. The park really gets jumping from early May through late July, when 150 species of migratory birds arrive here to nest and rear their young; this park is a wetlands habitat for nesting on the Pacific flyway. Hummingbirds are usually the last to leave, in August.

You can spend an enjoyable and relaxing several hours walking the interpretive trail, leaning over the river on the deck, and looking for birds. The park and its trails are open every day, 8 A.M. to sunset; the interpretive center is open for groups by appointment, or whenever the lone naturalist is present (775/334-3808).

RECREATION

Reno is a fantastic recreation destination for cool- and warm-weather sports and activities. It's a great biking town, with close access to some of the best skiing in the country. It also has some surprises—ballooning, for instance, is a popular non-casino attraction. There's plenty to keep kids entertained, as well, with excellent zoos and amusement parks close at hand.

Bicycling

Truckee River Bike Path is a paved cycling, jogging, and walking trail nearly the length of Truckee Meadows, right along the river most of the way. It's roughly 12 miles long, stretching between the eastern edge of Sparks (near the Vista Blvd. exit of I-80) through Rock Park (near the west edge of Sparks), Galetti Park (in east Reno), Idlewild Park (in central Reno), and finally to the Mayberry area (at Caughlin Ranch in west Reno). It's an idyllic ribbon of river, trees, and parks that snakes right through the middle of the city.

The most popular hill climb is to the top of **Geiger Grade** on Route 341 to Virginia City; it's a killer. Cyclists also work out on McCarran Boulevard between 4th and Skyline (though it's somewhat narrow). The streets of Reno–Sparks are in pretty good shape, but mountain bikes are preferred around town for their fat and cushiony tires.

Three places in Reno rent bicycles. **Truckee River Lodge & Bike Rental,** 501 W. 1st St., 775/786-8888, is near both downtown and the Truckee River. **Sundance Bike Rental** is based

downtown at the Sands Regency Hotel, 345 N. Arlington Ave. at the corner of 3rd St., 775/786-0222. **Snowind Sports,** 2500 E. 2nd St., is based at the Reno Hilton, 775/323-9463.

Ballooning

One of the most popular Reno events of the year is the **Great Reno Balloon Race,** which takes place in September. More than 100 balloons take to the atmosphere from Rancho San Rafael Park, starting very early in the morning. To go up in one yourself at other times of the year, call **Mountain High,** 888/GO-ABOVE, or **Sierra Adventures,** 775/323-8428. This is an experience that's nothing like anything you've ever done before—but it's only for early risers. The balloons take off around 8 A.M. in the winter and as early as 6:30 A.M. in the summer to avoid being caught in warm thermals as the air heats up.

Amusement Parks

The **Wild Island Family Adventure Park,** 250 Wild Island Ct., Sparks (take the Sparks Blvd. exit from I-80 and go north), 775/359-2927, has slides, pools, waves, and just all-around splashing during the summer season. There's also a three-story Scorpion ride, an 18-hole miniature golf course open year-round (weather permitting), kid-size racecars, and an arcade and fun center.

The waterpark is open every day in summer, from around Memorial Day to Labor Day. Normal hours are 11 A.M.–7 P.M., with shortened hours at the beginning and end of the season. Waterpark admission is $19.95 for everyone over four feet tall, $15.95 for those under four feet tall, free for ages 3 and under, seniors $4.95; after 3 P.M., admission is $9.95 for everyone.

The minigolf course and raceway are open Mon.–Thurs. 1:30–9 P.M., Fri. until 10 P.M., Sat. 11 A.M.–10 P.M., and Sun. 11 A.M.–9 P.M. Golf costs $5.50 for 18 holes, $6.50 for 36 holes. Indy car rides are $5, sprint car rides $3.

Bungee Jumping

The Ultimate Rush, 775/786-7005, operates bungee jumping all year round from its 180-foot tower in front of the Reno Hilton. It's open noon–10 P.M. daily; jumps cost $25.

Swimming

Reno has two indoor **public pools:** one at 240 Moana Lane (right off S. Virginia just north of the convention center), 775/334-2203; 2925 Apollo Way in a northwestern residential area, 775/334-2203. They both have public swim times afternoons and evenings. Sparks has the same at **Alf Sorenson Community Center,** at 1400 Baring Blvd., 775/353-2385. Outdoor pools are found at **Idlewild Park,** (775/334-2267, and **Traner Recreation Complex,** Carville Drive right behind Washoe County Fairgrounds, 775/334-2269.

Fishing

Idlewild Park in Reno has bluegill; Virginia Lake in Reno has brown trout. The Truckee River, running from Lake Tahoe through the heart of Reno, has rainbow and German brown trout. In Sparks, the newly developed Sparks Marina Park is stocked with rainbow trout. Pyramid Lake, 32 miles north of Reno, is noted for its cutthroat trout. Lake Tahoe, a 40-minute drive from Reno, has Mackinaws, rainbow and brown trout, and kokanee salmon. Fishing licenses are available at most sporting goods stores. (State fishing licenses are not required for Pyramid Lake, but a lake permit is required; 775/476-0555.) For the latest information on area fishing, phone the 24-hour **Fishing Hot Line,** 775/786-FISH.

Horseback Riding

High Sierra Stables, 775/972-1345, in Golden Valley, about a 10-minute drive northeast of Reno. Open 9 A.M.–7 P.M. daily, year round; rides by appointment only. **Sierra Adventures,** 2204 Dickerson Rd., 775/323-8928, will get you into the saddle for a scenic tour for about $149 each, which includes transportation from your hotel.

Golf

The Reno area is golf heaven, with 38 public golf courses within a 90-minute drive of downtown. The Reno–Sparks area has more than 10 courses, and another eight courses are just to the south in the Carson Valley. Information on golf courses and golf packages is available from area visitor centers and Chambers of Commerce. For a free Reno–Tahoe golf package brochure,

contact the Reno-Sparks Convention and Visitors Authority (RSCVA), 800/FOR-RENO, www.reno-laketahoe.com.

Zoos

Two zoos sit north of Reno on US 395 toward the California border. The **Sierra Safari Zoo,** 10200 N. Virginia St., 775/677-1101, is open every day 10 A.M.–5 P.M., but only from April 1 to October 31 (closed November to March); admission $5 adults, $4 children and seniors, and free for ages two and under (Mondays are free admission for families). This is Nevada's largest self-supporting wild-animal attraction, featuring 200 animals of 40 different species from aoudads to zebras, baboons to wallabies. Visitors can mingle with the tamer species. The mission statement of this zoo is "to foster compassion for and knowledge about animals and our environment by bringing people and animals together." Most of the animals, including the "big cats," have been hand-raised from birth. It's an exciting experience to actually interact with and touch the unusual animals here. To get to the zoo, drive eight miles north of Reno on US 395 to the Red Rock Road exit. Phone ahead if weather is questionable.

The **Animal Ark** is nearby, but less accessible, and purposely so. Aaran and Diana Hiibel live on 38 acres north of Reno, caring for orphaned and infirm wildlife, such as lion and tiger cubs, wolves, monkeys, and birds of prey. Animal Ark exists to provide permanent care in captivity to animals that cannot be returned to the wild, and is dedicated to helping create a bridge between humans and animals by increasing the appreciation of our natural world. Check out Wolf Howl Night, held on the Saturday night nearest the full moon, when participants view the park, attend a short lecture on wolves, observe wolf pack dynamics firsthand, and then join in a group howl. The Ark is open to the public from April 1 to October 31, Tues.–Sun. 10 A.M.–4:30 P.M., 775/970-3111, www.animalark.org; admission $6, children $4. To get there, take US 395 north to the Red Rock Road exit, turn right on Red Rock, drive 11.2 miles to Deerlodge Road, take a right and go another mile. The Ark is on the right.

SKIING AND SNOWBOARDING

Several downhill ski areas are within 45 minutes of the Reno Arch, and numerous ski resorts are scattered around Lake Tahoe no more than a hour and a half from town. Cross-country trails abound. Most resorts make snow when nature falls short; call their Snow Phones for current conditions. In addition to lodging and shopping, most resorts offer equipment rentals and ski schools. You can also buy ski packages, family packages, and interchangeable lift tickets for the North Shore downhill ski resorts. Cross-country packages are available, too. For detailed information, call the Tahoe North Visitors and Convention Bureau (530/583-3494 or 800/TAHOE-4U), or the Reno-Sparks Convention and Visitors Authority (800/FOR-RENO), www.reno-laketahoe.com, or the resorts.

Nevada

Of all the area resorts, the **Mount Rose—Ski Tahoe** resort is the closest to Reno, on Route 431, 22 miles from Reno. Mount Rose offers 1,000 skiable acres. Mount Rose has Tahoe's highest base elevation (8,260 feet), summit elevation 9,700 feet, five lifts, 43 runs and trails, and a 1,440-foot vertical drop evenly divided among beginner, intermediate, and advanced trails. Snowboarders are welcome. You can also rent equipment and take classes at the ski school. Shuttles are available twice daily from several of Reno's larger hotels and casinos. Call 775/849-0704 for specific information. Outside Nevada, call 800/SKI-ROSE; www.skirose.com.

Closer to Lake Tahoe, **Diamond Peak at Ski Incline** in Incline Village 35 miles from Reno bills itself as a family ski resort with great views of

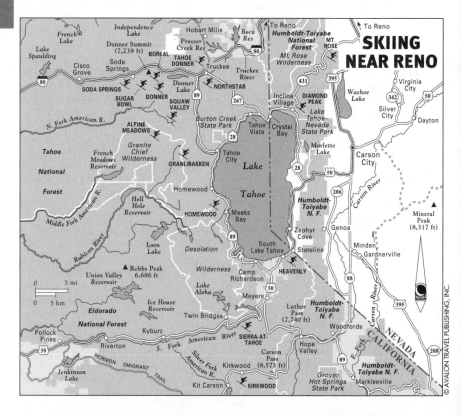

© AVALON TRAVEL PUBLISHING, INC.

the lake. With a summit elevation of 8,540 feet, it offers seven lifts and a vertical drop of 1,840 feet, fourth longest at Lake Tahoe. It also offers ski school and daycare. Call 775/832-1177 to reach the office, 775/831-3211 for the Snow Phone, and 800/GO-TAHOE or 800/TAHOE-4U for reservations. Diamond Peak also is known for its cross-country skiing. Off Route 431 five miles north of Incline Village, it offers 16 trails on 35 km of groomed track, one-third advanced, half intermediate, and the rest beginner.

The **Spooner Lake Cross-Country Ski Area** is on Route 28 a half-mile north of US 50, 775/887-8844, open daily 9 A.M.–5 P.M. Its 21 meadow and backcountry trails total 101 km, and include an 18 km round-trip to Marlette Lake. Call for info on ski schools and skating lessons.

South along the lake and 58 miles southwest of Reno lies the **Heavenly** resort on the Nevada–California state line. Heavenly has a summit elevation of 10,040 feet, a base elevation of 6,540 feet, a vertical drop of 3,500 feet, 4,800 acres for skiing, 24 lifts, 79 trails, and a ski school. Call 800/2-HEAVEN for reservations.

Across the Border

Climb the Sierra on I-80 and take Route 267 to reach **Northstar at Tahoe** 40 miles west of Reno. The resort, with a summit elevation of 8,600 feet, base elevation of 6,400 feet, and a vertical drop of 2,200 feet, has 11 lifts and is open to snowboarders. Its trails are half intermediate, and one-quarter each advanced and beginner. It also has a ski school with more than 100 instructors 65 km of groomed cross-country trails. Childcare is available on site. Call 530/562-1010 for information, 530/562-1330 for the Snow Phone, 800/GO-NORTH or 530/562-1010 for reservations.

Back on I-80, take the Donner State Park exit to reach **Tahoe Donner.** Northwest of Truckee on Northwoods Blvd. off Donner Pass Rd., this resort caters to new skiers and children. With three lifts, a summit elevation of 7,350 feet, and a vertical drop of 600 feet, its trails are split 50/50 between beginner and intermediate. Call 530/587-9444. Tahoe Donner also offers cross-

country with 32 trails and 65 km of track. Call 530/587-9484 for information.

The next resort west on I-80, also serving less-advanced skiers, is **Boreal,** just off the interstate. Take the Castle exit. It's known for night skiing, every night but Christmas Eve. It has nine lifts, summit elevation of 7,800 feet, a vertical drop of 600 feet, with nearly a third of its trails for beginners, and slightly more than half for intermediates. Call 530/426-3666. Associated with Boreal is **Soda Springs,** a resort set up for families. On old US 40, one mile off I-80 by way of the Norden/Soda Springs exit, it's open to the public weekends and holidays, available for rental other times. It has two lifts, summit elevation of 7,400 feet, a vertical drop of 652 feet, and its trails are split in much the same proportions as Soda Springs. Call 530/426-3666.

A bit closer to Reno, three miles from I-80 on the Norden/Soda Springs exit, is **Donner Ski Ranch.** It offers skiing for all abilities; its trails are half intermediate, one-quarter each beginner and advanced. It has six lifts, summit elevation of 7,031 feet, and a vertical drop of 750 feet. Call 530/426-3635 for info.

Close by is the recently expanded **Sugar Bowl** resort, with half of its runs catering to advanced skiers and nearly a third to intermediates. With a summit elevation of 8,383 feet, it has eight lifts, 58 runs, and a vertical drop of 1,500 feet. Call 530/426-9000.

Around the Lake

The famous **Squaw Valley** resort, site of the 1960 Winter Olympics, lies 45 miles west of Reno off Route 89, northwest of Tahoe City. Seventy percent of its runs are geared for beginners and intermediates. It has 33 lifts, a summit elevation of 9,050 feet, a vertical drop of 2,850 feet, and more than 4,000 acres of terrain served by lift in its 8,300-acre spread. It also offers a ski school, childcare, and cross-country trails. For information, call 530/583-6985, for reservations 888/545-4350, for Snow Phone 530/583-6955.

Closer to the lake on Route 89 and one hour from Reno is **Alpine Meadows.** Serving skiers of all abilities, it has 12 lifts, summit elevation of 8,637 feet, and a vertical drop of 1,800 feet. Its runs are one-quarter beginner, 40 percent intermediate, and 35 percent advanced. Its ski schools include lessons for the disabled. For information, call 530/583-4232 or 800/441-4423, for Snow Phone 530/581-8374 or 800/543-3221.

Just south of Tahoe City off Route 89 is Tahoe's oldest resort, **Granlibakken.** With one lift, a summit elevation of 6,500 feet, and a vertical drop of 300 feet, it's set up for beginners and families. Forty percent of its runs are beginner, the rest intermediate. Call 530/583-4242.

Farthest from Reno, six miles south of Tahoe City on Route 89, or 19 miles north of South Lake Tahoe, is the 1,200-acre **Homewood.** Known for its views of the lake, half its slopes are for the intermediate skier, with plenty set aside for the advanced, and 15 percent for beginners. It offers a daycare center, a ski school, and snowboarding lessons. With a summit elevation of 7,880 feet and a drop of 1,650 feet, it has 10 lifts. Call information 530/525-2992, Snow Phone 530/525-2900, lodging 800/TAHOE-4U.

ACCOMMODATIONS

With roughly 28,000 rooms to choose from, finding a bed in Reno–Sparks suitable to your taste and budget is child's play—except on weekends and holidays year-round, nearly every night in the summer, and during the many special events that happen here. On the Friday of Hot August Nights, for example, vacancy rates plummet and room rates skyrocket. But on a Tuesday night in February, you'll be welcomed everywhere like a long-lost high roller.

Reserving a reasonable room in Reno is somewhat akin to buying an airline ticket. If you book it far enough in advance you get a Super-Saver; as it gets closer to your travel date, you'll have to spring for regular coach fare; show up on any Saturday night and all that'll be left is first-class, one-way. Rates rise a minimum of 20 percent on Friday and Saturday nights for reserved rooms, and often up to 100 percent or a required two-night stay at the last minute. This is true for all the cities and towns in Nevada.

A reminder: Always ask to see the room first, and check it out carefully. Make sure the windows

open (and lock securely) and the air-conditioning works. Also, don't forget to ask about the telephone situation (if local calls are free and if long-distance access charges are imposed). Finally, be sure to ask if any coupons or funbooks are available, which often include substantial food and show discounts and gambling incentives.

Downtown Motels

There are plenty of motels right in the heart of downtown, near the casino action. They include the **Showboat Inn,** 660 N. Virginia St., 775/786-4032 or 800/648-3960, $34–100; and the **Golden West Motor Lodge,** 530 N. Virginia St., 775/329-2192, $35–175. Also are the **Easy 8 Motel,** 255 W. 5th St., 775/322-4588, with rooms starting at $29; the **Gatekeeper Inn,** 221 W. 5th St., 775/332-1730, $30–60; and **Season's Inn,** 495 West St. at the corner of 5th, 775/322-6000 or 800/322-8588, with rooms for $40–129. The **Bonanza Motor Inn,** 215 W. 4th St., 775/322-8632 or 800/808-3303, has rooms for $38–125. The **Stardust Lodge,** 455 N. Arlington Ave., 775/322-5641, has rooms for $30–85.

The quieter area near the Greyhound station is a good intermediate location—very near the downtown casinos, and yet with a more residential feel. Recommendable motels in this area include the **Truckee River Lodge,** 501 W. 1st St., 775/786-8888 or 800/635-8950, a nonsmoking hotel with 219 rooms for $48–180 (ask about weekly rates and bicycle rental), and the **Town House Motor Lodge,** 303 W. 2nd St., 775/323-1821 or 800/438-5660, with rooms for $39–45.

North of Downtown

The **University Inn,** 1001 N. Virginia St., 775/323-0321, opposite the university, is a bit removed from the hubbub of the downtown casino area although it's actually only a few blocks north. Its 170 rooms go for $30–200.

South of Downtown

Just south of the Truckee River is the good **Executive Inn,** 205 S. Sierra St., 775/786-4050, with rooms for $55–90 (ask about weekly rates). Further south, more removed from the downtown area, are **Quality Inn,** 1885 S. Virginia St., 775/329-1001, with rooms for $67 and up; and **Motel 6,** 1901 S. Virginia St., 775/827-0255 or 800/466-8356, $40 and up.

West of Downtown

The blocks just west of downtown are also a bit quieter, while still being near the casinos. Motels here include the **Gold Dust West Casino & Motor Lodge,** 444 Vine St., 775/323-2211 or 800/438-9378, with rooms for $29–109; the **Reno Travelodge,** 655 W. 4th St., 775/329-3451 or 800/578-7878, $29–199; and the **Donner Inn,** 720 W. 4th St., 775/323-1851, $30–60.

East of Downtown

La Quinta Inn, 4001 Market St., at the Plumb Lane exit of US 395 (exit 65), 775/348-6100 or 800/531-5900, has a fine reputation. Its 130 rooms go for $59–149, and there's a family restaurant, too. Just off I-80, at the Wells Ave. exit, are a **Motel 6,** 1400 Stardust St., 775/747-7390 or 800/466-8356, with rooms for $40 and up, and a **Days Inn,** 701 E. 7th St., 775/786-4070 or 800/448-4555, $30–140.

Downtown Budget Hotels

Most of the older hotels are convenient and adequate, if not classy. Some bathrooms are down the hall, some are in the room. Around the Greyhound depot are the **El Cortez,** 239 W. 2nd St., 775/322-9161, $20–60, and the **Windsor Hotel,** 214 West St., 775/323-6171, $40–85. Each has parking available in parking lots across the street.

Suites

The suite on the 12th floor of the **Atlantis Casino Resort** is the least expensive of the lot, but it could cost more. The tropical theme is implemented with rattan, palm fronds, and floral prints throughout the bedroom, living room, and bar; there's also a black-marble whirlpool tub in the bedroom (and a phone in the bathroom, standard in suites). The **Sands Regency Hotel/Casino** offers a suite on the 17th floor with a stunning view out of floor-to-ceiling picture windows. It comes complete with sunken living room, free-standing fireplace, full kitchen, and marble whirlpool tub.

The 16th-floor suite at the **Peppermill Hotel Casino** has three TVs, gold bathroom fixtures, velvet-bolstered bar (very comfortable), and a pool-size whirlpool tub as close to the bed as you'd ever need. The large walk-in shower converts to a steam bath at the snap of your fingers. Reno's newest hotel, the **Siena,** has the Floor dei Nobili dedicated to its suites. The 29 1,200-square-foot rooms are styled in Tuscan romance and offer the usual amenities, such as down comforters on the beds and superb views of the Truckee Meadows.

John Ascuaga's Nugget charges similar rates for its top-of-the-line (literally: it's on the 29th floor) suite. Sauna, marble fireplace, and a whirlpool tub that could fit your whole extended family. Nice desert view to the east.

Bed-and-Breakfast

The **South Reno B&B,** 136 Andrew Ln., 775/849-0772, is out in the countryside about 12 miles south of Reno. There's plenty of privacy, peace and quiet; it has a large grounds with lots of lawn and trees, the owners' cattle and horses are in a field off from the house, and the swimming pool is great in summer. Upstairs room (with bath) is $60–70.

Romantic

One motel stands apart from the madding crowd. The **Adventure Inn,** 3575 S. Virginia just south of Moana, 775/828-9000, was built by one of the owners of the Atlantis, who wanted to treat his wife to an exotic motel room. Theme rooms here include the Jungle, Bridal, Roman, Adam and Eve, Tropical, Bordello, Cave, and Space suites. All come with round or heart-shaped beds, "rainforest" showers, free limo rides within 10 miles, and complimentary champagne. Prices range $59–300.

CAMPING

The closest place to pitch a tent to downtown Reno is at **Chism's Trailer Park,** 1300 W. 2nd St., 775/322-2281 or 800/638-2281. The closest places to spend the night outdoors are all about

30 miles from Reno. By far the best spot to pitch your tent is at **Davis Creek Park,** a Washoe County facility, 19 miles south on US 395. **Lookout Campground** is 18 miles northwest of Reno beyond Verdi in California. **Warrior Point Park** is at the end of the paved road on the west side of Pyramid Lake.

RV Parking

The oldest private campground in Nevada, opened in 1926, is **Chism's Trailer Park,** 1300 W. 2nd St., 775/322-2281 or 800/638-2281; it's right along the Truckee River just west of downtown. It's also the shadiest, with towering trees and lush landscaping. A lot of the park is occupied by permanent mobiles, but there are enough overnight sites to make it worth checking out. Also, it's the closest place to downtown to pitch a tent. There are a total of 152 spaces, but only 28 for motor homes, all 28 with full hookups; six are pull-throughs. Tents are allowed. Accessible restrooms have flush toilets and hot showers; public phone, sewage disposal, and laundry are available. The fee is $10 for tents, $18.50 for trailers and RVs.

The largest RV park in the area, not surprisingly, is **Reno Hilton KOA,** at the Reno Hilton, 775/789-2147 or 888/562-5698. It's parking-lot camping; some sites overlook Hilton Bay (a square pond in the original gravel pit where there's a driving range). Note that it's right on one of the two approaches to Reno–Tahoe airport. There are 210 spaces for motor homes, all with full hookups, and 42 pull-throughs. Tents are not allowed. Accessible restrooms have flush toilets and hot showers; sewage disposal, laundry, groceries, video rentals, and a heated swimming pool are available. The stay limit is 28 days. The fee is $33–39 per vehicle.

Reno RV Park, 735 Mill St., 775/323-3381 or 800/445-3381, has four rows of parking off of two narrow alleys, all back-in sites. It's the closest to downtown Reno. It's an older part of town: hospitals, medical offices, and the police station are all nearby. Security is beefy, with a high wall and gates in and out. Harrah's sends its shuttle around Friday through Monday. There are 46 spaces for motor homes, all with full hookups.

Free-standing tents are allowed, but not tents that require stakes. Accessible restrooms have flush toilets and hot showers; public phone, sewage disposal, and laundry are available. The fee is $27 for two people; cheaper in winter. Good Sam and AAA discounts are offered, as are more economical weekly and monthly rates.

Keystone RV Park, 1455 W. 4th St., 775/324-5000 or 800/686-8559, is on the western edge of the downtown business district. The front section opened in 1993, the back (which fronts an 18-room motel) opened in 1992. It's parking-lot camping, with a few trees and a little grass. The casinos are about eight blocks away, so the Keystone fills up fast for the nonstop events in Reno between Memorial Day and Labor Day. There are 104 spaces for motor homes, all with full hookups, no pull-throughs. Tents are not allowed. Accessible restrooms have flush toilets and hot showers; sewage disposal and laundry are available. The fee is $22 for two people. Good Sam discounts offered.

Shamrock RV Park, 260 Parr Blvd. (from I-80, take the Virginia St. exit and go north about two miles, turn right on Parr and drive down the hill; the park is on the right), 775/329-5222 or 800/322-8248, was new in 1985, but it's so clean you'd think it opened last week. It sits in a little bowl with earthen walls in an industrial part of town. It's big, all paved, and has trees and shrubs between wide sites. The recreation hall has exercise equipment and a full kitchen. It's two blocks from the small but popular Bonanza Casino. A mile south is Rancho San Rafael Park, the largest park in the urban area. Two miles south of that is downtown. There are 121 spaces for motor homes, all with full hookups, 75 pull-throughs. Tents are not allowed. Accessible restrooms have flush toilets and hot showers; sewage disposal, laundry, groceries, a small playground, and a heated swimming pool are available. The fee is $30 per vehicle. Good Sam discounts offered.

Bonanza Terrace RV Park, 4800 Stoltz Rd., 775/329-9624, has 80 spaces for $22.40. **River's Edge RV Park,** 1405 South Rock Blvd., Sparks, 775/358-8533 or 800/621-4792, is an idyllic setting for an RV park, right on the Truckee River. You have immediate access to many miles of paved riverside biking and hiking trails. It's lush and well shaded. It also happens to be right on the eastern landing route for Reno–Tahoe airport, so big commercial airliners fly 300 feet overhead. But if you can stand an occasional jet engine or two, River's Edge is one of the nicest RV parks around. There are 164 spaces for motor homes, all with full hookups; 98 are pull-throughs. Tents are not allowed. Restrooms have flush toilets and hot showers; sewage disposal and laundry are available. The fee is $30–35.

Victorian RV Park, 205 Nichols Blvd. off Victorian Ave., Sparks, 775/356-6400 or 800/955-6405, provides RVers with access to the pool and arcade across the street at the Thunderbird resort. There are 92 spaces for motor homes, all with full hookups; 46 are pull-throughs. Tents are not allowed. Accessible restrooms have flush toilets and hot showers; sewage disposal, laundry, groceries, a heated pool and spa are available. The fee is $21. Good Sam, AAA, and AARP discounts offered

Boomtown RV Park, off I-80, Verdi, 775/345-8650 or 877/626-6686, is a large, self-contained area below the casino, with wide spaces, some greenery, and its own pool. You'll never lack for knowing the time, with the Boomtown clock tower right above. Inside the hotel are the Family Fun Center, featuring an 18-hole indoor miniature golf course, an antique carousel, a motion-simulation theater (the only one in northern Nevada), and video games galore. There is also a steakhouse, a buffet, and a 24-hour coffee shop. It has 203 spaces for motor homes, all with full hookups; 132 are pull-throughs. Tents are not allowed. Accessible restrooms have flush toilets and hot showers; sewage disposal, laundry, groceries, video rentals, a heated swimming pool, and two spas are available. The fee is $27.15 for two people. Good Sam and AARP discounts offered. **Bordertown RV Resort,** 19575 US 395 N., 775/677-0169 or 800/218-9339, near, not surprisingly, the state border, has 50 sites that cost $22 per night.

FOOD

Restaurants aren't nearly as numerous in Reno–Sparks as they are in Las Vegas, but food,

especially in hotel-casino restaurants, is just as much a loss leader in northern as it is in southern Nevada. Restaurant prices are heavily subsidized by casino earnings. Many people come to Reno and Sparks not for the slots or tables, not for the shows or recreation, but for the food alone.

Note that things change fast around here. It's not uncommon for an entire casino to change, let alone a restaurant in a casino, or a particular dish, or a particular price. The buffets, especially, change times, prices, and themes frequently. The following listings have been selected for reliability as much as quality and value, but use them only as a, you know, guide. Always call first to make sure where you want to go is still there and what you want there is still available.

The **Reno-Sparks Menu & More,** a free magazine published seasonally and available at all the usual free-paper news racks and visitor centers, gives current news and listings for all the Reno–Tahoe area casino restaurants, plus other food news.

Top Picks

Odette's is classy and usually crowded. It serves salads, sandwiches, and quiches, and a large variety of espresso, coffee drinks, and fountain treats. For breakfast, try a veggie-brie omelette or Belgian waffle. If it's really busy, you can almost always find a seat or two at the counter. 4935 Energy Way, 775/857-2828, Mon.–Fri. 9 A.M.–4:30 P.M., Sat. 10 A.M.–2 P.M. for cake pick-ups only.

Josef's Vienna Bakery, Café & Ceramic Studio takes top honors every year as the best bakery in the "Best of Reno" according to the *Gazette-Journal* voting. It bakes pastries, danishes, croissants, rolls, muffins, cookies, and breads, all served with coffee. Or have some muesli with fresh fruit and yogurt for $3. If it's clement, eat outside at the sidewalk tables. In the Moana West shopping center, 933 W. Moana at the corner of Lakeside Dr., 775/825-0451. The bakery is open Mon.–Fri. 7 A.M.–5:30 P.M., Sat. 8 A.M.–4 P.M., Sun. 8 A.M.–3 P.M. The café is open weekdays 8 A.M.–5:30 P.M., Sat. 8 A.M.–4 P.M., Sun. 8 A.M.–3 P.M.

Deux Gros Nez (Two Big Noses) is one of the funkiest little cafés in Reno, and proud of it. Above the Hermitage Gallery (look for the purple staircase), this place is renowned for its excellent fresh vegetarian food, such as flavorful pasta and rice dishes and focaccia, quiches, cakes and pies, coffee and teas, soups and sandwiches, all between $3 and $6. It is one of the last unreconstructed hippie-type establishments that remain in Reno, but that doesn't at all deter the lawyers, bankers, and socialites from patronizing the place. 249 California St., 775/786-9400, Mon.–Fri. 6 A.M.–midnight, Sat. and Sun. 7 A.M.–midnight.

The **Little Waldorf Saloon,** operating since 1922, is the oldest restaurant in Reno, if not Nevada. The walls here are chockablock with photos, plus wildlife prints, big-game trophies (including an Alaskan brown bear), ducks, birds, guns, and the like. Several big- and small-screen TVs are dotted around the room, one on each end of the long bar. Eggs start at $3.50; a four-egg omelette is $5.25. Burgers and sandwiches start at $5, and diner-type dinners start at $9. 1661 N. Virginia, open 24 hours, 775/323-3682.

Rapscallion has an interesting interior—lots of wood, some of it walling in very private dining alcoves, attractive bar, stained glass. Lunch is served Mon.–Fri. 11:30 A.M.–4 P.M.; sandwiches run $5–7. Dinners, served 5–10 P.M. nightly, start with escargot, calamari, or Cajun coconut prawns and continue with salads and fish and beef. Good food, good prices, attentive yet unobtrusive service, very popular. 1555 S. Wells, 775/323-1211, Mon.–Sat. 11:30 A.M.–4 P.M., daily 5–10 P.M., Sun. brunch 10 A.M.–2 P.M.

Cafe Soleil, serving gourmet California/ Mediterranean-style cuisine, is one of Reno's most popular upscale restaurants. The menu features tempting seafood, filet mignon, pasta, and vegetarian dishes for $14–26, and there's an extensive wine list. The restaurant is up on a hill, with a good view of the city; decor features an open kitchen where you can see the food being prepared, and a big wood-fired oven is great for winter warmth. Located a bit out of town, it's worth looking for. 4796 Caughlin Pkwy. at McCarran Blvd., about 3.5 miles south of I-80, 775/827-3111. Open every night 5–9:30 P.M. (Fri.–Sat. until 10 P.M.), with Sun. brunch 10 A.M.–2 P.M.

Casino Quick Bites

The **Cal-Neva** takes the prize, hands down, for the best snack bar in town. Bulldogs Sports Deli, 775/323-1046, on the third floor in the far corner of the sports book serves a big fat frankfurter and a bottle of Heineken for $1.50; Cal-Neva claims that it sells more Heineken than any other single location in the country. Other great deals are the burgers, roast beef sandwiches, and fries. The Sports Deli is open daily 11 A.M.–7 P.M.

Baldini's, in Sparks, is nearly unbeatable for lunch and dinner specials. You can enjoy a deli sandwich and a beer or soda, or a hot dog, for cheap. 865 S. Rock Blvd., 775/358-0116, daily 9 A.M.–10 P.M. The **Gold Dust West** is similar, with cheap specials: spaghetti, burgers with topping bar, steak and eggs, and usually a big steak special, all with salad bar. W. 5th and Vine, 775/323-2211, daily 6 A.M.–10 P.M.

There's a fast-food court at the **Peppermill,** in the northwest wing. You have plenty to choose from: Mexican, Italian, Chinese, and American. Everything (even a big prime rib dinner, baked potato, and veggie) is inexpensive. Very comfortable seats to boot. 775/826-2121, daily 8 A.M.–10 P.M.

The fast-food court downtown is Choices at the **Eldorado.** This is actually a step above fast food, served cafeteria-style. Choose from Mexican, Chinese, Italian, and American, with a full bakery and ice cream counter. 775/786-5700, daily 7:30 A.M.–8 P.M. Tivoli Gardens, 775/786-5700, at the **Eldorado** is head and shoulders above your usual coffee shop. With food from every continent (with Vietnamese and Thai specialties), plus wood-fired oven pizza and 24-hour breakfasts, you'll have a harder time choosing here than at Choices.

The Purple Parrot, 775/825-4700, at **Atlantis** points to the fact that "coffee shop" in a casino is a misnomer. Though it's open 24 hours and everything on the menu is inexpensive, the Parrot serves up everything from a bacon cheeseburger and club sandwich to halibut steak and shrimp louie. With a coffee shop comp for two, you could teach 'em a lesson easy.

The Shore Room, 775/786-5151, in the newly refurbished **Holiday Inn Hotel** at Center downtown overlooks the Truckee River. Other than that, it's basic café fare. Try the house special Tahoe Sandwich.

The Farmhouse coffee shop, 775/356-3300, at **John Ascuaga's Nugget** in Sparks is famous for its Awful Awful Burger, a half-pound burger served with a full pound of fries and all the trimmings. For just $3.50, it's awful big and awful good. (Both the Reno and Sparks Nuggets serve Awful Awful burgers and have since they were both opened in the '50s by the same owner.) The Country Store is the other coffee shop at the Nugget. The Sparks Nugget actively competes with the Eldorado for the best hotel food in town; it has incredible seasonal festivals such as the Best in the West Nugget Rib Cook-off. Open 24 hours.

Not surprisingly, the coffee shop, 775/358-8888, at the **Alamo Truck Stop** just off I-80 at the Sparks Blvd. exit is a good place to get an honest and filling meal. The menu is tractor-trailer size, the prices are extremely reasonable, the phones at the booths are always busy, and the fried chicken is about as good as it gets. But the real treat here is the potato dishes. Bakers are available 24 hours a day, home fries are thick and hearty, and the Potatoes Piled High will hold you for eight hours easy. Open 24 hours.

Diners

Johnny Rocket's, at the **Reno Hilton** (775/789-2000) near the race and sports book, is one of the few '50s-style diners at a hotel-casino in Reno. It ain't cheap, but it is authentic, with a black-and-white-checked floor, red Naugahyde booths, and individual juke boxes at the counter and on the tables. Try the big burgers with the works, veggie burger, chili dog, chili fries, malts, shakes, floats, hot fudge sundaes, and apple pie à la mode. The fries are brought first; the waitress pulls a bottle of ketchup from her apron and fills up a paper basket. The straw act is pretty cool, too. Open Sun.–Thurs. 10 A.M.–11 P.M. and Fri. and Sat. until 2 A.M.

The diner at the back of the little **Nugget** (775/323-0716) in downtown Reno isn't retro; it's a classic. Eighteen red stools face the counter and another 18 face the back wall. The Awful Awful burger is two meals. Every Wednesday

you can get an eight-ounce prime rib with all the trimmings for a great price. Or fill up on a dollar beer and free popcorn at the bar. Open 8 A.M.–11:45 P.M. More old-fashioned shakes and burgers await at Mel's: The Original Diner, 775/337-6357, at the **Sands.** Open 24 hours.

Breakfast

At **Cal-Neva,** 775/954-4540, the $1.49 breakfast has been voted the "Best of Reno" and no wonder! This is the *$5.99* breakfast at Denny's. This fill-er-upper comes with two eggs, ham or bacon, hash browns, toast, and coffee, and is served at the Top Deck on the third floor. Cal-Neva serves more than a million of these eye-openers every year, which averages roughly 3,000 a day. It's crowded on weekend mornings (try the counter if there are one or two of you), so sign up at the Top Deck on the third floor, then wander around the slots, pits, and books. From midnight to 7 A.M. this breakfast is an even better deal—$0.99. If the $1.49 breakfast isn't to your liking, how about a cube steak and eggs, top sirloin and eggs, oatmeal, and orange juice? Open 24 hours.

The food court, 775/826-2121, at the **Peppermill** has a good three-egg-and-bacon deal. Open daily 8 A.M.–10 P.M. The **Sundowner** serves up steak and eggs 24 hours a day in the coffee shop, 775/786-7050. The **Silver Club,** 775/358-4771, up the street from the Treasury in Sparks, serves a $2.50 breakfast with a half-pound of ham and two eggs in the coffee shop. Open 24 hours.

Steaks and Prime Rib

At **Cal-Neva,** 775/323-1046, the Top Deck coffee shop (open 24 hours) and Copper Ledge steakhouse (open for dinner) serve a recommendable eight-ounce prime rib; it's thin but consistently tender and tasty. You can also get a 12-ounce cut. You'll see these advertised all over town on billboards.

The Steakhouse at **Harrah's** (775/786-3232) is highly rated by restaurant reviewers (as well as by UNR professors who like to hang out there for lunch). Downstairs from the main casino, order your sandwiches, liver, filet, or lamb 11 A.M.–2 P.M. Dinner prices are high: peppersteak, filet,

20-ounce T-bone, salmon, sole, steak Diane, and more; daily 5–10 P.M.

At the Steakhouse, 775/331-1069, at **Western Village** in East Sparks, there's an early-bird special: prime rib or New York strip costs $9.95 with all the trimmings and fixings 4:30–6 P.M.—one of the best steak deals in town. Especially since this is a pretty fancy steakhouse. Open until 10 P.M.

As always, the **Eldorado** has a fine entry in the field: its Prime Rib Grill and Rotisserie, 775/786-5700, on the mezzanine. The salad bar has been judged the best in town by independent experts. Entrées are grilled or spit-cooked in the open kitchen. Filet, blackened rib steak with peppercorn sauce, prime rib, and spit-roasted lamb, chicken, fish, all in the $12–16 range. You can get the prime rib, pork, lamb, or chicken, along with the salad bar, for $8.99 with the early-bird special Open Wed.–Sun. 5–6:30 P.M. (the salad bar costs $8.50 by itself and is worth it). Open until 10 P.M.

The Steakhouse, 775/356-3300, at **John Ascuaga's Nugget** in Sparks has been around a long time. More than three million steaks have been served since the joint opened in 1956. For lunch, you can get a chicken breast, reuben, or New York steak sandwich, among others, along with salmon or seafood fettuccine. Dinner entrées include prime rib, steak, lamb, veal, chicken, duck, salmon, swordfish, and pasta. Open Mon.–Thurs. 11:30 A.M.–2 P.M. and 5–10 P.M., open at 11 A.M. Fri.–Sat., and for dinner only on Sun. from 5–10 P.M.

Seafood

And speaking of fish, the Oyster Bar, 775/356-3300, at **John Ascuaga's Nugget** is one of the best places to eat shellfish this side of San Francisco. This restaurant has been in operation for 35 years, and several of the waitresses have been there almost as long. You've never seen so many big clams in the red and white chowders, and the oyster, shrimp, and combo pan roasts are *loaded* and delicious. You can also get king salmon, prawns, scampi, oysters on the half shell, seafood cocktails, louies, cioppino, and sandwiches. Open daily 11 A.M.–10 P.M.

The other good casino seafood restaurant in town is Atlantis, 775/825-4700, at the **Atlantis.** The theme here is underwater, and the decor is sea cave, with the tallest aquarium you've ever seen and a rippling ceiling. Half of the menu here consists of piscatory pleasures, while the other half is meat. Seafood fettuccine, king crab legs, halibut, steamed mussels and clams, surf and turf, and more. Open 5–10 P.M. Be sure to also check out the Atlantis' Oyster Bar on the Sky Terrace overlooking Virginia Street. Diners will find a wide range of chowders and other shellfish specialties that are prepared in the exhibition kitchen. Open daily for lunch and dinner beginning at 11:30 A.M.

If it's Friday or Saturday night, head to the **Eldorado** for its seafood buffet, 775/786-5700, with all-you-can-eat cracked snow crab legs and peel-and-eat shrimp, half a dozen ocean entrées, big salad bar, and fancy desserts, including made-to-order cherries Jubilee.

Kokopelli's Sushi, 775/329-0711, is tucked inside the popular Art Gecko's at **Circus Circus.** It's Reno's first sushi offering to appear inside a Reno casino, and so far, the place is getting good reviews for their handrolls and other delicacies. Open for lunch and dinner. Fairchild's Oyster Bar, 775/687-8733, at the **Silver Legacy** rounds out the seafood offerings with strong entries for fresh seafood, crab cakes, and hearty oyster pan roasts. Open daily for lunch and dinner at 11 A.M.

Buffets

The best buffets in Reno are found at Atlantis, John Ascuaga's Nugget, and the Reno Hilton. There's a steak buffet nightly at the Silver Club. Those at Harrah's, the Peppermill, and the Sands will fill you up with no particular joy, though no particular despair either.

The **Atlantis**'s lunch and dinner buffets, 775/824-4433, have one feature that's duplicated at only two other buffets in the state (the Rio and Fiesta in Las Vegas): a Mongolian barbecue, where your vegetables and meats are stir fried on a round grill. It also has a specialty salad buffet with Caesar and hot spinach salads made to order. There's also a long salad bar, plenty of variety, and an excellent selection of desserts. Also open for breakfast.

Lunch, dinner, and Sunday brunch only are served at **John Ascuaga's Nugget** Rotisserie buffet, 800/648-1177. The food here is consistently good, especially the salads and desserts. If you're there on Tuesday and you like chocolate, you'll think you went to heaven, since it's chocolate dessert night.

At the **Reno Hilton,** the Lodge Buffet, 775/789-2000, is like eating at the El Tovar near the South Rim of the Grand Canyon. It's the most spacious buffet in town and has a large variety of salads and entrées. Impressive are the peel-and-eat shrimp along with snow crab legs and claws, lobster linguini, peppers and shrimp, Szechwan scallops, pecan chicken, Grand Canyon chili, and big desserts. Open for breakfast, lunch, and dinner.

There's an all-you-can-eat steak dinner buffet called Victoria's, 775/358-4771, at the **Silver Club** in Sparks that's very popular with locals. The room is small, cramped, and tumultuous, and the buffet part is kind of ordinary (corn on the cob, baked beans, spaghetti, garlic bread, baked potato), but let's face it, the steak's the thing: all you can eat, cooked to order, fair-sized boneless New York slabs.

View

The highest restaurant in town is The Top, 775/322-1111, on the 21st floor of the **Golden Phoenix.** The view from the restaurant and bar up here is obscured a bit by a surrounding deck. But inside it's a very comfortable and classy establishment. The restaurant also features the Ultra Lounge nightclub. Open Tues.–Sun. 6–11 P.M.

Basque

The original Basque boardinghouse and dining room is at the **Santa Fe Hotel.** Longtime residents swear by the Santa Fe, which opened in 1949. On busy nights, the big barroom in front is packed with people waiting to be seated (in waves) at the family-style tables in the dining room. The food is plentiful and hearty, the wine carafes are bottomless, and the service is feisty. For an interesting view, stand across Lake Street and see how the Santa Fe, which refused to sell out, seems an island of 1950s' Reno-Basque culture floating in the 1990s' Harrah's ocean. 235 Lake St., 775/323-1891, open for lunch ($8) Wed.–Fri. 11 A.M.–2 P.M., dinner ($14 adults, $7 children 12 and under) every night except Mon., 6–9 P.M.

With Basque food, it's a good idea to call ahead to find out what the entrées of the evening are. If the Santa Fe doesn't entice, try **Louis' Basque Corner,** just down the street from the Santa Fe. Bring an appetite and a half to this family-style spot to enjoy the soup, salad, beans, french fries, bread, wine, and ice cream that accompany the rotating entrée, generally a choice of lamb, steak, or chicken. If you're prepared to sit at tables with strangers and have a good time, you'll leave both downtown Basque restaurants satisfied and socialized. 301 E. 4th St., 775/323-7203. Lunch ($9.95) Wed.–Fri. 11:30 A.M.–2:30 P.M.; a six-course dinner ($19.95) nightly, 5 P.M. –9:30 P.M.

Basque gets a gourmet spin at **Restaurante Orozko,** 800/648-1177, at John Ascuaga's Nugget in Sparks. The entrées have a Mediterranean influence, and the room features walls painted to resemble the Basque countryside, enough to make owner and Basque-American John Ascuaga a little homesick. Open Wed.–Sun. 5–9 P.M.

Italian

The Eldorado's **La Strada,** 775/786-5700, is not only one of the top Italian restaurants in Nevada, but also in the country: it has been named among the nation's top 25 Italian and has won the *Wine Spectator's* Award of Excellence. All the pasta is handmade on the premises, and the pizza is so good that they ought to open a take-out place. Everything is baked in wood-fired brick ovens. Start off with a little carpaccio, then go on to spaghetti marinara or other pasta dishes. The ravioli is excellent (spinach, seafood, or regular). Chicken comes picatta, marsala, arrosto, parmesana, and saltimbocca. You can also get T-bones, scaloppine, and fish. A 30- by 5-foot mural on the back wall depicts the Ferrari-Carano vineyards in Sonoma County's Alexander Valley. Open Fri.–Tues. 5–10 P.M.

With La Strada right across the street, Harrah's had to do something different to make **Cafe**

Andreotti, 775/788-2908, a success. It succeeded. The create-your-own-pasta menu offers a selection of six pastas and six sauces. You can also try Andreotti's pizzas, pasta specials, manicotti, chicken, veal, scampi, or snapper. Or sample the calzone: a big half-moon of delicious pizza dough, bursting its seams with vegetables, cheese, and meats. Open nightly 5–10 P.M.

Another classic hotel Italian dining room is **MonteVigna** at the Atlantis, a posh room with cuisine—and a 4,000-bottle wine cellar—to match. 775/825-4700, open nightly at 5 P.M.

If you're looking for a great place to take a date, try the romantic **Romanza,** 775/689-7474 or 800/648-6992, at the Peppermill. Romanesque sculptures, a sky painted on the ceiling, dramatic lighting, and lush fabrics and furnishings make this dining room and special-occasion no-brainer. The menu covers the Italian gamut and also features dishes cooked in a wood-fired oven. Open nightly at 5:30 P.M.

Johnny's Ristorante Italiano has a nice little bar is on the right, and the big red-leather booths are quite conducive to settling back and enjoying your ravioli, lasagna, chicken cacciatore on polenta, or seafood platter. 4245 W. 4th, 775/747-4511, dinner Tues.–Sat., 5–9:30 P.M.

Reno also has two other favorite Italian restaurants. **Luciano's,** 719 S. Virginia St., 775/322-7373, is open Tues.–Thurs. 5–9 P.M. and Fri.–Sat. 5–10 P.M. **LaVecchia,** 3501 S. Virginia St., 775/825-1113, is open for lunch Mon.–Fri. 11 A.M.–2 P.M., and for dinner every night starting at 5 P.M.

Mexican

The Vineyard, 775/331-1069, is a Mexican-Italian restaurant at Western Village off I-80 in Sparks. Good chips and salsa and filling entrées. Open daily 4–9 P.M.

Miguel's, 1415 S. Virginia St., 775/322-2722, is one of the original Mexican restaurants in Reno, pleasing patrons for more than 30 years. It's very bright and friendly; excellent service, authentic, and inexpensive. One of the highlights of Reno. Open Tues.–Thurs. 11 A.M.–9 P.M., Fri.–Sun. 11 A.M.–11 P.M.

A couple of blocks south of Miguel's is **El**

Borracho, 1601 S. Virginia St., 775/322-0313, the other original Reno beanery. Relaxing interior, 11 interesting shrimp dishes (salads, cocktails, stew, brochette, ceviche), plus the usual tostadas, enchiladas, burritos, and other specials. Open daily 3:30 P.M.–11 P.M., closed Tues. **Bertha Miranda's,** 336 Mill St., 775/786-9697, has a deservedly good reputation among locals for great Mexican food. Open every day, 10 A.M.–10 P.M.

Micasa Too regularly wins "Best Mexican Restaurant" in the *Gazette-Journal* poll. There's always a huge crowd waiting to fill up here; luckily, the bar is as big as the restaurant, and the usual 30- to 45-minute wait is painless. Micasa Too has two locations in Reno: 2205 W. 4th St., 775/323-6466, and in south Reno at 3255 S. Virginia St., 775/825-3005. Both are open every day, 11 A.M.–11 P.M.

Chinese

Palais de Jade, 960 W. Moana, 775/827-5233, is the ritziest Chinese restaurant in town, in an extremely tasteful room done in mostly black and white, quite understated and elegant. It's won the best Chinese food category in the newspaper poll seven years in a row. All styles of Chinese food are represented, with the mu shu, cashew, and kung pao you've come to know, along with some scallop and lobster dishes and specials. The food is delicious and the service lively. Highly recommended. Open daily 11 A.M.–9:30 P.M.

Soochow, 656 E. Prater, 775/359-5207, is the yang of Palais de Jade's yin. A plain old neighborhood Chinese restaurant out in Sparks, favored by couples with kids for the inexpensive family dinners, starting as low as $5 per person for six or seven courses. Shrimp with snow peas for $4, pork egg fu yung for $3.75, and hot-and-sour soup for $4.25 gives you the idea. Open Mon.–Sat. 11 A.M.–9:30 P.M., Sun. 4–9:30 P.M. **Yen Ching,** 565 W. Moana, 775/825-2451, falls somewhere between the Palais de Jade and Soochow in terms of price, character, and quality. Open daily 10:30 A.M.–9:30 P.M.

Among the casinos, for Hong Kong cuisine try the upscale **Golden Fortune,** at the Eldorado, 775/786-5700; open Tues.–Sat. for dinner starting at 5 P.M. **Asiana,** 775/789-2268, at the Reno Hilton offers California-Asian fusion dishes, which means, of course, that they also have a sushi bar that's available for an all-you-can-eat option. Open Wed.–Mon. for lunch and dinner. Harrah's Reno offers the **Lucky Noodle Bar,** 775/786-3232, which is open for lunch and dinner.

Japanese
Ichiban, 210 N. Sierra, 775/323-5550, is a great place to take the kids, who love the spectacle of theatrical Japanese short-order chefs dicing and slicing, stirring and frying, on private *teppanyaki* grills (kids menu and kids drinks, too). Adults like Ichiban as well, for the pampering—hot fragrant towels and warm sake instantly do the trick. You choose steak, shrimp, scallops, chicken, lobster, or a combo thereof to be prepared with vegetables at your counter. Good location, walkable from everywhere downtown. Open daily 4:30–10 P.M.
Kyoto, 915 W. Moana in the Moana West Shopping, 775/825-9686, is a fine little Japanese barbecue house serving yakis, tempura, sushi, and special Kyoto steak. Open Mon.–Sat. 11:30 A.M.–2:30 P.M. and 5–9:30 P.M.

Other Asian
Trader Dick's, at John Ascuaga's Nugget, 775/356-3300, is one of the oldest restaurants in town, featuring Polynesian (mostly Chinese- and Japanese-style) cuisine in a low-lit, South Seas ambience; dark and leafy, it's a good place to feel enveloped by a sultry Polynesian evening. It's open for lunch, when you can get sandwiches if you're not in the mood for pork chow mein, teriyaki chicken, or stir-fried shrimp. The dinner menu lists steak, prime rib, king crab, and duck along with Chinese pepper steak, cashew chicken, and lobster and shrimp Cantonese. Have a mai tai, cha cha, chi chi, aku aku, zombie, wahine, Molokai Mike, or Rangoon Ruby at the bar, topped by the largest aquarium in town. Open Sun.–Thurs. 5:30–9 P.M. and Fri.–Sat. 5–10 P.M.

A local favorite is **Cafe de Thai,** 3314 S. McCarran, at the Mira Loma Shopping Center, 775/829-8424. *Everything* here is out of this world, all concocted by chef Sakul Cheosakul, a Thai trained in his native cuisine as well as at the Culinary Institute. Try the satay or papaya salad appetizers or the super-hot Oriental sausage salad; the *tom kha kay* soup is like swallowing purity. The wok dishes are superb and reasonably priced: garlic pepper pork, peanut beef, basil chicken, and the curries are spicy. Veggie dishes are delicious, as is the pad Thai. Highly recommended. Open Tues.–Sat. 11:30 A.M.–10 P.M.

For Vietnamese, head for the **Golden Flower,** 205 W. 5th St. at the corner of Arlington St., 775/323-1628. Choose from 17 different kinds of *pho* (traditional beef-noodle soup), along with the must-eat imperial rolls and shrimp stickers. Most entrées are around $8–10. Open daily 10 A.M.–9 P.M.

European
Adele's, 425 S. Virginia St., 775/333-6503, is one of Reno's finest restaurants. The sheer volume of menu choices (33 appetizers and more than 50 entrées) makes for a daunting selection, but let it be said that you can get practically anything you can imagine at Adele's. The number of fish dishes alone would make any Seattle restaurant jealous. For dinner, try your choice of chicken, duck, veal, lamb, beef, pork, fish, sushi, and pasta, and that's just on the menu; the waiter will describe the dozen or so evening specials. Dinner entrées start at $20 and can go as high as $80; steaks are around $27. Open for lunch Mon.–Fri. at 11:30 A.M. and for dinner (daily except Sun.) at 5 P.M. Dinner service stops at 10 P.M., but the bar stays open until midnight, with a late-night menu. There's live entertainment on Friday and Saturday nights, starting around 9:30 or 10 P.M.

At **Bavarian World,** 595 Valley Rd. at 6th St., 775/323-7646, the name says it all. You walk into a big German deli and grocery store, stocking everything from rye bread and strudel to a big selection of swiss chocolate and a lot of unusual boxed and canned foods. The big festive restaurant in back, with an Octoberfest-size dance floor, is a surprise considering the plain warehouse exterior. It serves schnitzel, sauerbraten, a vegetarian potato pancake, and other German dishes, all for $8–18. Open Tues.–Sat. 8 A.M.–8:30 P.M.

Wine Bar
The Siena has introduced another first to the Biggest Little City: a wine bar. **Enoteca,**

Reno and Tahoe

877/SIENA-33, tucked into the basement of the resort, features a wine bar with 35 wines for sampling by the glass and more than 300 wines for sale by the bottle.

INFORMATION AND SERVICES

The **Reno-Sparks Convention and Visitors Authority** (RSCVA), 1 E. 1st St. at Virginia St., 775/827-7600 or 800/FOR-RENO (800/367-7366), www.renolaketahoe.com, carries loads of useful tourist literature, brochures and other information; be sure to ask for the excellent *Travel Planner,* published annually. Call their 800 number for a recording of entertainment, casino activities, golf and ski packages, conventions, entertainment, and special events, and to access the Reno-Sparks Convention and Visitors Authority (RSCVA) hotel reservation service. A separate website, www.rscva.com, gives current information on conventions. Open Mon.–Fri. 8 A.M.–5 P.M.

The RSCVA operates two visitor information centers in Reno, both convenient for picking up brochures, visitors guides, maps, and answers to questions. One is the **Reno Downtown Visitor Center** in the lobby of the National Bowling Stadium, 300 N. Center St., 775/334-2625, open every day 9 A.M.–5 P.M. The other is the Visitor Center at **Meadowood Mall,** 5000 Meadowood Mall Circle in south Reno, 775/827-7708, Mon.–Fri. 10 A.M.–9 P.M., Sat. 10 A.M.–7 P.M., Sun. 11 A.M.–6 P.M.

You can also stop off at the **Sparks Information Center and Chamber of Commerce,** at the corner of Pyramid and Victorian Aves., 775/358-1976, www.sparkschamber.org, Mon.–Fri. 8 A.M.–5 P.M. year-round and 9 A.M.–5 P.M. summer weekends.

For **University of Nevada** information, stop in at Jones Visitor Center, right on the Quad, open daily 9 A.M.–5 P.M., or call 775/784-4865. The university's campus operator and general information number is 775/784-1110.

Marriage and Divorce

The County Clerk's office is in the courthouse, S. Virginia and Court Sts., 775/328-3274, www

.co.washoe.nv.us/clerks/marriage, open daily 8 A.M.–midnight. Bring your I.D., your betrothed, and $55 cash or credit/debit card for your license (no blood test, no waiting period). Then get married in any one of Reno's dozen wedding chapels (prices start at $150); most are bunched up on the strip, along W. 4th, and around Court and S. Virginia.

To just get married cheaply, with no muss and no fuss, go to the **Commissioner of Civil Marriages,** 350 S. Center St., 775/337-4575. In Reno–Sparks, the County Clerk doubles as the Commissioner of Civil Marriages. She appoints deputy commissioners whose sole function is to marry people. Just show up at their office with your license and $50 cash or Visa or MasterCard Thursday to Monday 9 A.M.–6 P.M. (closed for lunch 1–2 P.M.), and in 10 minutes you're hitched. On busy days you might have to wait a little for a couple or two ahead of you.

If it ultimately doesn't work out, one (or both) of the divorcing parties must be able to prove they have been a resident of Nevada for six weeks. **Ace Paralegal,** 2765 Wrondel Way, 775/825-1212, types up the court documents for you for $150, then sends you down to the courthouse to file; filing costs another $150. **Divorce Nevada Style,** 775/747-6921, prepares and files all documents for a fee starting at $100 for a simple divorce. Fees can be higher at either place, depending on circumstances; the fees mentioned here are for a simple divorce. You don't need to come in to either place personally, if you prefer not to; they can handle the whole thing for you by mail.

Libraries

The extensive **Washoe County Library** is at 301 S. Center, 775/785-4190. Open Mon. 10 A.M.–8 P.M., Tues.–Thurs. 10 A.M.–6 P.M., Fri. 10 A.M.–5 P.M., Sat.–Sun. noon–5 P.M.

A good place to find the Nevada books that are checked out of the Washoe County Library is at the **Truckee Meadows Community College Library,** 7000 Dandini Blvd. off US 395 about 10 miles north of downtown, 775/674-7600. Open Mon.–Thurs. 8 A.M.–7 P.M., Fri. 8 A.M.–4 P.M., Sat. 10 A.M.–4 P.M.

Bookstores

Reno's best community bookstore is **Sundance,** in the shopping center on Keystone and W. 4th, 775/786-1188. Open Mon.–Fri. 9 A.M.–9 P.M., Sat. and Sun. 10 A.M.–6 P.M. **Waldenbooks** in Meadowood Mall, way down S. Virginia at McCarran Blvd., 775/826-5690, is open Mon.–Fri. 10 A.M.–9 P.M., Sat. 10 A.M.–8 P.M., and Sun. 11 A.M.–6 P.M.

The **Barnes & Noble** superstore, with more than 150,000 titles, newsstand, and coffee bar, is at 5555 S. Virginia, 775/826-8882. Open daily 9 A.M.–11 P.M., Sun. until 10 P.M. **Borders Books, Music & Cafe,** 4995 S. Virginia St., 775/448-9999, is another huge store. Open Mon.–Thurs. 9 A.M.–10 P.M., Fri.–Sat. 9 A.M.–11 P.M., and Sun. 9 A.M.–9 P.M.

Maps

Oakman's, 634 Ryland, 775/786-4466, is a big art, crafts, office, and drafting supply store; in the back corner are many raised-relief maps ($18) and USGS topo maps. Open Mon.–Fri. 8 A.M.–5:30 P.M., Sat. 10 A.M.–3 P.M., At **AAA,** 199 E. Moana Ln., 775/826-8800, pick up their uniformly fine maps of Reno–Sparks and Nevada. Open Mon.–Fri. 8:30 A.M.–5:30 P.M.

TRANSPORTATION

Reno is 15 miles east of the California border. The Reno–Sparks area is served by two major highways: I-80, which crosses the country from San Francisco to New York; and US 395, which runs from southeast Oregon briefly through Nevada (from Reno to Topaz Lake), then heads south through California down to near Los Angeles.

The **Greyhound** bus terminal is at 155 Stevenson between W. 1st and 2nd, 775/322-2970 or 800/231-2222. Buses depart roughly 24 times throughout the day and night, with services south to Las Vegas (via Carson City), west to Sacramento, Oakland and San Francisco. In Sacramento there are connections heading south to Los Angeles and north to Redding, Portland, and Seattle. Eastbound buses head out I-80 to Salt Lake City, via Winnemucca and Elko. **K-T Bus Lines** operates between Reno and Las Vegas, arriving and departing from the Greyhou... pots on both ends.

Public Rural Ride (PRIDE),775/348-RIL. operates buses seven times a day, 6:30 A.M.–7 P.M., between Reno and Carson City. Fares are $3 adults, $2 youth, $1.50 seniors, including free transfers to Reno's city bus system, Citifare. In Reno, the bus operates from the local bus terminal at the corner of Center and 4th Streets downtown, opposite the National Bowling Stadium.

Amtrak, 775/329-8638, or 800/USA-RAIL, runs cross-country rail service on the transcontinental line laid through Nevada in 1869. Its *California Zephyr* passes right through the middle of downtown Reno (blocking traffic twice a day for 5–10 minutes). The depot, 135 E. Commercial St. at Lake St., is across from the north side of Harrah's parking building. The train stops in Reno once daily in each direction, heading west to Sacramento and Emeryville (in the east San Francisco Bay Area), and east to Salt Lake City, Denver, and Chicago; this train stops in Nevada in Reno, Winnemucca, and Elko. Amtrak also operates several buses daily between Reno and Sacramento, to connect with other trains there, including the *Coast Starlight* train going south to southern California and north to Oregon and Washington. The depot, open daily 8:30 A.M.–5:30 P.M., has the air of a real old downtown train station, which it is—built in 1925, it became Reno's fifth and last depot.

Nearly six million people pass through **Reno–Tahoe International Airport** every year; the airport is served by Alaska, Allegiant, America West, American, Continental, Delta, Northwest, Skywest, Southwest, Shuttle by United, TWA, and United.

Conveniently located, the airport is only a 10-minute drive from downtown; take US 395 south to the airport exit. Or catch the Bell airport shuttle, 775/786-3700, every 30 minutes (on the half hour) at the baggage-claim area, operating between the airport and the major downtown hotels; $2.65 one-way.

A Citifare bus route, number 13, operates between the airport and the Citicenter bus depot, downtown at 4th and Center Streets opposite the National Bowling Stadium. On weekdays

ery half hour from around
M., with hourly service on
A.M.–1:45 A.M. On Sun-
ns hourly, from around
rares are $1.50 for adults,
youth and $0.75 for seniors. Call
775/348-7433 for current info.

Getting Around

Reno's local bus system, **Citifare,** operates 24 hours a day on 24 routes around downtown all the way out to the four corners of Truckee Meadows. Fares (exact change) are $1.50 one-way, youth $1.25, seniors $0.75. For info call 775/348-RIDE. All routes start and end at the Citi-Center Transit Center, 4th and Center Streets.

All of the standard rental car companies operate out of the airport, which makes it convenient if you're flying in and out, though you'll have to join the throngs there if you're not.

If you don't want to deal with the airport, some of the **rental car** companies also have offices in town. Avis has a rental desk at the Reno Hilton, 800/648-5080, in addition to its desk at the airport, 775/785-2727. Enterprise has an office downtown at 4th and Vine Streets, 775/328-1671, and in south Reno at 2208 Kietzke, 775/826-2442, in addition to its desk at the airport, 775/329-3773. Dollar has an office downtown at the Golden Phoenix, 225 N. Sierra St., 775/348-2812. Hertz has a desk at the Silver

Legacy, 407 N. Virginia St., 775/325-7593, and an office at 1567 Vassar St., 775/785-2650, in addition to its desk at the airport, 775/785-2554. Budget has an office at 1595 Marietta Way in Sparks, 775/785-2545, in addition to its desk at the airport, 775/785-2545.

Alternatively, some companies will come to where you are to pick you up when you rent a vehicle, a convenient service. **Tahoe Casino Express,** 775/785-2424 or 800/446-6128, provides service between the Reno airport and Lake Tahoe's south shore casinos. Fare is $20 one way, $36 round trip.

Tours

Frontier Charters, 775/331-1147, offers a daily guided bus tour departing Reno at 9 A.M., heading over to Lake Tahoe with stops at Squaw Valley, Emerald Bay and South Lake Tahoe, then stopping at Carson City, then Virginia City, and arriving back at Reno at 5:30 P.M. The tour costs $34. **Scenic Tours,** 775/826-6888 or 800/828-7143, is a friendly, locally owned tour company offering a similar tour, departing Reno daily and heading for Truckee, Lake Tahoe, Carson City, Virginia City, and then back to Reno. The cost of $49 per person includes breakfast and lunch; on a special promotional deal, you can save $15 if you phone their local number and book the tour yourself. Locals recommend this tour. **Sierra Nevada Sightseeing,** 800/822-6009, also has tours.

Lake Tahoe

Lake Tahoe, 12 miles wide, 22 miles long, with 72 miles of shoreline and averaging 1,000 feet deep, is the largest alpine lake in North America and the 10th-deepest lake in the world. Tahoe's 122 million acre-feet are enough to cover all of California with a foot of water, and its 40 trillion gallons of water could supply every human on the planet with a shower a day from January through August. Its water clarity is rivaled only by Crater Lake in Oregon and Lake Baikal in Siberia, and you can clearly see a dinner plate sitting 75 feet beneath the surface. Its greatest depth is 1,645 feet, and

Tahoe drops 1,400 feet straight down from the shoreline at Rubicon Point (in California). The great depth and volume of water and its constant movement from lake bottom to top preclude Tahoe from ever freezing.

The lake lies in a huge bowl, almost completely surrounded by the granite Sierra Nevada (on the west) and the granite Carson Range (on the east). During the Oligocene (about 25 million years ago), the immense Sierra were uplifted: Tilt, faults, and erosion caused massive slippage along the new slopes, sinking the land and creating the Tahoe Basin. Five million years ago,

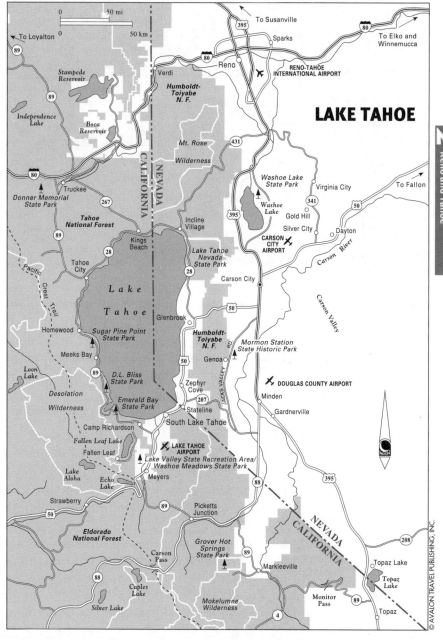

LAKE TAHOE

© AVALON TRAVEL PUBLISHING, INC.

COURTESY OF THE NEVADA COMMISSION ON TOURISM

Lake Tahoe

volcanic activity at the north end sealed the basin. Rainwater and snowmelt filled it.

During the Wisconsin Ice Age 10,000 years ago, the vast Lake Valley Glacier marched into the area, extending feeder ice rivers into the lake, including one that carved out Emerald Bay. Eventually the glacier retreated, the ice melted, and the lake level rose hundreds of feet, forcing an outlet through the porous volcanic seal at the northwest end—now the Truckee River.

Tahoe's watershed encompasses 520 square miles, including more than 60 inlets from tributaries, and a single outlet, the Truckee River. The river drains the lake at Tahoe City, where a dam regulates the water flow. The top six feet of the lake is reservoir, which supplies water for the Reno–Sparks metropolitan area, Fallon agricultural irrigation, and Pyramid Lake fisheries. The river flows north through Truckee, California, then cuts east through Reno, then finally empties into Pyramid Lake at Nixon, nearly 100 miles northeast.

The lake's denizens consist mainly of big mackinaw trout; the largest mackinaw caught in recent memory was in 1974 and weighed in at 37.5 pounds. Kokanee trout (a variety of landlocked sockeye salmon) are smaller, both in numbers and size. And there's some talk of trying to reestablish the great Lahontan cutthroat trout in Tahoe and its spawning areas.

Of the lake's 72 miles of shoreline, 29 are in Nevada; of its 122,200 acres of surface area, 31,700 are in Nevada. The vast majority of recreational opportunities—beaches and picnic areas, marinas and launching ramps, golf courses and stables, camping and skiing—are in California. The casinos, of course, are only in Nevada.

Shoreline roads go all the way around Lake Tahoe. The full 72-mile circle can be driven in about 2.5 hours, but you could easily spend a very enjoyable day doing the drive, stopping off at many beautiful places all along the way. A free pamphlet called *The Most Beautiful Drive in America* outlines the many attractions of the drive; it is available at all area chambers of commerce and visitor centers.

HISTORY

Washo Indians gathered on the northern shoreline each spring for at least 5,000 years to harvest the teeming trout, partake in leisurely water

DON'T DROWN IN LAKE TAHOE

Every year, an average of three people drown in Lake Tahoe, and another 10 or so are rescued from almost-certain death. Though it looks tame and inviting, Lake Tahoe is cold and clear and has strong currents, a potentially deadly combination. The average surface water temperature is no more than 60°F; near the shoreline it warms up to 68°—still cold. Numbness is an immediate danger, and hypothermia can set in after 20 minutes in 60° water. The clarity of the lake renders distance and depth deceptive, which can get you into trouble fast. And strong currents can result from heavy runoff from snow-pack-fed creeks. People are swept out from the shore—and they don't last long in the cold water.

In addition, Tahoe doesn't give up its dead. The lake is so cold that it prevents gases from forming that would raise the body to the surface. Take common-sense precautions about going into Lake Tahoe if you want to come out again.

By this time, word of the area's incomparable beauty had been carried far and wide by the traffic between the Comstock and the California coast. The lake's first resort and the insatiable logging and fishing industries were established at Glenbrook in the mid-1860s. By 1870, only 500 Washo could be counted. By the 1890s, the lake was nearly fished out, and 50,000 acres of forest had been cut (out of the total 51,000): half a million cords, 750 million board feet. Most of this lumber was manhandled into the lake, pulled by steamer to Glenbrook or Incline, railroaded to Spooner Summit, then shot down flumes to mills at Washoe Valley and Carson City. Delivered to Virginia City first by freighters and then by the V&T Railroad, the forests of Tahoe were killed, then buried in the monumental maze of square-set tunnels far below Mt. Davidson.

Recent Developments

Meanwhile, luxury hotels began opening to cater to the kings and queens of the Comstock. A narrow-gauge short line reached Tahoe City from the transcontinental stop at Truckee in 1900, and the first automobile arrived in 1905. Paved roads reached the lake in the 1930s, transforming this playground of the rich into one for everybody.

Still, the Tahoe Basin managed to maintain a kind of pristine second-growth remoteness well into the 1950s, with a total year-round population of under 3,000. But then Tahoe's development began in earnest with several water, power, and subdivision schemes. Small reasonably priced hotels attracted more and more visitors and private ownership of more and more shoreline encouraged an influx of residents. Harvey Gross and Bill Harrah built casinos at South Shore, land values skyrocketed, and the 1960 Winter Olympics at Squaw Valley completed Lake Tahoe's rise to a world-class year-round vacation and recreation destination. After the Olympics, development began to spiral out of control.

Finally, in 1965, the League to Save Lake Tahoe was formed, which spurred the creation of the joint Nevada–California Tahoe Regional Planning Authority (TRPA) in 1969. The planners now have a very tight rein on growth, enforcing what could be the strictest development

sports, and ceremoniously thank the spirits for their benevolence and abundance. The Washo spoke a Hokan dialect, separating them ethnologically from their Paiute neighbors, members of the Uto-Aztecan linguistic group. The Washo name for the lake was Da Ow A Ga, meaning "Edge of the Lake"; it is generally considered the forerunner of the name Tahoe. Another possibility for its etymology, however, is the Spanish word *tajo,* meaning "sheer cliffs." At contact, there were an estimated 3,100 Washo people. In *Rabbit Boss,* Thomas Sanchez's sprawling novel about this tribe, two Washo men first laid eyes on *them* (whites) by witnessing an episode of Donner Party cannibalism. Intense.

Pyramid Lake Paiute drew a map for John C. Frémont in 1844; he followed the Truckee River and spied the lake, which he named Bonpland, after a famous French explorer-scientist. Both California and Nevada approved the name Bigler, after the third California governor, but the head federal cartographer vetoed the choice simply by leaving it off the official map. He then consulted an expert in the Washo tongue, who suggested Tahoe.

restrictions in the United States. The TRPA set ecological "thresholds" to hold the line on the deterioration of the environment-water and air pollution, traffic congestion, forest management, and development. A complete moratorium on building permits was in force in the mid-'80s; since then only a small amount of construction has been allowed.

Needless to say, this has created a large-scale controversy. Developers and people who own "unbuildable" lots harbor resentments, often liti-

gious, against the TRPA. Environmentalists, on the other hand, are rabid about the thresholds, to the point where some are calling for the creation of a Sierra Nevada National Park. Unlike most such battles, so far the hard-line control-growthers hold the stronger cards.

Drought and Flood

Lake Tahoe is the main reservoir for the entire Truckee River water system: Reno–Sparks municipal water, Sierra Pacific hydroelectric water,

TAHOE RIM TRAIL

The Tahoe Rim Trail is a magnificent 165-mile trail encircling Lake Tahoe. Following the ridges and mountaintops that circle the lake, the trail winds through national forest, state park, and wilderness lands, passing through a variety of vegetation zones and providing spectacular views. The trail passes through thick conifer forests and wildflower-filled meadows, and skirts the shores of pristine alpine lakes. The trail offers something for everyone, with stretches ranging from easy to difficult, a number of loop trails, and an average grade of 10 percent. Hiking, horseback riding, and skiing are allowed on all parts of the trail; mountain biking is allowed on specified portions.

The idea of a trail circling Lake Tahoe was dreamed up in the early 1980s by the Forest Service Recreation Officer at Tahoe, and the nonprofit Tahoe Rim Trail Association (TRTA) was organized in 1981. The trail was designed to link up with 50 miles of the Pacific Crest Trail that travels along the west side of the Tahoe wilderness. Work on the trail, performed entirely by volunteers, began in 1983, and a year later, the TRTA had attracted 50 members. By 1988, 1,500 members had helped clear 30 miles of the trail, working strictly between May 1 and October 15. In 2001 the final section was completed, and the entire trail officially became a loop.

You can easily do a part of the trail by beginning at any of nine trailheads, or if you are ambitious you can do the whole circle and become a member of the "165 Mile Club." Camping is permitted along most of the trail, allowing extended trips into the solitude of backcountry and wilderness regions; the numerous trailheads give day users abundant opportunities to do smaller portions of the trail and explore the beauty of the mountains. On the Nevada side, trailheads include the Spooner Summit trailhead (US 50), the Kingsbury trailhead (two miles north of Hwy. 207) and the Tahoe Meadows to Spooner Summit trailhead (Hwy. 431). California-side trailheads include the Brockway trailhead (Hwy 267), the Tahoe City trailhead (one-eighth mile north of Hwy. 89), the Barker Pass trailhead (Blackwood Canyon Rd., four miles south of Tahoe City), and, on the south side of the lake, the Big Meadow trailhead (Hwy. 89), and the Echo Lakes and Echo Summit trailheads (US 50).

Trail maps are posted at the trailheads, but users are urged to carry maps with them on the trail. A detailed map is available at the Tahoe Rim Trail Association's office in Stateline for $10; it can also be mail-ordered, or ordered over their website.

There are lots of opportunity for involvement with the Tahoe Rim Trail Association. You can join a trail construction or maintenance party, buy a TRT T-shirt, volunteer in a variety of capacities, or "Adopt a Mile," among other possibilities. Contact Tahoe Rim Trail Association, 948 Incline Way, Incline Village, NV 89451, 775/298-0012, fax 775/298-0013, www.tahoerimtrail.org.

California and Nevada Fish and Game water, U.S. Fish and Wildlife water, Pyramid Lake Paiute fisheries water, and (some) Truckee-Carson Irrigation District water. The dam at Tahoe City (6,229 feet) regulates the six feet of reservoir water above the lake's natural rim (6,223 feet). The drought, in its ninth and last year in 1995 (with a one-year respite in '93) greatly diminished the winter snowpack in the Tahoe Basin, which supplies more than 60 percent of Lake Tahoe's water. The lake level dropped below its natural rim in July 1991, and except for a brief trickle in spring 1993 and 1995, not a drop of water flowed into the Truckee River. Downstream storage (Donner Lake and Stampede, Boca, Prosser, and Independence reservoirs) fell to precipitously low levels in the summer. Finally, the lake dropped to its lowest level (6,220 feet) in recorded history.

But a couple of wet winters (1996–97) replenished the rez, and in fact filled it a little too full. In January 1997, lake water started pouring over the dam, out of control. The Truckee River flooded over its banks for most of its 100-mile length, submerging downtown Reno under up to five feet of water in some places and causing hundreds of millions in damage. But that's life in the desert.

Scientists at Reno's Desert Research Institute have studied tree stumps found in 25 feet of water at Baldwin Beach. Their rings indicate that they lived 200 or so years, and carbon-dating puts them living 5,000–6,300 years ago. This could mean that large old trees once grew along the shores of a lake much more depleted by drought than today. Tree rings and pack rat middens (crystallized balls of vegetation the rats assemble for nests using urine as an adhesive) support a theory that the eastern Sierra have sustained a number of 30- to 40-year droughts (the latest believed during the 15th and 16th centuries). The researchers postulate that since instruments began to keep records within the last 100 years, our climatic cycle could be much wetter than the norm. Meaning that the nine-year drought might only be the beginning and the heavy winters of 1996 and 1997 were brief respites.

STATELINE/ SOUTH LAKE TAHOE

South Lake Tahoe could be the quintessential California–Nevada bordertown, a representation not only of the strange glue that binds the two together, but also of the discrete elements that differentiate each from the other. The California side of town is an elephantine freeway exit ramp, taffy-pulled into an elongated frontage road. Literally hundreds of low-rise motels, fast food spots, service stations, shopping centers, and apartment, condo, and professional complexes all jut up like warts from one continuous asphalt parking lot, cars crawling all over it. On the Nevada side of the border are the half dozen or so casinos, as contained and vertical as the California side is widespread and horizontal. Beyond the high-rises north along Nevada's east shore is the wilderness.

Harveys

Harvey Gross's Wagon Wheel was the first bona fide casino at South Lake. Gross was a meat wholesaler in Sacramento who supplied the beef to the restaurants and resorts at the lake in the 1940s. Gambling on growth, he and his wife Llewellyn bought some property near the California state line across from two existing slot joints. They started in a one-room log-cabin saloon with six slot machines, three blackjack tables, and a six-stool snack bar, and quickly added a dozen more slots and a gas pump out front—the only one at the time on the old Lincoln Highway (US 50) between Placerville and Carson City.

Harveys grew steadily, quietly, for 30 years. Then, in August 1980, a bomb placed on the property in an extortion attempt exploded, causing extensive damage but no loss of life. (The whole fascinating story of the bomb is recounted in *Nevada—True Tales from the Neon Wilderness* by Jim Sloan). Harvey Gross died in 1983, and the hotel was owned solely by his family until early 1994, when Harveys went public. Also in 1994 Harveys celebrated its 50th anniversary on July 18 by burying a time capsule containing Harveys, Lake Tahoe, and Nevada memorabilia, along with 1990s products such as a cellular phone, and a Tahoe water sample and analysis. The capsule will be reopened in the year 2044.

Today, Harveys is a 740-room hotel, largest on the lake; the $87 million Lake Tower was completed in 1992. The casino is also monumental at 52,500 square feet; a wooden "path" helps you to navigate the casino easily. On the back wall of the poker room is the world's largest **hand-tooled leather mural,** commissioned by Harvey Gross in 1946. It re-creates a scene from Virginia City at the height of the Comstock, taking some liberties with the characters and setting. Read the description of the damage it sustained during, and the restoration it received after, the bombing incident. The resort also is now part of the Harrah's Entertainment Group, which owns Harrah's, the Rio, and the Showboat in Las Vegas.

Unusual for a Nevada hotel-casino, the front desk is on a level lower than the casino, under a two-story chandelier, so you don't have to lug your suitcases by the blackjack pit. Harveys has six restaurants, plentiful bars and lounges, and a tunnel under US 50 that connects with Harrah's.

Harrah's

Harrah's is one of the country's top-10 hotel-resorts, earning four diamonds from AAA. This is luxury pure and simple: Each room has two full bathrooms, with a phone and a TV in each, along with a minibar and great mountain or lake views from the picture windows. The 65,000-square-foot casino has 1,300 slots and 170 table games; each pit area has a different theme, such as the Sports Casino and the Classic Rock Casino (where the tables are named after rock stars and the big sound system plays, you guessed it, classic rock). The health club has steam rooms, hot tubs, and complete exercise facilities. Reflections: The Spa, which offers an array of beauty treatments, reflects the lake's emphasis on pampering its visitors. The kids' arcade was tripled in size and is now a "family fun center," and families also enjoy the hotel's unique dome-covered swimming pool. Finally, in a rare microcosm of this schizophrenic town, the hotel-casino is in Nevada, the parking lot in California.

Horizon Casino

This hotel-casino opened in 1965 as the Sahara, built by Del Webb, who at the time owned the Sahara and Mint hotels in Las Vegas. Webb, a Phoenix contractor, first arrived in Las Vegas in 1946 to build Bugsy Siegel's fabulous Flamingo. In 1951, he was hired to build the Sahara in return for shares in the hotel. By the time Webb opened the Sahara Tahoe, he was one of the largest hotel-casino operators in the state. The name was subsequently changed to the High Sierra. Gradually, the Del Webb Corp., still based in Phoenix, divested itself of its Nevada holdings; when it sold the High Sierra to a Kentucky real estate investor, William Yung, for $19 million cash in early 1990, the sale ended a highly successful 44-year run.

Yung's Wimar Tahoe Corp. changed the name to Tahoe Horizon and spent $12 million on remodeling. It shows in the marble, brass, and glass. Now called the Horizon Casino Resort, the property has the brightest and airiest casino on the lake. It also has the GameWorld arcade and an eight-screen movie theater.

Caesars Tahoe

Like Caesars Las Vegas, Caesars Tahoe is a fine carpet club. This hotel is the newest in Stateline (opened in 1980) and has 440 rooms; the casino is only vaguely reminiscent of Caesars Las Vegas, with Corinthian columns and an 18-foot-tall statue of Augustus Caesar that greets you as you enter. The indoor pool is something to see: rock borders, a big rock waterfall with a tunnel you can swim through, and poolside dining at the Primavera Italian restaurant. After a day on the hiking trails or slopes, Caesars Spa provides a variety of relaxing treatments. As for dining the fashionable Stone St. Bar and Grill replaced the tired old Planet Hollywood, and in addition to the four other restaurants and buffet.

Bill's

This casino (owned by Harrah's and named after Bill Harrah) is low-roller heaven for Tahoe. You can't exactly call it a sawdust joint, but you will find a low-key, low-roller atmosphere. It also has a gaggle of $3 blackjack tables, even on the weekends (also one roulette and one crap table), and even a few penny slots. Hearty eaters should explore Bill's Roadhouse restaurant, which serves a 22-ounce steak (if you manage to finish one, you get your picture posted on the Wall of Fame).

Recreation

The **Round Hill Pines Beach & Marina** is on a half-mile-long sandy beach two miles north of the casinos and a half-mile north of the Round Hill Shopping Center. Facilities include a large deck area, a heated swimming pool, a tennis court, volleyball courts, horseshoe pits, barbecues, a deli, and a bar. Activities include water-skiing, fishing, parasailing, and private lake tours. **H2O Sports,** 775/4155 or 775/588-3055, rents Sea-Doos, kayaks, Sea Cycles, and paddleboats. Guided two-hour Sea Doo Excursions to Emerald Bay depart in the morning. Also here are the **Don Borges Water Ski School,** 530/541-1351, and **Mile High Fishing Charters,** 775/588-4155 or 530/541-5312.

The *Tahoe Star,* a 54-foot luxury yacht operated by Harrah's, offers cruises on the lake including an Emerald Bay Cruise ($38, children $23), a Historic East Shore Cruise ($38, children $23), and a Sunset Cocktail Cruise to Emerald Bay ($38; no children). Phone 775/586-6505 or 800/729-4362 for reservations.

You can fly a hot-air balloon right over Lake Tahoe with **Lake Tahoe Balloons,** 530/544-1221 or 800/872-9294.

The **Shore Line Ski and Sports,** 259 Kingsbury Grade, 775/588-8777, rents mountain bikes, mountain boards, inline skates, and off-road and inline skateboards in summer, skis and snowboards in winter. Electric touring bikes can be rented from **Leif and Jana's,** based at the Horizon Casino, 775/901-1360.

Sleigh rides, hayrides, and carriage rides are offered by the **Borges Family,** departing from near the casinos; 775/588-2953 or 800/726-RIDE.

Several fishing guides are available around the lake, including **Tahoe Sportfishing,** 775/586-9338 or 530/541-5448, **O'Malley's Fishing Charters,** 775/588-4102, and **Mile High Fishing Charters,** 530/541-5312.

Accommodations

Caesars Tahoe, 55 US 50, 775/586-4694 or 800/648-3353, www.caesars.com, has 440 rooms for $89–225 a night. **Harrah's Lake Tahoe,** off US 50, 775/588-6611 or 800/HARRAHS, www.harrahs.com, has 532 rooms for $119–209 a night. **Harveys Resort Hotel & Casino,** US 50 and Stateline Ave., 775/588-2411 or 800/HARVEYS, www.harrahs.com, has 740 rooms that range from $119–209 weekdays, $89–299 weekends. **Horizon Casino Resort,** off US 50, 775/588-6211 or 800/648-3322, www.horizoncasino.com, has 539 rooms that range from $99 to $169 a night. And the **Lakeside Inn & Casino,** US 50 at Kingsbury Grade, 775/588-7777 or 800/624-7980, has 124 low-rise motel rooms ranging $79–139 a night.

The **Pine Cone Resort,** in Nevada right on the highway about five miles from the state line, just north of Nevada Beach, 775/588-6561, has condo-like rooms, with kitchenettes and fireplaces, for $85–95 in summer, $75–85 off-season. The road's a bit noisy in the daytime but quiets down in the evening.

Food

Harveys: Downstairs on the tunnel level is Cabo Wabo, open daily 11 A.M.–10 P.M., with Mexican dishes and specialty drinks made from Sammy Hagar's infamous Cabo Wabo tequila. The lounge portion of the restaurant features live entertainment. Upstairs in the casino, the Sage Room steakhouse opens nightly at 6 P.M., just as it has for nearly 50 years. Harveys also has a Hard Rock Café and the casual Carriage House. Seafood lovers can get their fill at the resort's Pacifica Seafood Buffet.

The top of the lot is the four-diamond Llewellyn's, named after Harvey Gross's wife. This reasonably priced gourmet room on the 19th floor has the best lake views of all the restaurants at Stateline, with two-window alcoves and three levels of tables. If you're in the mood for the view but not an elaborate meal, relax in the Peak Lounge and order up an appetizer, salad, or bowl of soup. Llewellyn's also hosts a Sunday champagne brunch.

Harrah's: There's an excellent deli, the North

Beach, in the southwest corner of the sprawling casino. Friday's Station steakhouse on the 18th floor with a lake and mountain view opens daily at 5:30 P.M. On the other side of the top floor is the Forest Buffet, with concrete tree trunks and brass-leaf branches, and a gorgeous panorama to the south. Harrah's answer to Llewellyn's at Harveys is the Summit on the 16th floor, open Wednesday through Sunday at 5:30 P.M., a beautifully appointed room with balcony dining, mountain views, and everything à la carte. Bill's Roadhouse Cafe has some of the least expensive food at a casino at Stateline. This place is casual, cramped, and crowded on weekends.

Caesars: This place has the Broiler Room steakhouse, Primavera Italian restaurant poolside, the Stone St. Bar and Grill, a Subway, and the Roman Feast buffet serving breakfast, lunch, dinner, and a Sunday champagne brunch. Club Nero is Stateline's hot spot, opening at 8 P.M. with DJ music and a laser show. By the way, according to Mario Puzo in *Inside Las Vegas,* Emperor Nero was not fiddling while Rome was burning. He was shooting dice and losing.

Information

The **Tahoe-Douglas Chamber of Commerce Visitor Center** is directly across the parking lot from the Shell station on the ground floor at the Round Hill Shopping Center about a mile north of Stateline, 195 US 50, 775/588-4591, www.tahoe chamber.org. This is an attractive and highly useful little place, with fine exhibits, pretty photographs and posters, tons of information and brochures on everything from casinos to nature trails to ski packages to weddings, coupon booklets, and a reservation service; it also sells T-shirts, books, and video postcards. Open daily 9 A.M.–5 P.M.

The California strip of US 50 west of the border is lined with motels; for more information, contact the **Lake Tahoe Visitors Authority,** 1156 Ski Run Blvd., South Lake Tahoe, 530/544-5050, www.virtualtahoe.com; open Mon.–Fri. 8:30 A.M.–5 P.M. To make reservations or request free materials, call 800/AT-TAHOE. Its *Lake Tahoe Travel Planner* has a good amount of useful information, including a lodging guide.

Also on the California side is the **South Lake Tahoe Chamber of Commerce,** 3066 Lake Tahoe Blvd., 530/541-5255, www.tahoeinfo.com, with heaps of useful brochures, magazines, etc. It's open every day but Sunday 9 A.M.–5 P.M. Another excellent source of information about the California side of the lake is Kim Weir's *Moon Handbooks Northern California.*

EAST SHORE
Nevada Beach

This large U.S. Forest Service beach, day-use area, and campground, only two miles north on US 50 from Stateline (and take a left at Elk Point), is one of the most popular beaches along the lake. Open May 1 through mid-October, its parking lots are spread well apart, which spreads out the people, too. There's a $5 per vehicle entrance fee for day use.

Nevada Beach Campground is one of the most popular beaches and campgrounds on Lake Tahoe; this place fills up fast. Make reservations as far in advance as possible (up to 240 days); if you don't have a reservation, you can show up at 9 A.M. to see if someone left early. Checkout time is officially 2 P.M., but many campers spend a few extra hours on the beach and then leave. A good method is to pay the $5 for the day, hang out on the beach, then every so often take a walk through the campground to see what's vacant (see the campground host to pay for first-come, first-served sites). The camping is under the trees, shared equally by tenters and RVers. The beach is a two-minute walk. There are 54 campsites for tents or self-contained motor homes up to 35 feet. Piped drinking water, flush toilets, picnic tables, grills, and fire pits are provided. There is a campground host. The maximum stay is 10 days. Reservations are recommended, 877/444-6777; for more info call the park office at 775/588-5562. The fee is $22 and $24 per campsite. A pretty walk or aerobic run from here is north up Elks Avenue to Elk Point, a fairly exclusive residential neighborhood overlooking Zephyr Cove.

Round Hill Beach Resort

Another little ways up the round on the left is a

SAM CLEMENS VISITS TAHOE

Sam Clemens arrived in Carson City on the Overland Stage in July 1861 with his brother Orion, who had been appointed Secretary to James Nye, governor of the new Nevada Territory. Sam, in his self-appointed position as secretary to the Secretary, quickly found that he "had nothing to do and no salary." Heeding the call of the wild, he and a friend therefore set off on the Bigler Toll Road up to Lake Tahoe.

At this time, from their encampment, they could hear "a sawmill and some workmen" at Glenbrook, "but there were not fifteen other human beings throughout the wide circumference of the lake." They posted notice of their timber ranch and felled a few trees to inaugurate it.

They found a small skiff and rowed it upon the water—"not merely transparent, but dazzlingly, brilliantly so." They fished, read, smoked, hiked, and heard no sounds "but those that were made by the wind and the waves, the sighing of the pines, and now and then the far-off thunder of an avalanche. The view was always fascinating: "the eye never tired of gazing, night or day, calm or storm; it suffered but one grief, and that was that it could not look always, but must close sometimes in sleep."

Still, they never required any paregoric to effect such a sleep. For there was "no end of wholesome medicine" in the life they led for those few idyllic weeks on the shores of Lake Tahoe. "Three months would restore an Egyptian mummy to his pristine vigor and give him an appetite like an alligator," Clemens enthused in *Roughing It*. He did, however, qualify his statement, lest any readers infer any exaggeration, with "I do not mean the oldest and driest mummies, of course, but the fresher ones."

Forest Service sign for this marina; you twist and turn down to the beach, where it's $7 to park (check in at the snack bar). There's a small beach area and you can rent Sea-Doos. Sit on the deck or stroll out the dock; this is mostly a boat zone.

Zephyr Cove

This is an action-packed small marina a few miles north of Nevada Beach on US 50; its long pier is home base for the MS *Dixie II* paddlewheeler and *Woodwind II* sailing vessel. You can also arrange sailing and fishing charters, sailboarding, Jet-Skiing, boating, parasailing, horseback riding, and marrying. There's also a bar and grill, resort, and RV park and campground.

The original *Dixie* started her illustrious career on the Mississippi in 1927 and was brought to Tahoe in 1947 to become a floating casino. Legal squabbles over ownership prevented the *Dixie* from fulfilling that mission, and she sank under mysterious circumstances in shallow water off Cave Rock in 1949. The boat was raised in 1952, but didn't start tour cruises until 1972. The *Dixie I* made an estimated 17,000 trips on the lake in 22 years, but repairs necessary to pass the 20-year Coast Guard inspection in 1993 would have cost nearly $2.5 million. Instead, the owners decided to dry dock *Dixie I* and build *Dixie II* from scratch.

The *Dixie II* has a carrying capacity of 550 people (compared to the *Dixie I's* 360). It cost $4 million to build at a shipyard in LaCrosse, Wisconsin, and was shipped to Tahoe in four pieces in spring 1994. The main deck has a dining area for 200 and the galley; the upper deck is also enclosed for dancing and cocktails (and the captain's cabin). The "hurricane deck" is open-air, and hosts the snack bar and pilothouse. A variety of cruises depart from the cove year-round, starting at $26 for the two-hour Emerald Bay trip, up to $55 for the 3.5-hour dinner-dance excursion. Call 775/589-4906 for info and reservations.

The 55-foot *Woodwind II* catamaran sails from Zephyr Cove with up to 50 passengers, several times daily, from March or April through October, weather permitting. Eastern Shoreline and Happy Hour cruises cost $26 adults, $12 ages 4–13; the Sunset Champagne Cruise costs $32. Call 775/588-3000 or 888/867-6394, or visit www.tahoeboatcruises.com, for reservations and current info. The same company also operates a 41-foot, 30-passenger trimaran, the *Woodwind I*, departing from Camp Richardson on the south side of the lake and cruising to Emerald Bay.

For a cruise with a more historical bent, the company also offers outings on classic wooden motor yachts, the *Tahoe* (which departs from Zephyr Cove) and the *Safari Rose* (docking at Tahoe Keys Marina). The yacht cruises take passengers to either the Thunderbird Lodge Historic Site (the *Tahoe*) or the Hellman-Ehrman Mansion (the *Safari Rose*). Both offer guided walking tours of the fascinating properties (the Thunderbird Lodge was recently restored and added to the National Register of Historic Places). The *Safari Rose* also offers a six-hour, around-the-lake cruise that includes breakfast and lunch. Cost for all cruises is $95 adults, $49 ages 7–12; lunch included.

Zephyr Cove Resort Marina, 775/588-6644, rents open bow runabouts, ski boats, cruisers, deck boats, pedal boats, canoes, kayaks, electric Sunkats, water-skis, wetsuits, and more. Reservations are a good idea.

Hop a horse at **Zephyr Cove Stables,** 775/588-5664: one-hour ride $30, one-and-half-hour $45, two-hour ride $60, dinner ride $45.

A snack shop offers burgers, and a bar and grill restaurant overlooks the pier. A free shuttle runs back and forth to the casino area. Finally, after an exciting day on the water with your honey, why not get married at **Lakeside Chapel,** 775/831-6419?

In winter, the **Zephyr Cove Snowmobile Center,** 775/589-4908, is the largest snowmobile touring center in the USA, with more than 100 Ski-Doo Touring E snowmobiles, including single ($89) and double ($139) rider machines. Tours depart four times daily.

Then spend the night in one of Zephyr Cove Resort's rooms, 778/589-4907. The resort was built in the early 1900s and much of the original architecture and charm remain. A variety of accommodations includes six rooms in the lodge that sleep from two to six; there are also bungalows, cabins, cottages, studios, and chalets. Rates start at $60 and ascend to $260.

You can also camp or park an RV across the highway from the lodge at **Zephyr Cove RV Park,** 775/589-4907, a recently renovated campground under the pine trees. There are 93 spaces for motor homes, all with full hookups; seven are pull-throughs. There are also 57 tent sites. Restrooms have flush toilets and hot showers; public phone, sewage disposal, and laundry are available at the park.

Reservations are recommended for the summer, especially on weekends. The fee is $15–20 for tent sites ($100 for the week), $25–48 for RV sites ($150 per week). If you need a shower you can grab one for $3. Note: Discount coupons for Zephyr Cove's many attractions are ubiquitous. Get $5 off horseback rides and motorboat rentals, $4 off the *Dixie* cruises and **Whirlwind** rides, $4 off T-shirts, and two-for-one soft drinks or beer at the Sunset Bar and Grill.

Lake Tahoe–Nevada State Park

Continue north on US 50 four miles to **Cave Rock,** one of Tahoe's legendary landmarks. One tunnel through it dates from the early 1900s, another dates back to prehistory, fashioned by the Great Spirit with a spear. This is one of only three tunnels (that you can drive through) in the whole state; the others are on I-80 east of Carlin and the new airport access in Las Vegas. Just before you reach the tunnel, there's a turnoff for a parking lot, lakefront picnic area, and a boat launch, with Cave Rock towering overhead. Day-use fees are charged at Cave Rock beach: $6 per vehicle, or $2 for bike-ins and walk-ins.

In another four miles is the Glenbrook historical marker. Glenbrook was the site of the first non-Washo settlements at Lake Tahoe, dating from 1860. Friday's Station opened that year a few miles above Glenbrook along the Placerville Road to Genoa over Kingsbury Grade. A year later, A. W. Pray established a sawmill at Glenbrook, and in 1862, the Lake Bigler Toll Road connected Friday's Station to Carson City by way of King's Canyon, the route US 50 follows today. Finally, in 1863 Tahoe's first hotel was constructed at Glenbrook. Glenbrook is a small residential area with a country club.

Just beyond is the intersection of US 50 and Route 28. A right onto US 50 crests Spooner

Summit and heads down to Carson City. Go left to continue north up the east shore of the lake.

Almost immediately, you enter Lake Tahoe–Nevada State Park. It preserves three miles of shoreline, plus a 10-mile-long stretch of the wooded Carson Range, and adjoins Toiyabe National Forest. There's a lot of wilderness to explore here, with elevations between 6,200 and 8,900 feet, on several high-country trails. Most flora is second growth, at most 120 years old: pine, fir, cedar, and aspen to 7,000 feet, red fir and lodgepole pine above. Countless birds and rodents live here. The black bear population is increasing hereabouts as well.

Turn right into Spooner Lake parking lot; $6 to park, $2 to bike or walk in. Stroll down to the lake. An easy 2.3-mile nature trail circles the lake, taking about an hour; keep an eye out for birds and wildlife. A hundred feet to the left is a post that marks the five-mile trail through North Canyon to Marlette Lake, which still supplies water to Virginia City, just as it has for 120 years; the moderate 10-mile round-trip trail takes about four to six hours to traverse. Fishing is not allowed at Marlette Lake, due to hatchery operations. The trail continues 11 miles to the far trailhead at Hidden Beach; it has become part of the Tahoe Rim Trail. The Hidden Beach to Twin Lakes trail, a moderate five-mile round-trip hike, takes around four hours. Fishing at Spooner Lake is catch-and-release only; the lake is stocked with trout.

In summer, activities at Spooner Lake include hiking and mountain biking on the **Flume Trail.** This ride, an exciting singletrack 1,600 feet above Lake Tahoe, is one of the most scenic rides anywhere, providing spectacular views of Lake Tahoe; the trail follows the path of an historic flume line that once provided water to the silver mines of Virginia City. Most mountain bike parties begin at Spooner Lake; take North Canyon Road to Marlette Lake dam (six miles, 800 foot gain) and follow the historic flume line 4.4 miles to Tunnel Creek Rd. From there you can return to Spooner Lake, a 21-mile round trip, 3–5 hours; descend 1,600 feet (2.5 miles) to Route 28, a 13-mile one-way trip, 3–4 hours. Take a backcountry loop back to Spooner Lake (24 miles round trip, 4–6 hours); or a different backcoun-

try loop back to Spooner Lake via the Tahoe Rim Trail (22 miles, 2,000-foot gain). Nevada's Division of State Parks published a pamphlet with a basic map and information about these trails, called *Lake Tahoe Nevada State Park Backcountry;* look for it at the state park office, 775/831-0494, or at the Incline Village/Crystal Bay Visitors and Convention Bureau.

You can bring your own bike and use the **Flume Trail Shuttle Service** ($10 per person) to bring you back up to Spooner Lake, or rent a bike for $39, from the **Spooner Lake Outdoor Company,** 775/749-5349.

In winter, Spooner Lake has 101 km of groomed cross-country-skiing trails spread over 8,000 acres with skiing for beginners up to experts. The **lodge** is right off Route 28, open daily 8:30 A.M.–5 P.M. Trail fees range from free (under 7 or over 70) to $18, and ski rentals from $1 to $17.50. Lessons are also available. Call 775/887-8844 for conditions or 775/749-5349 for more info.

Spooner Lake does not have facilities for camping, but **Spooner Lake Cabins,** 775/749-5349 or 888/858-8844, www.spoonerlake.com, offers self-contained cabins with fully equipped kitchens for $95–275 in summer and fall, $149–319 in winter.

Eight miles north of this area is **Sand Harbor,** the main beach in the park. An arm of land, crowded with pines and boulders, juts into the lake. On the south side lies a gorgeous crescent beach—long, sandy, and sunny. Because of the spit, and the prevailing winds and currents, the swells are occasionally high enough to surf (foam boards are best; fresh water is not as buoyant as salt). The term often used to describe the water temperature is "bracing." The water reaches its highest temperature during the last two weeks of July: 68°F on the surface.

The north side of the spit is a different lake entirely: calm, clear, rugged with rocks, little beach. Known as Diver's Cove, it's a great spot for snorkeling and boulder hopping.

Sandy Point at the end of the spit has an excellent three-quarter-mile nature trail with interpretive displays in summer (left of the first parking lot). It takes an easy half-hour and is well worth the time for the close look at the lake ecology. Pick up free handouts at park headquarters near the entrance.

Sand Harbor has a wheelchair-accessible boardwalk, three large parking lots, bathrooms, group picnic facilities, lots of water fountains, and no concession stands. This is good for limiting litter, but bring everything with you, except bottles (prohibited). Get there early on weekends. It's open June through August daily from 8 A.M. on, closing at 9 P.M.; May through September until 7 P.M.; October through March until 5 P.M. Entrance costs $8 per vehicle, $15 for boat launching, or $2 for walk-ins.

During the summer Sand Harbor is the site of a fine music and drama festival in an excellent venue with a new $2 million outdoor stage. Held every summer since 1978, the North Tahoe Fine Arts Council sponsors four days of music in mid-July and a **Shakespeare Festival** during the entire month of August. Call 800/74-SHOWS to order tickets and for current details; you can also buy tickets at the Incline Village Visitors Center.

Another mile and a half brings you to Memorial Point overlook and parking lot. From here, it's just under a mile to the state park's **north trailhead,** which is unmarked but obvious at a fire track between two posts. You can also park a quarter mile farther on the north side of the trailhead just beyond the park boundaries, but here you're competing with cars to Hidden Beach and from the south residential section of Incline Village. The trail starts climbing quickly up the granite slopes of the Carson Range. It's a hour to Tunnel Creek Station (one and a half miles), another hour (one mile) to Twin Lakes, and one more hour to Hobart Creek Reservoir, where you loop back past Red House camping area to Tunnel Creek. Or walk across the park down to Spooner Lake, 16 miles, at least 10 hours. Two hike-in **campgrounds,** Marlette Peak and North Canyon, are available in the backcountry; each has around 10 campsites, all first-come, first-served; 775/831-0494 for info.

Hidden Beach is a half-mile-long stretch of prime Tahoe shoreline, where nude bathing and skinny-dipping are de rigueur. The U.S. Forest Service in 1992 bought 41 acres hereabouts for $7 million from the Trust for Public Land, which

acquired the property from William Bliss. Since 1982, the Trust has bought up and protected nearly 11,000 acres of Tahoe real estate, at a cost of nearly $90 million. How to get to Secret Harbor is kind of a secret, but here's a hint: Grab a parking space near other cars on the stretch between the north edge of the state park and the south edge of Incline Village, then bushwhack through the under- and overgrowth down to the lake.

INCLINE VILLAGE

Drive around town. Head up Ski Way to the town's own (public) ski area, or down Country Club Drive past the Hyatt Regency. Go right on Lakeshore Drive to check out one of the most valuable and scenic two-mile stretches of real estate in Nevada. Tool around the town's own golf courses, tennis clubs, beaches, and ski resorts, then stop in at the chamber of commerce for some super-slick local brochures. If you haven't quite gotten the idea that Incline Village is, well, prosperous, consider this: For a town of just under 8,000 year-round residents, there are more than two dozen real estate agencies and *300 agents,* five banks, and four title companies. Incline Villagers make up 3 percent of the population of Washoe County and pay 10 percent of the total property tax the county collects.

This area has been inclining upward since 1874, when the Great Incline Tramway was completed on Incline Mountain (it started at Tramway Drive at the far south end and oldest part of town, then passed through what's now the Ponderosa Ranch). This high-wire act rose 1,400 feet in elevation in only 4,000 feet of distance, for a straight-up grade of 35 percent. Two 12-foot wheels powered by a 40-horsepower steam engine hoisted log-loaded flat cars up to the summit, where they were shot down a flume, milled in Washoe Valley, and freighted to Virginia City. The empty car going down counterbalanced the loaded one going up, using technology that was later employed in San Francisco's cable cars.

By the early 1890s, the Comstock was dead and every single tree within 10 miles of the incline had been cut down. The operation ceased;

TREES ARE STILL DYING FOR THE COMSTOCK

Only 100–125 years ago, 50,000 acres of virgin forest around Lake Tahoe, mostly sugar and Jeffrey pine, cedar, and some fir, were clear-cut, then milled, shipped, and buried forever in the shafts, drifts, stopes, and tunnels of undermined Mt. Davidson. The big Jeffreys were what the loggers were after, and they took them all, leaving only a few firs, which provided the seeds of today's forest. The second-growth fir has regenerated the lake's forests, but they are completely lacking in diversity, age, size, and therefore health.

Furthermore, these young trees have overpopulated their habitat, and fir, unlike pine, is extremely drought-intolerant, which has left most of the forest susceptible to attack by fir beetles. Since most of the lakeside is also thickly settled, fire, which thins the forests naturally, has been suppressed, and conservation policies strictly inhibit logging activities. Combine all these factors and you'll understand why so many of Tahoe's trees are dead or dying.

Though some tree die-off is beneficial to the health of the forest, the recent ravages are unprecedented. Tahoe National Forest officials estimate that 25–33 percent of the trees in the 200,000-acre Tahoe Basin are dead or dying, and half the forest, roughly four million trees, is in grave danger from the drought and insects. Of course, the danger is only relative to people, houses, and to some extent wildlife. The natural cycle of a forest is growth, decay, fire, and regeneration. Native Americans found it not inconvenient to live with fire, simply moving their settlements to escape the danger. White settlers, however, built houses that couldn't easily be moved out of the way of the flames and therefore saw forest fires as destructive. For the last 100 years, the lack of fire has been the one element preventing the forest from recovering its health.

On the other hand, it's possible that the beetles are doing fire's work for it by thinning the forest. The insects also supply food for birds and other predators. Soon, predator populations will increase and eliminate the beetles. Then it'll rain. And a new forest will emerge. Nature could be providing a cycle to cope with the human suppression of fire.

Since late 1995, California and Nevada forestry crews have cleared 11,000 acres of fire hazards, but that's only 25 percent of the highly susceptible areas. Even so, the danger of wildfire mounts, since the dead trees that fall to the forest floor increase the danger. "Defensible space"—landscaping maintenance and clearing dead trees from privately owned land to protect houses—is the buzzword of the day, but homeowners have been slow to clean up, which threatens their own, and their neighbors' property.

the post office at Incline Village closed in 1895. The north shore of Lake Tahoe remained remote through the 1950s, when the only life at Incline was a small trailer park (where Burnt Cedar Beach is today).

Then, in 1960, a real estate investor from Oklahoma started up Crystal Bay Development Company, bought 9,000 north-shore acres for $25 million, and designed a development for 10,000 people. The original layout is still very much intact, with mansions on the lake, chalets on the mountainsides, and condos on the flats, all surrounded by dense forest, thanks to strict tree-cutting regulations. The commercial zones stretch in a thin line along Route 28 and down Southwood Boulevard designed to prevent congestion and preclude the establishment of a town center.

The town of Incline Village is still privately owned. The "local government" is known as the Incline Village General Improvement District (IVGID), which manages the beaches, ski resort, golf course, recreation center, and forests. (The beaches are open only to local homeowners and their guests, who pay $5.) A movement has been gathering steam over the past half a decade to secede from Washoe County.

Incline is said to have the best weather on the lake: 300 days of sunshine a year, and the least accumulations of snow. Still, the population more than doubles in the balmy summer months. The Village has more outdoor-related stores—outfitters, ski and ski repair, sportswear, camping, running shoes, cycling, fishing, and the like—than anywhere in Nevada, and the majority of residents and visitors are decked out in sweats, warm-ups, bike shorts, ski suits, sailing gear, and Vuarnets. Which all makes it a little interesting to think that Incline Village is still in Nevada and not California, and in Washoe County to boot. It's as far away from Gerlach as it could possibly be—in every sense but one: The people are uniformly friendly and helpful, which makes Incline, same as Gerlach, a great place to visit.

The Thunderbird Lodge

This spectacular example of historic preservation just south of Incline Village is well worth taking the time to explore. The lodge was built in 1936 by the fabulously wealthy George Whittell, who earned his money the old-fashioned way: He inherited it. Noted Nevada architect Frederic DeLongchamps designed the lakeside beauty as Whittell's summer cottage, incorporating two master bedrooms, a great room with a movie screen, and extensive servants' quarters. Whittell, a noted playboy of his day, entertained guests in the "card house," a beautiful stone room that was connected to the house via a tunnel (and yes, you get to go through it!). Whittell also had a penchant for wild animals, and visitors can inspect the Elephant House, which once was home to the millionaire's pet pachyderm, Mingo. Although the property has been in private hands over the years, various public agencies have acquired it and the Thunderbird Lodge Preservation Society now oversees the maintenance and tour operations. Speaking of which, tours are available by reservation only, limited to 20 at a time. Visitors will find parking and shuttle pickup at the Incline Village/Crystal Bay Visitor Center, 969 Tahoe Blvd. in Incline Village. Shuttles depart on the hour Wednesday and Thursday 9 A.M.–2 P.M., and Fridaay and Saturday 9 A.M.–11 A.M. Tour prices, which include the shuttle, are $25 for adults and $10 children (K–12 grades); children under five are free, but strollers are not allowed. Visitors also can check out the property via boat tours from Zephyr Cove. For information, call 775/832-8750 or 800/GO-TAHOE.

The Ponderosa Ranch

Bonanza made its debut on NBC in September 1959, sponsored by Chevrolet. The show became the most popular and successful television program ever, eventually reaching 88 countries in 12 languages for a total of 400 million viewers—

Bonanza!

and this in the youth of the medium. It rendered Virginia City a household word, its effect on the ghost town's revival incalculable. It became as much a myth of its own as the myth of the American West itself: God's country, where a man is a man, his word is his bond, reason and justice prevail, and the good guys always wear white and win.

Some scenes for the show were filmed on location around Lake Tahoe, which gave Bill and Joyce Anderson the idea to buy ranch property near the north shore, call it the Ponderosa, reproduce the sets and props of the show, and charge admission. Immediately, the lines separating the global myth of the Cartwright family's ranch from the Ponderosa tourist attraction blurred into oblivion. In fact, even the writers and directors began believing it to be the mythical Ponderosa and filmed there frequently. The cast simply remained in costume to interact with the hordes passing through the gate. It was truly a unique episode in the history of television technology and its effect on consciousness. Not to mention one of the most brilliant marketing coups in Nevada history.

The Ponderosa Ranch, 775/831-0691, www .ponderosaranch.com, is open mid-April through October 31, daily 9:30 A.M.–6 P.M. (last tickets sold at 5 P.M.), $12.50 adults, $7.50 kids 5–11, hayride $2. From Memorial Day weekend through Labor Day, entertainment includes daily live Wild West shows, hay-wagon breakfast rides, and guided horseback rides (stables 775/831-2154). Another attraction is an "authentic" Old West town, with lots of fun attractions.

Casinos

Of the five casinos on the north shore, one is in Incline, the other four in Crystal Bay. No other hotel-casino in Nevada is so close to forest and lakeside. The state line on the north shore has a much less "religious" feel to it than the south shore, but a lot more "reverence." This tiny corner of the state would be California but for the casinos. Where else can you walk away from a crap table and into some manzanita?

Hyatt Regency, Country Club Dr. and Lakeshore, has 424 rooms. But you'd never know

it from the outside. The casino, along with its lodgelike interior with a massive stone fireplace, has high-limit games and a big-money atmosphere.

The **Tahoe Biltmore** and **Crystal Bay Club** are right on Route 28 a block before the Placer County, California, line. Both are homey compared to the places at the other end of the lake. Between them they have two dozen blackjack tables, and crap and roulette.

Jim Kelley's **Nugget** is a slot shop, as classy in its way as the Hyatt is in its. This could be the state's only redbrick casino, which fits in nicely at the lake.

But the pièce de résistance of north shore is the **Cal-Neva Resort Spa and Casino.** The nine-story hotel building sits on a narrow head of land at the edge of Crystal Bay; each of the 220 rooms has an impressive view. It's the only hotel-casino in Nevada that qualifies for the title of "lodge," with features such as a real log exterior, stone vestibule, and stone flooring. The lodge part of the Cal-Neva is in California; the state line runs smack down the center of the huge stone hearth (as well as through the middle of the swimming pool outside). Known as the Indian Room for the poignant display of and by the Washo, the lobby has a fireplace burning real wood, massive granite boulders topped with a big bobcat, wooden cathedral ceiling, and big-game trophies; take some time to absorb the graphically presented story of the Washo. Peek out the back door to see the Washo bedrock mortar in a stone boulder on the deck. The round barroom is also one of a kind. The round room is paneled in carved wood (below) and mirrors (above), with an attractive stained-glass dome overhead.

The Cal-Neva opened over Memorial Day weekend 1926. Supposedly, it operated as an illegal casino until 1931, when gambling was legalized in Nevada. Prohibition made barely a dent in its patrons' alcohol consumption. Frank Sinatra owned it in the 1960s when, legend has it, Marilyn Monroe met President Kennedy there (this is apparently apocryphal; Guy Rocha, state archivist, has thoroughly debunked the myth and insists that Kennedy never visited the Cal-Neva). The Gaming Commission revoked Frank's license for allowing Chicago's Sam Giancana to stay and play on the premises.

After that, the Cal-Neva (which has no connection to the Club Cal-Neva in downtown Reno) went into a slow decline, until it was closed in 1983 by the state for gaming violations. It reopened three years and $11 million later. The latest owner, Chuck Bluth, reduced the casino by 30 percent (possibly the only casino in Nevada that's *shrunk* in the past 25 years) to re-create the original lodge. Today, the Cal-Neva is once again a true Tahoe resort. In the past few years, the resort facilities have been expanding. Weddings and honeymoons now account for 30 percent of the Cal-Neva's business, same as the casino.

Accommodations

The **Hyatt Regency Lake Tahoe Resort & Casino,** 111 Country Club Dr. at Lakeshore Blvd., 775/832-1234 or 800/233-1234, www .laketahoe.hyatt.com, has it all: private beach, tennis courts, health club, bike and nature trails, boat rentals, golf, and 458 rooms that go from $180–235 (suites $500–850) off season, up to $245–320 (suites $600–1385) high season (June–Sept., and the Christmas season).

The **Cal-Neva Resort,** 2 Stateline Rd., Crystal Bay, 775/832-4000 or 800/CAL-NEVA, www.calnevaresort.com, has 220 rooms for $85–289.

The **Tahoe Biltmore Lodge & Casino,** 5 Route 28, 775/831-0660 or 800-BILTMOR, www.tahoebiltmore.com, offers 92 rooms from $59–159.

Inn at Incline, 1003 Tahoe Blvd., 775/831-1052 or 800/824-6391, www.innatincline.com, is just south of Country Club Drive. Its 38 mini-suites range from $69 to $189 a night, and it has a surprise in the basement: indoor swimming pool, hot tub, and sauna. In Crystal Bay, the **Crystal Bay Motel,** 24 Route 28, 775/831-0287, has 18 rooms for $40–125.

All Tahoe guides and travel planners list vacation rentals, apartments, and condos. But there is one special place in Incline Village, the only bed-and-breakfast on the east (and part of the north) side of the lake. **Haus Bavaria,** 593 N. Dyer Circle, 775/831-6122 or 800/731-6222, is a

two-story stucco-and-wood chalet built by a German couple in 1980. There are five guest rooms upstairs, each with a private bath, and a large sitting room with a woodstove. Breakfast is served by owner Bick Hewitt, a transplanted San Diego airline worker, who also provides passes to Incline's private beaches and indoor recreation center. Rates are $109–175.

Crystal Bay Food

Starting from the north end is **Soule Domain,** Stateline Rd. right on the border, west across the street from the Biltmore's parking lot, 530/546-7529. Open nightly 6–10 P.M., this is one of two non-casino restaurants in Crystal Bay. In a cozy log cabin complete with fireplace, wood fence, and shake roof, Charlie and Steven Soule serve untraditional American-Italian fare, with appetizers such as garlic ravioli with lamb and olive filling, shrimp scampi, softshell crab, shiitake mushrooms, and escargot. Salads include Caesar, Greek, or spinach, and an interesting grilled lamb and goat cheese. Entrées include fresh vegetables in a pastry shell with swiss cheese, herbs, and roasted garlic in a tomato cream sauce, fresh pasta of the day, rock shrimp (with sea scallops or with lobster and scallops), sliced chicken breast, vegan sautee, curried cashew chicken, New Zealand lamb, and filet mignon.

At the **Cal-Neva** is the Lakeview Room, with big picture windows overlooking Tahoe, open daily 7 A.M.–10 P.M. Be sure to check out the Circle Bar, with its massive stained-glass ceiling.

The **Biltmore** coffee shop is open 24 hours, and has a renowned $1.99 breakfast special with two eggs and meat. Daily specials include prime rib for $6.95, plus changing specials for each day of the week. The Biltmore also has the Pub and Grill and Aspen Cabaret, with 60 beers on tap, 30 different microbrews, finger food, darts, and pool tables.

Incline Village Food

The following restaurants are listed from north to south along Tahoe Boulevard.

The butcher counter at **Village Market** in the Village Center on Southwood sells good sandwiches. The **Grog n' Grist** on the corner of

Southwood and Tahoe, 775/831-1123, is a local lunch legend, sometimes cranking out 500 sandwiches a day from its big, bustling deli counter in the rear.

In the Christmas Tree Center is **Mofo's Pizza and Pasta,** 775/831-4999. Open daily 11 A.M.–10 P.M., it does subs, minipizzas, chicken wings, and entrées such as lasagna and pasta primavera.

A great place for breakfast and lunch is the **Wildflower Cafe,** 775/831-8072: eggs, burgers, and specials served on huge plates full of hearty food. This homey place has been a locals' favorite since 1984. Open 7 A.M.–2:30 P.M.

T's Rotisserie, 901 Tahoe Blvd., 775/831-2832, is tucked away in the little shopping center beside the 7-Eleven store and the Incline Cinema, but it's often full of locals who pack in for the delicious, inexpensive fare including unique rotisserie chicken and beef, big burritos, soft tacos, tostadas, Yucatan-style and soy-lime chicken, beef tri-tip, salads, and salsas. You can phone in "to go" orders. Open daily 11 A.M.–8 P.M., Sun. noon–8 P.M.

One of the only fast-food chains in Incline is a **Subway,** Village Blvd. just uphill from Tahoe Blvd., 775/831-3370. **Azzara's,** 775/831-0346, in the Raley's shopping center is great for Italian. Everything is delicious, and a bargain to boot. Open Tues.–Sun. 5–11 P.M. **Hacienda de la Sierra,** 931 Tahoe Blvd., 775/831-8300, is the favorite for Mexican, with medium prices, tasty food, and attractive decor. Open nightly, 4–10 P.M. **The Black Bear Coffee and Co. Bakery and Deli** 120 Country Club Dr., 775/832-7437, offers java, desserts, and sandwiches.

One of the standouts among Incline's culinary offerings is the **Big Water Grille,** Ski Way, 775/833-0606. Maple-smoked pork chops, green-tea smoked duck breast, grilled venison, and other creative entrées fuse perfectly with the relaxed atmosphere of the room, which overlooks the big waters of Lake Tahoe. Opens daily at 4:30 P.M.

The Hyatt has the 24-hour **Sierra Cafe,** 775/832-1234, an upscale coffee shop with a salad bar and seafood buffet weekends. There's also Ciao Mein Trattoria, open for dinner Wed.–Sun. 6–10 P.M., with Italian pastas and Chinese entrées. **Cutthroat's Saloon** has casual dining and live entertainment. The real fancy dining is across Lakeshore Drive at the **Lone Eagle Grill,** 775/832-3250, right on the lake. Lunch and dinner are served; there's also a Sunday champagne brunch 10:30 A.M.–2:30 P.M. If the food prices are too high, you can always sit and have a drink and enjoy the view.

Information

The **Incline Village/Crystal Bay Visitors and Convention Bureau,** 969 Tahoe Blvd. near the south end of town, 775/832-1606 or 800/GO-TAHOE, www.gotahoe.com, is open weekdays 9 A.M.–5 P.M., weekends and holidays 10 A.M.–4 P.M. It has a friendly, helpful staff and all the brochures and information you'll need, including everything from hiking trails and outdoor activities to restaurants and resorts.

The **library** is just north of the Christmas Tree Center, set back from the road a little, 775/832-4130. A sign points the way. This is a branch of the excellent Washoe County library system and has an admirably thorough Nevada shelf (against the right-hand wall). Also check out (so to speak) the historical black-and-white prints of Tahoe scenes through the years. It's very bright, often crowded, and has good long hours. Open Tues.–Fri. 9 A.M.–6:30 P.M., Sat. noon–5 P.M.

Virginia City

In the beginning was the word, and the word was gold. In reckless pursuit of the word, the whole wave of '49ers, the tens of thousands of gold-fevered stampeders, rushed to California, forever after known as the Golden State, entirely missing Nevada's Gold Creek and Gold Canyon and Gold Hill. But starting as early as 1851, a backwash of prospectors filtered east again to search the high desert for the precious word, and some prospectors stopped in Nevada on their way to California and stayed. At the time, this land at the edge of the eastern Sierra was referred to by the U.S. government as the western Utah Territory. The Latter-day Saints' administrators called it the Carson County Colony of the State of Deseret. The gentile (non-Mormon) settlers considered it eastern California. John C. Frémont considered it the western edge of the Great Basin Desert, which he'd explored and named only seven years previously. And the local prospectors referred to it as Washoe, after the Wa-She-Shu Indian tribe, for centuries the mountains' and desert's primary inhabitants.

HISTORY

Throughout the 1850s, a handful of hopefuls huddled over several Carson River creeks near present-day Dayton, panning a day's wages in summer and either hunkering down or heading out for the winter. Though the Grosch brothers, two young New Yorkers with a working knowledge of geology, mineralogy, and assay procedures, had an indication of the quality and immensity of the *silver* wealth in the vicinity, they both died suddenly in 1857, and their valuable information was buried with them. By around 1858, the placer gold in the river valley was depleted, and the prospectors fanned out. Some followed Gold Creek up Gold Canyon and settled a town called Gold Hill on Sun Mountain. A few hardcore miners, including James "Old Virginny" Finney (after whom Virginia City was eventually named), began digging *into* the ground in the spring of 1859; several

feet below the surface they struck quartzite containing serious gold.

Immediately, miners began digging in nearby canyons. Two Irishmen made their way up Six-Mile Canyon on the east side of Sun Mountain and located some color. After a few days of pulling out about $12 a day, Henry Comstock, a Canadian trapper, prospector, and blowhard, accused the pair of trespassing on his "ranch." Instead of challenging the preposterous claim, the prospectors gave Comstock a piece of nearby ground. Although none of the participants realized it at the time, the Comstock Lode had been found, claimed, and named.

The miners on Sun Mountain optimistically called their gopher hole the Ophir Mine, after the biblical land where the wealth of King Solomon was located. Yet they remained unaware of the real riches right beneath their feet. In fact, the more they dug, the more they got bogged down by a heavy blue-gray mud they'd never seen before. This mud polluted the quartz veins, settled quickly to the bottom of the sluice boxes, diluted the quicksilver—in general, seriously impeded recovery of the gold. The miners hated this mud with all their hearts. They cursed it and damned it and flung it aside. . . until, by happenstance, a visitor carried a chunk down to Placerville in July 1859 and had it assayed. The mud was found to contain $875 per ton in gold, and an incredible $3,000 per ton in pristine sulphuret of silver. The news spread immediately west and east, and a new rush began gathering steam. The Comstock Lode, Virginia City, and Nevada were about to explode onto the scene. The boom had begun.

Rush and Flush

An estimated 10,000 fortune-seekers remained poised on the west side of the Sierra Nevada in early 1860 until the passes cleared of snow, then swarmed over the ragged settlement on Sun Mountain that had waited out the winter. Many of these hopefuls, such as J. Ross Browne, preeminent travel and mining writer of his time,

VIRGINIA CITY

To Geiger Grade and Reno

■ CEMETERIES

● RV PARK

CARSON STREET

★ THE WAY IT WAS MUSEUM

■ POOL

■ PICNIC PARK

■ BASEBALL DIAMOND

To Six-Mile Canyon

MILL STREET

OPHIR PIT ■

★ MARSHALL MINT GOLD SHOP MUSEUM

A STREET

B STREET

C STREET

D STREET

HOWARD STREET

SUTTON STREET

MINER'S UNION

UNION BREWERY

BONANZA SALOON

STEWART STREET

PIPER'S OPERA HOUSE

SILVER STOPE

PIPER HOME ■

SILVER QUEEN

JULIA C. BULETTE RED LIGHT MUSEUM

UNION STREET

KENNEY & SPAULDING HOUSE ■

DELTA SALOON

BUCKET OF BLOOD SALOON

SITE OF ■ BIG BONANZA

COURTHOUSE

NEVADA GAMBLING MUSEUM

E STREET

F STREET

G STREET

VIRGINIA CITY VISITOR CENTER

■ PARKING LOT

1875 FIRE MONUMENT ■

PALACE SALOON

GOLD PANNING

TERRITORIAL ENTERPRISE

ST. PAUL'S ■

TAYLOR STREET

PONDEROSA SALOON MINE TOURS

MARK TWAIN BOOKSTORE

ST. MARY'S

VIRGINIA CITY RADIO MUSEUM

★ THE CASTLE MANSION

OLD WASHOE CLUB

VIRGINIA CITY MIDDLE SCHOOL

LIBERTY ENGINE COMPANY #1 MUSEUM

To Water Tanks and Mt. Davidson

CHAMBER OF COMMECE

PRESBYTERIAN CHURCH

WASHINGTON STREET

FLOWERY ST.

MACKAY MANSION

★ VIRGINIA AND TRUCKEE RAILROAD COMPANY

FOURTH WARD SCHOOL

CHOLLAR MANSION B&B ●

CHOLLAR MINE ■

SCALE NOT AVAILABLE

LORING CUT ■

To Gold Hill

© AVALON TRAVEL PUBLISHING, INC.

took a look and left. The conditions were rigorous to say the least, and only the hardiest and most committed men and women stuck it out in the early days.

During that summer of 1860, anarchy reigned supreme. Food, water, and fuel were perpetually scarce, though whiskey flowed from a dozen taps. The plushest living conditions were deplorable. Men slept in their gopher holes as much to get out of the wind as to protect against claim jumpers. Death was casual and commonplace. Several governments competed for jurisdiction. The original discoverers sold out to California speculators for a song. The mines, deepening under newly renamed Mt. Davidson (after a San Francisco silver broker), outgrew the technology available to keep them from collapsing.

In early 1861, however, a young engineer, Philip Deidesheimer, invented square-set timbering, which revolutionized hard-rock-mining support systems and allowed the Lode to be unloaded at depths whose lower limits no one would know for another 20 years. Quartz mills sprung up locally to refine the medium-grade ore. Steam engines replaced mule-powered hoisting equipment; steam pumps cleared the shafts

and stopes of water. The virgin forests of the eastern Sierra across Washoe Valley began to be systematically felled, freighted, and buried within the Comstock.

By 1863, square-set supports, stamp mills, territorial government, and polite society had ushered in the first golden age of Virginia City. Fifteen thousand residents clogged the steep eastern slope of Mt. Davidson in a boomtown the likes of which had never been seen before in the United States. Still, as the mines got deeper (to the 300-foot level) and the ore got richer, stock speculation and property litigation ran rampant, defining this early wildcat period of the development of the Comstock Lode. Thousands of claims—badly recorded according to vague laws enforced by Darwin's Theory—overlapped to the extent that the Comstock was "owned" in its entirety three or four times over. Hundreds of lawsuits clogged the territorial courts to determine rightful possession of a rat's maze of mines. Corruption in the courts became so pronounced that the distinction between judge and auctioneer was rhetorical. Speculation fever, heavy and sweaty, gripped the city. Stock certificates turned into the instant currency of the boom. The wildly

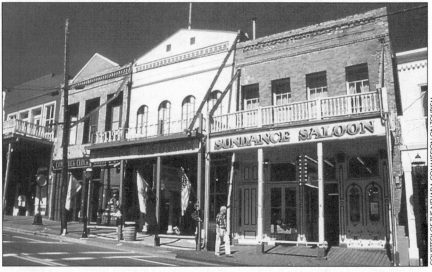

C Street

THE DEVIL AND J. ROSS BROWNE

John Ross Browne was one of the most prodigious travelers, prolific writers, productive illustrators, and improbable bureaucrats of his day. Born in Ireland in 1821, by the time he was 39 years old, he'd explored four continents, published three books, served as the official stenographer at the California constitutional convention, held jobs as a postal agent and customs inspector, regularly contributed articles to the popular *Harper's Monthly*, and become famous as one of the originators of the school of Western frontier humor. He was living in the Bay Area when "the cry of silver! Silver in Washoe!" was "borne on the wings of the wind from the Sierra Nevada" and "wafted through every street, lane, and alley of San Francisco."

Browne made his way on public transportation to Placerville and set off on foot over the mountains in the early spring of 1860.

In the course of a day's tramp we passed parties of every description and color: Irishmen, wheeling their blankets, provisions, and mining implements on wheelbarrows; American, French, and German foot-passengers, leading heavily laden horses, or carrying their packs on their backs, and their picks and shovels slung across their shoulders; Mexicans, driving long trains of pack mules, and swearing fearfully, as usual, to keep them in order; dapper-looking gentlemen, apparently from San Francisco, mounted on fancy horses; women, in men's clothes, mounted on mules or burros; whiskey peddlers, organ grinders, drovers, white-haired old men, cripples and hunchbacks, even sick men from their beds—all stark mad for silver.

He rested in Carson City, then took the stage to Silver City. On foot he approached Devil's Gate, and as he passed through, it struck him that there was something ominous in the sound of the name. "Devil's Gate—as in 'Let All Who Enter Here . . . ' But I had already reached the other side. It was too late now for repentance."

Browne found "every foot of the canyon claimed, and gangs of miners were at work all along the road, digging and delving into the earth like so many infatuated gophers." He also observed it a bit breezy. "Never was such a wind as this! Capsizing tents, scattering the grit with blinding force into everybody's eyes, and sweeping furiously around every crook and corner in search of some sinner to smite. It was the most villainous and persecuting wind that ever blew, and I boldly protest that it did nobody good."

During his inspection of the town, his worst forebodings upon passing through the Gate were confirmed.

The deep pits on the hillsides; the blasted and barren appearance of the whole country; the unsightly hodge-podge of a town; the horrible confusion of tongues; the roaring, raving drunkards at the barrooms; the flaring and flaunting gambling saloons, filled with desperadoes of the vilest sort; the ceaseless torrent of imprecations that shocked the ear on every side; the mad speculations and feverish thirst for gain—all combined to give me a forcible impression of the unhallowed character of the place.

After a few days, poisoned by the water, parched by the wind, appalled by the brutality, and deprived of sleep and sustenance, Browne departed Washoe, to "once more get clear of Devil's Gate."

fluctuating value of the famed "feet" of paydirt in one's possession turned paupers to princes and back to paupers in a single day.

Busts and Bankers

Toward the end of 1863, it seemed as if the silver edifice had reached so high that nobody could see the top of it. California capital was pouring into the mines and mills for equipment and payroll and the silver was shipped out in wagonloads to San Francisco. The *Territorial Enterprise* emerged as the trendsetter among a half dozen newspapers on the Lode; Samuel Clemens and William Wright adopted their pen names, Mark Twain and Dan DeQuille, as well as the frontier writing style popularized by J. Ross Browne.

Nevada became a state in 1864, and the five-year-old legal gridlock was unsnarled by a battery of new and unimpeachable federal appointees and elected officials. Right afterwards, however, the major mines hit rock bottom at 400 feet deep. Most of the wildcat operations succumbed to the Comstock's first bust. The stock market crashed. Mining in even the largest and most California-capitalized claims was suspended. The small-time quick-buck lawyers and scammers left town, to be replaced by the big-time, big-stakes bankers and swindlers.

William Ralston, president of the Bank of California, dispatched his functionary, William Sharon, to Virginia City to gain control of the desperate situation. Both had been born in Ohio in the 1820s. Both had started out in the riverboat business. Both were gamblers and empire builders. Sharon immediately began consolidating the bank's interests: buying out bankrupt claim holders for pennies on the dollar; approving loans liberally and accumulating collateral; exploring the shafts, tunnels and drifts; and conducting numerous and systematic assays. He studied geology, mineralogy, and ore bodies; the hoisting, pumping, and communications mechanisms of the mines and mills; timbering and teaming and transportation; the town's water and gas systems. Driven by determination, plus a natural greed and streak of ruthlessness, by the spring of 1865 William Sharon had emerged as the ultimate expert on

the Comstock, the possessor of the big picture, the maestro of the maelstrom.

For the next seven years, "Ralston's Ring" ruled the Lode. Sharon accumulated a huge monopoly of mines, mills, transportation, utilities, and stock. He unearthed bonanzas from the deepening diggings and became quite adept at manipulating the stock market to fleece the gamblers, little and large. Even the swindlers had never imagined a con game on such a grand scale. All Sharon had to do, for example, was quietly buy up the stock of an unproductive mine at $10 a share, then plant a rumor of a possible bonanza at that mine. This would drive the price up to $80, when he'd sell it off and fill the vault. In no time the vault itself was no longer large enough. In June 1867 the Bank of California moved into its new palatial headquarters at the corner of California and Sansome Streets in San Francisco. The building immediately earned the subtitle "The Wonder of the Silver Age."

Monopoly—Almost

In 1867 Sharon devised a plan to monopolize the two dozen reduction mills, scattered willy-nilly between Mt. Davidson and the Carson River. He allowed the mill owners to overextend their credit with the bank, then squeezed them till they suffocated. In the meantime, Sharon formed the Union Mill and Mining Company, and his tentacles closed around the remaining independent mines on the Comstock by withholding credit unless they refined their ore at his mills. Finally, he determined to control the transportation between the mines and the mills by constructing the Virginia & Truckee short line railroad from Virginia City to the Carson River and Carson City. From Carson City the train went north to Reno, where it connected with the Central Pacific railroad.

Only John Mackay, who came to the Comstock as a common miner in 1860 and climbed the ladder to become a major stockholder in some of the larger mines, continued to produce profits for anyone outside Ralston's Ring. With his partners James Fair, James Flood, and William O'Brien, Mackay began to beat Sharon at his own game, taking control of the Bank of California's Hale &

Norcross Mine from right under Sharon's nose. Their Kentuck Mine, too, paid dividends to its shareholders and enabled Mackay and Fair to play a hunch during the temporary bust of the early 1870s and quietly acquire the Consolidated Virginia Mine. They gambled again and followed a low-grade vein away from the main lode.

Both gambles paid off in 1873 when the Consolidated Virginia Mine, 1,200 feet beneath downtown Virginia City, hit the granddaddy of all Nevada orebodies. The ore was so rich that Mackay's Bonanza Firm made an even greater fortune manipulating the stocks a la Sharon and actually opened a bank of its own in San Francisco. This act helped precipitate a run on the Bank of California; William Ralston was forced out (and drowned that same day in San Francisco Bay). William Sharon took control of the bank.

The Great Fire of 1875 destroyed 33 blocks of Virginia City, including the 10-square-block downtown. But Big Bonanza money financed the rebuilding of Virginia far beyond its previous splendor. The peak year, 1876, saw 23,000 residents (half the state's population) celebrating the city's reemergence as if the bonanza would produce its riches forever. But within two years, the Comstock Lode had been pretty well played out. It took a few more years of gambling, speculating, and artificial stock highs and lows to convince the last die-hard investors of it. Estimates of the 20-year take (in 19th century dollars) range between $320 million and $750 million worth of precious metals, $100 million to $200 million of which had been from the Big Bonanza.

The 20th-Century Bonanza

The boomers packed their carpetbags and money pouches and blew town in search of new adventure, and Virginia City was left to die in the desert, like the hundreds of boomtowns created in its wake. But the Queen of the Comstock refused to succumb. A little further digging, a new cyanide process for recovering low-grade ore from tailings, and rising gold and silver prices all kept the Comstock on life-support systems into the 1930s. In 1935, the controlled price of gold was raised from $20 to $35 an ounce and Virginia City saw some renewed activity. The WPA paved C Street in 1937.

Around that time, Paul Smith, a mysterious New York hotelman, showed up and introduced the concept of merchandising and museums to the town. He opened the Museum of Memories in a section of the building that now houses the Bucket of Blood Saloon, hired all the local kids to scrounge artifacts from the dumps and attics, and displayed them—without much concern for authenticity (for example, an old top hat that one of the youngsters found became Sandy Bowers's own). He sold bags of sagebrush, conducted two-block walking tours to Piper's Opera House, and had the kids sell a booklet, *Drama of the Comstock,* for 15 cents to the tourists who happened to pass through.

The rigors of World War II caused a suspension in the mining, and by 1950 Virginia City seemed destined to dry up, fall down, and blow away. But Lucius Beebe and Charles Clegg, bon vivant authors from New York who wrote many popular histories of the American West and its railroads, fell in love with the town. They revitalized the *Territorial Enterprise* and sent copies out to friends around the world; they also helped revive the business district. The immensely popular TV show *Bonanza* renewed the aura around the town, with Ben Cartwright forever sending Joe, Hoss, Ben Jr., and Hop Sing to Virginia City for supplies, entertainment, Doc, and the sheriff. With tourists arriving in ever-increasing numbers, the few hundred residents, many of whom had been inspired by Paul Smith as kids, began to recondition the infrastructure, facilities, and attractions. Mining, too, continued, in fits and starts. Travelers quickly rediscovered Virginia City's boardwalks, saloons, mansions, mines, opera house, churches, cemeteries, and vistas. Today more than three million visitors a year drive up Geiger Grade or Devil's Gate to capture a piece of the glory of its past.

SIGHTS

With dozens of storefronts strung along five blocks of C Street, you could spend a long day just walking in and out of museums, saloons,

DANGERS OF ABANDONED MINES

There are plenty of old, abandoned mines around the Virginia City area, and around other parts of Nevada, too. Although entering an abandoned mine may seem tempting, DON'T DO IT! There's only one safe way to deal with abandoned mines—stay out, and not only that, but keep a good distance!

SHAFTS— The top of a mine shaft is especially dangerous. The rock at the surface is often decomposed, and timbers may be rotten or missing. It is dangerous to walk anywhere near a shaft opening—the whole area is often susceptible to slide into the shaft, along with anyone who might be walking by.

CAVE-INS— Cave-ins are an obvious danger. Areas likely to cave in are often difficult to recognize. Even minor disturbances, such as vibrations caused by walking or speaking, can cause a cave-in. If a person is caught, he can be crushed to death, or trapped behind a cave-in without anyone knowing he is there, in which case death can come through hunger, thirst, or gradual suffocation.

TIMBER— The timber in abandoned mines can be weak from decay. Timber that is apparently in good condition may become loose and fall at the slightest touch. A well-timbered mine opening can look very solid when in fact the timber can barely support its own weight. There is a constant danger of inadvertently touching a timber and causing the tunnel to collapse. Another danger is a winze—a shaft sunk inside a tunnel. In many old mines, winzes have been boarded over. If these boards have decayed, a perfect trap is waiting.

LADDERS— Ladders in most abandoned mines are unsafe, vertical ladders especially so. Ladder rungs may be missing or broken; some will fall at the slightest weight because of dry rot.

BAD AIR— "Bad air" contains poisonous gases or insufficient oxygen. Poisonous gases can accumulate in low areas or along the floor. A person may enter such areas breathing the good air above the gases, but the motion caused by walking will mix the bases with the good air, producing a possibly lethal mixture for him to breathe on the return trip. Because little effort is required to go down a ladder, the effects of bad air may not be noticed, but when climbing out of a shaft, a person requires more oxygen and breathes more deeply. The result is dizziness, followed by unconsciousness. If the gas doesn't kill, the fall will.

WATER— Many tunnels have standing pools of water which can conceal holes in the floor; pools of water are also common at the bottom of shafts. It is usually impossible to estimate the depth of the water, and a false step could lead to drowning.

EXPLOSIVES— Many abandoned mines contain old explosives, which are extremely dangerous and should never be handled. Old dynamite sticks and caps can explode if stepped on or even just touched.

RATTLESNAKES— Old mine tunnels and shafts are among the favorite haunts of these creatures to cool off in summer, or to search for rodents and other small animals. Any hole or ledge, especially near the mouth of a tunnel or shaft, can conceal a snake.

RESCUE— Attempting to rescue a person from a mine accident is difficult and dangerous for both the victim and the rescuer. Even professional rescue teams face death or injury, although trained to avoid all unnecessary risks. If someone needs to be rescued from an abandoned mine, call the county sheriff, who can organize a rescue operation.

RESPECT SIGNS— Fences, barricades, and warning signs are there for your safety. Mine owners have constructed these safeguards at their expense, for your protection. Disturbing or vandalizing them is dangerous.

—from pamphlet *Dangers In and Around Abandoned Mines,* published by Nevada Bureau of Mines and Geology, University of Nevada–Reno eateries, and shops from the near end of the street to the far end, then back up the other side. And that doesn't include the mine tours, mansions, opera house, churches, train and trolley rides, and hiking around. In short, Virginia City is so full of history, adventure, excitement, and curiosities that it's too hectic to do it all in one visit. Either plan on going full bore from sunup to sundown or hit a half-dozen highlights in a casual day trip.

For a look at the conditions in which the lowliest miners worked, the richest executives lived, and the whole spectrum of Comstockers was entertained, the top three attractions are an Underground Mine tour, the Castle, and Piper's Opera House.

Underground Mine Tour

The heart and soul of Virginia City was the Comstock Lode. Two mine tours allow you to get under the ground and see what the miners saw. Most authentic is the tour of the **Chollar Mine,** the last of the Comstock's old original mines. The Chollar Mine was the fifth highest in production, producing over $18 million in gold and silver, and this tour shows you the real thing, with the square set timbering, ore, old tools and equipment, and knowledgeable, experienced guides. The Chollar claim was filed in 1859, production started in 1861, and the mine was worked for almost 80 years, until it closed in 1942. It was reopened in 1961 for tours, 100 years after its first began producing, and has been giving tours ever since.

Guided walking tours of the Chollar Mine go over 400 feet into the mountain, take 30 minutes and cost $6 adults, $2 children age 4–14. The mine is open every day from Easter to the end of October; hours are noon–5 P.M. from June to August, with shorter hours in spring and fall (may be 1–4 P.M.). The Chollar Mine, 775/847-0155, is not far from the center of town; you can get there by going downhill from C to F Street, turning right (south) on F and just keep going for about a half-mile, or, head south from town on C Street, turn left (east) onto the truck route just past the Fourth Ward School, and follow the road around.

Virginia City's other mine tour departs from the rear of the **Ponderosa Saloon** on C Street. The mine tunnel snakes 315 feet from the rear end of the saloon into the Best and Belcher diggings, whose paydirt yielded 55 percent silver and 45 percent gold. Displays include gold-rich ore, the powder room where "monkeys" (young boys) worked, square-set timbering, minerals under black light, and all the heavy buckets, drills, winches, and rods the miners used to muck the rock, tunneling six to eight feet a day. The guide enumerates myriad dangers: the perpetual threats of cave-in, fire, scalding steam and water, the terrible heat and bad air, not to mention the back-breaking, head-knocking, bone-crushing work itself. At $4 per day (the equivalent of $232 today), the miners were well paid, considering that most hard-rock miners around the world earned less than a dollar a day; still, this tour is graphic evidence that the Comstock miners earned every penny. At the far end, the guide might light two candles and kill the overheads. If he blows out the candles (early-warning signal of gases or lack of oxygen), you'll be back in 1873! The only inconsistency in the authenticity is the 52-degree temperature; you could take a jacket, but don't really need one. Tours operate here all year round. In summer, from April to mid-October, they operate 10 A.M.–5 P.M. Winter hours, from mid-October through March, are 11 A.M.–5 P.M. daily. Tours take 25 minutes and cost $4.50 adults, $1.50 children under 12; 775/847-0757.

The Castle

This elegant mansion, on B Street up the hill a block from C Street, a little south of Taylor along Millionaire's Row, is so superlative that even guidebookese hyperbole fails to touch it; after this tour, the Mackay, Chollar, Bowers, and governor's mansions seem low rent. The history of this 16-room "castle" is absolutely charmed. It escaped the 1875 fire, was sold only twice in its 120-odd years with all its original furnishings, and was never refurbished. What a house full of priceless antiques! Built in 1868 by Robert Graves, superintendent of the Empire Mine, the tour is nothing less than a lesson in 19th-century European fine craftsmanship. The list is endless: English steel-cut prints, olivewood shutters, 14-foot (plus leaves) walnut dining-room table, French wallpaper, bronze statues, gold-leaf mirrors, Italian marble fireplaces, mouldings, alabaster urns, hand-painted Dutch vases, original wall paint, spectacular Czech rock-crystal chandeliers, Belgian linen lace, German walnut guest-room set. Notice the "fainting couch" in the living room, the rosewood headboard and the unique Czech lamp in the master bedroom, and the Heidelberg burl circassian walnut sideboard in the dining room.

Everything was shipped from Europe around the tip of South America to San Francisco, by riverboat up the Sacramento River to Knight's Landing, upriver from Sacramento, and then by wagon over the Sierra. Graves lived in it only for four years, then sold it to the Blauvelys of Gold Hill Bank, who lived here for 44 years. The banker sold it to the McGuirks, whose descendants still live in the home. The castle is open

COURTESY OF THE NEVADA COMMISSION ON TOURISM

a taste of Europe on B Street

daily 11 A.M.–5 P.M., Memorial Day weekend through October; $4.50 adults, $2 students, $0.25 ages 6–12; 775/847-0275. Leave your camera in the car; no photographing allowed.

Piper's Opera House

On the corner of B Street and Union is Virginia City's well-preserved, nearly restored theater. John Piper built this building in 1885, after the first two opera houses burned. It has canvas walls (for acoustics), balconies, chandeliers designed to throw patterns on the ceiling, the original round-backed chairs, the railroad spring-loaded floor (dancer enhancer), and a stage raked higher in the back-from which the terms "upstage" and "downstage" originate. Ads appear on top of the curtain. Three slotted sets (parlor, forest, and street) were rolled into and out of view by stagehands. Proscenium box seats are on one side of the stage. Signs inside tell of the performers who appeared here, who included Mark Twain, Harry Houdini, John Philip Sousa, Lillie Langtry, Al Jolson, and John Barrymore, among many others. Circles and keys painted on the floor date from when Piper's was used as a basketball court and roller rink in later years.

Tours are conducted 11 A.M.–4:30 P.M. every day from May through October, and 11 A.M.–4 P.M. weekends and holidays the rest of the year, weather permitting (groups by appointment, year round). Tours by donation; call for performance prices. Shows, concerts, and dances are presented here year round (daily at noon in the summer except Friday); phone the opera house (775/847-0433) or check with the chamber of Commerce for current schedules.

Museums

The following "museums" (the term is used liberally around here) are all on C Street.

The Fourth Ward School, 775/847-0975, at the far south end of town, was one of four public schools in the town at its peak. Built in 1876 for $100,000, it boasted many revolutionary modern conveniences: cut-stone foundation anchored with steel rods to the granite of Mt. Davidson; newfangled heating and ventilating technology; water piped to all four floors, including indoor drinking fountains. The last class graduated in 1936. The Nevada State Museum has set up an excellent exhibit on the ground floor in the form of nine "lessons," including highlights of Comstock history; mining technology (3-D viewing machine and models of a stamp mill and hoist works, and mine shaft and stopes); entertainment on the Comstock; women and immigrants in Virginia City; and many other informative signs and exhibits. Two classrooms across the hall have also been restored. One has all the desks, blackboards, and wood stove; the other has team and class pictures and other historical black-and-white photos. Notice how large the rooms are: At its peak, the Fourth Ward School had 1,000 students. The second floor has also been restored; a theater and art gallery occupy the classrooms, and there's an excellent exhibit about Mark Twain. The building is beautifully restored, and has a great view. Your $2 will help continue the restoration. Open daily 10 A.M.–5 P.M. May through October.

The **Way It Was Museum,** 775/847-0766, at the north end on C Street at Sutton, has a large array of Comstock mining artifacts, maps, and minerals, including working scale models of stamp mills, mines, Cornish pumps (all built by J. E. Parson of Oroville, California). Three "American Frontier" videos with Charlie Jones and Merlin Olsen, about the Comstock, Piper's Opera House, and Mark Twain, alone are worth the price ($3) of admission (children under 11 free). Also check out the scale model of the underground mine workings and Jim Fair's personal stamp mill. The Way It Was is open daily 10 A.M.–6 P.M. year-round, weather permitting.

The **Marshall Mint Museum,** 775/847-0777 or 800/321-6374, a combination museum-mineral-gold shop, is on the Reno side of town across C Street from The Way It Was Museum. It's owned by Texas mine magnate Hugh R. Marshall of Marshall Earth Resources, Inc. (MERI). The collection of gold, silver, other precious metals and minerals (some under black light), and art is definitely worth seeing. Feast your eyes on ivory, turquoise, malachite, jade, and lapis lazuli creations from around the world. The gold shop displays coins, gold nuggets, silver, and books

for sale. If you're at all into Comstock history, you probably won't be able to resist the Bonanza King silver medallions (all four go for just under $100). Marshall Mint coins and jewelry are minted and assembled on the premises; they also make personalized coins (you can design your own), and a series of "Angel of the Day" and "Our Lord and Savior" coins. The museum is open daily 10 A.M.–5 P.M.

The **Gambling Museum,** 775/847-9022, highlights the 150-year history of gambling in the West: Indian sticks and bones (dice), Mexican monte, faro, Chinese chips, an 1800s' Hazard Wheel, chuck-a-luck, and scores of antique slots. The history of cards and the cheating devices are interesting, as are the display of old U.S. currency and clear-glass slot machines. It's open daily 10 A.M.–6 P.M. April through October; 10 A.M.– 5 P.M. November through March; admission $1.

You can't go wrong at the museum in back of **Grant's General Store** next door to the newspaper office, with shelves full of old dry goods, an antique cash register, beautiful woodwork, and a barber shop replica—it's free. The "Victoriana" woodstove is one of the finest sights in Virginia City: It was fabricated for the 1904 World's Fair in St. Louis, Missouri, and embellished with silver and gold instead of the usual nickel and chrome.

The **Mark Twain Museum,** also called The Territorial Enterprise Museum, 47–53 South C St. in the center of town, 775/847-7950, is downstairs in the basement of the Territorial Enterprise Gift Shop. The museum displays 19th century printing technology, such as an 1894 linotype, old binding machine, and hot type cabinet. This was the pressroom for Nevada's oldest publication, which started up in Genoa in December 1858, moved briefly to Carson City, then in October 1860 settled down into a long and profitable run in Virginia City, with the likes of Mark Twain and Dan DeQuille keeping things lively. Twain's original desk is on display, along with some of his books and journals, and there's an interesting recording telling about Twain and his times in Virginia City. The museum is open every day, 10 A.M.–6 P.M., admission $1.

The **Comstock Firemen's Museum,** 775/847-0717, is in Virginia City's original firehouse, built in 1864. Not many buildings survived the big fire of October 1875, but this brick building is one that did. The old ladder trailer, 1856 Knickerbocker hand fire engine, and hose carriage are unique. The old fire extinguishers, model fire truck, helmets, and photographs, collected by the Virginia City Volunteer Fire Department, are definitely worth a good look, and a dollar or two donation. It's open daily 10 A.M.–5 P.M. May to October, then only on weekends.

The **Western Historic Radio Museumm,** 109 S. F St., 775/847-9047, www.radioblvd.com, looks like an ordinary house; you'll know it from the big statue of Nipper, the RCA Victor radio dog ("his master's voice"), in the front window. The museum entrance is in the rear. Whether you're a radio buff or not, this is a fascinating museum, with over 200 antique and classic radios on display, plus antique wireless (telegraph) apparatus, a ham radio room with vintage ham radios and a collection of QSL cards from around the world, and a collection of photos of famous old-time radio personalities, and several more statues of Nipper. Pride of place goes to an original, complete 1912 Spark Station, discovered in Reno in November 1999. Owners and curators Henry and Sharon Rogers will give you a guided tour of the museum, if you like. Radio buffs from far and wide contact the Rogers with radio issues, and for antique radio repair. The museum is open April to October, Monday through Thursday 11 A.M.–5 P.M. and Friday through Saturday 1–5:30 P.M. or by appointment; November to March, it is open "by chance or by appointment." Admission $2.50 adults, $1 children.

SALOONS

The **Crystal Bar,** C St. and Taylor, 775/847-7500, is the home of the Crystal Visitor Center, where the Virginia City Chamber and tourism offices are located. The crystal and gold-plated chandeliers are original, and many mementos line the walls.

The **Delta Saloon,** a half-dozen doors north, 775/847-0789, is as close to a casino as it gets in Virginia City, with rows and rows of slots and video poker (there are no table games in Virginia City), the Sawdust Corner coffee shop on one side and the Delta Gift Shop on the other. Be sure to traipse upstairs (if it's open) to check out the period carpeting, wallpaper, chandeliers, plus the bright skylights, four big banquet rooms, and restrooms. The Delta is also the home of the infamous Suicide Table against the back wall. Read its description if your curiosity is killing you. An interesting shrine to the Bonanza Kings is next to it on the wall. At the opposite end of the casino is an 1880s' world globe, built at a cost of $450 of rosewood (complete with mariner's compass) for Bonanza King James Fair. It's estimated that this unique globe is now worth $100,000.

A few shops north is the **Silver Queen,** 775/847-0440, home of a 16-foot-tall lady on the wall, with a dress of more than 3,000 silver dollars, a belt of 28 gold pieces, bracelet of dimes, and 50-cent-piece ring. Here are also some old Bally's slots and a great big back bar. The **Union Brewery,** across the street at the north end of town, was built in 1862; the exterior is original.

A few storefronts south of there is the **Bucket of Blood Saloon,** 775/847-0322. The Bucket, named after one of the hundreds of early licensed premises, is one of the most popular saloons in town, for good reason. It's light and airy, thanks to the big picture window in back overlooking Six-Mile Canyon. And it has a unique dice machine, the world's largest, which is so much fun it's addictive. Look up at the 50 old lamps, the portraits (such as of the Bowerses), and the great woodwork and brass rails.

Across the street and up the block is the **Ponderosa Saloon,** 775/847-0757, in the old Bank of California building. The highlight here (other than the mine tour; see above) is the original bank vault, with a half-inch steel-plate cage surrounded by two-foot-thick walls where Billy Sharon kept his spare change. Study the historic photos and the portraits of the early celebrities: Julia Bulette, James Finney, Henry Comstock, Sam Clemens.

South of there along the funny boardwalk is the **Old Washoe Club,** 775/847-7210, built in 1875 after the great fire. This was the local millionaires' hangout, frequented by Ulysses S. Grant, Thomas Edison, and Wyatt Earp, among others. The posh upstairs digs were accessed by the spiral staircase, still viewable in the back, which is listed by Ripley's as the longest spiral stairs without a supporting pole.

The **Bonanza Saloon,** 775/847-0655, has a big side room full of slots on a fine wood floor, plus an outdoor deck in the back with a coin-operated telescope and a large, faded, historical black-and-white photograph labeled with the features of the view.

SHOPS

Virginia City offers a handful of old-time photo shops: **Silver Sadie's Old-Time Photos, Priscilla Penneyworth's Photographic Emporium, Rotten Rowdie's Old-Time Photos,** and **Old Time Photos.** The props and costumes turn you into practically any kind of character from the roaring 1870s that you'd like to be: barmaid, piano player, cocktail waitress, cowboy and cowgirl, gunslinger. Priscilla's prices are representative: $13.95 each for 8 by 10 glossies with one person, $16.95 for two people, $19.95 for three people, additional copies $11.95.

Mark Twain Books, 111 S. C St., 775/847-0454, www.marktwainbooks.com, has an excellent selection of new, used, out-of-print and rare books, and specializes in books about Nevada, Western Americana, the Comstock Lode, Virginia City, and Mark Twain, plus Nevada travel guides, kids' books, postcards, and plenty more. Come in to take a photo with the lifelike dummy of Mark Twain, and check out the good selection of books by and about Twain and his years as a journalist here in Virginia City. The building is interesting, too; this is one of the oldest buildings on C Street, built in 1862. One of very few buildings to survive the Great Fire of October 1875, it survived because it is of stone and brick, whereas the other Virginia City buildings in 1875 were primarily constructed of wood. Ask for a leaflet telling the long and interesting history of the building; parts of it have been a livery stable, a bank, a hardware store and a museum over the building's long life.

A **panning for gold** operation can now be found beside the old Territorial Enterprise building. The gold mine is down a set of wooden stairs, at the bottom of a water wheel and sluice. It's $5 per person to wash out some specks of salted gold, which you get to keep. The prospector in charge is full of fascinating tidbits about the gold rush and good advice about the panning process. This is a very popular attraction, and draws a crowd of both onlookers and gold panners.

ENTERTAINMENT

For $3 you can take a 20-minute **tour,** 775/786-0866, on a replica trolley that looks like an old San Francisco cable car; in warm weather they use an open-air trailer pulled by a Ford tractor. It's a great tour, full of history and inside tips. Catch it at the parking lot next to the Bucket of Blood Saloon every half-hour 9 A.M.–5 P.M.; $3 adult, $1.50 children. While waiting, read the various plaques that grace the Centennial Monument in the parking lot.

Much more thrilling is a 35-minute jaunt on the **Virginia & Truckee Railroad,** departing from the railcar depot on F Street near Washington, just south of St. Mary's Church. A steam locomotive pulls an open car and caboose down to the red Gold Hill depot through tunnel number 4. Since there are eight trips a day between 10:30 A.M. and 5 P.M., you can disembark at Gold Hill and catch the next train back to Virginia. It's $6 for adults, $3 for children, and definitely worth it for the relaxation in the sun, the offbeat narration, and the sensation of going through the tunnel. The V&T runs daily from Memorial Day weekend till October 1, then weekends through the end of October, with possible weekday trains in October depending on weather and passenger load (call for info). Moonlight rides are given monthly on the Saturday evening closest to full moon, June through September. For more info, call 775/847-0380.

Events

The second weekend in September, more than 25,000 people have gathered in Virginia City for the **International Camel Races.** The race started in 1959 as a hoax (a long Virginia City tradition), when the editor of the *Territorial Enterprise,* Bob Richards, wrote a fictitious account of the city's camel races to fill a three-inch hole in the newspaper. The following year, Richards announced the races, and in fact challenged the staff of the *San Francisco Chronicle* to compete. Camels were leased from the San Francisco Zoo and celebrity riders participated (movie director John Huston won that first competition). The races are held in a racetrack on F Street; accompanying events include ostrich races, dances, parades, food, and more.

Other special events throughout the year include a **Cinco de Mayo Chili Cook-Off** on the weekend nearest May 5, **Outhouse Races** in mid-August, and the **Nevada Shakespeare Festival** at Piper's Opera House during July and August. The Chamber of Commerce, 775/847-0311, has information these and many other popular events held throughout the year.

The **Virginia City Outlaws** present an enjoyable, old-timey stunt show twice daily, at noon and 2 P.M., at Union and E Streets. Admission is $3 adults, $1 children.

Walking Tours

For tips on enjoyable explorations, pick up a copy of the *Walkers & Hikers Guide to Virginia City and The Comstock Area* ($2.95) from the Mark Twain Bookstore. The booklet details nine walks and hikes ranging from 2.1 to 10.8 miles in length, with practical tips, historical information, and points of interest noted for each walk and hike. Another useful booklet is the *Comstock Driving Tour/Virginia City Walking Tour,* also available at the Mark Twain Bookstore.

ACCOMMODATIONS

The **Comstock Lodge,** 875 S. C St., 775/847-0233, has 14 rooms priced from $48–65. All the rooms are done in period antiques; the room comes with coupons for a breakfast special at the Delta Saloon. The **Sugarloaf Mountain Motel,** 430 S. C St., 775/847-0551 or 866/217-9248, has 14 rooms for $50–90.

The **Chollar Mansion B&B,** 565 S. D St., 775/847-9777, is a three-level, fire-engine-red brick 13-room, 125-year-old Victorian mansion. It served as the lodging and offices of Isaac Requa, superintendent of the rich Chollar Mine. Twelve-foot-high ceilings, men's and women's parlors, and a total of 40 stairs in the house are just a few of the features befitting of Requa's station. Other structural elements are even more intriguing. The kitchen pantry was once the paymaster's booth, where an armed banker doled out the miners' $4 a day in coin; a sliding teller's window connects to the kitchen. The company vault, with its arched brick roof, stone floors and walls, and mine-tunnel entrance, is now the wine cellar. There are two guest rooms on the main floor, a suite on the ground floor, and a two-room cottage for rent. Rates range $75–125.

The **Virginia City RV Park,** Carson and F Sts., 775/847-0999 or 800/889-1240, www.vcrvpark.com, has been here since early 1988. It's down the hill on a bluff; to get there, turn downhill at Carson Street and drive three blocks to F Street. Some sites overlook the cemetery. It's a bit cramped, but the bathrooms were recently remodeled and the showers have individual dressing rooms. The town park, with a pool and tennis courts, is right across the street. There's a large market here. Downtown Virginia City is a mere four-block walk. The park has 50 spaces for motor homes, all with full hookups; 2 are pull-throughs. Tents are allowed. Reservations are recommended through the summer (open year-round). The fees are $14 per tent site (includes a shower) and $23 for RVs (AAA and Good Sam discounts).

In Seven Mile Canyon, a mile from Virginia City, **Tyson's Canyon Ranch,** 775/847-7223, www.nevadaduderanch.com, offers a bed-and-breakfast luxury cowboy adventure, with many special ranch events including cowboy entertainment, longhorn cattle events and campfire hay rides. Five private guest cottages, each with private kitchen and romantic fireplace, cost $125–165 nightly.

FOOD

The **Firehouse Restaurant & Saloon,** 171 S. C St. at the south end of town, 775/847-4774, is a coffee shop and bar, open daily 7 A.M.–4 P.M. It serves a variety of inexpensive breakfasts and lunches. French toast $3.50, omelettes $6; for lunch there's a variety of burgers, barbecue, hot sandwiches and other good fare, all for around $6.50.

The café attached to the **Delta Saloon,** 775/847-0789, known as Sawdust Corner, is a justifiably popular place for breakfast or lunch 10 A.M.–3 P.M., and for dinner on Wednesday nights. It's airy, comfortable, friendly, has an authentic air, and seats 100;.

The **Julia C. Bulette Saloon,** 775/847-9394, has an espresso bar up front, the museum in the basement, and a full-service bar in back that's been remodeled: two large-screen televisions, nice ceramic-tile floor, pleasant restrooms. It serves burgers and bar food.

The **Bonanza Saloon,** 775/847-7005, serves $5 burgers, $6.75 Philly cheesesteak, $4.95 soup and sandwich, and the like. It has a few slot and video poker machines and a small gift shop in front.

The **Brass Rail,** 775/847-0304, offers balcony dining out back, with a great view over Six Mile Canyon. If you prefer, dine inside, with a gargantuan Alaskan brown bear overhead. The house specialty, a pot pie and cobbler special for $8.95, is a hugely filling meal with a choice of two meat pies and four fruit cobblers. They also make breakfasts, vegetarian selections, burgers, hot and cold sandwiches, etc. Open from around 9 or 9:30 A.M. to 6:30 or 7 P.M., or as long as customers are present. (Most restaurants in town close earlier; this is one place that stays open later.)

The **Palace Saloon,** 775/847-4441, has a row of tables between a row of stools at the bar and a row of leather goods at the emporium. Locals say the burgers here, for $4.95, are the best in town. Check out the ice-cream-and-liquor drinks at the bar.

Solid Muldoon's, 775/847-9181, serves the usual breakfast and lunch offerings and is open for dinner. Blackened prime rib, chicken marsala, halibut, scallops, and the like go for $9–12.

You'll certainly see, probably smell, and maybe even taste the fudge being slopped around on tables in the picture windows in front of **Grandma's Fudge Factory.** Similar is **Aunt Rosie's Fudge Store** next to Grant's General Store; notice the old Coca-Cola cooler. **Red's Old-Fashioned Candies & Deli Bar** makes good deli sandwiches in the back. **Comstock Cookie Company** sells cookies, cobblers, and ice cream (try the waffle cone), along with espresso, hot dogs, and soft pretzels. The cobblers are mouth-watering at $2.50, à la mode $3.95.

INFORMATION

The Virginia City **Chamber of Commerce,** 86 S. C St., 775/847-0311, www.virginiacity-nv.org, occupies the old Crystal Bar. The old bar, which was once home to the best mint juleps ever mixed, is worth a look around even if you're stocked up on brochures and information. It's open every day, 10 A.M.–4 P.M.

Carson City

In 1858, Abraham V. Curry was a 43-year-old businessman who, born near Ithaca, New York, had worked on the docks in Cleveland, the hills of San Francisco, and the boomtowns of the Mother Lode. According to Doris Cerveri's fine book *With Curry's Compliments,* he and some partners were in Downieville, California, when they heard that Brigham Young had recalled his Mormon settlers to Salt Lake City to help defend Deseret against a rumored invasion by the U.S. government. Curry immediately foresaw the po-

tential in the prime real estate at the eastern edge of the Sierra Nevada that the Mormons had abandoned.

Curry and his partners traveled to Genoa, where they found the price of land to already be both outrageous and nonnegotiable. So they continued to Eagle Valley just north of Genoa and bought 865-acre Eagle Ranch from John Mankin for $1,000. Curry put $300 down but Mankin, who was something of a crook, took the money and ran, never bothering to collect the other

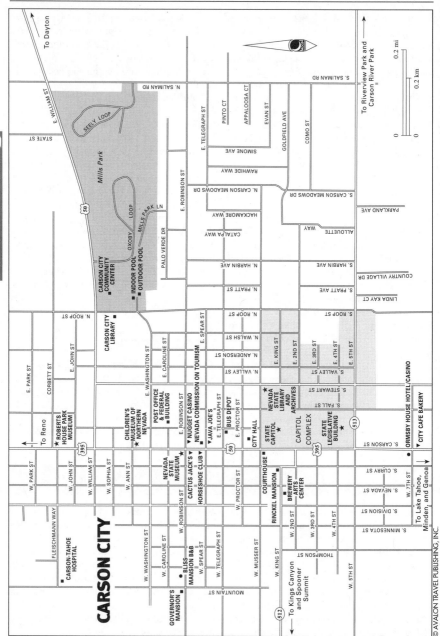

CARSON CITY

© AVALON TRAVEL PUBLISHING, INC.

$700. Thus, though discovery of the Comstock was still more than a year away and the "ranch" was little more than sand and sage, Curry had found the spot where he'd make his stand. Or maybe the spot found him.

HISTORY

The ambitious New Yorker knew he could never be content with a ranch. He immediately began promoting the desolate (though watered and scenic) valley as the eventual site of the state capital, which he named Carson City after Kit Carson. Nevada was not yet even a territory, let alone a state, and Eagle Valley could boast no more than a handful of residents and even fewer buildings. The local surveyor refused to plat a town site in return for ownership of "a full city block" of what at the time was desert scrub. The surveyor worked instead for an IOU (but soon became the first postmaster of Carson City).

Curry had him lay out wide city streets and a four-square-block area known to settlers as the Plaza, though Curry called it Capitol Square. Lots were sold dirt cheap to anyone who wanted them, including Major William Ormsby, a businessman fed up with Genoa. Curry used clay from the ranch to fabricate adobe bricks and constructed a few buildings in "town." He also discovered a large limestone outcrop near a warm springs on the property, which he used as a quarry; he dammed the springs and built a bathhouse, which attracted prospectors and travelers.

The winter of 1858–59 was especially severe and conditions in Carson City were still primitive at best, but Abe Curry possessed the faith of Job and he persevered. Spring arrived warm and fresh. That summer the Comstock was discovered mere miles east, and the rush was on. Thousands of frenzied miners and freighters and merchants and lawyers and scammers rumbled through Carson City's dusty (though wide) streets. Curry quickly located a claim high up on the Comstock, consolidated it with a Carson City butcher named Alva Gould, and sold his share to Californians for $2,000 (with which he traveled back to Cleveland to collect his wife and six daughters; his one son was already with him in Carson).

The Californians immediately became millionaires from the mine that forever carried his name, the Gould and Curry, and proved to be the richest ore body in the early days of the Comstock.

By 1860, the town's population had grown to more than 500. By the time Congress created the Territory of Nevada in 1861, burgeoning Carson City beat out Genoa and Virginia City for the territorial capital. Curry befriended fellow New Yorker James Nye, territorial governor, and helped induce him to convene both the territorial and the new Ormsby County governments at Carson. Finally, on Halloween 1864, Nevada became a state with Carson City its capital.

Power Attracts Power

By then, Uncle Abe, as he was henceforth universally known and revered for his civic spirit and generous soul, was Carson City's major landowner, contractor, hotelier, saloonkeeper, and road builder. He couldn't be content, of course, with mere prophethood and property, and quickly made another transition to politician: he acted frequently as sheriff, delegate to an early constitutional convention, and aide to Territorial Governor James Nye. Curry also saw the fulfillment of what one imagines to be his grandest ambition-philanthropy. He donated his hastily constructed Warm Springs Hotel for the first territorial legislature; the hotel being two miles from town, he transported the legislators in his horse-drawn streetcar—Nevada's first. Next, Curry sold his second hotel, Great Basin, to the government to serve as a courthouse and legislature; the Warm Springs building later became the territorial prison, with Curry as first warden. Prison labor quarried the limestone for many of Carson City's distinctive buildings, some still standing. In 1865, Carson City received federal approval to build a branch of the U.S. Mint, and Curry not only oversaw construction of the building, but also was appointed *its* first superintendent when it opened in January 1870.

Uncle Abe resigned his commission at the mint in September 1870 to run on the Republican ticket for lieutenant governor, a campaign that he lost. He then turned his attention to building the mammoth stone roundhouse and shops for the Virginia & Truckee Railroad. The Grand Ball, held to celebrate their opening on July 4, 1873, proved to be Curry's swan song. He was compelled to surrender to Nature's final summons in October 1873 from a stroke at age 58. All in all, Uncle Abe Curry had lived one of the richest lives of any early Nevadan, and had earned and maintained a reputation for being one of the most warm-hearted, civic-spirited, generous, and honest men during those turbulent times.

The 20th Century

The capital shared the boom–bust cycles of the Comstock over the next few decades, though never as severely, thanks to the business supplied by the burgeoning bureaucracy. Afterwards, except for the championship heavyweight prizefight between Bob Fitzsimmons and Gentleman Jim Corbett in 1897, Carson City settled down to the peaceful and purposeful community it has been ever since. The boxing match landed in Carson City after San Francisco elders caved in to public sentiment prevalent at the time against boxing and canceled it. Carson City elders felt no such squeamishness, and the 14-round bout attracted such large numbers of visitors and publicity that the legislators, most of whom had witnessed the prize-fight phenomenon first hand, put two and two together and came up with the Nevada tradition that evolved into legal gambling and prostitution, quick divorce and simple marriage procedures, nonrestrictive mining laws, and nuclear testing, among other unusual revenue-attracting efforts over the years.

Carson City became home to the Stewart Indian School, which provided vocational and higher education to thousands of native children from around the West for 90 years (though many people consider Indian schools such as the Stewart to be little more than government kidnapping and indoctrination). Carson City also partook of the turn-of-the-20th-century booms at Tonopah and Goldfield, thanks to the railroad connection and government participation. But the excitement was short-lived. From a high of 8,000 in 1880, the capital's population dropped to 2,000 in 1930. The 1931 gambling and divorce legislation prompted gradual growth,

to 4,000 in 1950, then doubling three times again over the next 30 years. Boom times revisited Carson throughout the '80s and into the '90s.

Carson City has roughly 56,000 people today. The State Prison, Gaming Commission, huge Department of Transportation, Commission on Tourism, Economic Development Department, and all the myriad state and federal agencies keep the cogs and gears turning. The Legislature meets for several months every two years.

Carson City could be thought of as the center of Nevada. The geographic center of the state is roughly 200 miles away, 30 miles southeast of Austin. Reno and Las Vegas are the financial and entertainment centers and are magnets for visitors and transplants. The claim of historic center rightly belongs to Virginia City. But Carson City is the *power* center, to which all the state looks for vision, leadership, and order (bureaucratic though it may be). And it's not only the obvious fact that Carson City is the state capital-center of *political* power. This calm, comfortable, pretty, and friendly town seems to sit atop a rare locus of *planetary* power. These emanations from the earth certainly infused its founders and partisans with a special zeal and authority. And they continue to infuse residents and visitors, who appreciate the city's excellent size, central location, friendliness, excellent facilities, and subtle sensation of powerful forces still at play just below the surface of this capital of the most unusual state in the country.

SIGHTS

Nevada State Museum

This is Nevada's premier museum, inside the old Carson City Mint, which operated between 1870 and 1893. After the mint closed, the stone building, erected by town father Uncle Abe Curry, served as a federal office building until 1933 when it was abandoned because of neglect. Five years later, Judge Clark J. Guild noticed a For Sale sign on the building and promptly mobilized a coalition, which included his friends, local residents, Senator Patrick McCarran, Nevada philanthropist Max Fleischmann, and the state Legislature, dedicated to repairing the building and outfitting it as a museum. It opened to the public on Nevada Day (October 31), 1941; a plaque on the north corner of the mint commemorates the event and leading players. The rear wing was added in 1959.

In 1990, the front wing (in the old mint building) was closed for safety reasons. Structural engineers found an uncemented rubble foundation and sandstone block walls held together with limestone mortar; a number of thin cracks ran clear through the walls. It's all fixed now, and better than ever.

Pay your admission, then head into the mint exhibit, which illustrates the entire coining process, from depositors' bullion through ingot melting, into gold and silver "cakes," which are rolled, annealed, and cut into blanks, then washed, weighed, and coined by the likes of the museum's huge coin press into $5, $10, and $20 silver and gold pieces. The mint produced $49.2 million from 56.6 million coins in its 23 years of operation, and you can see a sample of every coin minted here in a collection donated by the First Interstate Bank (which also has a fine money museum in Las Vegas). The mint wing also houses the silver collection from the USS *Nevada*.

Beyond is the dark and cool of the walk-through ghost town, narrated by a grizzled old prospector and his mule. On the second floor are more excellent exhibits. The Environmental Gallery is full of local fauna-great looks at a big black bear, bobcats, porcupine, big Lahontan cutthroat trout and cui-ui, and the Pyramid Lake pelicans and cormorants, plus eagles, owls, crows, falcons, hawks, and songbirds, shorebirds, small birds, scavenger birds, wading and diving birds, swans and geese. There's a skeletal ichthyosaur on the stairs.

The Earth Science Gallery is a geology lesson, including an underwater Devonian sea walkaround, seismograph, plate tectonics video, and Black Rock Desert diorama. The Archaeology Gallery in the next room displays projectile points and weapon sticks such as the atlatl, shells, tools, baskets, dioramas of a native mudhen drive, Great Basin camp, Pyramid Lake scene, pinenut harvest, salt mining, natural foods, and much, much more. The Changing Gallery is always a surprise.

The underground mine was re-created with timber, vents, and ores from once-active mines around the state. It's in the basement and has a very "low cap." It meanders through a large maze under the whole building and imparts a lifelike sense of working in tunnels underground. It leads to an exit; shield your eyes from the sun!

There's a big selection of Nevada books and museum gifts in the gift shop on the second floor. The museum, 600 N. Carson St., 775/687-4810, is open daily 8:30 A.M.–4:30 P.M., $3 adult, seniors $2.50, under 18 free.

Cross Robinson Street and enter the **Carson City Nugget** casino, where you can spend a few minutes drooling over the "world's rarest gold collection"—worth a cool mil, and 70 years in the collecting. The brochure explains how these specimens, completely unchanged by human hands, formed into such peculiar and stunning shapes.

The Capitol and Legislature

The state capital building, just south of the state library on Carson Street between Musser and 2nd, 775/687-5030, was built in 1870. Improvements, including the iron fence, were made five years later for $25,000; the library annex (now the controller's offices) was added onto the back of the building in 1905; the two legislative wings were constructed in 1913; and the whole original structure was gutted and restored in 1977 for $6 million.

A fine museum on the south side of the second floor, in the old senate chambers, displays a collection of Nevada artifacts. Just a few of the highlights include William Stewart's Wooten Patent Cabinet desk, an 1862 map of the Nevada Territory, the 36-star flag, architectural drawings of the Capitol from 1870, the silver trowel from the cornerstone ceremony, and the goblets used by Abe Curry and James Nye to toast statehood. Spend some time following the history of the building, especially the photographs of the gutted interior during restoration in 1977 and the installation of the new fiberglass dome. Whatever you do in the capital city, don't miss the Capitol room. In the old Assembly chambers down the hall is a display on the USS *Nevada*.

The Legislative Building across the plaza hosts

Reno and Tahoe

the legislators during January and February (and often into March and April, and sometimes into May and June) during odd-numbered years. As you're wandering around the building looking for the water fountains, peek into the Assembly (south) and Senate (north) galleries. During the other 660 or so days when they're not in session, you're all alone in the public galleries in air-conditioned meditative luxury.

Brewery Arts Center

Walk south a block to King, west a block to Division, then into the Brewery Arts Center, 449 W. King, 775/883-1976, weekdays 9 A.M.–5 P.M., free. Jacob Klein swept across the Sierra in the fateful spring of 1860 with the silver-crazed hordes to establish Nevada's first brewery in Carson City. Within four years, the dividends from the beer had built this establishment, which operated first by steam and then by lager till 1948 (with a hiatus during Prohibition). A display of Carson Brewing Company artifacts can be viewed here; tours of the historic building can be arranged. The Arts Center sponsors more than 100 classes and workshops in visual and performing arts, art exhibits, crafts fairs, concerts, plays, storytellers, and other cultural programs throughout the year.

Children's Museum of Northern Nevada

It took six years of fundraising ($400,000) and another year of renovating to unveil this children's learning center at 813 N. Carson (between Ann and Washington), 775/884-2226, Tues.–Sun. 10 A.M.–4 P.M., admission $5 adult, $2 kids 3–13. The museum is one block north of the Nevada State Museum, on the opposite side of the street. There are 25 exhibits in fine arts, humanities, and science, aimed at the 6–13 age group, but fun for the whole family.

Fire Museum

Warren Engine Co. No. 1 began as a volunteer firefighting fraternity in 1863 and has served Carson City uninterrupted ever since, making it the oldest volunteer company in the West (mostly professional firefighters now make up its ranks). That first year, 20 charter members

of the company raised $2000 at a fireman's ball to buy the first firefighting equipment in town: a Hunneman Engine built in the early 1800s and used by the Warren Engine Company of Boston. Later it was shipped around the Horn and worked in San Francisco and Marysville, California, before arriving in Carson City, where the company named itself for the Warrens of Boston. In 1913, on its 50th anniversary, the company bought a Seagrave fire engine, Nevada's first motorized fire truck. A new firehouse was built in the late 1950s at 111 N. Curry, with the upstairs devoted to a museum for all the memorabilia accumulated during the first 100 years. That station remained in service till 1994, when a new station was opened at 777 S. Stewart, 775/887-2210, open weekdays 8 A.M.–5 P.M., donation. Check out the 1913 Seagrave, the wild old goggles, masks, helmets, and caps, the 1870s two-wheeled hose cart, and the familiar Currier & Ives original prints of New York conflagrations. One of the firefighters will show you around; ask your guide to explain the trumpet trophies.

Historical Houses

The **Roberts House Park and Museum,** 1207 N. Carson St., 775/887-2714, is Carson City's oldest-built house—but the Gothic Revival–style house was not originally built here. It is believed that this is a "kit house," shipped from New England to San Francisco (possibly around Cape Horn), then transported by rail to Folsom, California (the trailhead for the Kingsbury Trail), and then hauled to Washoe City, where it was assembled in around 1859. In 1875 the house, home of James Doane Roberts and family, was moved to Carson City. Today the house has been restored and contains period furniture; guided tours include the story of who has lived in this house, and why the house is historically significant. It is open Friday through Sunday, 1–3 P.M., April through October; admission $1 donation.

Pick up the **Kit Carson Trail map** ($2.50) at the visitor center next to the Nevada State Railroad Museum (1900 S. Carson St.) for the historic tour of town. The flyer is beautifully illustrated and adequately written, though the tour, a bit too long to walk especially in the heat of high season, requires an accomplished navigator and careful attention to glimpse all the historic structures. You might read the map and choose the five or six houses that strike your fancy (the **Bliss Mansion,** for example, built by the Tahoe lumber magnate, or the **Stewart-Nye home,** home to both famous politicians). Or you could park on a corner with three or four of the houses nearby (around the **Governor's Mansion** at Mountain and Robinson, at Minnesota and Proctor, or at Spear and Nevada), and see them on foot. Whichever, do wander around these historic residential back streets; the stately old trees alone are worth every minute. A free pamphlet available at the Chamber of Commerce office outlines a simpler one-hour walk you can do around the historic area.

For historical reasons, you might want to make a pilgrimage to **Abe Curry's stone house,** 406 N. Nevada St., or **Orion Clemens' residence,** 502 N. Division, with its distinctive five-sided bay window. Clemens came to Nevada by Overland Stage in late 1860 to serve as secretary to newly appointed Territorial Governor James Nye. His younger brother Sam, better known to history as Mark Twain, accompanied him for the adventure.

The entire historical tour of Carson City encompasses 59 sites along the "blue line," a blue stripe painted on the city's sidewalks; 15 of the houses on the tour are "talking houses," which tell their tales on specific AM frequencies on the dial. Get all the info at the chamber of commerce.

Stewart Indian Museum

A visit to this campus of the Stewart Indian Boarding School is one of the highlights of Carson City. Thirty years after the complete dislocation of Nevada's Indian population, in 1890 U.S. Senator William Stewart secured federal funds to open this school, on a 240-acre campus site, with three teachers and 37 students. At that time, the federal policy was to "assimilate" Native Americans, which really meant "forced conversion" to white ways. The first students consisted of orphans, sons and daughters of tribal leaders, and children who were forcibly removed from their parents. In the early years, the school was run like a military boarding institution, with an emphasis on vocational skills and strict sanctions against observing traditional ways. Later the direction changed to academics and Native heritage. By the time the federal government closed the school in 1980 (budget cuts during the Carter administration), nearly 3,000 students had gone through the program.

The museum is in the former superintendent's home, 5366 Snyder Ave., 775/882-6929, www.stewartmuseum.com, open daily 10 A.M.–5 P.M.; donations pay operating costs. Exquisite woven blankets and rugs sell for $150–450. A large powwow is held every June; artists sell their work, 200 dancers perform, and photo ops abound.

The campus has a palpable spirit: the stunning 1930s polychrome stone buildings (dorms, classes, auditorium, gymnasium, churches, etc.), the gigantic shade trees planted as early as those downtown, the quiet. Some of the buildings now house the State Prison Administration offices, which lends a contrasting spooky air to the grounds. If you bring a picnic lunch and stay kinda close to the museum, you'll still sense the specialness of this spot, epitomizing the powerful soul of Carson City. To get there, head south on US 395 about three miles from downtown, beyond Raley's and Mervyn's, go left on Snyder Avenue. In about a mile, just beyond two churches, go right into the parking lot.

Nevada State Railroad Museum

The brainchild of Bank of California's William Sharon, the Virginia & Truckee Railroad was installed (almost completely by Chinese labor) on the 21-mile tortuous route (dropping 1,600 feet in 13 miles) from Virginia City to Carson City in less than a year (1869). In its 81 years of operation, the V&T became the richest short line (later connected to Reno) in the West. The Jacobsen Interpretive Center houses a number of painstakingly restored rolling stock, big and shiny and beautiful. The *Inyo* is the V&T No. 22 Baldwin steam engine, with the fireman and engineer working at the controls. The No. 4 passenger car has plush green seats and a smiling conductor. There's an incredible display of 15 model V&T engines and wood, coal, and mail cars assembled over 10,000 hours by George Lincoln Robinson

COURTESY OF THE NEVADA COMMISSION ON TOURISM

Nevada's Railroad Museum in Carson City

of Santa Barbara. Bulletin boards display text and photos of the restoration process for Caboose No. 9, Coach No. 4, and Boxcar No. 1005, with before-and-after pictures that you won't believe.

The gift shop as you walk in sells books, T-shirts, maps, caps, and a video. Two engines do a loop around the grounds during the summer ($1). One is No. 8, an 1888 Baldwin steam locomotive that chugs around the grounds, a couple of times a month, at five mph ($2.50 adult, $1 children). Seven to nine volunteers man the thing. The other is a regular motor car that runs regularly ($1 adult, $0.50 children).

The museum, 2180 S. Carson St. on the far south end of town, 775/687-6953, is open daily 8:30 A.M.–4:30 P.M.; admission $2 adults, free for ages 18 and under.

Carson Hot Springs

Head out Hot Springs Road (bear right when heading north on Carson St. at the Safeway north of downtown) and drive about a mile past a couple of traffic lights. Follow the road around to the right and there are the old hot springs on the left, 775/885-8844. Abe Curry built his Warm Springs Hotel next to these waters and ferried

the territorial legislators out here when they met at the hotel. Today, there's a pool with 100°F soft spring water (no sulfur odor, nor any chlorine; they drain the pool every night and fill it up again every morning, which takes a total of six hours), along with private hot tubs, masseuse, motel, RV parking, and restaurant. The facilities are open daily 7 A.M.–11 P.M.; $10 gets you use of the pool for all day (you can come and go). A private hot tub for two is $15 per person for a two-hour session. Massage is $45 for an hour and includes the use of the pool and spa. Carson Hot Springs is just the thing after coming into the big city from anywhere in outback Nevada.

Also at the site is Richard Langson's Racing Museum and Pit Stop Bar. Langson, a world-champion top-fuel dragster, displays his memorabilia, mostly photographs and models, along the walls of this comfortable premises. The restaurant and bar has come and gone over the years. At press time, it was just coming again.

CASINOS

The grand old man of Carson City hotels is **Ormsby House,** 600 S. Carson St. The hotel dates back, in various incarnations, to 1859, when it was opened by Major William Ormsby, who was killed in the Pyramid Lake skirmish with Numaga's Paiute in the spring of 1860. Immediately it was sold to one John Kooser, who expanded it. In 1872 it was expanded again, and was renowned as one of the fanciest hotels between Denver and San Francisco. In 1880 the name was changed to the Park Hotel, and the hotel operated into the 1920s, when it closed. It was reopened in 1931, after legalization of casino gambling, by the Laxalts, possibly the most famous Nevadan family. Paul Laxalt, governor, U.S. senator, and close friend of Ronald Reagan, built the existing hotel in 1972, then sold it in 1975 to Woody Loftin. Loftin engineered a multimillion-dollar expansion in late 1988, which shook its financial stability; two years later Loftin filed Chapter 11, and the Ormsby House struggled along for another year and a half, finally shutting its doors on 250 employees and owing more than $15 million to creditors. It remained closed until early 1995, when it was resurrected by a group of southern California developers. It's suffered, however, from short-bankroll problems ever since, and at press time was undergoing yet another renovation that included gutting the old hotel and revamping the casino.

Otherwise, **Carson Nugget** at 507 N. Carson St. is the main action downtown. This is one of four Nuggets opened by Idaho restaurateur Richard Graves in northern Nevada in the mid-1950s; two of the others are still in operation (one in downtown Reno and the other in Sparks). It has a dozen blackjack tables, along with roulette and craps. Not unlike John Ascuaga's in Sparks, this Nugget also boasts bingo, a big race and sports book, steakhouse, oyster bar, lunch and dinner buffet (no breakfast), and 24-hour coffee shop; the only thing it's missing are the elephants. Being the main action, it's always crowded with locals and some visitors, which gives it the typical air of casino excitement.

Carson Station/Best Western is the other main casino, which has been completely revamped and improved since its old Mother Lode Casino days. This is also a popular spot, especially at night when there's usually some jumping live entertainment. Carson Station has plenty of blackjack (with Las Vegas rules—the trend in northern Nevada these days), craps, roulette, keno, a sports book, coffee shop, and a good snack bar. The gift counter has a good selection of newspapers.

The newest Carson City offering is **Casino Fandango** at 3800 S. Carson St. The tropical-themed casino, complete with an indoor waterfall, has more than 600 slots and the requisite table games as well as the Rum Jungle buffet, the Palm Court Grill, a poker room, sports book and bar, espresso bar, deli, and live entertainment.

Cactus Jack's right downtown is not to be confused with Cactus Petes in Jackpot or Whiskey Pete's in Primm. It was opened in 1971 by Pete Piersanti of Cactus Petes fame (Jackpot); he sold it in 1989. The neon Senator out front waves cash (but is a bit too red for comfort). Inside is perhaps the most compact casino in the state, where the horseshoe bar is the largest feature, followed, in descending size order, by a U-shaped snack bar, tight aisles of slots, a four-table pit (three blackjack and one Let It Ride; one bj table is often shut down to host bingo of all things, right in the pit), a two-teller cage, and a mini–sports book.

Right next door is the **Carson Horseshoe Club,** not to be confused with the Horseshu across from Cactus Petes in Jackpot nor Binion's Horseshoe in downtown Las Vegas. It too is a slot haven—newer and darker than Jack's, and way less tightly packed, with some of the best snack bar prices in the state.

Slot World, 3879 US 50 E., 775/882-SLOT, is a slot machine casino open 24 hours, with a bar and a restaurant, the Caravan Cafe, open 6 A.M.–10 P.M.

The **Best Western Pinon Plaza Resort,** 2171 US 50 E., 775/885-9000 or 877/519-5567, www.pinonplaza.com, is one of Carson City's newer casinos. It's large and luxurious, with facilities including a full-service casino, the Fiesta Lounge with live entertainment, sports book and sports bar, a state-of-the-art bowling center, a steakhouse and saloon, plus swimming pool, sauna, hot tub, exercise room, and a 148-room Best Western hotel. This resort was voted the "Best of Carson" in 12 categories in a *Gazette-Journal* poll.

RECREATION

Mills Park, four blocks east on US 50 from US 395, is an excellent city facility with lots of recreation choices: big green shady lawn for stretching out and daydreaming, picnic tables and barbecues, tennis courts, horseshoe pits, indoor and outdoor pools next door at the community center with a big water slide (variety of hours; 775/887-2242), and the Carson and Mills Park Railroad (775/887-2523), a one-mile, 15-minute ride in toy passenger cars behind a 100-year-old steam engine on Carson & Colorado Railroad 30-pound track. The train runs from Wednesday to Sunday noon–6 P.M. in the summer and just weekends from noon–6 P.M. in the fall and winter; the ride costs $1.50, and a snack bar is open whenever the train is running.

Carson River Park, 775/887-2115, is on both sides of the Carson River, about four miles out of town. Heading south on US 395 from US 50, take a left (east) on E. 5th and drive right through the middle of the grounds of the state maximum-security penitentiary. Just the sight of the pen, roasting in the desert within high cyclone barbed-wire fencing and with gun towers in the corners, would be an effective deterrent to every boy between 15 and 25, the prime crime time. Cross Edmonds, take a right on Carson River Road, and head across the green valley down to the lazy river. Cross the little bridge and explore the network of dirt roads along it. Turn right (south) onto Mexican Dam Rd. and in about 1.5 miles you'll come to Mexican Dam. You can't go onto the dam itself (it's private property), but there's a fine one-mile trail along here, called the **Mexican Dam Ditch Trail.**

On the way to the river, you'll pass the **Silver Saddle Ranch Park,** operated by the BLM (775/885-6000). The park is on the south side of Carson River Rd., a quarter-mile north of Mexican Dam, between the river and Prison Hill; another section of the ranch is on the east side of the river. The intention for this park is that it remain undeveloped; you can walk down to the river on the old farm roads and just enjoy the quiet, open space. Open every day, 8 A.M.–dusk.

Alternatively, if you don't turn onto Carson

River Rd., you can continue straight ahead on East 5th Street until you come to **Riverview Park,** 775/887-2115, a lovely riverside park with a wetland area, exercise stops along a trail, and people walking their dogs.

Centennial Park, 775/887-2115, is one of the largest municipal recreation facilities in Nevada. It's off US 50 east of town to the south, along Centennial Drive. It boasts several softball and soccer fields, many pleasant and shady picnic sites, tennis courts, and a public golf course with driving range and clubhouse. This is the place for a long walk after a soak at Carson Hot Springs and a meal at Garibaldi's, and before hunkering down for some craps at Carson Station.

ACCOMMODATIONS

Be sure to have reservations if you're planning to stay in Carson City on a Friday or Saturday night, when every room in town is usually booked up.

A good room-dining-gambling package that's been around forever is at the **City Center Motel** (room) and the **Carson Nugget** (food and gambling). For $46, you get a room for two, two buffet dinners, four cocktails, four dollar tokens, and some miscellaneous coupons–a very good deal. You can get a second night for an additional $37. Call 800/338-7760 and ask for the "Good Times Package." The City Center Motel is at 800 N. Carson St., 775/882-1785; prices for "room only" are $28–54 for the 78 rooms.

First place to try if you're looking for a potentially inexpensive room is the **Frontier Motel,** 1718 N. Carson, 775/882-1377, with rates as low as $25 a night—and as high as $179. Also try the **Pioneer Motel,** 907 S. Carson, 775/882-3046, $28–70. Rates start at $30 at the following motels: **Carson City Inn,** 1930 N. Carson, 775/882-1785; **Best Value Motel,** 2731 S. Carson, 775/882-2007, and **Downtowner Motor Inn,** 801 N. Carson, 775/882-1333. For slightly more uptown digs, head for the **Super 8 Motel,** 2829 S. Carson, 775/883-7800, $29–150; **Nugget Motel,** 651 N. Stewart, 775/882-7711, $45–55; the **Mill House Inn,** way down at 3251 S. Carson, 775/882-2715, with rooms for $45–75; **Holiday Inn Express,** 4055 N. Carson St., 775/283-4055,

$75–129; **Best Western Trailside Inn,** 1300 N. Carson St., 775/883-7300, $39–149; **Days Inn,** 3103 N. Carson St., 775/883-3343 or 877/231-1574, $43–145; **Plaza Hotel,** 801 S. Carson St., 775/883-9500 or 888/227-1499, $46–76; or the **Hardman House Motor Inn,** 917 N. Carson, 775/882-7744, $62–99.

The **Best Western Pinon Plaza Resort,** 2171 US 50 E., 775/885-9000 or 877/519-5567, www.pinonplaza.com, has 148 spacious, luxurious rooms that range $50–150, and there's also an RV park. If you're a golfer, ask about their "Golf Getaway" packages, starting from $55 per golfer midweek.

For a truly exceptional place to stay, check out the **Bliss Mansion Bed & Breakfast,** 710 W. Robinson St., 775/887-8988 or 800/887-3501, opposite the Governor's Mansion. Built in 1879, this magnificent state historical landmark was completely renovated and restored in 1994, and is decorated with Victorian museum-quality furniture and art. The four upstairs guest rooms, each with private bath, are $175 per night; reservations required, adults only.

Camping and RV Parking

Camp-N-Town RV Park, 2438 N. Carson St., 775/883-1123, is aptly named: It's right in downtown Carson City, a 15-minute stroll to the Capitol, State Museum, and casinos, and across the street from a large shopping center. It's relatively quiet for such a central location, behind the 49er Motel. And it's shaded by the tall trees that help give downtown Carson its charm. It has 157 spaces for motor homes, all with full hookups; 38 are pull-throughs. Tents are not allowed. Restrooms have flush toilets and hot showers; a public phone, sewage disposal, laundry, groceries, a game room, a bar, and a heated swimming pool are available. Reservations are recommended for summer weekends; the fee is $28 for two people.

Comstock Country RV Resort, 5400 S. Carson St., 775/882-2445, has a great location just south on US 395 past the intersection with US 50. There are 163 spaces for motor homes, all with full hookups; 133 are pull-throughs. Tents are allowed. Restrooms have flush toilets and hot showers; public phone, sewage disposal, laun-

dry, groceries, a game room, and heated swimming pool and spa are available. Reservations are accepted; tent sites and RV spaces $32.

The **Piñon Plaza Resort RV Park** is beside the Piñon Plaza Resort Casino, 2171 US 50 E., 775/885-9000 or 877/519-5567, 2.5 miles east of downtown on US 50. RV spaces are $24, with AARP, AAA, and Good Sam discounts available. No tents allowed. Prices include use of the pool at the hotel.

Three public campgrounds are within easy striking distance of the capital. **Dayton State Park** is 13 miles east on US 50. **Davis Creek** and **Washoe Lake State** parks are 15 miles north in Washoe Valley.

FOOD

Carson City has a large range of restaurant fare for a town its size, from the $0.89 breakfast special at the Horseshoe to the $50 chateaubriand at Adele's.

For the cheapest food around, patronize the snack bar at the **Horseshoe Club** downtown, 775/883-2211. Good breakfast, lunch, and graveyard specials; open 24 hours. **Cactus Jack's** Corner Cafe, 775/882-8770, has been remodeled and the prices are a little higher since.

Perhaps the best place in the whole state to get breakfast or a true old-fashioned blue-plate-special diner meal is at the **Cracker Box,** 402 E. William (US 50 one block east of Carson St.), 775/882-4556, open daily 6 A.M.–2 P.M. This is the real deal, with an eight-seat counter and tables for 50 in a squat green-and-white box of a building. The grill cooks are straight out of the '40s, the waitresses out of the '60s. The basic breakfast has the thickest meatiest bacon this side of Macon, a big pile of home fries with bits of pepper and onion, and large eggs cooked *exactly* the way you order them; the orange juice is freshly squeezed (and comes in two sizes: "not very small" and "huge!"). The egg dishes are the mainstay, but the menu also bursts with burgers, hot sandwiches, and daily specials, all in the $3 to $8 range. It's a classic.

Heidi's, 1020 N. Carson St., 775/882-0486, serves big breakfasts and diner lunches to crowds of locals and passers-through at good prices. Its long north and south walls are now graced by detailed trompe l'oeil murals: The south wall's is a V&T steam engine with cattle pusher pulling out of the Engine House (a historic stone building constructed by Abe Curry and torn down amid controversy in 1992); the north wall's is a view of the desert from inside the Engine House. Heidi's also has branches in Reno, Minden, and South Lake Tahoe. The same folks run the popular **City Cafe Bakery,** 701 S. Carson, 775/882-2253, which is a little bit of San Francisco in Carson: six kinds of brewed coffee, along with espresso and cappuccino, big sandwiches, muffins, rolls, and breads (honey wheat, rye swirl, sourdough).

Juicy's hamburger joint, corner of Winnie and N. Carson, 775/883-5600, has some of the best burgers in western Nevada. The burger and fries will ensure that you don't think about food for at least a few hours. Eat in air-conditioned and house-planted comfort, or take out for a picnic at Stewart Indian Museum and campus.

Right in downtown Carson City is **Garibaldi's** Italian restaurant, 775/884-4574, weekdays 11:30 A.M.–2 P.M., nightly from 5 P.M.–10 P.M. It's a cozy little room, with an eight-seat bar, about a dozen tables, six ceiling fans, and all-wood decor. For lunch, the pasta (homemade) is in the $8–10 range (the vegetarian lasagna is down to earth; the spaghettini with shrimp and capers in a lemon-rosemary sauce is orbital), or try the meat pies (rabbit and vegetables, for example) or the veal-meatball sandwich for $8. Dinner pastas run $11–15, and the eggplant, veal, chicken, Italian sausage, New York steak entrées are $12–19. Another good Italian option downtown is **B'S-ghetti's,** 318 N. Carson St., 775/887-8879, which is open for lunch and dinner.

Station Grille and Rotisserie, 1105 S. Carson, 775/883-8400, open for lunch Tuesday to Friday starting at 11:30 A.M. and dinner starting at 5 P.M., has an open kitchen, murals of fruits and veggies, echoing stone tiles, and great food. The $9 rotisserie chicken (with soy and lime) is the play here, or you can get California-style wood-fired pizza ($8), grilled ravioli or cioppino ($10), along with blackened shrimp, leg of lamb, and other interesting dinner entrées. For lunch, the Grill serves mesquite-grilled burgers turkey en-

chiladas, pizza, and smoked chicken and avocado salad in the $8 range.

Red's Old 395 Grill, 1055 S. Carson St., 775/887-0395, is a fun barbecue restaurant with great decor and great food, very popular with locals. Lunch and dinner are served every day from 11 A.M.–10 P.M. (dinners $12–25), both inside and out on the barbecue patio.

The **Nugget,** 775/882-1626, has lunch and dinner buffets, a Saturday breakfast buffet and Sunday brunch buffet. The Nugget's oyster bar features white chowder, crab sandwich, seafood cocktails, combo pan roast, and louies. Its Steakhouse has entrées in the $9–17 range. The coffee shop is open 24 hours; you can call the above number and be connected to a recording about the changeable specials in the coffee shop and steakhouse.

For some of the best Mexican food anywhere, pull up an appetite at **El Charro Avitia,** 4389 S. Carson, 775/883-6261. At El Charro, opened in 1978, the seafood enchiladas, burritos, and gorditas are worth the drive from Tahoe or Reno. Or try the Taco Nacionales, with chicken, cream cheese, and almonds. The tamales are stuffed with barbecued pork, the mini-fajitas are a steal, as are the three-item combos, and the guacamole shrimp cocktail is to die for. It's open Sunday to Thursday 11 A.M.–9 P.M., Friday 11 A.M.–10 P.M., and Saturday 5–10 P.M.

Other good Mexican restaurants include **Mi Casa Too,** 3809 N. Carson St., 775/882-4080, voted best Mexican restaurant by locals in the local newspaper poll, and **Tito's,** 444 E. William St. (US 50), 775/885-0390, all serving lunch and dinner.

For Chinese food, try **Ming's Chinese Restaurant,** 202 Fairview Dr., 775/882-8878, or the **Panda Kitchen,** 2416 US 50 E., 775/882-8128. All serve lunch and dinner. The **Water Wheel Restaurant,** 4239 N. Carson St., 775/883-7826, has Chinese and Japanese offerings, including some respectable sushi. The restaurant is open for lunch and dinner.

For the finest dining in Carson, where the power brokers broker their power, head for **Adele's,** 1112 N. Carson St., 775/882-3353. This gourmet restaurant is in the 19th-century house of Nevada Supreme Court Justice Murphy, and is extremely elegant in all its Second Empire appointments (read about it on the dinner menu). Inside, the bar is in the living room and several tables are in the dining room, with Victorian-style carpet, stained-glass windows, and fine lamps. "Lite" meals served in the bar—clams, oysters, sandwiches, omelettes—start around $10. Full-blown dinners in the dining room start at $18.50 and go up to $50; they're far too numerous to even mention. Suffice it to say that practically anything you want that's in season is available at Carson City's finest restaurant.

You can break the Starbuck's habit with one stop at **Java Joe's,** 319 N. Carson St., 775/883-4004, a funky little coffeehouse inside a historic building that once housed a mortuary. The coffee drinks are superb, and the scones, pastries, and sandwiches are worth the stop. Open for breakfast and lunch and evening coffee.

INFORMATION AND SERVICES

The **Chamber of Commerce,** 1900 S. Carson, 775/882-1565, www.carsoncitychamber.com, is downstairs in the building next door to the Railroad Museum. It's open weekdays 8 A.M.–5 P.M. Pick up local maps and handouts. If you're from out of state, collect a free funbook for the casinos. The chamber sells some books, T-shirts, and souvenirs. It also answers general questions about the area, offers relocation and starting business packets, and brochures on area lodging, dining and special events.

Upstairs in the same building, the **Carson City Convention & Visitors Bureau,** 1900 S. Carson St., 775/687-7410 or 800/NEVADA-1, www.visitcarsoncity.com, open weekdays 8 A.M.–5 P.M. and weekends 10 A.M.–3 P.M., is another good place for visitors to ask questions. Call ahead and they'll send you a visitor packet.

The **Nevada Commission on Tourism,** in the historic brick Paul Laxalt State Building at 401 N. Carson St., 775/687-4322 or 800/237-0774, www.travelnevada.com, has information on the entire state of Nevada. The two offices mentioned above are the places to go for information about Carson City; this is the place to come for information on the rest of the state. This state office's goal is primarily to promote tourism in Nevada's rural areas. Here you can pick up brochures on all of Nevada and its territories, events around the state, the Nevada Scenic Byways brochure, regional brochures, Great Basin National Park brochures, and a good state map. The office is open weekdays 8 A.M.–5 P.M.

Books and Maps

The **Carson Ranger District** office is at 1536 S. Carson St., a block north of the Railroad Museum, 775/882-2766; open weekdays 8 A.M.–4:30 P.M. The staff is extremely helpful, with good literature, maps and information on Mt. Rose, Lake Tahoe, and the Humboldt-Toiyabe National Forest, the national forest which comprises all the national forest land in Nevada in many different places. The office also sells maps and a number of useful books and other items, unusual for a Forest Service office. Ten percent of the sales goes back to the Carson District for recreation and wilderness programs.

The **Carson City Library,** 900 N. Roop next to Mills Park, 775/887-2247, opens at 10 A.M. Monday to Saturday, staying open until 6 P.M. Friday, Saturday, and Monday; until 9 P.M. Tuesday to Thursday.

If you're serious about your maps, head to Room 206 of the **Nevada Department of Transportation** building, 1263 S. Stewart St., 775/888-7627, for the graphics and cartography department. Beautiful huge prints grace the foyer; beautiful huge maps are for sale upstairs. Pick up the catalog, plus mileage and public transportation maps free; huge state maps, poster-size city maps, enlarged area maps and quad maps, plus the excellent *Nevada Map Atlas* are available.

At the **Gaming Commission,** 1919 E. College Pkwy., 775/684-7750, you can buy a number of publications about the casino and slot industry, including thick printouts of regulations and lists of locations. But the booklet *Gaming Nevada Style* is free and explains most of it in English.

Transportation

Public Rural Ride (PRIDE; 775/348-RIDE) operates buses nine times a day, 6:30 A.M.–7 P.M., between Carson City and Reno. Fares are $3 adults, $2 youth, $1.50 seniors, including free transfers to Reno's city bus system, Citifare. In Carson City, PRIDE bus stops are at the Wal-Mart on the south end of town, at the Nevada Department of Transportation (1263 S. Stewart St.) in the center of town, and at the K-Mart on the north end of town.

Greyhound and **K-T** long-distance buses depart from the Carson City bus depot at the minimart of the Frontier Motel, 1718 N. Carson St., 775/882-3375. Direct buses go to Reno, Las Vegas, South Lake Tahoe, Sacramento and Los Angeles, with connections to other places.

Unless you've got a private plane or are chartering one, you won't need information about the Carson City Airport; no regularly scheduled flights service the capital!

Carson City has three rental car companies: **Enterprise,** 1001 S. Carson St., 775/883-7788; **Hertz,** 3550 S. Carson St. (at the Mazda dealership), 775/841-8002; and **U-Save Auto Rental,** 2001 US 50 E., 775/882-1212.

GENOA

Genoa (pronounced juh-NO-uh) is the oldest town in Nevada, settled by Mormons in 1851 after an advance party had established a trading post here a year earlier to service the Emigrant Trail. The first settlers returned to Salt Lake City extolling the valley's scenic, agricultural, and commercial virtues. Brigham Young assigned a mission to colonize this western outpost of the Utah Territory. The settlement, known as Mormon Station for its first five years, was the site of the first house, first public meeting, first written records, first land claim, and first squatter government in what would soon be Nevada.

In 1855, Young dispatched a prominent Mormon judge, Orson Hyde, to administer the colony, along with another 100 settler families. By then, the fertile surrounding valleys had already been homesteaded by gentiles, and Mormon Station, which Hyde renamed Genoa (in honor of the birthplace of Christopher Columbus), was thriving. But in 1857, all the Mormons were recalled by Brigham Young to help defend Salt

Lake City from an imagined invasion by the U.S. government and Genoa began its downhill slide from prominence.

The Latter-day Saints expected to be paid for their property, which was quickly claimed by gentile residents. After years of failed attempts to be reimbursed for the land, structures, and businesses, Orson Hyde finally placed a curse on gentile Genoa. "You can pay [$20,000] and find mercy, or despise the demand and perish!"

It's arguable that the curse succeeded; since then, Genoa has suffered some serious setbacks. When Abe Curry tried to buy a plot of land in Genoa, he was sent packing, so he went off to start his own town. Immediately after the discovery of the Comstock, Curry's Carson City, with a much more advantageous location to serve the Lode, eclipsed Genoa. The *Territorial Enterprise,* established in Genoa in 1858, moved to Carson City, then Virginia City. And although Genoa became the seat of Douglas County in 1861, the post office moved into Carson City the same year. Next, in 1879, some Genoa boys played a prank on a town resident, Lawrence Gilman, who immediately bought a plot from homesteader John Gardner at the southern end of Carson Valley, and moved there in a huff. Gilman's new settlement, Gardnerville, proved a much better location to serve the farmers of Carson Valley and the miners on their way to strikes farther south. A bad avalanche hit the town in 1884, and a flood in 1891.

In 1910, a fire consumed most of what was left of Genoa and in 1916, Minden took away the Douglas County seat. The curse seemed to fade after that. In the late 1940s, the state rebuilt the original Mormon station and fort. That attraction (and others), along with the beautiful setting, historical significance, and mushrooming tourism, have turned Genoa into a popular destination, especially as a day-trip from Carson City, 12 miles north. And today, Genoa is actually a growing suburb of the capital, with large new houses surrounding the historical center of town.

However, some residents still fear the effects of living under Orson Hyde's hex. One local tried to organize a curse-lifting ceremony to coincide with the unveiling of a new historical marker at the Mormon fort in 1991. But nobody seemed to know how to do it.

Sights

First stop should be at the **Genoa Courthouse Museum** across from the park, 775/782-2555, open daily May to mid-October, 10 A.M.–4:30 P.M.; admission $3 for adults and $2 youth. The building, a courthouse from 1865 to 1916, then a school till 1956, has been a museum since 1969. Eye-catching artifacts in the eclectic collection include: model stamp mill, beautiful Washo baskets, nine-inch "escape" keys from the replica prison cell, luxurious burgundy velour furniture in the pioneer parlor, and valuable first-day issues displayed in the original post office. Upstairs is the courtroom. Snowshoe Thompson, legendary Scandinavian mail carrier, gets a display case, as does the Ferris wheel, invented by George Ferris, who grew up in a house still standing in Carson City. An entire room is devoted to the Virginia & Truckee Railroad. From the museum book rack, pick up a copy of the *Genoa-Carson Valley Book* ($3), 100 pages of coverage of this whole neck of the woods.

Stroll across the road to **Mormon Station State Historic Park,** 775/782-2590, the site of Nevada's first permanent nonnative settlement, The stockade replicates one built by the earliest settlers to keep livestock—it's doubtful they were much afraid of the timid Washo. A small museum displaying relics of pioneer days is housed in a replica of the original 1851 trading post; take some time to read the signboards and check out the copy of the *Territorial Enterprise* from January 1, 1859, published here before it moved on to more silvery press rooms. The museum and park are open May through mid-October, every day 9 A.M.–5 P.M.; donation.

Down the road in town is **Genoa Bar,** which accurately claims to be Nevada's oldest operating thirst parlor (since 1863). Have a beer and read the newspaper story about the place—more than you ever wanted to know, including the names of the first two bartenders.

South of the courthouse is the old **Masonic Hall,** built in 1862, and added onto in 1874. The **Genoa Country Store,** built in 1879, is one of the great country stores in Nevada, with an interesting assortment of cards, bottles, flags, hats, and jams, plus a wooden Indian, Coke and beer, and a soda fountain with ice cream, frozen yogurt, and snacks. The **Volunteer Fire Department** was built in 1960, but the old **Town Hall** next door is more than 100 years old; the bell tower and porch were added in 1977.

Candy Dance

Genoa is also the scene of one of the oldest annual events in Nevada, the Genoa Candy Dance. This dentists' delight originated in 1919 when the town was trying to raise funds to install lights on the streets of the town. The fundraiser started out as a dance and midnight dinner, and eventually turned into a bake sale after the Genoa matriarchs mixed up batches of fudge to sell by the pound to the partygoers. The candy proved to be the star of the show, and the Candy Dance tradition began. Now having celebrated the more 80 years, the proceeds from the Candy Dance pay for most of Genoa's town services.

The Candy Dance takes place the third weekend of September. An arts and crafts fair is held Saturday and Sunday 9 A.M.–5 P.M.; up to 300 vendors set up booths with candy, food, and crafts at Mormon Station, the town park, and the Volunteer Fire Department. On Saturday night, a buffet dinner is held at the old fire station (next to the country store) and the dance takes place at the town hall (next to the old fire department).

More than 4,000 pounds of candy-plain, nut, and mocha fudge, almond roca, nut brittles, dipped chocolates, divinity, mints, almond clusters; 35 different kinds altogether-are sold during the two-day fair. For more information, call 775/782-8696.

Practicalities

Genoa boasts two bed-and-breakfasts. The rates at both B&Bs include the use of Walley's Hot Springs. **Genoa House Inn,** Nixon St., 775/782-7075, was built in 1872 and is a National Historical Place. It features three guest rooms upstairs, one with a whirlpool tub, the other with a bilevel shower stall, and one downstairs. Linda and Bob Sanfillippo run the inn; he's the

Genoa town maintenance man, and she's famous far and wide for her homemade cinnamon rolls. Rates are $120–165.

Just up the street from the Genoa House is the **Wild Rose Inn,** 2332 Main St., 775/782-5697. This three-story Queen Anne Victorian was built in 1989 as a B&B by Sandi and Joe Antonucci. All five guest rooms have private baths. One is on the main floor. Three are on the second floor, which features a circular plan in which none of the rooms share a wall–very private and quiet. The third floor has the inn's suite, with a full, twin, and trundle bed, sitting room, and long bath. Rates are $115–180.

The Pink House, 775/783-1004, is unmistakable. Serving dinner Tuesday through Sunday 6–10 P.M. (bar opens at 5 P.M.), the restaurant and bar are in a two-room guest cottage and bunkhouse on the property of the actual Pink House, around the corner on Genoa Lane. This is one of, if not the, oldest houses in Nevada, having been built in 1855 on a site up the hill a piece at today's Mill Street by Captain John Reese, the earliest non-Mormon settler at Mormon Station, and therefore Nevada. A man named Johnson bought the original structure in 1870 and moved it, using wood planks, a

winch, and manpower, to its present location. He also painted it pink. The house changed hands only twice before Walt and Nora Merrell bought it in 1971 and opened the restaurant and bar; new owners took over in 1994. The menu is full of meat, king crab and halibut, chicken, and "the best rack of lamb in Nevada," according to the host. All are in the $15–20 range. Dinners come with a mountain of other food: onion soup, Caesar or spinach salad, and baked potato.

The **Inn Cognito,** 202 Genoa Ln., 775/782-8898, serves dinner and drinks every night except Tuesday; the bar opens at 5 P.M., and dinner is served from 6–9 P.M. (until 10 P.M. Friday and Saturday nights). Make your reservations early for this extremely popular restaurant, one of the finest in western Nevada. The meals here are slightly more expensive than the Pink House's. Try the veal dish of the evening, calamari amondine, scallops pommery, or any one of the many daily specials. Save room for dessert, included. Dinners run around $17–40.

Walley's Hot Springs

This splendid resort is just over a mile south of Genoa on Route 206/Foothill Rd., 775/782-

Walley's Hot Springs

COURTESY OF THE NEVADA COMMISSION ON TOURISM

8155 or 800/628-7831. The springs have hosted a hotel since 1862. David and Harriet Walley opened a $100,000 spa at springs along a fault whose water reached 160°F. In 1895, after falling into disrepair, the resort was sold for $5,000. The original hotel burned in the 1920s, and was rebuilt in the late 1980s with no expense spared and attention paid to every last detail. Today, it's a beautifully landscaped, luxurious, and reasonably priced hotel-spa.

Cabins can be rented for $90 to $110. The rates include use of six mineral pools, large heated swimming pool, separate steam rooms and saunas, and weight rooms. You can also get a massage, play tennis, take exercise classes, or just use the facilities for the day ($20); open every day, 6 A.M.–10 P.M.

The restaurant and bar are in a large and beautiful stone-and-wood lodge. The restaurant is open for dinner Tuesday through Saturday, 5–9 P.M., and once a month for Sunday brunch.

MINDEN AND GARDNERVILLE

Lawrence Gilman, a refugee from the curse of Genoa, in 1879 bought nearly eight acres of land on the East Fork of the Carson River from John Gardner, who'd homesteaded the southern Carson Valley since 1861. He moved a building there from Genoa and opened the Gardnerville Hotel. He also opened a blacksmith shop and saloon, which served the local ranchers, and the miners and freighters heading from Washoe to the doings at Esmeralda (Aurora, Bodie, and the borax country south). In the 1880s, a number of Danish immigrants settled in Gardnerville; their Valhalla Hall became the social center of the valley. Then, at the turn of the 20th century, Basque sheep ranchers swelled the ranks, both human and ungulate, of Carson Valley, doubling the number of sheep in the valley from fewer than 10,000 in the late 1890s to more than 25,000 in 1925. Basque boardinghouses flourished in Gardnerville and their legacy is alive today.

In 1905, the Virginia & Truckee Railroad extended its line from Carson City down to southern Carson Valley to service the farmers and freight their produce to market. The right-of-way was provided by Henry Fredrick Dangberg, a rancher in residence from the early days of Mormon Station who owned 36,000 acres. Dangberg was the first to grow alfalfa in Nevada and he married Margaret Ferris, sister of Carson City's George Ferris, who invented the Ferris wheel. Dangberg Senior died in 1904, and Dangberg Land and Livestock Company, run by his three sons, established a town to capitalize on the railroad depot. They named it Minden for their father's birthplace in Westphalia, Prussia.

A tidy little town with square blocks and a central plaza was laid out around the V&T depot. Within 10 years, Minden scooped the county seat from Genoa, and got a $25,000 courthouse in 1915. Gardnerville got the high school the same year. Minden developed its residential aspect while Gardnerville developed its businesses. In the 1930s, both towns claimed a combined population of only 500. But in the 1960s, the area got an economic boost when Bently Nevada, maker of electronic instruments, moved into the old Minden flour mill and creamery buildings.

Only two miles apart, Minden and Gardnerville have grown contiguous over the years, with most of the action strung along both sides of US 395 for several miles. A major subdivision called Gardnerville Ranchos south of the towns was one of the fastest growing neighborhoods in western Nevada, doubling its population to nearly 8,000, in the 1980s. Modern times caught up to the twin towns in late 1991, when the mail was delivered to houses for the first time.

It's worthwhile to wander the thin strip of back streets on each side of the highway; you'll get an instant sense of Minden's tranquil European charm and Gardnerville's farm-to-market tradition.

Sights

Starting at the north end of Minden and heading south on US 395, you pass the Carson Valley Inn; at the stoplight, notice the big **flour mill** and **butter company** buildings, now occupied by the Bently Nevada Corporation, along with its several buildings behind. Don Bently heads Bently, which produces rotating and vibration-monitoring and measuring machinery. Don Bently was named Nevada Inventor of the Year in

1983, and 10 years later was awarded the Vibration Institute's Decade Award.

Continue down to the **C.O.D. Garage** and the rest of the brick buildings on Esmeralda Street in old downtown Minden. The garage is the oldest continually operating car dealership in Nevada, founded in 1910 as a Model-T dealer by Clarence O. Dangberg (C.O.D.), who immediately hired Fred "Brick" Hellwinkel as his mechanic. In 1916, the Minden Inn was built nearby, and Dangberg built a parking garage for its patrons, complete with a newfangled semi-automatic "car shampooer." He also became a Goodyear tire distributor, and in 1919 replaced the Model Ts with Buicks and Chevrolets. In the 1920s, the C.O.D. Garage expanded to a full block between Esmeralda Street and the highway. In the 1930s, Brick Hellwinkel began taking shares in the business in lieu of pay, eventually achieving ownership. The Union 76 sign on Esmeralda makes for one of the great art-deco photo ops in Nevada.

Follow Esmeralda Street north again a few blocks, past **Minden Park,** laid out by H. F. Dangberg across from his house for the pleasure of his workers. The **courthouse** is at the top of the street at the corner of 8th.

Heading south into Gardnerville, you pass the old high school building (which later became the junior high), built in 1915. The Carson Valley Historical Society spent several years restoring the building, which is now the **Carson Valley Museum and Cultural Center,** 775/782-2555. Inside you'll find the East Fork Artists Coop art gallery, a children's art museum, natural history and agricultural exhibits, a Basque exhibit, and an exhibit on the Washo tribe. Outside are picnic areas. The museum is open Tues.–Sat. 10 A.M.–4 P.M. Admission is $3 adults and $2 kids.

Casinos

The big action in the twin towns is at **Carson Valley Inn,** US 395 in Minden, 775/782-9711, opened in 1984. The popularity of this spot has been reflected in a decade's worth of almost continuous expansion, from a small casino on the highway to a classy hotel, with blackjack, craps, roulette, lots of slots, sports book, plus two bars,

Katie's 24-hour coffee shop, Fiona's steak and seafood restaurant (in the building next door), Michael's steak and seafood restaurant (in the casino), kids arcade, wedding chapel, RV park, and a motor lodge. It's definitely the biggest action of any kind between Reno and Mammoth Lakes on US 395.

Sharkey's on US 395 in Gardnerville, 775/782-3133, is as small as the Carson Valley Inn is large, and as unusual as CVI is typical. In fact, Sharkey's ranks right up there with the most interesting casinos in the state. The late Milos "Sharkey" Begovich learned the gambling business at his parents' boardinghouse in the California gold country. He worked as a pit boss at Harrah's Tahoe in the 1950s and '60s, and one night ran up a lucky streak on a blackjack binge at Harvey's, across the street, into six digits. He used the money to buy a stake in the Tahoe Nugget, which he operated for five years, then sold in 1969. He used that money to buy the Golden Bubble in Gardnerville and changed the name to Sharkey's Nugget. It's mostly slots, with three blackjack tables and keno.

But the gambling is secondary to the real attraction here. Every inch of wall space is packed with paintings, prints, posters, and photographs of gambling, horse racing, boxing, movies. Check out the huge woven back side of the one-dollar bill, and the large-format black-and-white photo of the 1910 Johnson-Jeffries fight in Reno. Stroll around to also look at the rooms full of antiques and saddles. You can't help being an oblivious tourist in this place—leaning over slots, bumping into people, getting the amused glance from some and the cold eye from others. Sharkey's one-of-a-kind memorabilia collection, his legendary generosity, and his huge prime-rib dinners can all be observed in the coffee shop behind the casino. First, look at the long line of commemorative and appreciative plaques in Sharkey's name on the left wall as you walk into the dining room. In the Rib Room is a fantastic collection of portraits of American Indians-handsome and dignified—by F. K. Young of Sparks. In an ironic twist, George Custer peers out over them all from the corner above the door. If you're going to eat here, the prime rib is famous far and wide.

Heritage Tours

Heritage Tours, the creation of a fifth-generation Carson Valley native and her daughter, offer fun and informative tours of the Carson Valley (as well as the Lake Tahoe region), visiting more sites of interest than you would have thought would be here, with plenty of interesting stories. Tours operate year-round, with a minimum of two persons; cost is $25 per hour for tours for one to four persons. Contact Laurie or Shannon Hickey, 1456 Foothill Rd., Gardnerville, 775/782-2893.

Recreation

Four golf courses grace the Carson Valley: **Carson Valley Golf Course,** 1027 Riverview Dr., south of Gardnerville, 775/265-3181; **Golf Club at Genoa Lakes,** Jacks Valley Rd., Genoa, 775/782-4653, listed among the Best Courses in America in 1995; **Sierra Nevada Golf Ranch,** 2901 Jacks Valley Rd., Genoa, 775/782-7700, in the Sierra Nevada foothills on a former cattle ranch; and the **Sunridge Golf Club,** 1000 Long Dr., Carson City, 775/267-4448, five miles south of Carson City at the north end of the Carson Valley.

A well-established glider-ride company, **Soar Minden,** 775/782-7627 or 800/345-7627, has been taking people soaring since 1978. The scenery is breathtaking, and there's no engine noise to interfere (though the wind does whip up pretty good). The most popular flight is the Mile High Flight ($125/200 for one/two people); other popular flights include the Lake Tahoe View flight ($95/160), the Emerald Bay Excursion ($210/275), and an aerobatic experience ($175). Introductory flying lessons are $150. Soar Minden operates out of Douglas County Airport, three miles north of Minden. To get there, heading south from Carson City or north from Minden on US 395 and turn east on Airport Road. Soar Minden's office is at 1138 Airport Road, at the entry to the airport parking lot; look for the sign saying "glider rides."

Accommodations

The **Carson Valley Inn,** 1627 US 395, Minden, 775/782-9711 or 800/321-6983, has 153 rooms for $55–189. Next door is the **Carson Valley Motor Lodge,** same phone numbers, with 76 rooms for $45–75. Behind the Inn is **Carson Valley RV Resort,** same phone numbers. It's parking-lot camping, but is surprisingly quiet for being so close to the highway. There are 59 spaces for motor homes, all with full hookups; 26 are pull-throughs. Tents are not allowed. Accessible restrooms have flush toilets and hot showers; public phone, sewage disposal, laundry, groceries, and gas are available. The stay limit is 14 days during the summer months. Reservations are accepted; the fee is $27–30 (Good Sam, AAA, and seniors-over-50 discounts available).

Other motels in Minden include: **Holiday Lodge,** 1591 US 395, 775/782-2288 or 800/266-2289, $30–48; and **Minden Best Western,** 1795 Ironwood Dr., 775/782-7766 or 800/441-1234, $55–90.

Gardnerville motels include the **Westerner,** 1353 US 395, 775/782-3602 or 800/782-3602, at $32–65 the least expensive of the bunch; **Sierra,** 1501 US 395, 775/782-5145 or 800/682-5857, $36–70; and the **Village,** 1383 US 395, 775/782-2624, $32–48. Another good option is the Historian Inn, 1427 US 395 N., 775/783-1175 or 877/783-9910, which has 35 rooms for $59–99.

The **Jenson Mansion B&B,** 1431 Ezell St., Gardnerville, 775/782-7644, is the local bed-and-breakfast. It's in one of the great public mansions in northern Nevada, built in 1910 in a combo Southern Colonial and New England architectural style. It has 12-foot ceilings, a huge Great Room, and four guest rooms on the second floor. Now under new ownership, it's expecting to re-open in fall 2004; call for current info.

Food

Minden–Gardnerville is Basque-food country, with one of the most famous and oldest (1909) Basque restaurants in the state. **The Overland Hotel,** 691 Main St., 775/782-2138, has been in Basque hands for decades. Lunch is served 12–2 P.M. ($12) and dinner 5–10 P.M. ($16), closed Monday. No menus—just choose between a few entrées and then watch the food pile up on the table.

Also try the **J&T Bar and Restaurant** down the street at 760 S. Main, 775/782-2074, for a Basque family-style experience: open Monday to Saturday for lunch 11:30 A.M.–2 P.M., dinner 5–9 P.M. ($19.50).

Sharkey's coffee shop is open 24 hours: bacon and eggs and omelettes, burgers, club sandwiches, big plates of delicious beef stew and dinner rolls for a mere pittance, veal, and shrimp. Sharkey's is famous for prime rib. Recommended.

Fiona's belongs to the Carson Valley Inn and is therefore just as classy: pleasing little tropical atrium with a koi pond, high ceilings, and impressive stonework. It's open for dinner daily 4:30 P.M.–9:30 P.M. and for Sunday brunch 9 A.M.–2 P.M. The play here is the salad bar, nearly as nice as the one at the Eldorado in Reno. Otherwise, the menu is full of the usual steak and seafood, with some interesting chicken (Cajun, pecan, or teriyaki) and pasta plates, mostly in the $14–20 range.

Petrello's Italian Restaurant, at the corner of US 395 and Esmeralda in downtown Minden in the historic district, 775/782-4410, is in the same league as Fiona's. It's open for lunch Tuesday to Friday 11:30 A.M.–2:30 P.M., dinner nightly 5–9 P.M. ($10–23), and Sunday brunch 9 A.M.–2 P.M. ($4–10).

Information

The Carson Valley Chamber of Commerce and Visitors Authority, 1513 US 395, Suite 1, Gardnerville, 775/782-8144 or 800/727-7677, www.carsonvalleynv.org, has information on the entire Carson Valley. It's open weekdays 8 A.M.–5 P.M.

TOPAZ LAKE

This undiscovered little gem, like its famous big sister to the north, sits half in Nevada and half in California. It's also fringed by the mighty Sierra, and has a state line lodge just across the Nevada border on the US highway. Unlike Tahoe, however, Topaz is a man-made water-storage basin, which impounds water from the West Walker River for recreation and irrigation of farms in Lyon County's Smith and Mason valleys. It's also more of treeless desert scene than forested Tahoe.

So in a sense, Topaz Lake is a hybrid of Lake Tahoe, Pyramid or Walker lakes, and Lahontan or Rye Patch reservoirs.

The Walker River Irrigation District, created in 1919 to manage the river, built a feeder canal from the West Walker River into a dry lake bed, renamed Topaz Lake, in 1921. An outlet tunnel was dug in the rim of the lake, allowing the river to continue on its way through Smith and Mason valleys and into Walker Lake. The Army Corps of Engineers built a rock-face wall in 1937 that added 15,000 acre-feet of storage for a total of 60,000. At its deepest, Topaz Lake is 100 feet.

Topaz Lake Park

Topaz Lake Park is one of two county parks with a campground in Nevada (this is a Douglas county park; Davis Creek Park is a Washoe County facility). It's a big spot, with a mile of beachfront. The RV sites are up the slope a little, and there's a grassy playground for the kids. There are 140 campsites for tents or motor homes up to 35 feet; 29 spaces have water and electric hookups and 13 are pull-throughs. Piped drinking water, flush toilets and showers, sewage disposal, picnic tables, grills, and fire rings are provided. The maximum stay is 14 days. Tent sites cost $8 and are first come, first served; RV sites cost $10 and can be reserved up to a year in advance. It's usually full on the weekends with anglers; the lake is stocked twice a year with trout. Call 775/266-3343 for information on the park and fishing, or 775/782-9828 for camping reservations. To get there, from the intersection of US 395 and Route 208, drive south on US 395 to the lake. At the sign, turn left and drive one mile (the last little bit is dirt) to the campground.

Topaz Lake Lodge and RV Park

This resort, 775/266-3338 or 800/962-0732, provides all the indoor recreation, accommodation, and supplies. Open year-round, the Lodge's casino has a good-size pit with a half dozen blackjack tables, plus crap and roulette tables. The long bar upstairs has a great view of the lake, the Wellington Hills, and Desert Creek Peak beyond. The 101 rooms at the lodge cost $50–63. The RV park next door has full hookups, plus showers and cable TV. The general store is open 24 hours; use your Shell card for any and all purchases. Check out the trout trophies hanging on the front wall: four- to five-pound browns and a seven-pound cutthroat (the average fish weighs three pounds and is 18–20 inches long). Trout are caught mostly between January and March, and the Lodge sponsors a trout derby from New Year's Day through the middle of April.

The Lakeview coffee shop is open 24 hours, and there's a buffet Friday and Saturday nights 5–9:30 P.M. There's also a nonsmoking steakhouse, open for dinner Friday, Saturday, and Sunday nights, 5:30–9:30 P.M. There's also a service bar and a big dance floor.

The RV park is next to the lodge. It has 36 spaces for motor homes, all with full hookups; 6 are pull-throughs. Tents are not allowed. Accessible restrooms have flush toilets and hot showers, and public phone, sewage disposal, groceries, and heated swimming pool are available. Reservations are recommended for summer; the fee is $24.

To get there take US 395 18 miles south of Gardnerville; it's three miles beyond the intersection of 395 and Route 208 east (38 miles to Yerington).

Reno and Tahoe

Northern Nevada

North of Sparks for a little more than 30 miles, you drive through sandy valleys hemmed in by desiccated hills where the most color in the country is found in the names: Pah Rah Range, Hungry Valley, Dogskin Mountain. Then you round a bend, crest a rise, and there, confronting startled eyes, is a hallucination. A huge lake stretches before you, its stark desert setting unlikely, its turquoise water improbable, and its stone pyramid, rising out of the depths, as perfect as Cheops. Its shorelines are smooth and treeless, its inlets gentle and graceful, its beauty strange and unsettling. And there's not a house, condo, cabin, motel, hotel, restaurant, nor even a parking lot in sight. As you descend to its edge and reach a tentative, unbelieving hand toward it, the cool clear water finally convinces you that it's as real as you are, and not a desert mirage after all: You've reach Pyramid Lake. But continue on, and the landscape become almost lunar, as you enter the Black Rock Desert.

As your encircle the northern region of Nevada, you'll find small towns and growing cities—from Fernley, Lovelock, Winnemucca, Elko, Wendover—surrounded by staggering natural beauty—Battle and Ruby Mountains—that remind you that you couldn't be farther away from the lights and noise of Las Vegas.

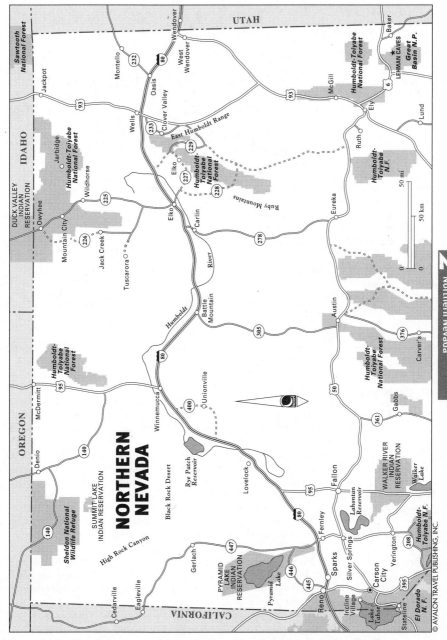

Northern Nevada

© AVALON TRAVEL PUBLISHING, INC.

Pyramid Lake

Pyramid Lake has been called the most beautiful desert lake in the world. It's one of the largest freshwater lakes in the western United States: 27 miles long, 9 miles wide, 370 feet at its deepest, 3,789 feet above sea level, with a water temperature fluctuating between 75°F in summer and 42° in winter. Its source, the Truckee River, leaves Lake Tahoe, travels 105 miles—down the east face of mighty mountains, through thirsty cities, and across reclaimed desert—then trickles into the southern delta of the lake, which has no outlet. Large Anaho Island juts up off the eastern shore slightly south of the pyramid, providing breeding grounds for the majestic American white pelican and other shorebirds. Jagged pinnacles stand sentinel over the northern end, where hot springs drain into the lake and a steam geyser vents from a rusty wellhead. Great Lahontan cutthroat trout grow to 15 pounds, and the endemic cui-ui sucker fish haunt the ancient depths. Nearly half a million acres of lake and surrounding desert are enclosed by the Pyramid Lake Reservation, a sacred area managed and preserved by its traditional Paiute caretakers.

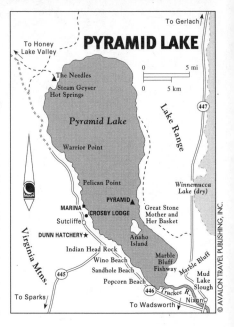

HISTORY

Pyramid Lake is the larger vestige (Walker is the smaller) of great Lake Lahontan, which covered much of the western Great Basin only 50,000 years ago. Glacial incursions during the ice ages of the previous two million years touched Nevada only in the high ranges, but the accompanying cold, wet climate created and supported this giant prehistoric body of water. An incredibly complicated inland sea, with its digitated branches spreading between, around, and over the basins and ranges, Lahontan stretched from McDermitt in the north and Honey Valley in the west to Hawthorne in the south and the Stillwater Range in the east. Its surface spread for 8,600 square miles at an average depth of several thousand feet (75 times larger and 10 times deeper than Pyramid Lake).

The climatological warming and drying trend that's prevailed since the last ice age, which ended roughly 15,000 years ago, has been shrinking the vast lake, smaller and shallower, shallower and smaller, down to this "minor" remnant. And unless a new ice age arrives, it'll continue to shrink until sometime in the not-too-distant future, when the Truckee River will echo the fate of the Humboldt and Carson Rivers, which both disappear, white and sour, into a desert playa that was once an improbable turquoise lake.

Paleo-Indians of the Lovelock period 11,000 to 4,000 years ago dwelled in lakeside caves, wore pelican-skin robes, chipped arrowheads from obsidian, carved fishhooks from deer antlers, and fashioned fishnets, baskets, even duck decoys from willow and tule reeds. It's undetermined whether the Lovelock people abandoned the area, were driven away by encroaching Paiute, or evolved into the Paiute. Many similarities exist between the two cultures, particularly their basketmaking styles.

the most beautiful desert lake in the world

The Paiute term for themselves is Neh-muh, or Numa. A nomadic people, the Numa gathered at Ku-yui Pah (Cui-Ui Waters) at spawning time, when the cui-ui and the gigantic and Lahontan cutthroat trout (actually a kind of landlocked king salmon—averaging 30–35 pounds) were easiest to catch.

The Americans Arrive

John C. Frémont, famous explorer, surveyor, and cartographer, entered the northwest corner of Nevada in late 1843, heading due south from eastern Oregon. He lingered briefly at High Rock Canyon, camped at the base of the Granite Range, and skirted the Black Rock Desert, about which Frémont wrote in his diary, "Appearance of the country is so forbidding that I was afraid to enter it." He and his party marched south in early 1844 along the edge of the Fox Range, beyond which they climbed a hill where "a sheet of green water. . . broke upon our eyes like the ocean. . . For a long time we sat enjoying the view [of the lake] set like a gem in the mountains." Frémont named the lake for the smaller of its two islands, which "presented a pretty exact outline of the great Pyramid of Cheops." Continuing south,

Frémont and his men encountered Paiute in a village near present-day Nixon. There, they were served up a feast of "trout as large as the salmon of the Columbia River. . . the best-tasting fish I had ever eaten." The explorers went on to name and map the Carson and Walker Rivers, then crossed the Sierra into California.

Only 15 years later, in January 1859 just before the discovery of the Comstock Lode and the establishment of Virginia City, an estimated 1,700 Numa congregated at the lake to fish and socialize. Chief Winnemucca was there with 300 of his clan; his son Numaga (Young Winnemucca) and his 300 Kuyui Dokado (Cui-Ui Eaters), whose territory encompassed the lake, hosted the gathering. At the same time, roughly a thousand white settlers and prospectors occupied traditional Numa land in what would soon be western Nevada.

Troubles between the nomadic Indians and the migrating whites were well underway. The Numa had determined the newcomers to be disrespectful people. Whites took prized ground with little or no regard for Indian claims or subsistence. They killed the game, felled the trees, wasted native food. They practiced indiscriminate

CUI-UI FISH

The endangered cui-ui (kwee-wee) is a sucker fish that lives only in Pyramid Lake. A prehistoric species, cui-ui inhabited Lake Lahontan for tens of thousands of years; as the inland sea slowly evaporated, these fish of the deep were able to survive at the bottom of the little Pyramid Lake remnant.

Cui-ui grow as large as seven pounds and can live 40 years. They spawn between the ages of 12 and 20, as early as April and as late as July, when they swim upstream as far as 12 miles west to lay their eggs. In the old days, before the Derby Dam water diversion lowered the lake level, the Paiute spearfished and snagged them at the mouth of the delta during the spawn. The WPA's *Nevada—A Guide to the Silver State* reported:

Now that the flow into the lake has been curtailed by upstream storage, the fish runs have practically ceased. Cui-ui schools circle through the shallows near the river mouth, searching in vain for spawning grounds, and pelicans step in and gorge themselves.

The cui-ui were nearly extinct by the 1940s. They managed to recover slightly in 1952 with one of the largest spawning runs (120,000 fish) in recent history. But compared to the millions of cui-ui that spawned in past, the population was decimated, prompting the federal government to list the fish as an endangered species in 1967. Another large run was recorded in 1969 (110,000 fish), but only a handful of cui-ui spawned between 1976 and 1982, and a census in 1984 counted only 150,000 of them. No cui-ui spawned between 1987 and 1992. Tribal members voluntarily stopped eating them in 1979.

In the early 1970s, federal courts directed that water in Stampede Reservoir be used exclusively to benefit the cui-ui. A small pulse of fresh reservoir water is released as early as January to tickle the spawning instinct; the pulse reaches its peak by April, which helps the fish reach the spawning grounds. The fresh water also incubates the eggs and helps the microscopic larvae to swim back to the lake.

The Marble Bluff dam and fishway were built in 1976 to stop the erosion of the riverbank, which threatened the stability of Nixon, just upstream. The dam

violence against the native peoples along the Humboldt River Trail. And they disrupted the natural order and sacredness of things, without giving anything in return. Still, the Northern Paiute, a strong, industrious, and peaceable people, knew the futility of waging war on the whites. In 1855, Chief Winnemucca had negotiated the Treaty of Friendship with federal Indian agents, in which it was agreed that tribal laws would be invoked to punish criminal acts by Paiute, and white justice would likewise deal with breakers of its own law. This treaty also defined territories, which were further delineated by the agents in 1859 as a precursor to the Pyramid Lake reservation. These agreements managed to keep the two peoples friendly for five years—until the discovery of the Comstock Lode.

The vast horde of fortune-seekers bound for Washoe in the spring of 1860 knew little, and cared less, about the Treaty of Friendship. Thousands of them overran prime Numa pinenut land in the Virginia Range and cui-ui spawning grounds along the Truckee River. Tensions mounted. Finally, an unfortunate spark touched off two pitched battles in the brief Nevada Indian wars. In May 1860, traders at Williams Station on the Carson River kidnapped and abused several Numa women. The Indians avenged the *also protects critical cui-ui spawning habitat. Some cui-ui will use the three-mile clay-lined fishway, which resembles an irrigation canal with a number of terraces known as ladders, but many won't. During large spawning runs, the fish jam the entrance to the fishway and some are smothered before they can be gathered onto a large elevator platform, which raises them up to the river and washes them into it. In 1993, after one of the wettest winters and springs in the century, so many fish struggled onto the elevator that it couldn't lift them, and 3,000 died. Officials had to load nearly 5,000 cui-ui into trucks, drive them past the fishway, and drop them back into the river.*

After the failure of the fish elevator, the federal government in 1996 allocated $2.5 million to redesign the Marble Bluff dam, fishway, and elevator. The project was underway in August 1997.

Two good water winters—1995 and 1996—and an astounding winter in 1997 have improved things considerably for Pyramid Lake and its cui-ui. In August '97, the lake was up 14 feet from three years earlier. At an elevation 3,809 feet above sea level, the lake hasn't reclaimed the high water mark of the early '80s (3,820 feet), but its current level still is one of highest since the early years of the century.

Aided by high water and other factors, more than 250,000 cui-ui spawned in the spring '97 run (a 50-year high). The Cui-ui Recovery Team now estimates the total adult cui-ui population at one million. John Jackson, director of water resources for the tribe, says downlisting the cui-ui's position on the Endangered Species List from endangered to threatened is under consideration.

Recently, members of the tribe have been able to get a taste now and then of this favored traditional food. An agreement with U.S. Fish and Wildlife allows the tribe to harvest and consume a small number of cui-ui, whose gills are removed and sampled by USF&W to test fish health and water quality. The tribe distributes the harvested cui-ui to elders and others on the reservation.

crime by killing the traders and burning the station. The incident spread hysteria and bloodlust through Washoe, and a ragged troop of volunteers set out on an ill-conceived, ill-prepared, and ill-fated retaliatory expedition.

Numaga, six-foot-four, fluent in English, son of great Chief Winnemucca (The Giver), spoke eloquently against engaging the whites in a fight. He led his Kuyui Dokado to meet the irregulars and sent a rider with a white flag to arrange a powwow. But the excited avengers shot at the rider and then blindly chased the Paiute into a ravine, where the Indians turned and slaughtered them. A month later, a force of regular troops from California pursued the Kuyui Dokado and exacted two Paiute lives for every white life lost.

Two years later, Territorial Governor James Nye met with Chief Winnemucca near the site of the second battle, where they exchanged gifts and spoke of peace. But another 12 years passed before President Grant in 1874 proclaimed Pyramid Lake and the surrounding desert an official reservation. Thereafter, a typical combination of unfortunate factors inhibited economic development. The continual replacement of Indian agents precluded consistent government relations. Federal appropriations proved remarkably insufficient. "Entrymen" (white squatters) appropriated prime agricultural acreage—at the big bend of the Truckee River, for one. Then the Central Pacific Railroad placed a division station at the southern edge of the reservation at Wadsworth in a 600-acre landgrab that is still, after more than 120 years, in dispute. At the time, however, a quarter of the reservation's inhabitants were coaxed to Wadsworth to work as laborers and housecleaners.

Water Troubles

After the diversion of the Truckee River in 1905 at Derby Dam to irrigate farmland around Fernley and Fallon, the water supply to the lake diminished systematically, depleting its fisheries and causing frequent irrigation problems for the Paiute farmers and ranchers. The lowered inflow created a silty, swampy delta where the river joined the lake, preventing the big Lahontan cutthroat from spawning. That, along with massive overfishing, rendered the trout almost extinct by the 1930s, further exacerbating the financial instability of the reservation. (In 1975 the Paiute began to stock the lake with purebred cutthroat, and today 15-pound trophies are not uncommon.)

The depth of the lake dropped continually throughout the 20th century; the surface level has been reduced nearly 100 feet. Diverting the river for reclamations and urban growth upstream has sidetracked much water from reaching the lake and increased the amount of pollution finding its way there. In addition, during periods of long-lasting drought such as occurred in the 1990s, the surface level of Lake Tahoe, source of the Truckee, falls below its natural rim. With all flow of Tahoe lake water into the river cut off, river water is prevented from replenishing the system's reservoirs in California, as well as Pyramid Lake at its terminus.

The Truckee-Carson–Pyramid Lake Water Rights Settlement Act (a.k.a. the Negotiated Settlement) was signed into law in November 1990. It settled nearly all the major water conflicts in western Nevada, allocating 90 percent of Truckee River water and 80 percent of Carson River water to Nevada (the rest to California). It allowed Westpac Utilities (the Reno–Sparks water company, a division of Sierra Pacific) to store 39,000 acre-feet of its own water in Stampede Reservoir, which is controlled by the Pyramid Lake Paiute, for drought or emergency conditions. In exchange, the Paiute received $25 million for the Pyramid Lake fisheries program, plus $40 million for economic development. In addition, conservation plans in the municipal water district were to be implemented, including the controversial retrofitting of all the houses in the Reno–Sparks area with water meters. Enough water rights were to be purchased to maintain 25,000 acres of Lahontan Valley wetlands and to improve the spawning potential of Pyramid Lake trout and cui-ui. The Army Corps of Engineers was mandated to prepare a plan for the rehabilitation of the lower Truckee River to restore natural spawning grounds.

The only major player along the Truckee–Carson water system that was not directly included in the Negotiated Settlement was the Truckee–Carson Irrigation District (TCID). Though the farmers of Fallon and Fernley would certainly disagree, Elmer Rusco in an article in the *Nevada Public Affairs Review* (1992, No. 1) wrote that the Settlement "does not worsen the situation of the TCID but simply confirms what existed before its passage." However, in another critical defeat for the Fallon farmers in June 1994, the federal Interior Secretary of Water and Science ruled that unclaimed water from the Truckee River (the overflow that isn't shunted off to reservoirs, ranging from 200,000 acre-feet in a dry year to more than a million acre-feet in a flood year) cannot be diverted to the reclamation project; it must be allowed to run its course into Pyramid Lake.

One of the first concrete accomplishments of the Negotiated Settlement was the Truckee River Operating Agreement, a pact that allows the tribe, the TCID, and various state and federal agencies to achieve the goals of the 1990 settlement by storing and exchanging each other's water throughout the lakes and reservoirs of the Truckee watershed. Prosser, Boca, Stampede, Independence, and Marlette reservoirs, in addition to Lake Tahoe, fall under the agreement.

The improvement of water quality on the lower Truckee is the goal of yet another working agreement that evolved from the Negotiated Settlement. The water-quality agreement calls for the tribe and Sierra Pacific Power Company to work together to purchase water rights in the watershed from the TCID and others. New ownership is viewed as a first step toward protection, enhancement, and rehabilitation of the entire river. Where the West and water are concerned, however, things move slowly.

While the deluge of January '97 left the reservoirs along the Truckee brimming and raised the level of Pyramid Lake to a 15-year high, it took scant pressure off the region's water users. With the drought years of the last decade still fresh in people's minds, water-conservation measures remained in effect, partly because such measures are mandated by the Negotiated Settlement.

Since 1975, the Paiute have operated the Dunn Hatchery at the lake. The hatchery has stocked Pyramid and Walker lakes with native cutthroat trout and have helped the cui-ui to spawn.

Friends of Pyramid Lake was founded in 1982 to unite citizens concerned about the lake's future. The group produces a newsletter and organizes forums, field trips, and other educational activities to increase awareness of the challenges, and the pleasures, of one of the most beautiful desert lakes in the world, and also organizes an annual triathlon at the lake. For more information, contact Friends of Pyramid Lake, P.O. Box 20274, Reno, NV 89515-0274, 775/323-6655.

ANAHO ISLAND

Anaho Island floats in Pyramid Lake like a giant sombrero, with a wide brim and a high crown. For centuries this 600-foot-tall island provided a breeding ground for the largest colony of American white pelicans in the United States. Because these birds—clumsy and comical on the ground, majestic and dignified in the air—have such sensitive nesting instincts, they have long been considered a symbol of the wild country, a measure of its wildness. Predictably, the numbers of nesting pelicans on Anaho Island have dropped dramatically in recent years, almost to the point of disappearance.

Pelicans could be the easiest birds in the world to recognize. Their creamy white feathers, black-tipped wings with 10-foot spans, and huge orange bills cause them to stand out in the crowd of cormorants, herons, terns, ducks, geese, gulls, hawks, owls, and smaller species that, several months a year, call Anaho home. For thousands of years, tens of thousands of these creatures have migrated to Anaho from Southern California and western Mexico in the spring to set up housekeeping in this makeshift pelican city. A pair of pelicans settle into a nest, barely a hole in the ground softened perhaps with some dry grass and sage twigs. Into it the female lays two eggs, incubating them for a month with the webs of her feet. The male flies off every day to bring back a fish dinner. After hatching, the chicks mature quickly, reaching flight growth in two months and full growth (15–20 pounds) by migrating time in the fall.

Contrary to common conception, pelicans do not store fish in their large beaks. (The pouch stretches or contracts to control body temperature.) They swallow the fish (traditionally tui chub and carp from Winnemucca Lake—now dry—just east over the Lake Range), then regurgitate and redigest them. Pelicans, in fact, are the true bulimics of the animal kingdom, vomiting their food in the face of intrusion or danger. They're so skittish that fast-growing chicks confronted by chronic emotional distress can't hold their food down and will starve to death. Adult pelicans, startled by noise, will abandon their nests, leaving their eggs to fry in the hot desert sun, if the gulls don't eat them first. Unprotected days-old chicks, too, will quickly succumb to starvation, exposure, or predation.

In 1913, President Woodrow Wilson signed a bill preserving Anaho Island as a bird sanctuary, and today it's a 750-acre national wildlife refuge. In 1948, 10,000 pairs of pelicans nested here; by 1968, only 5,000 were showing up. In 1988, an all-time-low 350 pelican couples arrived to breed, from which a mere 50 chicks matured.

Since then, the numbers have improved dramatically. The solution was simple: a big inflow of water into the lake (and the Stillwater marsh country 60 miles southeast, traditional feeding grounds for the pelicans). Nature saw fit to end the drought in 1995 and supply the area with all the fresh water it needs—until the next drought.

FISHING AND BOATING

Fishing season for cutthroat trout is from October 1 to June 30. Record cutthroat are generally 15–20 pounds. Fishing permits cost $6 a day, or $32 for the season; boating fees are the same. (If you're going to fish from a boat, it's therefore $12 per day, or $64 for the season.) If you buy a fishing permit, you don't pay the reservation's $7-per-vehicle day-use fee. (Otherwise, for nonfisherfolk visiting the lake, there's a $7-per-vehicle day-use fee and $9 camping fee.) If you catch a cui-ui, you have to release it unharmed immediately; the penalty for being caught with an endangered species is a $10,000 fine (and very bad publicity). Fishing and boating permits are available at the Pyramid Lake Marina and at the Pyramid Lake Store, near the entrance to the reservation.

You can bring your own boat, or rent one at the Pyramid Lake Marina. Two small locally owned companies operate fishing charters on the lake. Lex Moser of **Pyramid-Tahoe Fishing Charters,** 775/852-3474, comes highly recommended by locals, who say his trips are a lot of fun. He offers fishing trips on Pyramid Lake from mid-October to mid-May, and on Lake Tahoe from early May through late October. George Molino, owner of the Pyramid Lake Store, operates **Cutthroat Charters,** 775/476-0555, with fishing trips on Pyramid Lake from October 1 through June 30.

While you're here, visit **Dunn Hatchery,** 775/476-0500, up the hill from town, to learn about the Paiute tribe's Pyramid Lake fisheries. It's open Mon.–Fri. 8 A.M.–4:30 P.M. First examine the displays on prehistory, history, tufa, fishing, and past problems and future solutions in front of the main hatchery. Then a Paiute employee will show you around the work area. These hatcheries are considered among the most advanced and successful in the world. A million cutthroat (and a handful of cui-ui) are planted yearly in Pyramid and Walker Lakes. Pregnant fish are captured and artificially spawned at the Marble Bluff fishway. The fertilized eggs are brought to the hatchery and incubated; they hatch in one to four weeks. The fry are then "ponded" in 60 small or three large freshwater tanks. After a year, they're planted in the lakes. You'll see the numerous ponds, the incubation chambers, and the rock-filtration room.

Then head around to the back building to check on the much more specialized and intimate cui-ui hatchery. This operation provides a graphic representation of how difficult it is to artificially breed these ancient suckers. Good spawning runs make the breeding program a little less critical.

The **Numana Hatchery,** 775/574-0290, on Route 447 about 10 miles south of Nixon and eight miles north of Wadsworth, also grows cutthroat trout and gives tours. If there are just a couple of people, you can show up any day from 8 A.M.–4:30 P.M., visit the visitors' center and see the fish. Large groups must make tour arrangements at the main office, Pyramid Lake Fisheries, 775/476-0500.

CAMPING

Go down the hill and around the corner from Crosby's for the **Pyramid Lake Marina,** 775/476-1156, where there's a ranger station, a minimart, a small museum, and an RV park (all under private, rather than tribal, ownership). Stop off at the ranger station or minimart and pay $6 per vehicle for a day-use permit, which applies to everyone visiting the lake, even if they're just passing through. The ranger station is open every day, 8 A.M.–5 P.M. Next door, the store is open daily 7 A.M.–7 P.M. weekdays and 6 A.M.–8 P.M. weekends. It's similar to Crosby's, but bigger and brighter. There's also a snack bar.

Also here at the marina is a 44-site **RV park** with a Laundromat, flush toilets, showers, and a dump station ($5). All RV spaces are pull-throughs, with full hookups. Tents are not allowed. Camping fees are $15 a day, $100 a week, and $330 a month. Dry camping along the lakeshore costs $9 a night; this covers your $6-per-vehicle day-use fee, too.

Two miles north of Sutcliffe is **Pelican Point,** with a boat ramp, good beach, Sani-Huts, and probably several tents right on the water. Farther north on the pavement (Route 445), you pass many turnoffs and dirt roads down to the shore—the sites aren't exactly "secluded" (little shade, no facilities), but there's plenty of opportunity to be by yourself on the beach. The pavement runs out in eight miles at **Warrior Point Campground,** which has a phone (might work), picnic shelters, drinking water, barren campsites, and little else. Camping fee is $9 per vehicle.

INFORMATION AND SERVICES

A day-use fee of $7 per vehicle is charged for those visiting the lake and/or the marina. You can camp anywhere around the lake; the camping fee of $7 per vehicle *includes* your day-use fee. Additional fees are charged for fishing and/or boating on the lake. Permits can be purchased at the Pyramid Lake Store, just inside the boundary of the reservation if you're coming from Reno, and at the Pyramid Lake Marina, where permits are available at both the store and the ranger station.

Just inside the boundary of the reservation at mile 23 is the **Pyramid Lake Store,** 775/476-0555, open every day 6 A.M.–6 P.M. (6 A.M.–6 P.M. in winter). Here you can stock up on last-minute fishing and boating supplies, pay your day-use or

camping fee, and buy fishing and boating permits. **Cutthroat Charters** operates fishing charters from the store through the Oct. 1–June 30 season. Boat storage in a fenced compound can be arranged for a fee.

In the settlement of Sutcliffe (also spelled Sutcliff) off Sutcliff Dr., you'll come to **Crosby's Lodge,** 775/476-0400. The expanded bar has slots, video poker and large screen TV. The lodge, grocery store/gift shop, and gas pump are open 7 A.M.–10 P.M. most days, opening a bit earlier (6:30 A.M.) on Saturday and Sunday, closing a bit later (9 P.M.) on Friday and Saturday nights. Four cabins, and additional kitchen-equipped trailers, are available for $48–112; a house is available for $95 a night, and RV spaces with full hookups are $20.

The gravel road north starts out fairly well graded—35–40 mph. In another half mile is a flat site on an attractive inlet; two miles from there is one of the few forested and green areas on the lake. Horses graze in the grass.

For further information about Pyramid Lake, the reservation and the businesses or other features found here, a good resource is the **Pyramid Lake Paiute Tribal Council,** 775/574-1000. The office is open Mon.–Fri., 8 A.M.–4:30 P.M.

Black Rock Area

On Route 447 heading north, you'll see the **Lake Range** on the west and the dry bed of Winnemucca Lake on the east. Known as Little Lake of the Cui-Ui by the Paiute, this transient body of water came and went often throughout the ages, since its depth was dependent on the overflow of the Truckee. In 1876, for example, a gravel bar partially blocked Pyramid Lake from the mouth of the river, which emptied much of its mountain and desert water into Winnemucca Lake to a depth of 85 feet. After the Derby Dam diversion in the early 20th century, Winnemucca Lake received a continually diminishing supply of water. In the mid-1930s, the WPA's *Nevada* reported that "it is only in wet years that it contains any water," though "many geese and ducks live in the

bordering tule marshes." Since then, the lake has dried up completely, leaving only a few tufa sculptures and a long playa. See if you can imagine a big blue lake out there. The **Nightingale Mountains** rise up from its extinct eastern shoreline.

This road is pencil straight; you can put it on autopilot for both the accelerator and steering wheel. Twenty minutes north, the tufa begins appearing on the west side of the road; keep an eye out for **Tufa Snoopy.** Thirty miles north of Marble Bluff you can clearly make out the old shoreline at the north edge of Winnemucca Lake. The **Selenite Range** picks up where the Nightingales leave off; Mt. Limbo's **Purgatory Peak** rises to 7,382 feet. North of it, **Kumiva Peak** scrapes the sky 900 feet higher. About 40 miles north

BURNING MAN

The Black Rock Desert is the scene of a huge yearly event called **Burning Man.** A 40-foot, 1,500-pound wood sculpture is erected in the area each year over Labor Day weekend. At the end of the weeklong festival, the Man is burned. The symbolism is about construction and destruction, ambition and futility, and just plain getting wild on the playa.

What started as a fringe event by a bunch of fringe characters has evolved into a spiritual celebration for modern times. Whatever Burning Man has become, it certainly has grown in terms of the number of people it attracts—in 1998 the gathering attracted an estimated 15,000 participants, in 2004 35,000. In recent years the community—known as Black Rock City—that springs up on the playa outside Gerlach, is, temporarily, one of the 10 largest towns in Nevada. Huge art installations, bizarre art cars, all-night music parties, massive geodesic domes, lights everywhere—and of course, lots and lots of fire—are the hallmarks of the party in the playa. So too are naked people and drugs.

Since no commerce is allowed—except at the café and ice station— "burners" have to haul everything they need in (and out) with them, though everyone is encouraged to share with others. However, there's a lot of infrastructure. The city is mapped out on arcs of streets, in which theme camps and individual participants set up elaborately decorated sites. Black Rock City also has its own constabulary (the Black Rock Rangers), radio stations, daily newspapers, village lamplighters, and fire, emergency, and sanitation departments.

Bikes are the primary mode of transportation. Still, taking the leap at Burning Man provides a lesson in survival: Scenes from the parched playa often resemble *Mad Max Beyond Thunderdome.* Everything and everyone is constantly covered in a thin, brown coat of alkaline dust. Most participants carry dust masks and goggles with them at all times; dust storms blow through the city, knocking over tents and installations, without warning. Daytime temperatures can soar to over 100°F; it's been known to freeze at night.

The event takes place on federal BLM land. There's a hefty admission fee (usually $175–250), part of which goes to the BLM. Ticket prices increase throughout the year, so it pays to buy tickets well in advance.

Organizers promote the festival as an experiment in temporary community, where participants can shed the fetters of society and stretch the ordinary limits of life. But organizers put a lot of effort into trying to make Burning Man a peaceful and safe experience, and although police are present, citations are rare. Participants are required to take away everything they brought in, and volunteers stay for weeks to return the Black Rock Desert to its pristine condition. After a while, no trace can be found in the desert to show that the event ever took place.

Burning Man takes place every Labor Day weekend (late August to early September), outside Gerlach. Contact Burning Man, P.O. Box 884688, San Francisco, CA 94188-4688, 415/TO-FLAME, www.burningman.com.

---

of Nixon, you'll pass a turnoff with sign pointing right to Empire Farms, a company which dries and packages dehydrated garlic and onions. Burns and Phelps, another local company, grows garlic for seed in the area.

The valley narrows as it ushers you into **Empire,** a thin strip of green along the highway backed by the southern edge of the great **Black Rock Desert.** Giant mineload trucks haul dusty, chalky-white salt into the U.S. Gypsum plant here, passing flatbed 16-wheelers hauling out heavy loads of sheetrock. The mine is a little east

up in the Selenite Range. The mine and mill employ around 125 people.

On the corner of Route 447 and Empire Road is Empire Distributing Company grocery store and a Mobil station. Take a left onto Empire Road passing the sheetrock plant. Empire is a shady, breezy, comfortable company town four blocks wide and four long. Cruise up and down the streets to get a glimpse of company housing, the community pool and park, a nine-hole golf course (free and open to the public), and tennis and basketball courts.

Just beyond Empire is the green oasis of Gerlach huddled directly below distinct **Granite Peak,** more than 9,000 feet tall, the southernmost peak of the Granite Range.

GERLACH

Gerlach, at first glance, is a tiny town that serves as a division point for Southern Pacific Railroad as it chugs through northwestern Nevada. (The sign going into town lists the population at 350, but locals say the entire population of Gerlach, Empire, and the outlying ranches probably doesn't add up to that. The figure on the sign hasn't changed as long as anyone can remember, and folks insist there are only about 100 people on the Gerlach General Improvement District's tax rolls.) But as soon as you stop to consider that Gerlach is the largest settlement in an area of probably 10,000 square miles— from Reno to the south and Lakeview, Oregon, to the north, from Susanville, California, to the west, and Winnemucca to the east—the town takes on a much greater significance. Gerlach, in fact, claims the only gas station, slot machines, restaurant, and motel in Nevada's vast northwest corner. It's also the gateway to the famed Black Rock Desert, where the world's land speed record was set in 1983. And it's a friendly, comfortable town in its own right, boasting the best ravioli in the state, a surprising variety of house architecture, a cool pottery ranch, and one of the most dramatic views imaginable of a railroad snaking across a desert. Gerlach's clever motto, "Where the Pavement Ends and the West Begins," could very well be no brag, just fact.

This area was settled by native peoples for its good spring water, wild food, and plentiful shelter. More recently, pioneers paused at the springs here, marking the end of the Black Rock Desert and the beginning of the arduous journey through High Rock Canyon.

Louis Gerlach began ranching in this area around the turn of the 20th century. A few years later, the Western Pacific Railroad laid tracks along the northern route out of Winnemucca, crossing Desert Valley and the Jackson Mountains, then skirting the edge of the Black Rock and Smoke Creek deserts (then crossing Beckwourth Pass north of Reno and dropping down into Oakland). Gerlach was founded as a rail division point in 1906, named for the ranch.

Rocket Cars and Land-Speed Records

The most exciting times in Gerlach are the land-speed record-setting events on the Black Rock playa, which happen every so often. It all started in October 1983, when Project Thrust was rained out of the Bonneville Salt Flats on the other side of the state near Wendover. Driver Richard Noble and his team of Brits relocated their rocket-car operation to the Black Rock Desert northeast of Gerlach. They set up a 10-mile straightaway on the flat cracked-mud playa (another dry lakebed of vast Lake Lahontan), with a 10-mile overrun—in case the braking parachutes failed to deploy. Noble cranked up the Rolls Royce Avon engine (with afterburners) of *Thrust II,* the rocket car, and attained a speed of 633.606 mph, finally breaking Gary Gabelich's 13-year record of 622.407 mph, set at Bonneville in 1971. The residents and racers adopted each other, and a great time was had by all. In fact, a second record was set when a crewmember towing an outhouse to the raceway hit 70 mph, establishing a world speed record for portable toilets.

Gerlach's rush over speed was rekindled in summer 1997 as Noble the Brit and former record-holder Craig Breedlove (407 mph in 1966) of the United States made plans to face off on the Black Rock playa in the first-ever head-to-head challenge for the land-speed record. By August '97, the Noble and Breedlove camps had received permission from the BLM to construct a dozen parallel 15-mile tracks on the playa. Plans called for the teams to leapfrog from track to track in a succession of speed trials throughout September (or until the start of rainy season, whichever came first).

The BLM imposed a series of conditions on the racers intended to address complaints from the Paiute tribe about possible damage to cultural sites, environmentalists over possible impacts to wildlife, and history buffs concerned about the proximity to nearby emigrant trails. The ever-popular Black Rock simply isn't as remote as it was in 1983. In the '90s, the speed with which your permit is issued can be as important as the speed of your vehicle. Breedlove blamed the failure of his attempt at Noble's record in 1996, in part, on a last-minute appeal that postponed his run into the windy season. His hopes, though luckily not his brains, were dashed when a gust lifted the nose of his *Spirit of America* rocket car (clocked at 677 mph), sending him careening through the world's fastest—and longest!—U-turn. Setting a record requires a car to make one run down the track, refuel, and return within 60 minutes. Official speeds are averaged from the elapsed time, minus the midway pit stop. So even though he exceeded Noble's record by over 40 mph, Breedlove's 1996 time didn't count.

A month before the 1997 event, the Breedlove and Noble camps were downplaying any hint of a personal or international rivalry as hard as the media was playing it up. Their respective representatives said both men were eyeing the record— and the 741.4 mph sound barrier—not each other. The fact that both teams ended up in the Black Rock at the same time, however, seemed designed to boost public and corporate (read: sponsorship) interest in the event. The pressure was on to burst through the Mach 1 sound barrier (750 mph) by a land vehicle in '97 to coincide with the 50th anniversary of Chuck Yeager's first supersonic flight.

Breedlove, a 62-year-old grandfather, was set to pilot *Spirit of America,* which boasts a single jet engine with afterburners from an F-4 fighter that can deliver 48,000 horsepower. Incidentally, that's more horse than all the formula racers in the 1995 Indy 500 combined. Noble (also in his 60s and now an organizer and front man) enlisted Andy Green, a Royal Air Force pilot, to take the wheel of *Thrust II,* a sinister-looking twin-jet design. Resembling a jet fighter without wings, the thing looked capable of accelerating to Mach I and more.

Craig Breedlove's team began test runs on the Black Rock on September 6, two days before Noble's. *Spirit of America* was clocked at 330 mph before engine problems delayed further runs till Sept. 19, when Breedlove hit 381 mph. After more technical (and financial) problems,

Breedlove's car was clocked at its top speed of 531 mph on October 12.

Noble's team arrived at the Black Rock with the 10-ton *Thrust II* on Sept. 8 and the race was on. The first run was made on September 8; on September 10 the car reached speeds of 428 and 517 miles per hour. For the next two weeks, problems with the suspension, power converter, hydraulic system, computer, and weather postponed the British team's quest. On September 22, *Thrust II* completed two runs at 618 and 653 mph, but they didn't count toward breaking the record because they weren't within an hour of each other. The next day, Green revved the car up to 693 and 719 mph, but again missed the record books on the same technicality as the previous day. On Sept. 25, it finally became official: two runs of 700 and 728 mph within an hour of each other set the new land-speed world record at an average of 714 mph, 80 mph faster than the previous record.

But Noble's team didn't rest on its laurels, not by a long shot. On October 14, 1997, one day before the 50th anniversary of Chuck Yeager's breaking of the sound barrier in a jet, *Thrust II* achieved supersonic speeds of 760 and 764 mph, breaking the sound barrier on land for the first time in history. When the speed of the rocket car exceeded Mach 1, it let off a light sonic boom; much of the noise was absorbed by the acoustically soft desert. It didn't, however, set a new record—the runs were 61 minutes apart.

Practicalities

The reason that **Bruno's Country Club** in Gerlach, 775/557-2220, has been called the "social center of northern Washoe County" can be summed up in a single surprising word: ravioli. These big fat fatties, swimming in old-country meat sauce and covered with home-cured imported cheese, go for a bargain $11.80. Bruno's starts serving breakfast every day at 5 A.M. and finishes dinner at 9 P.M.

The adjoining bar has video poker and blackjack and reel slots, along with photographs of the racers and local artwork. The bar also serves as the front desk for **Bruno's Motel,** 775/557-2220, which has 40 units for $30–55, next to the Texaco.

Just up the street is another **Joe's Gerlach Club** and the **Miner's Club** next to Bruno's café round out the licensed premises.

Gerlach made a splash in the Reno newspaper in 1992 when two Washoe County sheriff's deputies showed up to enforce some law and order in unruly Gerlach (or that's the way the paper made it sound). Between Empire and Gerlach, there are six bars for fewer than 400 people. After 80 years generally outside the clutches, suddenly townspeople started getting busted for DUI at a very accelerated rate: 35 arrests in 14 months. (It's a two-hour ride to jail in Reno.) Note that the deputies' jurisdiction covers 3,500 square miles around this corner of the state. Unless you're driving drunk around town, you're definitely on your own out here.

Speaking of which, **Bruno's Shell** station is at the south end of town, last gas till Eagleville (80 miles) or Denio (110 miles). You can pick up local brochures here.

Sixty miles north of Gerlach, the **Soldier Meadows Guest Ranch & Lodge,** Soldier Meadows Rd., Gerlach, NV 89412, 530/233-4881, www.soldiermeadows.com, is a working cattle ranch with a 600,000-acre range. Guests

can go horseback trail riding, or ride out with the cowboys to join them in their ranch activities; the ranch is popular with hunters, too. The ranch lodge has 10 guest rooms. Lodging alone costs $45 per person, per day, or $75 per day with all meals included.

THE BLACK ROCK DESERT

In *Hiking the Great Basin,* John Hart observes that, overall, the Great Basin Desert is not generally referred to as "the desert." "That word," he writes, "is reserved for sections that stand out as barren among the barren, wastes among wastes," among which the "Black Rock Desert, at least one million acres in extent, is second only to the Great Salt Lake Desert." In short, this is a desert's desert, a landscape of unique barrenness and beauty, solitude and plentitude, danger and freedom. It's a vision so forbidding that as eminent an explorer as John C. Frémont, on his way to discover Pyramid Lake, was afraid to approach it. Yet thousands of westbound pioneers crossed it in awe and agony, on the Lassen-Applegate Cutoff from the main Emigrant Trail. And it was the scene of Nevada's fiercest fighting between Indians

COURTESY OF THE NEVADA COMMISSION ON TOURISM

Black Rock Desert geyser

and white settlers. Today, the Black Rock, largest playa in North America, is a magnet for rockhounds and history buffs, hikers and pilgrims, landsailors and hotrodders, UFO nuts and other nuts. Doug Keister, author and photographer of a book called *Black Rock: Portraits on the Playa,* says, "I see the playa as the world's largest stage. It's so pure and clean that anything you put on it becomes significant."

Indeed. Drive down onto the playa (a broad mud plain, another dry lake bed of ancient Lake Lahontan) and accelerate for miles without bothering to steer (but only after you've checked on conditions in Gerlach—you're looking for dry dry dry, because when wet the playa is an impassable sump). The edge of a shimmering lake that you seem to be hurtling toward is always just ahead. But wait! What's that black thing out there? Looks like a motorcycle, or maybe it's one of those jet cars on a collision course! Nah, it's too big and standing still—a cow? What's a cow doing on a silt bed, halfway between nothing and nowhere? But the black thing keeps looming bigger and bigger until you pass it at 65 mph, and oh . . . it's a beer can.

Then the surface starts feeling like thin ice, which you're always just about to crack through and fall deep into a dense mud bog. Now the other cars' tracks are racing up to you, crossing under you in a flash, then disappearing behind you—while you're standing still. Even the illusions are on a grand scale.

The Black Rock encompasses a million acres, split into two forks by the encroaching thrust of the Black Rock Range, the volcanic outcrop that gave a bearing to an estimated 30,000 emigrants who crossed the desert between 1849 and 1870. Because of its remoteness and hard surface, the Black Rock section of the Emigrant Trail is the best preserved in the west, and conservation groups want to set aside large tracts as a National Conservation Area, with interpretation and a visitor center.

To get onto the Black Rock, take the right-hand fork just north of Gerlach and continue on the paved road that travels along the upper edge of the playa; in several miles an obvious entrance ramp presents itself. Late spring through

fall is the safe season for cruising the cracked desert; winter it's too muddy. The first time you get out there you'll understand exactly why the root of playa is "play," and you'll be hooked.

The best descriptions of this country, and its unlimited hiking potential, are found in *Hiking the Great Basin.* For a group experience, contact the **Reno Gem and Mineral Society,** 480 S. Rock Blvd., Sparks, 775/356-8820, a hobby club which holds monthly meetings and conducts monthly field trips. If you're soloing, be careful! This place is treacherous, and people die out here every year. It's very easy to get lost, and if your car breaks down, you might be in serious trouble. If you're planning to explore the Black Rock in any depth for an extended period, it's recommended that you carry detailed topo maps and a compass; five gallons of water per person per day and emergency food for a week; sunblock, first-aid kit, warm clothes, and some portable shade; two spare tires, tools, a hand winch, rope and chain, shovel, axe, extra gas, belts, hoses, and fluids; and a CB radio. Many people actually tow an extra car in. Finally, don't forget Session Wheeler's classic *Black Rock Desert.*

The paved road, Route 34, continues northeast, leaving Washoe County and entering Pershing County. Ten miles past the first access to the playa is a second. The road cuts north for a bit and then back west, reentering Washoe. Sixteen miles out of Gerlach the pavement ends, and you can kiss it goodbye for many a long mile.

HIGH ROCK CANYON

After the pavement ends, the gravel road starts out relatively smooth, and you can run 50 mph for a short while. This is ranching country, with alfalfa fields, ranch houses under big cottonwoods surrounded by cypress windbreaks, and frequent cattle guards. The road slows you down to about 35 as it grows narrower and twisty turny. Short stretches of pavement on bridges over creekbeds give you just enough time to say "Ahhh" before it's back to rough riding. A few miles past the second access to the playa is a turnoff (right, signposted) onto another gravel road for Summit Lake Indian

Reservation, Rainbow Opal Mine, and Soldier Meadows Ranch B&B.

As you get deeper into the Granite Range, the road deteriorates further, down to 25 mph in places, then back up to 40 on a long flat smooth stretch. Just before the end of the straightaway, 35 miles from Gerlach, is a second main fork in the road: Route 34 veers off to the west toward Vya, while a very ugly road runs northeast to High Rock Canyon. You can get up to 20–25 mph on this one-lane primitive dirt road for about a mile and a half, and then it turns dire: chuckholes, washboards, grass in the middle of the lane, sage scratching both sides of the car. It gets worse. You creep across stretches with big rocks in the road, up and down deep gullies and washes, and thick sand. Five or ten miles an hour max. Then it gets worse. Only if you have a high-clearance 4WD vehicle should you even consider taking this little canyon excursion.

After a while, you come to an intersection. Bearing left you'll enter **Little High Rock Canyon.** There's a very narrow jeep track into this canyon-better hiking than driving. The left fork leads to more creeping toward the main show. Finally, two hours and 15 miles from the turnoff, three hours and 50 miles from Gerlach, you reach the BLM-brown sign for High Rock Canyon.

It's still another couple of hard miles to the start of the long series of canyons that make up High Rock. But then there you are, three hours and 17 miles from the fork, at 800-foot-high sheer walls of polychrome volcanic rock. The dark basaltic rock near the top of the walls is from the last volcanic activity, somewhere around 15 million years ago, when massive lava flows obliterated the landscape and laid down a uniform layer of tuff. The bright red band below the dark rock is the fine layer of soil that was turned red when the hot lava flowed over it. The beige bands below are ash deposits from earlier volcanic eruptions. Adding to the Kodak potential are the lichens growing on the rock—chartreuse, sageleaf green, rust. Those majestic birds with the huge wingspans soaring on the updrafts are golden eagles; you might also see falcons, hawks, and great horned owls.

John Frémont, as usual, made the first recorded passage through High Rock Canyon in 1843, and described it in his diary. In 1846, the Applegate brothers, following Frémont's directions, blazed a trail through the canyon, which Peter Lassen, in 1848, used to lead a wagon train from near Winnemucca on the main Emigrant Trail to Goose Lake in the northeast corner of California.

A pull-out in the middle of the first (and most spectacular) canyon has firewood, campfire rocks, and a cozy carbon-covered cave. Driving through, you almost think there are two canyons, one under the high rock walls and the other under the sage towering over the road. You can look straight out of the car window and see the root structure of the shrubs.

The road slows down to about one mile an hour, because of the rocks, dips, ruts, creek crossings. It's kind of dusty, too. This is both the High Rock road, and the high-rock road. Actually, "road" is a bit too optimistic a description; it's really a jeep track, no place for anything but a high-clearance, heavy-duty-suspension, 4WD vehicle.

Getting out is no less painful. The grass you drive over is taller than the car. You cross creeks, four-wheel over hillocks, and hope that nobody comes in the opposite direction (nobody does). You might feel like one of the long-distance automobile pioneers in the first decade or two of the century, who had to rely on directions from people who didn't know what they were talking about, maps that lied deliberately to get them to come through towns, and roads that were probably in even worse condition than this one.

If you're really into this country, you can carry the appropriate topo maps, which will let you know about side trips to historical sights, such as cabins, pioneer graffiti, and old emigrant camping grounds. Along the main track is a lone cabin, where there's a pullout if it gets dark and you need to stop for the night, or if you want a break from the psychic tension and physical pounding you get from the trail. The surface improves around 25 miles from the entrance to the canyon; it's back up to 20 mph, with some cattle around.

At the next fork in the road, go straight; you'll have to open and close a wire gate behind you. From there you climb up to Stevens Camp, the only place on the road with potable water. At Stevens you cut around to the northwest and drive for another little while at around 25 mph, till you come out on Route 8A—wide, smooth, 45 mph, a bit slippery and washboardy from the gravel, but it might as well be black velvet compared to the past 35 miles. Phew!

Take a left; Vya is 20-odd miles west. At Vya bear right, and head north up Long Valley to the entrance to Sheldon National Wildlife Refuge.

SHELDON NATIONAL WILDLIFE REFUGE

Like the American bison, pronghorn once roamed the west in the millions, but within 100 years of the first mountain men entering Nevada, overgrazing, hunting, disease, and deliberate poisoning had decimated their numbers to the verge of extinction. One pocket of pronghorn holdouts remained in the far remote corner of northwestern Nevada. In the early 1920s, Edward Sans, state director of predator control and a representative of the U.S. Biological Survey, began a campaign to carve a pronghorn refuge out of the large ranches in that corner of the state. He lobbied the Washoe County Commissioners, the federal land agencies, and the New York conservation societies and big-game clubs. The Boone and Crockett Club donated $10,000 for the effort, in return for naming the refuge after its leading member, Charles Sheldon, a hunter, explorer, and writer who had studied and reported on the pronghorn over the years.

By 1928, ranch land had been purchased and President Herbert Hoover set it aside as a refuge. Audubon Society experts and money managed the 34,000 acres until 1933, when the young refuge was officially taken over by the federal Department of Biology, forerunner of the Fish and Wildlife Service. Edward Sans was appointed director. By 1937, seven additional parcels had been acquired, expanding the refuge to 575,000 acres. Since then, programs have been implemented to manage the antelope, mule deer, and burros. The highway across the refuge was completed in 1962; bighorn sheep were introduced in 1968.

Today, the pronghorn at the refuge have regenerated to a winter population of 3,500. They are more dispersed in summer, as they range widely for food and water. In the spring and summer many antelope leave Sheldon for the Hart Mountain Refuge across the border in Oregon. Best time to spot them is in the morning and evening, though because they feed during the day (a boon to hunters), you might see them anytime. Early in the morning, especially, you can see hundreds of these graceful and skittish creatures all over the park. They're very fast and they'll keep a distance between themselves and your car, but when they feel safe, they'll resume their camel walk, their bouncing over the sage as if on springs, bobbing their heads back and forth and flashing their white rumps.

The western **ranger's residence** is a little past Bald Mountain summit: a beautiful stone house built in 1934 and a shop next door. Pick up a map and a brochure (if there are any) at the information signpost where you enter the refuge, coming in from US 140.

Continuing east, it's one fine dirt road, though narrow. You can go about 35 mph, but you'll probably want to poke along at 25. At the top of a gentle grade, you get a nice overlook of **Swan Lake Reservoir.** If the pronghorn are out at all, there could be scores of them on the flats south of the lake. Then you turn north, into unusual country for Nevada: high volcanic plains, vast and rolling, good for spotting wildlife. Little humps above the plateau carry names such as Sage Hen Hills, Round Mountain, and Blowout Mountain; flattop crests are called Bitner Butte, Big Spring Butte, and Gooch Table. You cruise along, then around, Rubble Ridge and come to **Catnip Reservoir** and a primitive campground (firepit, picnic table, outhouse, no fishing). You leave Washoe and enter Humboldt County, a little beyond which is a junction. Route 34 ends and 8A, the southern route that forked off at Vya, rejoins; if you've come up through High Rock Canyon and headed around via Vya, you've just completed 300 degrees of a circle.

You enter Humboldt County as 8A climbs a low rise between Fish Creek Table and Fish Creek

PRONGHORN ANTELOPE

The pronghorn *(Antilocapra americana)* is unique. It's endemic to North America and is not related to any other antelope, deer, elk, goat, or sheep. Its name is derived from its horns, which are pronged like the tines of a fork. But these horns, which grow to be about a foot long and only on the males, are more like antlers, as they're shed after mating season in the fall, and regenerate completely by the next July.

Pronghorn bucks stand three feet high and weigh between 100 and 150 pounds. The does have tiny button horns slightly larger than their ears; the females weigh up to 80 pounds. Both males and females are reddish-brown, with a black band from the eyes to the nose, white throat and stomach, and a white rump patch whose hairs bristle when the animal senses danger. The horns and hooves are jet black.

The rut is quite a bit more vicious than is normally known in ungulates, always bloody and occasionally deadly. A dominant buck will acquire three to eight does in his harem. The does give birth in the spring, usually to twins, but sometimes to single kids. The kids weigh four to six pounds at birth, and it takes only a week for them to be able to run 20 miles at a clip, fast enough to outrun a coyote or bobcat.

Special glands give off an odor repugnant to flies and mosquitos. Two pointy hooves, as opposed to the usual four, provide firm traction and good protection against predators. The resolution of their eyes, extremely wide-set and sharp, has been compared to eight-power binoculars. But mostly these animals are *fast*, having been clocked in a dead run at close to the 65 mph. Big livers store abundant glucose for bursts of speed and long-distance endurance.

But two fatal flaws quickly doomed the pronghorn after the arrival of settlers. First, they're diurnal, and move about in the light. Second, they're as curious as cats and want to get to the bottom of anything out of the ordinary, such as a red flag waved by a hunter. In addition, the pronghorns' vast western grazing and watering habitat was fenced; they were killed en masse by hunters, settlers, even trains; and they were poisoned to eliminate wolves and bears. By 1913, when Charles Sheldon estimated their numbers, fewer than 15,000 pronghorn remained. Today, pronghorn in the antelope refuge number approximately 3,500, the largest concentration of this unique animal in the world.

Northern Nevada

Mountain. There's no sign, but a change in county road crews is evident as you're forced to slow to 20–25 mph. Razor-sharp shards of obsidian glisten on the roadbed. Locals say the road eats tires, so watch it. But in five miles is US 140, the Winnemucca-to-the-Sea Highway, which means pavement, glorious pavement.

Going left brings you, eventually, to Lakeview and Medford, Oregon, and finally to Crescent City, California. But those are other authors' states. Instead, take a right toward Denio. A half mile east is a turnoff to Big Springs Reservoir Campground. Beyond, the road descends to Virgin Valley, where a long, straight, flat plateau points at the road like some cosmic freight train—the *Nevada Road Atlas* calls it **Black Ridge,** the USGS two-degree map **Railroad**

Point. US 140 runs along Thousand Creek and then leaves the Sheldon Refuge. The Pine Forest Range is straight ahead.

Heading toward Denio on US 140, about 10 miles north of Denio you'll come to a sign pointing out the turnoff to the Virgin Valley Campground and Hot Springs. Another sign advertises the Royal Peacock Opal Mine, with recreational opal mining for a fee. A good gravel road takes you one mile to the campground—and back into the refuge—past the Dufurrena Ponds. The free campground has about eight loosely defined spaces with fire pits and tables, pit toilets, and a tap for drinking water. The ponds offer fishing for bass and perch; state regulations apply.

A group called **Friends of the Refuge** has done an excellent job fixing up the place. The stone-rimmed hot pool has a fresh gravel bottom and the adjacent showers, in an old stone building, are clean and in good repair. At about 85°F, it's more of a warm springs, really, but welcome nonetheless. A colony of guppies lives in the lightly mineralized water. Some are fantails with orange, yellow, and blue spots, just like the ones you had in your aquarium as a kid.

All in all it's a nice place, marred only by the halogen lights outside a nearby ranch house and the minimal privacy afforded by the open campsites. In summer, you'll fall asleep to a serenade given by bullfrogs, which load the two dozen or so ponds in the area. While you're out and about, check out **Thousand Creek Gorge,** visible on the left on the drive in to the campground. A two-mile hike or drive from the Virgin Valley Campground leads you to the mouth of the gorge and a trail that meanders past ponds and willows in the shade of redrock walls 300 feet high. Signs of wild burros are everywhere. You might think you're in Moab around sunset as the evening light burnishes the cliffs a coppery gold.

Camping

Looking for more amenities? Driving eight miles farther into the refuge on the same road brings you to the **Royal Peacock Opal Mine,** 10 miles in from the highway. The RV park here, open May 15 to October 15, offers tent camping for $4 per person, 18 RV sites with full hookups for $18, and four fully-furnished trailers for $50 a night, to which you need bring only your food (reservations suggested). Hot showers are available to non-guests for $4 per person, and there's a Laundromat, gift shop and rock shop, too. You can dig for opals here at the mine, for a fee: $85 per day to dig in virgin ground, $35 per day to dig in the tailings, and you keep all the opals you find. This is a working mine; the black fire opals found in this valley are Nevada's state gemstone, and other types of opals are found here, too. Contact Royal Peacock Opal Mine, 775/941-0374 (winter 775/272-3246), www .royalpeacock.com.

There are approximately a dozen primitive camps in the refuge, most of which have vault toilets. The campsite at **Virgin Valley** has public hot springs and a tap providing drinking water. The other campsites have no drinking water. No camping reservations are accepted. All sites are free. Contact Sheldon National Wildlife Refuge, 541/947-3315.

Fernley and Lovelock

These two small farming towns are a nice change of pace from the barrenness of Black Rock and the hubbub of Reno. Fernley finds itself an "alternative crossroads" town. Downtown is intersected by two branch roads to major routes US 95 and US 50. (The "real" highways cross in downtown Fallon.) Lovelock is directly off the highway, yet it retains its small-town fell. Both are a good base of operations for northwestern and west-central Nevada, compared to the higher prices and lower vacancies of Reno–Sparks, especially on weekends. So whether you're passing through on a shortcut or just looking for a different place to go or stay, check out friendly Fernley and Lovelock. They're good alternatives.

FERNLEY

Fernley was founded in 1905 as part of the Newlands Reclamation Project, which once irrigated as much as 60,000 acres of desert between Fernley Valley, hemmed in on four sides by the Truckee, Virginia, Pah Rah, and Hot Springs mountains, and Lahontan Valley 30 miles east. Up until the early 1960s, Fernley remained a small trade center for the local ranchers and farmers, as well as the terminal of a branch line of the Southern Pacific that ran up the west shore of Pyramid Lake and on into Sierra logging areas. The arrival of Nevada Cement Company in 1964 improved the town's economy (though deteriorated its air) and completion of the high-speed freeway to Reno drew it closer into a suburban orbit.

Truck Inn

This is more than one of the biggest truck stops in the state. It's almost an entire Fernley suburb. Opened in 1982, the Truck Inn occupies a 40-acre lot, 35 of them designated for tractor-trailer parking. Consolidated Freightways has a terminal here. There are also a 26-unit RV park, holding corrals for livestock in transit, a motel, two casinos, spa, barbershop, dentist, repair shops, truck wash, scales, maxi mart, bar with live entertainment, coffee shop, and phones in the bathrooms and at the truckers' counter in the diner. Check out trucker haul of fame, the trucker memorabilia covering the walls. A couple of recent high-tech additions are the telephone-debit-card machine and computerized truck scheduling in the maxi mart. If you just want the quick in and out, stop off at the Winner's Corner minimart with Exxon station just off the exit ramp. Truck Inn, 485 Truck Way, 775/351-1000, www.truckin.com, has 43 motel rooms for $27–43. RV spaces are $10 a night, with weekly and monthly rates available.

Practicalities

Other than the Truck Inn, as you come into town from Wadsworth or the west, the first motels are the **Lazy Inn,** 325 Main St., 775/575-4452 or 800/682-6445, lazyinn.net, $30–60, and the **Lahontan Motel,** 135 E. Main St., 775/575-2744, $30–45. At the east exit (48) are **Super 8,** 1350 W. Newlands, 775/575-5555 or 800/800-8000, $58–75, and the **Best Western-Fernley Inn,** 1405 E. Newlands, 775/575-6776 or 800/528-1234, $50–100.

If you're hungry, there are a few options. On Main Street downtown is **La Fiesta,** 775/575-1800. Across the street is the **China Chef.** El Guadalajara on Center Street, 775/575-7735, also serves Mexican dishes. On is **Moe and Mary's Wigwam Cafe,** open 5 A.M.–9 P.M., another venerable and popular Fernley eatery, serving breakfast until 11 A.M., a good salad bar for lunch and dinner, and big portions of everything.

For quickie road food, try the coffee shop at the **Truck Inn** (open 24 hours). **McDonald's,**

opened in 1992, is nearby. For a picnic, stop at **Fernley Desert Park** just south of downtown on Alt. US 95.

There's a poker table at the **Truck Inn,** as well as two blackjack tables and one crap table. There are also two blackjack tables at **Sturgeon's,** and lotsa slots at both.

The **library,** 775/575-3366, is behind the Fernley Complex on the east end, open Mon., Wed., and Fri. 10 A.M.–6 P.M., Tues. and Thurs. 10 A.M.–8 P.M., and Sat. 11 A.M.–4 P.M.

The **Fernley Chamber of Commerce** is at 70 N. West St., 775/575-4459, www.fernleynvchamber.com, and is housed in the town's first schoolhouse, built in 1910. An intriguing business that has taken up residence in Fernley is a massive shipping center for Amazon.com.

LOVELOCK

Lovelock (pop. 2,280) is a pleasant old farming community, with big houses and trees surrounded by well-kept lawns, neat green alfalfa fields, and the rugged West Humboldt Range hemming in the valley to the south, the Trinity Range to the north. The town is named after George Lovelock, a Welsh quartz miner who came to California by way of Australia and Hawaii in 1850, at age 26. He worked for a while in San Francisco, Sacramento, and Oroville, then homesteaded a ranch in Humboldt County, Nevada, in 1861. In 1866 he bought 320 acres at Big Meadows and took title to the oldest water rights along the Humboldt River—just in time to donate 85 acres to the Central Pacific Railroad in return for naming the new railroad town after him, plus other terms that the railroad never fulfilled. "Uncle George" kept busy for the next 40 years with agricultural, mining, and business ventures, raising eight children, and voting Republican. He died at age 83 in 1907 after a three-day bout with pneumonia—reportedly the first sick days of his life—that he caught while out in the country, prospecting.

The rich land and good grass attracted cattlemen and ranchers; by the early 1900s reservoirs on the Humboldt irrigated 8,000 acres. But the supply of river water, never dependable, seemed to diminish

THE ROAD TO LOVELOCK CAVE

Lovelock Cave was discovered by teenagers in 1887, though it was not explored until 1911 when guano miners excavated 250 tons of bat scat, uncovering numerous Indian artifacts in the process. The 160-foot-wide by 40-foot-deep cave, created by Lake Lahontan, served as a shelter to aboriginal inhabitants around 2000 B.C., and was the first Great Basin site to be excavated by archaeologists. The artifacts—which include baskets, textiles, and the famous Loveland cave duck decoys—are exhibited at museums around the country.

The route from downtown Lovelock to Lovelock Cave has been declared a "cultural back country byway" by the state. Begin at the Marzen House Museum on the southwest side of town. Drive northeast through town and then turn right on Main Street. Go two blocks and turn right on Amhearst. After the park the road becomes South Meridian/Route 397. The first half of the 20-mile route takes you through irrigated fields. After crossing the Humboldt River, the road changes to dirt. This byway is at its best is summer and early fall.

year by year as settlers for several hundred miles to the east diverted more and more of the precious Humboldt. Finally, in 1933 the Bureau of Reclamation lent the Lovelock Irrigation District $1 million—$600,000 to buy upstream water rights and $400,000 to build Rye Patch Dam. The dam was completed in 1936, and its reservoir, when full, provides irrigation water to 40,000 acres of the Lovelock Valley. Almost all the farmland is cultivated for grain to feed livestock. In addition, the Lovelock Seed Company is one of the top alfalfa seed growers in the world.

Edna Purviance is Lovelock's claim to Hollywood fame. She grew up in town, then moved to San Francisco, where she was discovered by Charlie Chaplin. They appeared in 40 movies together and she was the leading lady in Chaplin's famous *The Tramp*. They were lovers on and off for decades, but never married. She remained on the Chaplin payroll till she died of cancer in 1958 at age 62.

In 1919 Humboldt County was halved, and Lovelock became the seat of new Pershing County, named after the famous World War I general, and last of 17 counties created in Nevada. Pershing encompasses 6,000 square miles, roughly twice the size of Connecticut. Mining supports a large segment of the economy these days, with a large diatomaceous-earth mine and plant and several gold and silver mines nearby.

SIGHTS

The commercial district stretches between Exits 105 and 107 of the interstate. Start your tour of Lovelock at the **Pershing County Chamber of Commerce,** 350 Main St., 775/273-7213, for brochures and information. Be sure to check out the **Marzen House Museum,** 775/273-4949, open daily 1:30–4 P.M. (closed Monday). Stroll around this restored house, built by Colonel Joseph Marzen, a German farmer and rancher who moved to Lovelock in 1876 and proceeded to become the area's major grain and livestock producer. Originally the Big House on Marzen's 3,400-acre ranch, the museum is packed with an amazing collection of memorabilia, much of it affectionately labeled with the names of the donors. Noteworthy are the pump organ from Unionville, a 1923 atlas, a turn-of-the-20th-century carpet sweeper, a big map of Lake Lahontan, which once covered the area, and a great wide-angle shot of downtown Lovelock in 1913. Upstairs, rooms are devoted to agriculture, mining, stock certificates, and much more. Chat with the friendly volunteer, help yourself to Chamber of Commerce handouts, and leave a small token of appreciation.

Continue east along Cornell Avenue, old Hwy. 40, to 8th Street; take a right and go one block down to Broadway, the old business street along the tracks. Go left by the Bernd Hotel, Lovelock's oldest (now a rooming house), Ranch House and Walks Place bars, and the abandoned Red Depot. Cross Main Street to the old railroad depot and assay office, both closed and boarded up. Felix's Bank Club, once the main casino in town, is also boarded up at the corner of Cornell and Main.

Take Main Street back across Cornell for the **Pershing County Courthouse,** one of only two round courthouses in the country. A park with picnic tables and a jungle gym is in back, between the courthouse and library. Also here is the Lovelock Memorial Swimming Pool, with two diving boards, one fairly high, and a kiddie pool.

Head north (right) on Central a mile through irrigated farmland, take your first left onto Pitt, and go by aptly named **Lone Mountain** in one-half mile, just past where the road curves around. Take a right onto the unmarked gravel road and kick up dust for a mile, till you come to the long line of low tufa formations. Park and get out into the desert a little by hiking the few hundred yards to and around the calcareous remnants of Lake Lahontan, familiar formations in northwestern Nevada. Hawks and owls peer down from atop the towers. Take winding Lone Mountain Rd. back to town past the mountain and cemetery.

Seventeen miles south of town is **Leonard Rock Shelter** which has tall tufa with petroglyphs; excavations in the early 1950s by UC Berkeley archaeologists recovered artifacts at the rock's base that were later carbon-dated to approximately 4000 B.C.

Accommodations

I-80 through northern Nevada wasn't completed until 1983, and Lovelock was one of the last towns to be bypassed; for a long time the traffic light at Main and Cornell was the only one on the highway between New York and San Francisco! This also accounts for the dozen or so motels along Cornell Ave.; until a mere 15 ago, all the interstate traffic had to drive right by them. The Desert Plaza, 1435 Cornell, 775/273-2500, $35–55, has 30 rooms. The Super 10, 1390 Cornell, 775/273-1666, has 10 rooms for $26–37. The **Cadillac Inn,** 1395 Cornell, 775/273-2798, offers 12 rooms for $20–42. **Sturgeon's Ramada Inn Casino,** 1420 Cornell, 775/273-2971 or 888/234-6835, has 74 rooms for $40–55. Two motels are on Dartmouth Ave.: the **Covered Wagon** at 945, 775/273-2961, $32–45; and the **Sierra** at 14th St., 775/273-2798, $20–42.

The **Lazy K Campground and RV** is at 1550 Cornell, 775/273-0577; from exit 105 off I-80, go north to Cornell Street, then take a right (east) for a mile to the campground. The Lazy K was a KOA for years, till it closed in 1994. It was reopened in 1995 and has been restoring it to its prior glory. It's right off the freeway, but luckily, the large trees and landscaping hold down the noise—because this is the only camping in Lovelock. There are 49 spaces for motor homes, 30 with full hookups and 9 pull-throughs. There are 10 tent sites in the trees. Restrooms have flush toilets and hot showers; laundry, groceries, deli and bar, and playground are available. The fee is $12 for tents, $22 for RVs.

Food

Sturgeon's is at the west end of town, 775/273-2971. There's a stuffed mountain lion on display (shot in 1970 on Mt. Tobin). Two blackjack tables operate at night, or try your luck at the video poker bar. Catch a bite anytime at the 24-hour coffee shop, which has surprisingly good and reasonable food. You also can check out La Casita, 410 Cornell, 775/273-7773, which is open from

6 A.M.–8:30 P.M. Henry's Station, 1005 W. Broadway, 775/273-1010, offers sandwiches and ice cream served up in a restored railroad depot.

Information

Pershing County Chamber of Commerce, 350 Main St., Lovelock, 775/273-7213, is open Mon.–Thurs. 9–2 P.M. **Pershing County Library,** 775/273-2216, just north of the courthouse, is open Mon.–Tues. 9 A.M.–5 P.M., Wed. 9 A.M.–8 P.M., Thurs. 10 A.M.–8 P.M., and Fri. 10 A.M.–5 P.M.

Winnemucca

Winnemucca has always been an overnight stop on a variety of long-distance journeys. A traditional crossroads for Indians, mountain men, pioneers, and miners, the site of Winnemucca was originally named French Ford after a Frenchman, Joe Ginacca. Ginacca began a ferry service across the river for pioneers along the Emigrant Trail who opted to take the secondary Applegate-Lassen Cutoff into northern California and Oregon. By 1865, minerals had been located all around the area, a small hotel stood near the ferry stop, and a bridge was built to ease the crossing. French Ford kept growing as a supply center for the trail and local mines and ranches and was a logical stop for the Central Pacific Railroad, which arrived in fall 1868. Railroad company officials promptly renamed it Winnemucca, in honor of the famous Paiute chief.

After several years of steady growth, a battle erupted between Winnemucca and declining Unionville for the Humboldt County courthouse. Unionville put up a good fight. A writer for the Unionville *Silver State* wrote, "The principal production of Winnemucca consists of sand hills, vapid editorials, and a morbid hankering for the county seat." But Winnemucca gained the courthouse in 1873.

A large Chinatown sprouted after the railroad was completed, and Basque shepherds settled around Winnemucca to labor on ranches and herd sheep. As usual, the Chinese were hounded away and little remains of their time here, but the Basque influence is still evident in the town's restaurants and cultural events. George Nixon, a telegraph operator on the Central Pacific, opened his first bank here and began a financial empire that stretched to Tonopah and Goldfield and a political career that stretched to Washington. In September 1900, Butch Cassidy's gang rode into town and stole $32,000 from Nixon's bank. Some disagreement exists as to whether Butch himself was in attendance (but probably not).

Winnemucca maintained a passable level of prosperity in the early 20th century, thanks to the railroad. The construction of three highways—US 40, Winnemucca-to-the-Sea Highway, and I-80—reinforced Winnemucca's status as a crossroads town. The population, however, remained steady at no more than 3,000 until the mid-1980s. At that time, Winnemucca's population and economy, like Battle Mountain's and Elko's, exploded in conjunction with a large new surge of mining activity—gold, silver, dolomite, and specialty limestone—in the area. Since then, the population has more than doubled, and Winnemucca has visibly burst its small-town boundaries, spreading north into Paradise Valley and south into Grass Valley.

Even so, by all reports and personal experience, Winnemucca has retained its old-time homey and friendly feeling for the newcomers, as well as for the visitors continuing to pass through town as they've done for at least the past 145 years or so. It's also still a service center for a large chunk of northern Nevada, mostly the ranching and farming country from Lovelock to Denio and McDermitt to Battle Mountain. Winnemucca has been making a name for itself as the Buckaroo Capital of the country, with the Buckaroo Hall of Fame located right downtown. And locals feel they have now hit the retail big time after getting a K-mart in 1996 and a Wal-Mart in 1998.

DOWNTOWN SIGHTS

At the main intersection downtown, on the corner of Winnemucca Boulevard (locally known as Main Street) and Melarkey Street, is an eight-foot-diameter cross-section of a **redwood tree trunk,** which washed ashore in Crescent City, California, in 1964. The townspeople there thought it appropriate to present a slice of it to the people of Winnemucca to mark the beginning of the Winnemucca-to-the-Sea Highway, which ends in Crescent City. The grassy square it stands in front of was the **Nixon Opera House.** This historic building was built in 1907 by George Nixon, who wanted to leave Winnemucca a memorial when business compelled him to move to Reno. It served as a theater and community center for nearly 80 years, till it was condemned in 1984. In 1991 the state Legislature earmarked $582,000 and townspeople raised another $300,000 for its restoration. Then it burned to the ground in July 1992. Arson. Now there's a hole in the heart of Winnemucca that will take a long time, if ever, to fill.

On the corner of "Main" and Bridge Street is the **East Hall** of the Convention Center, which houses the **Chamber of Commerce,** 30 W. Winnemucca Blvd., 775/623-2225, www.winnemucca-nv.org. It's open Mon.–Fri. 8 A.M.–5 P.M., Sat. 9 A.M.–noon and 1–4 P.M., and Sun. 11 A.M.–4 P.M. Pick up 10 pounds of photocopied histories, town practicalities, brochures, and tabloids. You can also buy books, postcards, and T-shirts.

While you're here, stop in to see the **Buckaroo Hall of Fame and Western Heritage Museum,** 30 W. Winnemucca Blvd., open weekdays 8 A.M.–5 P.M. This collection of cowboy art and gear is the outgrowth of the Western Art Round Up, held in Winnemucca every Labor Day weekend since 1982. Inductees to the Hall of Fame must have been born in the 19th century and worked as a cattleman within a 200-mile radius of Winnemucca. Many legendary local cowboys are commemorated here, as is the buckaroo lifestyle.

To get to **Riverview Park,** head north on Bridge St. and go under the freeway and across the river. This is an old well-shaded part of town

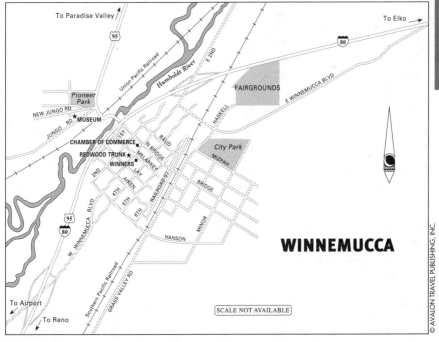

and a fine place to have a picnic or just a drink and watch the river flow.

From the Convention Center, walk north on Bridge Street, the main business district, toward the venerable **Winnemucca Hotel.** This is the site of the first bridge across the Humboldt, around which old downtown Winnemucca grew up. The Winnemucca Hotel is the oldest building in the city, built in 1863, one year before Nevada became a state. If you're not planning to come back later for a drink or meal, stop in at this old Basque bar, restaurant, and rooming house; notice the collection of international currency above the bar, and the old cash register.

On the other side of Winnemucca Boulevard **St. Paul's Catholic Church** is at the corner of 4th and Melarkey. Built in 1924, it has elements of baroque, Romanesque, and Spanish mission in the architecture.

a typical sight in Winnemucca

Across the street is the building that houses the Winnemucca city offices, 49 W. 4th St. Built in 1921, this was the first federal building erected in Winnemucca. It housed the post office, which had a large, fine *Cattle Roundup* mural, painted in 1942. When the post office moved in the 1990s, it took the beloved mural along. You can see it in the new post office location, 850 Hanson St. at the corner of Grass Valley Rd., 775/623-2456; open Mon.–Fri. 8:30 A.M.–5 P.M.

From the city offices corner, go south a block and west a block to the **Winnemucca Grammar School** at the corner of 5th and Lay, built in 1927, worth a look from the outside. A block or so south on Lay St. is **Railroad St.,** once the town's commercial center. A couple of original bars are down the block. At the corner of 6th and Bridge is the **Shone House,** built in 1901 by Thomas Shone, who was the keeper of the Station Toll House; the old frame rooming house has been restored to its original two-story splendor, complete with a verandah shading the sidewalk and a balustraded porch on the upper floor.

Heading south across the tracks on Bridge St., make a left onto Haskell, go two blocks to Mizpah, and take a right into **City Park:** big, green, shady, kiddie playground, two tennis courts, and an indoor pool—all right across the street from Humboldt General Hospital, in case you overexert yourself.

You can do a fine walking tour around town by following the route shown in the pamphlet *Take a Walk Through History,* which you can pick up for free at the Chamber of Commerce office.

The Chamber also has a flyer with information about the **Bloody Shins Trail,** a BLM trail about three miles east of town. At an elevation of 4,540 to 5,200 feet, it has hiking, mountain biking, and equestrian loop trails for beginners (seven miles), intermediates (12 miles), and advanced (24 miles). Another BLM trail, the Blue Lakes Trail, is further afield. Further information on both trails is available at the BLM's Winnemucca Field Office, 5100 Winnemucca Blvd., 775/623-1500.

Special events are held throughout the year. Events include a Mule Show and Races (July), Junior Rodeo and USTRC Grassroots Team

Roping (July), Nevada All-Around Working Cowhorse Championship USTRC—Northwest Finals (August), and Tri-County Fair and Stampede (Labor Day weekend, September). One of the best events is the Shooting the West photography seminar (March) during which award-winning, national photographers offer tips, slide shows, contests, and other events for pro and amateur photographers.

Humboldt Museum

Take Melarkey north under the freeway, then over the river and railroad tracks up to Pioneer Park. Take a left into the parking lot and visit the Humboldt Museum, 775/623-2912, open weekdays 9 A.M.– 4 P.M., Sat. 1–4 P.M. (donation recommended), closed Sat. during winter. The building was originally St. Mary's Episcopal

Church (1907), which stood on 5th Street until it was moved to 4th in 1917, then up to its present location in 1976 onto city-donated land. The old church houses Winnemucca's first piano (from the Winnemucca Hotel), a square grand piano brought to Winnemucca in 1868, Indian relics from Lovelock Cave such as projectile points, Paiute handicrafts, an Edison talking machine, paintings of the Jungo Hotel and Golconda School, posters of Charlie Chaplin and Edna Purviance, and a scrapbook from *The Winning of Barbara Worth,* starring Gary Cooper, Ronald Coleman, and Vilma Banky, filmed 30 miles west of Winnemucca at the edge of the Black Rock Desert in 1926.

The newer rear building boasts a beautiful floor, a wall-length mural of what downtown Winnemucca looked like around the turn of the

ALEXANDER VON HUMBOLDT

As you've probably gathered by now, the area around Winnemucca is Humboldt Land. You've got Humboldt County, Humboldt Mountains (plus East and West Humboldt Mountains), Humboldt National Forest, Humboldt Sink, Humboldt Mining District, Humboldt Trail, and of course Humboldt River. So who was Humboldt, anyway, and how did his name become attached to so many important features in northern Nevada?

The first white man known to have stumbled on the river was Peter Skene Ogden in 1829, and his humble name for it, Ogden River, stuck at least until 1833, when Joseph Walker followed its entire length west through Nevada, and continued from there into California. But it appeared on Bonneville's 1837 map as Mary River. John C. Frémont designated it the Humboldt River in 1844 in honor of Alexander von Humboldt. And the Humboldt River it has remained.

Alexander von Humboldt was born in Berlin in 1769. He received a college education in mining technology and advanced quickly in his field. At the age of 27 he inherited a substantial sum of money, with which he embarked on a scientific expedition that ranged from Venezuela, Cuba, and Colombia to Mexico and the United States. He

collected botanical, zoological, geological, and astronomical data, studied Pacific Ocean currents, the Cuban plantation economy, and pre-Columbian cultures. He climbed to 18,000 feet in the Andes, surveyed the headwaters of the Amazon, followed ancient Inca trails in Peru, and sipped mint juleps with James Madison in Washington, D.C.

Humboldt settled in Paris in 1808 and began publishing the reports and results of his travels and inquiries. The subsequent 30-volume, 12,000-page encyclopedia earned him an international reputation as a "one-man institution," at the same time that it ruined him financially. Humboldt then embarked on several years of diplomatic missions for Frederick William III of Prussia, traveled through Siberia at the invitation of Czar Nicholas I, and finally settled down to a position as lecturer and author in Frederick's court in Berlin.

For the last 30 years of his life, Humboldt concentrated on his five-volume *Kosmos,* an epic survey of the Earth and universe. In it, he attempted to determine, through scientific knowledge, man's place in the cosmic order. Alexander von Humboldt died in Berlin in 1859, at the age of 90. Frémont did northern Nevada a great service by naming the country after such an illustrious and erudite figure.

20th century when Butch's gang robbed the bank, plus a pump organ from Paradise Valley, couches from Unionville, and an original, hand-inked, mint-condition survey map of Winnemucca from 1867. The antique auto collection includes a 1901 Merry Oldsmobile, the county's first car. An old grain store in the grounds serves as a thrift shop to raise funds for the Historical Society.

CASINOS

Red Lion Inn, 741 W. Winnemucca Blvd., 775/623-2565, is an interesting little place. It's like a midget casino—with everything that the big ones have except in miniature: red and blue border neon outside and upside-down pyramid lights above the main entrance; lots of slots; four blackjack tables and a roulette wheel around a tiny pit; little lounge right in the middle of the floor with a big-screen TV; little coffee shop with salad bar; even minichandeliers lighting the place—all stuffed into a space the size of Harrah's Tahoe ladies' room.

The **Model T** casino and truck stop at the west end of town on Main St., 775/623-2588, has six blackjack tables, including one offering multiple action. The Model T also has plenty of slots (even some 10-centers), a good coffee shop, and a lounge with country-western groups playing Thurs.–Sat. 9 P.M.–3 A.M. There's also a three-story motel. Jump out of the first-floor back-corner room windows right into the pool. The room comes with a free breakfast at the coffee shop.

Winners, right downtown on the corner of Winnemucca Blvd. and Melarkey, 775/623-2511, is the biggest casino, the only one with a crap table. Its big lounge has high-tech duos and trios playing Top 40 nightly, usually with some energy and a good beat.

Legends lounge and casino, 775/625-1777, owned by Winners, is the newest gaming house in town with 104 slots and three tables—two offer blackjack and one features Let It Ride. The complex also has a Holiday Inn Express motel and a Dos Amigos Restaurant inside.

Sundance Casino, downtown across from the Chamber of Commerce at Bridge and Main, 775/623-3336, is, except for the only poker table in town, all slots, including a video poker bar.

ACCOMMODATIONS

Twenty-two lodging houses offer a little more than 1,000 rooms in Winnemucca, so you shouldn't have too much trouble finding a suitable one. But pay close attention to all the changes that the rates can go through: summer and winter, weekend and weekday, two people in one bed or two beds, etc.

The **Red Lion Inn & Casino,** 741 W. Winnemucca, 775/623-2565 or 800/633-6435, www.redlionwinn.com, is the largest, with 105 rooms at $69–109.

Scott Shady Court, 400 1st St., 775/623-3646, has a cozy setting off the main drag, and a big luxurious indoor pool. The motel stands on part of the Scott family's old dairy farm, converted to the original campground and cabins in 1928. One of 70 rooms goes for $35–75.

Motel 6, 1600 W. Winnemucca on the far west end of town, 775/623-1180 or 800/466-8356, is next, with 103 rooms at $40–50. Next up is the **Model T Quality Inn,** 1130 W. Winnemucca, 775/623-2588 or 800/645-5658, www.modelt.com, with 75 rooms in the $45–75 range. Across the street is the **Best Western-Gold Country Inn,** 921 W. Winnemucca, 775/623-6999 or 800/346-5306, www.westernescapes.com, with 71 rooms at $84–104.

Other **hotel/motel** possibilities include: the Best Western Holiday Motel, 670 W. Winnemucca, 775/623-3684 or 800/262-8901, www.westernescapes.com, 40 rooms, $49–69; Days Inn, 511 W. Winnemucca, 775/623-3661, www.westernescapes.com, 50 rooms, $59–79; Holiday Inn Express, 1987 W. Winnemucca, 775/625-3100 or 800/HOLIDAY, 72 rooms, $55–89; Santa Fe Inn and Suites, 1620 W. Winnemucca, 775/623-1119, 74 rooms, $25–60; Super 8, 1157 W. Winnemucca, 775/625-1818 or 800/800-8000, 50 rooms, $47–111; the Pyrenees Motel, 714 W. Winnemucca, 775/623-1116, 46 rooms, $35–63; and Winners Hotel and Casino, 185 W. Winnemucca, 775/623-2511 or 800/648-4770, www.winnerscasino.com, 120 rooms, $35–49.

RV Parking
Hi-Desert RV Park, 5575 E. Winnemucca Blvd.,

775/623-4513, is one of the larger and nicer RV stopovers for I-80 travelers, with grassy sites and good shade. The game room has a pool table, video games, and a TV; a weight room and hot tub are by the pool. A casino shuttle provides free 24-hour transportation to downtown. There are 137 spaces for motor homes, all with full hookups. There are 80 pull-throughs and 11 tent sites. Accessible restrooms have flush toilets and hot showers; laundry, groceries, video rentals, game room, and heated swimming pool are available. Reservations are recommended June through September; the fees are $17 for tents, $24 per vehicle, and $3.50 for noncampers to take a shower. Good Sam, AAA, and AARP discounts.

Winnemucca RV Park, 5255 E. Winnemucca Blvd., 775/623-4458 or 877/787-2755, has been in the same location, about a mile east of downtown Winnemucca, for more than 20 years. The trees are mature, there's plenty of grass (nice tenting area), and the spaces are spacious. There are 132 total spaces for motor homes, 83 with full hookups. Tents are allowed. The fee is $22.50 for two people in an RV, $17 in a tent. Good Sam and AAA discounts.

Model T RV Park, 1130 W. Winnemucca Blvd., 775/623-2588, is in the parking lot of the Model T Casino, lending a somewhat urban setting for this RV park. There are 58 total spaces for motor homes, all with full hookups, all pull-throughs. No tenters need apply. Restrooms have flush toilets, hot showers; laundry, convenience store, and seasonal pool are available. The fee is $22 per vehicle. Good Sam and AARP discounts.

FOOD

Winnemucca Hotel, 95 Bridge St., 775/623-2908, is the second-oldest hotel still operating in Nevada today. The back bar is also one of the most beautiful in the state, with a large display of international currency above. Rooms for rent (mostly to boarders) and Basque food is served family-style: lunch noon–1 P.M. Mon.–Fri. ($6), dinner 6:15–9 P.M. Mon.–Sat. ($13).

For Basque dining, also try the **Martin Hotel,** Railroad and Melarkey, 775/623-3197, open for lunch 11:30 A.M.–2 P.M. Mon.–Fri., and for dinner nightly 5–9 P.M. Lunch costs $5–9. The full family-style dinner costs $14–22 including wine and dessert; an a la carte menu is also available, from which you can select dinners from $6–18. This is a sprawling old hotel, with a cozy bar up front, the dining room on the side, and a small all-purpose room in the rear. Good Basque food, too.

A newer Basque restaurant in Winnemucca is **San Fermin,** 485 W. Winnemucca Blvd., 775/625-4900. A young Basque/Basque-American couple, Jesus Flamarique and Alicia Garijo, have reinvigorated this cuisine with culinary news from the Old Country. Together they run a top-notch operation. It's open for dinner Mon.–Sat., 5–9:30 P.M., with family-style dinners for $15–18. Hard-core traditionalists should be warned that each party gets its own table and that there's smoking in the bar only.

The Griddle, 460 W. Winnemucca Blvd., 775/623-2977, opens every day at 5:30 A.M. and closes Mon.–Fri., around 1:30 P.M., around noon on the weekends. This is the best and most popular coffee shop in town—the food (try the *huevos rancheros*) is fast and friendly, though the waitresses are a tiny bit bashful. It's also one of the oldest restaurants in Winnemucca, having been owned by the Aboud family since 1961.

Winners, Model T, and **Red Lion** casinos all have 24-hour coffee shops. **Grandma's,** the fine dining room in Winners, is open for dinner nightly from 5–10 P.M. For barbecue there's **Bridge Street Bar B-Que,** 245 Bridge St., 775/623-1155, open Tues.–Sat. 11 A.M.–9 P.M. and Sun. noon–6 P.M. **Ormachea's Dinner House,** 180 Melarkey St., 775/623-3455, is another local favorite offer casual cuisine.

The Bakery, 227 S. Bridge St. across from the chamber, 775/623-3288, has been a local institution since 1935. It moved to its present location in 1946; the oven installed at that time is still as good as new. It's open Tues.–Sat. 4 A.M.–5:30 or 6 P.M., closed Sun.–Mon.

Winnemucca has its share of fast food: Round Table and Pizza Hut, Arby's, Taco Time, and Subway, all on Winnemucca Boulevard. **Route 66,** 329 E. Winnemucca, 775/623-2763, has a fountain and grill; the food is a step up from the usual galloping grub: burgers, sandwiches,

Northern Nevada

chicken, etc. Good Mexican food can be found at **Las Margaritas,** 47 E. Winnemucca Blvd., 775/625-2262, is another good Mexican restaurant, open daily 11 A.M.–10 P.M.

INFORMATION AND SERVICES

Park Cinemas, 740 W. Winnemucca Blvd., 775/623-4454, opened in 1986 and remains the only theater between Sparks and Elko. It shows first-run features weeknights and matinees on weekends.

Winnemucca has a fine **library,** at the corner of 5th and Baud, 775/623-6388, open nice long hours. The Nevada section is in its own room in solid wood cabinets—great for anything from browsing to serious research. Sheri Allen, a fifth-generation Humboldt County resident, has been head librarian for more than 25 years; her great-grandfather was the first mayor of Winnemucca.

Humboldt County Hospital is located at E. Haskell and Mizpah, 775/623-5222. The **Greyhound** office is at 665 Anderson St., 775/623-4464. **Amtrak,** 800/USA-RAIL, blows through town once daily in each direction. The minidepot is located at 209 Railroad St.

TO BATTLE MOUNTAIN

Heading east again on the interstate from Winnemucca, Paradise Valley stretches far and wide to the north, the Santa Rosas bordering it on the west and disappearing toward the left-hand horizon. The road hooks around the top of the big Sonoma Range through its northern badlands, then turns southeast. There's a **rest area** on the westbound side at Exit 187, Button Point. Leaving Golconda, the highway makes a short but steep climb up Edna Mountain to Golconda Summit (5,145 feet). There's a rest area at the top, and you can catch a glimpse of Osgood Peak. Then you cruise along Edna's shoulder for awhile, and drop down her thigh into Pumpernickel Valley, with Buffalo Mountain's skirts hemming it in on the southeast, and the broad Humboldt River valley opening wide on the northeast.

As you head southeast, the skyscraping stacks of Sierra Pacific Power Company's huge Valmy Power Plant are visible a few miles north. This 500-megawatt generator, completed in 1985, burns nearly two million tons of Utah coal annually.

Battle Mountain, the mountain, sits alone and square southeast of the road. The tail of the Sheep Creek Range points off to the northeast. The long Shoshone Range, still running north all the way from just this side of Tonopah, sits dead ahead to the right and left. Battle Mountain, the town, squats in the middle of the northern edge of the Reese River Valley, extending north all the way from the south side of Austin.

Battle Mountain and Vicinity

Emigrants were attacked near this spot by Shoshone in 1861; the pioneers regrouped and counterattacked the Indians in the hills southwest of town. The mountain was named for the battle and the town was named for the mountain. But it could just as easily have referred to the miningmen battling the mountains themselves, wresting minerals from the reluctant earth.

The Central Pacific, fresh from Winnemucca, arrived in 1869, coinciding with a rush to Copper Canyon nearby. Mining and the main line attracted three more railroads and even a phony navigation company. The Nevada Central ran a spur line straight down the Reese River Valley 90 miles to the old mines at Austin. The Battle Mountain and Lewis Shortline ran 12 miles to Lewis, operating a total of a year and a half. Western Pacific arrived around the turn of the 20th century. And the Reese River, a suitably long but unsuitably shallow waterway, provided clever eastern promoters the means to bilk unwary investors with stock in the only steamship company in Nevada's history—and a crooked one at that.

A new boom erupted in the late 1960s, when the Duval Company reopened the Copper Canyon operation, initiating a resurgence of mining in the area, for gold, copper, silver, turquoise, iron, mercury, and barite. (Battle Mountain is the barite capital of the world.) And after coveting the county seat for 110 years, in 1980 Battle Mountain, at one end of long thin Lander County, finally usurped the courthouse from Austin, at the other end.

The McCoy/Cove Mine, operated by Echo Bay Minerals south of town, has been in operation since the 1980s and for a number of years was the major employer in town, employing 500 people and recovering millions of ounces of silver, along with hundreds of thousands of ounces of gold. Several other gold and silver mines in the vicinity also helped sustain Battle Mountain's population at around 7,000 residents. By late 2000, however, after several major mine layoffs, the town's population was down to 3,600 people, and a third of the houses in town were up for sale. Nevertheless, unlike many places in Nevada where the mining boom-and-bust cycles mean the birth and death of towns, here in Battle Mountain, both the growth and decline in population have been accomplished without compromising the graciousness of its traditional small-town character. Battle Mountain remains a pleasant small town with a slow pace of life.

Unlike other towns along the Humboldt River, Central Pacific, US 40, and I-80 corridor, downtown Battle Mountain hasn't budged for over 120 years. Front Street still fronts the railroad yards, with most of the businesses (and no vacant storefronts) lining the opposite side of the thoroughfare.

SIGHTS

Battle Mountain has two exits off I-80, on the east and west ends of town. Heading east into Battle Mountain from Exit 229, you pass the inevitable smoke shop and head downtown to the main intersection, Front and Reese. Take a left and cross the tracks. At the corner of N. Reese and N. 1st is the **VFW Park.** It's shady and has picnic tables and kids' apparatus—a pleasant place for a stretch, a bite, or a rest.

On the south side of town, the **Lander County Courthouse** is at Humboldt and S. 3rd. At Broad and 6th (Route 305 toward Austin) are the **Civic**

Center, with the Chamber of Commerce office and library. The **Chamber of Commerce,** inside the Civic Center building at 625 S. Broad St., P.O Box 333, Battle Mountain, NV 89820, 775/635-8245, battlemtncc@hotmail.com, www .battlemountain.org is open Mon.–Fri. 9 A.M.– 4 P.M. in summer, 8 A.M.–4 P.M. in winter. In the lobby of the Civic Center is a rack of brochures, both local and statewide. The **Library** next door, 775/635-2534, is open Mon. 11 A.M.–5 P.M., Tues. noon–6 P.M., Wed. 2–6 P.M., Thurs. 4– 8 P.M., Fri. noon–4 P.M., Sat. 10 A.M.–2 P.M., closed Sun.

The **Trail of the 49ers Interpretive Center,** 453 N. 2nd St., 775/635-5720, is a tribute to the pioneers who traveled through this area heading west. It is estimated that from 1828 to 1869, around 200,000 immigrants passed through here, with a particular swell around 1849 with the California gold rush. The immigrant route followed the Humboldt River, much as I-80 does today. You are invited to live the experience with the immigrants, here at the center. Open Mon.– Fri. 10 A.M.–5 P.M., Sat. noon–4 P.M., or by appointment; donation.

Battle Mountain has a **Museum site** in town on Broyles Ranch Rd., opposite the Gold Strike Lanes bowling alley, off I-80's exit 231. For a long time the town had the land for the museum, but no museum to put on it. But in October 2000, the historic **Old Ranch Cookhouse** was being moved onto the site, and work was to begin to make this the home of the town's new museum. The town was all excited about it; phone the Chamber of Commerce to see how progress is coming, or stop by.

ACCOMMODATIONS

Coming in from the westside exit (229), you pass the **Broadway Colt Service Center,** with minimart, truck stop, café, and motel. The motel, **Battle Mountain Inn,** 650 W. Front St., 775/635-5200 or 800/343-0085, offers 70 rooms for $49–69, continental breakfast included. Next up is the **Big Chief Best Western,** 434 W. Front, 775/635-2416 or 800/528-1234, with 58 rooms for $35–55. Others include the

Owl Club, 155 S. Reese, 775/635-2444, with rooms for $30–35, and the Nevada Hotel, 36 E. Front, 775/635-2453, with five rooms for $17–27. The Bel Court Motel, 292 E. Front, 775/635-2569, has nine rooms for $20–30. And the three-story Comfort Inn, 521 E. Front at the east exit, 775/635-5880 or 800/626-1900, has 71 rooms for $59–79. There's also a Super 8 at 825 Super 8 Dr., 775/635-8808, 54 rooms, $60–77.

Broadway Flying J RV Park, 650 W. Front St., 775/635-5424, has 96 spaces for motor homes, all with full hookups; 79 are pull-throughs. Tents are allowed. Accessible restrooms (in the truck stop) have flush toilets and hot showers; public phone, laundry, and groceries are available. Tent and RV spaces are $15; non-campers can shower for $5.

Nature-loving campers will like the Mill Creek camping area, 19 miles south of Battle Mountain off Route 305, heading towards Austin. It's a small, shady, secluded little camping area beside Mill Creek, with trees and a footbridge across the creek. There are no hookups, and no running water, but the price is great—free.

FOOD AND CASINOS

The Owl Club is the main action downtown, 72 E. Front, 775/635-2444. The dining room is open Fri.–Sat. 6 A.M.–11 P.M., Sun.–Thurs. 6 A.M.–10 P.M.—save room for a piece of pie. The casino has lots of slots, a three-table blackjack pit, and three big screens. The Nevada Hotel on the same block, 36 E. Front, 775/635-2453, has a diner (open 7 A.M.–9 P.M.), slots, and blackjack.

The Hide-A-Way, 872 Broad St., 775/635-5150, specializes in steaks and seafood. For Mexican food, locals rave about El Aguila Real, 254 E. Front St., 775/635-8390, with delicious

medium-priced Mexican fare, open 11 A.M.–9 P.M. every day.

The Broadway Colt Restaurant, 650 W. Front St. at the Broadway Colt Service Center at the far west end of town, 775/635-5424, open 24 hours, is a nice, bright, airy coffee shop serving good food, with daily specials. The casino next door has expanded from two rows of slots to more than 100 machines.

Mama's Pizza is next door to the Comfort Inn on the east side of town, 515 E. Front, 775/635-9211, open 11 A.M.–9 P.M., Sun. until 8 P.M.

INFORMATION AND SERVICES

Check with the Chamber of Commerce for current info on gold mining tours in the area. Barrick, Newmont, and Cortez are the major mines here, and there are also a number of smaller mines.

Battle Mountain's major annual event is the Pony Express open road car race, with cars racing down Route 305 from Battle Mountain to Austin. It's held every summer; the Chamber of Commerce has details. The Old Spice Festival is an annual summer event. The idea came about after a *Washington Post* writer declared Battle Mountain the "Armpit of America." Turning the other cheek, so to speak, the town decided to capitalize on the publicity. The rest—and the marketing plan—came easily.

At the Human Powered Vehicle bike race held in fall 2002, Canadian Sam Wittingham, of the Varna bicycle team from Vancouver, Canada, clocked in at a speed of 81 miles per hour, beating the previous world record of 68 mph.

For sundries, magazines, prescriptions, and whatnot, stop in at Mills Pharmacy, 990 Broyles Ranch Rd., 775/635-2323. The Battle Mountain Swimming Pool, 560 Altenburg Ave., 775/635-5850, is open June through August.

Elko

The Elko area's history generally parallels that of all the towns along the Humboldt River. Peter Skene Ogden blazed the trail in the 1820s that the emigrants from the east followed to California; miners created a demand for goods that the railroad fulfilled; when cars came into their own, the long-distance highway followed the railroad right-of-way, which the superhighway ultimately replaced.

Elko itself was founded at the same time the Central Pacific arrived in the area: very late in 1868. The company laid out a town site for a division point and sold lots for $300; the origin of the name "Elko" is obscure, but is believed to be a lyrical form of "elk."

Immediately, Elko turned into a major supply and freighting center for the eastern Nevada mining boom—from Tuscarora, 52 miles north, to Hamilton, 140 miles south. It also became the seat of huge new Elko County (which remains today larger than Massachusetts, Connecticut, and Rhode Island combined), and site of the first University of Nevada. Elko suffered the inevitable boom-bust cycles throughout the rest of the century and lost the university to Reno. Cattlemen grazed large herds on public lands around the county, but the mercilessly severe winter of 1889–90 wiped out most of the stock. Soon afterward, the Basque sheepherders showed up.

Clashes between the buckaroos and Basques over public grazing lands occasionally became violent and necessitated state and federal legislation to control matters. The arrival of the Western Pacific passenger trains in 1907 helped lift Elko from its doldrums, and the Victory Highway (US 40) began delivering more travelers in the early 1920s. In addition, Elko was selected as a stop on the transcontinental airmail route. At first administered by the feds, when the routes were turned over to private carriers, Valmy Airlines (a forerunner of United) made the first commercially scheduled airmail flight, from Pasco, Washington, to Elko.

When gambling was legalized in 1931, Elko started up its casino industry in the venerable Commercial Hotel. Newton Crumley, who'd owned hotels in Tonopah and Goldfield, and a saloon in Jarbidge, had bought the Commercial six years earlier. The Crumleys followed the lead of Raymond and Harold Smith of Reno by making the new gambling accessible and acceptable to the masses. But the Crumleys went an important step further and began to book big-name acts to do the floor show in the lounge. A rousing success, this began the tradition of headliners and floor shows in casinos.

Since then, Elko has prided itself as a can-do sort of town. The people of Elko managed to relocate the railroad tracks from between Commercial and Railroad streets downtown to out by the river—something that no other town along the northern Nevada main line, not even Reno, has managed to accomplish. When Elko wanted a community college, it got one. Kids' parks? No problem—the town raised the money and built them with volunteer labor. Downhill skiing? Someone bought a hill, dug a well for snowmaking machinery, and put in a rope tow. Museum? Convention center? Cowboy gatherings? Yup—they're all here.

In the past 15 years, however, Elko has really taken off. The resurgence of gold mining around here doubled every number in Elko's demographics between 1987 and 1990; mining now accounts for nearly 40 percent of the economy, with gambling and retail filling in the rest. Elko embraced the boom with its customary aplomb. Housing? It takes 30 days to approve a new subdivision and another few months to complete one; the houses are filled before the paint's dry. Doctors? At one point, a $10,000 reward was offered for anyone who coaxed a physician to Elko. In 1993, Elko was named the "best small town" by Norman Crampton, author of the *The 100 Best Small Towns in America*. According to the U.S. Census, Elko County ranks second in Nevada for average household income, at $54,000 a year; this puts Elko in the top 10 percent of the country.

Elko is the largest town between Salt Lake City (237 miles east) and Sparks (nearly 300 miles

Northern Nevada

ELKO

To Salt
Lake City

535

80

FLAGVIEW RD.

CONVENTION DR

CONVENTION
CENTER

CITY HALL

BALL PARK
COMPLEX

MOREN
WAY

City Park

GOLF COURSE RD.

NORTHEASTERN
NEVADA MUSEUM
★

SHERMAN STATION,
ELKO CHAMBER
OF COMMERCE AND
VISITORS' CENTER

HOLIDAY INN EXPRESS
HOTEL & SUITES

HIGH DESERT INN

ELKO SHOPPING
PLAZA

BEST WESTERN
GOLD COUNTRY
MOTOR INN &
CASINO

40

RED LION INN &
CASINO

ELKO CO.
FAIRGROUNDS

SENIOR CITIZEN
CENTER

ELKO COLONY
INDIAN RESERVATION

NORTHERN
NEVADA COMMUNITY
COLLEGE

COLLEGE AVENUE

COUNTY
HOSPITAL

RAILROAD ST

COMMERCIAL ST

RIVER ST

WATER ST

AMTRAK
STATION

12TH ST

RIVER

To Spring Creek
and Lamoille

227

LAMOILLE HIGHWAY

SCALE NOT AVAILABLE

COURT
HOUSE

WESTERN FOLKLIFE
CENTER

STOCKMEN'S
CASINO

Humboldt

6TH ST

COURT ST

5TH ST

4TH ST

3RD ST

ELM ST

THE MAP
HOUSE

COMMERCIAL
HOTEL & CASINO

40

POST
OFFICE

W SAGE ST

MOUNTAIN CITY
HIGHWAY

NEVADA DEPARMENT
OF WILDLIFE

IDAHO ST

MAIN ST

ELKO AIRPORT

40

225

RALEY'S

SHILO INN

To Mountain City

80

To Reno

© AVALON TRAVEL PUBLISHING, INC.

west), and between Las Vegas (400 miles south) and Twin Falls (173 miles north)—an area roughly comparable in size to New England. It's the fourth most populated locale in Nevada, behind Las Vegas and Reno and their vicinities, and Carson City. It has regularly scheduled air, rail, and bus services, an interstate passing by, one of the finest museums in the state, the Cowboy Poetry Gathering, and some of the most irresistible outdoor recreation anywhere. It also has the most legal brothels in the country. And in one of the stranger twists in local mythology, Hunter S. Thompson, master of hallucinatory journalism, published a cover story in *Rolling Stone* called "Fear and Loathing in Elko," in which Thompson smashes into a herd of sheep on I-80 outside of town and rescues Judge Clarence Thomas and two prostitute companions whose car was totaled by the same sheep. This unlikely team proceeds to have a string of wild and drunken adventures as dark and mean as the inside of Thompson's head. (Anyone interested should find the January 23, 1992, issue; a more twisted view of northern Nevada you will never read.)

SIGHTS

This booming town has a brash, modern, frontier energy all its own. It's easy to slip into Elko's strong stream of hustle and bustle, which seems to keep pace with the cars and trucks on the superhighway, the freight and passenger trains chugging right through town, and the planes landing at and taking off from the airport. Yet Elko also has a warm, homespun vitality to it. Coming into Elko after a long drive from any direction is like stepping up to a blazing campfire on a cold desert night. And you seem to return to Elko again and again, after playing around for a while in the Rubies or up around Jarbidge, or just passing through on your comings and goings. So get to know Elko. Within and around it is everything you could need or want from a major Nevada town.

Northeastern Nevada Museum

This remarkable museum, at 1515 Idaho St. toward the east end of town, 775/738-3418, is open Mon.–Sat. 9 A.M.–5 P.M. and Sun. 1–5 P.M.

It is one of the largest, finest, and most varied collections in the state, so plan to spend at least an hour or two perusing the highly informative and artistic exhibits and displays, musing over the many books in the gift shop, and schmoozing with the friendly volunteers and staff.

The Ruby Valley Pony Express Cabin out front was built in 1860. Relocated from Ruby Valley, about 60 miles south, it's now the oldest structure in Elko. Inside the museum, sign the guest register and go into the room on the right, with rotating art and photo exhibits, an old mud wagon, and Bing Crosby's Levi tuxedo (one of two ever made). There's also a Basque display and video, and a display case of photos of downtown, with an emphasis on the Commercial and Stockmen's.

On the other side are big exhibits on local wildlife (birds, bighorn, bobcat, badger, black bear, beautiful butterflies), mining and minerals, railroads, and buckaroos, along with a pioneer kitchen, type shop, and schoolroom. The Chinatown display is exotic, with its abacus, game book and chips, and salt-glazed stoneware, as are the Indian baskets, points, and beads. A new wing, the Wannamaker Wildlife Wing, is impressive, with animals from around the world beautifully displayed. Another highlight is an exhibit of the Spring Creek Mastodon bones.

But perhaps the most relevant piece in the place is the display on mining, which features the Newmont Company's promo slide show about microscopic gold mining along the Carlin Trend, so rich and extensive that some say it won't be mined out till the year 2030. Watch how the ore is blasted, scooped, hauled, dumped, vibrated, separated, crushed, limed, conveyed, ground, pulped, thickened, settled, leached, cyanided, charcoaled, stripped, steel-wooled, retorted, acid-treated, inductothermed, poured, and bricked—all to recover microscopic specks of gold; it requires up to 100 tons of paydirt to process a single ounce. Marvel over the 100-ton dump trucks with their 10-foot-diameter tires that dwarf good-sized truck drivers, and all the equipment that is used to make Nevada the number-one gold-producing state in the nation.

The gift shop sells historical and local-interest books, Basque and local cookbooks, along with some art and jewelry. Museum admission is $5 adults, $3 seniors and youth (ages 13–18, $1 children (age 12 and under). free for everyone on the last Sunday of each month.

Sherman Station

Next door to the museum is the historic Sherman Station, another very interesting place to visit. This group of five historic buildings, built of logs at various times between 1880 and 1903, was part of the historic homestead of Valentine and Sophie Walther, who homesteaded 600 acres on Sherman Creek in Huntington Valley, about 60 miles south of Elko, in 1875. The main house, a large two-story, 4,800-square-foot structure, is full of interesting historic exhibits, and also houses the Elko Chamber of Commerce and visitors' center. The other, smaller buildings are a historic blacksmith shop, schoolhouse, creamery (now housing a cowboy emporium), and stable (home to a company offering carriage tours of Elko). 1405 Idaho St., 775/738-7135 or 800/428-7143, is open year-round, Mon.–Fri. 9 A.M.–5 P.M. and Sat. 9 A.M.–4 P.M., with additional Sun. hours in summer, 11 A.M.–3 P.M.

Around Town

Between Sherman Station and the Northeastern Nevada Museum is the large and shady **Elko City Park;** around it are picnic facilities, a childrens' playground, tennis courts, ball fields, Convention Center, swimming pool, community college, fairgrounds, city hall, public schools, and cemeteries. Take Court St. (one block north of Idaho) back downtown to view a number of **historic houses.** Mostly brick, with big lilac trees blooming and perfuming in mid-May, the oldest is on Court Street near 4th, refurbished and now inhabited by Chilton Engineering. The map store next door on the corner was the first schoolhouse in Elko, built in 1869; buy topo maps here.

Drive north of town up the bluff through a nice residential neighborhood to the interstate; coming back to town, the Ruby Mountains stand out—high, jagged, snowy. Continue down to the river; the footbridge over it at South Water and 9th Streets could have been designed by a 15-year-old thrasher.

Make sure to stop off at **J. M. Capriola's,** one of the largest cowboy outfitters in the state, on the corner of Commercial and 5th, 775/738-5816, open Mon.–Sat. 9 A.M.–5:30 P.M. Guadalupe S. Garcia was born in 1864 in Sonora, Mexico, and moved to San Luis Obispo, California, when he was three; there he did a long apprenticeship at a saddlery. He moved to Elko at age 32, where he proceeded to become one of the West's most renowned saddle makers, winning every award in the book, outfitting American celebrities, international *vaqueros,* and local buckaroos by the thousands. Guadalupe died in 1937 in Monterey, California, but not before Joe Capriola completed his apprenticeship with Garcia and opened this shop. Downstairs, ranch and Western wear, boots, and hats are sold; check out the artwork on the stairway and the tools of the buckaroo trade upstairs, where craftsmen handmake saddles, bits, and spurs.

Western Folklife Center

The Pioneer Saloon opened in 1868, and the Pioneer Hotel was built in 1912 on the same site, at the corner of Railroad and 5th Streets, at a cost of $50,000. In 1981, the hotel was gutted and renovated for $2 million.

In 1991, the Western Folklife Center (WFC), sponsor of the Cowboy Poetry Gathering, received a grant generous enough to buy the Pioneer Hotel and move lock, stock, and barrel from Salt Lake City to Elko, where the Poetry Gathering had been held since 1985. The ground floor houses a gift shop full of tapes, CDs, and books of cowboy poetry and musi; posters and photos from Poetry Gatherings; and songbooks full of the music of Gene Autrey, Roy Rogers, and Dale Evans from the heyday of cowboy culture. The old mahogany bar has been restored for functions, workshops, and performances, which spill over to, or in from, the Music Hall next door. Now that the WFC is home for good in Elko, it can present year-round programs; call for current info.

The Center is at 501 Railroad St., 775/738-7508 or 800/748-4466, tbaer@westernfolklife.org, www.westernfolklife.org. Admission to the center is free. The gift shop is open Tues.–Sat.

10 A.M.–5:30 P.M. Administrative offices on the third floor are open Mon.–Fri. 9 A.M.–5 P.M.

Newmont Gold Company

Witness first-hand what's igniting Elko's boom with a visit to a working gold mine in the area. Newmont Gold Company, 775/778-4068, offers mine tours from 9 A.M. to noon on the second Tuesday of each month. Reservations are first-come, first-served; it's a good idea to reserve at least a week ahead. Children 12 and older are welcome, accompanied by an adult. Transportation is provided, and tours are free.

CASINOS

The **Commercial Hotel** downtown at 345 4th St., 775/738-5141, has been around for nearly 130 years, which makes it the third oldest hotel in the state (behind the Gold Hill and the Winnemucca). The White King on display here is the largest polar bear exhibited in Nevada (which isn't saying much) and probably the country (which is). This guy stands 10 feet, four inches, and weighs more than a ton. Too bad he had to be killed. The Commercial used to feature a fascinating series of portraits (by Lea McCarthy, 1958) and biographies of two dozen of the Wild West's most famous gunfighters, but now only a few portraits (*sans* bios) hang in the coffee shop. Of the two casinos downtown, the Commercial is more the sawdust joint, with six blackjack tables, one Caribbean stud, and lots of nickel slots and video poker.

Across the plaza is **Stockmen's** (not to be confused with Stockman's, in Fallon), 340 Commercial, 775/738-5141, which has old downtown carpeting, a big pit with craps, roulette, and blackjack, a popular sports bar, and a good dining room (see below).

The **Red Lion Casino,** on the east end of town at 2065 Idaho, 775/738-2111, is the big fancy joint in Elko. This place is more of a big-city's gambling house than a town's, with its long luxurious pit (including two each crap and roulette tables, plus lots of blackjack), comfortable sports book, big lounge with dance floor, gourmet restaurant, and buffet.

The Red Lion also runs a charter airline service, called the **Casino Express,** on Boeing 737s from all around the country, the closest thing to an old-fashioned junket as you'll find in Nevada these days. Casino Express delivers to the Red Lion thousands of "green-button" people a month, who pay upwards of $150–200 for two or three nights and round-trip airfare. You have to show somewhere around $350 in cash to qualify; there's no gambling requirement, but your play is monitored once you get here, which will affect your future junket prices. The planes are cramped and crowded, but there's some action: $500 is given away.

Across the street is the **Best Western Gold Country Motor Inn & Casino,** 2050 Idaho St., 775/738-8421, with three blackjack tables, some slots, and a big 24-hour coffee shop.

ENTERTAINMENT AND EVENTS

The action, as you'll quickly discover, is at the three big hotels. Nevada-style entertainment started right here in the **Commercial Hotel;** check the Round Up Room for your dancing and listening enjoyment. **Stockmen's** also has the country, and can get swingin' with the right players and audience. The **Red Lion Inn lounge,** Club Max, has a big dance floor and bar bands that can get the rock 'n' roll crowd movin' and groovin'. The hotel also offers occasional headliners, such as the Oak Ridge Boys and others. The **Crystal Theater** five-plex is at 676 Commercial St. at 7th, 775/738-5214.

Elko SnoBowl is Elko's ski and winter recreation area, six miles north of town via 5th Street, 775/738-4431. With a north-facing slope, a base elevation of 6,200 feet and a maximum elevation of 6,900 feet, it offers good skiing even when there's no snow in the valley. The ski hill is served by two rope tows and a chair lift. Saturday ski lessons are offered for children and beginners; more advanced skiers can try the expert run. Sledding and snow tubing are also popular. Skiers can compete in the SnoBowl Fest in February. A Snack Shack is open during ski season. A shuttle bus leaves hourly, on the hour, from the end of 5th Street.

"IN 45 YEARS"

by Peggy Godfrey

I've learned to see the mountains
as more than stone and mud
Come to know my neighbors
as more than flesh and blood
I've grown to see the work I do
as more than passing time
Poetry means more to me
than getting words to rhyme.
I'm now aware each day is more
than getting on with life
I see myself as more than just
my role as mom or wife
Life offers me a framework
like bones stripped bare and white
What I can do is flesh them in
with muscle, love, and light.

Peggy Godfrey is a rancher in Colorado and a perennial star of the annual Cowboy Poetry Gathering held in Elko in January. "In 45 Years" is reprinted with permission from *Write 'Em Cowboy,* Elliot Publishing.

Elko is a lively community with enjoyable events happening throughout the year; the Chamber of Commerce should have details on all of them. The **Cowboy Poetry Gathering,** 775/738-7508 or 800/748-4466, takes place in the last week of January. In April there's the **Spring Creek Ranch Hand Rodeo,** 775/753-6295. June brings the **Golf Tournament and Mining Expo,** 775/738-4091, and the **Lamoille Country Fair,** 775/753-6410. In July there's the **National Basque Festival** held on the Fourth of July weekend, 775/738-5386; the **Silver State Stampede Rodeo,** 775/738-3118, and **Art in the Park,** 775/738-1553. In September, the **Elko County Fair, Livestock Show and Parimutuel Horse Racing** provide entertainment for Labor Day weekend, 775/738-3616, and there's also the **Kiwanis Buckaroo Breakfast,** held in Elko City Park. October

events include the **Nevada Day Parade,** 775/753-7991, and **Octoberfest,** 775/738-4187. In December are the **Nurses' Bazaar,** 775/738-5414, the **Christmas in the Nighttime Skies** fireworks show, 775/738-8011.

ACCOMMODATIONS

Being the biggest town for several hundred miles in every direction and a boomtown to boot, Elko can be a tough place to get a room, especially in the summer and on weekends year-round. Still, Elko has more than 1,800 rooms, so if you call even a day or two in advance, you'll probably be able to come up with an adequate place to stay in your price range.

The biggest hotel in town is the **Red Lion Inn & Casino,** 2065 Idaho, 775/738-2111 or 800/545-0044, www.westernescapes.com. It has 223 nice big rooms, which go for $39–109. A block east is the next largest lodging in Elko, the **High Desert Inn,** 3015 Idaho, 775/738-8425 or 888/EXIT-303, with 171 rooms at $39–89 and an indoor swimming pool. Across the street from the Red Lion is the **Best Western Gold Country Motor Inn & Casino,** 2050 Idaho, 775/738-8421 or 800/621-1332, with 151 rooms at $59–119. **Best Western Elko Inn Express,** 837 Idaho, 775/738-7261 or 800/528-1234, has 49 rooms at $49–79 and an outdoor pool. **Ameritel Inn Elko** is at 1930 Idaho, 775/738-8787 or 800/600-6001, with 109 rooms at $65–150 and an indoor pool.

The **Motel 6,** 3021 Idaho, 775/738-4337 or 800/466-8356, at the east end of Idaho St. is tried and true, with rooms for $35–50; even though it's the fifth largest lodging in Elko with 123 rooms, it fills up fast. Reserve early. The back rooms at **Towne House Motel,** 500 W. Oak St., 775/738-7269, at the corner of Idaho and W. Oak on the west side, are far enough off Idaho to be relatively quiet. Attentive managers, too; $32–63. The **Centre Motel,** 475 3rd St. across Idaho from the Commercial, 775/738-3226, has a fine location and is amazingly quiet in the bargain. Great TV sets, and from the windows you get good neon—the Commercial, Stockmen's, and the Thunderbird; $30–50. The

Elko Motel, 1243 Idaho St., 775/738-4433, is also a good deal at $32–45; the rooms are old and small but clean.

The Shilo Inn is at 2401 Mountain City Hwy. in the Raley's shopping center, 775/738-5522 or 800/222-2244; its 70 rooms ($69–120) are all suites, with microwave, fridge, and wet bar; there's also a fitness center with steam, exercise equipment, and an indoor pool (with three indoor pools, Elko has the most of any town in Nevada).

Stockmen's Hotel-Casino, 340 Commercial St., 775/738-5141 or 800/648-2345, has 140 rooms at $33–75. A few other possibilities include the Hilton Garden Inn, 3650 E. Idaho St., 775/777-1200, 84 rooms, $69–149; the Holiday Inn Express, 3019 Idaho St., 775/777-0990, 77 rooms, $70–100; Oak Tree Inn, 95 Spruce Rd., 775/777-2222, 120 rooms, $49–79.

Other places to try include: Budget Inn, 1349 Idaho St., 775/738-7000, $30–65; Park View Inn, 1785 Idaho St., 775/753-7747, $40–60; Manor Motor Lodge, 185 Idaho St., 775/738-3311, $30–55; Super 8, 1755 Idaho St., 775/738-8488 or 800/800-8000, 74 rooms, $40–70; and the Thunderbird Motel, 345 Idaho St. right downtown, 775/738-7115, $49–79.

The friendly Once Upon A Time B&B, 537 14th St., 775/738-1200, mjohnson@elko-nv.com, operated by Michael and Madeline Johnson, is walking distance to downtown. The three guest rooms are $65–95, including full breakfast.

RV Parking

Double Dice RV Park, 3730 E. Idaho St., 775/738-5642, is a full-scale urban RV park atop a hill in East Elko (the Daily Free Press newspaper offices are next door). The park has its own bar and lounge, complete with video poker, slot machines, and sandwiches and burgers for sale (or catch the shuttle down the hill to town). The Double Dice makes its showers available to non-campers: $3 for 20 minutes. There are 140 spaces for motor homes, all with full hookups, and 55 pull-throughs. Tents are allowed. Reservations are recommended in summer. The fees are $17 for tent sites and $28 for RV sites. Good Sam discounts.

Best Western Gold Country RV Park, 2050 Idaho St., 775/738-8421 or 800/621-1332, is

right in the thick of the urban action at the east end of Elko; the RV park is behind the Best Western Gold Country motor inn. There are 26 spaces for motor homes, all 26 with full hookups. Tents are not allowed. Laundry and heated swimming pool are available. Reservations are recommended; the fee is $22 up to two people. AARP discounts.

Cimarron West RV and Trailer Park, 1400 Mountain City Highway, 775/738-8733, is a busy little complex just up the street from the airport and down the street from the Raley's shopping center. There are several spaces for overnight motor homes, all with full hookups (there are a total of 100 spaces, but some are occupied by permanent residents). No tents are allowed. Here you'll find a full-service minimart with ice cream parlor and slots, 24-hour restaurant, video rentals, gift store, service station, and drive-through car wash. Reservations are recommended (without reservations, especially in the summer, forget about staying here). The fee is $17 per night.

Valley View RV Park, 6000 E. Idaho St., three miles east of town, 775/753-9200, is open all year and has 100 pull-through spaces that can accommodate motor homes up to 50 feet long. Facilities include Laundromat, showers, children's playground, dog walking area, barbecue areas, and there's plenty of grass and trees. Tents are allowed. RV spaces with full hookups cost $15, tent spaces $8; weekly and monthly rates also available.

FOOD

Not surprisingly, the main theme in this cow town is beef—at coffee shops, diners, burger joints, steakhouses, and Basque restaurants.

Of the four Basque dinner houses in Elko, three are strung along Silver St., one block south of Idaho behind Stockmen's. The Star Hotel Basque Restaurant, 246 Silver St. at the corner of 3rd, 775/753-8696, is the oldest. It opened in 1910 as a Basque boardinghouse with 11 rooms (built for $11,000); business was so brisk that another dozen rooms were added in 1913. Since then, the Star has been owned by a succession of Basque innkeepers, the latest since 1989. Typically, the seating is family style, and the food bowls full of soup, salad, beans, veggies, fries, and bread are bottomless; entrées include selections such as trout, pork, lamb, steaks, even *bacalao* or salted cod. It's open for lunch Mon.–Fri. 11:30 A.M.–2 P.M., dinner Mon.–Sat. 5–9:30 P.M.

The **Nevada Dinner House** at 351 Silver St., half a block east between 3rd and 4th, 775/738-8485, offers Basque dining with regular restaurant seating. Open for lunch Tues.–Fri. 11 A.M.–1:30 P.M., dinner Sat.–Sun. 5–10 P.M., Tues.–Fri. 5:30 P.M.–9 P.M.

Biltoki, 405 Silver St., is half a block east on the corner of 4th, 775/738-9691. This is the least expensive of the three, with the most specials: lomo, beef tongue, lamb stew, along with lamb chops, Spanish omelette, and the usual steaks, with full dinner costing around $11–20. Open for dinner nightly, 4:30–10 P.M.

Toki-Ona (Come To This Place), 1550 Idaho St. across from the museum, 775/738-3214, is open every day, 6 A.M.–9:30 P.M., serving breakfast, lunch, and dinner.

In the Raley's plaza is **9 Beans and a Burrito,** 2525 Argent Ave., 775/738-7898, economical and popular with locals, especially at lunchtime. It's open Mon.–Sat. 7:30 A.M.–9:30 P.M., Sun. 8:30 A.M.–8:30 P.M. **La Fiesta** at 780 Commercial St., 775/738-1622, is another local favorite, serving lunch specials and dinner. Topping the menu in price is steak and lobster. Open every day, 11 A.M.–10 P.M. **Dos Amigos,** 1770 Mountain City Hwy., 775/753-4935, is another Mexican restaurant popular with locals.

The **Stockmen's** and **Commercial** casinos downtown, 775/738-5141, each have a 24-hour coffee shop. The Red Lion Inn & Casino has the 24-hour **Coffee Garden Restaurant & Buffet,** the only buffet in town, with buffets for breakfast, lunch and dinner. Lunch and dinner themes are different every day; on Friday, the dinner buffet features international choices with a Friday seafood buffet. The breakfast special goes 24 hours: two eggs, bacon or sausage, and biscuits and gravy. The Red Lion is at 2065 Idaho St., 775/738-2111.

Misty's, also at the Red Lion Inn & Casino, is the first-class dining room hereabouts. Try out appetizers such as shrimp royale and crab cakes, a Caesar salad for two, or treat yourself to a filet mignon Diane or angel pasta pescatore with shrimp and lobster. Open weekdays 5–10 P.M., weekends 5–11 P.M.

JR's Bar & Grill, in the Best Western Gold Country, 775/738-8421, features the only rotisserie-grilled meats in town, plus an array of tasty meat and pasta dishes. Have breakfast, lunch, or dinner at this local favorite. Open 24 hours.

For a slightly exotic combination of Chinese and buckaroo, try the popular **Elko Dinner Station,** 1430 Idaho, 775/738-8528. It serves chow mein, fried rice, moo goo and egg foo, steaks and seafood, and special dinners synthesizing the two. Open 11 A.M.–9:30 P.M., closed Mon.

Savary, 217 Idaho across from Zapata's, 775/738-0488, offers casual fine dining in a house with a long history that's described on the menu. It's a comfortable place, with five dining rooms, three fireplaces, bar and lounge area. The eclectic menu offers a wide range of choices; the emphasis is on fresh foods, with a Mediterranean and Southwestern flair. Open for lunch 11 A.M.–2 P.M. ($6–11) and dinner 5–9 P.M. ($9–20), every day except Sun.

If you're tired of road swill or are simply a coffee snob, Cowboy Joe serves espresso and sweet snacks. **Cowboy Joe's Downtown,** 376 5th St., 775/753-5612, is open Mon.–Fri. 5 A.M.–5:30 P.M., Sat. 5:30 A.M.–3 P.M., Sun. 7 A.M.–noon. The shop carries unique gifts and souvenirs.

INFORMATION AND SERVICES

Started in 1907, the **Chamber of Commerce,** 1405 Idaho St., 775/738-7135 or 800/428-7143, www.elkonevada.com, is Nevada's oldest. It's open Mon.–Fri. 9 A.M.–5 P.M. and Sat.–Sun. 10 A.M.–4 P.M. Located in the historic Sherman Station, the office has a goodly amount of information, brochures, and free newspapers. The town boosters working here are a friendly, efficient, and busy bunch. Much of their work involves sending out relocation and employment information to people (hundreds of requests come in each day) eager for a stake in Elko's continuing economic boom. Requests were coming

in so fast and furious that they finally had to start charging ($5) to offset the skyrocketing printing and mailing costs; they recommend viewing their website, which displays a lot of the same information.

The **library,** Court and 7th Streets, 775/738-3066, is open Mon.–Tues. 9 A.M.–8 P.M., Wed.–Thurs. 9 A.M.–6 P.M., Fri.–Sat. 9 A.M.–5 P.M. A big wall of bookcases is full of Nevadana; ask the librarian to open them up for your edification.

The **Bookstore,** in the Rancho Plaza Shopping Mall, 1372 Idaho St. at 13th, 775/738-5342 or 800/580-5342, is the area's primary book source, with a large selection of new and used books, magazines, paperbacks, local-interest and Louie L'Amour books. Open Mon.–Fri. 8:30 A.M.–5:30 P.M., Sat. until 5 P.M., closed Sun. For maps, check out **The Map House,** 421 Court St., 775/738-3108, chilton@chilton-inc.com, carrying USGS maps, Rand McNally maps, and others.

The **U.S. Forest Service** office, 2035 Last Chance Rd., 775/738-5171, www.fs.fed.us/htnf, is open Mon.–Fri. 7:30 A.M.–4:30 P.M. Stop here to check on road conditions in the Rubies and up around Jarbidge, and to pick up maps, information sheets on trails, camping, and fishing, and to get personal recommendations; information and maps are available especially for the Ruby Mountains, Mountain City, and the Great Basin National Park. **Elko General Hospital,** 2001 Errecart Blvd., 775/738-5151, has a 24-hour emergency room.

City Slicker Tours, 775/738-5642, based at the Double Dice RV Park in Elko, offers all kinds of trips and tours in the surrounding area, including Elko, Landers, Eureka and White Pine counties. To mention just one example: their half-day tour of Lamoille and the Lamoille Canyon costs $65. They also offer a number of full-day tours ranging further afield. Operated by Marv Churchfield, a rancher whose family has lived in the area since 1891.

Eagle's Nest Station, 775/744-4370, 15 miles south of Elko, offers wagon rides in summer, sleigh rides in winter, meals, cowboy music and poetry, and a log art gallery. Lunch rides and sunset steak supper rides are also offered (minimum

four persons). Transport is available from Elko, to bring you out to the ranch and take you back to town, with magnificent views along the way. The Eagle's Nest is open year round, except for a short time in spring and fall if there are muddy conditions. Camping is also available here on the ranch, except during fire season: $8 per night, $10 with shower, $15 with shower and ranch tent.

For full-service summer horseback pack trips, fishing and hunting trips, photography, or backpacking, call Bill Gibson of **Elko Guide Service,** 775/744-2277. Gibson and his guides have a lot of experience in the outdoors around Elko, and are licensed to operate on the federal lands in the vicinity.

Other local licensed outfitters serving the Rubies and beyond include **Nevada High Country Outfitters & Jaz Ranch** in Lamoille, 775/777-3277; **Ruby Valley's Secret Pass Outfitters,** 775/779-2232; Prunty Ranch Outfitters, 775/738-7811; **Humboldt Outfitters** in Wells, 775/752-3714; and **Hidden Lake Outfitters** in Ruby Valley, 775/779-2268.

TRANSPORTATION

The **Greyhound** depot, 775/738-3210 or 800/231-2222, is at 193 W. Commercial St. Three eastbound and three westbound buses a day pass through.

One **Amtrak** train comes through daily in each direction. They stop at two shacks on either side of the tracks. Get there via the 12th Street overpass, and follow the signs. If you're getting off late at night, hike up to the bridge and take a right to Idaho St.—something will be open. Call 800/USA-RAIL (800/872-7245) for schedules and fares.

The **Elko Regional Airport,** on Mountain City Highway at the west end of town, is open 5:30 A.M. to 9 P.M. The airport is also known as Jess Harris Field, after an Elko County sheriff and aviation pioneer of the 1920s. Historical black-and-white photos and captions line the wall behind the luggage carousel. The men's room has wonderfully high sinks for us long-legged dudes. Regularly scheduled air service is provided by **Delta Connection-SkyWest Airlines,**

775/738-5138 or 800/453-9417, connecting Elko with Reno, Salt Lake City, and Ely/St. George. Then there's **Casino Express Airlines,** 775/738-1826 or 800/258-8800, with economical round-trip excursions to/from Elko (origi-nating in other places, or outbound from Elko), with flights serving 90 locations in the USA, with more than 60 flights a month.

Enterprise, 775/753-2333 or 800/325-8007, is the option for rental cars in Elko.

The Ruby Mountains

Head south down either 5th or 12th Streets in Elko; they join across the river and become Route 227. A bit south of town, you crest the **Elko Hills** at Elko Summit (5,773 feet) and head east toward the northern Ruby Mountains, some-times called the "Alps of Nevada." You go by **Spring Creek,** Elko's southeastern suburbs. The area features an 18-hole, par 71 golf course and 19th Hole Bar and Restaurant, a trap and skeet club, and the Horse Palace Event Center. The 62,000-square-foot Horse Palace, built in 1976 to entertain prospective homebuyers in the new suburb, hosts rodeos, horse shows, concerts, and other local events.

The majority of commuter traffic turns off on the three Spring Creek exits, and one to Pleas-ant Valley. Then it's just you, the ranchers, and the Rubies. In another five miles is the turnoff (right) to Lamoille Canyon. Instead, take a detour first into Lamoille, a wonderfully picturesque valley town nestled right into the western base of this rugged and gorgeous range.

LAMOILLE

Lamoille Valley originally provided an alternative route to the denuded Fort Hall main stretch of the California Emigrant Trail. Pioneers cut south from Starr Valley near Wells, traveled along the western foot of the East Humboldts on a well-worn Shoshone trail, availed themselves of Lam-oille Valley's water and forage, then rejoined the main trail near Elko. The first homesteaders set-tled here in 1865, and within a few years a small

the alps of Nevada

COURTESY OF THE NEVADA COMMISSION ON TOURISM

Northern Nevada

village grew up around the farms and ranches. The post office arrived in 1883, but it took another 50 years for an actual road to reach the valley. Even then, Lamoille continued to hang on to its isolation for yet another 30-odd years, until 1965, when Lamoille Canyon was developed as a scenic area by the Forest Service.

A favorite place in Lamoille is the **Pine Lodge,** on Route 227 as you enter town, 775/753-6363. The lodge was built in 1947 and has been expanded over the last 10 years into the operation of today. It has three hotel rooms, at $65 each. Next door is the restaurant and bar, in a beautiful cabin representative of its stunning setting; check out the trophies and fantastic wildlife photography. The restaurant, a steak-and-seafood dinner house, is open Tues.–Sun. (closed Mon. at 3 P.M. and dinner is served 5–9 P.M.

Also in town is **O'Carroll's Bar & Grill,** 775/753-6451. Food is served every day, 8 A.M.– 4 P.M.; the bar stays open till 1 A.M. **Swisher's General Store,** 775/753-6489, is open every day, 8 A.M.–7 P.M.

The **Presbyterian Church** on the corner where the pavement runs out has a fine steeple and stained glass and might be the most heavenly located house of worship in the state—very close to God.

Red's Ranch, Country Ln., 775/753-6281, offers ranch accommodation on a beautiful Lamoille ranch. Activities include horseback riding, swimming, hiking and skeet shooting, and there's a spa; in winter, Ruby Mountains Heli-Skiing ski trips operate from the ranch. It has 10 rooms, each with private bath; reservations required.

SKIING

The Rubies are a mighty range, 100 miles long, with nearly a dozen peaks over 9,000 feet. They can receive 400 inches of snow in the upper elevations, and are snow-patched year-round. In 1976, three partners from Alta, Utah, were granted permission by the Forest Service to operate a heli-ski service in the Rubies, and a year later they were in business. Joe Royer, the youngest and most energetic of the three, subsequently took over the whole operation. Today,

Ruby Mountain Heli-Ski, 775/753-6867, www.helicopterskiing.com, is still owned by Joe and Francy Royer. They offer three-night ski packages, Mon.–Wed. or Fri.–Sun., which include lodging at Red's Ranch, all meals, ski rental, helicopter rides, guide service, and a guarantee of 39,000 vertical feet of skiing. With a maximum of 16 skiers, flying in groups of four guests per guide, they do an average of seven runs a day in fairyland frosting. The season runs from late January through early April. Make your reservations far in advance; for the 2004 season, package prices were $2,995 per person. With a 1,500-square-mile terrain, 3,000 vertical feet of virgin deep powder, and a chopper ride to the best conditions, this is the ultimate in skiing.

HIKING

The **Island Lake Trail** heads off north for two miles to 9,672 feet; the trailhead is just off to the right at the fork near the entrance to the parking lot. The 40-mile **Ruby Crest Trail** heads off south from the far edge of the parking lot; looking up at the top of the mountain, you'll see a prominent V-shaped saddle just down to the left of what can only be called "Bald Eagle Crest." That's Liberty Pass.

The trail starts out in forest primeval, and you start heading up fast into the cirque. You cross three creeks on nice Forest Service bridges, then pass **Dollar Lakes** (9,600 feet). Before you know it you're at **Lamoille Lake** (9,740 feet), where signs point the way. A hiker in fair shape can make it here in 40 minutes. From there you keep going up, twisting and turning toward the pass. **"Bald Eagle Crest"** defines itself into beak and head, shoulders, wings, and, even in late August at the end of the heat and sun, some snow patches that you could imagine to be the wing tips. Finally, another 40 minutes above Lamoille Lake, you reach **Liberty Pass,** at 10,450 feet, and get to see the other side. Which predictably is even more beautiful than the side you just climbed. **Liberty and Favre Lakes** await those with more time and energy, as does **Harrison Pass,** 30 miles and several days from the parking lot.

THE "YOSEMITE OF NEVADA"

If you go back a mile toward Elko from Lamoille and turn left up Lamoille Canyon, you'll be on the **Lamoille Canyon National Scenic Byway,** a 13.5-mile road that takes you straight into the heart of the Ruby Mountains. These metamorphic mountains occupy a sacred place in the hearts of most Nevada hikers, climbers, skiers, photographers, picnickers, and writers. Wettest of the high ranges, they combine the best aspects of the nearly 250 other discrete ranges in the Great Basin—long (100 miles) and thin (10 miles), tilted, and geologically labyrinthine—with dramatic features all their own. Glacial ice has played a large part in their erosion, with U-shaped valleys, cirques, kettles, valley-bottom moraines, and glacier-swept cliffs. This rainmaker range also supports lush vegetation, including large alpine tundra. In addition, the 8,800-foot level is accessible by car, and you can follow a good trail, through some of the most beautiful mountain country in the West, for days.

After long debate and some controversy, in 1989 the Ruby Mountains were designated one of 14 official wilderness areas in Nevada, fourth largest with 90,000 acres. The Ruby wilderness area, which along with the East Humboldt wilderness area comprises 25 percent of the local U.S. Forest Service ranger district, is mostly in the higher elevations of the mountains.

Lamoille Canyon Road runs around **Ruby Dome** (11,249 feet), highest peak in the range. Massive, skyscraping outcrops loom high overhead on both sides of the canyon in two continuous lines up the road. Rock sculptors would be kept busy for 10 lifetimes carving the busts of all the U.S. presidents, vice presidents, *and* secretaries of the interior on the faces of these cliffs. Explanatory signs along the way describe the glacial features. In the winter, the road often closes to cars but is alive with snowmobilers and cross-country skiers.

© AVALON TRAVEL PUBLISHING, INC.

The hiking season starts around June 15 and lasts roughly 12 weeks. Weekdays you'll meet a few other people, but weekends you're fending off crowds, especially on the first few miles. Backpackers, however, can leave the crowds far behind on any number of explorations to high-country lakes (many filled with trout) and isolated canyons.

For detailed and up-to-date information on campgrounds, hiking trails, and road conditions in the Rubies, call or write the U.S. Forest Service, Ruby Mountain Ranger District, 140 Pacific Ave., Wells, 775/752-3357. Office staff will send you a copy of *A Guide to the Ruby Mountain Ranger District* (very informative) and all kinds of other brochures and pamphlets about the area.

PICNICKING AND CAMPING

Driving up Forest Service Rd. 660, **Powerhouse** (6,200 feet) picnic area at the mouth of Lamoille Canyon has one group site and four single-family picnic tables, BBQ grills, and pit toilets. There's no water, however. Day-use fee is $5 per vehicle.

Thomas Canyon Campground (7,600 feet) has 40 paved sites; 30 have tent pads, there are five double-family sites, and four pull-throughs. Facilities include picnic tables, barbecue and fire pits, vault toilets, and pump water. The campground is officially open late May through October, but they try to keep a loop open all year, depending on climate conditions. The campground is situated in a spot in the canyon where downhill is due west, and the sun setting beyond the valley turns the rugged ridges a distinct ruby hue (the mountains, however, were named for its garnets). Sunrise is right over the cirque, imbuing the canyon with golden and magic light. Single campsites cost $14, double sites $20. Reservations can be made in summer; for reservations phone 877/444-6777. For further information, contact U.S. Forest Service, Ruby Mountains Ranger District, 140 Pacific Ave., Wells, 775/752-3357.

Terraces, at 8,400 feet on the other side of the road (left), is for picnickers only; it has picnic tables, barbecue and fire pits, vault toilets and potable water. $5 parking fee per vehicle.

Twenty-nine miles from Elko up 660 is **Roads End** picnic area (8,800 feet) and the trailhead for Island Lake and the Ruby Crest Recreation Trail. The area has one picnic site, water, and toilets; no fee.

SOUTH FORK RESERVOIR

The **South Fork State Recreation Area** is at the South Fork Dam, 16 miles south of Elko on Route 228. The dam, constructed between 1986 and '88, is made up of a million cubic yards of earth, which dammed South Fork Creek roughly 10 miles from the Humboldt River. The reservoir, when full, stretches 3.5 miles, covers 1,650 surface acres and impounds 40,000 acre feet of water. The reservoir is surrounded by 2,200 acres of wildlife-filled meadowlands and rolling hills. Swimming, boating, fishing, hunting, wildlife viewing, camping and picnicking are popular activities here. The Nevada Department of Wildlife stocks trout and bass; the park is known

for its trophy-class trout and bass fishery. Facilities include a campground, trailer dump station, boat launch, and picnic area. The 24-site campground, with showers and running water but no hookups, is on the reservoir shore, about two miles from the dam; camping costs $10, maximum 14-day stay. Or you can camp anywhere else you like around the park, outside the developed campground; this costs $5 per night, and you can come to the campground to shower. Day use of the park costs $4 per vehicle. The park is open year round, but winter access may be difficult due to extreme cold and snow. Access is off Route 228, roughly 10 miles south of the intersection with Route 227. Contact South Fork State Recreation Area, 353 Lower South Fork Unit 8 Spring Creek, 775/744-2010.

Twelve miles south of Elko and half a mile from the South Fork reservoir, the **Ruby Crest Guest Ranch,** Spring Creek, 775/744-2277, also the home of the Elko Guide Service, offers a wide variety of activities including horseback trail riding, summer horseback mountain pack trips, fishing and hunting trips, sightseeing and photography trips, and nature tours. Winter activities include cross country skiing, snowmobile trips, ice fishing and chukar hunting. Ranch vacations are a specialty, with accommodations ranging from a room at the ranch, to rustic log cabins at the base of the Ruby Mountains, to tent camps.

RUBY MARSHES

South of the reservoir, visit **Ruby Lake National Wildlife Refuge,** open every day from an hour before sunrise until two hours after sunset. This is an unusual sight for the Great Basin Desert— a freshwater bulrush marsh, host to a large variety of birds, fish, and mammals. Within the 38,000-acre refuge, created in 1938, is a network of ditches and dikes built to manage the riparian habitat. More than 200 species of birds, including trumpeter swans, canvasback and redhead ducks, cranes, herons, egrets, eagles, falcons, and small birds are found in the refuge in a normal year, along with five types of introduced trout and bass.

The water is collected up on the porous slopes and peaks of the southern Rubies, then is flushed out at the bottom from more than 200 springs into **Ruby Lake**. Ruby Lake, and **Franklin Lake** farther north, once covered 300,000 acres 200 feet deep in this valley, but are now down to fewer than 3,000 acres, lowest level in 30 years. In 1986, before the drought, the largest bass harvest on record occurred, with 300,000 fish caught; by 1992, the catch was down to a few thousand. In 1994, after eight years of drought, the normal six-to-seven feet of water was down to two feet. Precipitation returned, however, during the winters of 1995–97 to what passes for normal and so did lake and fish catches. Refuge officials say both are at normal levels now—"normal" including quite a bit of fluctuation in this desert environment.

Take a left at **Bressman's Cabin** onto the causeway to see the birds and birders, fish and fishers. Make the big loop around the marsh and rejoin the road at the south end of the East Sump.

Heading south on county road 767, the **South Ruby Campground** (6,200 feet) has 35 gravel sites, water, toilets, and an RV waste dump ($5 fee). Most sites have tent pads; $12 per night. Near the Gallagher Fish Hatchery, sites are on a rise overlooking the marsh. Campsite reservations can be made in summer; for reservations phone 877/444-6777. For further information on this campground, contact U.S. Forest Service, Ruby Mountains Ranger District, 140 Pacific Ave., Wells, 775/752-3357.

Two miles south of here is **Shantytown**, a small settlement that dates back to the 1940s, when the BLM leased half-acre parcels hereabouts for $5 a year. In 1967, the BLM sold off the parcels for $499; they now go for around $30,000. Shantytown has no services.

Heading back north, the **Wildlife Refuge Headquarters** is open weekdays 7 A.M.–4 P.M., Mountain Time. Brochures describing the refuge, wildlife, and fishing and boating regulations are available in a rack on the front of the office; they'll send you some brochures, if you like. Call 775/779-2237 for further information.

Rather grandly named, **Harmon's Ruby Lake Resort** is on the main Ruby Valley road, one mile north of the Harrison Pass junction. It's not a "resort" a la Las Vegas or Lake Tahoe, but it is a friendly place with a few amenities, including a store, gas station, bar, café, trailer spaces and rooms for rent. The six rooms (two share a bath) and sharing a community kitchen, are $30 a double. The 10 trailer spaces, all with full hookups, are $15. It's not a good setup for tents, but if tenters show up they won't be turned away; cost is $10 for tents. Public showers are $3. The café is open the same hours as the bar: noon to 9 P.M. every day. Contact Harmon's Ruby Lake Resort, 775/779-2242.

Continuing north on the gravel road you pass **Franklin Lake,** then travel a long way back to the pavement. Route 229 forks 15 miles east to connect with US 93, or 33 miles north to join I-80 at Halleck. You can also get back by traveling on a gravel road for 11 miles north to Deeth, 12 miles east of Halleck on I-80.

Wells

A spot a little northwest of the present-day town of Wells was once a famous camping site on the Emigrant Trail. Called Humboldt Wells for the dozen springs providing fresh water and grass, it was the easternmost source of the Humboldt River. The Central Pacific established a division point nearby, around which the town, shortened to Wells, slowly grew up. You can easily trace the evolution of the business district, from 7th Street at the railroad tracks to 6th Street along old US 40 to the developing exit ramps on I-80. Wells seems to have embraced each transition in a concerted effort to keep up and grow with the times.

Mining and ranching have also long contributed to the local economy. The WPA's *Guide to Nevada* has a story about the brutal winter of 1889–90, when most of the cattle froze or starved to death. "Wealthy stockmen went bankrupt almost overnight, and some were forced to begin all over again as cowboys. A Negro camp cook, looking over the dismal scene, exclaimed, 'Lawd, how your snow done equalize society!'"

Wells has also suffered its share of diversity in the past 15 years or so. In the early 1980s, a con man named Michael Wilwerding set up shop in Wells, claiming he could revert used tires back to oil. He got all kinds of tax breaks and state aid money, and even produced a small amount of oil. But the site turned out to be primarily a dump for highly toxic liquid wastes, and Wells received the first Superfund money in Nevada to clean up the mess. More recently, Sierra Pacific proposed to develop a $4 billion, eight-plant, 250-megawatt, coal-fired power complex nearby, but the deal fell through.

Still, Wells has rebounded admirably, and in the past few years a new shopping center at the west exit of I-80, a Flying J truck stop at the east exit, an industrial park, and a subdivision south of town have been built.

Wells is not only a crossroads town, hosting the intersection of I-80 and US 93. It is also a border town of sorts. Technically, Jackpot, 68 miles north on US 93, gets the travelers right after they enter Nevada from Idaho, and Wendover, 60 miles east on I-80, gets them from Utah. But Nevada border towns in general, and the above two specifically, exist for one reason: gambling. Room rates are high, vacancy rates are low. Wells's accommodations are cheaper and decidedly more available. Also, as a junction town, Wells has excellent travelers' and truckers' facilities. So if a casino at a real border town isn't your final destination, it might be worth it to drive the extra 60–70 miles to Wells—the nearest junction town to two borders.

SIGHTS

Start out at the "historic district" on 7th Street along the tracks, the most abandoned and intact railroad row on the entire original Central Pacific line. The **Bullshead Bar** on the corner opened as a log hut on Christmas Eve 1869; the last incarnation still stands, though it's closed. Since the last edition of this book, **Quilici's,** an interesting old general store—at the same location since the late 1880s and owned by the Quilici family since 1928—closed.

The **Wells Bank,** across Lake and up the block, opened in 1911; Morris Badt, Wells's first merchant (1876) was its original president. The **Nevada Hotel** on 6th St. is also a relic, turned into a movie theater until it closed. The **Coryell Residence,** at the corner of 9th and Lake, is the oldest house in town, and an old house on the other corner was built out of railroad ties.

A lot of the downtown area is being renovated now, including the historic **El Rancho Hotel.** There is also now an art gallery. A free brochure has been published to lead you on a self-guided walking tour of the downtown historic district, with plaques identifying the various historic buildings; pick one up at the Chamber of Commerce or at area businesses.

Between Lake and Clover Streets and 4th and 1st, is the municipal, educational, and recreational center of town. The city park provides picnic tables and grills, playgrounds, tennis, baseball fields, basketball courts, and a heated swimming pool.

BY LIGHT OF CASINO

A unique feature of the Silver State is that gambling houses tend to prosper most at her outer edges, hugging the state line so tightly that no sooner does the highway traveler pass the silver and blue point-of-entry marker than he is instantly blinded by the glare of 10,000 colored light bulbs. It's said that night pilots often navigate by the light of these commercial beacons and rumored that Nevada is the only state whose shape is discernible from outer space, thanks to her iridescent outline.

—Richard Menzies, *Nevada* magazine, June 1984

The **Old West** and **Luther's** bars downtown have slots. The **4-Way** truck stop has a gang of slots and a three-table blackjack pit. The **Ranch House** casino is still closed. The new kid on the block is **Lucky J's Casino** at the Flying J truck stop on the south side of the interstate at US 93: two blackjack tables and some slots.

The California Trail Historic Back Country Byway, beginning 25 miles north of Wells off US 93, consists of 96 miles of gravel roads in the extreme northeast reaches of Elko County. An information kiosk near the Winecup Ranch, four miles off the highway, tells of the trail's history, when over 200,000 emigrants passed this way heading for California in the 19th century. The 96-mile-long byway follows the emigrants' route for over 40 miles. Trail markers are placed along the way to show visitors where the actual trail was; trail ruts can still be seen in many places. The BLM Field office in Elko, 775/753-0200, has information on the route.

ACCOMMODATIONS

The old hotel downtown, the **Old West Inn,** 455 6th St., 775/752-3888, is pretty inexpensive, with 10 rooms for $20–24. The **Lone Star Motel,** 676 6th St., 775/752-3632, and **Shell Crest Motel,** 573 6th St., 775/752-3755, ranges $24–39. The **Best Western Sage Inn,** 576 6th St., 775/752-3353 or 888/829-0092, was re-

modeled a few years ago and charges $57–95. The **Rest Inn Suites,** 1509 E. 6th St., 775/752-2277 or 800/935-5768, across from the 4-Way next to Motel 6, has 57 rooms and minisuites with microwaves, fridges, hair dryers, and remote-control TVs, $35–53.

Mountain Shadows RV Park, 807 S. Humboldt Ave., 775/752-3525, is one of the coziest, cleanest, and friendliest RV parks on the interstate through northern Nevada. Dick and Chickie Smith took it over in 1993 and improved the bathhouse and laundry, planted trees, and spruced up the landscaping. There are 38 spaces for motor homes, 33 with full hookups and 13 pull-throughs. Tents are allowed and noncampers can take showers for $5. Reservations are recommended Memorial Day to Labor Day, especially for pull-throughs. RV sites cost $19.50; tent sites are $14 (10 percent AARP, AAA, Good Sam, and senior-citizen discounts). Open Mar. 1–Nov. 15.

Crossroads RV Park, 734 6th St., 775/752-3012, open April to October, has 24 RV spaces with full hookups. Tents are not allowed. Eight miles west of Wells, the **Welcome Station** at I-80's Exit 343, 775/752-3808, is open June to November and offers 35 spaces. Tents are allowed. RV sites cost $17, tent sites $14.

FOOD

The **4-Way** at the east exit has a 24-hour coffee shop, with the usual road food and a 40-item salad bar. On the other side of the interstate, **The Cookery** restaurant at the Flying J truck stop, 775/752-2400, is also open 24 hours and has an all-you-can-eat breakfast, lunch and dinner buffet. Also at the east exit ramp to Wells is a Burger King.

For groceries, stop at **Stuart's Deli and Bakery,** 647 Humboldt Ave. at the west exit ramp, 775/752-3215, open Mon.–Sat 7 A.M.–9 P.M., Sun. 8 A.M.–8 P.M.

INFORMATION AND SERVICES

Wells is a good place to wait for the sun to go down if you're heading west. The interstate aims directly toward the fiery orb, setting into your very eyes, and everything other than the blinding sun is shadows. Scary driving for 20 minutes or so.

The **Chamber of Commerce** is at 395 6th St. at the corner of Lake St., in the Kelly Kreations building; 775/752-3540, coc@well-snv.com, www.californiainterpretivecenter.com. Open Mon.–Sat. 7 A.M.–4 P.M. When the office is closed, you can pick up extensive tourist information in the lobby area; it's accessible 24 hours, seven days a week.

You can also stop in at **City Hall,** 1279 Clover Ave., 775/752-3355, and read the bulletin boards and rifle the info rack. Next door, the **library,** 775/752-3856, 196 Baker St., is open Mon.–Wed. and Fri. 11 A.M.–5 P.M., Thurs. 1–5 P.M. and 7–9 P.M.

The Forest Service office for the **Ruby Mountain Ranger District,** 140 Pacific Ave., 775/752-3357, is open Mon.–Fri. 7:30 A.M.–4:30 P.M. Pick up maps, trail guides, and general information on the Rubies and East Humboldts, read the proclamation by Teddy Roosevelt naming Ruby National Forest in 1906, and check out the picture of Hole in the Mountain Peak.

Many events take place in Wells all year round; the Chamber of Commerce has details. On Memorial Day weekend, **Senior Pro Rodeo** is a four-day event with contestants competing for points towards the National Finals in Reno. The **Wells Annual Fun Run Car Show,** held the last weekend of July, includes street dances, drag races, burn-outs, show-and-shine, and fireworks. The Race to the Angel in September is a bike/run from Wells to Angel Lake, a 2,800-foot climb over 13.1 miles.

EAST HUMBOLDTS

The 13-mile road from Wells to Angel Lake makes a lovely drive, especially in spring when the fields along the way are full of wildflowers. It's so pretty that it has been designated an official scenic route: the **Angel Lake Scenic Byway.**

Go under Wells's west exit ramp, then take a right at the sign. A paved road climbs up into the East Humboldt Range above **Clover Valley,** with beautiful high views down onto the lowlands, and beautiful low views up at the high-

lands. Pretty **Angel Creek Campground** is seven miles along in a little gully. The campground loop road, too, is paved: 18 campsites for tents or self-contained motor homes up to 40 feet, piped drinking water, vault toilets, picnic tables, grills, and fire rings provided. Angel Creek Campground is private, shady, and 15 minutes from Wells; camping costs $12 per site. They try to keep this campground open all year, depending on snow conditions; the running water is turned off in winter.

Another steep mile and a half up, a trail goes left four miles to **Winchell Lake.** The road twists and climbs for another two miles, then ends at the **Angel Lake Campground** (8,378 feet) alongside a pretty alpine lake at the bottom of the cirque: 26 campsites, half a dozen outhouses, and a large picnic area share the bowl. Camping costs $14 per site; day use $5. The lake itself is over a small rise (you could almost spend the whole night without knowing it's even there). This campground is open only in summer, from around mid-June to early September, depending on snow and weather conditions.

For both Angel campgrounds, contact Ruby Mountain Ranger District, 140 Pacific Ave. (P.O. Box 246), Wells, NV 89835, 775/752-3357.

Look east; several ranges disappear into the distance. Look south and up; **Chimney Rock** stands out prominently. **Grey's Peak** is 10,674 feet.

A trail up to **Grey's Lake** and beyond leaves from the horse-unloading parking lot at the east end of the cirque. This trail receives little to no maintenance and peters out frequently. Take along *Hiking the Great Basin* by John Hart for a good trail description.

Clover Valley

US 93 runs south from Wells along the magnificent eastern scarp of the East Humboldts. Ten miles south, Route 232 makes a loop west of the highway through luxuriant Clover Valley, which competes with Washoe Valley's Franktown Road at the eastern base of the Sierra for the number-one spot on Nevada's list of the most prime real estate.

You start out heading west toward a hump in the middle of the valley that looks like a hound dog with his chin on the floor and his haunches in the air. Then you turn south and drive through a truly bucolic scene—venerable trees towering over two-story, 100-year-old ranch houses with horses, cows, and goats grazing in the greenery, and creeks, defined by shrubs, snaking away from the sheer mountain walls.

Hole in the Mountain

About six miles from the highway is a distinct right turn onto a narrow 4WD track up into **Lizzie's Basin,** below the East Humboldt's highest mountain (11,276 feet). The phenomenon from which the peak derives its name accounts for one of the strangest and most compelling summits in the west. Roughly 300 feet below the peak is a large (30-by 25-foot) natural window in the weak and thin marble of the mountaintop. This cyclopean eye, staring east and west, was known as Taindandoi ("Hole In The Top") to the Shoshone, and Lizzie's Window to the early settlers, named after the first local to mention the hole.

As you cruise along Clover Valley, especially at sunset, the light shining through the window below the peak is a superlative sight in a land full of superlative sights. The pavement, oddly, runs out after about 15 miles, right where the road turns east again to meet up with US 93. But it's only for a mile, at 40–45 mph. Ely is 121 miles south.

TO WENDOVER

Back on I-80 heading east out of Wells, you cross broad **Independence Valley** and then climb the wall ahead of it, the **Pequop Range.** When you crest the summit (6,967 feet-highest point on I-80 in Nevada), you'll be looking ahead at the **Toana Range.**

The Oasis exit (378) puts you on Route 233. **Oasis** is just that, a tiny settlement dedicated to travelers through the desert. A ranch hereabouts in the 1880s was called Oasis; in the 1930s, there was a telephone and a Red Cross station on old US 40. A two-story hotel and gas station were built in 1946 to accommodate servicemen en route to and from Wendover; the hotel was renovated in 1982. Today, Oasis has a population of roughly 25, what might be the smallest post office in the country (with antique postal boxes), a café (with reputedly delicious pies), a gift shop full of crafts and souvenirs, and a gas station. A new paint job helps Oasis stand out on the north side of the highway.

If you head northeast on Route 233, the first place you'll come to is **Cobre,** the division point between the Southern Pacific main line and the Nevada Northern from Ely. Farther along, 24 miles from Oasis and I-80, is **Montello,** in pretty Tecoma Valley just east of the big Toano Range. With a population of only around 100, Montello is not big, but it's very friendly. At one time, Montello was a railroad town, where crews were changed on the trains to/from Ogden, Utah; there was a round house here, opposite where the motel is today, and the town had a population of 5,000. Now, however, the crews are changed in Elko, and Montello has only a skeleton crew of about five railroad workers. Today, Montello is a cattle ranching community. There are only four ranches, but one of them, the Gamble Ranch, is a huge million-acre ranch extending all the way from I-80 up into Idaho. Otherwise, most of Montello's residents are retired; some of the younger people work in casinos in Wendover, about 50 miles away.

Montello has one **motel.** The sign out front says The Pilot, but nobody ever calls it that—they call it simply "the motel." It's operated together with the **Montello Gas & Grocery,** 775/776-2428; the 10 motel rooms cost $25–38. For food, check out the **Cowboy Bar,** 775/776-2466; try the huge Cowboy Burger with fries, for $5.60, comes highly recommended. Food is served every day, 8 A.M.–8 P.M.; the bar stays open later. The **Saddle Sore Bar,** 775/776-2564, opens at 11 A.M., and they also operate a laundry.

Around 20 or 25 miles outside Montello, the **Sun Tunnels** is an unusual attraction. Built by a European sculptress, at summer solstice the tunnels turn pink inside at sunrise; a number of Europeans come out to see it.

Back on the interstate, I-80 drops down into Goshute Valley, then climbs again into the Toanas. From there, you descend into **Pilot Creek Valley,** with climactic Pilot Peak rising to 10,714 feet above it.

Pilot Peak

Named by Frémont in 1845, this is one of the most beautiful and historic mountains in Nevada. Pioneers along the Emigrant Trail focused on it during their brutal 50- to 90-hour ordeal of crossing the blazing Great Salt Lake Desert. Finally arriving at Pilot's base, just over the Nevada line, they found water and grass, the knowledge of which sustained them during the three-day desert dash to the mountain, and the presence of which replenished them for the next leg to Humboldt Wells.

Pilot is a classically conical mountain, wooded across the waist, with a long and tapered *bajada* beckoning to the salt flats in the southeast. It also slopes off to the northwest, pointing to California and the promised land. As it stands there, tall and alone, it seems a proud mountain— proud of its handsomeness, proud of its heritage of hospitality, and proud of its unique location, providing, more so than all of the hundreds of Great Basin peaks, a hopeful and nourishing welcome to travelers of past and present, to the golden sands of Nevada.

Wendover

Wendover sits on the western side of what was once Lake Bonneville, which covered a large area of northwestern Utah to a depth of 1,000 feet. The lake had no outlet, and as it shrank, and then disappeared (except for what is now the Great Salt Lake), it deposited a smooth layer of salt and other minerals in the lowest point of the Bonneville basin—where the salt flats are now—roughly 16,000 years ago.

The Central Pacific bypassed this area by 30 miles to the north in the late 1860s, but the Western Pacific pushed a railroad across the salt flats in the early 1900s. Wendover was founded to supply water to the railroad (piped in from Pilot Peak springs, 25 miles west), the only stop with water on the main line for 100 miles.

In 1914, the anonymity of this sleepy railroad village, with its roundhouse, saloon, and railroad-tie cabins, was lost forever. Speedsters discovered the advantageous features of the flats; one Teddy Tezlaff set the first land-speed record driving a Blitzen Benz just under 142 miles an hour and put Wendover in the media and on the map.

Highway 40 arrived in the mid-1920s, the start of Wendover's destiny as a travelers' oasis. William F. Smith, a young entrepreneur, opened a gas station and garage to service the border traffic, and over the next several years added a café and bungalows. In 1931 the state issued him one of the first gambling licenses, which has been in the family ever since; today his son, Jim Smith, holds the license.

Wendover Air Force Base was created in 1940. At 3.5 million acres, it was one of the largest in the world. Pilots, navigators, and bombardiers learned their skills over this range, and the crew of the *Enola Gay,* which dropped one atom bomb on Japan, trained here.

Potash (potassium chloride) has been mined from the flats over the years for use as fertilizer; magnesium chloride, a by-product of potash processing, is used in refining sugar beets. And speed freaks have kept coming back with hotter and faster wheels. Jet cars such as the *Meteor, Green Monster,* and Craig Breedlove's famous *Spirit of America* set and reset records; Breedlove was the first to break the 600-mph mark. (The first jet car, the *Flying Caduceus,* is on display at the National Automobile Museum in Reno.) Gary Gabolich's *Blue Flame* set a record in 1970 of 622 mph, which held for 14 years, until Richard Noble broke it on the Black Rock Desert. Weather permitting, racing takes place every year for a week in August and a week in September.

Today, Wendover, like Jackpot, is a booming border town. Straddling the Utah state line, Wendover's backyard is a shimmering, carbon-arc-white expanse of earth, so white that even in the summer's scorching heat, the surface remains cool. Another weirdness is that the heat waves and blinding silver reflection do strange things to radio and TV signals. Another: the bases of telephone poles on the flats become permeated with salt water; when the water evaporates, the salt crystals expand, swelling and splitting the poles. Fierce thunderstorms are caused by the rising heat, but then everything dries and brightens in a matter of minutes. Against such a backdrop, the big hotels, bright lights, and Wendover Will are as inviting to modern-day travelers as Pilot Peak, on the western horizon, ever was to the pioneers of the past. Note that Wendover is on Mountain Time; move your watches ahead one hour.

BONNEVILLE SPEEDWAY

The white state line is painted across Wendover Boulevard between the Stateline and Silver Smith; Wendover Will points at it with two moving arms. As in South Lake Tahoe, the big hotels are on the Nevada side, and the low-rise services line the main street of the state next door (Utah).

To drive on the **salt flats,** take I-80 into Utah, get off at Exit 4, then head five miles northeast. Obey the signs carefully if you don't fancy digging your wheels out of the mud or walking out for a tow truck, and watch for jet cars whizzing around at 500 mph.

Three weeks of official races are held on the flats. **Speed Week** has occupied the third week in August since 1948; 350 cars and motorcycles participate. **World of Speed** is a month later, with 100 cars and bikes. The **Bonneville Salt Flats World Finals,** held in October, is when the really fast cars come out. The race course has to be prepared from scratch every year, as "temporary Lake Bonneville" inundates the flats with six inches of water from November to May. The water's movement levels the desert, and a landplane scrapes the surface (clearing an area 80 feet wide, 10 miles long, between black spray-painted lines). This leveling of irregularities is important, I'm told, for vehicles traveling 350 mph or so on the ground.

The whole speedway encompasses 28 square miles: 3,700 feet wide and 13 miles long, of which about half is normally used in speed trials. The speedway is managed by BLM, which works closely with the Utah Salt Flats Racing Assn. (801/785-5364) and Southern California Timing Assn. (714/783-8293).

CASINOS

Start where it all started in Wendover, at the Smith properties right at the state line. The **State Line Nugget** casino, 775/664-2221, is Wendover Will's joint. This hotel not only has everything, it's all in very fine taste, as well: three crap and roulette tables, two dozen blackjack tables, a comfortable and classy sports book (downstairs), couple of snack bars, dinner buffet and weekend brunch, gourmet restaurant, and a big lounge. In 1997, the State Line did a $60 million expansion, adding 241 rooms, restaurants, an atrium, and additional gambling space.

Take the spiral staircase behind the front desk to the walkway over Wendover Boulevard—nice view. The **Montego Bay Casino and Resort,** Stateline's sister hotel, 775/664-9100, is in the same classy vein as the State Line Nugget. The casino is a casino is a casino. A small showroom puts on headliners and minirevues, and there are also a snack bar, a deli, and dinner buffet and weekend brunch.

The exterior of the **Peppermill,** 775/664-2255, is understated and pleasing; inside is the largest casino in Wendover. It has 1,000 slots and a single-zero roulette wheel. It also has the same red-and-blue-neon, silk-flower decor that it's famous for. The Cabaret bar is similar to the Reno Peppermill: high stage above the bar, video poker within and along the perimeter, even a dance floor.

The Peppermill bought Mac's Casino in the mid-1990s and transformed it into the **Rainbow,** 775/664-4000, a scaled-down version of the Peppermill in Reno with a rain forest motif and lots of neon. The Rainbow has 1,000 slots, 20 tables for blackjack and craps, a restaurant, and a buffet. Two new towers give it a total of 298 hotel rooms.

The **Red Garter,** 775/664-2111, has expanded: the old part of the casino is still dark, small, and usually jammed with people having a good time; the new wing is big, bright, and airy, with a bunch of slots, a sports bar and real bar. The casino has a 106-room hotel; a hallway leads to the Super 8 motel desk.

ACCOMMODATIONS

Wendover has more than 1,500 hotel and motel rooms, and there are another 540 on the Utah side to accommodate the overflow (Motel 6, Western, Bonneville, Heritage, Salt Flat Inn, and Days Inn). The big show is between the **State Line,** 100 Wendover Blvd., 775/664-2231 or 800/848-7300, and the adjacent **Montego Bay,** 775/664-2221 or 877/MONTEGO, with 740 upscale hotel rooms between them, for $29–175. **Nevada Crossing,** 1035 Wendover Blvd., 775/664-2900 or 800/537-0207, has another 137 rooms at $25–95. At the **Peppermill,** 680 Wendover Blvd., 775/664-2255 or 800/648-9660, www.peppermillwendover.com, rooms go for $25–90. **The Rainbow,** 1045 W. Wendover Blvd., 775/664-4000 or 800/217-0048, www.rainbowwendover.com, has 298 rooms for $25–90, and the **Red Garter,** 1225 W. Wendover Blvd., 775/664-2111 or 800/982-2111, has 106 rooms for $22 and up. And then there's the **Super 8 Motel,** 1325 Wendover Blvd., 775/664-2888 or 800/800-8000, with 74 rooms for $29–110.

Wendover KOA Campground, is just south of the Red Garter at 651 N. Camper Drive, 775/664-3221 800/562-8552; take exit 410 off I-80 to Wendover Blvd., then turn right and go approximately a half mile to Camper Drive and turn left. This big bustling RV park is on the southern edge of town, between the back doors of the Red Garter casino and the front door of the desert. The handy casino shuttle will pick you up and drop you off. It's the only place in town to pitch a tent. Proprietor Mike Cappa also has seven cabins for rent, each sleeping four people, for $30; one larger cabin sleeping six costs $50. There are 150 spaces for motor homes, 72 with full hookups and 85 pull-throughs. Tents are allowed and showers are for sale to noncampers for $5. Minimart and gift shop, heated swimming pool, playground, tetherball, volleyball, basketball, horseshoes, miniature golf course, rec room with slot machines and video games, meeting room, and bike rentals are available. Reservations are recommended, especially for the cabins. Camping fees are $17–25 for RVs, $13 for tents. Good Sam and KOA discounts.

The other RV park in Wendover is **State Line RV Park,** 775/664-2221. This RV park, though in Utah, is connected to the State Line casinos, just on the other side of the parking terrace. The park is graveled and has a few small trees. Overnighters get the use of the hotel's heated swimming pool and two tennis courts. Campers also are provided with the casino funbook and a discount coupon for the Wendover Golf Course. There are 56 spaces for motor homes, all 56 with full hookups; no pull-throughs. Tents are not allowed. Reservations are recommended. The fee is $17–19 per vehicle (10 percent Good Sam discount). To get there, take exit 410 off I-80, go left and drive a mile on Wendover Boulevard. Just across the Utah state line, go right on 1st Street and continue for one block.

FOOD

The **Stateline, Peppermill, Rainbow,** and **Red Garter** all have 24-hour coffee shops. The breakfast special at **Nevada Crossing** is best: $1.99 for two eggs, bacon, and hash browns, served 24 hours (a holdover from its truck-stop bygone days).

Wendover is a snack bar kind of town. All five major casinos have at least one snack bar, and they're all good and cheap. The one in the sports book downstairs at the Stateline is the most comfortable.

The **Peppermill** has three buffet meals a day, while the **State Line** has a dinner nightly and weekend brunches. The Rainbow casino has the **Rainforest Buffet.** The State Line offers fine dining in the **Salt Cellar,** open Sun. and Tues.–Thurs. 6–11 P.M., Fri. and Sat. until 11, closed Mon. Appetizers include delicious king-crab quesadillas and mussels; entrées include linguini, prime rib, salmon, veal, lobster fettucine, venison medallions, and steaks.

Over the Rainbow at the Rainbow also is open 24 hours, with a daily breakfast special. Dinner starts at $9 and climbs to $37 for steak and lobster. There's a good selection of dinner pasta dishes.

TO ELY

Alternate US 93 runs 60 miles south to where it rejoins US 93. Just south of town, the Utah Air

Force testing range must have a bunch of unexploded ordnance that could go off with just a little vibration or contact, which would explain the Danger Zone signs on the barbed-wire fence every 100 feet along the road for miles.

About 15 miles south of town is the turnoff for Blue Lakes, frequented by local scuba divers. You can see the lakes from the highway; they look a mile away, but after five miles of the very rough (20–25 mph) dirt road, they still look a mile away. In three more miles, they're still another mile. You might make it all the way in a low-clearance vehicle, but I didn't. Got stuck in a wash, had to shovel and struggle and sweat for a while. One of those cases where the eyes are bigger than the tires.

You travel over White Horse Pass (6,550 feet), right through the middle of the White Horse Range, part of the Goshute Mountains, then cross Antelope Valley, heading toward the Antelope Range. After climbing them, you drop down into **Steptoe Valley,** a straight shot south between the Schell Creek (east) and Cherry Creek (west) ranges; the latter drops off, and then the Egan Rangestarts up. You're coming into Pony Express country here, and cross the trail (signposted).

At Schellbourne is a bar, café, and motel; a rest area across the road has a Pony Express trail marker, and a historical sign commemorating this junction. From here it's another 40 miles in a straight line due south to Ely.

Central Nevada

In the early 1920s, the US 50-Lincoln Highway Association was actively competing against the US 40—Victory Highway Association for automobile traffic across Nevada. The northern Victory Highway had the edge: It was the first and always the more popular route for travelers, after Peter Skene Ogden and Joseph Walker pioneered it in the 1820s and '30s. It came to be known as the Emigrant or Humboldt Trail, and was used by the vast majority of pioneers who crossed Nevada in the 1840s and '50s. The central route, however, had its advocates. Jedediah Smith had blundered across it in 1827, almost dying of thirst, on one of the bravest and most desperate explorations of the American West. After Smith's horror march, however, it was nearly 30 years before a trail was surveyed through central Nevada by Howard Egan, then mapped by Captain James Simpson four years later, in 1859. The Overland Stage, Pony Express, and transcontinental telegraph all used the shorter central route. But the Central Pacific Railroad opted for the Humboldt Trail, which put an end, as early as 1870, to passage through the central state on long-distance public transportation.

Rough wagon ruts were developed between the major towns along both trails, but when the newfangled horseless carriage necessitated actual roads and when the new breed of automobile adventure traveler began to go *distances* on them, constructing statewide highways was an idea whose time had come.

Central Nevada

CENTRAL NEVADA

UTAH
NEVADA

NEVADA
CALIFORNIA

CALIFORNIA
NEVADA

To Wendover

To Wells

To Carlin

To Battle Mountain

To Las Vegas

To Las Vegas

Osceola
Baker
Ursine
Echo Canyon State Park
Dixie National Forest
Kershaw-Ryan State Park
Beaver Dam State Park
Rainbow Canyon State Park
Snake Range
LEHMAN CAVES
Great Basin National Park
Schell Creek Range
Pioche
Panaca
Caliente
McGill
Ely
Lund
Ruth
Egan Range
Cherry Creek
Humboldt-Toiyabe National Forest
Diamond Mountains
Eureka
Humboldt-Toiyabe N.F.
White Pine Mtns.
Currant
Grant Range
Pancake Range
Quinn Canyon Range
DUCKWATER INDIAN RESERVATION
Duckwater
LUNAR CRATER
Warm Springs
Simpson Park Mountains
Humboldt-Toiyabe National Forest
Monitor Range
Belmont
Round Mountain
Carver's
Toquima Range
Austin
Toiyabe Mountains
Shoshone Mountains
Manhattan
Tonopah
Goldfield
Lida
Berlin-Ichthyosaur State Park
Ione
Paradise Range
Desatoya Mountains
Clan Alpine Mountains
Dixie Valley
Stillwater Mountains
Gabbs
Monte Cristo Range
Coaldale Junction
Basalt
Inyo National Forest
Lovelock
Carson Sink
Fallon National Wildlife Refuge
Stillwater N.W.R.
Stillwater
Hazen
Fallon
WALKER RIVER INDIAN RESERVATION
Schurz
Walker River
Walker Lake
Luning
Mina
Hawthorne
Aurora
Humboldt-Toiyabe National Forest
Pyramid Lake
Reno
Carson City
South Lake Tahoe
Lake Tahoe
Tahoe National Forest
Eldorado National Forest
Topaz Lake

25 mi
25 km

© AVALON TRAVEL PUBLISHING, INC.

Immediately, every town wanted a highway. Savvy promoters began publicizing routes through *their* towns, whether or not the road to and from was maintained, had services, or even provided the most direct line from the last town to the next. Soon, individual boosters formed associations with neighboring towns and counties. These routes, in pre-roadmap days, still often followed three points on a square to get from the first to the fourth. Finally, government surveyors stepped in and brought some order and logic to the routes. Like the railroads before them, the highways made or broke the fortunes of many small towns in Nevada.

Defense Highway

The Victory Highway (US 40) followed the tortuous river route through northern Nevada, 400-odd miles between Utah and California, by way of Elko, Winnemucca, and Reno. The Lincoln Highway (US 50) followed the telegraph through central Nevada 370 miles by way of Ely, Eureka, Austin, Fallon, and Lake Tahoe. The competition between the two was sometimes good-natured and sometimes heavy-handed.

In the early years of long-distance auto travel, the Lincoln Highway held its own against the Victory Highway. In June 1931, a one-day traffic count at the junction of the two roads in Fernley revealed 181 cars turning onto the central route and 141 cars taking the northern route. But then the battle heated up: the Victory Highway Association installed signs designating its road the "Main Line" across Nevada, and the Lincoln Highway Association set up shop at Jim Smith's gas station in Wendover to try to divert westbound traffic to the central route.

The signs proved more successful than the service station; a traffic count in 1939 at Wendover showed that of nearly 3,000 cars, a few more than 700 turned south, while the rest continued on US 40 west across northern Nevada. More significant, of 2,000 cars with out-of-state license plates, only 500 headed for the central route. A year later, US 40 was designated a national defense highway, which gave it priority over other roads in the state in terms of expenditures for improvements.

The Lincoln Highway Association now realized it couldn't beat 'em, so it joined forces with the victorious Victoryites, along with Utah and Wyoming road associations, to promote the central route across the U.S. West, as opposed to the southern route (New Mexico and Arizona) and the northern route (Montana and Idaho). Eventually, the multistate organization expanded into Nebraska, Iowa, and California, and named the lengthening route the "49er Trail." The interstate highways' time had come.

The Interstate System

The Highway Act of 1956 called for the improvement of the national defense highways and construction of connecting interstates for a total of 41,000 miles of transcontinental superhighways. I-80 was designed to follow the US 40 route across the 49er Trail. That introduced a new form of competition, now among the half-dozen or so towns along the new highway in northern Nevada; each town promoted itself as the best service stop for the high-speed tourists and travelers.

It took more than 25 years for I-80 to be completed through Nevada while, in the meantime, US 50 traffic continued to decline. In 1983, the last stretch of superhighway was completed, finally bypassing Lovelock. Only three years later the old Lincoln Highway's fortunes had plummeted to the point where Eastern writers and editors were calling it the country's loneliest road.

The completion of I-80 and the dubious publicity might've set back a lesser foe. Indeed. The story goes that *Life* magazine ran an article admonishing travelers as to the lack of services on US 50 through Nevada, suggesting they avoid the road entirely. The article inspired a lighthearted and extremely successful advertising campaign by the Nevada Commission on Tourism. Far from being apologetic about it, the state publicists actually celebrated US 50's remoteness, challenging adventuresome drivers to get off the beaten interstate and *rejoice* in the loneliness. The magazine editors hadn't planned it, but they had given an unwitting shot in the arm to the 65-year-old traffic competition between the central and the northern routes across Nevada.

Ely

Explorers Jedediah Smith and Howard Egan, mapmaker James Simpson, the Pony Express, and the transcontinental telegraph all passed through this neighborhood between 1827 and 1861. In 1863, small-scale gold and silver mining began in the Egan Range, while it was still part of Utah Territory. In 1866 Nevada's eastern boundary was moved one degree east, which incorporated the Egan District. A year later, Treasure Hill on Mt. Hamilton created a stir, attracting the "requisite 10,000" (more likely half of that) boomers. When White Pine County was carved out of vast Lander County in 1869, Hamilton became the county seat. *Borrasca,* the final bust, came to Treasure Hill in 1878. Hamilton's courthouse burned in 1885. And the county seat transferred to Ely in 1887. Becoming the county seat fully doubled the population—to 160 people.

HISTORY

It had long been known that major copper deposits were there for the taking, but the task, especially during Nevada's 20-year depression (1880–1900), remained too unwieldy. Gold and silver could be mined and refined with hand tools and small machines and hauled away in the form of valuable bullion on mule trains. But copper meant *tonnage:* Every 60 pounds of raw copper required dumping 25,000 pounds of tailings and smelting 6,000 pounds of ore and was worth roughly $10. Only big bucks could buy and bring in the giant equipment required for mining, crushing, smelting, and shipping the astronomical quantities of paydirt, ore, and refined copper.

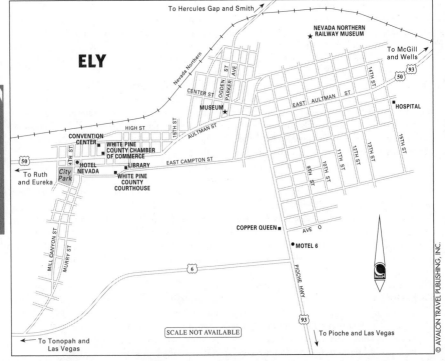

Typically, however, it was a couple of little guys who got the ball rolling. David Bartley and Edwin Gray, copper miners from California, appeared in September 1900, secured a grubstake, and started digging into a hill in the Egan Range just up from Copper Flat. They went 300 feet in and 200 feet down and discovered the richness and vastness of the deposit.

In 1902 Mark Requa, son of renowned Comstock superintendent and Eureka railroad builder Isaac Requa, took a $150,000 option on the claim, raised money from Eastern financiers, and by 1904 had organized the Nevada Consolidated Copper Company. Requa laid out a town site east of Ely, calling it (naturally enough) East Ely where he planned to build the big copper smelter. He also surveyed a railroad, Nevada Northern, from East Ely to the mine, growing deeper six miles northwest, as well as from East Ely 90 miles north to the Southern Pacific main line at Cobre (Spanish for "copper"), 30 miles east of Wells. He even managed to refine the first copper ore. By 1906, however, Requa had been bought out by the eastern investors. Within two years the original mine had been opened into a pit and the immense smelter had been located at McGill, 12 miles north of Ely, instead of at East Ely, much to the chagrin of local land speculators and developers. The Nevada Northern Railroad operation, however, remained based in East Ely, and track connected it with the pit at Ruth, the smelter at McGill, and the main line at Cobre.

Thus began Nevada's longest-lived and most prolific mineral venture, lasting a full 70 years. In 1909 six million dollars' worth of copper left White Pine County; by 1926, profits from the operation were recorded at nearly $50 million. Meanwhile, Utah's Kennecott Corporation had taken over production, and the pits kept growing. The granddad Liberty Pit expanded to more than a mile long, half a mile wide, and 700 feet deep. The dizzying descent to the bottom eventually required 14 miles of track. In 1940, the WPA *Guide to Nevada* predicted that the "copper supply can be mined profitably for another 50 years." In the mid-1960s the mine hit the billion-dollar milestone. But the ore started to thin, profits began to sag, and new pollution regulations finally shut the mine down in 1979. The WPA guide was only off by 10 optimistic years.

The smelter closed a couple of years later, and the railroad ceased operation for good in 1982. Ely's population, which had peaked in the late '50s at 12,000, dropped by the mid-'80s to just over 7,000. Unemployment in the county reached a depressed 25 percent.

But in 1986, local politicians, the Chamber of Commerce, and the newly formed White Pine Historical Railroad Foundation convinced Kennecott to donate the railroad property and equipment to the town; the trains have been running and the yard has been a museum since 1987. In addition, Great Basin National Park was created 70 miles east, and a new state prison was built just outside of town. A few gold and silver mines are operating in the area. Los Angeles Power and Water influence extends all the way out here; it owns the main line from Cobre to McGill, which it plans to use to deliver coal to the White Pine Power Project, a 1,500-megawatt power plant near Cherry Creek, 45 miles north of Ely.

A big new copper mine, BHP Mining, created an economic boom when it opened here in 1996; when it closed in 1999, it created somewhat of an economic bust. Today, Ely has a population of around 4,500 souls.

Ely has certainly benefited from the US 50 Loneliest Road campaign. But this town is much more than merely a stop on an old 3,000-mile highway (from just west of Washington, D.C. to Sacramento), 10 percent of which crosses Nevada. Intersecting US 50 here is another east-west highway, US 6, as well as the north-south US 93, one of the longest roads in the Americas. Its route through eastern Nevada, more than 500 miles from Jackpot to Boulder City, seems to have as much claim on Ely as US 50. Indeed, there's so much to do in and around Ely—copper pits, working railroad museum, Kennecott company town (McGill), Cave Lake State Park and Duck Valley, charcoal ovens, the Schell Creeks, Lehman Caves, and Great Basin National Park—that this is not a place just to pass through on any road. Here is one of Nevada's preeminent destinations all by itself.

Central Nevada

TWO HIGHWAYS: LONELY VERSUS EXISTENTIAL

U S 50 may be "the loneliest road in America," but loneliness, by definition, can only be felt in relation to other people. You might feel a bit forlorn on US 50, as cars from the other direction whiz by occasionally and as you pass or are passed by another car in your lane every so often. However, since US 50 is an east–west road, the scenery provides plenty of company as you cross a dozen mountain ranges and valleys, several quite imposing. Ely, Eureka, and Austin are perfectly spaced, an hour apart, for services and the human connection. And though it's a major haul from Austin to Fallon, the desert is so vast and the sky so boundless that it's as easy to become part of it, and expand into it, as it is to disregard it and contract into yourself. It's really a matter of choice. Wanna be lonely? Fine. But the road certainly doesn't require it of you.

But if US 50 can be lonely, then US 93, the other long road through central Nevada, can catalyze a deep existential *aloneness*. Since US 93 is north–south road, you drive through seemingly endless straight valleys, with the same few mountain ranges hemming you in for a hundred miles at a stretch like some sort of police escort. Wells, Ely, and Caliente are a long two hours apart, and talk about deserted! You can drive for hours at a time and not see another car on *either* side of the road. No choice there. You really are on your own. And after you've traversed the nearly 500 miles from Jackpot, even if your sanity is still intact, you're dumped right into the heart of psychedelic and mind-altering Las Vegas. US 50 gets the ink, has the history, and is a fine and dandy alternative to the mile-blurring impersonality of I-80. But for that bittersweet cosmic abandonment, it doesn't hold a candle to US 93.

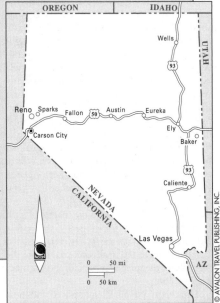

© AVALON TRAVEL PUBLISHING, INC.

ORIENTATION

Ely has the most road numbers per highway sign in Nevada. US 6 and US 50 run together from the Utah border 75 miles east through town, where US 6 cuts southwest (to Tonopah) and US 50 continues west (to Eureka). From the south, US 93 joins up with 6 and 50 just before Connors Summit over the Schell Creeks, and all three routes run together till the big intersection in East Ely. You might want to study a map, then drive around town a bit to get your bearings and sense of direction.

If so, start out on the west side, driving south of downtown on Murry St. through pretty Murry Canyon, site of Ely's original settlement. US 6 in-

tersects at the top of the hill, from where you can drive east (left) to US 93, then north back into town. Or just return on Mill St., one over from Murry. Then take a right (east) on Aultman (US 50 West) and cruise through the 1880s' townsite. The central square is a nice place to relax and watch Ely go by: little duck pond and fountain, big trees in the park, and the students coming and going from White Pine Middle School, built in 1913, right across Aultman.

Continue to the intersection with 6-50 East and 93 South. Here, Aultman turns into East Aultman, in East Ely on the townsite laid out by Mark Requa for the smelter and railroad in 1906. The depot is at the top of 11th, at A Street.

Be sure to take a drive around downtown Ely on Aultman St to see the murals in Ely's downtown mural project. By summer 2004, 11 murals had been completed, and there may be more, by the time you are reading this book.

Finish up your driving tour by heading north on Ogden St. at White Pine County Museum, through the 'burbs, and out into the west side of Steptoe Valley in back of town. In three miles the pavement ends, and two miles from there is **Hercules Gap**, a natural passage through the Egan Range between Steptoe and Smith valleys. Two miles north of the gash is a state maximum-security penitentiary, opened in 1989, which has a national reputation for the degree to which it educates its inmates.

NEVADA NORTHERN RAILWAY

This "museum" encompasses the entire Nevada Northern railyard, 1100 Ave. A in East Ely, 775/289-2085 or 866/40-STEAM, www.nevada northernrailway.net. The tour, one of the most thrilling in the state, takes you through the most complete and authentic working remains of any short line railroad in the country, if not the world. And then you get to ride on it!

When the Nevada Northern suspended operations in 1982, the company and workers at first thought it was temporary; layoffs had happened several times before. So they just left everything the way it was, figuring it would start up again, sooner or later. After three years, though, the workers received their severance checks, which made it final. Yet all the equipment still sat there like the day they'd walked away from it. By then the townspeople had started to come out of the shock of the loss and began a campaign to take over the operation.

Kennecott was prevailed upon to donate the depot, administration and dispatch office buildings, freight warehouse, yard, and even the 1910 Baldwin steam engine (Old No. 40). Later it also threw in 32 miles of usable track, all the machine shops, roundhouse, rolling stock, McGill depot, and the buildings along the entire Cobre route. The whole donation has been conservatively estimated at $45 million. Altogether there are over 30 buildings here from the 1906-1907 era, including an old water tower and sand and coal bins.

The museum is open year-round. Hours are Mon.–Sat. 8 A.M.–5 P.M. and Sunday 8 A.M.–2 P.M. (closed Tues.). Tours are given upon request and cost $3 for everyone ages five and up. You start out at the old depot, built in 1907 for $12,000 with local sandstone (from Currie). Check out the ticket office and big historical black-and-white photos. The depot is actually separate from the rest of the museum. It's state owned and operated, and so far has received $100,000 worth of restoration; another $180,000 will complete the job of restoring the depot to its original 1907 appearance. Sean Pitts, late of the White Pine Public Museum, is the curator.

From the depot you walk by the freight barn (oldest building in the complex, dating from 1905), past the bus barn and master mechanics offices, and then into the engine house, where most of the equipment is stored: locomotives, cabooses, a passenger coach, a rotary steam-driven snowplow, a steam crane, and track-repair cars. Next stop is the rip-track building, or car-repair shop. Here is the home of the 1910 Baldwin steamer (Ghost Train, or Old No. 40). This steam engine was restored in 1939 and almost immediately retired after Nevada Northern passenger service was discontinued, having transported nearly five million people over a 35-year period. It was as good as new, but the steamer was mothballed in the coach shop and not used for 45 years (except when brought out for special occasions), till it was resurrected in 1985 for the tourist train rides. Your guide helps you up into the cab and explains the valves, gauges, faucets, pipes, boiler, and controls with which the engineer and fireman get the danged thing stoked and rolling. Behind the Ghost Train are a converted flatcar, a Pullman sleeper, and a passenger car (used for the food concession).

Finally, you wind up in the transportation building, which has a small gift shop. By now you're itching to fire up a train and light out for the territory.

COURTESY OF THE NEVADA COMMISSION ON TOURISM

Ely's railyard museum

Rides

Daily between Memorial Day and September, the No. 40 and the No. 93 (restored in 1993) steam engines or the diesels No. 109 and No. 105 pull passengers on the Keystone and Hiline routes. The Hiline diesel is brought out for a trip to McGill 11 miles north. (Schedules may change from year to year, so call ahead.) The Keystone ride parallels Aultman Street a bit up the hill, for a great view of downtown and Ely's red-light district. Then it parallels US 50 through Robinson Canyon and passes through Tunnel No. 1, blasted out in 1907. The canyon broadens into Lane Valley, where the train goes by the Lane City ghost town, site of the original strike in 1869. The steamer then runs up to the copper-tailing mountains just this side of Ruth, then turns around. The 14-mile round trip takes 90 minutes and uses a ton of coal and 1,000 gallons of water.

The Hiline trip is a relaxing ride as the train rocks gently to and fro on its trip north toward McGill along a low eastern rise of the Duck Creek Range above Steptoe Valley. The locomotive switches from the front to the back of the train, then pushes the passenger cars ahead of it till the end of the track just before McGill—stand at the front of the open car in front of the train at this time!

Each of these train rides takes approximately two hours. Tickets for the train rides cost $20 for adults, $15 ages four to 12, and free for kids under four. A snack bar in the last car sells drinks and munchies. The museum also offers a variety of special event train rides, including a 4th of July Fireworks and Barbecue Train, Sunset at Steptoe, and Ely After Dark. During the off-season, the railway offers special weekend rides, such as the Polar Express train (based on the children's book) on the weekend after Thanksgiving and the first weekend of December; call for current information, schedule, and prices. Advance reservations are required.

You can also charter the equipment for special runs. You can even rent the engines by the hour and receive instruction on driving the damn things. Advance reservations are definitely required, and you must do it on days of operation. Call or write for schedules and reservations.

The gift shop is in the depot and is open during museum hours. It sells mostly T-shirts, railroad books, videos, odds and ends, and munchies for the train trips.

Finally, you can join **The Nevada Northern Endowment** and help preserve and restore this unique piece of history by becoming a member of the White Pine Historical Railroad Foundation; call 775/289-2085.

SIGHTS

The Nevada Northern Railway is *the* things to see and do in Ely, but there are a handful of other worthy attractions in and around town.

Bristlecone Convention Center

Around the corner from the chamber of commerce, the convention center houses a framed display of the cross section of a bristlecone pine. The 4,900-year-old tree, "Prometheus," was cut down by the National Forest Service and the bark dated in 1964; recorded history is traced through the rings all the way back to 1450 B.C., when Moses led the exodus out of Egypt, and beyond to 3000 B.C., when the pharoahs built the pyramids. The whole story of Prometheus, which when cut down was determined to have been the oldest living creature on the planet, is recounted in Jim Sloan's excellent *Nevada—True Tales from the Neon Wilderness.* 150 6th St., 775/289-3720.

White Pine County Public Museum

Opened in 1959, this is an eclectic and fun museum. Outside is Nevada Northern rolling stock, along with the original Cherry Creek depot, which was transported to the museum in 1991 and is slowly being restored. Inside is crowded with an array of items-everything from a petrified dinosaur footprint to an 1891 bicycle. Highlights include a big map of the county with corresponding black-and-white photographs, 1917 xylophone, mine-timbering model, 1876 cannon from Taylor, and a beautiful display of wood artistry-bowls, boxes, candle holders-by a late Elyan, A. Earl Preston. Study the schematic of the Ruth copper mine-what a pit! The museum displays a large collection of dolls, more than 300 types of minerals, turn-of-the-century furniture, and much more. A great introduction to Ely, you can also pick up maps and brochures here, plus buy postcards, souvenirs,

and books. 2000 Aultman, almost to East Ely, 775/289-4710, open daily 10 A.M.–5 P.M. (closed Tues.–Wed.), donation.

Also check out the gallery of historical black-and-white prints in the hallway between the **Jailhouse** casino and restaurant. Some great shots of Riepetown, Cherry Creek, and Hamilton, plus an interesting retrospective series on William Curto: eight frames of the evolution of his drayage company between 1912 and 1972. Curto lived to be 99 years old.

Success Summit Loop

North on US 93 six miles past McGill, follow the long white pipeline running for nine miles from Duck Creek Reservoir parallel to the highway along the lower slope of the Duck Creeks. The pipeline delivered nearly 300 million gallons of water to the smelter and still supplies all the town's water. Kennecott still owns the pipe and the water and in 1994 threatened to shut off the flow to the town in order to redirect it to a 3,500-acre project to restore Steptoe Valley (covering mill waste with dirt and vegetation). After an uproar in the town, the company decided to use non-potable water for the restoration. The original pipe, built in 1907, was replaced with the metal pipe in 1929. It delivers 380 gallons of cold pure water to McGill per minute.

Take a right on Route 486 and head through **Gallagher Gap,** on the other side of which the road cuts south. Beautiful **Duck Creek Ranch** is three miles off to the right, and **Bird Creek** Forest Service campground is off to the left, up into the Schell Creeks. This is a classically beautiful eastern Nevada ranching valley, with **Timber Creek** Forest Service campground four miles east, and **Berry Creek** campground five miles east from the junction at the end of the pavement. The road now turns rocky and rough (20 mph, some places 10). In a few miles you come to an unmarked fork in the road-go right. You descend into Boneyard Canyon, then up to aptly named Success Summit (you haven't slid off the road, hit a cow, ruined your suspension, had a flat tire, gotten lost . . .). Great views, too. This is where Nevada's largest elk and deer herds are found, so keep an eye out for them; they are most often seen in early mornings and evenings, or at night. Now you switch back about a dozen times and descend, along Steptoe Creek, to **Cave Lake State Park** where, after 25 miles and a couple of hours, is pavement, smooth, silky, quiet, l pavement.

Cave Lake State Park

This is one of the most beautifully situated parks in Nevada. Perched high in the Schell Creeks (7,300 feet), the emerald lake is backed by a sheer slope and stocked with rainbow and German brown trout. An earthen dam maintains the lake depth at an average 20 feet, 60 feet at the deepest. Two campgrounds combine for a total of 36 sites. The main camp at the lake has 20 sites, along with toilets, running water, and dump station. The Elk Flat camp across the road was completed in 1990 and competes with Wildhorse State Recreation Area for the best public showers in Nevada; campsites are $14 nightly per vehicle, first come, first served. With more than 100,000 visitors to this park yearly, these sites fill up fast. But a spot somewhere is usually available. Call 775/728-4460 for further info.

A trailhead at the main entrance leads to a five-mile interpretive trail, which winds through the piñon-juniper forest to meet up with Cave Creek Rd., and is popular with hikers and mountain bikers. A small cave yawns across from the sign that marks the park entrance. Even if you don't have several hours to spare on yet another rough gravel road making the loop over the summit and down through the Duck Creeks, be sure to at least come this far. You won't be disappointed, or even inconvenienced.

Ward Charcoal Ovens

Coming down from Cave Lake, take a left (south) onto US 93/50/6 and go a few miles to the historic sign for the Ward Charcoal Ovens. Take a right (west) onto a good gravel road (40 mph) and go six miles to Cave Valley Road. Turn left and enjoy the view of the ovens lined up in the desert, hemmed in by a digitated ridgeline.

For thousands of years, man has known that charcoal, the residue of campfires, burns at a much higher temperature than mere wood. The ancient Egyptians used the pit method to produce charcoal. They filled a pit with 100 cords of wood, covered it with sod, and let it smolder for two to three weeks; this created 3,000 bushels of charcoal. Some time later, the mound method, which piled wood in a conical mound with vents, improved production. When brick kilns were invented in 1820, they were the first technological breakthrough in the charcoal industry in 2,000 years.

The Ward Mining District was discovered in 1872 by Thomas Ward. A San Francisco company began digging in 1875. These six charcoal ovens, the largest in Nevada, were built in 1876 to supply the smelter attempting to refine the complex lead-silver-copper ore. The mills shut down in 1879, a big fire razed the town in 1883, and the post office closed in 1887. Only a quarter-million dollars in silver was reportedly recovered. The kilns, however, having been built by a master mason, survived it all, plus another 100 years of the elements, vandalism, practical jokes, shelter for cattle, sheep and horses, and Ely teenage partying.

Each oven is 30 feet high and 25 feet wide at the base, with a door, window, and chimney hole. Thirty acres of piñon and juniper were cut into 35 cords of wood and stacked in the kilns; the openings were shut with iron doors and a fire was started. By controlling the fire with small vents around the base of the ovens for roughly 12 days, tenders charred the wood to perfection and then smothered the fire by closing all the vents. Each oven yielded 300 bushels of charcoal.

For now, this is an otherworldly scene, with six large one-eyed jacks standing guard over history, speaking a silent language that only Gary Larson can understand. In the near future, however, it won't be so cosmic. Nevada State Parks recently constructed an 18-site campground nearby. Fees are $10 per night. There are tables, toilets, and grills. Call 775/728-4460 for information. Take Cave Valley Road almost all the way back to Ely.

ENTERTAINMENT

The **Central Theater** is at 145 W. 15th in back of Grand Central Motel, 775/289-2202. If you get

Back in the day, the Nevada Hotel was the tallest building in Nevada.

the chance, see a movie here, just for the experience of walking into the cavernous room. This is one of Nevada's few remaining movie houses that someone forgot to turn into a 16-plex!

A girl of your choice (if not of your dreams) at the **Stardust Ranch** will happily supply a memorable half-hour or so. She's up at 190 High St. at 1st, 775/289-4569, at the west end of town.

Casinos

The main action in Ely is at the corner of Aultman and 5th. The **Hotel Nevada** dates from the early 1920s, and was once the tallest building in the state. Sit down at one of four blackjack tables or nourish the hungry slots with your pocket change. The bar is especially lively at times.

Across the street, the **Jailhouse** is all machines; the restaurant here (see the Food section, further along) is highly unusual and worth a look. Up the block is the **Collins Court.** It opened in the spring of 1992 and shut down not long thereafter, the owners bailing out the back door at midnight.

Out on the Pioche Hwy., the **Copper Queen** has slots, both vertical and horizontal, but no table games. It's the only casino in the state that

shares a room with the motel pool. Chlorine Queen. There's no craps in Ely. In fact, there isn't a crap game for nearly 500 miles in eastern Nevada between Jackpot and Las Vegas on US 93 (Wendover is on *Alt.* 93 and Mesquite is on I-15).

The **Holiday Inn Prospector** opened out on the Pioche Hwy. in 1995 with 50 slots in the lobby and a café.

ACCOMMODATIONS

Nearly two dozen lodging houses offer more than 650 rooms at quite reasonable rates. Most of the older and less expensive places are bunched along Aultman between 3rd and 15th Streets; some newer ones are on US 93 South (Pioche Highway).

The six-story **Hotel Nevada,** 501 Aultman St., 775/289-6665 or 888/406-3055, www.hotel-nevada.com, is among the oldest hotels in the state, and has an appropriate exterior with neon slot machines and a big die-cut Unknown Prospector, a combination of the two most enduring and recognizable images of the state's regional identity. This 105-room hotel also has some of the best rates in town. Rooms start at

Central Nevada

$20/25 a single/double; higher-priced double rooms cost $38 and $48. The fifth and sixth floors are nonsmoking.

Across the street is the **Jailhouse,** 500 Aultman St., 775/289-3033 or 800/841-5430, www.ely-jailhouse.com; it added 22 rooms in 1996, and now offers a total of 61 "cells" at $45–75. There's also now a weight room and a whirlpool tub.

The **Ramada Inn/Copper Queen Casino,** 805 Great Basin Blvd., 775/289-4884 or 800/851-9526, has an interesting lobby. Walk around the front desk; the slots stand between it and the pool/whirlpool tub. Have a drink downstairs in the barroom, or walk upstairs and lounge on the deck. This is the only casino in Nevada that has a pool in the middle of it; I call it the Chlorine Queen. Rates for the 65 rooms are $55–125. **Motel 6,** 770 Ave. O, across from the Copper Queen, 775/289-6671 or 800/4-MOTEL6, is the largest joint in town with 99 rooms for $32–45.

The **Four Sevens,** 500 High St. right behind the Jailhouse, 775/289-4747, was the newest motel in town, until the Holiday Inn was built; it has 40 rooms at $35–60. The **Holiday Inn,** 1501 E. Aultman, 775/289-8900 or 800/HOL-IDAY, was completed in early 1995 with 61 rooms and the Prospector Casino, $56–105.

Steptoe Valley Inn Bed and Breakfast at 220 E. 11th St., just up 11th St. from the Nevada Northern depot, 775/289-6991 or 877/289-6991, was built in 1907 as the Ely City Grocery. It was completely restored in 1990 by Jane and Norman Lindley, who paid careful attention to all the Victorian details: paint, wood trim, tile, marble, fixtures, glass, etc. As of May 2004, the inn had new owners, Paul and Ronnie Branham, who plan to keep the property open year-round. The inn features a library, lounge, and upstairs verandah. Five guest rooms named after Ely pioneers go for $81–99 with a full breakfast; all have private baths and balconies. The Branhams awaken their guests with the aromas of freshly baked breads, pies, and pastries in the on-premises bakery, the fruits of which are available to the public after 9 A.M.

Another small bed-and-breakfast is the Hillside House, 410 Dickerson, 775/289-7927, which offers two rooms in a modern house with a full breakfast, private sitting room, and deck. Guests have full run of the house, although they share a bathroom. Pets are welcome (the house has a doggie door), but the home is strictly nonsmoking. Rates are $75 for one and $85 for two.

Other **motels** include: Best Western-Main, 1101 Aultman, 775/289-4529, 19 rooms, $42–100; Best Western-Park Vue, 930 Aultman, 775/289-4541, 21 rooms, $53–70; Deser-est Motor Lodge, 1425 Aultman, 775/289-4321, 18 rooms starting at $28; Great Basin Inn, 701 E. Aultman, 775/289-4468, $27–65; White Pine Motel, 1301 Aultman, 775/289-3800, 28 rooms starting at $27; **El Rancho,** 1400 Aultman, 775/289-3644, $28–48; **Grand Central,** 1498 Lyons, 775/289-6868, $32–36; and **Elk Ridge Motel,** 1550 High, 775/289-2512, $25–45; Bristlecone Motel, 700 Ave. I, 775/289-8838 or 800/497-7404, 31 rooms, $38–50; Fireside Inn, McGill Hwy., 775/289-3765, 15 rooms, $39–45.

RV Parking

Valley View RV Park, 65 McGill Hwy., 775/289-3303, opened in 1976 and is now one of the most mature RV parks in Nevada—and the tall trees, lush grass, and double-wide RV sites are there to prove it. It's quiet, friendly, and convenient to US 93 heading northbound from Ely. There are 46 spaces for motor homes, all with full hookups, and 12 pull-throughs. Tents are allowed. Accessible restrooms have flush toilets and hot showers; public phone, sewage. Reservations are recommended spring through fall, especially for the pull-throughs. RV sites are $21, tent sites $15. Good Sam discounts.

West End RV Park, 50 Aultman St., 775/289-2231, is on Ely's main drag, a three-minute walk from the Nevada Hotel and the Jailhouse Casino. The trees are large enough to shade the whole park. Sometimes West End fills up with long-termers, but you should try your luck if you want to be right in the thick of things. There are 11 spaces for motor homes, all with full hookups, but no pull-throughs. Tents are not allowed. The fee is $12 for two people.

Holiday Inn/Prospector Casino RV Park, 1501 E. Aultman St. on the east side of town,

775/289-8900, has 13 spaces with full hook-ups (six spaces are pull-throughs) for what must be the best price in Nevada: The first night is absolutely free, and succeeding nights are $10. Guests are welcome to use the swimming pool at the Holiday Inn next door, and receive drink coupons, a free $1 roll of nickels for use in the casino, and a 10 percent discount at the casino restaurant, open daily 6 A.M.–10 P.M. No tents allowed. All the spaces are first come, first served; the park often fills up by early afternoon.

KOA of Ely, three miles south of Ely on the Pioche Hwy., 775/289-3413 or 800/562-3413, is the largest RV park in all of eastern Nevada. Mature cottonwoods rim the perimeter and Chinese elms line the sites. Ward Mountain of the Egan Range broods directly behind the park, which sits up above the valley a little, so at night you can look down at the lights of town. There are 100 spaces for motor homes, most with full hookups; 38 are pull-throughs. Tents are allowed (a separate grassy area). Groceries, playground, and volleyball are available. The fee is $20–25 for RVs, $15–18 for tents. KOA and Good Sam discounts.

FOOD

Hotel Nevada, 500 Aultman, has a 24-hour coffee shop open daily 6 A.M.–9:30 P.M. A new sensation (for most of you) awaits at the hotel's **Jailhouse Dining Room**—cellblock dining behind bars; 775/289-3033, open for dinner 5–9 P.M. Try the Inmate Special, chicken Alaska (with crab) for $16.50. It also serves prime rib, ribs, halibut, shrimp, Cajun and teriyaki chicken, all around $16. The dining alcoves are designated by cell numbers, completing the theme. This is a great example of a negative cell.

The **Steptoe Valley Inn B&B,** 220 E. 11th St., 775/289-6991, offers a full bakery that is open to the public after about 9 A.M. For Mexican food, try **La Fiesta,** on Hwy. 93 N., about two miles north of Ely, at the Fireside Inn, 775/289-4112, open 11 A.M.–9 P.M. every day. Here you'll find

lunch specials for $5 and combo dinners starting at $7.75, with entrées going up to $17 for lobster and shrimp. Recommended.

The Copper Queen, on Pioche Hwy. near town, has **Big J's,** 775/289-4884, open 6 A.M.–10 P.M., well known for its home-baked bread, big steak dinners, and Sunday buffet brunch. The dining room and lounge were tastefully remodeled in 1990, though the banquet room in back was wisely left alone.

Silver State Restaurant, 1204 Aultman, 775/289-8866, is as classic a '50s diner as you'll ever see, right down to the orange vinyl booths and counter seats. No slots, no credit cards, no change for the Laundromat, no checks accepted; just good coffee shop grub, along with Mexican (served 2–9 P.M.) and steaks.

Finally, for a real old-fashioned treat, stop in at **Economy Drug,** 7th and Aultman, 775/289-4929, open Mon.–Fri. 9 A.M.–6 P.M., Saturday 9 A.M.–5 P.M., and pull up a stool at the soda fountain. Milkshakes, floats, ice cream sodas, freezes, and splits start at $1, and they use real milk, ice cream, and soda.

INFORMATION AND SERVICES

The White Pine County **Chamber of Commerce,** 636 Aultman, www.elynevada.net, open Mon.–Fri. 8 A.M.–5 P.M., stocks an abundance of brochures, visitor's guides, maps, and answers to questions. The **library** is next to the courthouse on Campton, 775/289-3737, open Mon.–Thurs. 10 A.M.–6 P.M., Friday 10 A.M.–5 P.M., first and third Saturdays 10 A.M.–4 P.M. *Big* Nevada section, two of everything; glance through *White Pine Lang Syne* by local historian Effie O. Read (1965).

For a map unique in Nevada, stop in at the front office of **Valley Motors,** 807 E. Aultman in East Ely, 775/289-4855: a score of USGS two-degree maps (1:250,000).

Ely Bus (775/289-2877), with a terminal at 426 Campton, offers service around town. Call for rates and schedules.

Central Nevada

Great Basin National Park

The 77,000-acre park, officially designated in October 1986, is the only national park in Nevada. It was carved out of Humboldt National Forest and surrounds Lehman Caves National Monument. National Park status was first proposed in 1922, when Lehman Caves was designated a National Monument, but the idea was heartily defeated by a powerful lobby of mining and ranching interests from the remote area. A second movement gained momentum in the late 1950s, but local opposition this time included miners, cattlemen, loggers, hunters, and even the Forest Service. A 28,000-acre Scenic Area was the result of a compromise on the 150,000-acre park proposal; the paved road up to 10,000 feet on Wheeler Peak was laid right afterward, in 1961.

Finally, in the mid-1980s, after Kennecott closed and unemployment in White Pine County reached 25 percent (same number as the population decline), the White Pine Chamber of Commerce resurrected the issue. This time, the political climate was favorable, and another broad compromise was worked out: Boundaries were drawn to exclude private mining land, grazing was permitted, and the 174,000-acre park proposal was whittled to its present 77,000 acres.

The nation's 47th national park and one of the smallest, Great Basin receives an average of 90,000 visitors a year. It gets crowded on weekends during the short peak season, and late arrivals can be turned away from the cave and campgrounds. (All the park's campgrounds are first come, first served, but you can make advance reservations by phone for the cave tours-a wise idea, for summer weekends.) But many visitors treat the park as a detour, just a day-trip, and view the caves, drive to the peak

overlook, and then are on their way. Since it's extremely remote from urban areas and interstate highways, there's little of the carnival atmosphere that pervades many other national parks, especially in the West. For anyone used to the circuses at Yosemite, Grand Canyon, and Yellowstone (among other) national parks, this place most of the time seems like solitude personified.

Great Basin National Park was created to preserve and showcase a preeminent example of the vast Great Basin ecosystem, which covers parts of five states and occupies nearly 20 percent of the land area in the continental United States. And indeed, the Snake Range packs a more diverse

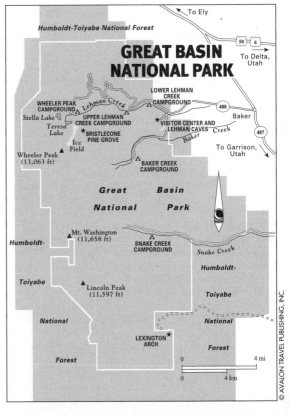

ecology into a discrete mountain range than any of the other 250 ranges in this vast western desert. All five Great Basin life zones occur in the roughly 8,000 feet from the valley to the peak, second-highest point in Nevada. The range contains the only permanent, glacier-like ice in the state. It boasts a large forest of 3,000- to 4,000-year-old bristlecone pines, the oldest living creatures on the planet. Within the quartzite limestone are corridors of caverns that have been carved by God and water for millions of years. What's more, the major attractions are eminently accessible: a road to 10,000 feet, highest in Nevada, day-trip trails to the peak, ice, and bristlecones, and rough 4WD tracks to the most solitary backcountry. The air is fresh, the views are grand, and the vibe is reverent in this hallowed temple of peaks, trees, caves, and wilderness.

Tiny Baker (pop. 55), five miles from the park entrance, is the nearest settlement; see the Practicalities section, further along, for services available in Baker. Ely, the largest town nearby, is a full 70 miles away by road.

SIGHTS

Head east out US 93/50/6, past Comins Lake and the cutoffs for Cave Lake State Park and the Ward Charcoal Ovens. Then you start to climb up into the pinon and juniper of the **Schell Creeks.** Right over **Connors Pass** (7,780 feet), the very big **Snake Range** comes into view. **Wheeler Peak** towers 3,000 feet above treeline, with permanent snow dropping down from the peak (13,063 feet). For a short distance, as you cross **Spring Valley** toward the Snakes, you're heading right at Wheeler Peak.

At Majors Junction, US 93 cuts south (right) at the fork, and you follow US 6/50 left. Continuing east, you drop into Spring Valley between the Schell Creeks behind and the Snakes ahead. The road up Spring Valley is an afternoon's scenic drive of its own.

A "short" cut goes right at the sign for **Osceola.** This very rough gravel road is passable, though just barely, with a low-clearance vehicle. You climb and climb straight up into the Snakes, and go by the cemetery and old gold pit. Some rusty mining

COURTESY OF THE NEVADA COMMISSION ON TOURISM

the oldest living creatures on the planet, the bristlecone pine, in Great Basin National Park

junk is lying around near the top, and headframes still stand. Placer gold was discovered here in 1872, and hydraulics were used to sluice out the nuggets and dust. *Arrastras,* primitive grinders, were employed in the early days. Later, a small stamp mill was built. In order to supply more water for the sluicing, a ditch was dug in 1889 around the mountain from Lehman Creek on the west side of the Snakes. The cost, $100,000, was never paid back in gold, as Osceola declined a year or two later, having produced $2 million in its 20 years. The rough road rejoins the highway on the east side of the mountains.

If you don't take the Osceola detour and stay on the main highway, you make a big loop north, through the low point of the Snakes, **Sacramento Pass,** at 7,154 feet. To the north **Mt. Moriah** rises to a peak 1,000 feet lower than Wheeler's. Nevada's fifth-highest peak, Mt. Moriah is now a designated Wilderness Area, one of the 14 created

Central Nevada

in 1989. It's 82,000 acres, and features the one-square-mile rolling-tundra Table at 11,000 feet, which is bordered by bristlecones. Hampton Creek Trail is a steep 15-mile round-trip hike to the summit of Mt. Moriah (4WD required); Hendry's Creek Trail is a 23-mile round-trip backpack up to the Table. For complete descriptions to and instructions for these trails, see *Nevada Wilderness Areas* by Michael White.

Turn off US 6/50 at the boarded-up Y Truck Stop onto Route 487. High country, low sage. Take a look-see around **Baker.** At a site just north of Baker, archaeologists have discovered the ruins of a settlement of the Fremont Indians, who were based in central and southwestern Utah around the time the Anasazi were predominant in southern Nevada. The Fremonts had the largest population of any native civilization in the area before and after, about 10,000 at its height. The Baker site is believed to be a western outpost of the agricultural Fremont. Like the Anasazi, they too disappeared from their western frontier around 1270, because of a 20-year drought in the area. Three pit houses, pottery, arrowheads, and artifacts have been found.

Now double back to the road up to the park. Keep an eye peeled for Sherman's whimsical roadside art gallery that extends from Baker to the park entrance. On the left is "Horse with No Name," a skeletal horse at the wheel of an old jalopy; on the right is "It's All Downhill from Here," a bony bike rider with flame-red hair, and several others. On the way back you'll want to track down Doc, a retired locksmith in Baker, just to hear him talk about his work.

Visitor Center

The park visitor center is open every day from at least 8 A.M. to 4:30 P.M., with the possibility of longer hours from Memorial Day to Labor Day. Contact the center with any questions about the park: 775/234-7331, www.nps.gov/grba.

Buy your tickets for the cave tour as soon as you enter the center, if you haven't already bought tickets in advance by phone. Allow time to study the exhibits on park flora, fauna, cave formations, and to enjoy the three-dimensional Landsat thematic image. You could easily spend an entire hour just looking at the books, slides, and videos.

Borrow a trail guide from inside and take the nature walk on the side of the visitor center. Stop off first at **Rhode's Cabin** to see the historical exhibit on the caretaking of the national monument. Then stroll the trail, stopping to read about juniper and pinon, mountain mahogany and mistletoe, limestone and marble, and cave entrances.

In front of the visitor center and down the hill slightly are some trees planted by Ab Lehman himself more than 100 years ago. The giant apricot trees flesh out a ton of very fine fruit—sweet, juicy, healthy—somewhat late in the season, perfectly ripe the second week of August. Help yourself; they're better than candy. The Park Service is cloning the apricots, and you'll also see apples, pears, peaches, and plums. An irrigation ditch off to the side is the only remnant, along with the fruit trees, of Lehman's homestead.

Various activities are centered around the visitor center; check the bulletin board or with a naturalist when you arrive. Next door to the visitor center is the gift and coffee-shop concessionaire, open April through October. At the **Lehman Caves Gift and Cafe,** 775/234-7221, the food is gratifyingly good, and the gift shop is well stocked with quality artwork, books, T-shirts, and the like. Quite a bit of the inventory comes from Nevada, some from the immediate area: silver and turquoise jewelry by Jan Everitt of Austin and Erman Blossom, a northern Paiute from Pyramid Lake; T-shirts by Virginia City's Tom Gilbertson, etc. On the café side, breakfast and lunch are served, and her homemade soups are distinctive and well-seasoned. Try the "incredible ice cream sandwich," a double scoop crammed between a giant pair of oatmeal cookies ($3.75), easily big enough for two or three people. The Great Basin Natural History Association operates a **bookshop** in the visitor center that benefits the park, 775/234-7270.

Lehman Caves

Five hundred million years ago, nearly everything, everywhere, for all time, had been under water. Nevada's sea was shallow, teeming with skeletoned

COURTESY OF THE NEVADA COMMISSION ON TOURISM

entering the Lehman Caves

creatures. The bottom turned into a graveyard for the little bones, which accumulated for eons, pressurizing into limestone. By 150 million years ago, the sea was out and the sandy desert in. Eventually the sand petrified into sandstone, which was metamorphosed into quartzite. Uplifting, tilting, and stretching 70 million years ago created the Snakes, mostly from quartzite, with a little limestone coming to rest at the eastern base of the range. Some molten granite was burped up near the joint, superheating the limestone into marble. Seepage dissolved the marble, opening up large caverns and long aqueducts for underground streams and lakes and springs. Then the water table dropped, leaving the caves high and dry. Now the seepage began to dissolve the surrounding limestone, depositing calcite, drop by drop, drip by drip, speck by speck, until the. . . things. . . started to grow, imperceptibly, inexorably, one-hundredth of an inch a year. Today, countless megazillions of calcite dribbles later, this is the classic Old Man Cave, with the

ornate and incredible stalagmites, stalactites, helictites, aragonites, columns, shields, draperies, bacon, popcorn, and soda straws to prove it.

Enter Absalom Lehman, in 1885. The legend is obscure, but Ab discovered the cave, explored it, altered it, and fostered it. The cave concessionaire changed a few times after Lehman's death in 1891, and the area became a national forest in 1909, achieving national-monument status in 1922. Additional changes have been made over the years, including entrance and exit tunnels and trail improvements.

Park Service personnel are putting together a proactive management strategy to protect the caves. The installation of a lighting system years ago resulted in unnatural algal blooms on some formations. Another problem is lint from visitors' clothing, which attaches itself to the cave walls—look closely at some of the formations and you'll see a fuzz coating. There is now a program in place to clean algae and lint from the cave on a regular basis.

The Park Service has also completed a resource survey on 30 other caves and rock shelters scattered throughout the park between the 8,000- and 12,000-foot level. A permit system allows people to visit some of the caves, while keeping others off limits. Contact the park's Resources Management department, 775/234-7270, for a permit to visit wild caves.

Cave tours are of varying lengths; options include a 60-minute tour ($6) and a 90-minute tour ($6). In summer, tours usually depart from around 9 A.M. to 3:30 P.M. every day (call for details); in winter, tours usually depart around four times daily. You can reserve space on a tour in advance, which is a good idea if you're planning a weekend visit. Call 775/234-7331, ext. 242, and put the admission fee on your credit card.

This is an excursion to the *inside*—inside the studio of a sculptor who's learned a thing or two during her 20-million-year career, and inside your own head, where the most dramatic macros and the infinite, intricate micros take their weird effects. Don't bother with the prosaic public names—West Room, Lake Room, Inscription Room, Palace and Talus rooms. Instead, let the formations trigger whatever's in the mind's eye.

Central Nevada

BRISTLECONE PINE: FAQ

Are bristlecone pines really the oldest living beings on Earth?

In 1964, only six years after Edmund Schulman of the Arizona Tree-Ring Research Group published an article in *National Geographic* announcing the discovery of bristlecone pines, a scientist doing research on Wheeler Peak found the tree called "Prometheus," later determined (when it was felled by the Forest Service) to be 4,900 years old. This ancient organism was older, by more than 1,000 years, than the most giant California sequoia. It predated the pyramids in Egypt by 1,200 years. In fact, Prometheus when it was cut down was only a bit more than 700 years younger than the date that the Old Testament gives to the birth of the world.

How do they live so long?

In his excellent and lyrical *Trees of the Great Basin,* Ronald Lanner comments that in the case of the bristlecones, "Adversity breeds longevity." Because these trees inhabit such a harsh environment—at the highest elevations, on exposed and rocky slopes, bearing the full brunt of the elements—they enjoy a suitable lack of competition; only limber pine and Engelmann spruce keep these timberline ancients company. Also, since the bristlecone stands are somewhat sparse, fire presents less of a danger to their lives. Finally, these slow-growing trees produce an extremely dense wood, which is highly resistant to infection, parasites, and decay. Carol Muench, in a 1967 article in *Nevada* magazine, expresses the irony that the "most tormented of species lives the longest."

How do they die?

A very little at a time! Even 3,000-year-old trees continue to be active reproductively and bear cones. Incredibly, the inexorable forces of erosion finally overtake their mountain habitat and expose the root system, which dries out and rots or becomes susceptible to fungus or parasites. The upper limbs connected to the lower roots then die off, one by one. Next, the wind and rain scour off the bark, leaving a bleached and polished trunk. Still, 90 percent of a bristlecone pine can be dead while, in Lanner's words, "a single sinuous strip of living bark connects the occasional live limb to the occasional live root." Also, an old bristlecone can stand for 1,000 or so years after dying off completely.

What does science learn from the mighty memories of these trees?

Thankfully, scientists have developed core-sampling techniques that enable them to "read" the rings without having to cut down the whole tree to do it. (Prometheus wasn't so lucky.) Bristlecones are sensitive to drought conditions, which restrict their ring formation. In this way these trees provide dendrochronologists a natural calendar of climatic events dating back to nearly 9,000 years ago, using long-dead trees. When you consider that scientific weather records have only been kept for the last 100 years, it becomes clear that the bristlecones add immeasurably to our knowledge. In addition, the trees can help us measure the action of erosion itself. Lanner writes, "Exposed roots of trees of known age have been used to estimate rates of mass wasting—the geological process that wears away mountains." And it's all right there to see, a mere half-hour walk from the parking lot at Wheeler Peak Campground in Great Basin National Park.

HIKING AND CAMPING

The park has four developed campgrounds: the **Baker Creek, Lower Lehman Creek, Upper Lehman Creek,** and **Wheeler Peak** campgrounds. The charge for staying at any of these is $10 a night, and all sites are first come, first served. All have drinking water during the warm months, and some have flush toilets. The Upper Lehman Creek campground has one handicap-accessible site, and the Baker Creek campground has two. The park also has primitive camping facilities along Snake Creek and Strawberry Creek Roads; campsites have fire grates, picnic tables and pit toilets, and are free of charge.

An excellent guide for this remote backcountry is *Hiking and Climbing in Great Basin National Park* by Michael Kelsey. Another book with a good chapter on Great Basin Park is *Nevada Wilderness Areas* by Michael Rose.

Baker and Johnson Lakes

Baker Road leaves the main park road just below the visitor center and heads south, then west, up to 7,000 feet. It's a good gravel road, 25 mph, through piñon and aspen, past massive stone outcrops. A little less than three miles from the main road is **Baker Creek Campground.** Three loops contain 32 sites (two wheelchair-accessible), with outhouses and running water (boil first). The choice spots are under big evergreens right on the creek. This campground is open from around May 15 to September 15.

A little more than three miles from the campground is **Baker Lake and Johnson Lake Loop Trail.** Both lakes are five miles from the trailhead, with a mile between, over Johnson Pass (10,800 feet) of Pyramid Peak (11,921 feet). Much of this area in the central and southern part of the park is generally accessible to high-clearance vehicles on dirt roads in from Route 487 near Garrison, Utah.

A well-graded gravel road heads into the southeast corner of the park from south of Garrison. At the end, a 1.7-mile trail brings you to **Lexington Arch,** a six-story natural limestone arch. Ask at the visitors center about the **Big Wash** hike. No permits are required for backcountry hiking or camping, but the Park Service strongly encourages you to fill out a voluntary backcountry registration form.

Lehman Creek and Wheeler Peak

Just below Baker Creek Road, down from the visitor center, take a left onto Wheeler Peak Road, and go up up up this mountain toward the peak. **Lower Lehman Creek Campground** at 7,500 feet has 11 sites, mostly used by trailers and RVs, and pit toilets. **Upper Lehman Creek Campground,** just up the road at 7,800 feet, has 24 tent sites on three levels of the slope. The upper Upper campground is on a creek; the trailhead for Wheeler Peak Campground leaves from here. The lower Upper campground is open year-round, the upper approximately May 15 to September 15. Both have drinking water available (in winter, water is available at the visitor center, if not at the campsites).

Continue climbing up this extraordinary road (RVs or vehicles over 24 feet not recommended). At around 8,500 feet are a couple of curves; then the peak, from treeline to summit, takes your breath away. At 9,000 feet the views, if possible, get better. Pause at the Serene Overlook, gazing right up into the glacial cirque. Keep climbing and climbing, with the peak ahead and the vast valley behind, till you get to the end of the road at the parking lot for the trailheads and the loop through **Wheeler Peak Campground.** The campground is 13 miles from the visitor center at a breath-catching 10,000 feet. It has 37 sites and pit toilets, open usually June through September.

Warm up your hiking boots on the **Theresa Lake** and **Stella Lake** trails, which you can do in an aerobic hour or a lethargic two. The grades are easy and the lakes are pretty and the peaks are mighty.

After acclimating on this loop, head up to the **bristlecones** and the **icefield,** two to three hours round-trip, though not especially strenuous. Signs point the way at the forks with the other trails. An interpretive trail circles the bristlecone sanctuary, where these ancient beings cling to life with the most tenacious yet precarious grip in God's Great Kingdom. The reverence here is palpable, and you'll unconsciously adopt a light step and a hushed tone as you move in awe through this divine forest. But don't be shy about caressing the trees—the barkless wood, polished for hundreds of years by the elements, invites touch, and not a hint of a splinter will you notice. The bottlebrush needles, likewise, are soft and sensual, surprisingly young feeling. The living parts of the trees are vital and triumphal, but even the dead parts are beautiful and immortal. This forest is exquisite proof that wood is one element that can remain aesthetic long after death, one which does not automatically demand to be buried.

Past the temple of the pines, the trail becomes steep and rocky and will tickle your ears with the bunches of scrunching underfoot. Tune in to this rock concert! In no time you enter the cirque, a hall of the mountain kings. It might be stretching it a bit to call the permanent snowpack here a "glacier"; there's not a touch of blue to it. But the parkies hereabouts are a little sensitive about their glacier. One of the many political skirmishes in the effort to name the area a national park was over whether the icefield was a true glacier. Ranchers and miners opposed to the park called it a snowfield. Park supporters rallied behind the little patch of ice. If Wheeler was the site of Nevada's only extant glacier, then it needed protection, right? According to the parkies, it has now been determined that Wheeler's ice does move, so a glacier, they say, it is. But anyone who's spent any time in Alaska or the Yukon might think it looks more like an ice cube.

Wheeler Peak Trail branches off from near Stella Lake and climbs 3,000 feet in four miles-steep, high, exhilarating. This trail is open all year, but in winter you'll need winter gear (i.e. cramp-ons) to traverse it.

ACCOMMODATIONS AND FOOD

The tiny town of Baker (pop. 55), five miles from the park entrance, has a couple of options

for accommodations and a bite. The **Silver Jack Motel,** 775/234-7323, has seven rooms at $39. The motel stays open April through October. Check out the gift shop and art gallery there. The Great Basin T-shirts, among other things, are original. Doc Sherman's copper, wood, and what-have-you sculptures are prominently displayed. Owner Bill Roundtree makes metal sculptures of western themes and his wife does the T-shirts. Three blocks up Route 488 toward the park, turn left to find **End of the Trail** operated by the same owners; it's a two-bedroom mobile home with a view, renting for $62 a night. The same owners also run **The Bunkhouse,** a cabin with kitchenette on the ranch, for $57 per night. Contact the owners at the Silver Jack Motel for info on all of these.

The **Border Inn,** 13 miles east of the park entrance on US6/50, smack on the Utah-Nevada line, 775/239-7300, has 29 motel rooms for $31–45, plus a restaurant, bar, slots, showers, laundry, and gas. The gas pumps are in Utah where transportation taxes are lower, which makes the gas here about 15 cents cheaper than in Nevada. Everything's open 24 hours a day.

Hidden Canyon Guest Ranch, 775/234-7267, is a lovely ranch down Big Wash Rd., about 15 miles south of Baker. Open in summer (June through September), by reservation only, it offers horseback riding, hiking, fishing and Western activities. Packages including lodging, all meals, activities and tour guides cost $125 per person, per day ($85 for ages 5–11). Lodging alone is $48 in tent cabins or in nice, big teepees. Camping is $9 per person, or $35 per family, in your own tent or small RV (long RVs cannot negotiate the road). In autumn and winter, the ranch opens for pheasant hunting; hunting packages are available including rustic lodging and meals, or hunters can rough it, or come out just for day hunting; phone for details.

The Toiyabes and Vicinity

Like the Ruby Mountains in northeast Nevada, the Snake Range in eastern Nevada, and the Spring Mountains in southern Nevada, the Toiyabe Range is the preeminent stretch of mountains in central Nevada. "Toiyabe" is a Shoshone word, variously translated as "Black Mountains," for the thick piñon, juniper, and mahogany cover, and "Big Mountains," for their length, height, steepness, and ruggedness. From Toiyabe Peak near Austin to Mahogany Mountain opposite Carver's, this mansard roof tops the exact middle of the state in a thin straight line more than 10,000 feet high for 50 miles. The southern slope extends for another 20 miles, tapering off into two squat legs (with feet), while the upper range elongates for another 50 miles, rising to a head at mystical Mt. Callaghan. Austin, at 6,500 feet one of the highest towns in Nevada, rests below the neck. To the south is the Toquimas and Monitor Valley and all its adjoining mining towns and ghosts towns.

AUSTIN

Austin's history reaches back to the days of the Pony Express. Silver was discovered in May 1862 by a recently retired rider in a small canyon in the Toiyabe Mountains, just up the hill from Reese River Valley, along the route of the express mail service. The "Rush to the Reese" got underway in early 1863, and by spring of that year a thousand claims had been staked in newly named Pony Canyon and on nearby hills. By summer, Austin, named after the Texas hometown of one of the original locators, was a bona fide boomtown.

Virginia City's International Hotel was dismantled board by board, hauled across the desert, and re-erected in downtown Austin. Lander County was created around Austin in 1863; it was so big that it occupied almost the entire eastern half of the territory. Eventually, Eureka, Elko, White Pine, and Nye counties were carved out of it (Lincoln County wasn't even part of Nevada yet). The *Reese River Reveille* went from a weekly to a daily in a matter of months. Three quartz

mills started up almost immediately. Prospectors fanned out into the far northern, northeastern, and eastern reaches of the territory, returning to town for supplies. Their indications triggered rushes to Belmont, Tuscarora, Hamilton, Eureka, Pioche, and later Tonopah and Goldfield.

Austin dogged Virginia City's output ounce by ounce in silver and history for the next 10 years. Roughly $50 million in gold and silver were recovered from the Reese District during its heyday, which lasted until around 1873. The Nevada Central Railroad, arriving in 1880, proved a bit late.

Austin is home to a number of classic Nevada legends, such as the Gridley Flour Sack that raised $250,000 for the Sanitary Fund (the Civil War's version of the Red Cross); the Sazerac Lying Club immortalized in Oscar Lewis's 1954 *The Town That Died Laughing;* and the Reese River Navigation Company, a phony steamship line.

Like everywhere else in Nevada, Austin experienced the long, melancholy decline of resources and population until quite recently, with this latest resurgence of mining. Turquoise and barium are abundant, in addition to the gold and silver.

Today, Austin has fewer than 300 residents, with no doctor, no pharmacy, and no barber shop. But it's still as central to Nevada's history as any other town of any size in the state. Its location, in addition, is 12 miles from the exact geographical center of Nevada. But Austin sits nearest to the heart of Nevada in *attitude*. Austin takes pride in offering the kind of personal liberty whereby "a person can do just about anything he sets his mind to so long as he doesn't step on anybody else's toes." With just 250 inhabitants in town, and two hours from Fallon and Tonopah and more than an hour from Eureka and Battle Mountain, stepping on anybody else's toes isn't easy.

SIGHTS

A two-minute drive at 10 mph along Main Street near the bottom of Pony Canyon takes you past almost everything. The town park is on the east

Central Nevada

SAZERAC LYING CLUB

F red Hart, editor of Austin's *Reese River Reveille* from 1873 to 1878, frequently found himself without anything "of a startling nature in the line of news" to print. This was a not uncommon predicament for editors of small frontier-town dailies, and it partially accounts for the tradition of 19th-century Western journalism, which incorporated elements of exaggeration, fantasy, satire, ribaldry, and just plain fiction, to fill up the column inches. Mark Twain, its most famous practitioner, summed it up with, "Never let the facts get in the way of a good tale."

According to Oscar Lewis in his book *The Town That Died Laughing*, one night, Hart, making his reporter's rounds, stopped into the Sazerac Saloon, where old-timers gathered to drink, smoke, and storytell. He overheard a description by one of the regulars about silver bars he had once seen in Mexico, which made a pile "seven miles long, forty feet high, and thirteen feet wide." The next day, strapped as usual for hard news, Hart printed a notice of the formation the previous night of the Sazerac Lying Club, which had unanimously elected Mr. George Washington Fibley as president.

It didn't take long for other Nevada and California newspapers to begin reprinting tall tales from the *Reese River Reveille* attributed to the Sazerac Lying Club, and from there news of the Austin institution spread far and wide. One story recounted the reason that a stage from Belmont had been delayed. Uncle John Gibbons, the driver, was en route when he seemed to be approaching a "thick bank of dark clouds," which in fact turned out to be a flock of sage hens. "'But boys, thar was more sage-hen obstructin' that road than I had reckoned on, and when them thar leader horses struck into them thar sage-hen, they was throwed back on the haunches just as if they had butted clean up ag'in a stone wall. As far's you could see thar warn't nothin' but sage hen; you could about see the top of the pile of 'em.'" Uncle John unhitched one of the horses and rode back to the station for help.

The hostler grabbed an axe, ready to "chop a road through the sage-hen." But a prospector there said, "'See here, boys, don't you think we could blast 'em out quicker'n we could chop through 'em?'"

The prospector "went up the hill and got his drills and his sledges and a lot of giant-powder cartridges and some fuse, and the rest of the blastin' apparatus, and then the whole raft of us started back for the place where the stage was; and when we got thar—well I wish I may be runned over by a two-horse jerkwater if there was a sage hen in sight as far's a man could see with a spy-glass. I hope you fellows is contented now you know what kept the stage late the other night.'"

This tale somehow made its way to Germany, where it was printed by the *Karlsruher Zeitung*. The article was forwarded back to Austin, where a German-speaking resident translated it into English.

In Austin, Nevada, America, there is a society whose object is competitive lying. . .
The lie which took the premium this year was told by Uncle John Gibonich. He
said that while riding post across the Valley of the Smoke there arose from the earth
a flock of geese so numberless that they blocked the road and shut out the light of
day. And in order that the blockade might be raised, and the royal mails pass on
their way, it was deemed useful to telegraph for a corps of sappers and miners from
the Government barracks, who mined a tunnel through the mass of geese, and the
post proceeded on its way.

edge of town as you come in on US 50; turn left on Nevada Street. Here you'll find kids' apparatus, outdoor pool (with the locker room in front), and some big trees with picnic tables underneath.

Coming from the east into town, the first business you reach is also the newest. Rick Crawford of **Tyrannosaurus Rix Mountain Bike and Specialties,** (known as **T-Rix**) 775/964-1212, www.t-rix.com, is trying to lead Austin to its rightful place in the mountain biking world: the top. This corner of the Toiyabes is chock full of all the things post-pavement pedalers demand: lung-searing hill climbs, heart-stopping downhills, and killer views. Problem is, no one knows it, even though Austin straddles US 50, the most direct route from California to the mountain biking mecca of Moab, Utah. Rick can rent, sell, or build you a bike. Rick also offers guided off-road bike tours of the Toiyabes. The refreshments served here, including espresso, latte, frozen or hot cappuccino, yogurt and other refreshments, are especially popular with European visitors longing for a good European-style coffee. The store is open every day, all year round.

Rick opened up shop in 1996, and a year later he was organizing his first American Mountain Bike Association race, T Rix Lost World Challenge. Since then, the event, held for a full weekend each August, has blossomed into the annual Claim Jumpers Mountain Bike Festival, a family event including a 27-mile mountain bike cross-country race on Saturday, a downhill race on Sunday, plus free racing and activities for children, barbecues featuring home-made ice cream, open swimming and a live band.

4 M's Gems and Jason's Art Gallery, 775/964-1346, is a retail outlet for a local turquoise miner, Mitch Cantrell. This store sells rocks and old bottles; Mitch also arranges rock hunting to his mine and wildlife-viewing excursions. **Nevada Blue Rock & Gem,** 775/964-2063, owned by Pancho and Joan Williams, carries a large selection of jewelry and gifts. Across from the courthouse, **The Trading Post,** 775/964-1348, has an extensive collection of rocks, old bottles, jewelry and gifts. There's a display of handmade dolls for sale in the office of the **Mountain Motel.**

You can't miss **Gridley Store,** a stone building on Main Street on the right coming into town from the east. The store was opened in 1863 by Rueul Gridley, whose name lives on in conjunction with a 50-pound sack of flour. Gridley paid off a losing bet by carrying the flour from his store to a bar across town, and then auctioning it off for a donation to the Sanitary Fund. The highest bidder auctioned it off again, then again, and again. Nearly $10,000 was raised by the end of the afternoon. From there, Gridley took the sack to Virginia City and repeated the process, then on to California and eventually the East Coast, raising $250,000 for Civil War relief. Gridley himself died penniless six years later. The house next to Gridley's store was originally the town brothel.

To get to **Stokes' Castle,** a curious attraction that could only be found in Austin, take a left on Castle Road at the west end of town, and follow a precipitous road about a half mile around to the back of the hill. This rare, three-story, stone "castle," built by mining baron Anson P. Stokes, has stood here like a sentinel for over 100 years. Incredibly, it was only occupied for a month or two in the summer of 1897. Still, it's a fine place to have a picnic, or stretch your legs in the piñon forest uphill, with a great overlook of Reese River Valley. You could camp here in a pinch.

Accommodations

There are a total of 39 rooms in Austin, none of which could be considered anything but utilitarian. Actually, things have improved some on the Austin lodging scene in the past few years: the Pony Canyon and the Lincoln Motel now have phones in the rooms.

The **Lincoln Motel,** 728 Main St., 775/964-2698, has eight-by-ten-foot rooms with a queen bed; you can sit on the toilet, wash your hands, shave, and brush your teeth all at the same time; $30–46. The rooms at the **Mountain Motel,** 902 Main St., 775/964-2471, occupy a single-wide trailer, with walnut paneling and gas heat; there are no phones in the rooms here, but the new owners seem to have fixed the crazy angles the rooms used to lean at. The Mountain is also the only inn in Austin that offers non-smoking rooms; $32–45. There are 10 rooms at the **Pony**

Canyon Motel, 775/964-2605, not a whole lot fancier than the others, $38–58.

You can rent the two-bedroom **Pony Express House,** 775/964-2306, for $35 a night (one room) or $70 a night (both rooms). The house is historic, built in the late 1860s. This is a "bed and fix your own breakfast."

Austin RV and Baptist Church on the right as you enter town, 775/964-1011, set at 6,900 feet, is the only RV park in Nevada that's connected to a church. The retired minister's wife, Donna White, leases the parking-lot RV park from the church (there are too many potential conflicts of interest for the church to be in the campground business); still, the RV office doubles as the Sunday school. Fee collecting is somewhat on the honor system (read the signs on the information board and drop the night's payment in the drop box on the front of the office). There are 21 sites, $17 for RVs (20 and 30 amp service available). Tent campers can use the large grassy area, $10. Hot showers and laundry facilities are available.

Adjacent to T-Rix on US 50 on the east end of town is the **Pony Express RV Park,** 775/964-2005, which offers 12 RV sites and four tent sites. On one side RVers have access to the amenities of the bike store, such as espresso and yogurt and on the other is the town park and public swimming pool. Rates are $12 for RVs and $8 for tents. Open May–Nov.

Food

Austin has two places to eat, each with unique charms. **Toiyabe Café,** 775/964-2220, is open Apr.–Oct. 6 A.M.–9 P.M. They close an hour earlier in the off-season. For breakfast try the green chile and Swiss or Spanish omelette, or bacon and eggs for. Lunch and dinner fare includes good soup and burritos, burgers, steak sandwich, and fish, beer and wine available.

The **International** café on the west side of town is in the second-oldest hotel building in Nevada (though lodging is not available). It's open 5:30 A.M.–9 P.M. and has good food. For a tasty filling meal, try the twice-baked potatoes with broccoli, bacon, and cheddar cheese for $3.95. Your basic burger runs $4.25, add $0.50 for cheese.

Information

The **U.S. Forest Service station,** on the west side of town overlooking the junction of Route 305, 775/964-2671, is open 7:45 A.M.–4:30 P.M. weekdays. It sells detailed maps ($2) and can advise you on hikes and the like.

The **Austin Chamber of Commerce,** 775/964-2200, www.austinnevada.com, has a large rack of brochures in the foyer of the courthouse; the chamber office upstairs is open most weekday mornings. Track down Wally Trapnell or Joy Brandt of the chamber for the latest Austin info. You can pick up brochures from the rack downstairs in the courthouse whenever the courthouse is open Mon.–Fri. 8 A.M.–5 P.M.

THE TOIYABE RANGE

Three peaks in the Toiyabes tower over 11,000 feet, with **Arc Dome** the highest at 11,788 feet. Another four peaks in the range rise over 10,000 feet. Big Smoky Valley accompanies the steeper eastern scarp from up near Austin to the bottom. The top of mighty Mt. Jefferson of the Toquima Range right across the valley actually looks down 200 feet at the crown of Arc Dome. This is one of the finest mountain scenes in the state. Reese River Valley faces the wetter western wall. Numerous creeks converge at the trough on the west side of the range to create the mudpuddle Reese River and fertile ranch land.

Frémont appears to have been the first European to set foot in **Big Smoky Valley** (1845); he named it after the late summer haze that partially obscured it. He followed it for three days, camping at Birch Creek, the hot springs, and Peavine. James Simpson passed along its northern edge in 1859 as he surveyed the central alternative route through the territory. After Austin attracted its horde of fortune seekers in 1863, prospectors crawled all over the Toiyabes, finding some minerals within the granite intrusions. Toiyabe City, Kingston, Canyon City, Geneva, Amador, and Yankee Blade all sprouted and withered at the finds.

Today, Arc Dome is the largest Forest Service Wilderness Area in Nevada at 115,000 acres. *Hiking the Great Basin* by John Hart covers a baker's-dozen hikes here in detail, including two for Arc Dome, several from Twin Rivers, Jett Canyon, and the 65-mile Toiyabe Crest National Recreation Trail. *Nevada Wilderness Areas* by Michael Rose covers seven hikes here, including two Twin River loops, Cow, Tom's, and Jett canyons, and the Toiyabe Crest Trail. If internal combustion is more your style, the roads down Big Smoky from Austin to Tonopah and up Reese River Valley from Ione Canyon to Austin provide two of the most breathtaking scenic cruises not only in Nevada but throughout the West.

Heading South

As you turn south on Route 376, 12 miles east of Austin, the first ridgeline you see is defined by Toiyabe Peak (10,793 feet) and Bunker Hill (11,474 feet). About 15 miles south of the junction is a turnoff into **Kingston.** In the late 1960s, a developer attempted to transform the ranch land around present-day Kingston into a town like Venice, California, with cobblestone streets, outdoor cafes, and upscale boutiques. It didn't happen. Today there's a little gold mining going on, supported by a small settlement; still, it's the third-largest population center, behind Battle Mountain and Austin, in Lander County.

You drive on pavement past the town and continue to where, predictably, the pavement ends on the way into **Kingston Canyon.** In another couple of miles is Kingston Canyon Forest Service campground, with 12 sites right on the creek at the lush bottom of the canyon, with big trees, and fat gooseberries in August; $7. A half-mile up the canyon is a small fishing pond; another half mile presents the trailhead to the Toiyabe Crest Trail. One more half mile brings you to the Forest Service station. And from there, the road travels right over the Toiyabes in the shadow of massive Bunker Hill, to connect up with the Reese River Valley road into Austin.

Continuing south on Route 376, you pass Sheep Canyon, Crooked Canyon, and Toiyabe Range Peak (10,960 feet), with a few 8,000- to 9,000-foot "hills" in between. Ten miles from the Kingston junction is **Smokey Joe's** gas station and minimart: clean restrooms, friendly service, and food.

South of there is a line of sheer granite walls, and I mean *straight* up and down. The valley just below is lined with ranches. The bottomland below that is another alkali bed of another ice-age lake. Roads head up into Summit Creek and Ophir Creek and Twin River below Toiyabe Range Peak (10,805 feet) to the old mining sites. Directly across the valley to the east in the Toquima Range loom **Mt. Jefferson's** three summits, all over 11,000 feet.

Carver's

Just beyond Darrough's Hot Springs (private, no sign) is Carver's. Jean and Gerald Carver homesteaded in the area in the early 1940s, then built a small restaurant and bar called, naturally enough, Carver's, halfway between Austin and Tonopah in 1947 right after the state road was cut. They served auto travelers and truckers, along with miners from the Round Mountain district just down the road. Twenty years later, as the mining continued in fits and starts, enough people had settled nearby that the name Carver's started showing up on state maps. And 20 years after that, when Round Mountain Gold cranked up the mining in earnest, Carver's found itself a full-fledged boomtown. The place that gave the town its name is now owned by the folks who run the International back in Austin. Retired now, Jean and Gerald are still nearby.

Today, Carver's consists of a big highway maintenance station, cafes, two gas stations, small shopping center, LDS temple, and firehouse. The **Jumping Jack Motel,** 775/377-2566, is the only motel between Austin and Tonopah. It has only 17 rooms, and sometimes fills up with vendors for the gold mine, so it's a good idea to phone ahead for reservations. Rooms are $40 single, $45 double. Be sure to stop in and have a look at the **Full Moon Saloon** to have a direct experience of why the words "bar" and "barn" are so similar. The Full Moon is party central for Big Smoky Valley, and serves lunch and dinner.

At Carver's the road turns to the southeast, aiming right at Round Mountain, where Round Mountain Gold Corporation's miners dig for gold and pile up overburden at one of the largest operations along a major road in Nevada. At the turnoff, the road to the right leads to **Hadley,** one of the largest company towns in Nevada. It's occupied by roughly 500 miners and their families, who pay $50 a month for their mobile homes. There are a 24-hour daycare center, an elementary and junior high school, a medical clinic, a swimming pool and rec center, and a golf course.

The **Round Mountain Golf Club,** 775/377-2880, operates the longest nine-hole course in Nevada. William Howard Neff, a top golf course architect from Utah, designed the par-36 course, which boasts three lakes. The course has a country club, café, lounge, cart rentals, and one of the best pro shops north of Las Vegas. There are two par fives, one 571 yards and the other 538. The course is open to the public; green fees run $11 for nine holes and $65 for 18. There's a paved airstrip 300 yards away (par 3?).

The **Smoky Valley Museum,** situated on Route 376 near Carver's, offers a glimpse at some of the area's mining and ranching history. The museum is housed in a 1935 schoolhouse, so you can check out the class ledgers and old photos. Open the second Wednesday of the month and by appointment, 775/377-2243. For more information about the area, contact the Greater Smoky Valley Chamber of Commerce, 775/377-1100, www.bigsmokyvalley.com.

ROUND MOUNTAIN AND VICINITY

Round Mountain is the name of the town, the hill it sits on, the circular tailings piling up around the pit, and the company doing the digging. All these "Round Mountains" provide an excellent history of the different forms of gold mining that have been practiced around the West over the last 140 years.

Round Mountain

Placer gold (waterborne deposits of sand or gravel containing minerals eroded from original bedrock), which washed down from ledges in the Toquimas into this valley, was discovered by prospectors from Goldfield in 1906. The gold occurred in small high-grade veins that could be dug out with hand tools and hoisted up with gasoline engines. Later, dry-wash machines worked the surface gravel deposits. A million dollars was recovered by the initial individual operators. In 1914, a larger syndicate laid a pipe

a history lesson on gold mining in Nevada: Round Mountain

across Big Smoky Valley from Jett Canyon in the Toiyabes to sluice the gold out of the lower-grade ore. In the mid-1920s, the Nevada Porphyry Gold Mine Company installed a dredge, which became the largest gold-gravel washing operation in the state's history.

A number of companies tried their hands at mining Round Mountain over the next couple of decades, till large equipment was installed in 1950. Huge power shovels scooped the paydirt into equally huge hoppers, which funneled it onto long conveyor belts. These belts, 36 inches wide and miles long, traveled at three miles an hour to stockpiles. From there, the ore was weighed and sent to crushers and washers, which could handle 500 tons an hour.

A lull in the mining quieted the area and nearly evacuated the town in the 1960s. But in the 1970s, a number of gold and oil companies began developing the lode; by 1977, the mine was processing 7,000 tons a day. In 1985, Echo Bay Ltd. bought in and began an extensive expansion, culminating in 1991 with a system that could handle 135,000 tons of ore every day. In 1983, the mine produced 92,000 ounces of gold leached from 3.6 million tons of ore at a cost of $265 per ounce; in 1990, the mine produced 432,000 ounces of gold from 16 million tons at a cost of $174 per ounce.

Today, the open pit is 8,000 feet long, 7,200 feet wide, and 1,200 feet deep. This microscopic stuff is mined on a scale that seems more like copper than gold; it takes 300 tons of ore to produce one ounce of gold. Twenty-eight-yard shovels, 23-yard excavators, 10,000-gallon water trucks, 190-ton dump trucks working at the bottom of the pit are dwarfed by its magnitude. But when those dump trucks come barreling by, with tires as tall as your house, and you think that it takes two full loads to make just one ounce of gold, you get a forcible impression of what "microscopic gold" really means. Still, say what you will about the ugliness of open-pit mines and the toxicity of the sodium cyanide leaching solution on the one hand, and the land use, employment, and economic benefits on the other: When you come right down to it, it's just a bunch of guys playing in the dirt.

You can't just waltz in and tour the operation, but you can tell from the size of everything as you drive by on Route 376 and Route 378 that this place means business. As you drive up Route 378 past the round mountain surrounding the pit, the colorful overburden is eye-catching: grays, reds, pinks, purples, even blues. The town of Round Mountain is up the hill past the pit and has a grand total of five, if that many, actual houses. The few dozen dwellings are mobile homes.

Manhattan

After gold was discovered in the shadow of Bald Mountain in the Toquimas in 1906, a rush from Goldfield got underway. The first excitement, financed by San Francisco capital, was prematurely aborted by the great earthquake that year, but Manhattan recovered in 1910. Successful placer operations necessitated the building of a large mill in 1912. Then rich paydirt was discovered in the lower levels of the hard-rock mine in 1915, and the mill had to be reconditioned. In the late 1930s, advanced gold-mining technology arrived in the form of a great gold dredge, an Alaska-size contraption that looked like a cartoon cross between an oversized houseboat and a crane. An endless conveyor on the dredge circulated dozens of steel buckets that scooped the gravel, conveyed it to the top end, and dumped it onto a revolving screen. The screen separated the larger rocks (shunting them off to the tailings piles), from the golden gravel, which was sifted by the screen onto riffles. There, quicksilver (mercury) gleaned the gold, forming an amalgam. The riffles were cleaned and the amalgam was further processed into bullion, which was assayed and shipped to the mint. The dredge operated for eight years. Manhattan produced $10 million in gold over its 40-year run. Houston Minerals started up the process again in the late '70s after gold was set loose to find its own worth on the international market, and Round Mountain Gold continues to run a comparatively small operation.

Today, Manhattan is a big-city name for a tiny, though attractive, village in a lovely canyon in the lower Toquimas. Driving up on Route

377, you pass the Manhattan pit. Old head-frames overlook the pit from the hill above; the company production plant is behind the pit on the other side. Manhattan town is up the road, with abandoned shacks, old houses, big trees, and a couple of bars. **Miner's Saloon** has video poker, bar food such as polish sausage, collectibles such as rocks, bottles, and jewelry, and apple trees outside. **Manhattan Bar** is darker, more rustic. Around 60 people live in Manhattan year-round. Route 377 continues past the water tank near the top of the canyon. There the pavement ends, and you drive over to the east side of the Toquimas 12 miles to Belmont.

This is a fun road, full of ups and downs, twists and turns, 30 mph. At the first fork, bear left. At the second fork, go right to hook up to the main gravel road from the original right fork off Route 376 just north of Tonopah. In a few miles you come to pavement, pass the big stack from the Belmont-Monitor mill, then cruise into Belmont.

Belmont

Silver indications were uncovered high up on the sunrise side of the Toquimas in 1865, in the lee of big Mt. Jefferson. The site, blessed by wood, water, and stone, was so attractive that after several initial names for the site, Belmont, meaning Beautiful Mountain in French, stuck. The rush was so great that 2,000 people lived in and around Belmont within a year. The mines and mills began producing millions of dollars of silver, and the state Legislature decided to move the Nye County seat from Ione to Belmont in 1867.

The courthouse, however, remained in a rented storefront for 10 years until a two-story building was completed in 1876. Ironically, by then the Belmont boom was as good as dead; the $22,000 courthouse opened the same year that the mines produced $11,000 worth of silver. Belmont continued to decline until most of the last 150 people left were county administrative employees. In 1905 the seat moved to Tonopah.

Still, Belmont had produced $15 million in silver during its 15-year heyday. Some excitement returned in the early 1900s on the aural edge of the Tonopah noise, but it was short-lived. Fire,

vandals, ghost towners, and entropy took their toll for the next 60 years, until the state stepped in to stabilize the courthouse building and protect the town as a park. Belmont was also declared a National Historic District, which eliminated further scavenging.

Today, Belmont's restored beauty is reminiscent of Unionville's a couple of hundred miles northwest. Fewer than 10 residents are full-time. Old and new houses are full of character and surrounded by well-tended yards. The courthouse (tours available in the summer) presides over it all. The ruins, too, are picturesque, but be aware that tramping in, around, and through them is trespassing, and the locals are very protective about their town. In fact, the town's only paid employee is a caretaker (he'll no doubt check you out in his Jeep).

The **Belmont Saloon,** which has been called the Queen of Nye County Ghost Towns, has been owned by Las Vegas refugee Dick Ashton since 1979. It's open only on weekends. But you can get a good look through the front windows, at the bar, taken from the ruins of an 1880s hotel up the street, 1940s jukebox, denim bar-stool covers, sardine-can ashtrays, '50s refrigerator, potato-sack ceiling, and the infamous "jug mug" atop the 1905 cash register.

Continuing on the Monitor Valley road for 17 miles brings you to a sign for **Pine Creek Campground;** follow the sign to the left and drive another 2.5 miles to the USFS camp. There are 26 sites and no fee. Catch trout in the stream. This is also your entrance to the 38,000-acre **Alta Toquima Wilderness Area,** containing the three-peaked Mt. Jefferson, at 11,941 feet the sixth highest mountain in Nevada. The Pine Creek Trail travels just under 14 miles to the South Summit and the ridgeline that connects it to the Middle and North summits. See *Nevada Wilderness Areas* by Michael Rose for all the details.

THE TOQUIMAS AND MONITOR VALLEY

Just after you turn south onto Route 376 from US 50 a dozen miles east of Austin, a dirt road immediately heads off east (left) toward the

Toquima Range. The dirt starts out rough (30 mph and a lane and a half) and gets worse (15 mph and a lane). Roughly halfway across the valley, a left turn (distinct though unsignposted) leads up to Spencer Hot Springs.

Spencer Hot Springs

This is a fine spot—with the Toiyabes stretching into the background and the Monitors reaching into the foreground and the big desert valley spreading out at your feet—for a hot soak. These springs are not only quite civilized and not too far off the beaten track, but also expertly "developed." The big pool at the top ledge is sandbagged, tastefully tiled with slate, and offset by a little wooden deck. Toward the road a bit is a big galvanized tub. Hot water flows from a pipe. Put the pipe in the tub to regulate the temperature. Then lie back, breathe deeply, and offer up a prayer of thanks from your nerve endings.

COURTESY OF THE NEVADA COMMISSION ON TOURISM

ahh!

The Reese River

Back on US 50 west, you drop down out of Austin onto the **Reese River Valley** flats, heading toward the **Shoshone Range,** still in national forest. Here you cross the raging Reese River. This perfect description appears in David Toll's well-written *Complete Nevada Traveler:* "The Reese at floodtide has barely the breadth of a man's wrist and the depth of his fingers. Stagecoaches forded it at a full gallop with only the suggestion of a bump, and in the dry season the Reese is even less spectacular." This one is from Jim Andersen's affectionately funny article in *Nevada* magazine: "The Reese River is a river in the same sense that Stokes Castle is a castle; you have to use a little imagination."

Still, it was a well-known and surveyed river in the 1860s, and appeared on all the contemporary maps to flow confidently north from south of Austin in the Toiyabes to Battle Mountain and the Humboldt River. It provided a perfect apparition for starting up a paper business, calling it the Reese River Navigation Company, and selling phony stock in it to unsuspecting investors. Great joke.

Pony Express

Just beyond the Reese are markers for the Pony Express Trail. US 50 generally parallels the Pony Express Trail through central Nevada, but this stretch, between Austin and Carson City, is full of reminders of this 18-month adventure that helped open up the West.

Pony expresses had been known as mail and message relayers since the time of Genghis Khan (1203–27), who is generally credited with inventing the system: small jockeys riding flying ponies between stations every 25 miles or so. Several pony expresses were established on the East Coast to carry correspondence and news in the 1820s and '30s. But the idea for the express route from Missouri to California originated in the imagination of California Senator H. M. Gwin on a cross-country ride to Washington, D.C., in 1854. The tensions of pre–Civil War politics in the following years prevented the government from acting on Gwin's proposals, so he turned to the freighting firm of Russell,

Central Nevada

Majors, and Waddell, which ran the Overland Stage from St. Joseph, Missouri (western terminus of American railroads), to Salt Lake City. At Gwin's urging, the partners, against their better bottom-line judgment, accepted the challenge. Within two months they had recruited several division agents, built nearly 200 stations in the remote, barren, and dangerous 700-mile stretch between Salt Lake and Sacramento, bought 500 horses, and hired a score of riders. The first 10-day run from St. Joseph to Sacramento was completed on April 3, 1860.

The efficiency, bravery, endurance, and dedication of the employees are legendary. In Nevada, each rider completed a 33-mile route, with a fresh horse every 10 miles. Riders carried a pistol, a Bible, and the *mochila,* or padlocked mailbag. The stations, in Sir Richard Burton's eyewitness words, were "about as civilised as the Galway shanty—or the normal dwelling place in Central Equatorial Africa." Maintaining fresh horses, food, water, and security at the lonely stations was a continuous life and death struggle. Several riders and many stationmasters were killed on the warpath.

But the miracle of delivering mail from St. Jo to Sac in 10 days, the singlemindedness of the operation to open up the West (even in the face of the financial ruin of the company), and the romantic vision of the Pony riders stirred the collective imagination of the entire nation. That the Pony was logistically able to operate year-round proved that telegraphs and railroads could do the same, and prompted the government to invest in those evolving technologies. Ironically, completion of the transcontinental telegraph line along the Pony's route in October 1861 spelled its immediate demise: the incredible land-speed records set by Pony Express riders across the West were still no match for the miraculous dispatch of communications through the wire.

Modern-Day Pony

If US 50 is truly lonely on this stretch, try driving 10 mph for a ways to get a feel for the one-horse-power speed of the "XP" riders. From the Reese River Valley, you climb up to **Mt. Airy Summit** (6,679 feet) in the Shoshone Range, at the west-

ern edge of this part of the Toiyabe National Forest. Drop into **Smith Creek Valley,** then climb up to **New Pass Summit** (6,348 feet) in the **Desatoya Mountains.** Just before you reach the pass, you cross into Churchill County. Then you come to a historical sign and the New Pass Station ruins of the Overland Stage Company, from 1861.

You next come down to **Edward's Creek Valley,** with the salty sediments of a dry lake. Here US 50 turns southwest, following the valley's orientation, with the **Clan Alpine Mountains** similarly oriented ahead. A historical sign explains how Colonel John Reese discovered the route through this valley. Chevron gas and road maintenance stations are at **Middlegate.** Overland Stage Station and Pony Express trail markers keep you company. You cross the Clan Alpines, and arrive at the junction with Route 361, a shortcut via Gabbs down to US 95 at Luning.

This route takes you through the **Broken Hills;** halfway to Gabbs you leave Churchill County and drive a mere two miles, across the thin northeast beak of Mineral County. Beyond is the extreme northwest corner of Nye County, roughly 275 miles from Pahrump at its southeast corner. Twenty miles from US 50 you cross broad **Gabbs Valley** on the ruler-straight, well-paved, and fast road, aiming right at the big wall of the Paradise Range. Two miles before the town of **Gabbs** is a turnoff onto Route 844 to Berlin-Ichthyosaur, Ione, and the Reese River Valley road back to Austin.

Berlin-Ichthyosaur State Park

Route 844 heads straight at the Paradise Range, then up into it. You switch back and forth into the piñon and juniper forest, and reach **Green Springs Summit** (6,947 feet). From the top is a classic Great Basin view of Ione Valley and the Shoshone Mountains across it. Cross the valley and bear left at the sign (and the new pavement) to the Berlin-Ichthyosaur State Park, 23 miles east of Gabbs.

As you're driving up into the Shoshones toward the park, try to imagine what it might've looked like 200 million years ago, when this was all shallow ocean and giant sea lizards ran the show.

Berlin is one of the best-preserved ghost towns in Nevada and has been a state park since 1955. Its earlier history belongs to the Union Mining District, located in 1863 by prospectors from Austin, and which included Union, Ione, Downeyville, and Grantsville. Its later history belongs to the Tonopah excitement at the turn of the 20th century, when Nevada Mining Company built a large mill here that operated for nearly two decades. Berlin's post office closed in 1918.

The park office (775/964-2440) is in the former mine superintendent's home, where you can pick up a brochure with a good map; the office is open irregular hours. If it's closed up, just up the road from there is a signboard with a map of Berlin in 1905. Up the hill are the ruins of the assay office, stagecoach stop, machine shop, and the hoist building over the main mine shaft. Down the hill a trail passes the sites of bunkhouses, a union hall, and a saloon; still standing are homes, shops, and the infirmary. The trail continues out to the cemetery.

The biggest building in Berlin, down by the road, is one of the last original mills in Nevada (the roof has been braced). Check out the tongue-and-groove joints and wooden pegs holding the whole thing together. Four big steam engines on the floor powered 30 stamps, and you can easily imagine the deafening din of metal on rock. For all that, Berlin produced less than a million dollars worth of precious metals between 1900 and 1907.

Take Primitive Rd. up from Berlin and go right into the **campground,** which has 14 sites among the pines and junipers, running water, and good outhouses; campsites $12, plus $4 entrance fee. A trail from site number eight leads a half mile to the **fossil shelter,** or drive up to it on Primitive Road.

Ichthyosaurs (ICK-thee-oh-saurs) swam the oceans from 240 million to 90 million years ago; these ancient marine reptiles swam in a warm ocean which covered central Nevada 225 million years ago. Fossils of these giant marine creatures were first found in 1928, but the extensive excavations took place in 1954. The dig uncovered partial remains of 40 individual ichthyosaurs. Apparently these sea dragons became stuck in shallow water, were beached by waves, covered by silt and mud, hardened into fossils, uplifted by mountain building, exposed by erosion, and finally discovered by researchers. Fifty to 60 feet long, weighing in at 50–60 tons, with 10-foot heads, nine-foot ribs, eight-foot jaws, and one-foot eyes, these creatures were great predators and even tangled with the big nothosaurs, other giant prehistoric fish. It's believed that Nevada's ichthyosaurs were the world's largest, and today they're honored as the official state fossil.

Outside the shelter, a sculpted relief of their probable size and shape appears on a big concrete wall carved in 1957. If the shelter isn't open when you're there, descriptive signs and big picture windows provide a self-guided "tour" of the skeletal features of the creatures. Inside, you'll see the remains of nine ichthyosaurs that seem to have all died together and were left where they were found; the shelter was built around them. You have to use a little imagination to visualize their size and shape from the fossils. There's also a cabinet full of fossils, a geologic timetable, a fossil dig, and a mural on the late Triassic landscape.

Park rangers offer three interesting tours. The 45-minute Fossil Tour is the only one offered all year round. From Memorial Day to Labor Day it is offered daily at 10 A.M., 2 P.M. and 4 P.M. From mid-March to Memorial Day, and from Labor Day until mid-November, this tour is offered Saturday and Sunday at 10 A.M. and 2 P.M. The rest of the year (mid-November to mid-March) the tour is offered by advance reservation only. Cost is $3 adults, $2 ages 6–12.

The 90-minute Berlin Town Site Tour is offered Memorial Day through Labor day, Saturday and Sunday at 3 P.M. The price is $3 adults, $2 for kids. The 60-minute Mine Tour is offered from May to September, Friday, Saturday and Sunday at 11 A.M. Cost is $3 for adults and $2 for kids.

The park is always open, 365 days a year. Travel may be impeded, however, by extreme winter weather.

Ione

Back down in Ione Valley, take a right (north) at the fork, site of Grantsville. In six miles is another fork: 29 miles to the left is US 50 at Eastgate, one mile to the right is the surprising town of Ione (pronounced EYE-own), founded in 1863. The mineral discoveries here catalyzed the creation of vast Nye County, and Ione had a brief moment in the sun as county seat, until Belmont took over in 1867. The nearby mines produced a million in gold and some mercury before *borrasca* in 1880. Revivals over the years lent a certain semi-ghost vitality to Ione.

A major resumption of gold mining in 1983 turned Ione into something of a showpiece. Though the half-subterranean log cabins with dead sod roofs predominate, the old schoolhouse was beautifully refinished into a general store, with wood shelving and cabinets and tasteful old lamps. Up the street the old post office was also renovated for use as the field office of Marshall Earth Resources, Inc. (MERI). Across the street is the town park. With its stone picnic tables, old London street lamps, scalloped concrete benches, white picket fence, trees from the 1860s, and swings and slides, this is an idyllic place for a picnic.

The **Ore House Saloon** (775/964-2003), built in 1864, provides refreshments to miners and tourists alike; ask here about renting a trailer overnight ($35, Ione's version of hotel accommodation), or overnight RV spots ($8). The saloon is fronted by another of Nevada's famous Unknown Prospector die-cuts. Pick up a *Historic Guide & Map* brochure, guiding you to Ione's historic buildings and explaining how Ione got its nickname of "The Town that Refused to Die."

Ione is famous throughout central Nevada for hosting a big blowout bash, **Ione Days,** every Labor Day weekend. Down-home rip-roarin' events include a greased pole climb, greased pig chase, horseshoe tournament, mud wrestling, shotgun shootout, turkey shoot, barbecue, Sunday pancake breakfast, live music and more; 775/964-2003 for info. The six criblike structures along Main St. are the remnants of retail booths from past Ione Days.

Continue through Ione Canyon across the Shoshones down into green Reese River Valley. Keep left (north) at the forks on this 35-mph dirt road. **Yomba** is a tiny Indian settlement and Forest Service district station. The valley is fairly well settled with ranches along the Reese River. The Toiyabes run straight and strong on the far east end, while the Shoshones chaperone the road on the near west end. Eleven miles south of US 50 you reach pavement-feels good. In an-

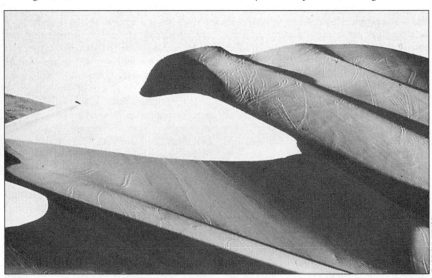

Listen for the vibration of sand crystals on this mountain, not to be confused with a bass guitar.

© JOE CUMMINGS

Central Nevada

other few miles is Route 722, the US 50 bypass; left goes 50 lonely miles to Eastgate, right heads eight miles back to Austin.

SAND MOUNTAIN

Back on US 50 at the junction of Route 361 to Gabbs, you continue west down into Fairview Valley, with Chalk Mountain on the north and Fairview Peak on the south. Pass under the *bajada* of Fairview Peak; a few miles east and south is the Naval Air Station Bombing Range, one of many around Fallon. You next pass between the Sand Spring Range on the south and Stillwater Mountains on the north, and drop down onto Fourmile Flat with the Bunejug Mountains to the south. See if you can pick out the site of an old salt mine from the 1870s on the flat.

Sand Mountain is known as a "seif" dune, for its sword shape. It's one of only a handful of dunes in the country that make a deep booming sound created by the vibration of crystals as the sands cascade down the slopes. The one-note bass guitar effect (50–100 hertz) is not to be confused, however, with dunes that make more common singing, ringing, squeaking, whistling, barking, and even roaring tones. This discontinuous deep rumble seems to hum most predictably on the hottest and driest summer evenings.

But even if you don't hear the dune, the one-hour steep round-trip hike provides an intense focusing of your auditory faculties. Concentrating on sound, you'll hear a faint "booming"—which turns out in a moment to be a fly buzzing by. Another "boom" starts from afar, and increases steadily in vibration, getting louder and louder, until. . . a helicopter appears over the hillside. If you listen very hard, you can almost hear the Navy jets taking off from the Air Station at Fallon 15 miles west. Clomping downhill, you think you hear a boom, like the sound of a rock plopping into deep water, but it turns out to be your heels landing hard on the sand.

If it's windy, which is often, the top of Sand Mountain is a tenuous place to be, but an amazing sight to see. Swirls of sand dance across the surface like gossamer presences, taking the shape of the wind. Long streams of grains rise from the ridge like smoke signals. Whole sections blow in a great uniform flow over the ridge and disappear. After such a show, you won't wonder how the dune was formed.

On the weekends, Sand Mountain gets crowded with off-road vehicles, from putt-putt four-wheelers to big buggies, sputtering up and down the dune like so many revved-up beetles. Someone might be renting rides if you're inspired to give it a whirl. Other people bring wide downhill skis, hitch a lift to the top, and slide straight down the coarse course. (Trying to turn immediately and dramatically slows the progress.) These sand skiers appreciate the absence of such impedimentia as trees, lift tickets and lines, ice, and variable conditions. Between the booming, the buggying, and the boarding, Sand Mountain is an entire recreational facility unto itself.

And there's more. A turn off the access road leads a half mile into **Sand Springs Desert Study Area,** a square mile totally enclosed by a fence (foot traffic only). Here you follow a couple of dozen guideposts along a trail, with 10 or so signposts describing different features of the desert: lizards, playa lakes, hand-dug wells, albino scorpions, scavenger scarabs, etc. The centerpiece of the stroll is the big Pony Express stationhouse ruins, buried in sand after its abandonment as a telegraph office in the 1870s, then rediscovered 100 years later by archaeologists. They excavated it and took the artifacts, but left the volcanic rock walls. Signs show the layout of and describe life at the station, where the food was gritty and the water so alkaline that the men had to add vinegar to drink it. A sign-in book is worth reading for the comments. Contact the BLM, 775/885-6000, for information.

Fallon

Natives from the prehistoric to the Paiute made gentle use of the Stillwater marsh for thousands of years before the mass western migration of Easterners in the 1840s and 1850s. At that time and for centuries previously, the lives of the Toidikadi (Cattail Eaters) band of Northern Paiute centered on the bountiful marsh, both for their physical needs—food, clothing, and building materials—and spirituality, which focused on the migratory cycles of the waterfowl.

Most of the emigrants, however, bypassed these wetlands on a delirious dash from Lovelock's Big Meadows to the Carson River, one valley west. The small station of Leeteville marked the end of this treacherous stretch of the Emigrant Trail, known as the 40-Mile Desert. Several miles west of present-day Fallon, Leeteville was more commonly known as Ragtown, either for the discarded mattresses and household goods strewn around the area or for the ragged clothes washed in the Carson River and laid out on the banks to dry. The Pony Express and Overland Stage also rode right through Ragtown.

Churchill County was created by the first territorial legislature in 1861, but the county seat changed towns twice before settling in the small farming community of Stillwater in 1867. Some mining (mostly soda and salt), some supply freighting (along a route between Virginia City/Carson City and Austin), and a little ranching ushered the county into the 20th century.

Reclamation

The area's early ranchers dug their own irrigation ditches, sometimes for miles, always by hand, from the Carson River to their homesteads. Enter Francis Newlands, a Nevada representative to Congress at the turn of the century and son-in-law of Comstock King William Sharon, himself once a senator. Newlands had water on the brain. The driving force behind the Reclamation Act of 1902, which created the United States Reclamation Service, Newlands

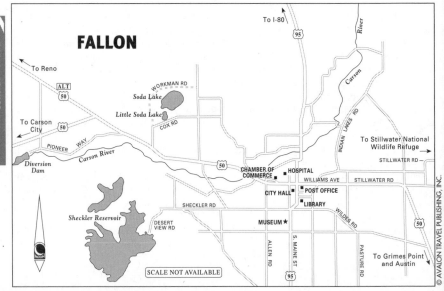

© AVALON TRAVEL PUBLISHING, INC.

made sure that the government's first reclamation project was an irrigation district in western Nevada, using water from the Carson and Truckee rivers. Workers began building the Derby Dam and digging the Truckee Canal in June 1903 to divert Truckee River water from nearly 32 miles southeast into the Carson River, and from there to the farms of the irrigation district.

Fallon was founded on pre-reclamation ranch land originally owned by Mike Fallon; he sold out to Warren William, a state senator who platted the town site, named Maine Street after his home state, started work on a courthouse, and then persuaded the Legislature to move the Churchill County seat there from Stillwater.

The Reclamation engineers grossly underestimated the amount of water needed to irrigate the planned 400,000 acres, and the agricultural project nearly died of thirst over the first 10 years. To rectify the situation, Lahontan Dam, built on the Carson between 1911 and 1915, impounded enough water to irrigate roughly 75,000 acres.

Cantaloupes and Fighter Pilots

Even with a reliable supply of water, the alkaline soil of Carson Sink had to be fertilized for years before profitable crops could be counted on. Beets failed. Heart O' Gold cantaloupes proved more successful, even enjoying a national reputation for 15 years. Turkeys, likewise, were briefly popular. But alfalfa endured as the major crop, and in a normal water year 30,000 acres of stock feed produce nearly 150,000 tons. Garlic, some vegetables and grains, and some Heart O' Gold cantaloupes are also grown. (Even as the number of melons grown in the vicinity drops, the number of people who attend the annual Hearts O' Gold Cantaloupe Festival grows. The Labor Day weekend event at the Churchill County Fairgrounds draws more than 20,000.)

The arrival of a small airfield in 1942 boosted the local economy. It closed after the war, reopened during the U.S. intervention in Korea, and now aircraft carrier-based-pilots are trained here. The Navy Fighter Weapons School, more popularly known as "Top Gun," moved to the airbase in 1996 from Miramar, California.

Describing Fallon as a land of extremes is, on the one hand, the worst cliche in travel writing. On the other hand, it's more true of Fallon than probably any other place in Nevada. Lush green fields in the middle of the dry beige desert are the most obvious contrast. The water itself actually becomes an attraction, and you can fill up an unusual day on a desert quest for the aquatic—at Stillwater Refuge, Sheckler Reservoir, Soda Lakes, and elsewhere. The marshlife—fish, birds, insects, reeds, and grasses—and the delicate natural balance of the fragile habitat stand in stark contrast to the mechanized reclamation process—dams, canals, ditches, and laterals.

The Navy (and Coast Guard) presence in the middle of the Great Basin Desert is an additional incongruity for Fallon, especially noticeable at Grimes Point petroglyph park, across the road from which the sleek bombers practice short take-offs and landings. But natural or unnatural, Fallon for almost 100 years has claimed, and rightly so, the title "Oasis of Nevada."

SIGHTS

Watching Top Gun pilots or viewing ancient petroglyphs—you can do both in Fallon.

Churchill County Museum and Archives

One of the state's top museums, this is a delightful surprise to stumble upon, at 1050 S. Maine, 775/423-3677, www.ccmuseum.org, open March–Nov. Mon.–Sat. 10 A.M.–5 P.M., (noon–5 P.M. on Sunday). December through February the museum closes at 4 P.M. Admission is free, but leave a donation in the box. In 1968, Alex and Margaret Oser, southern California philanthropists who owned land in Churchill County, bought an old Safeway building to donate to the county for the museum. Today the huge building is packed with fascinating exhibits; it'll keep you occupied an entire morning or afternoon.

A relief map near the entrance has push-button lights that locate the sights-mountain ranges, towns, Pony route, local attractions. Then check out the Audichron Company's time and temperature machine, known as "Molly." One of the highlights is the Paiute exhibits, with baskets, tule weavings, duck decoys, spears and points, moccasins and belts, and a huge tule desert shelter. Then spend some time reading all about the Hidden Cave excavation. The usual pioneer kitchen and bedroom are augmented by an unusual rumpus room with player pianos, organs, marxophone, Victor talking machine, and an old Kodak portrait camera. And the parlor has a library attached with a big vault door built in. Large glass cases contain ducks, minerals, guns, old cameras, dolls, china, purple glass and bottles, beautiful petrified wood, and leather postcards, to name just a few. One whole room in the back is occupied with quilts, one has a replica western schoolroom (check out the mounting instructions for the 1870s bike!), and another is full of old bank safes and vaults. Historical photos (for sale) tell the stories of settling the town, building the dams, and farming the land.

A gift shop sells a large stock of books, postcards, and gift items. The museum also sponsors tours of Hidden Cave, which originate at the museum; sign-ups start at 9:30 A.M. on the second and fourth Saturday of each month. Groups are limited to 30 people, and start at 10 A.M. It's a half-mile hike from the parking area to the cave. The price is unbeatable: the tours are free. For more info, call the museum. The museum also hosts a Time Portal program on the first and third Saturday during which visitors can learn to make crafts from the 1800s (a $1 charge covers materials, and drop-ins are welcome).

Naval Air Station and Sheckler Reservoir

Take either Maine or South Taylor streets for about five miles down US 95 until you see the sign for the Naval Air Station to the left on Union Lane. Go another few miles on Union till you get to the south gate. Then you can take a right on Pasture Rd. and a left on Berney Rd., or just a left on Pasture Rd., to view the runways on the other side of the high cyclone fence. Watching the planes taking off is the whole excitement *outside* the fence.

The Top Gun air combat school arrived in May 1996 from Miramar. Twenty-five pilot trainers are stationed at the base year-round. Ten trainees at a time are assigned to the school for 10-week flight and air-combat classes offered four times a year. F-18 Hornets and F-14 Tomcats can sometimes be seen engaging each other in mock dogfights over the Navy training area east of the Stillwater Range. Military operations are rehearsed here. Why here? One of the reasons is a climate where perfect weather prevails more than 300 days a year.

Scheckler Reservoir, with the **Dead Camel Mountains** in the background, makes another fine outing. Sandy tracks run right around the reservoir. A map is available at the Chamber of Commerce.

Grimes Point and Hidden Cave

Petroglyphs had a religious significance far beyond what we might think of today as doodling on rocks. The carving was a ritual performed by a shaman before a hunt, an event, or a life passage. The artwork at this site is considered to have been carved sometime between 5000 B.C. and A.D. 1500.

At Grimes Point you'll see one of Fallon's remarkable contrasts. You walk along a trail (just under a mile, with eight signposts), viewing with short eyes these scratches in rocks made by ancient people, while at the same time your long eyes are looking over at the airbase, with the cutting edge of technology roaring down the runway, taking off, and circling over your head in formation, one group right on the heels of the other. This prehistoric rock art site, one of the largest and most accessible petroglyph collections in northern Nevada, contains about 150 basalt boulders covered with carvings.

Two types of petroglyphs are visible along the trail: primitive Pit and Groove formations, created by striking the boulders heavily with a sharp stone; and Great Basin Pecked, which used flat stones to sand the shapes into the rock. You've also got your two styles, curvilinear and rectilinear, fancy names for lazy eights and stick figures. Some of the artwork's symbolism is obvious, a lot of suns, snakes, and people. But you'll also see pictographs that represent mushrooms, tic-tac-toe games, the Great

Lahontan butterfly, menorahs, spermatozoa, treble clefs, and even the Great Prophet foretelling the arrival of streamlined hook-and-ladder fire trucks. By the end of the trail, you'll be enough of a petroglyph expert to invent your own theories about their shapes, meanings, ages, and "scientific" descriptions.

Two signs for Hidden Cave are at or near the trailhead to Grimes Point. But once you start heading in the direction they point you to, the signs stop, sandy roads fork off every which way, and you're lost in the desert. Could be why they call it Hidden Cave. (The BLM has installed a information kiosk at the trailhead parking lot for Grimes Point and Hidden Cave. Signs along the trails are supposed to make it harder to get lost.) One alternative: sign up at the museum for the free guided tours every other Saturday. On the tour, you drive your own car to the cave site (about 15 miles), and hike a half mile in. A guide leads the group (maximum 30 people) around the loop of three caves, pointing out local petroglyphs, tufa, and obsidian. Signs mark the cave's features, some of the tools used for excavation, and the distinct pungence of bat guano. The tour takes two hours door to door. Congregate at 9:30 A.M. at the museum, leave at 10, and be back by noon.

Soda Lakes and Carson Dam

Heading west on US 50, take a right on Lucas Road, and follow it north, then around to the east where it meets Cox Road. Just before Cox turns north again, take a left onto a wide unmarked gravel road. Go up and over the hill, then down to Soda and Little Soda lakes. Unexpected islands of blue in a sea of beige, these lakes occupy the craters of basalt cones about 3,000 years old. They're fed by an underground tributary of the Carson River; after the dams and ditches were constructed, the lakes' water levels rose hundreds of feet. Before that, soda mined from the lakes supplied the Comstock mills, and won a gold ribbon at the Philadelphia Centennial Exposition in 1876. The rising water not only diluted the soda, but also drowned the mine and mill. Today divers and boaters use the lakes as recreational sites.

Continuing west on US 50, you can take a left onto Pioneer Way at Ragtown Station Sa-

loon. From here a back road (mostly paved) runs along the Carson, between big trees and fields of green. At the fork in the road, if you take a left, in about a quarter-mile you arrive at **Carson Diversion Dam,** where you could have a picnic if you brought any food. It's worth the five-minute detour even if you didn't. Then return to the fork, take a left, and climb up to US 50. Beautiful view on the way up. Or if you're coming in on US 50, turn off at the sign for the Carson River Diversion Dam and drive down a few hundred yards for the view—desert in the foreground, green alfalfa behind, the river behind that, and the mountains in the background.

Livestock Auctions

Every Wednesday starting at 10:45 A.M. at **Gallagher's Livestock,** 1025 Allen Rd., 775/423-2174, there's an event which, if you happen to be in Fallon or vicinity, it's worth stopping off to see. This livestock auction is one of the liveliest and largest in the West. They start with small animals, such as calves, pigs, and sheep, then move up to butcher cows, cattle, and horses starting at 1 P.M. and finishing sometimes well after dark. The auction takes place one block off West Williams behind Stillwater Plaza at the west end of town.

Top Gun Raceway

The Top Gun Raceway Motor Sports Complex continues to draw overflow crowds of spectators to the drag races from March through November. The 2,500-seat complex, owned and operated by Motor Sports Safety Inc., is located 15 miles east of Fallon on US 95. The track has state-of-the-art staging and timing equipment, lights for night racing, and a concession stand. For more info, call 775/423-0223 or 800/325-7448. The Rattlesnake Raceway, 775/423-7483, at Rattlesnake Hill one mile east of town on Rio Vista Drive, is also going strong. The stockcar dirt track is operated by the Lahontan Auto Racing Association. Saturday evening races start at 7 P.M.

Fallon Air Show

FAS is the town's contribution to northern Nevada's "Aerial Triple Crown," along with the Great Reno Balloon Race and Reno's National

Championship Air Races. The spring event, which draws 50,000 annually, takes place at the Naval Air Station. The show features the Blue Angels, the USAF's world-famous precision jet team. The show and parking are free. The date of the event varies; call the county Chamber of Commerce at 775/423-2544, www.fallonchamber.com, for dates and info.

Stillwater National Wildlife Refuge

After a long reclamation and conservation effort, Stillwater is one of the most productive refuges in the country. In a good year, 80,000 shorebirds—pelicans, but to the 12,000 swans, several thousand pintails, canvasbacks, teals, and other ducks, the large colony of nesting white-faced ibises, plus 161 other species—will rest and nest in this area, which is also a National Hemispheric Shorebird reserve. There are 50–100 native occupation sites, dating back more than 5,000 years. For further information, contact the Stillwater National Wildlife Refuge Headquarters, 1000 Auction Rd., Fallon, 775/423-5128.

Lahontan State Recreation Area

Drive nine miles west from Fallon to the cutoff of the Carson Hwy. (main US 50) toward Carson City; in another eight miles is the entrance to the Lahontan State Recreation Area. A wide gravel road runs down and across the Carson River to the ranger station at the entrance, where you pay $4 per vehicle for day use, $8 with a boat, $10 per vehicle for camping, or $14 for camping with a boat. Follow the road around to the junction and take a right to get to the day-use picnic area and beach right at the south side of the Lahontan Dam.

Lahontan boasts 25 picnic, camping, and swimming beaches at three different locations. From this part of the reservoir, you follow the gravel shore road southwest past 10 separate beaches; number seven has wheelchair access. There are 40 campsites for tents of self-contained RVs up to 30 feet long, along with piped water, flush toilets, showers, picnic tables, grills, and fire pits. No reservations are accepted, and sites are $10 a night. For information, contact Park Headquarters, 16799 Lahontan Dam, Fallon,

NV 89406, 775/867-3500. Or contact the park's Silver Springs Ranger Station, 775/577-2226.

ENTERTAINMENT

The **Depot** has mostly nickel keno and poker slots, plus a blackjack table or two. **Stockman's** has a big dance floor and stage, large-screen TV, and rock videos. A band plays Top 40 six nights a week. On Saturday at least eight blackjack tables and a crap table operate, and the crowds can be magnificent. At the same time, the **Nugget**, right at the big corner downtown, has the military men hovering around lots of tables and tons of slots. Dancing to sides spun by the DJ is not unlike a contact sport. Here, the rough-and-ready Seabees and flyboys provide another Fallon-type contrast to the sedate family-oriented farm town.

ACCOMMODATIONS

More than a dozen motels give Fallon a total of 559 rooms, which can be hard to come by on weekends year-round or every night in the summer. Several are strung along US 50 (Williams St.) west of town, with one to the east. A couple are on US 95 (Taylor St.) north of town, with one south.

Holiday Inn Express, 55 Commercial St., 775/428-2588 or 800/HOLIDAY. All 59 rooms ($69–129) come with a continental breakfast, and it has indoor and outdoor pools, sauna, whirlpool tub, and other amenities.

The **Bonanza Inn & Casino,** 855 W. Williams, 775/423-6031, is the main action in the center of town, with 75 rooms at $40–50. Other Fallon **motels** include the Best Western/Fallon Inn, 1035 W. Williams Ave., 775/423-6005 or 888/466-6005, $55–98; Overland Hotel, 125 E. Center St., 775/423-2719, $21 nightly or $75–85 per week; Fallon Motel, 390 W. Williams, 775/423-4648, $32–80; **Lariat,** 850 W. Williams, 775/423-3181, $39–60; **Value Inn,** 180 W. Williams, 775/423-5151, $35–65; Microtel Inn, 1051 W. Williams, 775/428-0300 or 888/771-7171, $45–95; **Comfort Inn,** 1830 W. Williams, 775/423-5554, $56–119; Motel 6, 1705 Taylor St., 775/423-2277 or 800/4-MOTEL6, $40–75; Oxbow Motor Inn, 60 S.

Allen Rd., 775/423-7021, $42–65; Western Motel, 125 S. Carson St., 775/423-5118, $39–61; and **EconoLodge,** 70 E. Williams, 775/423-2194 or 800/553-2666, $68–149.

Fallon also has the historic **1906 House B&B,** 10 S. Carson St., 775/428-1906, www.geocities.com/Eureka/1219. It's a lovely Queen Anne Victorian house with turret and wrap-around porch, furnished with all Victorian period furnishings. When the owners bought the house, they were told it had been built in 1906, hence the B&Bs name; it was only later that they found out the house was actually built in 1904. It has two guest rooms, sharing one bath; prices are $65 per room, including full breakfast.

Hub Totel RV Park, 4800 US 50, 775/867-3636, is right on the main drag four miles west of Fallon. Hub Totel isn't a play on Tub Hotel, by the way; the "Hub" refers to wheels and "Totel" is a contraction of Towing Motel. There are 44 spaces for motor homes, all with full hookups, all pull-throughs. Tents are allowed. Laundry and rec room are available. The fees are $12 for tent sites and $23 for RVs. Good Sam discounts available.

There's also the **Fallon RV Park,** 5787 US 50, 775/867-2332. Of the two Pepsi-Coke RV parks west of Fallon on US 50, this is the nicer. The trees are larger, the grass is greener, and the spaces are wider. But it costs a couple of dollars more. There are 44 spaces for motor homes, all with full hookups; 20 pull-throughs. Tents are allowed. Tent sites are $12; RV spaces cost $23.

Other RV parks include the **Bonanza Inn RV Park,** 855 W. Williams, 775/423-6031, which has 20 sites, and the **Cold Springs RV Park,** 523 US 50, 775/423-1233, with 10 spaces for $12 on weeknights and $15 Fri.–Sat. The nearest state park camping is at Lahontan State Recreation Area.

FOOD

The **Depot Casino,** 875 W. Williams, 775/423-3233, serves good homestyle cooking at its 24-hour **Depot Diner. Stockman's Casino,** 1560 W. Williams, 775/423-2117, also has a **24-hour coffee shop** with daily specials for the hearty appetite, plus the more up-market **Angelica's** for fine dining. At the **Nugget,** 475 W. Williams,

775/423-3111, **Aniceta's** is another place for homestyle cooking.

La Cocina, downtown at 125 S. Maine, 775/423-6166, is open Mon.–Fri. 11 A.M.–9 P.M., Sat. and Sun. noon–9 P.M. The place is friendly and serves what may be the numero-uno-supremo tostada in Nevada, if not the solar system. Order sour cream, guacamole, peppers, and meat to add in, and unless two of you are very hungry and sharing the small tostada, you might as well ask for a take-out container right up front. The basic tostada is $4.25 ($5.25 with meat). The large one runs $9, but you no longer get a T-shirt if you finish one by yourself. On the Mexican side of the menu lunch runs $4–5, while dinner ranges from $6–10. La Cocina is vegetarian-friendly: There is absolutely no meat or lard in the rice and beans.

The **Waterhole,** 111 S. Allen Rd. behind the Stillwater Plaza, 775/423-3051, offers Western-style dining, with steaks, seafood, and Mexican dishes. It's open weekdays 11 A.M.–2 P.M. and 5–10 P.M. (closed Tues.), Sat. and Sun. 5–10 P.M.

The **Golden Rice Bowl,** 1760 W. Williams, 775/423-7078, is a popular Chinese restaurant open every day 11 A.M.–9:30 P.M. Next door, the **Pizza Hut,** 1770 W. Williams, 775/423-1123, is open 11 A.M.–11 P.M. daily, Fridays and Saturdays until midnight. For Italian, there Armando's, 310 S. Maine, 775/428-1198.

INFORMATION AND SERVICES

The **Churchill County Chamber of Commerce,** 100 Campus Way, is off Auction Rd. (off US 50) up by the tracks, 775/423-2544, www.fallonchamber.com, open Mon.–Fri. 9 A.M.–5 P.M. You can pick up a good map of Fallon and vicinity here, and collect the latest accommodations chart.

The **Churchill County Library,** 553 S. Maine, 775/423-7581, is open Mon., Thurs., and Fri. 9 A.M.–6 P.M., Tues.–Wed. 9 A.M.–8 P.M., and Sat. 9 A.M.–5 P.M. Its Nevada room overflows with interesting books and reports. A used bookstore is next door.

Churchill Community Hospital, 801 E. Williams, 775/423-3151, has a 24-hour emergency room.

Hawthorne

In 1881, the Carson and Colorado Railroad, managed by H. M. Yerington, chose a spot near Walker Lake's southern tip to serve as its freighting station for nearby mines and boomtowns. In doing so, Yerington deliberately snubbed a town 57 miles northwest, which had recently renamed itself Yerington to flatter the manager into locating the station there. Possibly as a practical joke against the town of Yerington, which until the renaming had been called Pizen Switch, the new town was named after an assistant manager of the railroad, W. A. Hawthorne. Once the railroad had been installed, the town layout was modeled after Sacramento's. Lots were sold at an auction for $100 apiece.

Hawthorne's fortunes were directly proportional to the boom-bust cycles of the railroad, mines, and county politics. Aurora had been in decline for a decade and Hawthorne replaced it as Esmeralda County seat in 1883, only to lose it 20 years later to booming Goldfield. But it regained the seat when Mineral County was cleaved off Esmeralda in 1911. The Southern Pacific took over the Carson and Colorado in 1904, and its new track bypassed Hawthorne by seven miles. Possibly in another joke, the new station was named Thorne. A fire in 1926 nearly finished off the town, leaving fewer than 200 residents. But in a strange quirk of fate, the Naval Ammunition Depot in Lake Denmark, New Jersey, also went up in flames that same year, necessitating its relocation from the major East Coast population center to some remote location in the West. Thanks in large part to the tireless efforts of Nevada Senator Tasker Oddie, Hawthorne was selected as the site.

Subsequently, Hawthorne's fortunes rose and fell with the country's war involvements. During WW II, the barracks town of Babbitt was built to accommodate the sixfold increase in population; after the war, the population dropped and Babbitt became a plywood ghost town. (Today, no more buildings are left in Babbitt.) US 95 ensured a steady flow of traffic, and in the '70s and '80s Hawthorne expanded its travelers' services: casinos, lodging, restaurants, and Walker Lake recreational opportunities.

SIGHTS

Hawthorne is completely surrounded by thousands of thick concrete bunkers and pillboxes. Like sand creatures out of Frank Herbert's *Dune,* these magazines take the shapes of whitehead-like pyramids, stubby worm segments, camouflaged caterpillars, and long gray slugs. They're filled with bullets, bombs, grenades, mortars, mines, depth charges, missiles, and other conventional ammunition and ordnance, steadied and readied for when the Army calls. Ironically, this depot of death and destruction has for the last 65 years stabilized Hawthorne's previously precarious existence; the very same arsenal that moment by moment could conceivably wipe Hawthorne off the face of the Earth finally put it on the map for good.

Hawthorne is just a short drive from a number of attractive places, including Walker Lake, mentioned above. It's also a short drive from the eastern gateway to Yosemite, the historic ghost town of Bodie, and Mono Lake, across the border in California. Lovely desert mountains surround the town, and the nighttime skies are alive with stars. The town's memorial rose garden features many rows of roses landscaped with paths, benches to rest on, and a babbling fountain. The views from the top of Lucky Boy Pass are spectacular, spanning 50 miles from north to south and showing the unique beauty of a desert lake.

Mineral County Museum

If you happen to be passing through at the right time on the right days, be sure to stop in at the Mineral County Museum. This is a big barn of a building, with numerous interesting historical displays. First check out the big painting of Hawthorne's history commissioned for the country's bicentennial: everything from Cecil the Serpent to chromate-green bombs. Also for the bicentennial, the townspeople created a quilt now on display. The post office exhibit displays a letter from 1883 with a two-cent stamp, and a letter addressed to H. M. Yerington, the big cheese around here in the early years. The locksmith exhibit has keys from the Gold Hill Jail. There's an apothecary exhibit from Golden Key Drugs. There's lots of mining equipment, including a three-piston stamp-mill crusher, and lots of stories, including how the collection of Spanish-mission bells was discovered. Recommended.

The museum is at 10th and D Sts., on the right just as you enter town from the north, 775/945-5142. From April to November the museum is open Tues.–Sat. 11 A.M.–5 P.M.; in winter, from December to March, it's open Tues.–Sat. noon–4 P.M. Admission is free; donations are welcome.

Hawthorne Ordnance Museum

The newest attraction in town is the Hawthorne Ordnance Museum, which highlights what was manufactured over the years at the Army Ammunition Plant. The museum showcases a few big guns, but it's mostly torpedoes and other now-nonexplosive pieces of military history. The museum, 925 E St., 775/945-5400, is open Mon.–Fri. 10 A.M.–5 P.M. and Sat. 10 A.M.–2 P.M.

Walker Lake

Thirty miles long and three to eight miles wide, this pristine high-desert limnological lodestar is actually just a piddling pond left over from ancient Lake Lahontan, which once covered 8,400 square miles of western Nevada and eastern California; Pyramid Lake, 100 miles north, is the other remnant. In addition, the health of Walker Lake is in serious jeopardy these days, experiencing problems similar to, though worse than, Pyramid Lake. Still, this is deep-blue relief for eyes accustomed to the beige basins and gray ranges that surround it for scores of miles. And it's been a welcome sight since the earliest explorations. While seeking the mythical San Buenaventura River, which was widely assumed to run through the vast western desert to the sea, both Jedediah Smith and Peter Skene Ogden came across the lake in the late 1820s. The lake's namesake, Joseph Walker—a surveyor with John Frémont's expedition—himself stumbled upon the lake, dying of thirst, in 1833.

Farmers around Bridgeport and in Antelope Valley (43,000 cultivated acres), in Smith and Mason Valleys (80,000 acres), and on the Walker River Paiute Reservation (2,100 acres) divert

COURTESY OF THE NEVADA COMMISSION ON TOURISM

Central Nevada

waterskiing in the desert at Walker Lake

the river water for agriculture. Walker River carries an average of 406,000 acre-feet, of which the farmers along the way are entitled to 200,000. It's estimated that riverbank trees and other flora drink up another 103,000; that leaves 103,000 acre-feet for the lake. But Walker Lake loses 136,000 acre-feet, or 3.7 feet in elevation, every year to evaporation alone. As the lake level drops, dissolved solids, such as minerals and salts, become more concentrated and kill off the microscopic zooplankton that feed the fish, and algae increase, depriving the lake of oxygen. The Walker Lake Working Group (WLWG) is trying to get everyone to conserve water to ensure that Walker Lake survives.

Aurora

Gold was discovered in the midst of these stray volcanic peaks (the Brawleys) just east of the southern Wassuks in 1861, several years before the California-Nevada border here had been clarified. Both territories claimed the rich mining town, and both established county seats and municipal administrations, on each side of town. In 1864, when the new state was surveyed, Aurora was placed inside Nevada, and the Mono County offices had to move to Bodie, the notorious camp next door.

Sam Clemens stopped off at Aurora to try his luck, suffered a series of setbacks, and consoled himself by submitting freelance correspondence to the *Territorial Enterprise*. At his darkest moment, a letter arrived from Virginia City, offering him a job as the newspaper's city editor for a princely $25 a week. There Sam Clemens became Mark Twain.

Aurora rivaled Virginia City in size and population just before statehood, but the former's heat was about to dissipate, while the latter's was just warming up. Aurora produced more than $20 million in gold in roughly seven years, till *borrasca*. But it kept hanging on; the WPA guide reported in 1940 that "Aurora shows signs of coming to life, maintaining a remarkable resistance to complete abandonment." Until right after the war, that is, when a contractor from Southern California dismantled the deserted brick buildings. Scavengers grabbed the rest.

To get there from Hawthorne, continue straight on Main Street (Route 359) at the intersection where US 95 turns left. This is the highway around the eastern slope of the Wassuks on **Whiskey Flat** and through a small saddle in the **Anchorite Hills** to California and Mono Lake. You'll see a turnoff on a gravel road to **Lucky Boy Pass,** up to which you start climbing immediately. Dow Corning ran a silicate mine up here, and you might find it hard to imagine big semis full of minerals barreling down off this grade. Finally you come to the pass at 8,000 feet elevation, where you can see for miles into the East Walker River Valley. From there, you head down to the Aurora Crater and around to Aurora town site. Little remains.

RECREATION

The north quarter of Walker Lake is owned by the Walker River Paiute, the middle half by BLM, and the south quarter by the Army Ammunition plant. Speed-boat races, fishing and derbies, water-skiing, swimming, and camping are the main sports on the lake.

Sportsman's Beach is 15 miles north of Hawthorne, along the west shore below US 95; 17 sites, outhouses, tables, and shelters, free. **Walker Lake State Recreation Area,** 775/867-3001, is two miles south at **Tamarack Point.** It has 12 picnic sites, outhouses, and the lake's only boat ramp.

Best **fishing** for the two- to three-pound cutthroat trout stocked in the lake is in March and April. Fishing derby prize-winners are generally four to six pounds. Like many lakes, Walker is no exception when it comes to giant serpents. Cecil is the 80-foot-long monster that hides in the lake's ancient depths. Although he's less than benign in Paiute legends, to the children of Hawthorne, Cecil is friendly and is always well represented in local parades.

Loons visit Walker Lake twice a year. Roughly 700 in April and 1,000 in October drop in to eat and mate on their migrations. The Nevada Division of Wildlife conducts **loon tours,** boat trips out onto the lake to see and hear the loons, every year in April. For information, contact the

Nevada Division of Wildlife, 380 W. B St., Fallon, 775/423-3171; open Mon.–Fri. 8 A.M.–5 P.M.

On the Walker River Paiute Reservation, The Four Seasons market is where you get the permits you need to fish ($5), boat ($8), and camp ($5) at the **Weber Reservoir** located on the reservation six miles west on the road to Yerington. Over the years the reservation acreage has been chipped away for mining and recreation, but the Paiute people continue to maintain a strong tribal organization and unity. The tribe celebrates its Pine Nut Festival in September, drawing thousands of participants from around the West, and hosts a rodeo in June.

At the nine-hole **Walker Lake Golf Club,** 775/945-1111, open 8 A.M. until dark, green fees run $14 for 18 holes. Add $2 on weekends. The bar serves simple snacks like hot dogs and chili. It's at the Army base, about three miles north of Hawthorne, between town and Walker Lake.

ENTERTAINMENT

The **El Capitan** is the big casino in Hawthorne, with plenty of slots, four blackjack tables, a crap table, and free coffee. It opened in 1943 during the boom years of World War II, and locals owned it all the way up to 1989, when International Gaming Technology bought it. IGT sold the El Cap several years later to Summit Casinos, which also owns the Silver Club in Sparks, the Topaz Lake Casino, one in the Caribbean, and which would be the perfect corporation to buy, finish restoring, and reopen the Goldfield Hotel. An exhibit case displays memorabilia from the El Cap over the years near the side entrance of the casino.

ACCOMMODATIONS

The big action is at the **El Capitan Resort & Casino,** 540 F St., 775/945-3321 or 800/922-2311, with 103 low-rise rooms across the street at $49–55. The next largest is **Best Inn & Suites,** 1402 E. 5th St., 775/945-2660 or 800/237-8466, with 39 rooms at $60–80. If you're looking for the inexpensive, try **Rocket Motel,** 694 Sierra Way, 775/945-2143, $22–25; **Monarch Motel,** 1291 E. 5th., 775/945-3117, $28–50; **Holiday Lodge,** 5th and J, 775/945-3316, $30–38; **Hawthorne Motel,** 720 Sierra, 775/945-2544, $24–27; **Covered Wagon Motel,** 1322 5th St., 775/945-2253, $25–40; **Sand N Sage Lodge,** 1301 E. 5th St., 775/945-3352, $30–50; and the **Anchor Motel,** 965 Sierra, 775/945-2573, $25 and up.

Scotty's RV Park, 5th and J Sts., 775/945-2079, has 18 spaces for motor homes, all with full hookups; 17 pull-throughs. Tents are not allowed. The fee is $14 per vehicle. Just down the street is the **Frontier Overnight RV Park,** 5th and L Sts., 775/945-2733, with 27 spaces for motor homes, all with full hookups; all pull-throughs. Tents are not allowed. The fee is $13. The Frontier has been here since 1977. It's got some trees and fairly wide spaces.

At Walker Lake Village, **Cliff House Restaurant and Motel** rooms are on the beach (though the water is pretty far away these days, especially when you compare it to a dozen years ago when the motel had to be closed because of flooding). The rooms go for $49 and the cabins for $70. Some people like to rent all 12 rooms to have their own little private beach (there are eight cabins). For room reservations, call 775/945-5253.

Camping on the lake is available at the **Desert Lake Campground,** US 95 at Walker Lake, 775/945-3373. Open from Mar.–Nov., the campground has 25 sites with full hook-ups. Tents are allowed.

FOOD

Maggie's, 758 E. Main, 775/945-3908, serves breakfast, lunch, and dinner every day from 7 A.M.–9 P.M. Maggie bakes all her own breads, biscuits, and pies; in fact, just about everything on the menu is made from scratch. This place has the best salad bar for miles around; the all-you-can-eat soup and salad bar costs $5.50 for lunch and $6.95 for dinner and is included when you come for dinner. Breakfast here runs $3–8, lunch $4–8, and dinner $7–15, including the all-you-can-eat soup and salad bar. Local favorites are the honey-dipped fried chicken and the chicken-fried steak. You can dine outside on the patio. Maggie's won the state's Governor's Tourism Award in 1996, Business of the Year in 2000, and many other awards.

The **Idle Hour,** 1302 5th, 775/945-3716, is a popular steakhouse. **Happy Buddha,** 570 Sierra Way, 775/945-2727, and **Wong's,** 923 5th, 775/945-1700, serve Chinese.

The **El Capitan** casino has a coffee shop that is open 24 hours, with daily lunch and dinner specials. **Joe's Tavern** is across the street from the El Cap. It's a bar, dance hall, casino (slots and one blackjack table), and general hangout owned by the Viani family. Joe Viani was a beloved Hawthornite and state assemblyman; Joe Junior now runs the joint. Check out the mining artifacts, the bell from the Candalaria schoolhouse, the big scale, and the resolution noting the passing of longtime Nevada resident Grandma Julie Viani. There might be live entertainment weekend nights.

The **Cliff House Restaurant and Motel** is in Walker Lake Village, down the road toward the lake. The restaurant has been well known for a quarter-century for its fine food and views. The restaurant and bar are open Wed.–Fri. 11 A.M.–10 P.M. and Sat.–Sun. 6 A.M.–10 P.M. The prawns and crab are renowned, the lobster is Australian rock, and the beef is milk-fed center cut. Make dinner reservations at 775/945-5253.

INFORMATION

The **Mineral County Economic Development Authority,** 932 E St., 775/945-5896 or 877/788-LAKE, www.hawthorne-nevada.org, will gladly supply you with fact sheets, business directories, and the like. It's open Mon.–Fri. 8:30 A.M.–5 P.M. The **Mineral County Chamber of Commerce,** 314 5th St., 775/945-2507, also stocks local information but is only open Wednesday afternoons.

The **library** is at 1st and A, 775/945-2778, open Mon.–Fri. 10 A.M.–6 P.M. and Sat. 10 A.M.–2 P.M.

Stop in at **Gun and Tackle,** 898 Sierra Way, 775/945-3266, to ask about fishing and recreation on Walker Lake.

TO TONOPAH

Back on US 95, the highway runs 24 miles to the junction of Route 361 to Gabbs. If you're going this way, Route 361 is well paved, and provides a straight shot into the Gabbs Valley Range. The road turns east to crest **Calvada Summit** (6,130 feet), then turns north again to cross **Petrified Summit** (6,246 feet). Sheer sandstone walls and jagged ridges up here. Also up here is the Santa Fe gold mine, with big dumps and a plastic water pipe feeding the operation. From there it's a straight shot through **Gabbs Valley** into Gabbs.

Luning and Mina

Back on US 95, the road runs 24 miles to **Luning,** through the long tail of Soda Spring Valley, between the Gillis Range on the north and the **Garfield Hills** on the south. The Southern Pacific Railroad tracks run right through town, which has been settled since the 1870s. The area produced silver through the 1890s, then copper and lead in the early 1900s.

US 95 cuts south from Luning, still along narrow Soda Springs Valley, with the **Gabbs Valley Range** keeping it company on the east. Eighteen miles from Luning is the town of **Mina,** at the end of the Southern Pacific's Hazen branch. The town, in fact, is a creation of the Southern Pacific Railroad, which built its own settlement rather than deal with an unscrupulous landowner from Sodaville, a few miles south. Mina was once a major rail junction for the Southern Pacific, Tonopah and Goldfield, and an S.P. narrow gauge to California.

Before the Tonopah and Goldfield Railroad reached the Southern Pacific at Mina nearby, **Sodaville** was the most important town between Reno and Tonopah. Here, all travelers and freight transferred to stages and wagons for the 70-mile ride to Tonopah, a ride so dusty that a joke survives to this day about a man who had to take a shovel at the end of the ride to distinguish fellow passengers from his wife. The ride *from* Tonopah was made more bearable by the presence of warm springs at Sodaville. But the birth of Mina ensured the death of Sodaville.

Strung out along the highway, Mina's business district consists of a gas station and mini-mart, two motels, a café, bar, and RV park. **Jackson's** gas station and market is on the highway. The other motel, with the bar and café, is across the road at the **Silver King,** 775/573-9703. At the southern edge of town, the **Sunrise Valley RV Park,** 775/573-2214, offers shady RV spaces with pull-throughs for $22; ask for Good Sam and AAA discounts. Tents are allowed, and there's a small store on the premises.

Salt and Borax Country

Five miles south is the **Tonopah Junction** at a site once known as Rhodes. This is the center of numerous surrounding salt marshes, with Rhodes Salt Marsh on the left a bit north of the intersection. Prospectors from Aurora and Bodie drifted south into this neck of the desert in the early 1860s and discovered the Rhodes, Teels, and Columbus salt flats. Soon, freighters were snaking toward Aurora, Virginia City, and Austin full of salt used in refining silver ore. This is the time and place in Nevada history during which camels, imported from North Africa, were used to cross the 100 miles of arid land to the mills. A few years later, silver was discovered at **Candalaria,** due south of the Tonopah Junction in the Candalaria Hills.

Route 360 heads southwest from the junction with US 95. A dirt path five miles down the road heads west (left) to **Marietta,** where borax was first mined on a large scale. Frank ("Borax") Smith, a salt miner in Columbus, spotted borax in 1873 at Teels Marsh, which soon became the most important borax mine and mill in the world. Borax previously was used in pharmaceuticals and mined exclusively in Europe, and the development of these large deposits overwhelmed the small market. But Smith was a promoter as well as a miner, one of the first American industrialists to recognize the value of a full-scale advertising campaign. Subsequently, borax became a household word as an abrasive cleanser. The operation here lasted for 20 years until a more profitable type of borax was discovered in Death Valley, California, to which Smith relocated his mines and mills and went on to further popularize the product with the outlandish 20-mule-team wagons. Borax is still used today, but its primary use is in fiberglass. Secondary uses include glass and ceramics, pharmaceuticals, and cosmetics. Soap accounts for a mere 15 percent.

In another four miles, a road cuts off east (right) to Candelaria, which produced $20 million worth of gold, silver, and copper through the 1870s. Take the seven-mile paved road to the ghost town past vast tailing piles that are being revegetated by the Candelaria Mining Company. Owned by the Kinn Ross Company, a subsidiary of Arman Hammer's Occidental Petroleum, Candelaria Mining has been mining gold and silver in the area since the late 1970s. The mill and office complex look prosperous and somewhat ominous standing behind a huge sign warning unauthorized visitors not to approach. The mine shut down in the late 1990s. The ruins of the bank and mercantile, both built of native stone, look impressive even without most of their doors and some of their walls (the bank is the one with the tall steel doors). Two shacks of rock and wood built into the hillside slouch nearby. Just up the road on the left is the mill, or rather its sprawling stone foundation. A dozen other foundations, poking through the scrub, are visible from the road. This would be a fun place to explore if it weren't for the no-parking and no-trespassing signs everywhere.

Back on US 95, it's 14 miles to **Basalt,** at the junction with US 6, which continues west over **Montgomery Pass** (7,132 feet) in the **White Mountains. Boundary Peak,** at 13,143 feet, is the highest spot in Nevada.

US 95 from Tonopah Junction runs 21 miles southeast to **Coaldale Junction.** The Candalaria Hills on the west give way to the Columbus Marsh. The **Monte Cristo Range** is on the east. These unusual volcanic mountains sport layers of ash and lava atop floodplains and lake beds in a maze of gullies and soft rounded hills reminiscent of badlands. The treeless slopes are amazingly colorful, with pastel purples, browns, yellows, even whites, and a pink so fiery that it glows any time of day. The highway follows the crescent-shaped range south by Coaldale, then east to **Blair Junction** with Route 265 to

Silver Peak, then north along its eastern leg halfway to Tonopah.

At Coaldale Junction, US 95 splits off from US 6 west, which goes into California past Boundary Peak. This is the second-largest "town" in Esmeralda County (behind Goldfield). It boasts a motel, café, and bar with slots and gas, open 24 hours. From here it's six miles to Blair Junction,

from where it's 21 paved miles to **Silver Peak,** on the edge of Clayton Valley in the Silver Peak Range. This boomtown had one of the most up-and-down cycles of all the mining camps in the area, producing nearly $9 million in silver during its heyday. Thirty-four miles east of Blair Junction, across Big Smoky Valley, is Tonopah, just inside the Nye County line.

Tonopah

The boom at Austin in the mid-1860s sent prospectors into the rugged and remote desert south through Big Smoky Valley. The discoveries at Ione prompted the state legislators to designate it the seat of new Nye County. A bigger boom at Belmont, 50 miles southeast, was reason enough to move the county seat only three years later.

HISTORY

Through the last two decades of the 19th century, mining all over Nevada was a bust. One particular miner took to hay ranching in Big Smoky Valley near Belmont. Jim Butler was born at the Mother Lode in California and had been a prospector and miner from Austin to Hamilton and back for decades. In the first spring of the 20th century, Butler left his ranch to inspect a mine optimistically called the Southern Klondike, 100 miles south of Belmont. Legend relates that he camped near a spring he knew called Tonopah (Shoshone for "Small Water"). Next morning, Butler awoke to discover that his burros had wandered away. He found them up on what was soon to be called Mizpah Hill. There, he noticed likely looking quartz floaters. Following them up the hill to the vein, he packed a few samples in his saddlebags. Another legend tells a different story: that he was led right to the vein by Indian prospectors. Whichever, Butler continued to the Klondike diggings, which didn't interest him; he showed the rock to the miners there, but it didn't interest them.

Butler then returned to Belmont, where he was faced with two challenges: getting the rock assayed and baling hay. He showed the rock to a young lawyer from New Jersey, Tasker Oddie,

who sent it to Walter Gayhart, principal of Austin High School and a backyard assayer. When the results of Gayhart's testing reached Belmont, Butler and Oddie found themselves owners of some very valuable, silver-rich rock.

Here, legend again overcomes fact. One story claims that Butler was a lackadaisical miner and rancher who hung around Belmont all summer to watch his hay grow. Butler's wife Belle, so the story goes, had to drag him back to Tonopah to stake a few claims. But a better version might be that word of the valuable ore started to get around, and Butler deliberately delayed his return, using the hay harvest as an excuse, to diffuse the rush and maintain personal control of the property, of which only he knew the location. In the fall, he snuck off with his wife and Tasker Oddie and laid out the ground.

The Year of 112 Handshakes

Whatever the truth, as soon as Butler showed up at Tonopah, miners immediately descended on the place wanting a piece. Butler and Oddie worked out an amazing system of verbal leases, wherein the leaseholders would pay 25 percent in royalties for the right to work the ore till the end of the year. Out of the 112 handshake agreements made, not one formal contract was signed and not one lawsuit was ever filed. Times were hard that first winter, with everything, especially water, scarce. But by the spring of 1901, the rush was on and all the boomtown rats arrived to serve the feverish miners, who were trying to recover every last cent of silver from their leased holes before the deadline arrived at the end of the year. On New Year's Eve, the miners surfaced, brushed off, and celebrated both their own prosperity and the beginning of Nevada's most promising silver strike in 25 years. On January 1, 1902, a Philadelphia mining venture paid Butler more than $300,000 for all the leased property, incorporated the Tonopah Mining Company, and hired Oddie as general manager.

Jim and Belle Butler bought a big ranch at Inyo, California, and moved there in 1903. Butler invested his fortune in property and hotels around central and southern California. Tales of his generosity, simple lifestyle, and fancy French car and chauffeur are legendary. Belle died in June 1922, and Jim followed her that December.

The Fall and Rise

The silver bonanza (along with the gold strike in Goldfield) initiated a resurgence in mining ac-

tivity that, from Tonopah's good location, reached all corners of the state. It also created men who would attain the highest positions of power, both statewide and nationally, over the next 50 years. Tasker Oddie, George Nixon, George Wingfield, Key Pittman, and Patrick McCarran—governors, senators, financiers—were all closely identified with Tonopah–Goldfield.

The heyday years were heady until the mines began to play out around 1915. Nearly $150 million worth of silver had been removed. Tonopah's population fell to under 2,000, and mining ceased completely at the start of World War II. The Tonopah–Goldfield short line stopped running in 1947.

Bonanza Highway (US 95) traffic, the Army Air Base south of town, and the Nye County

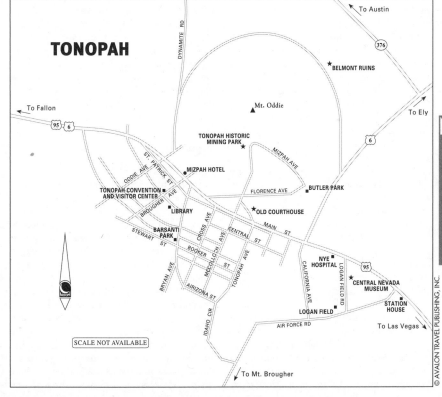

TONOPAH

SCALE NOT AVAILABLE

© AVALON TRAVEL PUBLISHING, INC.

Central Nevada

seat kept the town alive into the early 1950s. Howard Hughes himself was an admirer of, frequent visitor to, and sometime investor in Tonopah in the 1950s, before his years as the world's most famous recluse. When Hughes married Jean Peters in March 1957, he did it in Tonopah. Also, when he set up shop on the ninth floor of Las Vegas's Desert Inn and proceeded to spend $300 million between 1966 and 1969 on Nevada hotels, casinos, airports, TV stations, and land, a large part of the $10 million with which he bought mining property was centered on Tonopah and Round Mountain.

Finally, in the mid-1970s, the price of gold was deregulated and the oil embargo was taking its toll on the black-gold companies, which saw an opportunity in the yellow-gold business. Houston Oil bought up the Hughes property around Tonopah and began a new mining boom.

Also, Anaconda Copper Company opened a large molybdenum mine and mill 25 miles north of Tonopah in the San Antonio Range in 1979. At its peak, the mine employed 450 people and processed up to 22,000 tons of ore a day, producing a million pounds of moly a month. Though the moly boom lasted only a few years (Anaconda shut down worldwide in the early '80s), the impact on Tonopah was significant. The landmark Mizpah Hotel, named after the boom's most valuable mine, was refurbished. A modern hotel-casino, Station House, opened. The town got its first supermarket, the Warehouse. A subdivision and parks were built, and the community recreation center went up. In 1999 an Australian company, Equatorial North America, came in and starting mining copper, which they are still doing today.

Tonopah Today

Today, the departments of Energy and Defense maintain the super-secret Tonopah Test Range, which is within the Nellis Air Force Range, whose northern border is only a few miles southeast of town. The Stealth fighter F117A, along with Soviet MiG jet fighters bought from defecting pilots, was test-flown here. The Air Force moved the Stealths to New Mexico in the early 1990s. Though the military has only a marginal impact on the local economy according to most people, Tonopah may be the only place in the world where shopkeepers smile when sonic booms shake windows around town. If the old merchants were still around, the din would probably remind them of the heady days when silver mines rumbled just two blocks off Main Street.

Of Nevada's several crossroads towns, Tonopah is the greatest. Austin, 117 miles north, might be more centrally located, but Tonopah has the roads. In a state that measures 400 miles from Reno to Wendover, 470 from Jackpot to Boulder City, and 710 miles from Laughlin to Denio, somehow Tonopah seems within only 200 miles of everywhere. Route 376 runs up Big Smoky Valley right into Austin, from where it's 90 miles into Battle Mountain—only 200 miles of traveling on good roads to fan out into northern Nevada. US 95 runs 200 miles into Las Vegas. US 95 and 395, with a few twists and turns on back roads, travel 234 miles into Carson City. US 6 runs 167 miles right into Ely, and Route 375 cuts south from US 6, for 190 miles to Caliente. Thus Tonopah makes a natural trip-breaking stop, usually for lunch, or dinner, or the night, whatever direction is your destination. It's a vital, energized town as well, with lots to see and do nearby.

SIGHTS

Central Nevada Museum

This large and varied museum, just off US 95 on the south end of town near Logan Field, 775/482-9676, is open Wed.–Sun. 10 A.M.–5 P.M., closed 1–2 P.M. (schedule is subject to change, so it's wise to call ahead); donations gratefully accepted. In 2004 the museum closed for a time to undergo a major overhaul of all the exhibits. The collections are the same but have received a good polish and freshening. Start out by wandering around the extensive outdoor mining exhibit: ten-crusher stamp mill, sheave wheel, double-deck hoisting cages. Also follow the boardwalk around the replica townsite, complete with headframe, pump station, wagon shed, shops, shacks, tent cabins, and outhouse. Many engrossing displays await inside as well. Check

COURTESY OF THE NEVADA COMMISSION ON TOURISM

The Tonopah Historic Mining Park gives homage to the town's history.

out the big Nevada flag, great black and whites of central Nevada towns and big color prints of abandoned mines, aerial views of Tonopah and maps of the state, purple bottle collection (manganese in the glass reacts to sunlight), animal-horn chair, lots of Shoshone artifacts including baskets, mining materials, Tonopah's first organ, a bootlegger's still from Prohibition days, a big old safe from the Belmont Courthouse, and more. Note the display concerning the early Tonopah Army Air Force Base, and the photos of the Stealth bomber.

The research room is available for modern-day digging, and for sale in the gift shop are books, historical journals, postcards, and possible gift items. After an hour or so here, you'll have a much better appreciation of the history of the town, and central and southwestern Nevada, which is sure to color the rest of your visit to Tonopah and beyond.

The 70-acre **Tonopah Historic Mining Park** on Mizpah Ave. is open every day, 9 A.M.–5 P.M. April–Sept. and Wed.–Sun. 10 A.M.–4 P.M. Oct.-March. Tours of the park are $3 single, $5 couple, and $7 family. The tour starts with a 15-minute video about the town's mining past. Afterward

you can walk around the Silver Top and Mizpah mines and other equipment and trappings.

Three other big mines—the Desert Queen, Montana Tonopah, and Northern Star—are located within the park, but are deemed too difficult or dangerous to approach. These mines pulled $150 million in silver out of the ground before they closed. You get to go inside the Mizpah and Silver Top hoistworks and warehouses, where spare parts and cases of core samples sit gathering dust pretty much the way they have since the mines shut down. The tour offers a close-up look at the snaking stopes and cracks where the lease miners removed the ore in their hustle to make their fortunes before their agreements with the mine owners expired. On the way over to the Mizpah you'll walk right across an exposed two-foot-wide vein of silver ore just like the one Jim Butler found in 1900. Curiously it was never mined. Peer into the 100-foot-deep crater of the Glory Hole site of a 1922 cave-in caused by mining too near the surface. No one was killed, but only because the collapse occurred at night. Miners returned to work the next morning to find the assay office in splinters at the bottom of the pit.

Central Nevada

The newest attraction is the "Underground Adventure," during which visitors can venture down a mine tunnel, called the Burro Tunnel, that leads to one of the original discovery stopes. At the end of the tunnel you step onto a viewing cage that hovers above a 500-foot-deep stope. The museum also now has an extensive mineral display, a replica mine office, and small equipment display.

The park also offers an excellent view of downtown Tonopah. Look across Main at the Silver Queen Motel and you'll see that the upper wing of the inn is built on the huge tailing pile from the Silver Queen Mine. The motel swimming pool sits above the old shaft.

Around Town

For a great view and to figure out the lay of the land, turn onto Air Force Rd. near the Station House, and drive one and a half miles away from town and up **Mt. Brougher** till you get to the No Trespassing chain-enough room to turn around. From up here, the overview of the little high-desert bowl of the **San Antonio Mountains** in which Tonopah sits reveals the unmistakable evidence of a boomtown, with its haphazard layout, piles of tailings, and headframes across the way on **Mt. Oddie.**

On the way down head to the left past the public school complex, past **Barsanti Park** with its tennis courts, swimming pool, and kids' playground, and wind down over to Brougher Avenue. Take a left and drive up to the old **K.C. Hall,** built in 1907 by Jim Butler's lawyer, George Bartlett. Later it was turned into a center for the Knights of Columbus. Around the corner on Stewart St. is the **Castle House,** one of the oldest buildings in town (1906) and Tonopah's own haunted house. The Mizpah is haunted too, but it's a hotel. The owners of the Castle House say their ghost, George, is friendly, but a little shy, only making himself heard when rooms are painted or furniture is moved. It's been said that the wife of the original owner, Arthur Raycraft, Tonopah's first banker, held seances in the tower room with a crystal ball. As for the ghost at the Mizpah, visitors staying on the fifth floor have reported a "diaphanous young lady dressed in red" who is said to be the spirit of a woman who vanished 80 years ago under mysterious circumstances.

Near the corner of Brougher and Summit streets are the chamber of commerce/convention center and the library.

Brougher St. joins Main right at the five-story bank and **Mizpah Hotel.** The Mizpah started life as a one-story saloon and grill on this location in 1905. A year later, it was hitched up to a team and dragged to another location to make way for the big hotel. The Mizpah opened in 1908, with all the mod cons, including electricity, private baths, and an elevator. Jack Dempsey, a laborer in the silver mines, took a job as a bartender-bouncer in the bar. He watched Wyatt Earp, still formidable in his fifties, down a few there. During the town's long decline, the Mizpah was sold several times; new owners installed the rooftop sign and remodeled the lobby in the early '50s. It was completely renovated in the late '70s, with no expense spared to re-create the splendorous appointments of its heyday. Today, however, it remains closed.

Around Mt. Oddie

Wander around the other (east) side of town, by taking Florence Avenue (behind Silver Queen Motel) to McCullough, continuing up to near the **Mizpah Headframe.** Located and named by Belle Butler (according to legend), the Mizpah was the richest of the Butler properties. **Butler Park** is up here, near the corner of Valley View and Mizpah Circle-picnic tables, bathrooms, a pleasant place for getting out of the car. Come back on Florence to go by the **County Courthouse,** built for $55,000 in the mid-aughts on land donated by the Tonopah Mining Company.

Heading out US 6 east of town, you go by the bowling alley. In a half mile, take a left on Ketton Road, and creep up to the foundations of the **Belmont,** a state-of-the-art, 500-ton silver-cyanide mill that operated from 1913 to 1923. This is another good place to get out of the car and explore.

Old Tonopah Cemetery

Ask at the chamber of commerce for directions to the Old Tonopah Cemetery. Opened for business in 1901, the cemetery is the final resting place for more than 300 early residents of the town, including the victims of the "Tonopah Sickness." To this day, no one knows what caused the epidemic that took the lives of more than 30 local miners during the winter of 1901–02. The outbreak caused a mass exodus from Tonopah that winter. Also buried are the 14 victims of the Tonopah Belmont Fire in 1911. Another is Nye County Sheriff Tom Logan, killed in a shoot-out at a brothel in nearby Manhattan. In 1911, a new cemetery was established a mile west of town when the old one became hemmed in by mines and the burgeoning boomtown.

ENTERTAINMENT

The big-town casino is at the **Tonopah Station** (775/482-9777) on the south end of town. This hotel-casino was built in 1982 in the midst of the latest boom in Tonopah, next to the Warehouse Market, Tonopah's first supermarket, which opened in 1981. The casino is cramped and crowded with slots, a small blackjack pit, and a mini-craps. A nice display of antique slot machines sits downstairs by the restrooms.

The **Banc Club** restaurant/bar/casino (775/482-5409), 360 N. Main St. on the west end of town, has slot machines and occupies a building that was once the Bank of America building. (Locals say it would have been named "The Bank Club," since it's in the old bank, except that Nevada law prohibits using the word "bank" in the name of a casino.) The site is the site of the old Tonopah railway depot, which burned down in 1981.

ACCOMMODATIONS

Tonopah has nearly 500 motel rooms, enough to accommodate most everybody at any time (except on the very busiest Saturday nights and during Jim Butler Days, the town festival that takes place the last weekend in May), and inexpensive enough that you don't have to worry about getting a good deal anywhere you go. All are located along Main Street from one end of town to the other.

The **Silver Queen Motel,** 255 Main St., 775/482-6291 or 800/210-9218, has 85 rooms at $31–45. The **Tonopah Motel,** 325 Main St., 775/482-3987, has 20 rooms at $27–33. Next up from there is the **Golden Hills Motel,** 826 Main St., 775/482-6238, $24–65. The **National 9,** at the south end of town, 775/482-8202, charges $30 and up for one of its 52 rooms. The **Clown Motel,** 521 N. Main St., 775/482-5920, is one of the newest, with 31 rooms starting at $27. **Jim Butler Motel,** 108 S. Main St., 775/482-3577, has 24 rooms at $31–55. The **Tonopah Station/Ramada Inn,** 1100 Main St., 775/482-9777, has 78 rooms priced at $49–120. The **Best Western Hi-Desert Inn,** 320 Main St., 775/482-3511 or 877/286-2208, has 62 rooms at $49–89.

Tonopah Station RV Park, 775/482-9777, is in the back-side parking lot of the Station House hotel/casino. It's not exactly shady, private, or quiet. It has 19 spaces for motor homes, all with full hookups. Tents are not allowed. Reservations are recommended, especially during the summer. The fee is $17 per vehicle.

The **Twister Inn RV Park,** 1260 Ketten Rd. half a mile east of Highway 6, 775/482-9444, has 13 RV sites for $14. Tents are not allowed. Good Sam and senior discounts available.

FOOD

If you've been traveling around southern Nevada for a while, you'll appreciate the choice of food in Tonopah.

The **El Marques,** across from the Tonopah Motel, is open Tues.–Sun. 11 A.M.–9 P.M., with $5–9 Mexican dinners, and a pleasingly dark and cool room.

The **Station House** has surprisingly good food at its 24-hour coffee shop. At the snack shop you can get tacos, burritos, burgers, chili, hot dogs, root beer floats, and milkshakes, and nothing is more than $5. **The Banc Club** also has a coffee shop, open 7 A.M.–10 P.M. daily.

Cisco's Tacos, 702 N. Main, 775/482-5022, is popular with the locals for its cheap good food, serving up ribs, tacos, pizza, and the like.

INFORMATION AND SERVICES

The **Tonopah Convention and Visitor Center** at 301 Brougher St. (P.O. Box 408, Tonopah, NV 89049), 775/482-3558, www.tonopah-nevada.com, is open Mon.–Fri. 8 A.M.–5 P.M.

Down the street on Summit is the **library,** oldest one still active in Nevada (since 1912), with a new library extension built in summer 2000; 775/482-3374. The **Nye General Hospital** is on the south side of town, 775/482-6233. Tonopah has two **laundromats:** one at the Tonopah Station, and another at the Texaco station.

DETOUR: HOT CREEK AND RAILROAD VALLEYS

On the south side of Tonopah, take a left (east) onto US 6. Heading toward this extremely remote section of central Nevada, you pass the bowling alley, the airport, and the entrance to the Tonopah Test Site. The flats of Ralston Valley give way to the southern edge of the Monitor Mountains, with the scene around the national forest sign *completely* devoid of trees. Stone Creek Valley leads to a convenient pass between the Kawich Range on the south and the Hot Creek Range on the north. At **Warm Springs Junction,** the minimart and bar are defunct, though the creek and springs are as bubbly, sulphury, and toasty as ever; follow the white-bordered stream around back and up the hill for the pool. US 6 cuts northeast beyond here, while Route 375 (the "Extraterrestrial Highway") heads southeast to join Route 318 at Hiko.

You drive along Hot Creek Valley, with the otherworldly Pancake Range hemming in the road to the east. In 25 miles is Sandy Summit (6,030 feet). A few miles past is the turnoff to the BLM Lunar Crater loop road.

Lunar Crater

Volcanism is one of Earth's most dramatic processes, and Nevada rests on one section of the most active belt of volcanoes in the world: the Pacific Ring of Fire. The Pancake Range is an excellent example of volcanism at work in Nevada, both recent and long past. During the Oligocene Epoch, 40 million years ago, a colossal episode of volcanism obliterated the existing Nevada landscape. Through fractures, fissures, and vents, an unimaginably titanic disgorgement of white-hot steam, ash, and particulate spewed up from the depths, burying the surface under thousands of feet of ash-flow sheets. The topmost sheet transformed the landscape into a single uniform layer. The **Lunar Cuesta (Field)** is an illustration of the welded tuft or fused volcanic rock that resulted from this cataclysm.

But the cinder cones, lava tongues, craters, and maars at Lunar Crater are manifestations of much more recent volcanism, only a few thousand years old. Take a right onto the Lunar loop road and drive three miles. Turn left at the sign to **Easy Chair Crater.** It's clear how this high-backed hole got its name. A 100-yard trail from the parking area leads up to the viewpoint. This could be a recliner—for the Man in the Moon; a sign points out some geology and the direction of lava flows. Within the turn of a neck and the roll of an eye is some amazingly diverse topography: pancake buttes, mashed-potato mounds, craters, cones, the cuesta floor, and the mighty Quinn Canyon Range in the background. The Apollo astronauts trained in this 140,000-acre lunar landscape.

Back on the good dirt road (35 mph, one lane), you drive another few miles and climb up to **Lunar Crater,** 420 feet deep and nearly 4,000 feet in diameter. This is a typical maar, formed when the violent release of gases reams an abrupt deep crater with a low rim. Unlike the crater behind it, which is the peak of a small cinder cone, no magma was ejected with the gases. But the old lava and ash flows were exposed by the explosion; the descriptive sign points them out.

Continuing the next eight miles toward The Wall, you drive on the east side of the loop along dry Lunar Lake. You won't wonder where or what The Wall is, and it needs no description here. Suffice it to say that Pink Floyd's eponymous double album is not only apropos, but essential.

The loop ends on the old US 6 asphalt; pick a convenient spot to four-wheel up to the highway. North of the highway is **Black Rock Lava Flow,** the most recent basalt ooze in the area, covering 1,900 acres. The lava cooled so fast that it's specked with green, red, and black glass.

Railroad Valley

US 6 continues northeast beyond the Pancakes through Railroad Valley, where oil was discovered in 1954 by Shell geologists. It was the first commercial-quantity oil located in Nevada. Previously, scientists thought the geology of the Great Basin was unfavorable for oil deposits, as they suspected that the "oil traps" were susceptible to the instability of the local earth. But steady (though small) production for the last 40 years or so has proved the early theory incorrect. From 1954 until the mid-'80s, Nevada produced fewer than 400,000 barrels annually. But in the mid-'80s, oil companies explored Nevada more thoroughly, looking for domestic reserves. Since then, they've drilled wells in Pine Valley (south of Carlin) and Grant Canyon (one of the gashes in the Grant Range off Railroad Valley). One well in Grant Canyon gurgles up 6,000 barrels a day. Most of this oil is processed into diesel fuel, kerosene, stove oil, and asphalt.

The **Quinn Canyon** and **Grant** mountains escort the road toward the intersection at **Currant.** Both these ranges are new wilderness areas (27,000 and 50,000 acres, respectively), and have been described as "true wilderness, a virtually trackless limestone massif capped by eight-mile-long Troy Peak." The ponds and springs at the western base of the long ranges make up the **Railroad Valley Wildlife Management Area.** In 1934, nearly 140,000 acres here were set aside as a migratory bird refuge, and as at Ruby Lake in northeastern Nevada, wells, dikes, and spillways have been built to control the water in the marsh. Gravel roads lead from US 6 into four management sections.

At Currant is the turnoff for the **Duckwater Indian Reservation.** Beyond is an unexpected canyon along Currant Creek. Currant Mountain, a 36,000-acre Wilderness Area since 1989, is "one of the most impressive mountain masses in the Great Basin," according to John Hart. It's also one of the least known and accessible, and entirely trailless.

GOLDFIELD

When Tonopah was still less than two years old and already the biggest boomtown Nevada had seen for a generation, Jim Butler grubstaked two young prospectors who'd seen rich ore on a small ledge about 25 miles due south. Just like Butler, they staked 20 claims, mined their first paydirt, and managed a small return. Unlike Butler, whose bread and butter was silver, the two miners had a fever. This was *gold,* by god, in the Silver State.

These guys dug in with a vengeance all winter long and finally attracted some expert attention in the late spring. Again like Butler, they proceeded to lease their remaining claims. One of these claims was the Combination, most profitable of all.

The mushrooming tent camp was at first named with a pun: Grandpah. When George Wingfield moved in with George Nixon's money, the boom was on. By then the ore had been found to be so rich that $5-a-day miners could "high-grade" $250 a day worth of nuggets—in shoes, secret pockets, hollow ax handles, and body holsters—then sell it to fences for cash. The town was laid out in September 1903, and with everyone so loaded, real estate prices quickly went through the roof.

The post office opened in January 1904 and the Goldfield *News* came off the hastily imported press in April. Large stone buildings were put up over the summer and the Tonopah-Goldfield Railroad arrived in September. The ore kept growing purer and the cash-$10 and $20 coins-heavier. When the mine owners ran out of patience with high-grading employees, they attempted to install changing rooms, which the miners resisted.

A national prizefight in the summer of 1906 was promoted by Tex Rickard, a well-known character from the Klondike–Nome rushes in Alaska five years earlier; he made so much money on this event that he was able to leverage it all the way to promoting prizefights at Madison Square Garden. The famous Nelson-Gans bout went a brutal 42 rounds. The publicity was priceless, and prizefights have been big business in Nevada ever since.

By 1907 Goldfield had surpassed the milestone 10,000 people. The one-two boom—silver in Tonopah and gold in Goldfield—was heard clearly around the country.

By the turn of the century, the violence between individuals in mining boomtowns had been replaced by corporate clashes between organized labor and company-hired goon squads. Goldfield's catalyst was a confrontation between labor (represented by the emerging International Workers of the World, or Wobblies) and management over high-grading and reduced wages. It came to a head when Wingfield and his owner cronies persuaded Governor Sparks to ask President Roosevelt to send in the Army to "maintain order and protect property." The military presence allowed the corporations to hire scabs and break the union. The federal troops were replaced by a new law-enforcement unit that became the state police. And the owners' power was complete.

Goldfield became the seat of Esmeralda County in 1907 (to the dismay of Hawthorne; but when Mineral County was carved out of Esmeralda in 1911, Hawthorne was made seat). The peak of the boom occurred in 1910, with just over $11 million in production and a population estimated at 15,000-20,000, largest in Nevada by far. But *borrasca* wasn't far behind. A flood in 1913 took the starch out of the town, Goldfield Consolidated closed in 1919, and the great fire of 1923 made it a near ghost.

Today, the population is roughly 400, though you're likely to find only a handful in town at any given time. Most of the residents mine gold in the desert, or work on the highway, at the air base, or in Tonopah. Several stone buildings, including the grand old fenced-in Goldfield Hotel and the high school, are remnants of the heyday. Still, the energy from that heyday was so strong that Goldfield is not a near-ghost town, but a near-ghost *city.*

Sights

Roll along US 95 into town, which rests in a bowl between **Columbia Mountain** of the **Goldfield Hills** on the east and the **Montezuma Range** on the west.

You can't mistake the **Goldfield Hotel,** built in 1908 for a cool half mil. It boasted 150 rooms and 45 suites with baths. Every room had a telephone, which was part of an ingenious fire-alarm

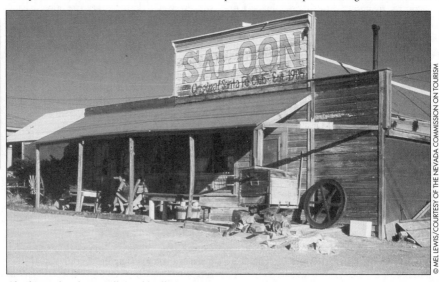

Oh, the stories these walls could tell!

system. The hotel possessed the first electric elevator west of the Mississippi. There were a pool and a billiard parlor, a separate gaming room for ladies, and the dining room was 40 by 80 feet. Opening night dinner featured oysters, caviar, filet mignon, vegetables from the hotel nursery, and ice cream; the cost, $2. The hotel passed through several hands before it finally closed for good in 1946; it's also changed hands several times since, but has never reopened. In 1986, a San Francisco investment company began to renovate the place, but never finished. Today, inside you'll find a construction job half-completed, and boxes and boxes of hotel supplies awaiting somebody else to come and tackle what appears to be one of the hardest jobs in Nevada.

The hotel, courthouse, high school, and several other stone buildings in town survived the big fire; some have historical markers on them, including the **Southern Nevada Consolidated Telephone Company** (1906–63). The huge **high school** is not an editorial comment on the American public education system, but rather a statement about the transience of boomtowns, no matter how permanent they appear during the boom.

The county **courthouse,** built in 1907, still serves all 1,300 residents in Esmeralda County, smallest in Nevada. You're welcome to tour the building, respectfully; if the courtroom is locked up, ask at the clerk's office to go inside. Do; it's worth the trouble to see the best preserved courthouse in the state, thanks to the original 1905 Tiffany lamps on the bench, the original brass, leather, and wood furniture and fixtures (100 seats), the judge's chambers behind, and the bighorn head overseeing it all.

Also check out the **Santa Fe Saloon.** A sign points the way from the highway—at 5th Ave., past a school, headframe, Joshua trees, single-wides, satellite dishes, and pavement, all in four blocks. If the Santa Fe Saloon could speak, it would tell you the whole long story of Goldfield. Which is not to say that it can't *talk;* anyone with eyes and a sense of history can understand its language. The sign and front door will take you back almost 100 years, to when Goldfield was only a few years old and this club was one of the requisite couple of dozen, competing against the likes of George Wingfield's hotel and Tex Rickard's saloon. The original wooden floors speak of muddy boots and shiny boots, dress shoes and spike heels, brooms, and mops. The back bar is one of the most lived-in in the state. The front page of the April 18, 1906, Goldfield *News* does speak, with the big headline about the San Francisco earthquake. But the best tale, the house special, is the magnificent, pieced-together black-and-white historical photo of Goldfield at its peak: biggest, richest, most powerful, and fanciest town in all of Nevada. The saloon won't speak about surviving the devastating fire in 1923, which razed 50 blocks, and it will only briefly mention the US highway that was pushed through town four blocks away. Last but not least, in fact the ultimate manner in which the Santa Fe Saloon symbolizes Goldfield, is that you can count on its being open. It's one of Nevada's quintessential soul survivors.

Practicalities

The **Mozart Club** serves cocktails, three meals with a small salad bar, and has slots—a pleasant rest stop. Stop in for a drink and a chat at the **Santa Fe Saloon,** and try your luck at the Jolly Joker antique poker-pinball machine (oldest in the state). Check out all the history on the walls. T-shirts are for sale. Someone interesting is sure to be sitting at the bar. The Santa Fe also has four motel rooms next door; $30–42, 775/485-3431.

Central Nevada

Warm Springs to Pioche

On the south side of Route 318 at its three-way junction with Route 375 and US 93 is Crystal Springs. The site was once a Paiute village, and served as a resting place for California-bound travelers. It was first settled by white men in the 1860s as a result of nearby silver discoveries. The settlement was declared the seat of Lincoln County in 1866, though it never had a population of more than a few dozen, and most of those were transient miners. Hiko became the county seat in 1867, and now nothing remains but the spring itself and a few surrounding cottonwoods.

At the junction of US 93 and Route 318, take a left toward Hiko, then another left onto Route 375. You start out heading southwest over the Mt. Irish Range, site of the Pahranagat Mining District (a few miles north). Stretch your legs and whatever else at **Horney's Rest Stop** just before Hancock Summit (elev. 5,592 feet). After a couple of soft downhill curves, the road cuts northwest like an arrow through Tikapoo Valley. This is lonely open-range country. (Nevada Department of Transportation officials say the highway only draws about 50 vehicles a day on average, though a great deal more show up twice annually when Rachel holds "UFO Friendship Campouts" for tourists looking for flying saucers.)

The road climbs up a bit into the Timpahute Range of the Worthington Mountains, not, as is generally believed, named after Cal Worthington, then over Coyote Summit (elev. 5,591 feet). Then you continue down down down into the big fertile Sand Spring Valley, with ranches, old farmhouses, and the town of Rachel.

Coming out of Sand Spring Valley, you climb up and over some foothills of the Quinn Canyon Range at Queen City Summit (elev. 5,960 feet). That's Reveille Peak standing at nearly 9,000 feet atop the Reveille Range across the big valley. The road cuts due north up Railroad Valley between the Reveilles and the Quinn Canyons. A good gravel road starts here, goes by **Nyala,** and past another dirt road that heads right into the heart of the Quinn Canyons at **Adaven,** an old mining town whose name is Nevada spelled backwards.

Just below Black Beauty Mesa, Route 375 cuts due west through Hot Creek Valley up toward the Hot Creek Range, where Rawhide Mountain tops out at 9,169 feet. Right at the base of this range ends Route 375 at US 6 and derelict **Warm Springs** (no services). Tonopah is 50 miles west.

ROUTE 318 TO CALIENTE

Hiko

A few miles north of the intersection with US 93 and Route 375 on Route 318 is Hiko (HY-ko). This is a small ranching hamlet spread along the highway for a mile or two behind range fencing. The silver strike in 1867 at Irish Mountain, 15 miles north of Hiko, was a flash in the pan compared to the silver strike in the Highland Range at Pioche in 1871. Amost overnight the population of Hiko moved to Pioche, as did the county seat, where it remains today. Hiko rests in the center of a pretty little basin with a string of ranches, a post office, the state's Key Pittman Wildlife Management Area, and Nesbitt Pond. A sign here warns that the next gas is 100 miles away in Lund.

Named to honor Key Pittman, a former U.S. Senator from Nevada known for his vigorous support of monetary legislation designed to assist the silver-mining industry of the West, **Key Pittman Wildlife Management Area** comprises two lakes, Nesbitt and Frenchy. The WMA is managed by a resident ranger, Bart Tanner, who is headquartered at his home in Hiko, 775/725-3521. The lower lake, Frenchy, is usually dry about half the year since it's used to supply irrigation water for the farms in the area. Frenchy Lake is reputedly named after an old sourdough miner who worked the old Logan Mines up in the Mt. Irish mountains to the west. North on Route 318 just under five miles is Nesbitt Lake, a beautiful lake that does not go dry. It's surrounded by tules, tall cottonwoods, and oak, and is inhabited by an abundance of wildlife (birds, small animals). When you come to the entrance to **Nesbitt Lake,** stop, open the cattle gate, drive in (close the gate behind you so you don't let grazing cattle out onto the road), then take a leisurely drive around the lake. You can park at several shady areas at the beginning of the road around the lake. Non-motor boats are allowed on the lake. There are no fees for picnicking or camping in this lush oasis.

Mt. Irish Archaeological Site and Logan

Directly across from Nesbitt Lake is a barbed-wire gate to a dirt road leading 18 miles up into the Mt. Irish Range and the Mt. Irish Archeological Site. The range and site are rich with ancient petroglyphs and other Indian artifacts. Up here you'll also find the remains of the old mining town of Logan. This is a dirt road and pretty isolated, so be sure to take water, a digging tool, a spare tire, and other desert survival equipment in case you get a flat or get stuck. It's a long walk back. Passenger vehicles can easily make the 18 miles to Logan, but avoid going off this road. All other access roads are strictly 4WD.

Continuing North

Route 318 runs northeast from Hiko through the Hiko Range along a route cut by the once-wet White River. You leave the Mt. Irish Range behind on the west and come into a basin hemmed in by the Seaman Range on the west and the North Pahroc Range on the east. For a little while you head directly toward Fossil Peak (6,486 feet), southernmost bump in the Seamans, then zig to the east. In about 15 miles, you come to **White River Narrows.** The White River isn't, but it is narrow; this is a state archaeological site. The walls, though not especially high, are sheer and pillared, and the road winds through them for a couple of miles.

From there the road continues north into big White River Valley. Here you leave Lincoln County and enter the far northeast corner of Nye County, about as far away from Pahrump as you can get. There's a turnoff on a gravel road for Gap Mountain (7,045 feet elevation), which is one of the southern peaks of the Egan Range. **Hot Creek Campground** is seven miles in from the highway; this is the southern access road to

the state Wayne E. Kirch Wildlife Management Area. Beyond that to the west is the mighty Grant Range, with Troy Peak rising 11,268 feet, within a Forest Service Wilderness Area.

In another seven or so miles, the road skirts the edge of the Kirch Management Area; there's a turnoff onto the northern access road. You continue up White River Valley, the big Egans ushering you along to the east. Just under 200 miles from Las Vegas is a turnoff onto a 30-mile gravel road to Currant on US 6, a shortcut to Duckwater and Eureka. Then you leave Nye County, enter White Pine County, and cruise into Lund.

Lund and Preston

Lund is one of the prettiest and well-kept little towns in central Nevada. It's named after Anthony Lund, a president of the Mormon church around the turn of the 20th century when the town was founded. Today, it's a typical farm and ranching center, the residential streets extending one block on each side of the highway, with a tractor dealer, rodeo grounds, and two schools (slow down to 15 mph on school days) in the middle. You first come to **Whipple's Country Store,** 775/238-5260, open Mon.–Sat. 7 A.M.– 7 P.M.; there's a telephone booth outside and the post office is next door.

Up the street is **White River Valley Pioneer Museum,** open daily. Stop in and have a chat with the dedicated local senior volunteer, and look around at the interesting stuff: old stock certificates, Valentines, typewriters, irons, quilts, and the first piano in the valley; old photos, including those of Lafayette Carter, one of the town elders, who donated the building. Out back is a log cabin full of cream separators, life-saving skis, and rusting equipment. A great place to stretch your legs, rest your eyes, and sign the guest book.

The main action is at **Lane's** café, store, fuel, public scale, and motel on the north side of town. The café is open 6 A.M.–9:30 P.M. every day but Christmas. The motel, 775/238-5346, has 15 rooms that go for $38 d.

A few miles north of Lund is the turnoff (left) onto a three-mile loop along a scenic farm byway through the farm village of **Preston.** Here is little

THE EXTRATERRESTRIAL HIGHWAY

While the federal government wishes everyone would go away, in April 1997 the Nevada Department of Transportation designated the desolate 92-mile stretch of Route 375 the "Extraterrestrial Highway," putting up four signs to that effect at a cost of $3,300. During the ceremony, Nevada Gov. Bob Miller quipped that some of the signs should be placed flat on the ground "so aliens can land there." Gov. Miller also commented that the designation shows Nevada has a sense of humor. This is UFO country, folks, and the town of **Rachel** is its headquarters.

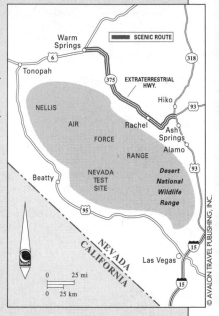

It all seems a little unlikely, when you cruise in from a remote stretch of state highway, that this tiny hamlet of 100 souls, a leftover development of the aborted MX missile project of the early 1980s, has been garnering almost as much publicity over the past few years as Las Vegas has. Rachel is in the center of a controversy that encompasses two Air Force facilities, government secrecy and security, military land grabbing, UFOs, toxic waste, and a computer programmer from Cambridge, Massachusetts.

It all started in 1989, when Bob Lazar, a former engineer at the Los Alamos labs in New Mexico turned Nevada brothel owner, told a Las Vegas newsman that he'd been working on extraterrestrial aircraft at a top-secret Air Force facility near Rachel known as Papoose Lake. His story, though yet to be confirmed, launched a media feeding frenzy that turned up Papoose Lake and a second previously unknown Air Force installation, Groom Lake (also known as Area 51), in the far northeastern corner of the vast 3.5-million-acre Nellis Air Force Range.

Meanwhile, UFOnauts from around the planet descended on Rachel, convinced that the answers to all their questions rested somewhere in the alkali flats of dried-up Groom Lake.

All the hoopla attracted the attention of one Glenn Campbell, a young computer programmer from the East. He made the pilgrimage to the now infamous "black mailbox" (29 miles south of Rachel serving the Medlin ranch), a landmark where UFO enthusiasts gathered to wait for ET. Campbell never caught a glimpse of any intergalactic spacecraft, but he did see fighter jets galore, taking bombing target practice over the nearby desert and simulating dogfights in the big sky. But it wasn't until the Air Force, under media scrutiny from around the world, denied that Groom Lake even existed that Campbell found his true calling.

Meanwhile, the Rachel townsfolk lined up on both sides of the UFO uproar, some claiming to have seen and been visited by UFOs, the rest convinced that any extraterrestrial worth his higher intelligence wouldn't be bothering with a dusty village in an unfriendly desert on a backward planet. But Pat and Joe Travis, owners of the Rachel Bar and Grill, changed the name to the **Little A-Le-Inn** (pronounced just like "alien") and redecorated it in an alien motif, with a giant wooden saucer outside and extraterrestrial trinkets (bumper stickers, doormats, cigarette lighters, and T-shirts) for sale inside. Try an Alien Burger or a Beam Me Up, Scotty (made from Jim Beam, 7UP, and Scotch). There are also 13 motel rooms here that go for $25–35 apiece.

Down the block from the Little A-Le-Inn is a single-wide trailer with a sign: Area 51 Research Center. This is Glenn Campbell's publishing and public relations outfit, where he cranks out a newsletter and meets with visiting media, whom he guides to vantage points overlooking Groom Lake, described in his manual, *Area 51 Viewer's Guide.*

According to what's been pieced together from the sketchy reports of local eyewitnesses, ex–Groom Lakers, and government whistle-blowers, the Groom Lake installation has field tested top-secret aircraft since the 1950s, including the U-2 spy plane, the Stealth series, the Manta craft used in the first Gulf War, and the rumored Aurora speed demon, which can fly at 5,000 miles an hour. Reports say that the three-mile long runway is the longest in the world. In the past year or so, some former employees of the base have filed a class-action suit, claiming that the Air Force's mishandling of toxic materials affected their health. Finally, the Air Force has applied for an additional 4,000 acres of land surrounding the base for security; this would effectively seal off all known vantage points of the facility that doesn't exist.

Current thought is that, as a result of the notoriety received by Groom Lake and Area 51, the Air Force has surreptitiously moved whatever was there to a more secret location, but maintains the illusion of security at Groom Lake to keep the curiosity and interest focused there where it can do no harm, rather than somewhere else where the truth may accidentally be discovered.

Central Nevada

more than farmhouses and fields, a creamery, cemetery, and a big piece of peace. In another eight miles you come to US 6; from there, Ely is 23 miles east.

Delamar

Back at the junction of US 93 and Route 318, heading to Caliente, US 93 cuts across Sixmile Flat, then climbs into the Pahroc Range. Climbing up to Pahroc Summit (just under 5,000 feet), you enter sage country, and then, oddly enough, pass through a forest of Joshua trees. Farther along, even more oddly, is a little interface zone with the Joshuas growing right next to the junipers—something you don't see very often in Nevada. Beyond there you head up into the Delamar Range.

About 24 miles east of Alamo, you come to a dirt road on the south side of the highway proclaiming Delamar 15 miles. This straight-arrow dirt road heading southwest is well graded and an easy passage for passenger vehicles. The broad Delamar Valley, one of the most striking in the state, is west of the Delamar Mountains. John and Alvin Ferguson made the first strike of record here in 1891. Using a monkey wrench, they broke a small piece of quartzite from a ledge, which proved to be high-grade ore. They named their claim the Monkey Wrench for the incident. On April 1, 1892, Frank Wilson and D. A. Reeves discovered the April Fool Mine in the same area. The town of Reeves was laid out below the mine, but the name was later changed to De Lamar (Delamar) when Capt. John R. De Lamar, a Dutch immigrant, purchased the group of mines in 1893.

Delamar was a principal gold-mining center that supported a thriving business district of stores, saloons, theaters, and professional offices. As many as 120 mule-drawn freight wagons were ceaselessly employed in importing supplies from the nearest railroad at Milford, Utah. Through 1908, the Delamar Mine had an estimated production of $25 million, even though it suffered from one of the worst working conditions in Nevada mining history. Improper ventilation permitted silica dust to waft continuously through the mines and mills with fatal results

for many of the workmen. Three months was enough to kill a miner in Delamar from silicosis, and the town became notorious as a widow-maker. This accounts for the large size of the cemetery here.

Today, nothing much remains at the site except old stone walls, a crumbling mill, and a large cemetery, from which many of the old tombstones have been stolen by souvenir seekers. The rock ruins, crowded as they are into the shallow canyon above the mine dumps, make a fascinating picnic site. Have no fears: none of the deadly silica dust remains.

From Delamar, you can continue southwest on the dirt road to Alamo, or return to US 93 to the north and drive on in to Caliente. Six miles from the Delamar turnoff you top **Oak Springs Summit** (6,237 feet). A campground a short distance off the south side of the highway has picnic tables, grills, and a green shady picnic area. It's a nice cool place at high elevation to enjoy a rest and a picnic, and to listen to Air Force jets streaking up and down Pahranagat Valley.

From here you start dropping down to Caliente. One last scenic treat awaits before town; Newman Canyon has high, sheer sandstone cliffs, some of them completely vertical and smooth. This is but a warm-up, however, to Rainbow Canyon on the other side of town.

CALIENTE AND VICINITY

Petroglyphs in Meadow Valley indicate that a native population used this lush region for hunting, traveling, and artwork. The first Anglo settlers were farmers and ranchers; the Culverwells bought a large tract in 1879. On this property Caliente was founded, and the Harriman-Clark Railroad War was waged.

This southeast corner of Nevada, too far to connect with the transcontinental main line in northern Nevada, was neglected by the railroads until late in the 19th century. In 1894, E.H. Harriman's Union Pacific surveyed a route between Salt Lake City and Los Angeles. At the turn of the century the Union Pacific's subsidiary, Oregon Shortline, resumed work on the route, laying track southward from Utah to Meadow

Valley. There, however, it was stopped short by William Clark's upstart San Pedro, Los Angeles, and Salt Lake Railroad, which claimed title to the narrow right-of-way south of the Culverwell ranch. Each company deployed thugs to interfere with its competitor's progress. The inevitable violence ensued in Clover Valley with shovels and axe handles—the only major confrontation between railroads in Nevada history. A federal judge sided with Harriman, who shortly thereafter reluctantly went into partnership with Clark. Beginning again in 1903, together they continued construction south toward the little ranch known as Las Vegas—along the dangerous Meadow Valley Wash. Caliente was created as a division point on the San Pedro, Los Angeles, and Salt Lake Railroad, thanks to the abundant water gushing out of springs near the Wash, which quelled the unslakable thirst of the steam engines.

Company row houses were built north of the repair shops and offices, and the new town enjoyed a continuous prosperity up through the '40s. The only disruptions were railroad related. The disastrous floods of 1907, for example, required a million dollars' worth of repairs, only to be washed away again in the terrible flood of 1910, which wrecked 100 miles of track. (Two million was spent after that to raise the roadbed; little damage recurred.) The branch line between Caliente and Pioche ran a full 60 years, 1907–67. The bell might have tolled for Caliente in 1948 when dieselization replaced steamification and the maintenance yards were moved to Las Vegas. But US 93 had already been built through town, three state parks were created nearby, agriculture continued to contribute, and the railroad never abandoned Caliente completely. Freight trains rumble through town regularly.

Today, Caliente has a vitality all its own. The streets follow an orderly company-town grid, with two main business streets downtown, one on each side of the wide railroad right-of-way. The hot springs for which the town was founded and named are one of the surprise treats in the state. That, along with the depot mural, Rainbow Canyon, and the singularly unstressed residents, makes Caliente (pronounced like the Spanish—but with an American West inflection: "cally," which rhymes with Sally, and "anti," as in freeze) an undiscovered gem in this southeastern-Nevada corridor full of undiscovered gems.

Sights

Start out at the **Union Pacific Railroad Station,** built in 1923 for $83,000, once the nerve center of the railroad, now the nerve center of the town. City Hall, the library (open Mon.–Fri. 9 A.M.–4 P.M.), and the Chamber of Commerce (775/726-3129, open usually Mon.–Fri. 11 A.M.– 2 P.M.) all share the lovely building. The pièce de résistance in the depot and town is the historical mural in the lobby. The big painting covers the history between 1864 and 1914 of the entire southern section of Nevada, from Pioche in the northeast to Las Vegas in the south and all the way up to Tonopah in the west—with a lot of detail. Locals Mary Ellen Sadovich and Rett Hastings designed and painted it. The depot is also open on Saturday and Sunday; stop in to the lobby and pick up the brochures from the info rack. Also check out the EPA's radiation-monitoring apparatus outside the depot; it comes complete with a printout of the level of microentgens for southern Nevada (almost always within the range of normal background radiation for the U.S.).

Lots of local buildings have been standing since 1905; consult the walking tour brochure. Wander around the two main streets. Near the corner of Market and Culverwell in back of town, the community church is an attractive historical structure. Also pass the Underhill rock apartments (take a right off Clover St. beyond town), built in 1907 and still in use. Union Pacific railroad row houses, standing grandly on Spring St. just north of town, were built in 1905; notice the two choices of floor plans.

Rainbow Canyon and Kershaw-Ryan State Park

Beginning at the intersection of US 93 and Route 317 at the south end of Caliente by the Mormon Church lies **Rainbow Canyon,** one of the most beautiful canyons in all of southern Nevada. Mark your mileage at this point because many of the most interesting sites can only be located by knowing the miles you've driven from this intersection. You come around the corner, pass under the first of many trestles, and then you're there, in this stunning and remarkable wash. The cliff rock is volcanic tuff, which settled over all of Nevada 34 million years ago; hot mineralized water flowing through cracks and faults accounts for the glorious colors: iron the reds and yellows, copper the blues and greens, manganese the black, and plain ash the white. Many elements combine to make this one of the most scenic (and least known) roads in the state: the dips in the road in the flood zones; the many railroad trestles and bridges; the idyllic ranches, farms, big trees, and creek; the petroglyphs and other historical sites; and of course the sheer and colorful canyon walls.

Two miles into Rainbow Canyon you come to **Kershaw-Ryan State Park,** a small park that was recently opened for the first time since it was destroyed by flash floods in the summer of 1984. The entrance to this gem is a well-marked graded dirt road leading east into a box canyon off Route 317. The park is open daily 8 A.M.– dusk, except on holidays in the winter months. No overnight camping is allowed, but this is a beautiful place to spend the day.

The park is 240 acres of cliff and canyon country, liberally shaded by groves of ash and cottonwood and laced with hiking trails. The rugged cliff walls enclosing the canyon are heavily overgrown with scrub oak and wild grapevines. The sound of running water is everywhere since the end wall of the canyon has a series of seeps that send water trickling down its face to be caught in a pond and little brook at its base. This protected canyon is early to feel spring returning and late to feel the cold touch of winter, making it a good place to visit during most of the year.

The park has modern restrooms amid a profusion of ivy and grass. The picnic area has tables and barbecue grills. Just above the picnic area is a small wading pool for children. Above that is a beautiful seep dripping water from the canyon wall in an undercut that creates a beautiful hanging garden of riparian plantlife including grapevines. Two short hikes (one a mile and the other a quarter mile) lead to other springs and

lush canyons. The fees are $4 per day, group use $15. The fine for failing to pay at the self-pay station is $2.

Continuing down Rainbow Canyon, at mile 3.8 you come to the **Old Conway Ranch,** which was turned into a public golf course that went bankrupt, but there's talk of it reopening in the future. At mile 5.0, you arrive at **Etna Cave.** Park on the right shoulder, walk under the train trestle, and follow the sandy wash though the tunnel for about 400 feet, then look up to the left on the tan cliff face. This site has been an archaeological dig since the 1930s when a profusion of Indian artifacts were found that document 5,000 years of native habitat. The artifacts are currently collecting dust in the basement of a museum in San Francisco, but efforts are being made to reclaim them for a Lincoln County museum. The San Francisco folk did not manage to make off with the abundant petroglyphs and pictographs carved and painted into the cliff face.

At mile 6.0 you come to the **Tennile Ranch.** Tennile sold the ranch to a Las Vegas man who conducts stress-management classes at the beautiful ranch house. The place is now called the Longhorn Cattle Company. At mile 8.7 you come upon the remains of **Stein Power Station,** a steam-generated power plant that supplied electrical power to the mines between 1902 and 1909. Farther up this road are the remains of the old Delamar pumping station and pipeline, which pumped water over the high cliffs to Delamar on the other side of the mountains to the west.

At mile 11.0 you come to a vantage point where you can view the few remaining pinion pines and juniper trees, which were much more abundant in the canyon prior to being cut down for fuel and building materials at the turn of the century. This stand has grown back after the intensive uses of the past.

At mile 14.7 watch for a turnoff to the left just after crossing under another railroad trestle. Park off the road and take a short drive (0.7 mile) up a good dirt road into **Grapevine Canyon.** Bear left at the fork. Park at the barbecue-pit area and enjoy a picnic under the shade of huge ash and hackberry trees. Walk back down the road about 100 feet, then follow the well-marked foot trail up the slope to some tuff overhang. You'll spot another abundance of petroglyphs and pictographs dating back thousands of years. More such artifacts can be found along the cliff face and on the south side of Grapevine Canyon.

At mile 17.5, just past the railroad bridge, look for a short dirt road on the right. Park and walk north along this access road about 400 feet. You'll see a small railroad tie structure and **Tunnel No. 5,** dated 1911–25. Look west and uphill from the structure. You should see several dark-stained talus blocks strewn along the hillside with petroglyphs of bighorn sheep carved on the top and sides.

At mile 19.9, park along the right shoulder of Route 317 and look for a boulder covered with petroglyphs. Across the highway lush willows dominate a wetland zone and protect the stream bank from erosion by flooding. They also provide food for deer, beaver, and livestock.

At mile 20.2 you come to **Bradshaw's "End of the Rainbow" Ranch,** which was established in the 1880s, and is the only ranch in the canyon still owned by family of the original settler. The pavement ends here. If your visit occurs in the fall, you might be able to pick a bucket of Jonathan or Delicious apples in the ranch's orchard. Check for a sign on the ranch gate for the dates when End of the Rainbow is open to the public. In another few miles Rainbow Canyon starts to peter out and becomes an ordinary desert wash in the summer months. The stream that you've followed all the way down the canyon either dries up or goes underground.

Elgin and Carp

The old railroad station of **Elgin** has been absorbed into the ranching community at the south end of Rainbow Canyon where the pavement turns to dirt. Little is left of the old station facilities. However, a few years ago the Bradshaw family finished restoring a 1921 one-room schoolhouse. Hours are irregular, but visitors can peek into the windows and enjoy the picnic table under the huge cottonwood.

Continuing down Rainbow Canyon along what is now a dirt road, you come to **Carp,** which was a station on the main line of the Union Pacific and a local community, first settled in 1907. Like Elgin, not much is left of Carp today: only the shells of two concrete buildings and the foundations of a few wood-frame houses. The place has become a garbage dump and milling place for free-range cattle.

This dirt road continues down the barren desert valley and comes into the back side of Moapa on I-15 about 35 miles later. All along this road are the remains of frequent Union Pacific way stations, but nothing else of much interest.

Kane Springs Valley Road

This road starts at the south end of Rainbow Canyon where the paved road turns into dirt and ends 38 miles (45–50 mph) southwest on US 93. It's a shortcut or a good circle tour for anyone traveling between Caliente and Las Vegas. It's also a great drive across high desert with clean clear air and lots of yucca. As you traverse the high-desert green valley running between the Meadow Valley Mountains on the south and the Delamar Mountains on the north, shut off your air-conditioning, open your windows, and taste, smell, and feel the desert. Don't seal yourself off from it. Toward the end the Sheep Range keeps growing bigger and bigger dead ahead.

Beaver Dam State Park

One of Nevada's loveliest and most remote state parks is accessed from Caliente. The park is so irrepressibly cheerful a place that the long dusty drive to get there is a small price to pay for a visit. The 2,393-acre park is set high in mountain pine forests. Hiking trails wind under the trees and cliffs and through the canyons. Spring-fed Schroeder Reservoir is stocked with fish and anglers may try their luck along the cottonwood-lined stream leading to the reservoir or in the small reservoir itself; no boating services or facilities have been developed, and vehicle access is limited. Swimmers are welcome to try the reservoir. There are picnic sites and developed campsites in the park ($9 per night). There are no visitor center or concessions; bring everything you'll need.

The well-marked turnoff for the state park is 5.3 miles north of Caliente on US 93. For the next 25 miles the well-graded dirt road climbs gently into pinion pine country. However, you can't travel faster than 35–40 mph because the road twists and turns a great deal and you don't know what's coming up around the next turn or over the next hilltop. After 14 miles you come to a fork in the road. Stay on the left branch to Beaver Dam. The right branch, which rapidly becomes 4WD territory, goes to the dry remains of Matthews Canyon Reservoir, then winds its way though the mountains south into Utah backcountry.

After another 4.5 miles you cross the Union Pacific tracks. Four miles later you come to the beginning of a steep incline down the side of Pine Ridge into Beaver Dam State Park. While it may look like a nail-biting ride, any passenger vehicle can make it with no trouble. From this point it's three miles to the campground. Do what the stop sign says (yes, a stop sign way out here) and register. The park is open year-round, weather permitting. Fees are $9 a day to camp and $4 for day use. Group use reservations are $15.

There are a number of campgrounds available with a total of 33 campsites. The first (to the left) is the best of the lot, with tables, grills, running water, porta-potties, cut and cured firewood, and camping spots for RVs. All the other campgrounds are much more primitive.

The road through the campground drops down a steep grade; at the bottom is parking and the trailhead for a half-mile hike along narrow trail to the Beaver Dam Reservoir, better known as Schroeder Lake. Passenger vehicles would do better not to chance the hill; park at the top and hike down instead. It's only a few hundred feet (of loose gravel) and you may have some trouble with traction coming back up.

The reservoir has a lot of over and undergrowth as well as a couple of rather large beaver dams. You can hike all the way around the dam and camp on the earthen dike, providing a beautiful view of both the lake and the stream and canyon below. There are numerous other hikes available in the area. The Hamblin Ranch is not far up canyon from the reservoir, or you can follow the wash from the dam down quite a ways and enjoy the lush flora and abundant fauna in the area.

Practicalities

Caliente has four motels with a grand total of 60 rooms. The **Rainbow Canyon,** 884 A St., 775/726-3291, charges $25–60; **Shady Motel,** 450 Front, 775/726-3106, charges $43–53; and the **Midway Motel,** 250 N. Spring St., 775/726-3199, charges $35–60. Or follow the signs across the railroad tracks north of town and stay at **Caliente Hot Springs Motel,** 775/726-3777 or 888/726-3777, where the hot spring baths are located. The room rate includes use of the baths; if you're not spending the night, you can use the baths from 8 A.M. to 10 P.M. for $5. These are spacious private cubicles with five- by five-foot Roman tubs, about three feet deep; fire-hydrant faucets fill them up in four minutes flat. This water, at 105°F, is so soft, so sulphur-free, and so seductive that you easily pass the pickling point. The baths are a bit frayed around the edges these days, but if you can look beyond some missing tiles, a little dirt in the tubs, and 20-year-old paint, you'll have a mighty good time.

Young's RV, is on US 93 behind the BLM office, 775/726-3418. Spaces are wide, with trees and grass at each. Facilities are limited, but it's right in town. There are 27 spaces for motor homes, all with full hookups; 16 are pull-throughs. Tents are allowed (separate grassy area). Restrooms have flush toilets and hot showers; sewage disposal is available. Reservations are accepted; the fee is $10 for tents and $14 per vehicle. **Agua Caliente RV Park,** 1000 N. Spring St., 775/726-3399, has 20 RV spaces; call for rates.

The **Knotty Pine** coffee shop is on Front St., open weekdays 6 A.M.–9 P.M., Fri. and Sat. until 10. A bar with pool table adjoins. Something typically local is bound to be going on inside. The **Branding Iron,** on Clover St. across the tracks, is similar, open 6 A.M.–9 P.M., Sun. until 2 P.M., closed Mon.; bacon and eggs $4.50, burgers $2.75, fried chicken $8, steaks $11. Foodtown supermarket is next door. There's also a **Pioneer Pizza** next to the Hideaway Bar and the Hansen Fine Dining restaurant, which is open in the evenings.

The Intellectual Cowboy is a great little bookstore down the street from Foodtown, open at 9 A.M.

PANACA

Drive north on US 93 through Meadow Valley between the Cedar Range on the east and the Chief Range on the west. After 14 miles the high desert turns amazingly green (in summer). Lush, irrigated fields of grains and vegetables, barns, farm equipment, stacks of hay, feedlots, long fences, and farmers frame the landscape, much as they have for 130 years. One of the oldest villages in the state, Panaca (pan-ACK-uh) was founded in 1864 by Latter-day Saints missionaries and colonists. The town's name was an anglicized version of *pan-nuk-ker,* a Southern Paiute word meaning metal or wealth. The Panaker Ledge was actually at Pioche, and the boomtown of Bullionville thrived slightly north of Panaca between 1870 and 1875 until it was supplanted by Pioche.

As usual, the two groups made uneasy neighbors, with the miners disrespectful of the Mormons' water rights, religious beliefs, and lifestyle, and the Mormons disapproving of the miners' lawlessness and faithlessness. Even so, a mutual dependence arose as the miners provided an excellent market for Mormon produce, and both groups defended a common interest against Indian threats. In fact, this yin-yang relationship between the valley farmers and the mountain miners was so complete that it's hard to write about one without the other; Pioche and Panaca today remain excellent reminders of that typical frontier tension. Of course, the boom at Bullionville—five mills and the narrow-gauge Pioche and Bullionville short line notwithstanding—lasted a mere half-dozen years. Pioche, as well, finally settled down to a semblance of law and order by the mid-1870s, and real quiet arrived with the inevitable decline of the mining boom.

Some serious dust, however, was stirred up after an 1866 survey revealed Panaca to be within Nevada's boundaries, not Utah's or Arizona's, to which the townspeople had already paid taxes. Panacans thought it unjust for Nevada to try and collect back taxes from them, and many left in protest. But the town itself persisted as it always had and always would, through the vagaries of desert, miners, Indians, tax collectors, and persecution. To pause here is to enter a timelessness felt nowhere so strongly in the rest of the state.

Sights

At the corner of US 93 and Route 319 is a Texaco station. Turn right from the highway and poke into town along Main St., which becomes four lanes downtown. You pass H & W Video and Mini-mart on the way in. Peek into the **Mercantile,** established in 1868 on the corner of 4th, then go up a block and take a left on 5th. Notice the Italian Victorianate house on the east corner; this was the second house of N. J. Wadsworth, a member of one of the founding families. On the west corner is an interesting redbrick house, built in 1871. Take the first left onto E Street, then mosey along past the gymnasium and ballfield, which dominate the town and where you'll find the whole populace during a basketball or baseball game, past the schools and church, all presided over by the incongruous but striking chalk formation known as **Court Rock.** This public square is a graphic example of how seriously this town takes its education, religion, and civic responsibilities. Go right at the stop sign across from the big two-story frame house. Take your first left on D Street, go to the end, and take a left onto 2nd Street at **Henry Matthews's home.** Look back for a view of this pretty house, built in stages. Go two blocks to Main Street; a right returns you to the highway.

Now go back to the corner of Main and 5th and take a left. Bear around to the right of the school athletic field, and stay on 5th after the pavement ends. Drive through the back of town, past big backyard gardens, some with tall corn growing in late summer, past some sand dunes, and head toward the tallest cottonwood tree about a half mile in the distance. This is **Panaca Spring,** whose warm sweet water is part of Meadow Valley Wash, which makes this farm valley possible. It's deep and warm, with kids swimming all hours, and a beautiful view of the valley and mountains beyond.

Cathedral Gorge State Park

Only a mile north of Panaca on US 93 and 165 miles north of Las Vegas is this state park, yet another unexpected delight on the run up eastern Nevada (which even Las Vegas, considering itself the gateway to such far-away and out-of-state places as Death Valley and the Grand Canyon, has yet to discover). Take a left into the park; at the fork a right goes to the gorgeous gorge, a left goes around to the campground. Like Valley of Fire, Cathedral Gorge (1,578 acres) is more a place to exercise the imagination than your legs and lungs. Simply put, it's a wash, a cut in the earth's skin, which over the eons has been weathered and eroded into a fantasyland. What separates it from countless other washes and gulches is that its walls are made of a chalky-soft suede-colored bentonite clay, which has created the pillars, gargoyles, wedding cakes, fortresses, hunch-backed men, dragons, palaces, melting elephants, and, of course, cathedrals. Baroque architectural elements—lacy, filigreed, fluted, and feathered—decorate its walls.

A million years ago, this valley was covered by a lake, into which streams washed silt, clay, ash, and other decomposed volcanic and igneous products from rock outcrops surrounding the valley. These sediments were eventually deposited on the lake bottom up to 1,500 feet deep, the coarser materials at the edges and the finer in the deep middle. Then faulting in the mountains at the southern end of the lake allowed the water to slowly seep away, carving the canyon deeper along the fault line. After the lake dried up and exposed the bed, the sun, wind, and rain did the rest.

More recently, some evidence shows the presence of Basket Maker Indians a few thousand years ago; the Paiute passed through. The wash was named, for obvious reasons, in 1894 by a local woman; in the 1920s, Shakespearean passion plays, local pageants, and fairs made use of the dramatic backdrop. The whole thing was designated a state park in 1935, along with the three other original Nevada state parks.

Park at the pullout near the signboard at the main part of the gorge. Notice the horizontal line running along the formation; the darker rock on top is compacted clay hardened by lime from decomposing limestone, while the light greenish rock below is the siltstone from the middle of the lake. The hard clay protects the soft siltstone from accelerated erosion, which is believed to have already worn away roughly 1,000 feet of deposits from the lakebed.

From here, hikes disappear into Moon and Canyon Caves, narrow passageways with walls so tight that they almost create natural bridges. Best time for pictures is in the evening, as the cliffs face west. A one-mile trail continues from the end of the paved road to under Miller Point Overlook; a four-mile nature trail leads through the desert and around to the campground; signs along the way identify plants and animals in the lower gorge.

Cathedral Gorge knows no real visiting season. It's open year-round. There is a visitor center at the entrance (built in 1996) that has interpretive exhibits and park information. Be sure to check out some of the ranger programs that cover topics ranging from bird-watching to stargazing. You'll also find a campground, shaded picnic areas in strategic locations, drinking water, restrooms, and the magic of your imagination.

The **campground** is a pleasant spot, with introduced Russian olive and locust trees. In spring, the Russian olives bear a little yellow flower in spring, which gives the susceptible locals a bad case of hayfever; birds love to eat the pea-size olives, but can't quite digest them. Elevation is 5,000 feet. There are 22 sites for tents or self-contained motor homes up to 30 feet; the two pull-throughs can handle longer. Piped drinking water, flush toilets, heavenly showers, sewage disposal, public telephones, picnic tables, grills, and fire pits are provided. The maximum stay is 14 days. Day-use fee is $4 and it's $14 to camp. Bundles of firewood are for sale for $2. Call the State Parks District Office in Panaca, 775/728-4460, for more information.

To Pioche

Another mile north from the main entrance is **Miller Point Overlook,** with a superlative view of the whole wash, plus four sheltered picnic tables, pit toilets, and explanatory signs.

The historical sign for **Bullionville** stands between the entrance and Miller Point. Beyond

Miller Point, the road begins to climb into the juniper forest on the slopes of the Highland Range. In a few miles you pass the Castleton Cutoff, then in three miles take a left at the fork to go up into Pioche.

PIOCHE

They came in waves from Virginia City across the corrugated Great Basin of central Nevada—prospectors in search of rich lodes, miners in search of eternal veins, speculators in search of boomtown profits, and camp followers in search of new lives to lead. First Austin in the Toiyabe Mountains in 1862, then Eureka in the Diamond Mountains in 1864, then Hamilton in the White Pine Mountains in 1868, and finally Pioche in the Highland Range in 1869 all mushroomed atop promising ore bodies in the rush to riches eastward across the new state.

Pioche (pronounced pee-OACH, and named after a San Francisco financier who bankrolled the original strike) quickly gained notoriety as one of the most dangerous towns on the western frontier, described in terms usually reserved for Bodie or Tombstone. Here, the distinction between law enforcement and law breaking was determined by your particular side of the gun. And since Pioche attracted the most violent and anarchistic frontier element, inevitably groups of "regulators" were organized to protect the various claims, which further contributed to the mayhem. Pioche's enduring (and dubious) claim to fame is the 40–50 men who died of violence or accident before anyone lived long enough to expire of natural causes. Records show that two men were punished during this time. And then, during a particularly rowdy celebration in 1871, a fire got out of control and touched off an explosion of 300 powder kegs, killing a dozen, wounding a score, and destroying nearly the entire town.

By the mid-1870s, after the Lincoln County seat was transferred from Hiko to Pioche and the population had increased to 12,000, some order had been established on the streets and in the mines. One explanation credits (or blames) the influx of women to the town; they married the miners and settled them down. In fact, it got to the point where men were afraid of "walking down the street for fear of coming home married," and the Single Men's Protective Association was formed in 1876 to help "the bachelors withstand the wiles of the fair sex."

Behind the scenes, meanwhile, unchecked corruption reigned supreme. In the freewheeling days at the peak of the boom, county officials developed a fondness for expenses (to build the courthouse, for example) far beyond their capacity to raise revenues. They floated bonds, printed local scrip, and quickly doomed the county to 70 years of debt. Part of the problem was that the citizens weren't interested in paying taxes, especially in the decline period of the late 1870s. This situation prompted the sheriff to assume tax-collection responsibilities, which helped line his and his cronies' pockets. The courthouse, which cost $26,000 to build in 1871, was finally paid off in 1938—at an accrued cost of nearly a million smackeroos.

Pioche's boom-and-bust cycles have continued ever since. Mines and short lines came and went; a small boom developed when cheap power reached Pioche from Hoover Dam just before World War II. The war effort also kept the mines open and producing manganese and tungsten. Since then Pioche has managed to stay alive in large part due to highway traffic, some mining, ranching, and farming. Historical signs and sites, the visitors center and library, two museums, the tramway structure, and a couple of motels and cafes will keep you happily occupied for an afternoon and complete your tour of the "Lincoln County Tri-Towns"—the orderly railroad company town, the virtuous Mormon farming community, and the rough-and-tumble mining boomtown—within an hour's drive of each other on US 93.

Sights

At the fork you have your choice of two routes: the higher, westerly road, newly paved and newly named Business 93 or Route 321, goes left into Pioche (6,060 feet up in the hills), and the lower, easterly one bypasses the town. The lower bypass runs under the tramway **buckets** suspended on the cable between the mine and the mill. The upper road takes you right to the **headframe** of the aerial tramway built by the Pioche Mine Company in 1923. The weight of the buckets carrying ore down to the mill helped propel the empty buckets back up to the mine. A five-horse-power engine (about the size of one that turns a large washing machine) got the whole thing going. According to the historical sign at the site, the cost of delivering ore to the mill by the tramway in the late 1920s was six cents a ton. Slide down to the 80-foot-high structure to see where the small motor turned the little pulley that turned the big pulley that hooked up to the small gear that turned the bigger and biggest gears that helped propel the cable and its dozens of buckets. The whole monstrous structure—headframe, gears, cable, and buckets—is in the very same place it's been since the tram was shut down for the last time, some 70 years ago. Climb around on it at your own risk, but if the risk doesn't bother you, it's jungle-gym heaven.

Stop in at the **Commerce Cottage,** at the top of Main St., 775/962-5544, open weekdays 11 A.M.–3 P.M., weekends 10 A.M.–2 P.M. (open May–Oct.), for a historical map and plenty of handouts on Pioche. Down Main Street from the visitors center is the **library,** open Mon.–Fri. 12–4 P.M. (Tues. 1–5 P.M.), 775/962-5244.

Next door is the **Lincoln County Museum,** open daily 10 A.M.–1 P.M. and 2 P.M.–4 P.M., 775/962-5207. This place has a fine collection of artifacts, which completely fills two large rooms. Most of the first room is occupied by mining material: pretty calcite and aragonite (like that from Lehman Caves), case after case of minerals from Lincoln County, a blacklight display, plus taxidermied birds, guns, medicines, 1910 embalmer's certificate, printing press, clocks, and invaluable bound books of the Lincoln County *Record* from 1920–60. The second room illustrates Pioche in its heyday, with black-and-white photos and a big map of town from the 1870s and '80s. Finally there are the obligatory pioneer kid's bedroom, a kitchen, plus antique pianos, organs, Wurlitzers. Admission is free, but this place is worth two bucks for sure.

Take Main Street through town. At the fork of Main and Pioche are the **Commercial Club** and **Amsden Building,** both of which by some miracle managed to survive fires, explosions, and gunfights, and are now two of the oldest buildings in Nevada. Two doors down from them is the old firehouse.

Next door is the **Thompson Opera House.** The interior still has the original footlights, seats, and scalloped picture frames, plus an adit to an old mining tunnel running out the back. Money to shore up the foundation has been raised, and the exterior received a facelift. Since Main St. was paved and designated Business 93, federal money for historical preservation has for the first time also been made available to the Opera House.

Down the street are the **Wells Fargo Building** and a **miner's cabin,** with the local historical signs in front. Take a right on Comstock St. to get to the cemetery, with its renowned Boot Row. Come back to Main and keep going down to the "new" courthouse; take a left in front, past Dinky, the little railroad engine that once could, to **Memorial Park,** which has kiddie toys, swimming pool, tennis courts, and RV parking. Also around town are the **antique store** and **craft and gift shop.**

Million Dollar Courthouse

This is one of Nevada's ultimate symbols of a boom–bust economy and mentality. Originally designed to cost $16,000, overruns forced the price up to $26,000 when it was finally completed in 1876. Discounted bonds to finance the construction immediately put the county deep in the red, from which it took nearly 70 years to recover. By 1890, officials had yet to make a payment on the principal, and interest had accrued to the tune of $400,000—nearly 70 percent of the assessed value of the entire county! The state refused to allow the county to default, and the commissioners refinanced the debt, by then $650,000, in 1907. They finally finished paying off the bonds in 1938, four years after the building itself had been condemned, and the same year a new courthouse was constructed.

It's open Apr.–Oct. daily 10 A.M.–4 P.M. Walk in, sign in, and the volunteer will take you around the building: through the historical photo room, sheriff's office, DA's office, and assessor's office.

Upstairs are the fire department's room, the judge's office, and the courtroom. The judge's bench and nearby chairs are original. From there you head out the back door to the jailhouse—the middle cell has the original bunk and leg iron. The jailhouse is possibly the most graphic evidence remaining of the tough hombres that hung around this town 120 years ago. New to the courthouse in 1994 was a series of large watercolors painted in the late 1800s and early 1900s by one R. G. Schofield, a watchmaker and jeweler by trade.

Echo Canyon State Recreation Area

This state park, with a reservoir and campground, is four miles east on Route 322 (or the Mt. Wilson National Backcountry Byway), then eight miles southeast on Route 86. This narrow two-lane road winds around and then drops fast into a beautiful and inappropriately named Dry Valley, part of the Meadow Valley Wash water system. You pass by well-irrigated and verdantly green alfalfa fields, and then approach the small earthen dam stretching across Echo Canyon on the far side of the valley. When you arrive at the park, take a right to get to the ranger station and group picnic area; drive straight ahead and past the earthen dam, which is about 40–50 feet high and holds back a fairly large body of water, to get to the campground. The **campground** has 33 big sites, lush with tall sagebrush, plus piped drinking water, flush toilets (turned off end of October), sewage disposal, public telephones, picnic tables under roofed shelters, barbecue, and fire pits; the fees are $4 day use, $10 per night camping, firewood for sale $2. The maximum stay is 14 days. The elevation is 5,300 feet. No reservations. Contact park headquarters at 775/962-5103 or the state parks district office, 775/728-4467.

The reservoir is fed from the northeast by a stream that flows through a long narrow farming community dedicated to growing hay. The canyon in which the park is set has high walls of volcanic tuff, which has been eroded and carved by time, wind and rain. The reservoir is stocked with rainbows and crappies (the campground has a fish-cleaning shed). Boating costs $6 per day.

The road continues into Echo Canyon up the wash, under big white sandstone walls-100 feet high with eroded pinnacles. It emerges in Rose Valley, another beautiful little basin full of alfalfa fields hemmed in by hills and canyon walls. At Rose Valley Ranch is a T-intersection: to the left, the road climbs a mile back up to Route 322; instead, go right through another lesser canyon into Eagle Valley for more of the same farm-canyon scenery.

Continue on this good dirt road all the way to **Ursine,** a stunning little farm town with huge cottonwoods and fruit trees, idyllic farmhouses, horses and sheep along the creek that runs right through, kids and dogs in the road. This is as bucolic and pastoral a village as you could ever imagine. You pick up the Route 322 pavement again at the far end of Ursine; take a right. **Eagle Valley Resort,** 775/962-5293, has 50 spaces for motor homes, 36 with full hookups and no pullthroughs. Tents are allowed (separate grassy area). The fee is $7.50 for tents and $11.50–15 per RV. The grocery store and bar (slots, video poker) are across the highway. Beyond the resort, You wind around **Eagle Canyon** past the precarious gravel- and slate-covered slopes of the White Rock Mountains until you reach Spring Valley Recreation Area.

Spring Valley State Park

Spring Valley has the same facilities as Echo Canyon: dam, reservoir, campground. A canyon cliff forms about 15 percent of the dam wall. This park is bigger and a bit more crowded. There's pretty good fishing (for rainbow and cutthroat trout) at the 65-acre reservoir—indicated by the large number of anglers around the lake. There's a five trout limit; the trout are three to four inches when released and grow three inches per year. Docking and launching facilities are available. The reservoir water is muddy, precluding swimming.

Horsethief Gulch Campground has 36 campsites for tents or self-contained motor homes up to 28 feet. Piped drinking water, flush toilets, showers, sewage disposal, fish-cleaning shed, public telephones, picnic tables, grills, and fire pits are provided. There's a seven-day limit, which many people, presumably, use up. Fees are $14 overnight, $4 day use, boating $6 per day, $5 firewood; there are a limited number of boats available for rent (call **Big Fish Boat Rentals,** 775/962-1405 or 775/728-4692). Ice fishing is growing in popularity here: Die-hard anglers bundle up and trek onto the reservoir, which freezes over for about two months in the winter. Contact park headquarters at 775/962-5102 or the state parks district office, 775/728-4467.

The road continues along the reservoir, though the pavement ends at the dam. The reservation gets marshy quite quickly, and then just like that it's gone. The road, the Mt. Wilson Backcountry Byway, keeps going and going and going (you'll need the *Nevada Map Atlas* to explore back here). The drive is gorgeous in the summertime.

Practicalities

Pioche has about a dozen or so motel rooms and a few hotel rooms. The **Hutchings Motel** is on US 93, 775/962-5404, charging $35 and up. The **Overland Hotel,** on Main St., 775/962-5895, charges $41; the bar here has an unusual antique interior.

The **Silver Cafe,** Main St., 775/962-5124, is open Sun.–Thurs. 6 A.M.–8 P.M. and till 9 P.M. Fri.–Sun.

Tillie's Mini Market and Tillie's Too offer groceries and sundries in town. If anything exciting is going on in town, it'll probably be at the Alamo Club; also look into the Nevada Club, which has 10 slot machines.

Know
Nevada

The Land

Half a billion years ago, Nevada rested underwater, the eastern half a narrow shelf that slanted westward into a deep ocean trench. Where Salt Lake City now sits was the shoreline; the equator passed nearby and the region teemed with tropical Precambrian life. Soft-shelled brachiopods, primitive trilobites, tiny spiny starfish, single-celled radiolaria, and algae all populated the tidal flats, reefs, lagoons, estuaries, and wide bays of the shallow sea. For roughly 150 million years, skeletons and sediments accumulated on the ocean floor and were pressurized into limestone. At least twice during the mysterious 300-million-year Paleozoic era, violent and titanic orogenies (episodes of uplift) raised the land, draining the sea and leaving towering mesas and alluvial plains. Gravity pulled the upland rubble into the low-lying basins, which sunk under their own weight, creating new lanes for the seawater to flow back. Then, toward the end of the Paleozoic in the period known as the Permian, supercontinental collision flattened massive ridges in the ocean, forcing the ocean into retreat again and, incidentally, triggering the first of the two near-global extinctions in the history of Earth.

This mass extinction of plants and animals extinguished most of the carbon, creating a superabundance of oxygen (which is usually bound up by carbon). Thus the oxygen resorted to rusting the ubiquitous ferrous iron in the Earth's crust, turning it red. During the Triassic period of the new Mesozoic era, 230 million years ago, the exposed and oxidized sediments eroded. Ferric red sands blew southward and collected in dunes, which petrified into sandstone mountains, to be sculpted in later eons by wind and water.

During the Jurassic, 175 million years ago, the fused supercontinent tore asunder, a cataclysmic megashear resulting in global-scale tectonics, which again caused the flooding of North America. This triggered what's known as the Nevada Phase of the Cordilleran Orogeny, a violently unstable and confused era. The earth squeezed together, folded, and thrust up from

the sea. Huge blocks of sediment faulted, tipped, and rose thousands of feet. Earthquakes shuffled the ranges like a deck of cards. Great crustal fissures cracked open. Molten lava, gaseous plumes, and hot springs spewed out, bearing solutions of gold, silver, copper, silica. Volcanoes blasted hot rock and ash from their bowels. During the greatest period of granite formation in Earth's history, the ancestral Sierra Nevada were raised. Flash floods gouged the mountains—leaching, oxidizing, concentrating the ores. Two families of creatures that had survived the Permian Extinction—marine and flying reptiles and dinosaurs—evolved, over the 165 million years of the Mesozoic, into giants. But then, 65 million years ago, another cosmic cataclysm, the Cretaceous Extinction, again erased almost all life and ended the Mesozoic, framing "an era of burgeoning creation," as John McPhee puts it, "within deadly brackets of time."

The Cordilleran Orogeny ended shortly thereafter, followed by the Laramide Igneous Gap, 25 million years of gradual erosion. Then, during the Oligocene, 40 million years ago, another colossal episode, this time of volcanism, obliterated the Nevadan landscape. Up through fractures, fissures, and vents spewed an unimaginably titanic disgorgement of white-hot steam, ash, and particulates, burying the surface under thousands of feet of ash-flow sheets, turning the topmost sheet into a single continuous and uniform plain.

Finally, 17 million years ago during the Miocene epoch, the continental collision course stretched and lifted the crust, bowing the vast volcanic-ash plain upward like an arch. The crust pulled apart, thinned, then crumpled into blocks that tilted and slid into each other—the high edges became the ridgelines of the ranges, the low edges V-shaped canyons. As they began to fill with eroded sediment, the canyons spread into basins, tilting the blocks further upward. Large cracks ripped open between the rising mountains and sinking valleys; the blocks still quake the land at the faults today, as the crust continues to adjust. Still spreading, the Basin and Range could very well be cracking open a new sea-lane, by way of the Gulf of California, the Salton Sea, and the Mojave Desert (the latter two already below sea level in places), and basins northward. California becomes an island. Nevada drowns again.

Meanwhile, erosion continues to litter the valleys with mountain material. Some ranges have been whittled down over the past 15 million years to a mere 12,000 feet. Others have been completely buried in their own shavings. Still other ranges are growing, as their blocks tilt more steeply. Some hills are really the peaks of mountains that extend thousands of feet below the surface, iceberg-style, resting on bedrock. Roughly 200 discrete ranges have been named in Nevada, 90 percent of them oriented northeast-southwest. The other 10 percent constitute what's known as a discontinuous fault zone—hooked, curved, folded toward all points on the compass. Collectively referred to as the Walker Belt, these individually scrambled mountains at the same time occur in a line, northwest-southeast, roughly 400 miles long, along the geologically uneasy California–Nevada state line.

Appropriately enough, the locale where the structural continuity is most disturbed, where the southwest-trending cavalcade jams up at a southeast-trending dead end, where a cosmic X marks the spot, is right there at the edge of Las Vegas Valley. To geologists, this phenomenon is known, with no apparent irony, as the Las Vegas Zone of Deformation.

The final uplift of the Sierra Nevada occurred roughly 10 million years ago; the rainshadow it cast transformed the terrain east of the great range of granite mountains into a wide desert. The Pleistocene, beginning a little less than two million years ago, ushered four great ice ages into history. Alternately warm and cool, the humidity remained constant. The soil was moist, rich, and full of minerals from decomposed lava. Forests of giant fir, pine, and sequoia towered over a lush undergrowth of moss, fern, and willow. Great lakes covered much of Nevada, mountain peaks poking out as islands. Lakeshore grasses and woodlands supported great Pleistocene fauna: sabre-toothed cats, ground sloths, tapirs, camels, two-horned teleoceras, three-toed horses, and four-horned antelope in warmer times; musk ox, woolly mammoth, bison, mastodon, and caribou in cooler. The last glacial epoch, the Wisconsin, expired roughly 15,000 years ago, inaugurating a warm dry climate that persists to this day.

TWO STATES IN ONE

Unlike Nevada's next-door-neighbor state to the west, whose demarcation between its northern and southern zones is variable, based as much on a state of mind as a point of geography, northern and southern Nevada can be pinpointed fairly specifically. Simply stated, Nevada's two deserts separate the state into its two distinct parts. Northern Nevada is usually considered to comprise everything within the Great Basin Desert, while southern Nevada occupies the Mojave Desert. The differences in the field probably wouldn't be immediately apparent to the untrained eye, but the two primary related factors are elevation and vegetation.

The base elevation of the Great Basin Desert ranges from around 4,500 to 6,200 feet, where the predominant vegetation is sagebrush. The Mojave's elevation in Nevada starts at 490 feet (the lowest and southernmost point in Nevada at the Colorado River near Laughlin) and ascends, in latitude as well as elevation, to the Great Basin; the predominant vegetation below 4,000 feet is creosote.

It isn't an exact science, but generally speaking, a digitated line can be drawn from around Beatty in the west to around Caliente in the east in terms of elevation, vegetation, and drainage to denote southern Nevada. The WPA's *Nevada* reported that roughly 15 miles south of Tonopah, "A distinct change in the vegetation is noted; northward is the sagebrush zone, southward the creosote bush. The line of demarcation between the zones is so sharp that in this area not a single piece of sagebrush is found within a few hundred feet south of it and not a creosote bush a hundred feet north."

Too, Caliente is surrounded by sage above 4,000 feet, but because its Meadow Valley Wash is drained southward into the Colorado system, it's generally considered not part of the Great Basin, whose drainage is internal, without an outlet to the sea. Of course, all the life zones are found on the mountain ranges of the Mojave, but the Great Basin does not lower itself to the Mojave's own zone.

Though the northern part of the state accounts for the vast majority of land, the southern part accounts for the vast majority of population. Roughly 80 percent of the real estate is in the north, and 80 percent of the residents are in the south. As for climate, the farther south you travel in Nevada, the hotter and drier it gets. Las Vegas has some of the least precipitation and the lowest relative humidity of any metropolitan area in the country; Laughlin, at the extreme southern tip of the state, is second only to Laredo, Texas, for the most record-high temperatures in the country.

Nevada's 110,000 square miles, or 70,264,320 acres, make it the seventh-largest state in the United States. The federal government owns nearly 60 million of those acres, or 85.28 percent of the total land area in the state. Of the federally claimed acreage, nearly 50 million acres are managed by the Bureau of Land Management, with just over five million acres controlled by the U.S. Forest Service. The military rules over four million acres, which it uses for bases, training grounds, and test sites, and that number is growing.

Tribal reservations, national wildlife refuges, and wilderness areas account for the remainder of the federal total. Twenty-four state parks preserve roughly 50,000 acres. The rest is privately owned.

THE DESERT

Great Basin

The Great Basin Desert is one of the major geographic features in the United States. It stretches 500 miles wide between California's Sierra Nevada and Utah's Wasatch Mountains, up to 750 miles long between Oregon's Columbia Plateau and southern Nevada's Mojave Desert, and makes up a large part of the Basin and Range Physiographic Province. John C. Frémont named the Great Basin in 1844 for a curious and unique phenomenon: internal drainage. None of the rivers that flow into this desert ever flow out. Instead, they empty into lakes, disappear into sinks, or just peter out and evaporate.

The Great Basin is not a basin at all. The image of a bowl-shaped depression between the two major mountain ranges couldn't be further from the truth. It's more like a square of corrugated cardboard inside a shallow box. Some of the interior ridges rise higher than the sides of the box. All of the ridges, no matter what their height, have troughs between them. This desert is not even *shaped* anything like its name might imply. Stare at the "Great Basin" map for a hundred years and you won't see a basin. Frémont did get one thing right in the name, though. It *is* great.

Roughly 75 percent of Nevada is occupied by the Great Basin Desert. At the same time, roughly 75 percent of the Great Basin Desert is in Nevada. Only a few thousand years ago, a large proportion of this desert was covered by great lakes left over from the wet Pleistocene. The earth is highly mineralized: copper, lead, iron, gypsum, salt, magnesite, brucite, diatomaceous earth, silver, and gold have all been mined in unimaginable quantities. But this desert's most unmistakable characteristic is the basin and range corrugation. There are upwards of 200 separate mountain ranges; most are oriented northeast-southwest, are between 50 and 100 miles long, and are separated by valleys of equal length. The average base elevation (where the basins meet the ranges) is 5,000 feet above sea level, slightly lower in the west, slightly higher in the east. The bottom of the basins here are higher than most mountains east of the Mississippi. The overwhelmingly predominant vegetation is sagebrush, the state flower. Piñon pine and juniper, mountain mahogany and aspen, fir, pine, and spruce inhabit the higher life zones, where many creatures, from field mice and jackrabbits to pronghorn and bobcat, reside.

Mojave Desert

At the southern tip of Nevada, the Mojave Desert borders the northern boundary of the great Sonoran Desert, which encompasses southwestern Arizona, southeastern California, Mexico's northwestern state of Sonora, and nearly the entire Baja California Peninsula. Ironically, the Mojave Desert is a basin, sluicing south, down to and out of the main drainpipe (the Colorado River). Elevations begin to plummet south of Goldfield on the west and Caliente on the east: down to Las Vegas at around 2,000 feet, then down to Laughlin at around 500 feet. The Mojave is not only lower, but also hotter and drier, than its northern Nevada counterpart. Its prevalent vegetation consists of creosote, yucca, and Joshua tree. Snakes, lizards, and bighorn sheep predominate.

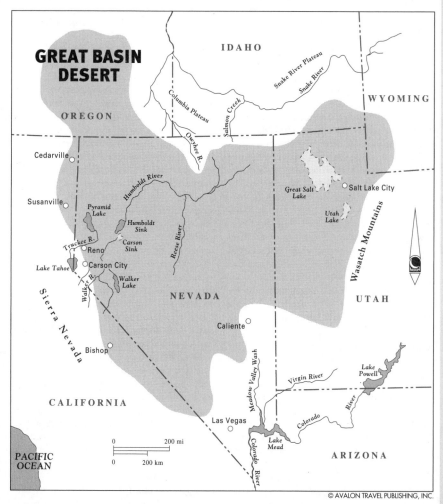

© AVALON TRAVEL PUBLISHING, INC.

Outside of the Deserts

Two tiny nondesert tableaux impinge upon Nevada: the sheer eastern escarpment of the Sierra Nevada from just west of Reno to just south of Lake Tahoe, and the little bit of north-eastern Nevada that separates the Great Basin from the Snake River Plateau in southwestern Idaho. Lake Tahoe sits in a mountain bowl at roughly 6,200–6,300 feet, its east shore (Nevada side) contained by the Sierra's Carson Range. These rugged, heavily forested (second growth) granite mountains drop precipitously into the desert; the Carson Range, right on the California state line, is the only part of northwestern and north-central Nevada that's outside the Sierra rainshadow. The Sierra are responsible for both the paltry rainfall to the east of them and the Truckee, Carson, and Walker Rivers that form from the runoff from the wet peaks. The summit of Mt. Rose in the Carson Range (10,778 feet) attracts more than 30 inches of precipitation in a normal year, while Washoe City, at Mt. Rose's eastern foot, receives less than five inches annually.

The jumbled U-shaped ridgeline of the Jarbidge Wilderness along the Nevada/Idaho border consists of eight peaks higher than 8,000 feet and three over 10,000. The Bruneau, Owyhee, and Salmon Rivers flow north from there into the Columbia drainage system. And the vast Snake River Plateau stretches from this part of northeastern Nevada north into infinity. These three anomalies abundantly substantiate that this corner of northeastern Nevada isn't the Great Basin anymore.

THE MOUNTAINS

Depending on who's counting and how, between 150 and 250 mountain ranges have been counted within Nevada's borders. Most were uplifted and eroded by similar forces; therefore, most share similar geological characteristics. These ranges were created by the tectonic pressure exerted on the western continental crustal surface from the strain of the Pacific plate edging north against the North American plate, right at the San Andreas fault. This colossal jostle has fractured the crust at numerous places; at the cracks, some chunks have sunk down, some have lifted up, and some have listed over. A typical Nevada range is approximately 50 miles long (but can stretch as much as 100–150 miles from one end to the other) and is 10 miles wide. Each is slanted: a long gentle slope on one side, and a sheer scarp on the other. Boundary and Wheeler, the two highest peaks, reach just over 13,000 feet. Mt. Moriah, Mt. Jefferson, Mt. Charleston, Arc Dome, Pyramid Peak, and South Schell Peak hover around 12,000 feet. A score rise higher than 10,000 feet.

In the early mists of time, Nevada was covered by a shallow inland sea, then a vast duney desert. Limestone and sandstone, respectively, remind us of those times, hundreds of millions of years ago. Limestone ranges occur primarily in eastern Nevada. From the Tuscarora Mountains to the Las Vegas Range, several dozen ranges are built from this ancient rock, laid down during the dim Paleozoic era, from 570 to 230 million years ago. The Schell Creeks, Egans, and Snakes around Ely are the best known and most representative of the limestone massifs; the Snakes contain Great Basin National Park, within which Lehman Caves provide a graphic lesson in mountain building and erosion. The sandstone ranges occur in the southern Mojave: the Spring and Muddy mountains, outside of Las Vegas. After the sea retreated, massive sand dunes covered the land. Chemical and thermal reactions petrified the dunes into polychrome sandstone; wind and water erosion sculpted it into the strange and wondrous shapes on view at Red Rock Canyon and Valley of Fire.

The granite ranges mostly cluster in the west-central part of Nevada around the most magnificent granite mountains of them all: the Sierra Nevada. Granite, the major mountain-building rock, is forced up into the crust as molten magma, then cools slowly. The Granite and Selenite ranges around the Black Rock Desert and the Pine Nut and Wassuk ranges around Topaz and Walker lakes are examples.

When magma cools slowly it forms granite; when it cools quickly it forms basalt and rhyolite.

The volcanics are the youngest and most active of Nevada's many types of ranges and mark the eastern edge of the famous Pacific Ring of Fire. The Virginia Range is one of the older, more eroded, and most mineralized of the volcanic ranges—having yielded hundreds of millions of dollars in gold and silver. The Monte Cristos west of Tonopah are an anomaly in the Great Basin—crescent-shaped, mazed by badlands, and brightly colored with pinks, purples, yellows, and whites. The Pancake Range is only a few thousand years old, and the Apollo astronauts used its Lunar Cuesta to simulate the craters, lava flows, and calderas of the moon.

The rest of Nevada's many mountain ranges are composites, exhibiting a great variety of granite, sedimentary, volcanic, and metamorphic signs. The Humboldts, Santa Rosas, Stillwaters, and Toiyabes are composite ranges; the Toiyabes have been called "the archetype of Nevada ranges."

THE RIVERS

As author John Hart has written, "Only two large areas of North America were unexplored by 1825: the interior of Alaska and the inner areas of the Basin." The first explorers were looking primarily for rivers, seeking their beaver pelts and drinking water. They also had it half in mind to find the mythical San Buenaventura River, believed to flow from the Rocky Mountains through the great unknown expanse of the west all the way to the Pacific Ocean.

Ten rivers of note snake around Nevada. The Truckee, Carson, and Walker flow in, while the Bruneau, Owyhee, and Salmon flow out. The Humboldt and Reese are born and die in the Great Basin. The state's southeast boundary is formed by the Colorado, which meanders for 150 miles along the edge. The Amargosa rises in the Nuclear Test Site, waters Beatty slightly, then flows underground to Death Valley. Seven of the 10 are dammed.

Only the Colorado was a large enough river to be served by riverboats. The legendary Reese, however, looked good enough on the early maps to foster one of the great scams in Nevada history:

a phony navigation company. The Humboldt was both the scourge (the highly alkali water was as good as undrinkable) and the salvation (both for its stock-feeding grasses and its trail along the riverbank) of thousands of pioneers. The Carson, Truckee, and Walker Rivers are life-givers and sustainers for most of western Nevada.

The Humboldt

Jedediah Smith came west from Wyoming in 1825, trapping beaver as he explored. He sniffed out a river in the great desert and named it Mary's, after his wife. Apparently, Peter Skene Ogden hadn't heard about that, because when he located it from the north in 1828 he named it Unknown River. Joe Walker, in spite of Ogden's name, found it and followed it in 1834. John Frémont was the last one to label it, in honor of a German scientist so eminent that not only did the name stick like glue, but the river trail, three mountain ranges, a mining district, a sink, and a county were named for him, too.

Originating in northeastern Nevada, it flows southwest, picking up runoff from the East Humboldts, Rubies, and a half-dozen mountain ranges north and south of it between there and Beowawe. It cuts northwest up to Winnemucca and back southwest into the Rye Patch Reservoir. Beyond the dam, it disappears into its own sour sink. The emigrants cursed its foul water and harvested all the vegetation from its banks, and reclamation projects dammed it to irrigate Pershing County. A railroad, U.S. defense highway, and interstate superhighway have been built next to it.

The Colorado

Nevada got lucky in 1866 when, only two years after its boundaries were surveyed, the state was allowed to extend its southern borders into Utah and Arizona territories. Nevada annexed 150 miles of the west bank of the Colorado River, along with Las Vegas Valley, the Muddy and Virgin Rivers, and Meadow Valley Wash. The Colorado is one big river, which had followed its own destiny for countless eons until the Bureau of Reclamation had a better idea. With a few smaller dams on lesser rivers to its credit, the Bureau of Reclamation took on the Colorado and plugged it with Hoover Dam. Davis Dam, 80 miles south of the Hoover and built in 1954, further controls this now-docile dragon in Nevada.

The Sierra Three

The Truckee, Carson, and Walker Rivers all flow east out of the Sierra and fan out northeast, east, and southeast, respectively, into western Nevada. The northernmost of the three, the Truckee River, emanates from the edge of Lake Tahoe and flows northeast. It provides all the water for Reno–Sparks and some water for the reclamations project in Fernley and Fallon. (Derby Dam, which diverts Truckee water to Lahontan Reservoir, was the Bureau of Reclamation's first dam, built in 1905.) The rest of the river water reaches its destination at Pyramid Lake.

The Carson River, which flows north to Carson City, then east between the Virginia Range and Pine Nut Mountains, at one time spread out into the desert within the large Carson Sink. Today, a dozen or so miles west of the sink, the Carson is backed up by Lahontan Dam and then sent by canal and ditch every which way to irrigate Fallon. For years little water reached the Carson River marsh at Stillwater National Wildlife Refuge, but that's beginning to change.

The Walker River flows north from two forks into idyllic Mason Valley. It passes Yerington, then makes a big U-turn around the Wassuk Range and heads south into Walker Lake. Bridgeport Lake (in California) dams the East Fork early on, and Topaz Lake dams the West Fork early on; Weber Reservoir backs up the Walker on the east side of the Wassuks, a little north of Walker Lake, its final resting place.

The Idaho Three

The Bruneau, Owyhee, and Salmon Rivers flow north from the area where the Snake River Plateau protrudes into the Great Basin. They empty into the Snake, which empties into the mighty Columbia River. The headwaters of the Humboldt cascade south from the Great Basin side of the plateau. This is a very active corner of Nevada for water—a real slice of the Pacific Northwest. The Owyhee is dammed at Wildhorse, the Snake is dammed in Idaho.

THE LAKES
Man-Made

Dams are the name of this game. Lake Mead is the largest man-made lake in the country. All it took was seven million tons of cement poured 700 feet high to hold back the ragin' Colorado. Lake Mojave is no slouch, but nothing to brag on, either: It's only restrained by an earth-filled 200-footer. Both Rye Patch (on the Humboldt) and Wildhorse (on the Owyhee) reservoirs are popular with anglers, boaters, and campers; South Fork Dam, completed in 1988, is the newest dam in Nevada, impounding 40,000 acre-feet of South Fork Creek 10 miles south of Elko; the state's newest park is there. Lahontan Reservoir (on the Carson) also has lots of campsites, in addition to the amazing network of ditches and canals through Fallon between it and the Carson Sink.

Man-Altered

The overflow from the Truckee River once drained out of Pyramid Lake and into Winnemucca Lake. It took only 30 years for large Winnemucca Lake to dry into a playa after the Truckee Canal diverted some river water over to Lahontan Valley. Today, 100 years later, Pyramid Lake has dropped to uncomfortable levels, the Fallon National Wildlife Refuge is gone, and the Stillwater National Wildlife Refuge is hanging on by a thread. But now it appears as if almost everyone—the feds, the state, the hatcheries, the power company, and the conservationists, though not the farmers, entirely—are starting to agree on how to satisfy all the various, and often conflicting, water requirements for the lakes, refuges, irrigation systems, and urban populations.

Ruby Marsh has a number of dikes and causeways around and through it; Pahranagat is less changed. Walker Lake, like Pyramid, has had its water diverted and its fishery devastated; this lake could be one of the most endangered in the West.

For sheer beauty, Lake Tahoe—logged out, fished out, dammed, silted, but now slowly returning to a fairly pristine condition—is unsurpassed. Except maybe by a few of those backcountry lakes way up in the Ruby Mountains.

CLIMATE

Two generalizations apply to Nevada's weather: It's hot in the summer and dry year-round. But because the state is so big—500 miles from the southern tip to the northern, more than 300 miles wide in the northern half—and mountainous, it experiences a great variety of local climatic conditions. Still, weather patterns can be generally distinguished between the north and south state.

The prevailing winds in the north state blow either from the west or the southwest (occasionally from the northwest in the winter). Most of the fronts blowing in from the warm and moist Pacific drop their precious precipitation on the *west* side of the high Sierra, watering the long, sloping, Central Valley–facing hillsides of California. This rainshadow effect alone is responsible for the relative dryness of the Great Basin Desert: an average of seven inches of precipitation a year. Still, the Sierra don't only take away. They also give back, in the form of runoff from the rains and snowpack. Several rivers that flow east out of the mountains supply almost all of the water demanded by the densely populated urban area of Reno-Sparks, the agricultural lands and wetlands of Fernley, Fallon, and Smith and Mason Valleys, and the fisheries of Pyramid and Walker Lakes.

The prevailing winds of the south state are southerlies, which, having already crossed the fierce Sonoran Desert, hold little moisture. Las Vegas is America's driest metropolitan area, receiving an average of three to four inches of precipitation a year. On top of that, the south state gets scorched seven or eight months a year. Temperatures in Las Vegas reaching 110°F are not uncommon in May and September; highs can rise to 115° in July and August. Laughlin can hit 120° and usually registers over 20 days a year

of the country's highest temperatures. (A record-high temperature for the state was recorded in Laughlin in June 1994: a sizzling 125°.) Luckily for Las Vegas and vicinity (in a historical sense, since Las Vegas was founded for its plentiful local water), the mighty Spring Mountains to the west grab some clouds and relieve them of their moisture, which then percolates into the water table. But for most of its water needs, southern Nevada relies on Lake Mead.

Other mountain ranges provide similar water-gathering services. The Sheep, Snake, Schell Creek, Ruby, Humboldt, Jarbidge, Independence, Santa Rosa, Toiyabe, Toquima, and Monitor Ranges, among others, all coax a little of life's sustaining fluid from passing clouds. Many peaks are snowcapped for nine months a year, and one, Mt. Wheeler in the Snake Range, has a permanent icefield. The Rubies help swell the Humboldt River, and runoff from the Toiyabes and Shoshones collects to create the Reese River. Many lush and gorgeous basins on each side of the highest mountain ranges—Washoe, Paradise, Independence, Clover, Spring, Big Smokey, and Steptoe valleys—support farms and ranches.

Cloudbursts and thunderstorms anywhere in the state, but mostly in the south, can dump more rain in an hour than many places receive in half a year. These torrential downpours tend to be extremely localized and dangerous, giving rise to raging and roiling waves that surge down gullies and washes and drainages that might have been dry for a decade. The "wet" season is December to March; summer storms and flash floods (known in Las Vegas as "monsoon" season) occur between June and August.

Since most of the state is around a mile high, winters can be surprisingly severe. The harshest locations for this season are northeastern Nevada from Jarbidge to Ely, with temperatures regularly dropping below zero and the snow remaining for four or five months, and even longer in some places. Central Nevada is similar. The western and southern sections, from Reno to Laughlin, luck out with milder and shorter winters, one reason that around 80 percent of Nevada's population lives in this "sun belt."

Flora and Fauna

FLORA

Creosote

The Mojave covers the southern quarter of Nevada, and the creosote bush covers the Mojave. Because of the extremely arid environment, these shrubs, which grow from two to 10 feet tall and sprout dull-green, resinous foliage, are widely scattered over the desert sand, occupying only about a tenth of the available surface. Creosote shares the Mojave floor with a variety of cacti, yucca (especially the easily recognizable Mojave yucca, also known as Spanish bayonet), and the Joshua tree, which is endemic to the Mojave. Creosote is sometimes referred to as greasewood and is closely related to saltbush, which grows at an elevation that's lower than the sagebrush zone in the Great Basin. Greasewood, saltbush, rabbitbrush, shadscale, and other plants with spiny stems and tiny leaves are highly adaptable to alkali soil; their presence generally indicates conditions unsuitable for agricultural cultivation. They grow in the 450- to 3,000-foot zone in Nevada, mostly limited to the Mojave in the south and the lowest points in the lowest valleys in the Great Basin.

Joshua Tree

This picturesque tree, also known as the tree yucca or yucca palm, is the largest species of the yucca genus. It can grow to 30 feet tall, with a stout body and boldly forking branches. It blooms bright yellow from March to May. The Joshua tree was named by Mormon pioneers, who imagined the big yucca's "arms"—imploring, slightly grotesque—to be pointing the way to the Promised Land.

Sage

Sagebrush is the state flower. It's also possibly the most memorable and enduring image of Nevada, along with neon, that travelers take home with them. The Great Basin Desert has been called a "sagebrush ocean"; the sagebrush zone, roughly 4,000–6,000 feet, could also be considered a "Lilliputian forest." Unlike shadscale and greasewood, sage grows in well-drained and minimally alkali environments. Healthy sage can grow 12 feet tall, with roots up to 30 feet deep. Tall sagebrush indicated fertile soil to farmers, promising good crops with proper irrigation. Thus, farmers considered sage a pest and cleared it with a vengeance. Emigrants cursed sage as the vilest shrub on Earth, more useless even than Humboldt River water.

It was the Indians for whom sage was the great provider. They chewed the young leaves and drank decoctions brewed from the buds as a general tonic. They dried, ground, and made a mud of the stems and used it as a poultice. They stripped the pliable bark from the tallest sage plants, near streams for example, and made robes, sandals, and other wear from the fiber. And they used the leaves and stems for insulation.

Covering a third of the desert surface, sage protects the earth from wanton erosion. It also gives shelter to snakes and small rodents that burrow under the bush, and feeds sage hens,

NEVADA STATE SYMBOLS

Animal: desert bighorn
Bird: mountain bluebird
Colors: silver/blue
Fish: Lahontan cutthroat
Flower: sagebrush
Fossil: ichthyosaur
Gemstone: blackfire opal
Metal: silver
Motto: "All For Our Country"
Nicknames: Silver State; Sagebrush State; Battle-Born State
Reptile: desert tortoise
Rock: sandstone
Semiprecious Gemstone: turquoise
Song: "Home Means Nevada"

squirrels, jackrabbits, and other fauna that eat the spring buds. Sheep, cattle, and pronghorn also nibble on the young leaves.

Sage has successfully resisted nearly all attempts at commercial exploitation. Except for fuel in the absolute absence of any other wood, this bitter and oily plant hasn't been found to fulfill any productive purpose. Most desert rats consider this just as well, since there's nothing quite so evocative of the desert as the silver-green sheen and pungent aroma of an ocean of sagebrush after a good rain.

Juniper

Utah juniper is the most common tree in the Great Basin. It grows on every mountain range and in some basins, too. Juniper is also the first tree that takes to a particular microenvironment; piñon follows later. Junipers grow to 20 feet and are sometimes as round as they are tall. They produce blue-green juniper berries (bitter but edible), pale green needles, and yellowish pollen cones. You'll normally see them between 6,000 and 8,000 feet.

Recent research has indicated that the Utah juniper has survived the radical climatic changes that the Great Basin experienced over the past 30,000 years. By cross-breeding with its cousin, the western juniper, the Utah juniper altered its genetic makeup and was able to live out the ice ages (the western juniper thrives in a cooler wetter climate, such as in the Sierra). Forestry paleontologists are comparing the DNA of Utah juniper seeds and twigs discovered in ancient pack rat nests with today's juniper to decipher how plants survive climate changes—as well as which local trees will live through the current global warming.

Like sage, juniper provided for many Indian needs. The Puebloans favored it as a building material, especially for the roofs of their structures. They used it as a savory firewood. They stripped, softened, and made the bark into baskets, rope, and clothing. Ronald Lanner, in *Trees of the Great Basin,* even reports that they smoked the inner bark in cigarettes. Once you learn to recognize this tree, you'll not only come to appreciate its shade, but also use it to gauge your elevation.

Piñon Pine

If juniper is the most prevalent, then piñon is the most popular tree in the Great Basin. Juniper is the lower-growing tree of the pair in the piñon-juniper zone, piñon is the higher. It's the only variety, of 100 different types of pine worldwide, that has a single needle—thus its nickname: singleleaf pine.

Piñon is a Spanish word for pine nut. The pine nut feeds small and big rodents, birds, deer, even bighorn and bear. It was the staple food for Great Desert native peoples, who harvested the nuts from groves that they considered sacred and ground them into flour, which they baked into biscuits, cakes, and a type of breadstick. Today, the Paiute and Shoshone continue to celebrate piñon harvest festivals in the early fall; new subdivisions, especially in northern Nevada, have been encroaching perilously close to the groves. Actually, gathering pine nuts is a popular pastime for many nonnative Nevadans in late September and early October; be sure you're not trespassing where you're picking, then let the cones dry in the sun, and roast or boil the nuts carefully.

Singleleaf pines were the preferred tree of the *carbonari,* the Italian charcoal burners. Most of the piñon woodlands of Nevada were clear-cut to produce charcoal for the silver smelters, to fuel the steam engines at the mines, and to burn in woodstoves for heat and cooking. But because of the piñon's popularity with birds, seeds were widely redistributed and the singleleaf pines have made a successful comeback.

Cottonwoods, willows, aspens, sagebrush, rabbitbrush, and Mormon tea, among other trees and plants, also grow in the piñon-juniper zone.

Other Trees

Starting at around 7,500 feet and going up to 11,000 feet or so are the trees that most people relate to the forest. In the Great Basin, the higher you go (up to a certain elevation), the wetter the environment, thus the bigger the trees. Ponderosa, Jeffrey, and sugar pine; white fir; and incense cedar occupy the lower reaches of the forest. Lodgepole and white pine and mountain hemlock inhabit the middle zone, at about

9,000 feet. Douglas fir, white fir, blue spruce, and Engelmann spruce top off the thick growth up to 10,000 feet. Limber and bristlecone pine trees survive and thrive at or above the usual treeline in the harshest environment known to trees of the Great Basin.

Foraging

Foraging for edible foods—though not as easy as it is in California, the Pacific Northwest, or even Alaska—can nonetheless be enjoyed in the Nevada desert. Many of these forageable wild plants are "escaped domestics," which grow around old ranches, settlements, even ghost towns. Raspberries and strawberries are sometimes found near remnants of civilization, though they also grow wild, mostly in damp woods or along steep well-drained slopes. They fruit in late summer (late August and early September). Wild asparagus is a good forage to stalk. It's easiest to spot in summer, when the shoots are tall; return to the spot the next spring to harvest the tender five- to seven-inch-high edibles. Roses grow above 5,000 feet in the sagebrush zone; look for five-petaled pink flowers on thorny stems in spring, and the orange-red hips in September. In well-watered areas, the hips are juicy and delicious on their own; dry and mealy hips are generally made into jams. Remove the pips and process the flesh. Finally, pine nuts are the traditional and ultimate forage in the Great Basin. Harvesting and preparing these thin-shelled, starchy seeds is almost a rite of passage for Nevadans.

FAUNA

Fish

Contrary to popular perception, Nevada is not just a great desert wasteland. In fact, nothing dispels the myth quite so forcefully as the fact that Nevada has more than 600 fishable lakes, reservoirs, rivers, streams, and creeks. (*Nevada Anglers Guide,* by Richard Dickerson, lists 162 of them, the ones with the best public access and that can take the fishing pressure without too much strain.)

The biggest fish are found in the biggest lakes. Mackinaw, a variety of Great Lakes trout, averages

20 pounds (the record is a monster 37-pounder); catch mackinaw deep in Lake Tahoe. Lahontan cutthroat, the "trout salmon" that so impressed John Frémont, grow to 15 pounds in Pyramid Lake; a 41-pounder is on display at the State Museum in Carson City, but it's a member of the original species, which is now extinct. The ancient cui-ui sucker fish is endemic to Pyramid. Lake Mead boasts an abundance of striped bass, and a regenerating population of the popular largemouth bass.

Seven-pound cutthroats, five-pound browns, and three-pound rainbows are fished from Topaz Lake and a number of ponds and streams in Nevada. One-pound golden trout are catchable in the lakes (especially Hidden Lake) high up in the Ruby Mountains. Rye Patch Reservoir near Lovelock was a favorite for walleye until the reservoir was drained in 1992.

Finally, one stream in Nevada, Desert Creek near Yerington, actually has Arctic grayling, a tasteless white fish well known to all anglers familiar with the lakes and streams of Alaska.

Lizards

Of 3,000 different kinds of lizards worldwide, Nevada has 26—15 or so of them in the Mojave Desert. Only two lizards of the 3,000 are poisonous and Nevada has one of them. The **banded Gila monster** is found in Clark and Lincoln counties between the Colorado and Virgin Rivers. Nevada's Gila monsters are nocturnal—most active right after dusk—though you might see one after a summer rain or on a cool day. They're also endangered.

The **chuckwalla** is nearly as common as the Gila is rare. This 16-inch vegetarian eats mostly blossoms and leaves and is found in Clark and Nye counties. The **desert iguana** is another vegetarian. The **Great Basin whiptail** is found anywhere from 2,000 to 7,000 feet. It's easy to identify, since its tail is twice as long as its body. Another tail by which to tell a lizard is that of the **zebratail,** which is banded with black and white stripes. It wags its tail as it flees, hoping to distract its predators. If a Gila, say, gets the tail, the zebratail grows another. But that would be a feat for the Gila, since zebratails are extremely fast and zig-zag when they run.

The **collared lizard** has a black-and-white band around its neck. It's generally seen around rocky terrain, hunting for grasshoppers, cicadas, and leopard lizards. It bites if handled. **Leopard lizards** are extremely common in northern Nevada, and prefer to hang around sage. They're easy to recognize, with thick spots all over their bodies and very long thin tails. If you creep quietly toward them, they'll tolerate you until you're very close before darting away. They also bite readily and are fierce predators.

The **horned lizard** is an unusual creature of the desert Southwest. It's black and tan and grows horns on the back of its head. Small spines cover the rest of its body. Ants are its favorite food. It relies on camouflage for protection, but will puff up and hiss if threatened.

The most common lizard of Nevada is the **Western fence lizard.** It's brown with bright blue stomach patches. Like the zebratail, it can shed its tail to escape danger, then grow another.

Since lizards, like all reptiles, are cold-blooded, you'll often see them sunning on rocks in the morning and evening. They need a body temperature of 104°F to be in full fettle. Too much heat, however, is fatal; during the hottest part of the day, they hide in the shade of shrubs, rocks, or burrows. And, of course, they hibernate in the winter.

SAFETY IN SNAKE COUNTRY

Though there are seven different types of rattlers in Nevada, a couple of them extremely venomous, your chances of seeing one in the daytime are narrow, your chances of being bitten by one are slim, and your chances of having a fatal encounter are statistically nil. Two Nevada deaths have been attributed to snakebites in the last 55 years. Only a dozen people a year die of snakebites in the whole country, and those people either generally teased or tried to handle a snake.

Rattlers are mostly nocturnal, though they do move around during the day. However, most daylight sightings turn out generally to be Great Basin gopher snakes. These are harmless guys, but they do make a hissing noise that might sound like a rattler.

The best way to protect against snakebites is by wearing hiking boots. Use caution when walking in rocky areas, around ledges, or near any area that might make a snake den. Try to keep night strolling to a minimum, and if you can't, be extra careful. If you bump into a snake, stay calm, stay still, and when you can, edge away. Experts recommend that you try for a soft footfall, so as not to disturb the snake's sensitivity to ground vibration.

In the unlikely event of a bite, stay calm; this slows the heart rate and prevents the poison from spreading as quickly. Keep the bite below heart level. If you can, try to ascertain what kind of snake bit you, but don't catch it; it could bite you again. A fang mark or two will be apparent, the area will swell and discolor, and it will hurt. Loosely bandage above and below the bite and wash it with soap and water. The old way of dealing with a snake bite, which some old—and young—codgers still subscribe to, was to take a sterilized knife, cut a quarter-inch incision between and slightly past the fang marks, then keep squeezing out the venom until you reach a doctor. But this technique removes only a small amount of poison. If you have one of the suction-cup snakebite extractors handy, you can try that. But the best thing to do is hightail it to a doctor.

Remember that snakes are as afraid, if not more, of you as you are of them. Because they'll sense your presence before you will theirs, they'll generally be long gone by the time you get to where they were. Caution is always the rule. But don't let the fact that you share the backcountry with snakes deter you from using and enjoying it.

Snakes

Like lizards, most snakes in Nevada are found in the Mojave. Several varieties of rattlers inhabit the Las Vegas area. The **Panamint** has a wide range (from Las Vegas to Tonopah) and a bad bite. The **Southwestern speckled** likes the mountains and washes around Lake Mead. **Western diamondbacks** are easy to identify, as their name implies, and it's a good thing, too, since they're especially ill-tempered, as well as being the largest of the seven species of Nevada rattlers. The **Mojave rattler** is sometimes mistaken for the diamondback, although the latter rattler has distinctive black and white tail rings. The Mojave is less nasty but its venom is 10 times more poisonous. The **sidewinder** is a small rattlesnake (around two feet long), known for the S-curve trail its slithering motion leaves in the sand. The **Great Basin rattlesnake** has the greatest range, covering more than half the state, from 5,000 to 10,000 feet in elevation.

The **mountain king snake** is not poisonous, likes riverbottoms and farmlands, and eats rattlers for breakfast; it's immune to the venom. Because it displays red and black bands, it's often confused with the highly poisonous **Arizona coral snake,** with its red and yellow bands. Though they're not supposed to exist in Nevada, coral snakes have been identified as far north as Lovelock and as far west as Carson City.

The **Great Basin gopher snake** is probably the most common and widely distributed serpent in Nevada and is active during the day. It's not poisonous; rather, it kills small mammals by constriction.

Desert Tortoise

The desert tortoise is the state reptile. It's unmistakable: hard shell and four fat legs, the front legs larger than the rear for digging burrows. Burrows protect them on hot summer days and when they hibernate throughout the winter. These tortoises eat grasses and blossoms in the early mornings and late afternoons. In June, females lay four to six eggs in shallow holes and then cover them with dirt. The eggs hatch in late September-early October. The tortoises can live to be 100 years old.

These days, however, most don't. In April 1990 the desert tortoise of the Mojave was listed as threatened, due to loss of habitat to agriculture, road construction, military activity, energy and mineral development, off-road vehicles, raven predation, and private collection. The tortoises are also victims of a upper-respiratory syndrome.

Birds

Nevada is one of the best places in the West to look for raptors—eagles, hawks, falcons, ospreys. The Goshute Mountains especially, between Ely and Wendover, are on the "flyway," or aerial highway, of up to 20,000 migrating raptors every year. In fact, HawkWatch International, 800/726-HAWK, has been monitoring the migrations over the Goshutes from the Pacific Northwest and Alaska since 1979: counting the individual birds among 18 different species, capturing birds to observe their health and size, banding birds to track their movements, and assessing their data to estimate population fluctuations. Recently, HawkWatch's count was the highest in a decade; it concludes that the use of DDT and other pesticides, to which raptors are especially susceptible, is diminishing.

Both bald and golden **eagles** are found in Nevada. Golden eagles stay year-round, mostly in the northern part of the state; bald eagles migrate here for the winter and like well-watered and agricultural areas.

Ospreys have wingspans approaching those of eagles and are related to vultures. Since they feed entirely on fish (they're also known as fish hawks), osprey are mainly observed feeding in the Reno–Tahoe rivers and lakes on their migration south for the winter.

Accipiters include **goshawks,** fairly large birds about the size of ravens; **sharp-shinned hawks,** about the size of robins; and **Cooper's hawks,** similar to sharp-shins. Since accipiter habitat is mostly in forests and heavily wooded areas, HawkWatch has found their populations to be on the wane because of extensive logging in the Pacific Northwest and western Canada.

Buteos are the hawks normally seen soaring above the desert. Among them are **ferruginous hawks,** which live in the juniper of eastern Nevada year-round. Common **red-tailed hawks** prey on lizards in the Mojave. **Rough-legged hawks** winter in Nevada, while **Swainson's hawks** prefer Nevada in the summer and then fly to South America for the winter, though they're fairly uncommon these days.

Sharp-eyed birdwatchers can also spot marsh hawks, kestrels, merlins, and peregrine falcons.

Pelicans have traditionally nested in large numbers at Anaho Island in Pyramid Lake. Their numbers had fallen dramatically because of the drought, reaching an all-time low of nine chicks in 1991, after a high of 10,000 in 1986. But they recovered in 1992 and 1993, producing 1,500 chicks each year. The pelican population is now back in the thousands.

Other shorebirds also nest at Anaho. The wildlife refuges at Ruby Marsh, Stillwater, Pahranagat Lakes, Railroad Valley, Kirch (south of Ely), and others are also prime bird-watching locales.

Mountain Lions and Bears

Predators and prey around the West are considered plentiful nowadays by experts, compared to their numbers during the first half of this century. Pronghorn, elk, deer, sheep, wild horses, and burros all have revived in the past 30 years or so. That's why mountain lions and bears have become more common in the mountains, both remote and inhabited.

Mountain lions aren't particularly shy of humans, but they're so elusive that they're not often seen. When one is, especially in a population area, it's trapped and relocated, and it makes pretty big news. Attacks on humans are rare, but not unknown. Also known as cougars, panthers (or painters), and pumas, mountain lion males weigh up to 160 pounds, females 100–130 punds As such, they're second in size only to bears as North America's largest predators. They hunt at night, taking everything from coyotes, mule deer, and bighorn sheep to beavers and even porcupines.

Likewise, **black bears** are more common in Nevada than most people might think. A De-

partment of Wildlife study a few years ago concluded that up several hundred bears live in Nevada, most in the Sierra, and the rest in Pine Nut and Sweetwater Ranges in western Nevada and up around Jarbidge in northeastern Nevada. These bears can be any color from blond to cinnamon to jet-black; nearly all have a white patch on their chests. The males can be six feet long and weigh 300–400 pounds, the females five feet long and up to 200 pounds.

Coyotes

Coyotes are the west's most common predator, and therefore its contemporary symbol of defiance. Coyotes are extremely smart and patient. They're fast, they reproduce readily and in large numbers, and they're utterly opportunistic, taking advantage of bumper crops of rabbits or vulnerable deer, even supplementing their diet with pine nuts. Coyotes have also pretty much lost their fear of humans and are occasionally seen in towns, looking for cats and dogs. They prey voraciously on domestic stock, killing an estimated 10,000 sheep and cattle a year in Nevada. The federal Animal Damage Control (ADC) hunts them all over the west, killing nearly 100,000 coyotes in 17 Western states every year.

Bighorn Sheep

The desert (or Nelson) bighorn is the state animal. It is smaller than its cousins, the Rocky Mountain and California bighorns, but has bigger horns, and is therefore highly prized as a big-game trophy. In fact, hunters have stalked this animal since records of such activities have kept track of such things; petroglyphs and pictographs, such as in Valley of Fire State Park northeast of Las Vegas, illustrate bighorn hunting. It's even believed that sheep comprised a larger part of Indians' diet than deer. More than 2,000 hunters apply for the 100 or so sheep tags distributed every year for Nevadans; 1,000 nonresidents compete for a dozen out-of-state tags.

Nevada is the only state in the country that can claim all three subspecies of bighorn. Desert bighorn inhabit south and central Nevada, Rocky Mountain bighorn occupy northeastern

COURTESY OF THE NEVADA COMMISSION ON TOURISM

Nevada's state animal

Nevada, and California bighorn live in north-western Nevada. An aggressive relocation program is underway; bighorn are trapped and redistributed throughout the state to ensure healthy populations.

The Desert National Wildlife Range, at 1.5 million acres, is the largest wildlife refuge outside of Alaska in the country. It was established to protect the desert bighorn, seen mostly in the Sheep Range, which stretches from just north of Las Vegas all the way up to near Alamo (along US 93). Desert bighorn have overpopulated the area around Lake Mead to the point where they can be seen grazing on the grass at Hemenway Valley Park, right in the middle of Boulder City.

Wild Horses and Burros

One of the great wildlife controversies in Nevada is over wild horses, also known as mustangs. Since passage of the 1971 Wild Free-Roaming Horse and Burro Act, the Bureau of Land Management has protected these horses and burros "as a symbol of the history and pioneer spirit of the West." This legislation was enacted, thanks in part to the efforts of Velma Johnson, a Reno secretary, to

put an end to the brutal business of the legendary mustangers. These cowboys chased wild horses, often with low-flying airplanes, roped them from flatbed trucks, and sold them to slaughterhouses as pet-food meat. Mustanging was graphically dramatized in the classic movie *The Misfits,* written by Arthur Miller, who took the six-week cure (got divorced) at the Reno clinic in 1956 and observed mustangers working around Pyramid Lake. Possibly the most famous movie filmed in Nevada *The Misfits* captured the last performances by Clark Gable (who died of a heart attack shortly after completing the picture) and Marilyn Monroe (who died of a drug overdose under mysterious circumstances in 1962).

Since 1971, the BLM has been in charge of rounding up wild horses. Everyone seems to agree that a definite limit to the population needs to be maintained. Ranchers insist that the horses destroy the range and pollute water sources. Herds of wild horses are occasionally found shot in remote ranching areas.

Some environmentalists note, however, that when the horses are removed, ranchers run twice the number of cattle that's appropriate for the particular area. Others claim that horses actually benefit the range, by allowing growth of shrubs and plants that provide forage for native species, such as pronghorn, bighorn, and mule deer. One expert, Joel Berger, studied horses for five years in the remote Granite Range north of Gerlach and concluded that horses account for minimal damage to the range. Still, he recommended that 90 percent of the wild horses be removed to protect the native species.

In a recent round-up from a 300,000-acre horse-management area east of Eureka, of nearly 1,500 mustangs, upwards of 1,250 were culled. Horses nine and younger were transported to Palomino Valley to be offered for adoption. Horses older than nine were released back into the wild. The BLM defended the process, claiming that the older horses can reproduce until they're 16 or 17 years old. But critics insist that by pulling out the young horses, the government is purposely weakening the herds.

Once the horses are removed from the range, the question is what to do with them. In 1985, for example, 19,000 horses were culled from the wild herds, but only 9,000 were adopted. Since then, the BLM has begun to cultivate the market, by matching particular kinds of wild horses to local preferences in the southern, midwestern, and eastern states. One way of dealing with a saturated wild-horse market is injecting a contraceptive vaccine into nonpregnant five-year-old or older mares; the contraceptive is effective for two years. Even environmentalists and animal activists support this project. Other possibilities include sterilization, establishing large horse sanctuaries, destroying horses that aren't adopted in, say, 90 days, and selling unwanted horses for meat to supply the many people around the world who eat horse meat as well as to supply the domestic pet-food manufacturers.

In the 1992 BLM census, Nevada was home to roughly 33,000 free-roaming horses, 60 percent of the nation's total 54,000. But a combination of factors, including the round-ups and drought, reduced the population by more than 30 percent to 23,000 in 1996. The population in early 2004 was 21,400.

In an agreement negotiated by the Fund For Animals and Animal Protection in 1997, the BLM admitted to major abuses in its adoption system, whereby people who adopted mustangs for $125 apiece sold them to pet food manufacturers at a profit. It turns out the BLM had lost track of 32,000 adopted horses since the program began; 90 percent of the mustangs adopted each year, the Fund claimed, wound up as pet food. The BLM agreed to monitor its wild-horse adoption program more vigorously.

Controversy and drought notwithstanding, it's a thrill to see free-roaming herds, which is possible in nearly any rural setting in Nevada.

Environmental Issues

WILDERNESS

To many Nevadans, *wilderness* is a dirty word, a negative concept. Wilderness means controlled access and use: reduced grazing and logging; regulated road building, mineral exploration, and mining activity—in short, general commercial restraint of the activities that most rural Nevadans rely upon for their livelihoods. All through the 19th century, after original settlement and statehood, the term "public-domain lands" was tantamount to "anything-goes lands," with no restrictions whatsoever on grazing, mining, road-cutting, polluting. Especially since the vast majority of Nevada land is desert, traditionally considered unattractive and useless, it belonged to whomever wanted it, with no thought to preserving it in (what environmentalists think of as) its "pristine state." At the turn of the 20th century, Theodore Roosevelt, a "preservationist" president, was elected, and Nevada became the object of some of the earliest environmental-protection and controlled-usage policies (the Ruby Mountains, for example). However, up until quite recently, only small isolated chunks of Nevada's federal lands were protected: Jarbidge Wilderness Area (1964) and Great Basin National Park (1986).

The federal government owns more than 80 percent of Nevada, with 70 percent in the hands of the Bureau of Land Management (BLM). Traditionally, mining and ranching interests have been far too strong to be overcome by any wilderness proposals. Recently, however, the mass migrations into Nevada's two urban areas, the increasing importance of tourism to the state's economic well-being, and the election of three Democrats (out of a possible four) to Congress in the late 1980s turned the tables. In 1989, 25 years after the passage of the Wilderness Act in 1964, empowering states to set aside peaks, canyons, forests, streams, and wildlife habitats in parks, the political stars were aligned properly for the federal government to designate wilderness areas in Nevada.

Original legislation proposed in 1985 by the House Interior Committee included 1.4 million acres of wilderness and recreation areas. In 1987, a bill sponsored by Congressman Harry Reid setting aside 760,000 acres of wilderness and recreation areas was passed by the House of Representatives, but was killed in the Senate by Chic Hecht, known as a booster for rural livelihoods. In the 1988 election, however, Hecht's Senate seat was taken by Richard Bryan, who supported a bill to set aside 600,000 acres. Finally, on December 5, 1989, the Nevada Wilderness Protection Act became law, designating 733,400 acres of national forest lands as wilderness areas in 14 separate locations around the state.

The largest is Arc Dome in the Toiyabe Range in central Nevada at 115,000 acres; the smallest is Boundary Peak, with 10,000 acres surrounding Nevada's highest mountain. The wilderness areas range from Mt. Rose (28,000 acres) and Mt. Charleston (38,000 acres) within an hour's drive of Reno and Las Vegas, respectively, to the remote and trackless Quinn Canyon (27,000 acres) and Grant (50,000 acres) ranges in eastern Nevada. Also included are the Santa Rosas (31,000 acres) in the northwest, East Humboldts (36,900 acres) and

Rubies (90,000 acres) in the northeast (along with the long-established Jarbidge Wilderness Area), Mt. Moriah (82,000 acres) and Currant Mountain (36,000 acres) in the Ely vicinity, and Table Mountain (98,000 acres) and Alta Toquima (38,000 acres) in central Nevada.

In July 1997, the first guide to Nevada's wilderness area's was published. *Nevada Wilderness Areas And Great Basin National Park—A Hiking and Backpacking Guide* by Renoite Michael C. White. The book covers a dozen wilderness areas, plus Great Basin, with a total of 56 trips. It's indispensable for anyone wanting to explore the highest peaks and most remote ranges, as well as some of the most popular and accessible areas of wilderness in Nevada.

Another guide in which some of the access and backpacking routes are covered in detail is John Hart's *Hiking the Great Basin*. For the latest government publications on the areas, contact the Humboldt and Toiyabe Forest Service headquarters. The Toiyabe Chapter of the Sierra Club (775/323-3162; www.nevada.sierraclub.org) publishes the *Toiyabe Trails* newsletter six times a year, covering Sierra Club activities, wilderness, water rights, and other Nevada environmental issues and publicizes group outings.

In 1976, Congress passed the Federal Land Policy and Management Act (FLPMA), which instructed the Bureau of Land Management (BLM) to examine its land holdings (which in Nevada amount to nearly 50 million acres) to determine the areas that had potential as official wilderness. The BLM selected 100 sites encompassing a little more than five million acres to study in minute detail, out of which 52 areas and 1.9 million acres were proposed as wilderness areas. The rest of the study areas were released from wilderness consideration.

The BLM's proposals add up to more than double the existing wilderness in Nevada, and the prohibitions, in some ways, are even stricter than in Forest Service wilderness. No mechanized vehicles are permitted (including bicycles) and mining is prohibited (except if the mines existed before FLPMA). As might be imagined, the mining and environmental industries disagree over the areas and their boundaries. But spokesmen for the groups seem to indicate that they'll be able to compromise on the extent of the wilderness, which Congress will then have to pass into law. The process is expected to take years, but in the meantime, FLPMA prohibits any development in the proposed wilderness areas. They're now protected by default and will remain so until the determinations are finalized by law.

The Wilderness Society is urging the federal government to use $15 million from the Land and Water Conservation Fund (provided by a share of the royalties from offshore oil production) to purchase Nevada land to be protected by the Forest Service. Most of the sensitive areas are near Carson City, Reno, and Las Vegas, in the Carson Range, along the Truckee River, and in the Spring Mountains.

NUCLEAR ISSUES

Nevada Test Site

This 1,350-square-mile chunk of the southern Nevada desert is a Rhode Island–sized area that's off limits to the public—but you probably wouldn't want to go there even if it weren't. Between 1951 and 1962, 126 atmospheric tests of nuclear weapons were conducted within the Test Site's boundaries. Between 1962 and 1992, another 925 underground explosions rocked the desert (add to that another 204 tests that the federal government admitted it conducted secretly).

It all started after American scientists and military planners found that nuclear test explosions over the Marshall Islands in the central Pacific were politically and logistically inconvenient, and they went looking for a more suitable location on the U.S. mainland. Nevada already had the enormous Las Vegas Bombing and Gunnery Range, and there was nothing out there, anyway, right? The first bomb, a one-kiloton warhead dropped from an airplane, was detonated in January 1951, initiating another bizarre episode in southern Nevada history, not to mention a deadly "nuclear war" conducted against atomic veterans and downwinders that continues to this day.

About one bomb a month was tested every

month for the next four years; after a two-year suspension of testing at the site (during which larger bombs were exploded again in the central Pacific), a bomb was blown off every three weeks until the first Nuclear Test-Ban Treaty was signed in the early 1960s, eliminating atmospheric explosions.

Set off just before dawn, the tests sometimes broke windows in Henderson (100 miles away). The fireballs could be seen in Reno (300 miles away). And the mushroom clouds tended to drift east over southern Utah. For most of the blasts, the Atomic Energy Commission erected realistic "Doom Town" sets to measure destruction, and thousands of soldiers were posted within a tight radius to be purposefully exposed to the tests.

In his classic *Been Down So Long Looks Like Up To Me,* Richard Fariña described it thus:

> *The sky changed, the entire translucent dome stunned by the swiftness of the shimmering atomic flash. The light drove their once tiny shadows to a terrifying distance in the desert, making them seem like titans. Then it shrank, the aurora crashing insanely backward, like a film in reverse, toppling, swimming into a single white-hot bulge, a humming lump, a festering core. It hovered inches above the horizon, dancing, waiting almost as if it were taking a stoked breath, then swelled in puffing spasms, poking high into the stratosphere, edging out the pale skyrocket vapor trails at either side, the ball going sickly yellow, the shock wave releasing its roar, the entire spectacle catching fire, blazing chaotically, shaming the paltry sun.*

> *In the echo, there was silence.*

And in a less rhapsodic but no less poignant description, K. J. Evans, in his story "A Hometown Grows Up" (*Nevada Day* magazine, 1987), wrote:

> *I recall an early morning in 1957, seated with my family around the breakfast table. Suddenly, an atomic blast lit up the sky. My mother stopped stirring the Wheatena, peeled back the curtain from*

the kitchen window and peered out. A faint rocking motion that failed to stir my kid brother, asleep in his high chair, accompanied the flash.

Dad arose and padded to the back door.

'A-bomb,' he grunted, and went back to blotting the bacon.

Indeed, far from disturbing the local health consciousness, at the time Las Vegas turned the blasts into public-relations events, throwing rooftop parties to view them. Moe Dalitz and Wilbur Clark planned the opening of the Desert Inn to coincide with a detonation; the former garnered more coverage than the latter. A silent majority certainly worried which way the wind blew, and a vocal minority seemed to contract a strange "atom fever": marketing everything from atom burgers to nuclear gasoline and appointing a yearly Miss Atomic Blast.

But in a recently published coffee-table book that gives a brand new dimension to the word horrifying, *American Ground Zero: The Secret Nuclear War,* author Carole Gallagher quotes a 17-year-old soldier who witnessed an aboveground explosion in 1957:

That cloud was like a big ball of fire with black smoke and some red inside, big, monstrous, almost sickening. . . It left me really sad, real apprehensive about life. . . That explosion told me I was part of the most evil thing I have ever seen in my life.

GIs were stationed as close to the blasts as was physically possible without killing them outright. Citizens in the path of the fallout wore "film badges" on their clothes to measure the amount of radiation they were subjected to. Livestock dropped dead fairly soon after the exposure. People involved with or in proximity to the tests have been dying of cancer and leukemia ever since. Today, exposed soldiers, residents of southwestern Utah, and their children are part of extremely high cancer clusters. For more than 35 years, the government steadfastly denied any connection between the deaths and the tests; the Justice Department spent untold millions of dollars fighting lawsuits brought by victims of the nuclear tests, primarily people who worked at the Test Site and people downwind of the tests in Nevada, Utah, Arizona, and New Mexico. Only in the past few years have the feds begun to consider the possibility that maybe, there could be a possibility of some cause and effect relationship between the two.

The Nuclear Waste Repository

Now the state is being asked to play host to yet another aspect of the nuclear industry—radioactive waste. Yucca Mountain, 100 miles northwest of Las Vegas, is the only site being considered to become the nation's permanent high-level radioactive waste disposal site.

In a power play involving the U.S. Congress, the states, the Department of Energy (DOE), and the nuclear industry, Nevada has been awarded the dubious honor of receiving spent, partially cooled, but highly radioactive fuel from nuclear weapons plants and 100-odd nuclear reactors across the country. In 1987, Congress mandated that the DOE conduct an in-depth study of the Yucca Mountain site over the next five years. In so doing, the nation put all its radioactive eggs in one basket.

Not actually a peak, Yucca Mountain is a six-mile-long ridge rising 1,500 feet above the Amargosa Desert. The proposed repository lies astride the Nevada Test Site, Nellis Air Force Range, and a BLM parcel. Adjacent to Death Valley, Yucca Mountain's rainfall measures only six inches per year, 95 percent of which evaporates or runs off the volcanic rock surface. The DOE believes it can deposit the rad-waste 1,000 feet below the surface and still maintain a 700- to 1,400-foot buffer of dry rock above the water table. This deep "unsaturated zone" was one of Yucca Mountain's most attractive features, since no other site under consideration could offer near the protection from groundwater and deep-aquifer pollution.

The dry desert ecology also helps to mitigate federal engineers' concerns regarding the length of time it will take before the casks that hold the spent fuel inevitably corrode and begin leaking beneath the surface of Yucca Mountain. No one expects the casks not to leak. Other features of the site that should make it unattractive to store nuclear waste include its proximity to volcanic craters and 32 earthquake fault lines; still another fault line was discovered in January 1994, amid quotes from geologists that Yucca Mountain is less a monolith and more a big piece of Swiss cheese.

The DOE maintains that the chance of an earthquake or volcanic eruption is slight. Tunnels at the NTS have withstood shocks from weapons testing for 25 years. Aboveground structures, such as the waste-handling buildings, would definitely be vulnerable should seismic activity affect the site. And seismic activities measured at the site have bolstered critics' claims that the site is at risk from earthquakes. The worst, in June 1992, was a 5.6-magnitude quake that rocked Little Skull Mountain, which is only 10 miles from the repository, causing roughly $1 million in structural damage to the Yucca Mountain Field Operations Center. Proponents, on the other hand, contend that the sizable jolt would have done much more damage had the area been as unstable as some believe. In any event, they say the repository would be built to withstand an earthquake with a magnitude of 7.0.

The transport of 5,000 shipments of highly radioactive fuel per year to Yucca Mountain is also a major concern to Nevadans. Based on the DOE's record of accidents in its nuclear weapons transportation program, opposition groups estimate the probability of 50 transport accidents *per year* involving radioactive waste on the nation's highways and railroads. Around 250 shipments per year would pass through the Reno-Sparks area alone, and only a few states would be spared because they are not en route from the various reactors and weapons factories where the spent fuel is now being stored.

Another concern: Critics have assailed the Yucca analysis process for containing less science than public relations. A long line of independent scientists has criticized the federal government for sugar-coating, white-washing, even falsifying data. After years of resistance, DOE finally agreed to an independent study of the site. At the same time, however, the feds have accelerated their efforts to determine if Yucca will be safe for 20,000 years as the deadline nears for taking title to the canisters of nuclear waste now stored at power plants around the country. The process for completing the dump is well under way. In 2001, after seven years of study, the DOE released its Preliminary Site Suitability report, which conclude that the proposed Yucca Mountain site would meet the Environmental Protection Agency's Radiation Protection Standard. A year later, the DOE issued its Final Site Suitability report recommending Yucca Mountain as the nation's nuclear waste dump.

Ignoring objections from Nevada Gov. Kenny Guinn and the state's congressional delegation, President George W. Bush (who, while campaigning in Nevada in 2000, had promised to base his decision on "sound science") quickly accepted the recommendation and forwarded the report to Congress for approval. In 2003, Congress voted to allow the DOE to proceed with a license application to the Nuclear Regulatory Commission, which is expected to make its decision by 2007.

While the DOE hopes to have the dump constructed and opened by 2010, the state of Nevada has filed more than a half-dozen lawsuits challenging the science, safety standards, site guidelines, approval process, and constitutionality of forcing one state to accept the nation's nuclear waste. In 2003, most of those suits were consolidated into one legal action, which is still under judicial review. Additionally, that same year previously unrevealed information about the proposed rail lines needed to ship the waste across the country and into Nevada began appearing in the media, which generated concern not only in Nevada but also in other states potentially affected by the shipments.

Citizen Alert, a statewide environmental organization working since 1975 to assure public participation and government accountability on issues affecting the land and people of Nevada, has in recent years focused on nuclear waste, nuclear testing, and Native American sovereignty. A good resource for information and education about these issues, Citizen Alert publishes regular newsletters. Contact Citizen Alert, P.O. Box 5339, Reno, NV 89513; 775/827-4200; www.citizenalert.org.

MINING REFORM

Under President Bill Clinton's administration, the General Mining Law of 1872, still in effect today, came under serious fire. The law, designed 126 years ago to hasten western exploration, gives miners the right to prospect hundreds of millions of acres of land that's ostensibly owned by the government, lease it for $2.50 to $5 an acre (prices set in 1872 and never raised), and dig up the minerals on the land without paying the government any royalties.

Congress has long been considering reforming the law, and in 2002 the BLM finalized extensive changes to mining regulations covered under the Federal Land Policy and Management Act. Amendments are still pending, although U.S. Interior Secretary Gale Norton has urged Congress to resolve longstanding issues with Mining Law reform.

RANGE REFORM

Farming and ranching are no different from mining when it comes to changing perceptions of land use based on environmental values as opposed to lifestyle and economic considerations. The argument on one side goes that alfalfa farming, for example, produces 1 percent of Nevada's gross state product, while using more than 85 percent of the available water. Range-reform legislation was passed by Congress in 1999, but the current administration is looking at revising it again.

On the other side, ranchers argue that so-called "federal" lands are owned and used by the *people,* more often than not third- and fourth-generation ranchers on the same land, who have a strong vested interest in the health of the land for their continued livelihoods and lifestyles. Farmers, ranchers, miners all believe that their very way of life is coming under attack and will soon be legislated out of existence by the powerful forces of urban environmentalism, which hold an almost religious conviction of returning the land to their vision of nature—an early 18th century ideal.

These are tough issues anywhere, but out here in a state that's owned almost in its entirety by the federal government, these are profoundly momentous, and divisive, concerns, which will affect the future of all Nevadans.

History

NATIVE PEOPLES

Excavation and carbon dating of artifacts discovered in a number of caves around the state have supplied evidence that primitive aboriginals occupied the region now encompassed by Nevada as early as 11,000 B.C. Bones taken from a cave near Winnemucca Lake and spear tips unearthed at Leonard Rock Shelter (south of Lovelock) attest to human presence along the shoreline of great Lake Lahontan between 10,000 and 7500 B.C. Basket remnants from the rock shelter are thought to have been woven around 5600 B.C.

At Tule Springs, an archaeological site near Las Vegas, indications are that Paleo-Indians also lived in shoreline caves at the tail end of the wet and cold Wisconsin Ice Age, and hunted Pleistocene mammals, such as woolly mammoth, bison, mastodon, and caribou, as early as 11,000 B.C. At Gypsum Cave, also near Las Vegas, remains of humans, horses, and even a giant sloth certify a hunter culture from 8500 B.C. Little is known, beyond these finds, about the earliest "Nevadans," but starting around 3,000 years ago, a picture of the local prehistoric people starts to emerge.

The Lovelock Cave was a treasure trove for archaeologists, who excavated darts and fishhooks, baskets, domestic tools, tule duck decoys, shell jewelry, and human remains dating from roughly 2000 B.C. It's known that Lake Lahontan was shrinking, and these water-based aboriginals had to evolve a new desert culture. The area's

COURTESY OF THE NEVADA COMMISSION ON TOURISM

petroglyphs at Grimes Point, near Fallon

later Paiute demonstrated similar basket-making skills, but it's unclear whether the people who used Lovelock Cave were their ancestors. Petroglyphs from around this period have been located in the vicinity (especially at Grimes Point near Fallon), but they raise many more questions than they answer about the lives of the Paleo-Indians.

Anasazi

In the southern regions, an Indian culture began to evolve around 2500 B.C. Known as Archaic Indians, these were a foraging people who lived and traveled in small bands, built rock shelters, used the atlatl (an arrow launcher), hunted bighorn sheep and desert tortoise, and harvested screwbean mesquite and cholla fruit. By around 300 B.C., the Basket Maker culture had arrived; these people too were foragers and lived in pit houses.

Long about the beginning of the common era, natives in Nevada's southern desert began to develop the first signs of civilization. They lived in close proximity to each other in pit houses (little more than holes in the ground with brush roofs), and evidence exists of cooperation during hunting and gathering chores. By around A.D. 500, these Anasazi ("Enemies of Our Ancestors") had developed pottery and bows and arrows, begun building more sophisticated dwellings with adobe walls, learned how to mine salt and trade with neighbors, and started to bury their dead. By A.D. 800, their civilization was at its peak: they cultivated beans and corn in irrigated fields, lived in grand 100-room pueblos, fashioned artistic pots and baskets, mined turquoise, and generally enjoyed a sophisticated lifestyle in the fertile delta between the Muddy and Virgin Rivers in what's now southeastern Nevada—an outpost in Las Vegas Valley was the first prehistoric architecture in Nevada. Around 1150, however, the Anasazi disappeared. No one knows for sure why, but speculation includes drought, overpopulation, disease, collapse of the economic underpinnings of the culture, or warring neighbors. Whatever, the Anasazi abandoned their pueblos and farms (one of the largest of which was uncovered in the 1920s and is now preserved at Lost City Museum in Overton).

Paiute, Washo, and Shoshone

The Southern Paiute claimed the territory that the Anasazi had fled, but they never regained the advanced elements of their predecessors' society. In fact, for the next 700 years, these Paiute remained nomadic hunter-gatherers. Some migrated north to populate the high desert (Northern Paiute), where they encountered the Washo and Shoshone peoples. All settled into a basically peaceful existence, adapting to the arid land. (Their fishing techniques, rabbit and sage-hen drives, pine-nut harvests, salt mining, foraging, tools and weapons, basket making, and shelters are graphically displayed in the Archaeology Gallery at the State Museum in Carson City.) For hundreds of years, the Washo of western Nevada, the Shoshone of eastern Nevada, and the Paiute of northwestern and southern Nevada developed and maintained cultures perfectly adapted to their difficult environments. Until, that is, the first white explorers from the east arrived. Within 40 years of contact, the Native American lifestyles had been destroyed.

EXPLORERS AND PIONEERS

The first white men to enter what is now Nevada were Spanish friars surveying a trail to connect missions between New Mexico and the California coast. Two expeditions, one led by Francisco Garces, the other by friars Escalante and Dominguez, explored the region, but only Garces touched the far southern tip of Nevada. Escalante and Dominguez, however, discovered a couple of large rivers running west from Utah and postulated a great waterway flowing from there to the Pacific. Thus the mythical San Buenaventura River, the one great river that flowed from the Rocky Mountains to the Pacific Ocean, was introduced into the frontier imagination. It took almost 70 years to once and for all bury the myth of this great river.

In 1819, a treaty between the United States and Mexico designated the 42nd parallel as the boundary between American and Spanish territories (today the borderline between Nevada and Oregon/Idaho). For the next 30 years, all the

American explorers, trappers and traders, mapmakers, gold rushers, and settlers who entered Nevada were technically illegal aliens. The 1848 Treaty of Guadalupe Hidalgo, following the Mexican-American War, ceded most of the Southwest, including all of Nevada, to the United States.

In 1826, Jedediah Smith led a party of fur trappers through the same country that Garces had crossed, and spent that winter in California. In the spring, he crossed the central Sierra Nevada and discovered the Great Basin Desert—the hard way. Smith's party struggled through the sand and sage with no water for days at a time, crossed a dozen mountain passes, stumbled into Utah, and reached Salt Lake an agonizing month and a half after leaving the coast.

A year later, Peter Skene Ogden entered Nevada from the north and trapped beaver along the Humboldt River. In 1829 Ogden returned to the Humboldt, then continued south, becoming the first white man to cross the Great Basin from north to south. Meanwhile, Kit Carson and company were following parts of the route laid out by the Franciscans, thereby helping to establish and publicize the southern Spanish Trail. In 1830, Antonio Armijo, a Mexican trader, set out from Santa Fe on the Spanish Trail. An experienced scout in Armijo's party, Rafael Rivera, discovered a shortcut on the route by way of Las Vegas's Big Springs, thereby making him the first nonnative to set foot on the land that only 75 years later would become Las Vegas.

Enter Joseph Walker. In 1833 he led a fur-trapping expedition west along the Humboldt and Walker Rivers through Nevada, crossed the Sierra into Yosemite Valley, spent the winter in California, then returned east along the same route in the spring of 1834. In both directions he encountered and fired upon the Northern Paiute—the first skirmishes between the races in Nevada.

In 1841, the famous Bidwell-Bartleson party became the first emigrants to set out from Missouri and enter California. Through a combination of dumb luck and good guides, these pioneers managed to follow Walker's route along the Humboldt, Carson Sink, Walker River, and over the Sierra. With them were the first cattle, wagons, and white woman and child to enter Nevada. Their success encouraged a few more staggered wagon trains to attempt the long journey across the uncharted western half of the country and stimulated the first official map-making expedition through the Great Basin.

Frémont and the Forty-Niners

In 1843, John C. Frémont, a lieutenant in the U.S. Army's Topographical Corps, was assigned the job of exploring and mapping much of what would become Nevada 20 years later; he also hoped to finally locate that elusive San Buenaventura River. Guided by Kit Carson, he marched west through the Columbia River Basin, then cut south into far northwestern Nevada. He "discovered" and named Pyramid Lake, followed the Truckee River for a spell, turned south and "discovered" the Carson River, and continued down to the river that Joe Walker had found. Frémont's party crossed the Sierra in January, glimpsing Lake Tahoe, then traveled south through California and reentered Nevada on the Spanish Trail, camping at Las Vegas. From there they continued through Utah, crossed the Rockies, and returned to Missouri. This initial trip resulted in the naming of the Great Basin—and the denaming of the San Buenaventura. Frémont returned to Nevada a year later, this time guided by Joe Walker himself, and further mapped the country. By then, several hundred emigrants had already crossed the great desert into California.

The famous Donner incident, in which an ill-fated pioneer party became snowbound in the Sierra and resorted to cannibalism to survive, slowed emigration temporarily. But one year later, in 1847, a mass migration of Latter-day Saints settled Salt Lake Valley, advancing civilization to the eastern edge of the Great Basin. A year after that, the Americans emerged victorious from the Mexican-American War and appropriated the rest of the West; fortuitously, only two weeks earlier, the country's first major gold had been discovered at Sutter's Mill. Roughly 500 people emigrated to California from the east in 1847. But over the next five years, nearly a quar-

ter of a million frenzied stampeders flooded the coast. Of those who took the Emigrant Trail through the vast Utah Territory, some stopped to pan the eastside creeks of the Sierra Nevada and found gold, while others settled just short of California in the verdant valleys at the base of the great range. Mormon advance parties set up trading posts to supply the travelers; the one established in Carson Valley (Mormon Station) in 1851 attracted other settlers, who turned it into the first real town in Nevada.

Genoa and Las Vegas

Over the course of the next few years, the population of the country around Mormon Station—Washoe and Carson Valleys, Johntown, Ragtown—started to grow. Traders, prospectors, wagon drivers, and homesteaders moved in. In 1855 this far-western corner of Utah Territory, administered from Salt Lake City, was designated Carson County and put under the direct administration of local Mormon officials and colonists. Mormon Station was renamed Genoa and became Nevada's first county seat.

Missionaries were also dispatched from Salt Lake City to civilize southern Nevada at a rest stop along the Spanish Trail known as Las Vegas, or the Meadows. They built a stockade similar to the one in Genoa, befriended the Paiute, nourished the travelers, and even began mining and smelting lead nearby. But tensions between the Mormon colonists and miners, meager rations, and the hardships and isolation of the desert caused the mission to disband.

In addition, Brigham Young, concerned with possibly going to war with the U.S. Army over autonomy, bigamy, and manifest destiny, recalled the Saints from Genoa. Their places were taken by the people who would soon become the first official Nevadans.

THE COMSTOCK LODE

Prospectors and gold miners had been crawling all over the Carson River and its creeks for almost a decade. Chinese laborers had even been brought in to dig a canal from the river to Gold Canyon;

their settlement became Dayton, second oldest town in Nevada. The prospectors were already following their noses up toward what could be the source of the promising placer pay dirt. Of the hundred or so ignorant and unwashed miners, only the young Grosch brothers, mineralogists and assayers from New York, knew of the gargantuan silver lode under everyone's feet. But they both died suddenly one winter, and their secret was buried with them.

Meanwhile, Abraham Curry bought a ranch and opened up a trading post in Eagle Valley, between the county seat at Genoa and the lumber mills at Washoe City. And Myron Lake bought a bridge over the Truckee River in the large basin north of Washoe. Lake had dreams of a boomtown, and Curry had dreams of a capital.

An expedition led by one Lieutenant Ives powered the steamboat *Explorer* up the Colorado River all the way to Black Canyon, and a surveying team led by one Captain Simpson blazed a trail through central Nevada as an alternative to the heavily trafficked road along the Humboldt to the north. Soon, Pony Express riders were galloping over the Simpson route, passing linemen stringing telegraph wire between poles. Several new roads were cut across the Sierra into California from the east side for the settlers at Truckee Meadows and Washoe, Eagle, Carson, Mason, and Smith Valleys.

Virginia City

In 1859, two Irish gold miners dug a hole around a small spring high up on Sun Mountain and struck the fabled daughter lode. The respectable quantities of gold, however, were encased by a blue-gray mud, a peculiar rock that polluted the quartz veins, fouled the sluice boxes, and diluted the quicksilver. But when a visitor to the diggings carried a bit of the mud down and had it assayed in Placerville, it was found to be nearly pure sulphuret of silver. A drunken prospector dropped a bottle of whiskey and baptized the ragged settlement on the eastern slope of Sun Mountain with the name Virginia after his home state. And a shifty, lazy, and scheming braggart made so much noise about *his* claim to the riches

that the whole outfit came to be named after him: the Comstock Lode.

The Comstock is still one of the largest silver strikes in the world. And Virginia City remains one of the most authentic and colorful boomtowns in the Wild West. Such was the enormous impact of the riches, the power, and the fame of this find that within a year Nevada had become its own territory. The capital was placed in Abe Curry's Carson City, and of the territory's nine original counties, six surrounded the Comstock.

Meanwhile, trading posts were established all along the Humboldt Trail, at Lovelock, Winnemucca, and Carlin, among others. Boomtowns such as Aurora, Austin, and Unionville were mushrooming up from the desert. Gold was also discovered at Eldorado Canyon on the Colorado, a short distance from Las Vegas. But Virginia City was the lodestar, the ultimate boomtown. In 1864, a mere five years after its discovery, the Comstock had earned Nevada statehood status. It also helped finance Lincoln's Union Army. (Nevada's two new senators cast the deciding votes to abolish slavery.) And the unearthing of tons of silver affected monetary standards worldwide.

The Roaring '60s

Abe Curry, founder of Carson City, not only got his capital, but he got the state prison and the federal mint as well. Myron Lake won a 10-year contract to collect tolls on his bridge over the Truckee at a bustling little site soon to be known as Reno. The new state's eastern and southern boundaries were pushed outward, swallowing a few chunks of Arizona and Utah territories, including 150 miles of the Colorado River. Alfalfa was on its way to becoming the star crop of Nevada agriculture. The mines of the Comstock, deepening to more than 500 feet, were greedily devouring virtually every tree within 50 miles for timber supports. And Virginia Town was quickly turning into Virginia City, the largest and loudest metropolis between Salt Lake City and San Francisco.

Silver was located at Eureka, 70 miles east of Austin, and Hamilton, 70 miles east of that.

Gold and silver were mined in Robinson Canyon, as well as Osceola, just west of the Utah border around today's Ely. The silver at Tuscarora opened up the northeast. A gold miner from Eldorado Canyon named O. D. Gass homesteaded Las Vegas Valley, squatting in the ruins of the Mormon fort. But the big news, in 1868, was the arrival of the Central Pacific Railroad—at Reno in May, Winnemucca in September, Elko in February 1869, and Promontory Point, Utah, in May, also hatching Lovelock, Battle Mountain, Carlin, and Wells as it went.

The Railroads

The transcontinental railroad across northern Nevada stimulated the building of numerous wagon roads to the north and south of it, interconnecting the whole top half of the six-year-old state. The Virginia & Truckee Railroad was laid from the mines at Virginia City to the mills at Carson City, then hooked up to the main line at Reno. Thousands of Chinese were abandoned by both railroads after construction was completed; every Chinatown in the state was hounded and persecuted out of existence over the next 15 years. The Indians as well, after numerous skirmishes and several major battles, were finally subdued, then left to fend for themselves, both on and off the few reservations set up to contain them. In the late 1860s and early 1870s, the Comstock hit the third or fourth bust of its boom-bust cycle, but in 1872, John Mackay's Big Bonanza gave Nevada a six-year $150-million infusion of cash. A disastrous fire in 1875 temporarily muffled Virginia City's boom, and although Big Bonanza silver restored it even beyond its previous splendor, the Comstock mines played out in the next few years.

By then Eureka was producing serious enough silver to rate its own railroad connection, the Eureka and Palisade, to the Central Pacific. The Nevada Central followed suit between the mines around Austin and the main line at Battle Mountain. Other short lines were laid from mines to mills, with boomtowns in between. But the demise of the Comstock quickly forced Nevada to its knees. From a population of nearly 60,000

within a 20-mile radius of Virginia City in 1876, only 42,000 people remained in the whole state 20 years later.

Between 1880 and 1900, it seemed every strike in the whole state played out and stayed out. No new ones appeared. The boomtown economy deflated into a shambles. A still-unbroken record snowfall and cold snap during the winter of 1889–90 wiped out the entire livestock industry. Silver politics became the pastime of choice: calling for the federal government to turn more of Nevada silver into circulating coins at the mint. This minor political wrangle ushered Nevada into the new century.

THE 20TH CENTURY

In May 1900, Jim Butler, once a miner in Austin and at the time a rancher outside of Belmont, located some very rich rock in the wilds of south-central Nevada. Butler's silver strike at Tonopah was the first news of prosperity in a generation. Two years later, Goldfield began booming even more loudly 25 miles south of Tonopah. Prospectors fanned out from there and located the Bullfrog, Round Mountain, and Manhattan districts. Railroads were slapped into place between Tonopah and the Southern Pacific (which had replaced the Central Pacific). The Tonopah & Las Vegas Railroad hooked up the new boomtowns in central Nevada to a new transcontinental railroad—the San Pedro, Los Angeles, and Salt Lake—that crossed the southern corner of Nevada; a new town, Las Vegas, was created in 1905 as a service station for the railroad from Salt Lake City to Los Angeles. Copper in unimaginable quantities was ripped from the earth in eastern Nevada at Ruth, smelted at McGill, and shipped to the northern Southern Pacific near Wells on the Nevada Northern Railway.

Nevada's population nearly doubled in the first decade of the 1900s. The newly established federal Bureau of Reclamation dug right in to divert Truckee River water out into the fertile desert around Fallon with the Derby Dam and Truckee Canal. Humboldt National Forest was created to manage the Ruby Mountains. The

Western Pacific Railroad was laid across Nevada in 1909: from Oakland, California, across the Black Rock Desert, then along the Southern Pacific route from Winnemucca to Wells, and then along a northern route to Salt Lake City. Short lines ran from Tonopah into California, from Searchlight to Las Vegas, from Pioche to Caliente, from Carson to Minden, from near Yerington to Wabuska, and elsewhere around Nevada. The railroads were in their prime, but they would last only one more generation. A company with the auspicious name of Nevada Rapid Transit had already built a road especially for automobiles between Rhyolite and Las Vegas in 1905. Floods in 1907 and again in 1910 knocked out hundreds of miles of track on both the northern and southern routes. And in 1913, the designation of Nevada Route No. 1 along the Humboldt, the first state auto road, spelled an end to the railroads' monopoly on automated transportation.

The Road

Also in 1913, Nevada passed its first motor vehicle law, the license fee based on the horsepower (any auto with more than 20 horsepower needed a license). In 1914, a highway between Los Angeles and Salt Lake, through Las Vegas, was begun; it took 10 years to build. The Federal Aid Road Act of 1916 allocated funds to stimulate rural road building, which sent Nevada on such a road-building binge that it had to establish a Department of Highways less than a year later. In 1919, this state agency laid a road down on top of the defunct Las Vegas and Tonopah right-of-way, the first stretch of the Bonanza Highway (US 95).

The Federal Highway Act of 1921 invested more money in building long-distance connectors. Over the next several years, the Highway Department improved old Nevada Route No. 1 by widening and grading it and laying down gravel. By 1927, the transcontinental Victory (US 40) and Lincoln (US 50) highways were complete; a national exposition was held in Reno to celebrate, for which that city's first arch was erected over Virginia Street. The roads had an immediate negative impact on the railroads; the downtowns along the tracks began their inexorable migrations, relocating along the highways.

The Crash

The stock market went down and out in 1929 and took Nevada's banks with it. The Great Depression was in full swing, but three events in the following two years did more to shape Nevada's urban history than any others: divorce residency requirements were lowered to a scandalous six weeks; wide-open casino gambling was legalized; and Hoover Dam was built. Divorces and gambling combined to focus a national spotlight on Reno, Biggest Little City in the World, and biggest big city in Nevada. Unhappily married celebrities waited out their six weeks until divorce in the spotlight of newspaper society pages around the country—dateline Reno. Raymond and Harold Smith, veteran carnies and fledgling casino operators, embarked on a national advertising campaign to polish the image of gambling; their "Harold's Club or Bust" billboards attracted the gamblers and thrill-seekers in droves. (The house advantage did the rest.) Las Vegas also hit the front pages: Best Town by a Dam Site. Construction workers from the dam flooded the Fremont Street clubs and Block 16 cribs on payday; after the Hoover Dam was topped off, many stayed. And when the first turbine at the dam turned, Las Vegas had as much juice as it would need to do what it so desperately wanted, and was destined, to do.

Midcentury Modern

A big Naval Air Station went in at Fallon, and an Army Air Base opened at Stead Field outside Reno. When the Army Airfield was installed near Las Vegas in 1941, it supplied the growing town with a steady stream of soldiers and prompted the opening of El Rancho Vegas and the Last Frontier Hotel on what would soon be known as the Strip. Basic Magnesium began mining metals at Gabbs and built factories and a town for 10,000 people at Henderson between Las Vegas and Boulder City. After the war, Mafia money and muscle, supervised by a "charming psychopath" named Benjamin Siegel, raised up and nailed down the ultimate one-stop pleasure palace.

Bugsy Siegel expanded the Las Vegas Strip, furthered the modern tourism industry, and ushered in a 20-year underworld siege of southern Nevada. Embattled state officials, caught in an unexpected squeeze play between federal heat and its growing casino revenues, slowly legislated systems of control.

Otherwise, the conservative moral sensibilities of 1950s' America did little to prevent Nevada from marching to its own unconventional drummer. In 1951, for example, Nevada welcomed the Nuclear Test Site to the state, enjoying the fireworks for 10 years (until they went underground, where they continued to go off until the most recent Test Ban Treaty). The hotel-casinos kept opening one after another, year after year, and the brothels were left the way they've always been. Divorces were granted as automatically as ever, and the Freeport Law, instituting tax-free warehousing, was passed.

Finally, Howard Hughes rode into Las Vegas on a stretcher and bought half a dozen of the most troublesome Mafia-owned hotels. This put the seal of corporate respectability on them and paved the way for Hilton, Holiday Inn, Ramada, MGM, and other publicly traded companies to run the industry. Nevada's gambling revenues have never looked back.

Nevada Today

These days, gambling has become the country's most explosive growth industry. In 1990, only two states had legal casino gambling; in 1998 fully 24 states had it, with more lining up every day to get it. With gambling now an acceptable pastime, where do all the small-time casino customers want to go? The big time, of course: Las Vegas. In 2003, upwards of 35 million wagered nearly $30 billion, earning Las Vegas $6.1 billion in pretax profits in Las Vegas alone. Growth continues every year. Statewide, gaming brought in a revenue of $9.5 billion in 2003. In addition, Nevada for the past 25 years, but especially over the last half-decade, has been the fastest growing state in the country. Also, Nevada has once again become the nation's number-one producer of precious metals (particularly gold).

These large reasons, and other smaller ones, have introduced the stress of success to Nevada. The state faces a bewildering combination of contemporary changes and challenges. Growth issues are typical: water rights and conservation; carrying capacities and social services; housing, employment, and education; utilities and infrastructure. The recent resurgence of gold and silver mining, as well as the long-established policies of grazing, road building, subdividing, and other forms of developing public lands, have put environmentalists on a collision course with the boomers. The irradiation of Nevada continues to raise pressing questions about the U.S.'s nuclear testing and waste policies, which also have a direct impact on the local debate about preservation and progress. Nevada continues to try to balance the old boom-bust propensities with the new social responsibilities, to maintain the traditions that have made and kept Nevada unique and great, while at the same time changing with the times to ensure its continued presence at the cutting edge of national morality and policy.

PROSTITUTION

It all started, in Nevada anyway, in Virginia City, where brothels opened long before any grocery stores. Anywhere from 150 to 300 dens of ill-repute were operating at its peak. And just as the miners fanned out from the Comstock to discover the mineral riches across the vast state, the women followed right behind. James Scrugham, governor of Nevada during the Roaring Twenties, wrote: "The camps were not for wives. They just couldn't put up with the roughness. On those slopes, where many tents and shacks had no heat, the cribs had stoves. They had pictures on the walls, and maybe a bottle of sherry (whiskey was not as refined). The miners, some coming in from a day in the drifts, some coming in from months of prospecting, hands calloused, boots worn, having smelled only sagebrush and sweat—why, the poor bastards knew that the one place they could get a welcome, a smile, a bed with springs, clean sheets, the smell of perfume, was the crib. These men had it all the same. Come evening, the miners, card sharps, high-talent guys, blacksmiths took the same walk down the street of whores."

Of course, conditions back then weren't exactly conducive to sanitation and health, especially for the women. "All night, men have pawed and used her and not one has given a damn about her feelings," wrote George Williams III, in *Rosa May—The Search for a Mining Camp Legend.* "She may start to drink hard, snuff cocaine, or take laudanum [an opium derivative], to ease the pain of her loneliness." Suicide rates, murder, and death from venereal diseases and poisons taken for contraception and infection took a heavy toll among mining-town prostitutes.

But prostitution was a frontier tradition, and in Nevada the frontier tradition refused to be tamed. The railroad towns adopted the mining-camp custom of keeping a house to satisfy the need of the crews, cowhands, sheepherders, travelers, or just to keep the single guys away from the married women and high schools. Tonopah and Goldfield had prostitution through the 20th century's first couple of decades. Reno had its complex of cribs down by the Truckee River, and Las Vegas had its Block 16, both remaining in operation up until World War II. Ely, Elko, Winnemucca, Beatty, Wells, even the state capital at Carson City, had their dens.

Though prostitution was not technically legal, it wasn't technically illegal either. It stayed acceptable on unwritten terms refined since the towns came into existence. A modest house on the edge of town displayed a small red light near the front door. A discreet madam kept the women off the streets and somehow prevented them from scandalizing or blackmailing the married men, bankers and lawyers, reporters and editors, politicians, even ministers, who availed themselves of their services.

World War II

Military bases sprang up in Nevada during World War II. Stead Army Base, just north of Reno, and Las Vegas Bombing and Gunnery Range imported thousands of soldiers, with the same need as the miners and ministers. But the War

Department quickly put a lid on it. The base commanders insisted that Reno and Las Vegas close up the brothels, and they never reopened, legally, anyway. Today, prostitution is officially illegal in Reno's Washoe County, Las Vegas's Clark County, Lake Tahoe's Douglas County, Carson City, and Lincoln County.

Joe Conforte

Meanwhile, in the northern part of the state, a man named Joe Conforte was openly challenging the vague mishmash of law that regulated the sex industry. By the time Conforte arrived in the 1950s, whorehouses had been around in Nevada for 100 years, and nearly 50 rules and regulations had been entered into the state statutes governing the brothel business. For example, no brothel can operate on a main street; no advertising is permitted; habitual clients can be charged with vagrancy; pimps are verboten; and all brothels must be at least 300 yards from a school or church. Basically, 50 convenings of the state Legislature had tiptoed around the issue, leaving it up to the counties to decide for themselves.

Joe Conforte had fought for official legalized prostitution in Reno (Washoe County) for years, doing battle with a crusading district attorney who finally succeeded in jailing Conforte for a number of years on charges relating to their disagreements. (For the whole sordid tale, see Jim Sloan's *Nevada—True Tales of the Neon Wilderness.*) But after serving his time, Conforte set up shop at a ranch, just over the Washoe County line in Storey County, known as Mustang. Eventually, the allegations of paying off all the county officials started to rankle him. By then, the Mustang Ranch was Storey County's largest taxpayer, which gave him a certain influence in county politics. In 1971, Conforte convinced the commissioners to pass Ordinance 38, which legalized prostitution, making Storey the first county in the country to do so. Lyon County, next door, quickly followed suit. Finally, in 1973, the Nevada Supreme Court upheld the right of counties with fewer than 50,000 people to license brothels. They're regulated by the sheriffs, district attorneys, and health department. (Several years ago, Joe Conforte retired and left Nevada; the Mustang has closed.)

Legalities

As of the year 2004, 10 of Nevada's 17 counties have legal prostitution, and there are currently 28 licensed brothels in the state. All legal prostitutes are checked weekly for sexually transmitted diseases, monthly for AIDS; the state health department oversees the weekly health checks. Health officials assert that there hasn't been a single case of an HIV-positive test while the woman was working at a brothel. In addition, not a single customer has been infected with the AIDS virus from a prostitute in a licensed brothel.

Prostitution is illegal in Las Vegas. Both the client and woman can go to jail, and although the women are arrested more often than the clients are, clients are taking a risk when they engage in illegal prostitution. Las Vegas police spend $3 million per year enforcing antiprostitution laws.

GOVERNMENT

Nevada's executive branch has six elected officials. The governor is elected to a maximum of two four-year terms. The current governor, Kenny C. Guinn, assumed office in January 1998, after former governor Bob Miller served nine years as governor, the longest stint in the state's history. The Lieutenant Governor, Attorney General, Secretary of State, Controller, and Treasurer all answer to the governor while in office and to the voters at election time. The state government's executive branch employs roughly 10,000 people.

The Nevada Legislature is one of the smallest in the country, with a 21-member Senate and a 42-member Assembly. It meets for 120 days (though it's often much longer) starting on the third Monday in January of odd years.

The Nevada Supreme Court's five justices are elected for six-year terms. Trials are conducted at nine District Courts, whose judges are also elected for six years. Municipal courts handle preliminary hearings on felonies, misdemeanors, and small claims. Most municipal judges are elected for four-year terms; some are appointed. There's no appellate level in Nevada's judicial system; to be appealed, cases travel from municipal or district court directly to the Nevada Supreme Court.

Nevada has 16 counties, plus Carson City, which is a consolidated "city-county." County governments consist of three to seven elected commissioners. Also elected are assessors, treasurers, clerks, recorders, sheriffs, and district attorneys. City Councils, headed by mayors, govern Nevada's 18 incorporated cities.

Economy

TOURISM AND GAMBLING

By the end of the fiscal year ending in June 2000, Nevada had 238 casinos with net gaming win of more than $1 million each, per year. Taxable gross revenues from these large casinos came to a total of $8.4 billion; their net profit was $877 million, for a 5.7 percent profit margin. Of the statewide total, Clark County casinos with net gaming win of over a million dollars each (144 casinos) had gaming revenue of $6.7 billion, with a net income of $712 million. Total gaming revenues in Nevada came in at $9.5 billion for the fiscal year ending in June 2000, up a full one billion dollars from the same date in 1999, when gaming revenues totaled $8.5 billion.

Tourism is by far the state's largest employer, accounting for 35 percent of all jobs. (In southern Nevada it's closer to 45 percent.) By the end of 1999 it was taking 229,543 tourism employees to shepherd Nevada's 45.5 million tourists through the state, up from 208,233 and 42 million, respectively, the year before. Nevada is number one in the nation in tourism jobs per capita, eleventh in the number of foreign visitors. Roughly 25 percent of the state's labor force works for casinos directly. Tourists generate nearly $3 billion in payroll, which equates with

CASINO CASH

Stop and think about it for a moment. Nevada casinos take nearly $8 billion a year from their customers. Eight thousand million. Eighty million $100 bills. Eight hundred million $10 bills. There's always a lot of talk about how much money enters casinos in the pockets of customers, and how much money is transferred from those pockets to the slot buckets and table drops and cashier drawers and counting rooms. But did you ever wonder what the *casinos* do with all that cash?

Nevada casinos average more than $20 million in daily cash receipts. That's more than two million $10 bills. What to do with it all? First, casinos employ numerous people, for three shifts round the clock, whose jobs are solely to do the hard (coin) and soft (bill) count: organizing, processing, recording, and storing the cash. These days, casinos don't even actually count the money; they weigh it, both coin and paper, on supersensitive scales that calculate the amounts within fractions of a penny. Then, armored cars transport the money to various banks for deposit. The casinos and banks work closely together, using high-tech computerized accounting systems to ensure the accuracy of deposits.

The banks then ship the cash, by armored car, to local central vaults, where it's counted again and stored. Any surplus cash (over and above the vaults' storage capacities) is transferred to California. Reno–Tahoe's cash is sent to San Francisco, Las Vegas's to Los Angeles. Again, high-security trucking is used for the transfers, either private armored-car companies or official Federal Reserve transportation. Occasionally, money is sent via insured mail.

At the California Federal Reserve, personnel separate out the old currency and destroy it. Sometimes new currency is added. Some of this money is sent to other regions of the country according to their cash needs, which are monitored by Federal Reserve officials. Presumably, a number of these same bills make it back into casino counting rooms.

$16,000 in revenue for every Nevadan, and more than $1,800 in taxes per capita.

Given these statistics, it's amazing to think that the state Commission on Tourism wasn't created until 1983. In 1981, Nevada spent $165,000 on promoting itself as a destination, compared to a national average of $2.5 million. By 1984, Nevada had already spent more than $3 million. By 1993, $5.8 million collected from room taxes throughout the state was designated for statewide tourism promotion. In 1999, promotion of tourism topped $138.9 million, and the Nevada Commission on Tourism estimated that the state received an additional $66 million of free publicity in newspapers and magazines throughout the country.

TAXES

Money magazine perennially ranks Nevada as having the third-lowest state tax burden in the country. The same prosperous and hypothetical family of four, which would pay $3,775 in state and local taxes in Nevada, would pay $1,694 in Alaska (number one), and $11,020 in New York (number 51). *Money* notes that Nevada's average 7 percent sales tax is higher than that of most states nationwide. Nevada also ranks third among 90 federal judicial districts in its percentage of IRS criminal prosecutions.

Analysts agree that Nevada has the second-highest taxing capacity in the country, while the actual taxes imposed are the third lowest. However, there's a price to pay for residents' taxes being subsidized by "export" or out-of-state taxes. Much of the General Fund is spent on tourist industry infrastructure, such as police and fire protection, parks and recreation, and visitor authorities and tourism agencies. At the same time, Nevada ranks low in spending on education and health care.

According to Census figures, the U.S. government spent $4,800 for every American in fiscal 1996. Thirteen cents of every dollar was spent in California, compared to half a cent of every dollar spent in Nevada. It's ironic that the federal government, which owns a larger percentage of Nevada than any other state, spends one of the least amounts per capita.

INCORPORATING

Nevada's corporation system is one of the most liberal in the country (it competes with Delaware). Benefits of incorporating in Nevada include no state corporate tax on profits, no state personal income tax, very little paperwork and a low filing fee ($125), and protection from personal liability and public scrutiny. In addition, a single individual can be the sole president, secretary, and treasurer. Nevada corporations can conduct their primary business out of the state. And most attractive of all, Nevada is the only state without a reciprocal agreement with the IRS to exchange tax returns, which legally ensures maximum privacy.

Madonna is the head of a Nevada corporation, Music Tours, Inc. Michael Jackson, Paul Simon, Prince, Chevy Chase, Rodney Dangerfield, and Diane Keaton all funnel their large incomes through Nevada corporations to legally avoid taxes and protect financial privacy; the state doesn't require income data, and it releases no information. A New York City cab company formed 50 corporations for every pair of cabs in its 100-taxi fleet; its liability is limited to 2 percent (unless a litigant wants to sue 50 companies). Ski resorts have done the same with ski lifts, oil companies with oil wells.

It's easy, it's cheap, and it's anonymous. It doesn't even require an attorney. The one necessity is a resident agent within Nevada who can receive mail and be served with any legal documents. Several service businesses help other businesses to incorporate in Nevada. Many incorporating companies provide such services. A good one is Laughlin Associates, 2533 N. Carson St., Carson City, 775/883-8484, www.laughlinusa.com. You receive a fat package explaining how to legally eliminate state income taxes, how

to judgment-proof a business, how to protect your privacy and estate, and more.

Nevada's Secretary of State office is another good source of information. They'll send you out a free packet of information on incorporating in Nevada, and on how to qualify to do business in Nevada. Contact Secretary of State, 202 N. Carson St., Carson City, NV 89701-4201, 775/684-5708.

MINING

Mining is Nevada's number-two revenue-generating industry. Upwards of $2.7 billion dollars worth of minerals are mined from Nevada every year, $2 billion of that consisting of precious metals, mainly gold and silver. Gold is the most valuable in its economic impact, but a long list of other minerals are also mined in Nevada.

Nevada is the United States's largest gold and silver producer, producing a whopping 74 percent of the nation's gold and 11 percent of the world's gold each year. If Nevada were a separate country, it would be the third-largest gold-producing nation in the world, South Africa being first and Australia being second; as it is, Nevada's gold production brings the USA in as the second-greatest producer of gold in the world, after South Africa.

More gold has been mined in Nevada in the past five years than was mined at the height of the California, Comstock, and Klondike rushes combined. In 1999, Nevada mines produced 8.3 million ounces of gold, down a bit from the all-time record year of 1998, when 8.9 million ounces were mined. (In 1850, at the zenith of the California rush, three million ounces were produced. The Klondike, Goldfield, and Montana mines produced five million ounces between 1900 and 1910. And the Comstock produced 8.3 million ounces of gold between 1864 and 1889.) In economic terms, the 1998 price of $300 per ounce meant that Nevada gold production earned $2.7 billion in 1998; in 1999 it earned $2.3 billion, with gold prices at $275 per ounce. In 2002 gold averaged $310 per ounce, while Nevada mines generated 7.73 million ounces. Overall, Nevada mines generated $2.7 billion

North America's physically largest gold mine, the Barrick Gold Strike Mine north of Carlin, is one of several Nevada mines that each produce over one million ounces of gold every year. Along with Newmont Gold's mines on the Carlin Trend in Eureka County (Nevada's second-largest mine), and the Cortez Mine in Lander County in the Carlin area (the state's third-largest), Nevada's gold mines account for 74 percent of all the gold mined in the United States.

Silver is mostly produced as a by-product of gold mining, somewhere between 22 million and 28 million ounces annually. (This is opposite of Comstock production, in which gold was a by-product of the silver mining. Just under 200 million ounces of silver were wrested from the Comstock.) Today Nevada has just one mine, the Coeur-Rochester mine near Lovelock, which is a primary silver mine; in all other Nevada mines today, silver is a by-product of gold mining. Nevada is the country's largest producer of silver, with 19.5 million ounces produced in 1999, down from the high of 25 million ounces produced in 1997. In 2002, production was down to 13.6 million. But it doesn't look like Nevada's slogan of The Silver State will change any time soon.

Mining directly employs around 8,860 workers in Nevada, down a bit from the previous 12,000; another 51,000 employees have indirect ties to the industry. However, along the "I-80 mining corridor" (between Winnemucca and Elko), one of three employees works for a mining company. In fact, Elko, where most of Newmont's and Barrick's employees live, closer to 40 percent of workers are employed by the mining industry, at an average annual salary of more than $60,000, which gives Elko on average the highest-paid workers in Nevada (the average state salary is $33,993). The total annual payroll for all miners comes to $552 million.

Mining companies pay a large share of state taxes: in 2002 mining paid $22 million in property taxes and $38 million in sales tax and $25 million in income tax, for a total tax contribution of $86 million.

Two useful websites for further information on Nevada's mining industry are: http://minerals.state.nv.us, and www.nbmg.unr.edu.

AGRICULTURE

In 1978 there were 2,400 farms in Nevada. In 2002 there were 3,000. The average size was 2,267 acres. Alfalfa is the major crop; other important crops include wheat and barley, alfalfa seed, garlic, onions, and potatoes. Hay crops as a whole account for well over half of all harvested acreage in Nevada. Nevada's total crop value came to $155 million in 2002. Farms employ 5,000 workers, 1 percent of the labor force.

There are approximately 1,700 cattle ranches in Nevada. Cattle production dropped dramatically in the 1980s, primarily because of bad publicity about red meat. But in the early '90s it became profitable again, primarily because of a strong ad campaign. The number of cattle on Nevada land remained generally steady throughout into 2000, fluctuating between a low of 490,000 and a high of 530,000; in 2003, there were 382,500 head of cattle in the state. Nevada ranchers are largely dependent on public grazing lands, primarily federal BLM lands, for at least part of their forage needs.

Nevada also is home to 95,000 sheep and 7,500 hogs, figures that have decreased dramatically from previous years. At one point, around the early 1930s, Nevada had 1.3 million sheep. But sheep ranching declined as it became less profitable, due in part to a reduction in demand for wool and in part to a change in consumer tastes in meat, moving away from mutton and lamb and more towards beef. In 1999 Nevada had 14,000 hogs, but by 2000 there was only one commercial swine operator left, with a count of 7,500 head. Poultry figures are so low that the Department of Agriculture quit keeping track of them.

People

DEMOGRAPHICS

According to official population statistics, Nevada's population topped 2 million for the first time in the year 2000: the 2003 figure came in at 2,296,566. A whopping 92 percent of Nevada's residents live in urban areas. Believe it or not, Nevada ranks third in the percentage of its population living in cities and towns (California is first, New Jersey second). Clark County is home to 1.6 million Nevadans—a remarkable fact considering the county was not established until 1909—while Washoe County is home to more than 300,000.

Nevada has been the fastest growing state for most of the past quarter century. Clark County, for example, has grown an astounding 350 percent in the last 25 years. Projections conservatively estimate another 300,000 moving into the Las Vegas area in the next five years. According to the U.S. Census Bureau, Las Vegas is the fastest-growing city in the United States, gaining over 470,000 people during the 1990s, bringing the Clark County population to 1,549,657 in 2002. Reno's population has more than doubled in the past 20 years; in 2002, Washoe County's population had reached 359,423. Even though Nevada has an overall population density of only around 18.2 people per square mile, Truckee Meadows is filling up fast and Las Vegas's water worries are growing. With 87 percent of the population living in urban areas, that means that only 13 percent of the population resides in all the rest of the state. That's a lot of wide open, sparsely inhabited space.

Statewide, Nevada has had a growth rate over the past 15 years of nearly 50 percent, highest in the country. Only 20 percent of Nevada's residents were born here; Nevada has the lowest proportion of native-born residents in the country. Of the 80 percent who migrate to the state, a third of them come from California.

Health

So many elements of Nevada are extreme that it tends to attract extremists. Nevada is always either a big winner or a big loser in terms of almost every behavioral characteristic, compared state by state, that somebody cares to count. Nevada wins large, and dubiously, in the health department with high numbers of deaths from heart disease and cancer.

THE NEVADA ALPHABET SCOOP

Those tall whitewashed letters on the hillsides above most of the towns in Nevada—who put them there? How? Why? When?

Similar letters are scattered all around the west. But Nevada's 30 are the most of any state. The first letter was put on a hill overlooking Berkeley, California, in 1905 by college students as an imaginative expression of school spirit. The sentiment found its way to the University of Nevada–Reno in 1913, when students constructed a huge N on Peavine Mountain above the campus, consisting of thousands of rocks, hundreds of gallons of whitewash (water and lime), and covering 13,000 square feet. The rage quickly spread to high school students around the state. Elko teens assembled their E in 1916; the Tonopah T went up in 1917; and Carson City (C), Battle Mountain (BM), Virginia City (V), and Panaca (L for Lincoln County) all had their own letters by 1927. Austin high schoolers finally put up their A in the early '50s, and Beatty's B dates back to 1971.

Lately, liability worries have prevented students from maintaining some of the letters. The R (for Reno High) on Peavine west of the big N, for example, is noticeably faded. In places, the task has been taken over by service clubs and alumni groups. In fact, the SV above Smith Valley has gone high-tech, and is now kept bright with an air sprayer powered by a portable generator. It'll take more than insurance premiums to jeopardize Nevada's 85-year tradition of sweater letters on hillsides.

Nevada has been distinguished by the number-one consumption of alcohol in the country for the past 15 years: 4.85 gallons per person. It also ranks number one in the most deaths from smoking-related diseases: 24 percent of all deaths in Nevada are caused by smoking. (By comparison, Utah checks in with 13 percent.) The large number of seniors who move to Nevada to retire might skew the statistic somewhat, but one of three Nevadans is a smoker. Nevada also claims the largest number of chronic drinkers in the country, twice the national average (alcohol is as good as free in casinos). Nevada's suicide rate is also two to three times higher than in the rest of the country, and leads the U.S. in senior suicides. It stands to reason that Nevadans pay the third-highest hospital bills. And Nevada has the nation's 12th-highest auto insurance rates; Las Vegas's are highest in the state.

Other Vital Statistics

The transience and low economic status of Nevadans, many attracted by a boomtown mentality to low-paying hotel and casino service jobs, are evident in a number of social categories. In 1990, the income of 10 percent of Nevadans was below the poverty level, a figure that is probably still about the same. Nevada has the highest rate of high school dropouts in the country: 15 percent or one in seven kids between 16 and 19. And those who go on to higher education have the second-highest loan default rate in the United States: more than one out of three. Voter turnouts also reflect the transience and carpetbagging nature of Nevada: 45th out of 50 with just under 50 percent of eligible voters going to the polls.

According to one study, Nevada's crime rate is seventh-highest in the country, and according to another, Nevada is the nation's fifth-most lawsuit-prone state (neither study takes into account the number of visitors who are in the state at any given time).

In the good-news department, only 5.4 percent of Nevada's population is without a telephone!

NATIVE AMERICANS

At the turn of the 19th century, four groups of Indians lived in what is now Nevada. The small Washo tribe lived in the west-central region around Carson City, Lake Tahoe, and the eastern Sierra. The Northern Paiute made a large section of western Nevada their home, from today's Humboldt to Esmeralda counties. The Southern Paiute occupied all of Clark County and the southeastern section of Lincoln County. The Shoshone were found in the east, from Elko to southern Nye counties.

The Northern Paiute (*pah* meaning "water" and *Ute* designating a Utah branch) called themselves *Numa,* and the Shoshone called themselves *Newe,* both meaning simply "the People." The name for the Southern Paiute was *Nuwuvi,* or "Peaceful People of the Land."

These different people shared many similar customs and lifestyles. They spent so much of their time gathering and preparing food in their harsh environment that they had little time or energy left to battle each other. The only time the small bands gathered into tribes was for cooperative hunting or harvesting efforts or to skirmish with neighbors or encroachers. Otherwise each band, a single-family unit or a group of no more than 100 individuals, was mostly autonomous. The resources of the local environment tended to dictate the size of bands; the Pyramid Lake Paiute, for example, was a large group with an abundant ecology. Its chiefs were famous. And the band was able to hold its own against the more warlike Pitt River bands from the north. Bands had headmen, and shamans, who were found to possess powers of prophecy, healing, or magic.

Traditionally, all the bands in a given area would come together several times a year for pine-nut harvesting, antelope hunts, and rabbit or mud-hen drives. Celebrations during the get-togethers included sports such as archery, races, and stick games, story-telling, and music and dance; some of the dances dictated courting rituals. The Washo, in particular, held large gatherings twice a year, once in the fall at the Pine Nut Mountains to harvest the pine nuts for their winter flour, and once in the spring at Lake Tahoe to fish.

The Family

Native peoples enjoyed extended family arrangements, usually including the maternal grandparents. Variations might consist of two wives and a husband (the second woman was adopted if she found herself alone for some reason) or two husbands and a wife. Sketchy accounts describe the society as having very little divorce, with no words for broken homes, orphans, or child abuse. Children were loved and well cared for, assimilating into the ways of the family and band, proving themselves worthy as they went along, learning skills and morality mostly from the grandfather.

Religion

Everything in nature, animate or inanimate, was embodied by a spirit. Fire, fog, even rocks were alive, and required an empathy equal to that for a wolf (good influence), coyote (bad influence), or a wife or husband (either). Dreams, omens, seasonal cycles and unnatural variations, prayers, and the powers of the medicine man all figured into Native American religion—which was as integral a part of their daily routine as eating and sleeping.

Lifestyle

The never-ending search for food in the somewhat barren desert dictated daily and seasonal activities. The native peoples had little need for shelter (except for shade) or clothing (except for a breechcloth and skirt) in the summer. In winter they stayed in a kind of teepee with a framework of poles and branches; grass or reed made up the roof, which had a hole in it for smoke from the fire. At that time they wore animal-skin robes, hats, moccasins, skirts, or sage-bark sandals and caps, and slept under rabbit-fur blankets. Colored clay was dabbed on as makeup and to ward off evil spirits, and bones, hooves, or traded shells provided jewelry for necklaces, earrings, or bracelets.

Mostly nomadic people, they had to carry everything during their frequent movements; a sophisticated basket technology evolved. Woven from split willow twigs, grasses, and cattail reeds (tule), conical baskets were used for transporting possessions or served as women's caps. Flat trays were used for winnowing seeds and sifting flour. Large pots were even used to cook in and to carry water—pitch from piñon pines, grasses, and mud kept them from burning or leaking. Decoys and snares were also fashioned from willow and tule twigs. Cradleboards attained a level of art. Properly shaped stones provided mortar-and-pestle tools for grinding, and drums, rattles, and flutes combined the use of baskets, skins, and grasses. In their knowledge and use of the local plants, the Indians were particularly ingenious. Everything had a use, and everything was sacred. They also fished and hunted rabbits, squirrels, antelope, mountain sheep, deer, ducks, and birds.

Contact

The first Anglo-Europeans who came into contact with the Shoshone, Paiute, and Washo Indians considered them to be slightly better than wildlife. They had no possessions, no houses, and hardly any clothes. As James Hulse writes in *The Nevada Adventure,* "The greed, brutality, and contempt of the white man destroyed much of the beauty of Indian life and prevented the Indians from entering the white man's culture." The Native Americans were on peaceful, even friendly terms with the first trappers and traders; Chief Winnemucca prophesied, and his daughter Sarah preached, that whites and Indians could live together with a mutual respect for each other and the land. But the wagon trains quickly put an end to the utopian vision. The migrating cattle ate all the Indians' grasses, loggers cut their sacred piñon pines; large areas were denuded of all the living things that the native tribes used to survive. Though the Nevada Paiute and Shoshone had no real organization for waging war, and Nevada histories are usually devoid of any but the largest armed confrontations (Pyramid Lake, Paradise Valley, Black Rock Desert, Battle Mountain), many skirmishes occurred, with some loss of life on both sides. Treaties were signed and violated and signed and violated. Within 25 years of the first wave of emigrants, the Indian spirit was broken, self-reliance was shattered, and dependence became the way of life.

Reservations

The first reservations in Nevada, Pyramid Lake and Walker Lake, were surveyed and set aside for the Paiute in 1859. Several others (Fort Mc-Dermitt, Moapa, Fallon, Owyhee) followed over the next 15 years. But as E. A. Hoaglund writes in his *Washoe, Paiute, and Shoshone Indians of Nevada,* "The early history of Indian reservations in America is generally one of confusion and mismanagement." A near total lack of direction, financing, facilities, equipment, education, understanding of the native experience, and compassion for their cultural dislocation colored a full 70 years of white-indigenous relations. The reservations were usually too small, the land too poor, and the populations too large. Also, the reservations continued to segregate the Indians from the mainstream. "The period from 1890–1934 was one of slow moral and physical decline [for the native peoples]. Many left the reservations and found work on ranches or the fringes of towns."

In 1887 the Dawes Act tried to disenfranchise the reservations in an attempt to ease assimilation into white culture. In June 1934, the Indian Reorganization Act began a process of redressing this tragic part of American history, by giving more money, land, cattle, and irrigation systems to the reservations. Self-government was made official by way of Tribal Councils. The 1978 Indian Self-Determination Act addressed the need for economic development. Slowly, the federal government has untangled the complex questions of land issues and begun to show some responsiveness to the simple question of human rights.

Self-Determination

In an interesting article in *Nevada* magazine (August 1989), Becky Lemon and Linda Johnson explain that since the 1960s, smoke shops have been the 24 Nevada tribes' primary revenue producers. Tribes buy cigarettes at wholesale prices, which include federal taxes. But instead of the high local taxes on smokes, the Indians charge a smaller tribal tax, which is reinvested in the tribal organization. Most smoke shops also display and sell arts and crafts.

But the tribes are beginning to require sources of revenue other than cigarette sales. And many have found the means. The Las Vegas Paiute, for example, have begun a large-scale resort development on reservation land 20 miles north of Las Vegas; when complete, there will be four golf courses and several hotel-casinos.

The Washo, whose reservation is in Gardnerville, raise cattle and own and manage feedlots. They're beginning to develop their own alfalfa farms to feed the cattle; what they don't raise, they buy from other Indian farmers.

The Yerington Paiute own a Dairy Queen in town and have gone into the laser ground-leveling business, relied on by local farmers. The Walker River Paiute opened a truck stop and tourist center near Schurz. The Fallon Paiute-Shoshone raise small game birds for hunting. The Pyramid Lake Paiute fishery has helped Pyramid Lake regenerate into one of the top cutthroat lakes in the West. The Indians raise funds from fishing, boating, and camping licenses. And they own and operate a marina in Sutcliffe.

The Reno-Sparks Colony's smoke shop is in a small shopping center, from which it leases space to other businesses. The smoke shop opened a second location on US 395 just south of Foothill Drive in Reno.

A good way to observe Indian traditions and customs in action is to attend any of a number of powwows put on by the different tribes over the course of the year. The dancing, drumming, traditional costumes, and intensity of the participants clearly indicate the commitment to "abiding," write Becky Lemon and Linda Johnson, "by the spiritual values of balance, harmony, and oneness with nature," while at the same time "initiating modern business practices."

BASQUES

The Basque people are the oldest ethnic group in Europe. Evidence of their continuous existence dates to 5000 B.C., a full 3,000 years before Indo-European people arrived. There are roughly three million European Basques, their homeland occupying the Pyrenees Mountain provinces of

COURTESY OF THE NEVADA COMMISSION ON TOURISM

Basque dancers in Elko

pastoralist life of the American West readily, particularly in northern Nevada. For nearly 50 years, Basque ranchers ran the largest bands of sheep in the country. They imported relatives, friends, and neighbors to herd sheep. Contract shepherds often took payment in lambs and sheep, with which they started their own ranches. Herders remained in the backcountry alone with their flocks all through the summer. It was an arduous and lonely life, being an immigrant in a strange and barren country, barely speaking the language or understanding the strange customs in the towns. But a prevalent aspect of the Basque national character is the ability to endure: Hard work, loneliness, and physical strength all add up to the measure of their self-worth.

Sheepherding was seasonal. Many newcomers were laid off in the fall after the animals were shipped to market and not rehired till spring lambing season. Some sheepherders remained on the ranches, but others drifted to the hotels run by Basques in the towns. These boarding-houses quickly became the center of Basque culture in the rural towns of Nevada. Shepherds old and young spoke their own language, played their own games, ate their own food, and kept company with their own countrymen and -women. Many married and remained in the towns, assimilating into the new culture. Some made their money and went home to Europe. Others stayed bachelors and lived out their lives at the inns. The Basque hotel was "a crucible of birth and death, joy and sorrow; a public establishment masking many private intimacies," writes William Douglass in *Amerikanuak: Basques in the New World.*

Oso Garria!

The Basque hotel is a legacy that endures. The Winnemucca Hotel, for example, is the second-oldest hotel in the state. Gardnerville's Overland Hotel dates from 1909, Elko's Star Hotel from 1911, and the Ely Hotel is from the 1920s. No traveler to Nevada should leave without experiencing a meal at a Basque hotel.

A Basque meal, especially dinner, is never taken lightly, nor is it a light meal. It consists of a

France (three districts) and Spain (four districts). The true origin of these people is a mystery. Some scholars maintain that similarities exist between Basques and Iberians (early Spanish neighbors); others believe that they share characteristics with the Irish and Welsh. Some Basques contend that they're descended from the Atlanteans!

Their language is unrelated to any other in the world, although researchers have tried to match it up with all of them—from ancient Aquitanian to modern Japanese. Though the Basques were never conquered, the Spanish and French have had a noticeable influence.

Basque argonauts migrated to Argentina, from where many made their way north, especially in the 1850s to the California gold rush. Following the silver exodus east to Washoe, they mined in Nevada until that work dried up. They then returned to a skill familiar from the old country: sheepherding. Basque sheepherders took to the multitude of courses served family-style: soup, salad, beans or pasta, french fries, and usually an entrée of chicken, beef, or lamb. Make sure to try a picon punch, made with Amer (a liqueur), grenadine, and topped off with a quick shot of brandy. Few of northern and central Nevada's towns are without Basque restaurants, where you're guaranteed a fine filling meal and a social experience. Raise your glass of picon punch and toast the house: *"Oso garria!"*

The Basque festival is the other enduring cultural tradition. Festivities include mass, folk dancing, strength and endurance competitions, a sheep rodeo, and the consumption of enormous quantities of red wine from the *bota* (the festival itself is an endurance contest!). The Basques are known for their world-class wood chopping, and the contestants compete in areas of strength and will. *Soka* and *tira* are the popular tugs-of-war.

Pelota is handball, of which jai alai is an offspring. Weight lifting and carrying are the real crowd pleasers. Annual festivals take place in most of the larger towns in northern Nevada. Check the events section of *Nevada* magazine in the summer.

Transportation

Getting There

Five main roads crisscross Nevada, three east–west and two north–south. I-80 takes the long northern route west across the shoulder of Nevada. US 50 cuts across the shorter waist of the state, joins up with I-80 at Fernley, then splits off to Reno or Carson City. US 6 travels along with US 50 in eastern Nevada for a while, then cuts south to Tonopah and out toward Fresno in California. US 95 zigzags south, then southwest, then south, then southeast for nearly 700 miles from McDermitt at the north edge of the state to Laughlin at the south. US 93 travels between Jackpot to Boulder City for 500 miles, but in a fairly straight line.

Greyhound bus routes connect Las Vegas with Carson City, Reno, Laughlin, and Mesquite; routes heading further afield from Las Vegas include routes to Los Angeles, Phoenix, and Salt Lake City, with connections to other places. Greyhound routes connect Reno with Carson City, Las Vegas, Winnemucca, and Elko, and places further afield including Sacramento, Oakland, San Francisco, and Salt Lake City.

Otherwise, rural bus lines are few and far between. Today, there are only two: **K-T Bus Lines** carries passengers between Reno and Las Vegas. Public Rural Ride (PRIDE) operates between Reno and Carson City.

Amtrak operates the *California Zephyr* train between Emeryville (in the east San Francisco Bay Area) and Chicago, stopping in Nevada in Reno, Winnemucca, and Elko. (Note that Amtrak no longer runs through Las Vegas.)

There are big airports at Las Vegas and Reno, fair-sized airports at Elko and Ely (each has four departures and arrivals a day), and 10 other airports attended either 24 hours a day or during daylight hours. Carson City is one of a handful of state capitals without regularly scheduled airline service.

If you're driving in, get in your car and make a beeline; having this book along will help no matter which way you go. If you're flying in, consider touching down in Las Vegas first. McCarran International is one of the easiest airports to access in the country and with a little research and planning, it can also be one of the cheapest. Reno is an hour by air from Las Vegas and nowhere in Nevada is more than 10 hours or so by car.

Getting Around

The best way is with your own car. Buses don't reach half the state. Distances are long and services are few and far between. You can find yourself on gravel a lot if you're adventurous, and if your steed is trusty, you can really get out there. That's the idea, isn't it? And if you want to get back from out there, you have to treat your car right. First of all, does it have a name? Give it one. Cars, like pets, prefer familiarity. Desert driving is hot, dusty, bumpy, and can be strenuous on your car. There's a whole lotta shakin' going on out there. Make sure it's had the best fuel, fluids, tires, parts, and care. Carry plenty of spare water and fluids, spare tire and jack, flashlight and flares, spare belts and hoses, tool kit, and shovel; baling wire and Super Glue often come in handy. Don't forget a rag or two.

Common-sense maintenance consciousness is required on the road. If the car gets hot or overheats, stop for a while to cool it off. Never open the radiator cap if the engine is steaming.

After it's sat, squeeze the top radiator hose to see if there's any pressure in it; if there isn't, it's safe to open. Never pour water into a hot radiator—you could crack your block. If you start to smell rubber, your tires are overheating, and that's a good way to have a blowout. Stop and let them cool off, too. In winter in the high country, a can of silicone lubricant such as WD-40 will unfreeze door locks, dry off humid wiring, and keep your hinges in shape.

Road Courtesy

The speed limits on most of the interstates and

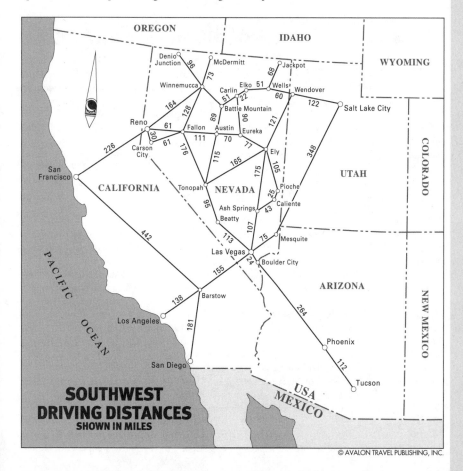

SOUTHWEST DRIVING DISTANCES
SHOWN IN MILES

© AVALON TRAVEL PUBLISHING, INC.

US highways outside of the cities and towns have been raised in the past couple of years—praise be the Lord! They're now 75 mph on Interstates 80 and 15, US 95 and 93, and a few state roads. You can drive 65 mph on the interstates in Reno and Las Vegas. Most passers—through drive upwards of 80–85 mph without worrying about being noticed by the highway patrol. Since the superhighways are two lanes in each direction, road courtesy isn't much of a problem; anyone wanting to go faster than you can zip around on the left, if not the right.

Passing is generally not a problem on the two-lane highways through rural Nevada; the solid and dotted lines are well maintained and long straight stretches through the valleys are conducive to safe zipping.

There are only a few long climbs up mountains on main roads in Nevada, and here passing can be a problem. The good news is that turnouts are common. The bad news is that some flatlanders and RV drivers don't know what turnouts are for. If you're pulling a heavy load, are nervous about mountain driving, or just have a slowpoke car, please pull over and let the drivers behind you pass.

Information

STATE AND FEDERAL GOVERNMENT AGENCIES

General Information: 775/687-5000
Nevada Commission on Tourism: 401 N. Carson St., Carson City, 775/687-4322 or 800/NEVADA-8, www.travelnevada.com
Nevada Division of State Parks: 1300 S. Curry St., Carson City, 775/687-4370, www.state.nv.us/stparks
Great Basin National Park: 100 Great Basin National Park, Baker, 775/234-7331, www.nps.gov/grba
Lake Mead National Recreation Area: 601 Nevada Hwy., Boulder City, 702/293-8947, www.nps.gov/lame
Bureau of Land Management: State Office, 1340 Financial Blvd., Reno, 775/861-6400, www.nv.blm.gov
Humboldt-Toiyabe National Forest: Supervisor's Office, 1200 Franklin Way, Sparks, 775/355-5311, www.fs.fed.us/htnf
Nevada Div. of Wildlife: 1100 Valley Rd., Reno, 775/688-1558, www.nevadadivisionofwildlife.org
State Library and Archives: 100 N. Stewart St., Carson City, 775/684-3360
Road Condition Report: 877/687-6237.

Maps

The biggest, most beautiful, and informative map about the land—mountains, rivers, lakes, and elevations—is produced by **Raven Maps,** 800/237-0798. It's available for $30 (paper) or $50 (laminated); call for a free catalog. The Nevada **Department of Transportation,** 1263 S. Stewart St., Carson City, 775/888-7627, also has wall-size maps of the roads, counties, and natural features. In addition, it publishes an indispensable *Nevada Map Atlas* of 127 quadrangle maps of the state, which include all the non-paved roads.

Nevada Magazine

The best general source of information about Nevada, this magazine has been financed by the state government since the 1930s. The "Nevada Events and Shows" section of the magazine provides comprehensive listings of things to do around the state; the website provides contact information for convention and visitors bureaus, chambers of commerce, events hotlines, and more. The main office is at 401 N. Carson St., Suite 100, Carson City, 775/687-5416, www.nevadamagazine.com.

Libraries

Every major library in the state has a Nevada room or a special collection of local-interest titles. But the three main libraries for researching specific aspects of the Nevada experience are the

Getchell Library on the University of Nevada–Reno campus, the Lied Library on the University of Nevada–Las Vegas campus, and the State Library in Carson City.

Taxes

The sales tax varies from county to county, but falls somewhere between 6 and 7 percent. Room taxes are higher, up to 9 percent in downtown Las Vegas (now paying for the Fremont Street Experience). The entertainment tax on shows around the state totals 17 percent: 7 percent sales tax and 10 percent entertainment tax. Check carefully what the tax will be on rental cars in Las Vegas. It can approach 21 percent: 7 percent sales tax, 7 percent use tax, and 7 percent airport tax.

Weights and Measures

The area code for all of Nevada is 775, except for Clark County (the Las Vegas area), which is 702. For directory assistance, dial 775/555-1212 or 702/555-1212. Nevada is mostly on Pacific time, same as California, Oregon, and Washington. Note, however, that the border towns of Jackpot and Wendover keep their clocks on Mountain time, same as Idaho and Utah.

Accommodations and Food

CASINOS

Nevada is one of the easiest and cheapest states in the country to travel in. Forty percent of its employees are in the service trades, 25 percent working directly in casinos. A casino can be a traveler's best friend. They're all open 24 hours and have lots of convenient parking, so you know right where to go for a bathroom and can get there post haste. Most have 24-hour coffee shops and bars, so you'll never go hungry or thirsty. The cashier will happily change traveler's checks and personal checks into cash, cash into coin and vice versa, and plastic to paper. There's usually a vacant motel room within walking distance. And of course they all have slots and most have table games, if you need a distraction and don't find it too oppressive or disorienting to go from white-line fever to three-reel or five-card fever. (Better is to walk around, stretch your legs, and take deep breaths.)

In interior Nevada, bona fide casinos can be few and far between. In towns such as Austin, Eureka, Battle Mountain, Carlin, Pioche, Caliente, Goldfield, Gerlach, and of course Boulder City (the only place in Nevada where gambling is illegal), you're on your own, especially late at night. But everywhere else in the state, all hours of the day and night, when you're in need of grub, caffeine, entertainment, or restrooms, casinos are a welcome sight.

Casinos are also good places to be careful around. Many people, including those who are on the road, stumble out under the influence of too much free booze. You've simply got to be on the defensive with everyone who's just walked out of a casino.

LODGING

There are upwards of 177,000 motel and hotel rooms in Nevada, with more being built all the time. In addition there are thousands of camping and RV sites. Taken on average, Nevada lodging, indoor and out, is among the least expensive in the country, subsidized as it is by attached casinos or competing against casino-subsidized rooms.

The absolute cheapest way to spend the night is also the most satisfying and soul nurturing: to camp out somewhere in the wilds of the vast Great Basin or Mojave. Pull off the pavement onto a graded dirt road, then pull off that into the real outback; set up your tent, watch for stray cows and rattlers, and commune with the desert and the sky. If you prefer some civilization, county, state, and national park and forest campgrounds charge up to $14; a few have showers. With a tent, you can also always pull into an RV park and pay no more, usually, than $12–18 for the night, which includes flush toilets and hot showers. Often RV parks will sell showers alone for $3–5.

The bargain-basement lodging, usually in old hotels right downtown, often costs as little as $20–25 for a double. The bathroom's down the hall, you don't get Showtime, the rooms are small and the walls are thin, but they're indoors and cheap. If you're diligent and don't mind inspecting and rejecting rooms, you can often find acceptable motel accommodations, with air-conditioning, cable, and a telephone, for $25–30 for two. If you're not shopping and don't mind spending $35–45 a night (on all but the busiest weekends during high season), you can pull into most any motel in Nevada and have yourself a room.

Las Vegas, Reno, Laughlin, Stateline, and Mesquite have high-rise hotels. Motels are more convenient for the quick in and out; hotels are more convenient for casinos, coffee shops, room service, pools, and big rooms. The hotel scene in Reno is fairly straightforward, though still a miniature version of the wacky world of hotel rooms in Las Vegas.

Summer is the high season, and some towns regularly sell out of rooms every night. Sunday through Thursday, you're pretty much guaranteed a room without a reservation if you check in early enough; it could be tight if it's late. On Friday and Saturday nights, it gets a little trickier. You've got a good shot at a room on Friday until around 6 P.M. and on Saturday until around 3. After that, every sign in the state says No Vacancy, and at the ones that don't, you don't wanna know how much they're charging. On Saturday later than midafternoon in Nevada—if you don't have a prepaid reservation for a Saturday night anytime during the year and you're not prepared to spend the night in the car, on the road, in a casino, or in a tent—your only play is to stop at the biggest motel you can find between 5 and 6 P.M. and wait around hoping for an unpaid reservation to become a no-show; you'll have the room if you're there. Otherwise, stay put wherever you spend Friday night—if they'll have you.

FOOD

In terms of food, Nevada is a land of extremes. There's either a gluttonous abundance of eateries (Las Vegas has nearly 850 restaurants, more than 100 coffee shops, 30 buffets, and hundreds of fast-food stops) or you're doomed to yet another bacon and eggs, burger and fries, or chicken-fried steak. In the larger towns that have any variety, you might find a Chinese restaurant, or if you're really lucky, a Mexican restaurant. In the northern half of the state, you can usually locate some good and plenty Basque food. And in the cities, choose from Italian, French, Chinese, Japanese, Vietnamese, Korean, Mongolian, Brazilian, Salvadoran, Indian, Greek, deli, and natural food.

Buffets are great for traveling—fill up in the morning and go until dinner, or have a big lunch and two small meals before and after. They're also perfect for children under 5; real young kids eat free, and you can have food in their mouths within 30 seconds flat of walking in if you do it right. If it's not a kid food emergency, I suggest you take a peek at the buffet before you pay to eat; just ask the cashier or hostess if it's all right. At the cheap buffets, the way to gauge taste by sight is simple visual recognition. Don't read the labels (if there are any), and see if you can tell what the food is. If the steam-table fare looks like gloppy casseroles and starchy sauces over mystery meat and fish, and if the salads appear to be straight from 55-gallon drums, just go next door and look at another buffet. Or if the heat lamps give the food an otherworldly amber glow, find one that's a little more, you know, down to earth. If you can't recognize the food by sight, the odds are overwhelmingly against that you'll be able to by taste. Still, for $3.99 for breakfast, $5.99 for lunch, and $9.99 for dinner (on average), if your buds have been completely McDonaldized and you're looking to shovel home the volume, what the heck.

Also take a good close look at the seafood buffets (often on Friday nights but sometimes held throughout the week), whether they're cheap or not. Here, the salmon steak, halibut, bay shrimp, steamed prawns, and clams are labeled, recognizable, even presentable, but often taste (if you can call it that) like a preposterous pile of insipid pollack.

If you're staying in Las Vegas or Reno for any length of time, it's handy to carry a hot plate and extension cord to cook your own store-bought meals. If you're out seeing the back-country and come into towns only occasionally, you'll probably have your camp stove, bulk dry goods, and freeze-dried food.

Drink

Always carry water! It's a desert out there. If you're hiking, have a canteen on your belt and a gallon jug on your pack. If you're driving, a five-gallon container will get you—or someone you happen upon—through almost any emergency. All supermarkets sell gallon jugs of spring water. Don't run out! You might also buy canned or boxed juices; try diluting the strong juice with half or more water: it gets the water in you, and it tastes nicely sweet.

The drinking age in Nevada is 21. If you're 21 or older, you can drink alcoholic stupefacients more readily and cheaply in Nevada than any other place in the country, if not the world. Every casino in the state and many bars remain open 24 hours and every casino in the state serves free drinks to players. The easiest way to get free beer or booze is to plop down at a video poker bar, buy in for a roll of quarters, and tip the bartender well. You don't even have to play: Simply buy in, get your comp drink, and cash out at the change booth. Then go next door and do it all over again. As Max Rubin says in *Comp City*, this technique "has carried many an alkie through some desperate nights in Glitter Gulch."

If you don't even want to buy in, ask any bartender about drink specials. In Las Vegas, $0.75 draft beers, $0.99 margaritas, $1.00 imported beer, and $1.00 well drinks are all common. Most of the casino bars outside of Las Vegas offer some variation of the same. Don't drink and drive. The life you save might be my own.

Gambling

Gambling and Nevada are inseparable in the national consciousness. No other state in the country is so inextricably linked to a single social, economic, recreational, and controversial activity. Indeed, the state's reputation since casino gambling was legalized for good has been predicated on Americans' *image* of gambling. For nearly the entire period, an irresistible torrent of public censure rained down on Nevada. The media, authorities, moralists, and sore losers accused and convicted the Silver State of being a haven for the underworld, petty criminals, crooked casinos, vice run amok, and general lowlife. The height of the heat centered on the 20-year period between 1946, when Benjamin Siegel, Las Vegas's most notorious gangster, built the seminal Flamingo Hotel, and 1966, when Howard Hughes introduced corporate respectability.

Since then, Nevada's image has taken a turn for the bettor. Today, state gaming revenues are $9.6 billion dollars a year, of which 60 percent are from the gambling losses of out-of-staters. Casino employment accounts for a full 25 percent of the jobs in Nevada and taxes on the house profits are responsible for 40 percent of state General Fund revenues. And that's just from gambling; the indirect effect of the massive tourism on the state's economy is incalculable.

Though it's not often credited for it, Nevada has contributed heavily to the growing legitimacy of various forms of gambling that exist now in 48 states: lotteries, bingo, off-track betting, video gambling machines, pull tabs, card rooms, and casinos. Casino gambling was legalized in Atlantic City in 1978, the first in the country outside of Nevada—and the last until Iowa riverboats came on line in 1991. Since then, casino gambling has become available on riverboats in Illinois, Indiana, Mississippi, Missouri, and Louisiana; in historic mining towns in Colorado and South Dakota; and on Indian reservations in a growing number of states. Gambling has become an accepted way to raise revenues without raising taxes, a sort of "painless user's tax." Certainly gambling

COMPULSIVE GAMBLERS

The vast majority of people who gamble do so for entertainment or recreation, to satisfy the primal urge of financial risk-taking for fun and profit. For them, losing is a sensation they can live with. But 3 to 4 percent of Americans who gamble are unable to simply walk away having had a good time. For them, gambling becomes compulsive, an addiction, a dangerous and deadly psychiatric disorder.

What makes a group of people turn to gambling for an escape is a matter of endless conjecture. A gambling disorder starts out as a euphoria derived from the initial excitement. For the particular people susceptible to it, gambling is a more satisfying sensation than any other. Whether it's the surging adrenaline of a crap game, the hypnotic trance of a video poker machine, or even the fast pace and high stakes of a securities market, as long as these people gamble, they're high. Stopping means coming down, and they need to gamble again to get back up. This dependence is particularly insidious, since the house advantage ensures that the longer they play, the more they lose. The more they lose, the more they start chasing losses. And herein lies the danger signal. Nearly all compulsive gamblers spend their own, and their families' savings. Three out of four sell or hock valuables and write bad checks. Almost half descend to theft or embezzlement. Finally, in the terminal stages of ruin, despair, fear, and shame, an estimated 20 percent of compulsive gamblers attempt suicide. Then and only then, if unsuccessful, do most addicts reach a point of seeking treatment.

However, public perception of compulsive gambling is 10 to 20 years behind that of alcoholism, for example. Though the ranks of addicted gamblers have swelled in the last few years, serious treatment remains hard to come by and is often a case of too little, too late. There are 600 Gamblers' Anonymous chapters nationwide, but only a handful of primary treatment centers (one in Las Vegas). Dr. Robert Custer, considered the father of compulsive-gambling treatment, says that compulsive gambling is the "most under-researched" psychiatric disorder, and the most deadly. "No other psychiatric disorder even approaches" a 20 percent rate of attempted suicide, he points out. Of the 35 states with lotteries, only Iowa earmarks a share (0.5 percent) of lottery revenues for a Gamblers' Assistance Fund. Ironically, by the time a compulsive gambler is ready for recovery, expensive treatment programs are often beyond his shattered resources. Governmental assistance, so far, hasn't been forthcoming.

is still generally considered frivolous by a great many Americans. It's also a highly addictive activity that has been called the deadliest psychiatric disorder. Yet its growing popularity shows no signs of abating. In fact, it was the most explosive growth industry in the country in the 1990s.

The Question of Honesty

In this cash-crazy business, everyone is afraid of everyone. The casinos have always been afraid of cheating customers and dishonest dealers and have evolved some of the most sophisticated security and surveillance technology, not to mention one of the heaviest envelopes of private muscle, this side of the Pentagon. As the benders, crimpers, hand muckers, and past-post artists of yesteryear have turned into today's sleight-of-hand artists, card counters, and computer-equipped players, the catwalks and one-way glass above the casino ceilings have given way to video cameras and recorders, in addition to all the bosses in the pit, the house guard, and outside security contractors.

The Nevada casino industry is not the most heavily regulated in the country. Atlantic City's is. But Nevada's is the most efficient and practical; New Jersey has been over-regulated to the extent that it's been difficult for Atlantic City casinos to succeed (though that's starting to change). Nevada, on the other hand, started with little to no regulation of casinos when gambling was legalized in 1931, then took more than 50 years to reach a middle ground

Know when to say "when."

where the regulation is sufficient to keep things honest, but also allow the industry to prosper. Mississippi, where nearly 50 casinos have opened in the past five years, copied Nevada regulations verbatim; in fact, in a few instances the Mississippi typists neglected to change the name of the state!

The Nevada Gaming Control Board, by way of its announced and unannounced inspections, owner and employee screening, and customer-complaint services, has dealt with the *state's* two main fears. The first is the house cheating the state, by underreporting the action, skimming the cash, and other various nefarious scams. The second is the house cheating the players. Here, the conventional wisdom is that with the astronomical number of people coming, the amount of money that they're risking (and losing), and the profits that are accruing, the casinos don't *need* to cheat the players; indeed they'd be crazy if they did: They'd risk losing what amounts to a license to coin money, thanks to the house advantage.

Casino Psychology

More than 35 million people sampled the excitement and temptations of Las Vegas alone in 2003,

with numbers of visitors continuing to grow every year. Inside the casinos are a dozen different table games and scores of gambling machines, free drinks, acres of dazzling lights, expert come-ons—in short, limitless choices designed to sweep you off your feet and empty your pockets. You have nearly 70 years of marketing history and a distinct mathematical disadvantage working against you. Every inch of neon, every cocktail waitress, every complimentary highball shares the same purpose: to confuse you, bemuse you, and infuse you with a sense of saloon-town recklessness. And that's where the house advantage kicks in.

The game of roulette best illustrates the house advantage. There are 38 numbers on the wheel: 1 through 36, plus 0 and 00. If the ball drops into number 23 and you have a dollar on it, the correct payoff would be $37 (37 to 1, which adds up to the 38 numbers). However, the house pays only $35. It withholds two out of 38 units, which translates to a 5.26 percent advantage for the house. Now, this 5.26 percent advantage can be looked at in different ways. Over the long haul, for every $100 you bet on roulette, you can expect to lose $5.26. Or, you'll lose your bankroll at a little less than four times the rate at roulette than on a pass line bet at craps, which has a 1.4 percent house advantage. But don't make the mistake of thinking that for every $100 you carry into the casino you'll only lose five bucks. Anything can happen in the short run. You can win 13 bets in a row and make a bundle, or you can lose all your money in one big bet. But the house advantage guarantees that you'll be a long-term loser at almost all the games in a casino, and that the casino will be long-term winner.

The house advantage is the single most important concept to be aware of to understand the well-known secret behind casino gambling. As soon as you're savvy to all its implications, and the varying percentages of the games, you'll begin to recognize the difference between a sucker bet, a break-even bet, and even an advantageous bet—which occurs more frequently than most people think. Then you can gamble in such a way that the percentages aren't so overwhelmingly unfavorable, and in that way you can make sure that your bankroll lasts as long as it possibly can against the omnipotent house advantage.

For First-Timers

If you've never learned to play, it's very wise to study up beforehand and practice, practice, practice. All these games move very fast, and if you try learning them as you play, you'll not only lose, but everybody will get very impatient with you, which is embarrassing. *Looking like* a piker is a technique that expert players use to slow down the game (to minimize risk) and to deflect the attention of and heat from the pit bosses (to make other advanced moves). But there's no upside to really not knowing what you're doing.

It's easy and fun to learn to play. Most casinos offer free lessons in all the games at specified times of day. In Las Vegas, lessons are sometimes advertised on marquees; signs are also posted in the casinos. Or ask someone in the pit about them. In Reno, one of the dealer schools (Reno–Tahoe Gaming Academy) is a good place to learn.

Loads of books have been written on how to play all the casino games. John Scarne's guides, though a little outdated, should be in most libraries. To really get into it, requests catalogs from the Gambler's Book Club, 630 S. 11th St., Las Vegas, 800/634-6243, www.gamblersbook.com. Huntington Press, 3687 S. Procyon Ave, Las Vegas, 800/244-2224, www.huntingtonpress.com, will send you a "boutique" catalog of the best gambling books and software.

Attitude

Don't ever let anyone tell you differently. In a casino, it absolutely *is* whether you win or lose. You *can* beat the casino, but *not* with any one of a thousand superstitions or "systems"; not with being cool, knowing all the rituals, looking like James Bond; not even with an above-average degree of competence at the games. The gambling professionals (there are maybe a few thousand true pros—defined as people who make their entire living at gambling—mostly in Las Vegas) are part mathematician, part probability theorist, part banker, part actor, and part martial artist. They play high-level blackjack (sometimes in teams) and rarely get caught; they pounce on progressive video poker machines when the meter goes positive; they enter all the big-money gambling tournaments (often in teams) and win regularly; they factor comps into the positive expectation; and they subscribe to the unlimited-bankroll school, which holds that "money management" is a crock. They take the big losses in stride and the big wins for granted. They eat, sleep, and dream gambling theory; they spend all their time in casinos; they carry a lot of cash and flash it when necessary; they throw big bucks at small edges; and sooner than later they go into gambling publishing, where the real money is.

The rest of us? Rank amateurs. We're supposed to be in it for the fun, the recreation value, and to some extent the dream of the once-in-a-lifetime jackpot (though that's only possible in bad-odds games such as keno and slots, which take your money a bit more slowly than a pickpocket). For us it's about spending the same money with which we'd buy tickets to a ballgame, a concert, an amusement park, for gambling. It's about maximizing our vacation budgets by taking advantage of the rock-bottom room, food, beverage, and entertainment prices in Nevada, plus the slot club and comp systems for the freebies that accrue to players. It's about risking our gambling bankrolls for the excitement and adrenaline of the casino, the camaraderie with fellow players, the interaction with the dealers and cocktail waitresses and bosses, and seeing how our luck is running lately. It's mostly about risking the pain of losing for the fun of winning.

In this case, the way to play is to set a limit and *not go over it.* Simple as that. Never sit down to play with money that you can't spend. That's one of the sure signs of degenerate gambling. And never try to chase your losses—another sign of the onset of problematic or compulsive gambling. Be a good loser. Be a good winner. Have some fun, get some comps. Oh, and good luck.

Comps

"Comps" is short for complimentaries, also known as freebies. These are travel amenities—free room, food, drink, shows, golf, limos, even airfare—with which the casinos reward their good players and entice other players into their joints. Comps come in many varieties. The easiest to get are free parking (in downtown Reno and Las Vegas parking garages, you're entitled to three to four hours of free parking with a receipt validated at the casino cage) and funbooks (which often contain coupons for free drinks, snacks, and souvenirs). For these comps, you don't have to play; you only have to walk into the casino to get them.

The lowest level comp for players is the ubiquitous free drink. It doesn't matter if you're putting one nickel at a time in a slot machine or laying down $5,000 baccarat bets, the casino serves you complimentary soft drinks, cocktails, wine, and beer.

The value of comps increases with the value of bets. The standard equation used by casinos to determine comps is: size of average bet times number of hours played times the house advantage times the comp equivalency. In other words, say you play blackjack, making $10 bets for two hours. The casino multiplies 120 hands (60 an hour) by $10 and comes up with $1,200 worth of action. It then multiplies $1,200 by the 2 percent house advantage

and comes up with $24—what the casino believes it will win from you on average in two hours of $10 blackjack. It then multiplies $24 by 40 percent (what it's willing to return in comps), so you're entitled to $9.60 in freebie amenities (in this case, probably a coffee shop comp for one).

Comps returned to big bettors enter the fabled realm of high-roller suites, lavish gourmet dinners, unlimited room service, ringside seats, private parties, limos, and Lear jets. Caesars has 10,000-square-foot apartments complete with butler and chef, private lap pool and putting green, monster hot tub, and grand piano. The Mirage will fly you to the Super Bowl, put you in box seats at the 50-yard line, and send you to a party with the Most Valuable Player. All you have to do is bet $25,000 a hand eight hours a day over a long weekend, or have a $5 million credit line.

Comps for $25 players might include casino rate on a room (generally 50 percent of rack), limited food and beverage, and line passes to the show. Hundred-dollar players qualify for full RFB (room, food, and beverage, meaning your whole stay is free) at some of the second-tier joints (Riviera, Stardust, and downtown), while the first-tier places (Caesars, Mirage, MGM) typically want to see $200–250 a hand for full RFB.

To enter the comp game, you must "get rated." This consists of identifying yourself to the casino cage (where you fill out a credit application and are entered "in the system," or given a file in the casino computer), a casino host (who will also put you in the system), or a pit supervisor (typically a floorman or pit boss, who will either look you up in the system or keep track of you on his or her own). If you're in the system, you simply identify yourself to the boss, who then fills out a rating slip, which records your time in, time out, average bet size, and a few other details. The data is entered into the computer and casino marketing determines what comps you're entitled to. If you're not in the system, you call the boss over and say something like, "How long do I have to play to get a coffee shop comp for two, or a gourmet room comp for two, or a show for two?" Then, if you fulfill his requirement, he'll write you a comp.

And herein lies the weakness in the comp tracking system. It's possible to trick the casino into thinking that you're a higher roller than you really are by practicing "comp wizardry." Casinos are especially vulnerable to attack on their comp systems, because your play must be observed by pit bosses. By slowing down the game (actually playing only 40 hands an hour, instead of the 60 the casino expects to deal), betting $25 when the pit boss is watching and only $10–15 when he isn't, looking like a loser, and employing other advanced moves can greatly minimize your risk and maximize your reward in the comp game. The book *Comp City—A Guide to Free Las Vegas Vacations* by Max Rubin is the best (and only) book on the spectrum of casino comps for table game players. It's highly recommended for anyone who plays blackjack for $5 a hand and up. It's also one of the funniest and savviest gambling books ever written.

That's the upper tier of the two-tier comp system. The lower tier encompasses the vast majority of casino players, who prefer the machines to the tables. And here we enter the world of slot clubs. Almost all casinos in Nevada have slot clubs, which are similar to the frequent-flyer clubs of the airlines. Slot clubs are free to join; all you do is sign up at the slot club or promotions booth usually located somewhere on the edge of the casino. There, you're issued a slot club membership card, similar to a credit card, which you put into a slot in the gambling machine that you play. Card readers in the machine track the amount of your action, e.g., the number of coins that you play. Once you play a certain number of coins, usually 20–40, you're awarded a point. And once you have a certain number of slot club points, you can exchange them for comps, just like a table-game player. Every slot club is different, so there's a science and an art to getting the most comp value out of the various slot clubs in the various jurisdictions around the state. The best (and only) book to read for your slot club education is *The Las Vegas Advisor Guide to Slot Clubs* by Jeffrey Compton.

Kids

No one under 21 can play in the casino. That's the law. People under 21 can walk through the casino, but the operative word here is *through*. Older kids on their own and younger kids with their parents must be moving along toward some destination. If you're with your kids and you stop somewhere in the casino for some reason, security guards not far behind will invite you to continue on your way. The guards will tell you that both you and the casino can be fined for having youths in a gambling area (this is so rare that you could argue the point, but it's not recommended that you get into a tussle with casino security guards).

You and your kids can stop in a gambling area only if you're standing in a line to see a show or enter a buffet that winds through the casino.

What about 19- and 20-year-olds who sit down and play? That depends on the casino. The conventional wisdom used to be that minors could play, but they couldn't win. In other words, a 20-year-old could feed the slots till he was broke, but if he hit a jackpot that required a slot host to fill out IRS paperwork (anything more than $1,200), for which he needed to see identification, the underage player not only wouldn't get paid, but he'd get the bum's rush out the door to boot. Court case after court case has upheld the casino's right to refuse to pay; in fact, if the casino did pay, it could get fined or lose its license.

These days, with more and more kids roaming around Las Vegas, some joints check ID religiously. Others don't. A few years ago, for example, Bally's found itself in a hassle with the Nevada Gaming Commission for dealing blackjack over a several-hour period to three underage players, one of whom was said to have looked 14 years old. After hearing that the boys lost upwards of $6,000, the parents of one of them complained to the Gaming Control Board, whose agents reviewed the videotapes of the game and recommended a heavy fine. They didn't, to be sure, require Bally's to return the $6,000. What if the boys had started winning those $100 bets? My guess is the pit bosses would have been all over them, demanding to see ID and kicking them out without further ado.

Suggested Reading

For an exhaustive bibliography of books about Nevada and gambling, see *Nevada—An Annotated Bibliography* by Stanley Paher (Nevada Publications, 1980); and *Gambling Bibliography* by Jack Gardner (Gale Research Company, 1980). Although both were published more than 20 years ago, they are still the most comprehensive general bibliographies available.

For a large number of Nevada titles published in the 20 years since the two bibliographies, contact **University of Nevada Press,** 775/784-6573 or 877/NV-BOOKS. **Huntington Press,** 800/244-2224, www.greatstuff4gamblers.com, Nevada's largest commercial publisher, is another fine resource.

For the best current books about gambling, request catalogs from the **Gambler's Book Club,** 800/634-6243, www.gamblersbook.com. Huntington Press publishes and distributes a number of books about gambling.

A visit to any bookstore specializing in Nevada themes will turn up many books on interesting Nevada-related topics including the California Trail, the Pony Express, Native Americans, the Basques (check out the University of Nevada Press's Basque series), ghost towns, and the natural history and geology of the Great Basin. Larger museums usually offer a good selection of Nevada-related books.

TRAVEL AND DESCRIPTION

Castleman, Deke. *Nevada.* Oakland, CA: Compass American Guides, 2000. Travel guidebook with information for travelers on everything from Las Vegas lights to the most remote ghost towns and nature spots, with color photos.

Dickerson, Richard. *Nevada Angler's Guide—Fish Tails in the Sagebrush.* Portland, OR: Frank Amato Publications, 1997. A handy, useful, and authoritative guide to 116 of the most accessible fishing spots in Nevada.

Glass, Mary Ellen, and Al Glass. *Touring Nevada: A Historic and Scenic Guide.* Reno: University of Nevada Press, 1983. An excellent guide, well organized into specific "circle tours" for people who are interested in the historical significance of the sights of Nevada.

Graham, Jefferson. *Vegas—Live and In Person.* New York: Abbeville Press, 1969. This large format, profusely photographed book lives up to its name. Graham's brief history carries him right up to Las Vegas live-games, high rollers, movers and shakers, entertainers, waitresses, bellmen, maitre d's, wedding chapel owners, and signmakers.

Grubbs, Bruce. *Hiking Nevada.* Helena, MT: Falcon Publishing, 1994. Good guidebook for hikes all around Nevada; includes maps.

Hall, Shawn. *Old Heart of Nevada: Ghost Towns and Mining Camps of Elko County.* Reno: University of Nevada Press, 1998. Identifies and locates the ghost towns and old mining camps of Elko County, and recounts their colorful histories. Divides Elko County into five easily accessible regions, lists the historic sites within each region, and provides directions to reach them.

Hall, Shawn. *Preserving the Glory Days: Ghost Towns and Mining Camps of Nye County, Nevada.* Reno: University of Nevada Press, 1999. Nevada's largest and least-populated county is also the site of many of the state's most colorful ghost towns and mining camps. A lively, informative record of Nevada's isolated interior, this book provides historical information on nearly 200 sites and a current assessment of each one, with clear directions for locating each site.

Hall, Shawn. *Romancing Nevada's Past: Ghost Towns and Historic Sites of Eureka, Lander, and White Pine Counties.* Reno: University of Nevada Press, 1994. History of 175 significant sites, with historic photos and an update on the present condition of each ghost town or landmark, and easy-to-follow directions to each one.

Hart, John. *Hiking the Great Basin.* San Francisco: Sierra Club Books, 1980. An indispensable guidebook for anyone wanting to explore the backcountry of Nevada. Wonderfully written, accurate and detailed, superb attitude.

Kelsey, Michael. *Hiking and Climbing in Great Basin National Park.* Provo, UT: Kelsey Publishing, 1988. The best book available on hiking Great Basin Park. Nearly 50 hikes with maps and photos for each.

Moreno, Richard. *Roadside History of Nevada.* Missoula, Montana: Mountain Press Publishing Company, 2000. Memorable tales of Nevada's places and people, written with a historian's nose for details and a traveler's sense of fun, with 140 photos and detailed maps showing how to get to every place mentioned. Written by the friendly, personable and knowledgeable publisher of *Nevada* magazine.

Nevada Road and Recreation Atlas. Medford, OR: Benchmark Maps, 2003. Comprehensive collection of detailed maps of the entire state of Nevada; includes listing of campgrounds, historic attractions, parks, museums, and geological sites.

Parr, Barry. *Hiking the Sierra Nevada.* Helena, MT: Falcon Publishing, 1999. Good hiking book for the Sierra.

Perry, John, and Jane Greverus. *Guide to the Natural Areas of New Mexico, Arizona, and Nevada.* San Francisco: Sierra Club Books, 1985. This handy book has information on 82 BLM, Forest Service, State Park, and state and federal Wildlife Department lands.

Prosor, Larry, and Richard Moreno. *Endless Nevada.* Las Vegas: Stephens Press, 2003. Marvelous blending of Nevada images by award-winning photographer Larry Prosor and the evocative essays of Richard Moreno.

Tingley, Joseph V., and Kris Ann Pizarro. *Traveling America's Loneliest Road: A Geologic and Natural History Tour through Nevada along U.S. Highway 50.* Reno: University of Nevada Press, 2000. A guide to geologic features and other points of interest along U.S. Highway 50 between Lake Tahoe and Great Basin National Park.

Toll, David W. *The Complete Nevada Traveler.* Virginia City, NV: Gold Hill Publishing Company, 1999. Subtitled "The affectionate and intimately detailed guidebook to the most interesting state in America," this guidebook offers narrative about places to visit around the state, with historic and recent black-and-white photos. An interesting book for visitors, but does not try to comprehensively cover nuts-and-bolts travel info such as places to stay, places to eat, transportation, etc.

White, Michael C. *Nevada Wilderness Areas and Great Basin National Park—A Hiking and Backpacking Guide.* Berkeley: Wilderness Press, 1997. If you want to explore any of Nevada's 13 rugged, remote, and primitive wilderness areas, you must have this book.

GAMBLING

Anderson, Ian. *Turning The Tables on Las Vegas.* New York: Vintage Books, 1976. "Ian Anderson" was a pseudonym for R. Kent London, a highly successful and anonymous card counter. Goes into extraordinary detail about playing and betting strategies, camouflage, interaction with the pit personnel, and maintaining a winning attitude. Required reading for aspiring counters.

Bass, Thomas. *Eudaemonic Pie*. New York: Houghton Mifflin, 1985. A true hippie adventure story about a group of physicists at U.C. Santa Cruz who invented a computer that fit in a shoe to beat the casino at roulette.

Castleman, Deke. *Whale Hunt in the Desert: The Secret Las Vegas of Superhost Steve Cyr*. Las Vegas: Huntington Press, 2004. Inside story on casino hosts who cater to high-stakes gamblers (known in the business as "whales").

Compton, Jeffrey. *Las Vegas Advisor Guide to Slot Clubs*. Las Vegas: Huntington Press, 2001. A must for anyone who plays any gaming machines, this is the only book that covers all the slot clubs of Las Vegas.

Ortiz, Darwin. *On Casino Gambling*. New York: Dodd, Mead & Company, 1986. One of the best-written and most useful how-to books for playing casino games.

Rubin, Max. *Comp City—A Guide to Free Las Vegas Vacations*. Las Vegas: Huntington Press, 2001. A former casino executive, Rubin quit his job to write this book, revealing the best-kept secrets in the casino industry about comps (free rooms, food, beverage, shows).

Scott, Jean. *The Frugal Gambler*. Las Vegas: Huntington Press, 1998. The world's preeminent low-rolling casino buster reveals her secrets for staying free at hotel-casinos, beating casino promotions, eating and drinking on the house, and getting bumped from airplanes and flying free.

Solkey, Lee. *Dummy Up and Deal*. Las Vegas: Gamblers Book Club, 1980. Written by a Las Vegan who earned a degree in urban ethnology and dealt blackjack for seven years as part of her "field study." Talks with great authority about the dealer culture, language, territorial domains, and the dealer relationship with the casino.

HISTORY

Cahlan, Florence Lee, and John F. Cahlan. *Water—A History of Las Vegas*. Las Vegas: Las Vegas Water District, 1975. Written by the longtime publisher of the Las Vegas *Review-Journal* and his reporter-wife, this is a sprawling, two-volume history of Las Vegas that "shows how its evolution as a city closely paralleled the development of its water."

Carlson, Helen S. *Nevada Place Names: A Geographical Dictionary*. Reno: University of Nevada Press, 1974. This classic book of place-name facts is spiced with plenty of history, folklore, and legend.

Demaris, Ovid. *The Vegas Legacy*. New York: Dell Publishing, 1983. By one of the coauthors of *The Green Felt Jungle*, this is a story, *very* loosely based on actual Nevada history, about a presidential convention taking place in Las Vegas and how the Nevada powers that be attempt to install their totally corrupt favorite son as the candidate.

DeQuille, Dan. *The Big Bonanza*. New York: Random House, 1980. The story of the discovery and development of Nevada's fabulous Comstock Lode, written by Mark Twain's friend and fellow reporter on Virginia City's *Territorial Enterprise* newspaper. An American classic, first published in 1876.

Dodd, Charles H., and Jeff Gnass. *California Trail: Voyage of Discovery—The Story Behind the Scenery*. Las Vegas: KC Publications, 1996. Well illustrated with excellent color photos, this book tells the story and follows the path of the California Trail, which stretched from Missouri to California. More than 200,000 immigrants passed through Nevada headed westward on this trail from around 1828 to 1869.

Findlay, John. *People of Chance—Gambling in American Society from Jamestown to Las Vegas.* Lincoln: University of Nebraska Press, 1986. Written by a Pennsylvania State University history professor, this incredible book is not only *the* best book on the evolution of American gambling, but also one of the great books on American history itself.

Ford, Jean, Betty Glass, and Martha Gould. *Women in Nevada History: An Annotated Bibliography of Published Sources.* Reno: Nevada Women's History Project, 2000. An excellent resource for finding out everything you ever wanted to know about women in the Silver State's history.

Hall, Shawn. *Connecting the West: Historic Railroad Stops and Stage Stations in Elko County, Nevada.* Reno: University of Nevada Press, 2002. Informative guide to historic railroad and stage stations in northeastern Nevada. As in his earlier volumes, Hall includes a history of each site along with historic and contemporary photos, directions, and maps.

Hulse, James W. *The Silver State.* Reno: University of Nevada Press, 1998. This cohesive and readable history provides students and general readers with an accessible account of Nevada's colorful history, exploring many dimensions of Nevada's experience and its peoples.

James, Ronald M. *The Roar and the Silence: A History of Virginia City and the Comstock Lode.* Reno: University of Nevada Press, 1998. This lively, thoughtful book chronicles the area's history from its earliest days through the early 20th century, when the lode finally gave out and the Comstock sank into silent decay, and up to the present, when Virginia City and its environs found new life, first as a community of bohemians and artists, and more recently as a tourist attraction.

Kasindorf, Jeanie. *The Nye County Brothel Wars.* New York: Linden Press, 1985. Spellbinding account of how an "outsider," who tried to open and run a brothel in Pahrump, ran afoul of the Nye County Sheriff's Department, District Attorney, established whorehouse owners, and their henchmen, and how his battle against harassment, arrest, attempted murder, low- and high-level corruption, white slavery, and racketeering eventually was taken up by the FBI and U.S. Attorney and tried in federal court.

Kling, Dwayne. *The Rise of the Biggest Little City: An Encyclopedic History of Reno Gaming, 1931–1981.* Reno: University of Nevada Press, 1999. The first 50 years of Reno's gaming and gambling industry, written by a long-time gaming executive and illustrated with historic photos.

Land, Barbara, and Myrick Land. *A Short History of Reno.* Reno: University of Nevada Press, 1995. An entertaining and anecdotal history of Reno's colorful past and the larger-than-life characters who left their mark on the city, illustrated with dozens of black-and-white photos.

Land, Barbara, and Myrick Land. *A Short History of Las Vegas.* Reno: University of Nevada Press, 2004. A lively history, illustrated with historic and recent photographs, telling the story of the Las Vegas area from the earliest visitors 11,000 years ago up to the present.

Laxalt, Robert. *Nevada—A History.* New York: W. W. Norton & Company, 1977. This is a very personal, lyrical, and selective account of the history and shape of the state by one of Nevada's best-known and best-loved writers.

Lewis, Oscar. *The Town That Died Laughing.* Reno: University of Nevada Press, 1986. The story of Austin, Nevada—rambunctious early-day mining camp—and its renowned newspaper, the *Reese River Reveille.*

McCracken, Robert D. *Las Vegas: The Great American Playground.* Reno: University of Nevada Press, 1997. Traces the city's history from its first Native American occupants more than 10,000 years ago to its present status as a premier tourist destination, illustrated with historical photos.

McDonald, Douglas. *Virginia City and the Silver Region of the Comstock Lode.* Las Vegas: Nevada Publications, 1982. Another in the long list of excellent historicals from Stanley Paher's press. Very well written and nicely illustrated.

Moehring, Eugene P. *Resort City in the Sunbelt: Las Vegas, 1930–2000.* Reno: University of Nevada Press, 2000. In this new edition, renowned historian Moehring provides a comprehensive history, description and analysis of Las Vegas's development since the 1930s, and also provides insight into the city's future. Indispensable for Las Vegas researchers.

Nevada—A Guide to the Silver State. Portland: Binfords and Mort, 1940. One of 50 books in the famous WPA American Guide Series, and 60 years later still indispensable to modern-day domestic historians and researchers.

Nicklas, Michael L. *Great Basin: The Story Behind the Scenery.* Las Vegas: KC Publications, 1996. One in a series of interesting books with excellent color photos on various places around the West.

Paher, Stanley W. *Nevada Ghost Towns and Mining Camps Atlas.* Reno: Nevada Publications, 2001. Contains 62 color maps with full aerial relief detailing the locations of ghost towns and historic sites throughout Nevada.

Paher, Stanley W. *Las Vegas: As It Began—As It Grew.* Las Vegas: Nevada Publications, 1971. This outstanding history, with hundreds of fascinating black-and-white photos and a half-dozen historical maps, covers in detail the popular history of Las Vegas from the Old Spanish Trail up through the building of Hoover Dam.

Ralston, Jon. *The Anointed One: An Inside Look at Nevada Politics.* Las Vegas: Huntington Press, 2000. Kenny Guinn was elected the governor of Nevada in a 1998 landslide, but the outcome was determined long before a single voter stepped into a polling booth. Written by Nevada's foremost political reporter, this book is a biting commentary on the inner workings of the Nevada political machine.

Reid, Ed, and Ovid Demaris. *The Green Felt Jungle.* New York: Pocket Books, 1964. The classic book in the Diatribe style of indicting Las Vegas as "a corrupt jungle of iniquity."

Reid, John B. and James, Ronald M. *Uncovering Nevada's Past: A Primary Source History of the Silver State.* Reno: University of Nevada Press, 2004. Useful historical research tool that contains a collection of first-hand accounts and major documents describing significant events in Nevada history.

Roske, Ralph. *Las Vegas: A Desert Paradise.* Tulsa: Continental Heritage Press, 1986. A spectacular picture book, affectionately written by a history professor at UNLV.

Shaner, Lora. *Madam: Chronicles of a Nevada Cathouse.* Las Vegas: Huntington Press, 1999. A first-hand look into Nevada's sex-for-money industry, written by a former madam.

Sifakis, Carl. *Mafia Encyclopedia.* New York: Facts on File Publications, 1987. Entries on scores of top underworld personalities and locales, including Las Vegas, Moe Dalitz, Bugsy Siegel, Gus Greenbaum, Virginia Hill, and Johnny Roselli.

Sloan, Jim. *Nevada—True Tales of the Neon Wilderness.* Salt Lake City: University of Utah Press, 1993. Eleven stories covering some of Nevada's biggest headline-grabbing events of the past few decades, written by a reporter and editor for the *Reno Gazette-Journal.*

Townley, John M. *Tough Little Town on the Truckee: Reno.* Reno: Great Basin Studies Center, 1983. Sprawling and brilliant book on Reno's environment and early history.

Vogliotti, Gabriel R. *The Girls of Nevada.* Secaucus, NJ: Citadel Press, 1975. One of the best books ever written on Nevada, including the complete rundown of prostitution issues, a great bio of Joe Conforte, and a stunningly unique history of Las Vegas.

Wolfe, Tom. *The Kandy-Kolored Tangerine-Flaked Streamlined Baby.* New York: Farrar, Strauss & Giroux, 1965. The Las Vegas chapter in this big book of essays is perhaps the classic look at the city as the ultimate expression of the new culture—glamour, entertainment, art-style—that emerged from 1960s' America.

BIOGRAPHY

Canfield, Gae Whitney. *Sarah Winnemucca of the Northern Paiutes.* Norman, OK: University of Oklahoma Press, 1983. Biography of the daughter of Chief Winnemucca, whose book *Life Among the Piutes* became a classic.

Garrison, Omar. *Howard Hughes in Las Vegas.* Secaucus, NJ: Lyle Stuart, 1970. Everything about this troubled, mysterious billionaire is gripping. But this book, centered around the four years Hughes spent sequestered on the ninth floor of the Desert Inn, is especially eye-opening, shedding light on the public events and private life of the recluse, as he set about to buy and redesign the city that may well have been "his true spiritual home."

Hillyer, Katharine. *Mark Twain: Young Reporter in Virginia City.* Reno: Nevada Publications, 1997. Tells the story Twain's life as a young reporter in Virginia City, which was the beginning of his literary career.

Hopkins, A. D., and Evans, K. J. *The First 100: Portraits of the Men and Women Who Shaped Las Vegas.* Las Vegas: Huntington Press, 1999. One hundred in-depth profiles of the men and women who helped transform Las Vegas from a desert watering hole to the city it is today. Produced by two staff writers of the Las Vegas *Review-Journal.*

Hopkins, Sarah Winnemucca. *Life Among the Piutes: Their Wrongs and Claims.* Reno: University of Nevada Press, 1994. Daughter of Chief Winnemucca, born around 1844, writes the story of her life and her people.

Seagraves, Anne. *High-Spirited Women of the West.* Hayden, ID: Wesanne Publications, 1992. Includes stories about the lives of several women important in Nevada's history, including Sarah Winnemucca, Jeanne Elizabeth Wier, and Helen Jane Wiser Stewart. Seagraves has written several good books about women in the West, all published by Wesanne Publications, including *Women of the Sierra* (1990), *Women Who Charmed the West* (1991), *Soiled Doves: Prostitution in the Early West* (1994), and *Daughters of the West* (1996).

Twain, Mark. *Mark Twain's Virginia City, Nevada Territory, in the 1860's.* Golden, Colorado: Outbooks, 1982. Reprint of material first published in 1872, with original illustrations, in which Twain tells of his journey across the continent by stagecoach in 1861 with his brother Orion, and their later adventures in Nevada, particularly Twain's sojourn as a newspaper reporter in Virginia City.

Twain, Mark. *Roughing It.* Berkeley: University of California Press, 1996. Twain's account of his life in the West, including his sojourns in Nevada, first published in 1868.

Williams, George III. *Mark Twain: His Life in Virginia City, Nevada.* Dayton, NV: Tree by the River Publishing, 1992. Tells the story of Mark Twain's time in Virginia City, with many stories of the town and historic photos. George Williams III has written many fine books about Virginia City, Mark Twain, and Nevada history, all available from the same publisher.

NATURAL HISTORY

Anderson, Steve, et al. *Ruby Mountain Flora: A Guide to Common Plants of the Ruby Mountains and East Humboldt Range.* Elko: Humboldt National Forest Interpretive Association, 1998. Excellent book for identifying plants, with fine color photos.

Clark, Jeanne L. *Nevada Wildlife Viewing Guide.* Helena, MT: Falcon Press, 1993. Guide to 55 sites around the state for viewing Nevada's varied birds, mammals, reptiles, and endangered fish, with maps, directions, and descriptions of both the wildlife-viewing areas and the animals, with excellent color photos.

Fiero, Bill. *Geology of the Great Basin.* Reno: University of Nevada Press, 1986. One in a comprehensive and in-depth series of a half-dozen large and beautiful books on the Great Basin.

Haase, John. *Big Red.* New York: Pinnacle Books, 1980. Towering novel about the building of Hoover Dam, from the point of view of Frank Crowe, the dam's chief engineer. As monumental and epic a book as the dam itself.

McPhee, John. *Basin and Range.* New York: Farrar, Strauss & Giroux, 1980. Another stunning job by this master author. Here he takes the entire history of geology and relates it to a drive along I-80 through northern Nevada, and manages to tell the tale in 215 pages. Breathtaking.

Ryser, Fred A. Jr. *Birds of the Great Basin.* Reno: University of Nevada Press, 1985.

Sigler, William, and John Sigler. *Fishes of the Great Basin.* Reno: University of Nevada Press, 1987.

Taylor, Ronald J. *Sagebrush Country: A Wildflower Sanctuary.* Missoula, MT: Mountain Press Publishing, 1992. Excellent book for identifying plants, with fine color photos.

Tilford, Gregory L. *Edible and Medicinal Plants of the West.* Missoula, MT: Mountain Press Publishing, 1997. Excellent book for identifying plants, with fine color photos.

Trimble, Stephen. *The Sagebrush Ocean: A Natural History of the Great Basin.* Reno: University of Nevada Press, 1999. This noted writer and photographer mixes eloquent accounts of personal experiences with clear explication of natural history, and his photos capture some of the most spectacular but least-known scenery in the western states. An excellent general introduction to the ecology and spirit of the Great Basin.

FICTION AND LITERATURE

McLaughlin, Mark. *Sierra Stories: True Tales of Tahoe.* Carnelian Bay, CA: Mic Mac Publishing. Volume 1, 1997; Volume 2, 1998. Stories about Lake Tahoe and the Tahoe area.

McMurtry, Larry. *The Desert Rose.* New York: Simon and Schuster, 1983. An affectionate and poignant little character study of an aging showgirl and her ties—men, daughter, neighbors, friends, and co-workers—that McMurtry wrote over a three-week period during a lull in the writing of his epic *Lonesome Dove.*

Puzo, Mario. *Fool's Die*. New York: Putnam, 1978. A sprawling, semi-autobiographical novel about a writer who starts out as an orphan, gets married and raises a family in New York, makes a pilgrimage to Las Vegas, and publishes a blockbuster novel that is turned into a box-office smash. Contains some of the best writing in fiction about a Las Vegas hotel owner and his right-hand assistant, scams on both sides of the gaming table, and casino color.

Puzo, Mario. *Inside Las Vegas*. New York: Charter Books, 1977. A short, stream-of-consciousness look at gambling, girls, and glamour by this famous novelist, himself a heavy, but not degenerate, gambler.

Thompson, Hunter S. *Fear and Loathing in Las Vegas*. New York: Random House, 1998. Thompson's classic novel.

Tronnes, Mike (ed.). *Literary Las Vegas: The Best Writing About America's Most Fabulous City*. New York: Henry Holt & Company, 1995. A collection of previously published articles about Sin City by two dozen of America's top wordsmiths: Tom Wolfe, Hunter S. Thompson, John Gregory Dunne, Joan Didion, Noel Coward, Michael Herr, and many more.

MAGAZINES

Las Vegas Advisor. Published by Huntington Press, 3687 S. Procyon Ave., Las Vegas, NV 89103, 800/244-2224, and. Monthly magazine covering where to go, where to stay, where to eat, entertainment, tournaments, special events and so on in Las Vegas. Subscribers get a coupon book offering valuable savings.

Nevada. 401 N. Carson St., Suite 100, Carson City, NV 89701-4291, 775/687-5416, www.nevadamagazine.com. Published continuously since 1936, this bimonthly contains an extraordinary amount of coverage on the 36th state, with proportionate attention paid to Las Vegas. Good writing and photography, great production, and the "Events and Shows" section alone is worth the subscription price.

Range. P.O. Box 639, Carson City, NV 89702, 775/884-2200 or 800/726-4348, www.range magazine.com. This quarterly magazine focuses on creating a public awareness about the positive presence of ranchers on the nation's rangelands.

Index

Hot Springs

amoeba contamination: 116
Blue Point Spring: 114
Boy Scout Canyon: 116
Carson Hot Springs: 206
Goldstrike Canyon: 116
Panaca Spring: 337
Rogers Spring: 114
Spencer Hot Springs: 301
Virgin Valley: 237
Walley's Hot Springs: 214–215
Warm Springs Junction: 324

Parks/ Wildlife Refuges

Skiing/Snowboarding

Trails

U.S.~Metric Conversion

1 inch	=	2.54 centimeters (cm)
1 foot	=	.304 meters (m)
1 yard	=	0.914 meters
1 mile	=	1.6093 kilometers (km)
1 km	=	.6214 miles
1 fathom	=	1.8288 m
1 chain	=	20.1168 m
1 furlong	=	201.168 m
1 acre	=	.4047 hectares
1 sq km	=	100 hectares
1 sq mile	=	2.59 square km
1 ounce	=	28.35 grams
1 pound	=	.4536 kilograms
1 short ton	=	.90718 metric ton
1 short ton	=	2000 pounds
1 long ton	=	1.016 metric tons
1 long ton	=	2240 pounds
1 metric ton	=	1000 kilograms
1 quart	=	.94635 liters
1 US gallon	=	3.7854 liters
1 Imperial gallon	=	4.5459 liters
1 nautical mile	=	1.852 km

To compute Celsius temperatures, subtract 32 from Fahrenheit and divide by 1.8. To go the other way, multiply Celsius by 1.8 and add 32.

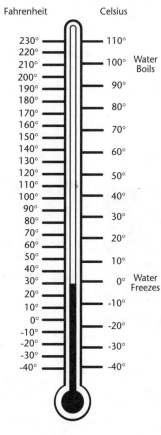

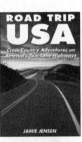

Keeping Current

Although we strive to produce the most up-to-date guidebook humanly possible, change is unavoidable. Between the time this book goes to print and the moment you read it, a handful of the businesses noted in these pages will undoubtedly change prices, move, or even close their doors forever. Other worthy attractions will open for the first time. If you have a favorite gem you'd like to see included in the next edition, or see anything that needs updating, clarification, or correction, please drop us a line. Send your comments via email to atpfeedback@avalonpub.com, or use the address below.

Moon Handbooks Nevada
Avalon Travel Publishing
1400 65th Street, Suite 250
Emeryville, CA 94608, USA
www.moon.com

Editor: Christopher Jones
Series Manager: Kevin McLain
Acquisitions Editor: Rebecca K. Browning
Updater: Carolyn Graham
Copy Editor: Ellen Cavalli
Graphics Coordinator: Deb Dutcher
Production Coordinator: Darren Alessi
Cover Designer: Kari Gim
Interior Designers: Amber Pirker,
Map Editor: Kat Smith
Cartographers: Mike Morgenfeld,
 Kat Kalamaras, Suzanne Service
Indexer: Rachel Kuhn

ISBN: 1-56691-595-3
ISSN: 1078-5426

Printing History
1st Edition—1989
7th Edition—March 2005
5 4 3 2 1

Text and Maps © 2005 by
 Avalon Travel Publishing, Inc.
All rights reserved.

Avalon Travel Publishing
An Imprint of
Avalon Publishing Group, Inc.

AVALON
publishing group incorporated

Some photos and illustrations are used by permission and are the property of the original copyright owners.

Front cover photo: © Deke Castleman

Printed in Canada by Transcontinental